ARTICLES ON ————————————————

COLONIALISM AND NATIONALISM IN AFRICA

A Four-Volume Anthology
of Scholarly Articles

Series Editors

GREGORY MADDOX
Texas Southern University

TIMOTHY K. WELLIVER
Bellarmine College

A GARLAND SERIES

SERIES CONTENTS

VOLUME
4

AFRICAN NATIONALISM AND REVOLUTION

Edited with introduction by
GREGORY MADDOX

GARLAND PUBLISHING, Inc.
New York & London
1993

Library of Congress Cataloging-in-Publication Data

African nationalism and revolution / edited with introduction by
Gregory Maddox.
     p.   cm. — (Colonialism and nationalism in Africa ; v. 4)
Includes bibliographical references.
ISBN 0-8153-1391-8 (alk. paper)
   1. Africa—Politics and government—20th century.
2. Africa—History—Autonomy and independence movements.
3. Nationalism—Africa—History—20th century.   I. Maddox,
Gregory. II. Series.
DT29.A34 1993
960.3—dc20   93-11080
                                 CIP

Printed on acid-free, 250-year-life paper
Manufactured in the United States of America

CONTENTS

SERIES INTRODUCTION

The study of African history as an academic discipline is a rather new field and one that still has its detractors both within and outside academics. The eminent British historian Hugh Trevor-Roper, now Lord Dacre, is once reputed to have said that African history consisted of nothing but "the murderous gyrations of barbarous tribes," while more recently the Czech novelist Milan Kundera has written to the effect that even if it could be proved that hundreds of thousands of Africans died horrendous deaths in the Middle Ages it would all count for nothing. At the very least, such views are a matter of perspective; for the 400 million or so people living in the nations of sub-Saharan Africa today history still shapes the rhythm of their destiny.

This collection of articles highlights for students and scholars the modern era in African history. It brings together published research on the colonial era in Africa, an era relatively brief but one that saw dramatic change in African societies. It highlights the ongoing research into the struggles for independence and social transformation that continue to the present. The authors of these articles eloquently rebut the Euro-centric bias of critics like Trevor-Roper and Kundera and claim for African societies and Africans their rightful place as agents of history.

The articles collected here cover the period between the "Scramble for Africa" in the late nineteenth century, when all but two nations in Africa became colonies of European powers, and the struggles to define the meaning of independence in Africa and throw off the last vestiges of white rule in the southern part of the continent. Such a concentration by no means implies that African societies before the late nineteenth century were tradition-bound or unchanging. They developed according to their own pace and played significant roles in world affairs from the days when West Africa provided a major proportion of the Old World's gold before 1500 through the era of the Atlantic slave trade. However, the colonial era created the modern map of Africa, and Africans transformed their societies politically, economically, and socially in the face of their forced integration into the world economy as producers of raw materials.

The articles in this collection chart the development of African historical studies. As the field emerged in the late 1950s and early 1960s, many historians sought to place the struggle by African peoples to liberate themselves from colonialism and racial domination within a historical tradition. Some scholars, inspired by T. O. Ranger's work, sought to link modern nationalist movements to resistance to colonial rule in the late nineteenth century. They also focused on the development of what they saw as a national consciousness that overlaid existing economic, ethnic, and religious communities.

The reaction to this approach was not long in coming within both African politics and historical scholarship. The ongoing struggles within African nations, often defined in ethnic terms, find their image reflected in early critical works such as those of Steinhart and Denoon and Kuper included here that question the development of national consciousness. More generally, as I. N. Kimambo of Tanzania has argued, there was a turn towards economic and social history that concentrated on the transformation and relative impoverishment of African societies under colonialism. Some scholars have gone so far in the search for the origins and meanings of community in Africa as to reject the modern nation state as of much use as a unit of analysis. Basil Davidson, one of the most influential pioneers in African historical research and a long time supporter of African liberation, has recently produced a volume that calls for a reconfiguration of African political life to fit the reality of African communities (*The Black Man's Burden: Africa and the Curse of the Nation State*). This collection demonstrates the competition between these views and the shifts that have occurred over the last three decades.

This collection intends to make available to students and scholars a sample of the historical scholarship on twentieth century Africa. The articles come mainly from Africanist scholarly journals, many of which had and have limited circulations. It includes some seminal works heretofore extremely difficult to locate and many works from journals published in Africa. It also includes some works collected elsewhere but shown here in the context of other scholarship.

The articles collected here represent a growing and distinguished tradition of scholarship. Some are foundation works upon which the field has built. Many pioneer methodological innovations as historians have sought ways of understanding the past. All go beyond the often abstract generalities common to basic texts. Taken together they reveal the diversity and the continuity of the African experience.

Several people have contributed greatly to this project. Leo Balk and Carole Puccino of Garland Publishing have guided it through all its stages. Cary Wintz was the catalyst for the project. I. N. Kimambo critiqued the project and made many suggestions. The library staffs of the Ralph J. Terry Library at Texas Southern University, the Fondren Library at Rice University, and the University Library of Northwestern University, and especially Dan Britz of the Africana Collection at Northwestern, provided critical help. Bernadette Pruitt did some of the leg work. Pamela Maack was always supportive, and Katie provided the diversions.

INTRODUCTION

Between 1954 and 1965, independence came for almost all African nations between the Zambezi River and the Mediterranean. South of the Zambezi, white domination remained intact, and even in the newly independent nations of "middle Africa" between the Sahara and the Zambezi, independence did not necessarily mean an end to economic dependence nor did it even always fulfill the political aspirations of its advocates. Kwame Nkrumah, who led the British colony of the Gold Coast to independence as the nation of Ghana, once described his policy as "seek ye first the political kingdom," while Julius Nyerere, who led the British colony of Tanganyika to *uhuru* (freedom in Swahili) and oversaw its merger with Zanzibar into Tanzania, described the struggle that lay ahead in 1961 as the country faced a serious food shortage as "fighting not man but nature." For many Africans the political kingdom did not necessarily yield the full fruits of victory and man as well as nature continued to leave some of the promises of African nationalism unfulfilled. "Flag independence," in Walter Rodney's dismissive phrase, often proved a false independence.

South of the Zambezi, of course, the struggle remained one of national liberation against white domination. The lynchpin of this situation was apartheid in South Africa. Militant Afrikaner nationalists who finally seized control of the South African state in 1948 not only intensified the already strong system of racial domination in South Africa, but, as independence approached elsewhere supported the maintenance of colonial rule in Portugal's colonies of Angola and Mozambique and settler dominance in the British colonies of the Rhodesias. Not only did liberation have to come from the barrel of a gun, but in many ways the liberation movements in southern Africa became more radical and revolutionary than their counterparts elsewhere.

The articles collected in this volume address both the problems and possibilities African nations faced as they won their independence. They explore the efforts at nation building after almost a century of politics of division. They chart the debates over the nature of liberation and the efforts by some Africans to move from political to economic independence. They also explore historiographic debates that arose out the emergence of an academic discipline of African history. A new future required a new past, one that emphasized the ability of Africans to make their own history.

The biggest political problem facing many newly-independent African governments in the first decades of freedom was national unity. Ideologically, most nationalist movements that contested colonial rule in the years after World War II had espoused some form of pan-Africanism as a basis for unity. African leaders only fitfully supported pan-African unity, creating the Organization of African Unity as a very weak body. However, in many cases the political mobilization of masses had often been along more sectarian lines. In Sudan civil war broke out almost immediately between the Arab, Muslim-dominated north and the less-developed, non-Muslim south, which has raged, off and on, to the present day. In Nigeria and the Belgian Congo (now Zaire), political parties, although for the most part dedicated to an expansive view of nationalism, did not even form a common front against colonial rule. In Nigeria, the existence of three major parties, each with a power base in one of the three regions of the country, delayed independence as they jockeyed for position and set the stage for civil war in the late 1960s as the southeastern region of the country, taking the name Baifra, fought to secede. In the Belgian Congo, the haste with which the colonial order disintegrated led to civil war as the movement with a base in the copper producing region of Katanga fought to secede from the country with the backing of mining interests and the white dominated regions of southern Africa. United Nations intervention in favor of unity, and western backing for the first African commander of the Force Publique over the more leftist central government of Patrice Lumumba, maintained unity under the dictatorship of Mobutu Sese Sekou.[1]

Even in nations where ethnic, religious or regional divisions were on the surface successfully overcome, important ideological differences made the goal of pan-African unity elusive. In many cases, African leaders and movements equated the anti-colonial struggle with a struggle against capitalist exploitation. The most ideologically coherent of such movements was the Tanzanian[2] leader Julius Nyerere's *Ujamaa* (familyhood in Swahili, translated as socialism), but many African nations developed their own forms, usually emphasizing nationalization of the "commanding heights" of the economy while allowing for continued smallholder production in the countryside.

Ujamaa went farther, but the experimentation with collective agriculture was quickly abandoned in the face of a dramatic fall in agricultural production.

On the other hand, many African nations sought to promote indigenous capitalism, even if their leaders used evasive language in describing their policies. Kenya, Ivory Coast, and Senegal all maintained close economic ties with the former colonial power and encouraged foreign investment. Such differences helped prevent a greater unity among the former Francophone colonies of West Africa and led to the break up of the East African Community between Kenya, Uganda, and Tanzania.

Given both the ethnic divisions and the extreme poverty most new African nations inherited from colonial rule, many African nations found themselves beset by instability from the beginning. For most, hastily cobbled-together multiparty political systems quickly gave way to some form of authoritarian rule. For many, starting with Zaire, military dictatorships became the order of the day. For others, nationalist leaders, arguing that multiparty systems promoted ethnic, religious, and regional divisions, created one-party states. Some, such as Tanzania, Senegal, or Kenya, remained fairly open systems, while others degenerated into despotism.[3] Despite occasional attempts to reinstitute pluralistic political systems, only in the early 1990s did there seem to be a sustained movement towards multi-party democracy.

The Cold War rivalry between the United States and the Soviet Union also played a part in both promoting instability and maintaining authoritarian rulers. The U.S. and France backed many corrupt regimes in the name of anti-communist unity. The U.S.S.R. supported the 1974 revolution in Ethiopia which overthrew one the world's oldest monarchies. The revolutionary government then proceeded to allow mass starvation in the country as part of its campaign against regional separatist movements.[4]

South of the Zambezi River the struggle continued to be more against man than nature. South Africa served as the hub, both economically and politically, of the region. The South African government supported the maintenance of Portuguese rule in Mozambique and Angola. It ruled South West Africa (now Namibia) directly in defiance of the United Nations which mandated that the former League of Nations Trust Territory be granted independence under majority rule. It supported the Unilateral Declaration of Independence from Great Britain by white settlers in Southern Rhodesia (now Zimbabwe) rather than see that country come under majority rule. Even the countries that became independent in the region under majority rule remained economically and to some extent politically dominated by South Africa.

South Africa's political dominance was based on its economic dominance. The Portuguese colony of Mozambique, along with the eventually independent nations of Malawi, Lesotho, and Swaziland, received most of its revenue from remittances from migrant laborers in South Africa. In Rhodesia, Botswana, Angola, and even Zambia much of the capital for mining operations and markets for agricultural products remained in South Africa. Even access to ports via railway for countries as far north as Zambia lay through South Africa.

With the notable exception of MauMau in Kenya, the struggle for independence in sub-Saharan Africa had been remarkably peaceful. Britain and France had realized, in Harold Macmillan's phrase before the South African Parliament, that a "wind of change" was blowing across the continent. They recognized both the economic and military costs of maintaining their empires along with the ideological inconsistency it represented in terms of the Cold War. In the south, whites fully intended to maintain their position, by force of arms if necessary. Nationalist movements in the nations remaining under white rule, then, turned to armed struggle during the early 1960s.

Guerrilla movements began perhaps initially with the shift of the African National Congress of South Africa to armed struggle under the leadership of Nelson Mandela. The ANC's rival in South Africa, the Pan African Congress, quickly joined it. Soon afterwards, movements in Angola, Mozambique, South West Africa, the Portuguese colonies of Guinea Bissau and Cape Verde, and Southern Rhodesia all fielded armed forces. Ironically, the South African struggle has remained the one in which liberation movements have had the least success militarily, although they may be on the brink of political success during the 1990s.

The successful liberation movements all shared one important element. They generally became more militant and Marxist-influenced than their counterparts to the north. Western conservatives often saw the material support received by these liberation movements from the Soviet Union and its allies as the reason for this difference; a realistic explanation lies in the more naked oppression in the remaining minority regimes. Cold War rivalries certainly enhanced the killing power in the region, and in Africa as a whole, and probably extended the conflicts; but their causes lay in racial domination in southern Africa.

Independence for Angola and Mozambique in 1975, for Zimbabwe in 1980, and Namibia in 1990 did not end the conflict in those countries. The victorious factions in Mozambique and Angola had received heavy Soviet backing. South Africa and the United States in turn backed anti-government movements in Angola and Mozambique throughout the 1970s and 1980s that effectively disrupted those countries. Zimbabwe under Robert Mugabe avoided the worst of that result in part by distancing itself from the Soviet Union and maintaining cordial relations with the United States while still supporting South African liberation movements politically.

During the 1980s, though, the South African government began to lose the ability to maintain its position both regionally and internally. International sanctions gradually began to disrupt its economy. Most importantly, grass roots organizations, eventually roughly unified under the umbrella of the United Democratic Front, succeeded in making large parts of South Africa ungovernable. In the early 1990s F.W. DeKlerk bit the bullet and began a process he and the Nationalist Party claimed would lead to majority rule. Progress has been slow, and the leading role of Nelson Mandela and the African National Congress has been under pressure from both left and right. On the right, the Inkatha Freedom Party, basically a Zulu national party, threatens a post-apartheid South Africa with the same type of ethnic turmoil that has struck some other African nations. On the left, the slowness of both political and, most importantly, economic reform, has seen support grow for more militantly nationalist groups like the PAC. The winds of change still blow.

NOTES

1. Crawford Young, *Politics in the Congo: Decolonization and Independence* (Princeton, 1965); and Conor Cruise O'Brien, *To Katanga and Back: A UN Case History* (New York, 1962).

2. Tanzania was formed after union between Tanganyika and Zanzibar in 1964. A revolution in Zanzibar at independence overthrew the Arab-dominated government of the Sultan and replaced it with a People's Republic. Instability and the threat of outside intervention led the revolution's leaders to accept union with Tanganyika.

3. See Ali A. Mazrui, "The Social Origins of Ugandan Presidents: From King to Peasant Warrior," *Canadian Journal of African Studies*, 8, 1 (1974), pp. 3–23, and Bert N. Adams, "Uganda Before, During, and After Amin," *Rural Africana*, 11 (1981), pp. 15–25, both collected in this volume, for a discussion on one such debacle.

4. See John Markakis, "The Nationalist Revolution in Eritrea," *Journal of Modern African Studies*, 26, 1 (1988), pp. 51–71, collected in this volume, for a discussion of one of those movements.

NATIONALIST HISTORIANS IN SEARCH OF A NATION
THE 'NEW HISTORIOGRAPHY' IN DAR ES SALAAM

by Donald Denoon, *Makerere University*
and
Adam Kuper, *University College, London*

THE EMERGENCE OF nation-based histories is perhaps an inevitable consequence of the foundation of national universities in newly independent African countries. One of the demands made of historians in that environment is to provide a history of the nation concerned, as a means of filling the gap left by the colonial-based historiography which commonly preceded independence. Historians in Tanzania are by no means uniquely circumstanced in this respect. What makes their work particularly interesting is the manner in which they have set about the task. The diligence and determination of past and present members of the History Department at Dar es Salaam has now produced a substantial corpus of Tanzanian and East African history. That work is characterized by a sufficient number of common concerns and approaches to make it perhaps legitimate to refer to a 'Dar es Salaam school' of historiography. The use of the term 'school' clearly runs the risk of attributing one member's opinions to everyone else, and of minimising the changes which take place in individual opinions. Nevertheless there are in fact common concerns and approaches, as will emerge from a detailed study of the literature produced. The literature amounts to a composite picture of Tanzanian history which has a striking internal consistency. That result stems partly from the unusual situation in which members of the department found themselves: namely that of a predominantly expatriate group, founding a new department in a newly independent country for which up to that time very little history had been written at all.

It is common cause that there was such a thing as a 'colonial-minded' historiography of Africa before independence, and that implicit is this there was often a strong element of racial arrogance. At the least this embodied the assumption that the only worthwhile topics for consideration were the interventions of more advanced external cultures upon an inert tropical Africa. So profoundly have these historians affected the climate of discussion that they have imposed upon more modern writers a sense of obligation to justify the study of the history of Africans. Bethwell Ogot, in the introduction to his *History of the Southern Luo*,[1] felt constrained to explain that the Luo have a

Dr Denoon, who lectures in History at Makerere and is at present on exchange at the University of Ibadan, took his doctorate at Cambridge University. Dr Kuper, who also read for his doctorate at Cambridge, was until recently a Lecturer in Social Anthropology at Makerere, and is now teaching at University College, London.

1. B. A. Ogot, *History of the Southern Luo*, Vol. I, *Migration and Settlement* (Nairobi, 1967).

329

1

history despite being African. As late as 1969 I. N. Kimambo and A. J. Temu, introducing *A History of Tanzania*,[2] believed that there was a need to insist that history happens among all peoples at all times. If African scholars even now feel so oppressed, how much more so the post-independence expatriates, often suffering a sense of guilt by racial association and anxious to dissociate themselves from their older colleagues? Inevitably, and to their credit, members of the new History Department in Dar es Salaam found themselves strongly opposed to earlier orthodoxy in East African historiography.

In seeking a new approach, historians could find inspiration in recent studies on the character of imperial expansion, which laid much greater emphasis than before upon the pressure of political forces in Africa and Asia outside the control of the European imperialist powers. Perhaps the most relevant in this context was Robinson and Gallagher's *Africa and the Victorians*.[3] That seminal work, asserting that British imperial policy in Africa was often a series of reactions to local factors within Africa—notably Egyptian and Afrikaner—provides a charter for the study of local pressures upon imperial and colonial officialdom. It seriously undermines the older orthodoxy which assumed that imperial power held most of the historical initiative most of the time, and instead demonstrates the importance of peripheral pressures even at the height of imperial strength. It should be noted, however, that the Robinson and Gallagher thesis operates on an empire-wide scale: the authors are content to ascribe the initiative in imperial affairs at various times to Egyptian, Afrikaner and Irish nationalists. A number of scholars have carried the approach further: European interventions in West and Central Africa, and to a lesser extent in East Africa, have been shown to be in part prompted and modified by the pressure of much more local developments within the continent.[4] But the scholars of Dar have gone further still: in giving primacy of attention to local initiatives within a particular territory they have made the diminution in scale more pronounced, more arbitrary and more decisive. This decrease in political scale is a characteristic to which we will recur. For the moment let us simply observe the new Department, poised in the early 1960s to challenge the entrenched orthodoxies. The fact that they were working in Tanganyika (and then Tanzania) is significant, in that they were surrounded by the activity of a highly articulate national political party, building a nation out of an ex-dependency. They were exposed to stronger ideological currents than scholars in many other independent countries, where national movements are less pervasive and dominant.

2. Kimambo, Temu *et al* (1969). See note 8 below.
3. R. Robinson and J. Gallagher, with Alice Denny, *Africa and the Victorians: the official mind of imperialism* (London, 1961).
4. See for instance J. Hargreaves, *Prelude to the Partition of West Africa* (London, 1963); C. Newbury, *The Western Slave Coast and its Rulers* (Oxford, 1961); Roger Anstey, *Britain and the Congo in the Nineteenth Century* (Oxford, 1962); R. P. Ceulemans, *La Question arabe et le Congo* (Brussels, 1960); R. Oliver, *The Missionary Factor in East Africa* (London, 1952).

The characteristics of Tanzanian ' nationalist ' history

For whatever reasons, the Dar es Salaam school have written history which can be described as nationalist.   Professor Ranger, the first head of the department, expresses the attitude eloquently in his introduction to *Emerging Themes of African History*,[5] the symposium resulting from the Congress of African Historians in Dar es Salaam in 1965.   Examining existing approaches to African history, he narrows the discussion to the two most likely to dominate future historiographic discussion: that of the ' Africanists ' and that of the Fanonesque radical pessimists.[6]   The predicted conflict is depicted in these terms:

> ' The historian who persists in treating national movements as something of genuine importance and formidable energy; who sees the African people winning their independence in the face of colonial reluctance and suppression; who believes that mass participation was at various points crucial; has to argue his case against a wide belief that national independence was an episode in a comedy in which the colonial powers handed over to their selected and groomed bourgeois successors and in which nothing fundamental was changed .... The Africanist historian .... will increasingly find his main adversaries not in the discredited colonial school but in the radical pessimists ' (p. xxi).

In this confrontation Professor Ranger takes the side of the Africanist, by which is meant the historian whose concerns include the study of nationalism. In practice, the frequent use of the term ' African ' is likely to mislead, since the recommended focus for historians is not the whole continent but African activity within national boundaries and generally for a national purpose.   The analysis repudiates not only a Fanonesque view, but also any view involving generalization on a scale larger than that of a nation—whether a world view, an imperial view or a continental approach.   The recommended approach, then, is African nationalist.

The extent to which that aspiration has been attained in Dar es Salaam may be grasped by a reading of Professor Ranger's inaugural lecture delivered shortly before leaving the Department in 1969, which surveys the work accomplished during his term as its head.[7]   The aims of the scholars in the department have been, to quote the title and to summarise the argument, to recover African initiatives in Tanzanian history.   The works referred to include *A Political History of the Pare*, by I. N. Kimambo; *A History of Tanzania*, edited by Dr Kimambo and A. J. Temu; *Tanganyika under German Rule* by John Iliffe; *Tanzania Before* 1900, edited by A. D. Roberts; and the various historical pamphlets produced by the Historical Association of Tanzania.[8]   Some of these

5.   Ranger *et al* (1969).   See note 8 below.
6.   See especially Frantz Fanon, *Les Damnés de la terre* (Paris, 1961) trans. as *The Wretched of the Earth* (New York, 1965).
7.   T. O. Ranger, *Recovering African Initiatives in Tanzanian History* (Dar es Salaam, 1969).
8.   For convenience, a short list of the main works belonging to, or associated with, the Dar es Salaam ' school ' is given at the end of this article.   Only short titles will be given in footnote references in the text.

3

works will be considered in more detail later.   For the moment it is sufficient to say that they do indeed reflect Professor Ranger's aim though to different degrees. The publication of *A History of Tanzania* in 1969 may be regarded as marking the attainment of the twin objectives : the recovery of African initiatives and the compilation of a coherent history of an East African nation.   Much remains to be done, of course, but at least outlines have now been laid down.   How have the objectives been pursued ?

Professor Ranger has identified a number of ' themes ' which have a strong claim upon the attention of an African historian; priority is allocated to only five.

First, it is necessary to confute the classic colonialist picture of pre-colonial Africa as essentially static though riven by bloody and pointless feuds.   In place of the old stereotype, the historian should observe the developing scale of trade and the expansion of plural tribal states, perhaps foreshadowing a general development towards a more sophisticated economy and large-scale political organization.

Second chronologically comes ' primary resistance ' to colonial rule, forcing the indigenous institutions further to expand their scale and scope.   To this topic the department has devoted considerable attention, and the ' new orthodoxy ' (to quote Dr Lonsdale)[9] has moved through several phases in interpreting resistance movements.   As Professor Ranger puts it,

' We have already come a long way past the simple treatment of African ' primary ' resistance as a demonstration that Africans did not acquiesce in the imposition of colonial rule and moved towards an approach that uses the great African resistances as a way of understanding the dynamics of late 19th century African societies. '[10]

The most recent and most sophisticated expression of conclusions upon this theme is to be found in the same author's chapter in Volume I of *Colonialism in Africa*, edited by Gann and Duignan.[11]   In this Dr Iliffe's distinction has been adopted, which divides the theme into African military endeavours during, and subsequent to, the colonial ' pacification '.   At the same time, ' collaboration ' is no longer so sharply distinguished from resistance, as a reaction to alien authority.

Third, and connected to the second theme, is the concern with messianic movements, ' witchcraft ' and the history of African churches.   Primary resistance (and particularly post-pacification resistance) was often expressed in messianic movements; and religious upheavals often marked the first adjustment to colonial authority.   Later on, church groups including breakaway and independent African churches often became the centres for new philosophies concerning the African's place in the new world.   These churches also provided new institutions in which people could exercise leadership.

9.   Lonsdale, ' Emergence of African Nations ', p. 201, Ranger *et al* (1965)
10.   Ranger, *Emerging Themes*, Introduction, p. xviii.
11.   Ranger, ' Reactions to Colonial Rule ', Gann and Duignan (1969).

Fourth come the ' new men '—the first generation educated within the colonial framework.   In one way or another they claimed positions of leadership and influence, often reforming or even displacing traditional authorities.   The ' new men ' sometimes worked in the colonial administration, but the new orthodoxy is more concerned with those others who were forming trade unions or other voluntary improvement associations, often coming into conflict with colonial authorities as a result.

Finally there is the search for the ' roots of nationalism '.   Since TANU is, amongst other things, a lineal descendant of the Tanganyika African Association, the main vehicle of the ' new men ' in the inter-war years, the roots of nationalism necessarily involve some consideration of the ' new men ' and their improvement associations.   A major problem is the extent to which, and the manner in which, the activities of the ' new men ' developed into recognizable modern nationalist movements.   From what is implied in other writings, it appears that the new orthodoxy would subscribe to the following view: that TANU, by uniting élite and mass Tanzanian nationalists, thereby created the modern nationalist movement which enabled the people to regain their independence.   That interpretation of the history of the nationalist movement is used as a springboard for the conclusion that anything which happened in what is now Tanzania becomes Tanzanian history; and also that it becomes part of the history of Tanzanian nationalism.

The connections between these themes are implicit in the description already quoted of the African historian ' who persists in treating national movements as something of genuine importance and formidable energy; who sees the African peoples winning back their independence in the face of colonial reluctance and suppression, who believes that mass participation was at various points crucial...' This is not simply an appeal to put the African back into African history.   The demand is for a history of African *national* dignity and self-assertion—in current political terms, for an African nationalist history, even if that involves an academic ratification of the Partition.

History being by nature a selective activity, it is not legitimate to complain that themes have been selected or omitted: but it is perhaps valid to point out that the omission of certain important factors may impair the power of the writings to convince the critical reader.   The approach outlined above does involve important omissions, and these must now be specified, and the consequences observed.   Two classical topics in African historiography are indeed not discarded.   Colonial policy (and particularly its local impact) and mission history are granted importance; and it is suggested that there is an urgent need to purge them of mythical elements.   But the play of cross-currents of influence within the African continent is ignored; and the discussion of the colonial impact —the ' non-African factor '—tends to pass over or specifically reject a number of highly relevant aspects.

Very rarely is it admitted that elements in Africa beyond the borders of

Tanzania have had any impact within.   Yet it seems reasonable to suppose that,
just as the long-range trade from Zanzibar and the East African coast had
consequences affecting at least the whole of Eastern Africa and large parts of
Central Africa as well, so local reactions to traders in the Congo, Uganda,
Malawi, Zambia and Mozambique are likely to have affected the activity of
traders and local people closer to the trading bases.   Again, there can be no
doubt that the resistance or the collaboration of Africans in other parts of the
continent on occasion had some effect upon African and colonialist activity in
German East Africa.   It would appear feasible to advance similar arguments
regarding many aspects of life in Africa during the colonial years, and especially
during the years after the Second World War.   Anti-colonial movements and
parties elsewhere in colonial Africa must surely have had a considerable bearing
upon the independence struggle in Tanzania.

If the influence of African developments from beyond Tanzania's borders has
been important, that of the ' non-African ' factor, operating from both within and
outside the territory, has also been so.   It is one thing to re-assert the continuity
of African societies and the role of African initiatives; it is quite another to play
down the significance of the colonial context within which they were worked out.

In particular, colonial economic policies may well prove in Tanzania, as they
have in Uganda and Kenya, to have been major determinants of the course of
political development.   For example, in colonial East Africa as a whole governments tended to demand that each district be self-sufficient economically; and
the consequent backwater condition, with the production and exchange of
foodstuffs on a purely local scale, is likely to have had a severe effect in diminishing the scale of political activity.   Land policy is another area in which colonial
decisions both central and territorial had a direct effect upon local society.
Modification of land-tenure systems, especially where this led to the alienation of
land to non-Africans, is an obvious example, and this occurred not only in
central Kenya and parts of Uganda, but also in Tanganyika.   Land policy,
again, was often linked with decisions governing the growing (or not growing) of
cash crops by Africans or by settlers, and these decisions often had a critical
effect upon local political and social development; revolutionary for instance in
Buganda,[12] inhibitory and frustrating for Africans in Kenya.   Sometimes
labour policy was of even greater significance.   Administrative decisions were
made and modified as to whether people should be drawn into cash or forced-
labour markets, and which mechanisms should be used to ensure a labour supply.
The history of Malawi is incomprehensible without reference to labour policies,
and the same may apply, to a lesser extent, in Tanzania.   Particularly, official
decisions often determined whether streams of migrant workers should flow
north to work for settlers, or south to work in southern African mines.   Central
Tanzania, until independence, appears to have been a watershed, where the

12.   C. Wrigley, ' The Changing Economic Structure of Buganda ', in The King's Men,
edited by L. Fallers (London, 1964).

demands of the north yielded to those of the south. This may, for example, be a factor towards explaining the difference between Africanist churches in northern and southern Tanzania.

In the economic field as in others the question of inter-racial and settler policies is a topic to which the current trend pays less than due attention. In these spheres African 'initiatives' strictly so-called had relatively little force; but such policies, and settler pressures in shaping them, often profoundly affected social and economic developments. These developments in turn were amongst the most powerful factors in producing African reaction—both in the colonial period and after independence. In Kenya the relative success of settler pressure for land alienation, for cheap labour, and for social and economic services to their own advantage, are recognised to have been crucial in sharpening the focus of African opposition to government. The role of such pressures in Tanzania was certainly slighter, but the whole question of racial issues is not one to be lightly set aside.

All of these manifestations of the 'non-African' factor call for study at several levels—local, territorial, metropolitan. First it would seem rewarding to study policy and politics at the level of the district. That study would include the establishment of the machinery of district administration and the recruitment of personnel to man it, adjustments in the structure and the function of that machinery, and the flow of policy decisions and their repercussions between administration and people. The techniques adopted by administrators in all these respects are likely to have had far-reaching effects. In parts of Uganda, as A. D. Roberts has demonstrated,[13] the effects were immense. Both Lonsdale and Ogot have shown the close interrelation between colonial local administration and politics in western Kenya.[14] To this it may be rejoined that similar research in Tanzania is only a matter of time. Yet in the introduction to the *History of Tanzania* the editors write:

'There has been no attempt to deal with colonial administrative structures. That is because our main interest has been on the African himself.'

Historians of political development within colonial dependencies, in any part of the world, would be rightly appalled at such a self-imposed limitation.

At the territorial level the role of colonial policy is more generally accepted by the new orthodoxy. There is, on the other hand, a somewhat narrow propensity to play down the effect of metropolitan policy. If it is indeed a minor factor in the history of a particular colony, this must be demonstrated, as Dr. Iliffe has sought to do for German metropolitan policy in Tanzania. In fact, in many of the fields referred to above—land policies, the encouragement or otherwise of settlement, labour policies—the metropolitan part was paramount. Most

13. A. D. Roberts, 'The Sub-imperialism of the Baganda', *J. Af. History* **3, 3** (1962).
14. B. A. Ogot, 'British Administration in the Central Nyanza District of Kenya, 1900-60', *J. Af. Hist.* **4, 2** (1963); J. Lonsdale, 'Some Origins of Nationalism in East Africa', *J. Af. Hist.* **9, 1** (1968).

important, the decision to decolonise was taken in the capitals of Europe. It may well be that African pressures were the most important factor in forcing the dislodgement of alien governments, but the question is not settled simply by asserting that there *were* African pressures. It was the assessment of these pressures in London, Brussels and Paris which counted, and the weight which they carried in the final decision to decolonize. At the very least, the timing of decolonization was determined in Europe; otherwise it is difficult to explain why the East African states should have attained independence in the order that they did: Tanganyika, Rwanda, Burundi, Uganda, Zanzibar, Kenya.

Obviously ' themes ' are never selected at random. The problems we have mentioned seem less pressing to historians interested above all in demonstrating African national initiatives and working back from the perspective of contemporary nationalist ideology. At this stage it is sufficient to note that many factors are pushed aside which, not only from other scholarly perspectives, but even for a full treatment of the theme they have chosen, may appear very important indeed.

This is not the place to embark on a full evaluation of the use of archival sources by members of the department. Indeed, given the wide popular readership envisaged for some of the publications under discussion, it would be unrealistic to expect detailed and critical references. Yet there are some indications of selectivity in the choice of sources.

The classic historians are rarely cited unless to be derided for some reactionary phrase or, occasionally, lumped together with amateur colonial writers to furnish a straw-man's thesis which can be contrasted with the ' new orthodoxy '. Take for example the following re-assessment of African independent churches:

> ' The African independent churches have sometimes been approached by writers, especially those belonging to the ' mission ' churches, as though they were an abnormality, almost a disease, which needed some special explanation, which might be diagnosed and perhaps cured. It seems to me to be more sensible to regard African independency rather as one of the many different forms of African Christian initiative. '[15]

The pamphlet from which this is taken, it is true, is addressed primarily to secondary school teachers, but the antithesis suggested is nevertheless unduly disingenuous. The old scholarly orthodoxy—dating from Bengt Sundkler's classic study, which appeared in 1948[16]—does treat independency as a rational social, organizational and intellectual response to colonial or settler Christianity. The misrepresentation of the state of scholarship creates the false impression that the new historiography is revealing new truths mischievously obscured by its predecessors.

15.   T. Ranger *The African Churches of Tanzania* (Nairobi, n.d.) p. 4.
16.   B. Sundkler, *Bantu Prophets in South Africa* (London, 1948).   See also B. A. Pauw, *Religion in a Tswana Chiefdom* (London, 1960); J. B. Webster, *The African Churches among the Yoruba*, 1888-1922 (Oxford, 1964).

There is also undue stress laid on publications, reports, and even *obiter dicta* of district commissioners, missionaries and modern members of TANU. It is all too easy to use selective quotations from these sources to obscure rather than to illuminate the period under discussion. They can readily be made to yield light relief, apocalyptic prophecies, or anachronistic—but convenient—judgements. Thus the meeting is described between a gathering of Zulu intellectuals and a radical white missionary in the closing years of last century, at which the Zulu rejected his leadership on the grounds that no white man was to be trusted. This, it is suggested, shows that they understood the continuity between pre-colonial and post-colonial resistance better than modern historians who distinguish between 'primary' and 'secondary' resistance.[17]

Finally, the members of the school show a certain shyness about using the work of the anthropologists who worked in Tanganyika during the colonial period. The social anthropologists were the main group of scholars active in colonial Africa; they worked in the vernaculars; and they published accounts of East African societies and social movements over many years. Not only are their ethnographies invaluable historical documents, but their interpretations would often be suggestive for the historian. The reason for this neglect appears to be the association of anthropology with colonialism. The Tanganyika administration was unusual in British colonial Africa in employing anthropologists as government servants.[18] Though more recent anthropological work has certainly been used, it has often been used unsystematically. In *Tanzania Before 1900*, for example, anthropologists have contributed particular chapters, but as amateur historians rather than anthropologists, and in any case their conclusions are somewhat at variance with the general conclusions presented in the introduction (see pp. 340-2).

Before turning to the texts themselves, it may be useful to outline the main points made so far. Even if the concern with the history of Tanzanian nationalism is accepted as a legitimate and important theme—among others—it has been undertaken too narrowly and too uncritically. It may be added that there has so far been little attempt at a close definition of the phenomenon being studied. The most precise is that laid down by Lonsdale, who offers the following definition of nationalist movements or parties in the context of colonial Africa:

'I have taken a nationalist movement or party to mean an organisation possessing three major characteristics: it must aim at the exercise or sharing of power at the colony's political centre; it is led by a political élite which is conscious of the aspirations of the masses, willing to articulate them; it possesses a popular following.... The difference between a nationalist organisation and earlier protest movements is that while the latter may possess certain of the above characteristics, they do not posses them all '.[19]

17. T. Ranger, ' Reactions to Colonial Rule ', pp. 320-21.
18. Is this why, when Professor Ranger does quote from the works of Monica Wilson, he refers to her, inaccurately, as a sociologist rather than an anthropologist ?
19. Lonsdale, ' Emergence of African Nations ', p. 201.

It will be noted that according to this definition a fully-fledged nationalist movement can only arise after the creation of a political élite, that is, comparatively late in the colonial period. As will be seen, however, even this definition goes beyond anything attempted by other writers of the ' school '; with the result that all manner of phenomena have been described as being related to, or precursors of, later nationalism. The precise historical relationship between nationalism and earlier events and trends, therefore, becomes almost impossible to establish.

The fundamental weakness of the Dar es Salaam ' school ', in fact, is the assumption that nationalism is the key to an understanding of Tanzanian history, at all times and with scant consideration for other factors involved. Once that basic assumption has been made, it is understandable that great efforts should be devoted to studying the development of nationalism; and the more work is done, the less likely is the assumption to be challenged. It may be reinforced by a tendency towards the selection of sources. The reader is often referred to colonial officials who found nationalism because they feared it (as McCarthy found communism) and to TANU leaders who found nationalism because they desired it. More important, however, the assumption tends to be reinforced by the selection of themes, since those that might throw doubt on the eternal efficacy of nationalism as a key to Tanzania's history have generally been avoided. The charge, in short, is not simply that nationalist history itself cannot be studied without fuller reference to the other factors we have mentioned: but that often these other factors—colonial land policies, the settler role, pan-African currents, the ' imperial factor '—continue to be valid and important themes in their own right which the ' nationalist ' preoccupation too lightly thrusts aside.

Some publications of the Dar es Salaam ' school '

We turn now to a consideration of some of the publications listed earlier in this article. Our conclusions from these reviews are: that nationalism is more often asserted than demonstrated, that the gulf between proto-nationalism and later nationalism has not been (and perhaps cannot be) bridged, and that a strong ideological commitment has often closed the writers' eyes to difficulties in their approach.

John Iliffe's *Tanganyika under German Rule*[20] started its life, in thesis form, under the title ' The German Administration in Tanganyika, 1906-11 '. The change is significant, in that the main focus is no longer on colonial policies, whether metropolitan or territorial, but upon the local situation. Its main purpose is (p. 1) ' to show that even the structure and operation of a colonial administration can be understood only if they are related to the insights which recent study of modern African history has made available. '

The book opens with an account of Maji Maji, the widespread African rising

20. Iliffe (1969).

which took the Germans unawares in July 1905.   Reversing the roles previously
allocated to the African societies and the German colonial authorities, Dr Iliffe
claims that the rising was 'the African initiative to which the "Dernburg
reforms" were the European response' (p. 7).   An important point of definition
must be noted at the outset.   The Tanganyika which is the subject of the book
deliberately excludes Rwanda and Burundi (and the Kionga Triangle); it is not
German East Africa, but what is now mainland Tanzania.   If the other colonial
boundaries are accepted as being relevant, surely Rwanda and Burundi—which
contained after all about half the population of the German colony—should be
included.   The diminution of scale is significant, and is further exemplified by
Dr. Iliffe's minimal references to Germany's other African problems, and to the
rest of colonial Africa.

It is somewhat contentious to describe Maji Maji as an initiative when it was
at the same time a consequence of other historical events and trends.   On the
evidence (pp. 22-3) the immediate cause was 'a specific grievance', namely the
compulsory cotton cultivation scheme.   The deeper causes described also throw
doubt on the validity of describing Maji Maji only as an initiative, though it was
certainly an initiative insofar as it involved innovation.   In one dimension, it
seems to be a reaction to new circumstances consequent upon German colonial
conquest and administration.   In another, it seems to be a continuation
(perhaps climax) of several developments originating in pre-colonial Eastern
Africa including for example the growth of the Kolelo cult, and the tension
produced by Ngoni divisions as against a continuing sense of common identity.
Historians are, of course, confronted with the problem that a chain of cause-and-
effect may stretch out infinitely, and are therefore often obliged arbitrarily to
decide where to start.   In this case, however, it is unusually arbitrary to present
Maji Maji first in the narrative, and to describe it as an initiative while it is also
a consequence of many earlier events, when the significance of Maji Maji looms
so large in the overall argument.

Yet certainly the argument would be strong if it were demonstrated that the
'Dernburg reforms' were undertaken solely, or mainly, in response to Maji
Maji.   But in fact the author himself traces several other contributory causes.
The appointment of Dernburg as Colonial Secretary was the result of the
Chancellor's perception of political tactics in Berlin.   Second, Dernburg's
decision to change various aspects of colonial policy was largely a result of the
'Hottentot election': he was indeed acting under African pressures, but of these
pressures the Maji Maji rising was less powerful than that generated by the
Herero and Nama risings in South-West Africa.   Maji Maji certainly had an
effect upon German colonial policy, but neither as directly nor as clearly as Dr
Iliffe claims.   Close concentration upon local events has led to the neglect of not
only the 'imperial' but also the wider 'African' dimension.

It may be questioned whether the high importance ascribed to African initiatives can be reconciled with the very considerable part played during this period

11

by the issue of European settlement and by settler pressures. About one third of Dr Iliffe's book is in fact devoted to these topics, and clearly the rise of settler power before 1914, and its abrupt curtailment thereafter, did have a great bearing on Tanzania's modern history. Certainly African pressures, and the official assessment of them—the fear of renewed rebellion for example—did influence the settler issue; but it is difficult to see how the white settlers could have been prevented from achieving a position similar to their Kenya counterparts during the Second World War, had it not been for the effect of European events upon the East African colonial situation. The argument admits the significance of settler pressures, but by presenting Maji Maji first and most prominently, it implies and asserts that its effects were greater than they seem to have been.

Tanzania Before 1900, edited by A. D. Roberts and published in 1968,[21] is a series of local histories linked together in a substantial introduction by the editor. In this Dr Roberts is on the look-out for characteristics common to the whole of Tanzania in the nineteenth century, so that the whole shall be greater than the sum of its parts. The statement of one key theme is worth close examination:

> ' One of these themes is the development of military and economic power rather than spiritual power as a basis for leadership, and the related emphasis on personal achievement and loyalty rather than kinship as a qualification for political office ' (p. xv).

As evidence are cited the careers of Ghendewa in Ugweno, the Chagga chiefs Sina and Rindi, Kimweri in Usambara, Kapuufi and Kimalaunga in Ufipa, Mirambo among the Nyamwezi, Nyungu ya Mawe among the Kimbu, and Mkwawa among the Hehe. The evidence proves rather less convincing. Ghendewa is described (p. 29) as a chief who partially stayed the destruction and fragmentation of Ugweno, but failed to do so effectively. He

> ' had the qualities of a man who could have restored the power of Ugweno and, perhaps, even enlarged his political influence. He spent a long time organising his people for military campaigns. He mobilised the resources of his country (especially cattle) in order to feed his army. Above all he made an alliance with Rindi, an arrangement which could have given him great advantage.'

Beyond that point, Dr Kimambo, the author of the chapter, resolutely refuses to move.

In the chapter on Usambara, we find Kimweri described (p. 10) as the ruler who, continuing to rule and to comprehend events in traditional ways, failed to prevent the break-up of his kingdom on his death. Semboja, not Kimweri, is described as ' a revolutionary figure ' in Shambaa politics, since he adapted to the new facts of political life in the region. Similarly, in the Kilimanjaro area,

21. Roberts *et al* (1968).

12

chiefs Sina and Rindi appear to have remained firmly rooted in the political culture. of the Chagga. Certainly they used any available instrument which came to hand—European travellers and administrators included—but in pursuit of good old-fashioned political authority as already understood and relished around the mountain.[22] Moving on to the Fipa chapter, we find that the careers of the two leaders he instances cannot convincingly be shown to have brought about major changes in political organization. The institution of appointive chiefs already existed, and Kapuufi came to power by conventional means. He became very wealthy partly by encouraging agricultural development and by the acquisition of firearms: but Dr Willis does not point to any change in the style of government as a result. Kimalaunga proves to be a military governor whose career resembles that of Mzilikazi, rather than of any of the other leaders mentioned by Dr Roberts. He was defeated first by the Nyika and then by the Germans, and although his power was certainly based upon his private army, he appears to have brought about no durable changes in Fipa political organization. The Fipa, like many other societies affected by the Mfecane, seem to have at least as many features in common with those other societies further south as they have with neighbours not so affected.

The last three examples—Mirambo, Nyungu and Mkwawa—come much closer to the pattern affirmed in the introduction. In Dr Roberts's own chapter, though, there is a sense of straining to find those ' roots of nationalism '. Of Mirambo's period, for instance, he has this to say, apparently without irony:

> ' Looking back on the course of Nyamwezi history, this blend of competition and co-operation involving so large an area of Tanzania, we can see how appropriate it was for President Nyerere to adopt the tune of Mirambo's war-song "Iron breaks the heads" as the tune of the song "TANU builds the nation". ' (pp. 144-5).

Even when the final three cases are conceded, however, some reservations must be made. First, the careers of chiefs without matching consideration of their followers and opponents provide a very slender basis for generalizations about the quality of political authority. Second, of the careers mentioned, only that of Nyungu ya Mawe resulted in institutional changes which survived the death of the initiator. Third, it is not clear whether the societies mentioned provide a typical cross-section: whether our attention is directed only to those societies which expanded rather than those which contracted; whether we are considering one phase of a repetitive cycle, or one phase of a larger development. Fourth, even if the overall pattern were fully established, it would not constitute a specifically ' Tanzanian ' trend. From Gingindlovu to Addis Ababa during the nineteenth century there are chiefly careers which exemplify Dr Robert's trends at least as well as those he has taken for his basis. The trends are neither

---

22. The editor is here drawing, not upon a chapter in the symposium, but on Kathleen Stahl's *History of the Chagga People of Kilimanjaro* (The Hague, 1964).

13

confined to nineteenth century Tanzania nor discovered uniformly within the area.   It is right to emphasize this point, for Dr. Roberts subsequently not only repeats his overall analysis, but does so in even stronger terms:

> ' The nature of political change in Tanzania can be summed up very briefly.   It consisted of a shift from religious to military power as a basis for political authority. '[23]

Though little further evidence is advanced in support of that statement, it is applied much more specifically as a national phenomenon.   But Dr Roberts still fails to establish a relationship between the trend which he claims to observe, and the geographical area upon which he projects it.

The most recent publication, *A History of Tanzania*,[24] deserves special attention, particularly as it includes contributions from so many members of the ' school '.   Under the editorship of Dr Kimambo and Dr Temu, several historians have attempted to synthesize material into a single coherent account of the history of the nation.   Little comment arises out of the first three chapters. Dr Sutton opens the first, ' The Peopling of Tanzania ', with the assertion (p. 1) that the Tanzanian nation ' is the product of a long historical process stretching back hundreds, even thousands of years, ' but he does not in practice attempt to Tanzanianize the australopithecines.   Dr Kimambo's second chapter, ' The Interior before 1800 ', likewise resists the temptation to impose homogeneity upon the area: when the people looked beyond the borders of what is now Tanzania, he follows them; when the focus of life was a region his account is regional.   Dr Alpers's third chapter, on the coast and the caravan trade, is also in general a careful and scholarly account of the subject.   Only in the first and last sentences is there a sense of straining after a nationalist effect.

Dr Gwassa's fifth chapter, dealing with German intervention and African resistance, is also powerful when it deals with research material, but less so when it moves to other topics. His account of Maji Maji, for example, is a very useful summary of research findings: but his summary (p. 122) of the relation between Maji Maji and later political developments is less convincing:

> ' The relationship between privileged and unprivileged groups (after the suppression of resistance and the establishment of colonial administration) falls outside this chapter.   It is sufficient to say here that such a phenomenon held a potential for conflict which in turn led to the beginnings of mass nationalism.   African resistance to German intervention provided posterity with something to think about and to emulate if necessary in the quest for lost independence.   Tanzanians strengthened the process of mass nationalism by building on past mistakes and successes. '

Yet almost half a century elapsed between the Maji Maji war and the next mass

23.   A. D. Roberts, ' Political Change in the Nineteenth Century ', in Kimambo, Temu *et al*, p. 58.
24.   Kimambo, Temu *et al* (1969).

movement in the area, namely TANU; and Dr Gwassa has himself observed elsewhere[25] that TANU recruiting was difficult in the Maji Maji area precisely because of the memory of the war and its suppression campaigns. Yet here he postulates a relationship even closer and more direct than the simple similarity of aim implied in President Nyerere's opinion (quoted on p. 118) that both were expressions of the people's desire to rid themselves of foreign domination.

Can it really be maintained, to turn to another point (pp. 86-7), that nationalism faced greater obstacles in Tanzania than in other African dependencies, because the territory was ruled in turn by two colonial powers? The change of master was common to the German territories of Togo and Kamerun, and—more significantly—to the three or four million people of Rwanda and Burundi.

The case of Rwanda and Burundi is relevant to another point made here also (p. 87)—that Tanzania's difficulties were increased by the sudden accelerating of decolonization. In the Belgian territories the increase in pace was even more sudden; and indeed throughout tropical Africa decolonization was hastened from the late 1950s onwards. Tanzania's experience was by no means unique in this.

The role of the 'new men', as the spearhead of the movement for African self-improvement, is the theme of the sixth chapter, by Dr Iliffe. He examines in particular the Tanganyika African Association, the first territory-wide organization to take up political objectives. He concludes that by 1945 (the end of the 'age of improvement') its achievements were three-fold: it 'kept the dream of unity alive and managed to preserve its own claim to be the legitimate embodiment of it;' it helped to co-ordinate local improvement associations throughout Tanganyika and Zanzibar; and 'it had come to see itself as a Tanzanian institution' (p. 157). Yet Dr Iliffe himself allows (p. 152) that it was only during the 1950s that Tanzanians 'chose territorial or national unity', and his evidence shows that the earlier 'unity' sought by TAA was pan-African as much as territorial. Not until the end of its career did it become national, by shedding its pan-African interests. Equally interesting is the evidence that the activities and aspirations of TAA were for long normally compatible with those of the colonial authorities. The author also makes the point that the appeal of Maji Maji 'was not to Tanzanians as Tanzanians, but to Africans as Africans.' If Maji Maji and TANU were indeed intimately related, this chapter does not establish that it was through TAA that the relationship operated.

Professor Ranger's seventh chapter, 'The Movement of Ideas, 1850-1939', also throws light upon the years between primary and early resistance on one hand, and the appearance of modern mass nationalism on the other. Here too the evidence quoted suggests that pan-African ideas were much more common than national ideas before the Second World War, and it is possible to conclude that the later emphasis upon national issues marked a diminution of scale. There is a tendency moreover to draw connections which are evocative rather than concrete. The claim for instance that the composition of the Revolutionary

25. In a lecture delivered at Makerere in 1969.

Council in Zanzibar was ' an excellent illustration of the sort of grass-roots pan-Africanism that Zanzibar developed ' appears to rest on little more than the fact that the Zanzibar labour force—within which the Council was formed—was drawn from a number of mainland countries. Similarly the possibility of a conjunction (during the First World War) between pan-Islamic and pan-African sentiments in East Africa is treated (p. 178) with a seriousness which its source— a single Kenya Secretariat minute of 1917—can hardly justify.[26] From this in turn is drawn a conclusion which is likewise evocative, and more sweeping than any evidence quoted would seem to warrant:

> ' Many historians of the period give the impression of Tanzania between the two world wars as very much cut off from the lively developments that were going on elsewhere .... Nevertheless the impression was a false one; there was much more going on in Tanzania and there was much more contact between Tanzania and other territories than these histories show ' (p. 179).

Chapter eight, ' The Rise and Triumph of Nationalism ', deals with a topic which is crucial for the whole Dar es Salaam interpretation. Whereas both Gwassa and Iliffe see the connection with early resistance as tenuous until late in the colonial period, which is the period Dr Temu deals with in this chapter, he casts aside their restraint. He writes :

> ' Our nationalism began with the onset of colonialism for it was then that, threatened with German invasion, the people of mainland Tanzania rose to defend their country against colonial invasion .... Tanzanians rose in different parts of the country at different times as and when the Germans threatened their independence ' (pp. 189-90).

Had the people really been Tanzanians at that time, or even Tanganyikans, ' their independence ' would have been one and indivisible, and therefore threatened simultaneously. But the evidence he adduces for the suggestion that nationalism does date from the conquest is less than conclusive. Lenin is called upon to testify that wars of resistance were nationalist ; so too (p. 191) is Ndabaningi Sithole :

> ' The Reverend Ndabaningi Sithole recognized two methods for realising African independence; that is, the non-violent and the violent method. President Nyerere early believed that if peaceful means of demanding the independence of Tanzanians failed, Tanzanians would not give up the struggle, but would instead adopt forceful means of gaining their independence from the British. Thus it is clear that these wars (of resistance) were expressions of nationalism .... Defeat did not mean humiliation on the part of the Africans who lost ; on the contrary it has now come to symbolize patriotism. '

26. For the significance attached to this minute, see also Lonsdale ' Some Origins of African Nationalism ', *loc. cit.*, p. 132.

16

It is not until after this rhetorical prelude that the author embarks on analysis. But he still goes back (p. 192) to Maji Maji as the key to continuity :

' In Maji Maji lies the connection between the early organisers and latter-day nationalists—both generations saw success in rallying and uniting the masses around them against colonialism . . . . The aim was and has been . . . to oppose the occupation of the country by alien authority and to replace it. Early generations sought to do this through force of arms while later generations, with the bitter experience of the former method, often tried other means but with the understanding that they would invoke the use of force if the method they adopted failed—hence Mau Mau in Kenya. '

The possibility that anti-colonialism may not necessarily be nationalist is not considered. Professor Ranger is then quoted to the effect that Maji Maji is comparable to the Shona-Ndebele rising. The only direct evidence adduced is a quotation taken from an interview with a elder in southern Tanzania within the last few years ; and this amounts to no more than a comparison between the process by which TANU spread from a central point to surrounding areas and the similar spread of the Maji Maji in the time of the rising.[27]

Apart from this, there is the fact that Lenin, Sithole and Professor Ranger have all commented on resistance movements ; and that Dr Gwassa's and Dr Iliffe's evidence is alleged to demonstrate the connection. Now there may indeed be connections between Maji Maji and later nationalism, but these connections, so far as the evidence in this chapter goes, exist exclusively in the minds of the later nationalists.

Both the final two chapters run on into the post-independence period and so somewhat beyond the scope of the present paper, yet it is worth noting that both Mr Mosare (on the Zanzibar revolution) and Dr Cliffe (on events leading to the Arusha Declaration) draw an important and valid distinction between political and real independence. If, as they insist, political independence in itself involves no essential change, then the pursuit of the origins of political nationalism is of less relevance to modern affairs than the previous chapters would suggest.

Finally, let us look at John Lonsdale's chapter, ' The Emergence of African Nations ' in *Emerging Themes of African History*. The author himself would perhaps deny that in his search for the continuities in African societies he was seeking to establish a ' missing link ' between the clearly defined nationalist movements of the end of the colonial period and the early phases of resistance :[28] but, read in conjunction with other works of the Dar ' school ', this is certainly the impression the chapter creates.

27. Quotation from Mzee Kipugo, who commented on the parallels: ' It is true that a source of salvation cannot hide itself from the people. ' Recorded in G.C.K. Gwassa and J. Iliffe, *Records of the Maji Maji* (Nairobi, 1968) I, p. 29.
28. Since returning from Dar es Salaam—where ' The Emergence of African Nations ' was first drafted—Lonsdale has carried his thinking further in his ' Some Origins of Nationalism ' article (*J. Af. History, loc. cit*); and also in the revision of his Ph.D. thesis on political development in Nyanza, now being prepared for publication.

' If the colonial period is to be seen as part of African history, the new orthodoxy must deny that Africans were "outwardly acquiescent and politically passive during the interwar years" ' (p. 207).

That is, if mass involvement at a conspicuously political level is absent, it must be sought out and found in social developments below the political surface.   Other writers, he notes, have shown a preference for the urban trade unions as the source of grass roots enthusiasms ; for Kenya he himself identifies the rural anti-colonial resentments of the 1950s as a crucial phase—but feels bound to explain the absence of such discontents earlier in the period.

' Here is another part of the explanation of the apparent African passivity in the inter-war years : it could well be argued that colonial administrations had not placed serious burdens on the peasant prior to these rural development schemes ' (p. 212).

Perhaps this may be regarded as a recognition that a full continuity of large-scale anti-colonial sentiment is not always to be found.   At all events, his Dar es Salaam colleagues—Gwassa, Iliffe and Temu—appear still to be convinced of the existence of a ' missing link ' between early resistance and TANU nationalism in Tanzania ; while Roberts would like to push back the roots of resistance on a national scale well into the nineteenth century.

Conclusion

So far, the criticism may be illustrated by analogy.   Let us assume that Dar es Salaam includes not only the surface area but also the earth beneath, right to the centre of the world.   A study of Dar es Salaam would therefore involve a study of the whole segment.   It would have to be assumed that each layer was related to the surface, rather than to equivalent layers under neighbouring cities. The new historiography in Tanzania makes similar assumptions, and the present surface area of Tanzania is assumed to unify not only the present but also the past, stretching back to the mists of man's origins.   The inclusion of Dr Sutton's valuable archaeological work lends unusual force to the maxim ' he who controls the present controls the past. '   Since the subject is assumed to have continuity and consistency, only those factors observable in the present can possibly be regarded as important in the past, and these are the factors which contribute towards the consistency and continuity of the whole.   Intruding groups by definition are of no greater relevance than a geological fault.   However, just as urban geography may mislead geologists, so observation of the present may mislead the historian.   The themes which have been selected and explored have been regarded from a rather narrow point of view : the world context, the wider African context, the imperial context, the district context, have all been subordinated to the national context.

The nationalist point of view, as Professor Ranger has indicated, would make little sense if nationalism in a particular state were either a very recent growth, or

18

only a surface phenomenon.   He anticipates, as we have seen, a great coming debate between his own school and the Fanonesque 'radical pessimists'.   There will certainly be other points of view as well, and it is worth enquiring whether the Dar es Salaam school is equipped to enter the debate.

Scholars who regard the outside world's interventions in Africa as having achieved more than nationalism, and who consider that colonialism has been replaced very frequently by neo-colonialism rather than national independence, are not likely to be convinced by the implication that colonial policy was of scant significance even during the colonial years.   They might well regard nationalist historians as providing pie in the past rather than an understanding of present problems.   Scholars who regard pan-African sentiment on the one hand, or particularist sentiment on the other, as having at times been more far-reaching in their effects than national sentiment, can still point to much evidence from the 1950s when many of the upheavals that profoundly affected the attitudes of colonial authorities were particularist rather than national in inspiration. Scholars who regard colonialism as a matter of interplay rather than simply imperial domination, can still argue that German policy in East Africa was influenced by African risings in South-West Africa ; that British policy in East Africa as a whole was influenced by Mau Mau, by Ghana's independence, and even by the independence of India and Pakistan.   They may well consider inadequate the apparent nationalist view that imperial policy in a particular African colony was determined primarily by events within that colony.   These are but some of the points of view likely to be expressed when a debate commences, and a reading of the publications of Dar es Salaam scholars does not disarm such other scholars in advance.

So far, nationalist historians have been protected by the fact that the ideological content and overtones of their writings are widely shared by other Africanist scholars.   The International Congress of African Historians held at Dar es Salaam in 1965 (and whose papers are published as *Emerging Themes of African History*) passed a series of resolutions.   Resolution 8 (p. 218) reads as follows :

'That an African philosophy of history which would serve as a liberation from the colonial experience must be a vital concern of all historians studying in Africa.'

We may perhaps consider this resolution to be the ideological charter of the writings.   It is tactically difficult to criticise the publications, since they raise the presumption that disagreement is either anti-national or anti-African.

One of the few people so placed as to be able to comment without fear of criticism on ideological grounds is President Nyerere.   According to press reports, when he was formally presented with a copy of *A History of Tanzania*,

'he called upon African historians to refrain from exaggerating historic facts about Africa simply because their alien counterparts played them down or excluded them from their writings in the pre-independence period .... He

said that impartiality was important in the production of a succint and authentic history of Africa. '[29]

Our point could hardly be made better, or more authoritatively.

To sum up, our argument is that the new historiography has adopted the
political philosophy of current African nationalism, and has used it to inform the
study of African history. That commitment inclines the school towards
rhetoric in defence of narrowly selected themes and interpretations, and the
stereotyping and total rejection of alternative views. We suggest also that the
basic assumption regarding the continuity and impact of national movements is
questionable, and is asserted rather than demonstrated. In short, this is
ideological history.

It is significant that Professor Ranger identifies the main threat to the ' new
orthodoxy' in another ideology, Fanonism. We hope that he is wrong. The
real threat should be from disinterested scholars. African history is too important to be left to politicians. The African historian should be committed to
writing the truth, rather than the politic half-truth. Future generations in
Africa will be better served if the highest standards of scholarship are maintained, than if a lesser burden of proof be required for African history.

29. *East African Standard*, 11 November, 1969.

A SHORT BIBLIOGRAPHY OF MAIN EAST AFRICAN WORKS DISCUSSED OR MENTIONED

ALPERS, E. A.: ' The Coast and the Development of the Caravan Trade ', *in*
        Kimambo and Temu (1969).

CLIFFE, L.: ' From Independence to Self-Reliance ', *in* Kimambo and Temu
        (1969).

GWASSA, G. C. K.: ' The German Intervention and African Resistance in Tan-
        zania ', *in* Kimambo and Temu (1969).

ILIFFE, J.: *Tanganyika under German Administration*, 1906-12 (Cambridge, 1969).
        ' The Age of Improvement and Differentiation, 1907-45 ',
        in Kimambo and Temu (1969).

KIMAMBO, I. N.: *A Political History of the Pare* (Nairobi, 1970). ' The Interior
        before 1800 ', *in* Kimambo and Temu (1969). ' The Pare ',
        in Roberts (1968).

KIMAMBO, I. N. and TEMU, A. J., (eds.): *A History of Tanzania* (Nairobi, 1969).

LONSDALE, J.: ' The Emergence of African Nations ', *in* Ranger (1968). Also
        published in a revised form in *African Affairs*, **67**, 266 (January,
        1968). ' Some Origins of Nationalism in East Africa ', *J. Af.
        History*, **9**, 2 (1968).

MOSARE, J.: ' Background to Revolution in Zanzibar ', *in* Kimambo and Temu
        (1969).

RANGER, T. O. (ed.): *Emerging Themes of African History* (Nairobi, 1968). *The
        African Churches of Tanzania*, (Nairobi, n.d.). ' The Move-
        ment of Ideas, 1850-1939 ', *in* Kimambo and Temu (1969).
        ' African Reactions of the Imposition of Colonial Rule in East

20

and Central Africa ', *in Colonialism in Africa*, edited by L. Gann and P. Duignan, (Cambridge, 1969).

ROBERTS, A. D.: ' The Nyamwezi ', *in* Roberts (1968). ' Political Change in the Nineteenth Century ', *in* Kimambo and Temu (1969).

(ed.) *Tanzania Before* 1900 (Nairobi, 1968).

SUTTON, J. E. G.: ' The Peopling of Tanzania ', *in* Kimambu and Temu (1969).

TEMU, A. J.: ' The Rise and Triumph of Nationalism ', *in* Kimambo and Temu (1969).

21

SOCIOLOGIE POLITIQUE
DE L'AFRIQUE NOIRE

I. WALLERSTEIN
Columbia University

Ethnicity and National Integration in West Africa[1]

Many writers on West Africa, whether academic or popular, assert that there is currently a conflict between tribalism and nationalism which threatens the stability of the new West African nations. In fact, the relationship between tribalism and nationalism is complex. Although ethnicity (tribalism) is in some respects dysfunctional for national integration (a prime objective of nationalist movements), it is also in some respects functional. Discussion of the presumed conflict might be clarified by discussing this hypothesis in some detail. Before doing so, it should be noted that we deliberately use the term ethnicity in preference to tribalism, and we shall preface our remarks by carefully defining our use of the term ethnicity.

In a traditional, rural setting, an individual is a member first of all of a family and then of a tribe.[2] The demands the tribe makes on him vary with the complexity of the tribal system of government,[3] as does the degree to which family and tribal loyalties are distinct. To a large extent, however, family and tribal loyalties support each other harmoniously.

---

[1] Revised version of a paper delivered at the Annual Meeting of the American Sociological Society, 1959.
[2] A tribe is what Murdock calls a community, and he notes: "The community and the nuclear family are the only social groups that are genuinely universal. They occur in every known human society..." (G. Murdock, *Social Structure*, New York, Macmillan, 1949, p. 79.)
[3] Statements on the typologies of tribal organizations in Africa are to be found in: M. Fortes and E. Evans-Pritchard, ed., *African Political Systems*, Oxford, 1940; — J. Middleton and D. Tait, *Tribes without Rulers*, London, 1958; — D. Forde, "The Conditions of Social Development in West Africa", in *Civilisations*, III, No. 4, 1953, pp. 472-476.

9

Under colonial rule, the social change brought about by European administrators and the process of urbanization has led to widespread shifts of loyalty. This process has been called "detribalization". Writers speaking of tribal loyalty often confuse three separate phenomena which it would be useful to distinguish: loyalty to the family; loyalty to the tribal community; and loyalty to the tribal government, or chief.[4] Often what a writer means by detribalization is simply a decline in chiefly authority. It does not necessarily follow that an individual who is no longer loyal to his chief has rejected as well the tribe as a community to which he owes certain duties and from which he expects a certain security.[5]

It may be objected that West Africans do not make a distinction between the tribal government and the tribal community. This is perhaps true in the rural areas but they do when they reach the city. For in the city they find that there are new sources of power and prestige which, for many persons, are more rewarding than the tribal government. Hence they tend to lose some of their respect for the authority of the chief. The tribe, however, still can play a useful, if partially new, function as an ethnic group. The *Gemeinschaft*-like community to which the individual belongs may no longer be exactly the same group as before; the methods of government are different; the role in the national social structure is different. This community, however, bears sufficient resemblance to the rural, traditional "tribe" that often the same term is used. In this discussion, however, we shall use "tribe" for the group in the rural areas, and ethnic group for the one in the towns.

Some writers have challenged the very existence of detribalization. Rouch, for example, says he finds instead "supertribalization" among the Zabrama and other immigrants to Ghana.[6] For as Mitchell has commented of another part of Africa: "People in

---

[4] We shall not discuss further the role of the family in West Africa today. We note here that it would be an oversimplification to suggest that family ties have drastically declined in the urban areas. In any case, the strength of family ties can vary independently of the strength of tribal ties.

[5] There are, to be sure, cases where the two loyalties decline together, and there is consequently severe anomy. Failure to distinguish this case from one in which primarily loyalty to the chief alone diminishes can result in much confusion. See this comment by Mercier in which he tries to clarify this confusion: "C'est dans cette minorité [la population saisonnière] que l'on peut parler réellement de faits de *détribalisation*, au sens de pure dégradation du rôle des anciens cadres sociaux. Au contraire, nous avons vu que, dans la population permanente, *les structures de parenté et l'appartenance ethnique* jouaient un rôle considérable." (P. Mercier, "Aspects de la société africaine dans l'agglomération dakaroise : groupes familiaux et unités de voisinage", p. 39, in P. Mercier et al., "L'Agglomération Dakaroise", in *Études sénégalaises*, No. 5, 1954.)

[6] J. Rouch, "Migrations au Ghana", in *Journal de la Société des Africanistes* XXVI, No. 1/2, 1956, pp. 163-164.

rural areas are apt to take their tribe for granted, but when they come to the town their tribal membership assumes new importance."[7] This is, however, a false debate. We shall see that quite often the group from which the individual is "detribalized" (that is, the tribe to whose chief he no longer pays the same fealty) is not necessarily the same group into which he is "supertribalized" (that is, the ethnic group to which he feels strong bonds of attachment in the urban context).

Membership in an ethnic group is a matter of social definition, an interplay of the self-definition of members and the definition of other groups. The ethnic group seems to need a minimum size to function effectively, and hence to achieve social definition.[8] Now it may be that an individual who defined himself as being of a certain tribe in a rural area can find no others from his village in the city. He may simply redefine himself as a member of a new and larger group.[9] This group would normally correspond to some logical geographical or linguistic unit, but it may never have existed as a social entity before this act.

Indeed, this kind of redefinition is quite common. Two actions give such redefinition permanence and status. One is official government sanction, in the form of census categories,[10] or the recognition of "town chiefs"; the other is the formation of ethnic (tribal) associations which are described more accurately by the French term, *association d'originaires*. These associations are the principal form of ethnic (tribal) "government"[11] in West African towns today.

Some of these ethnic associations use clearly territorial bases of defining membership, despite the fact that they may consider their

[7] J. C. Mitchell, "Africans in Industrial Towns in Northern Rhodesia", in *H.R.H. The Duke of Edinburgh's Study Conference*, No. 1, p. 5.
[8] Mercier observes: "Il faut noter également que, moins un groupe ethnique est numériquement important dans la ville, plus la simple parenté tend à jouer le rôle de liens de parenté plus proches." (*Op. cit.*, p. 22.)
[9] In Dakar, Mercier notes: "Un certain nombre de personnes qui étaient manifestement d'origine Lébou... se déclaraient cependant Wolof, preuve de la crise de l'ancien particularisme Lébou." (*Op. cit.*, p. 17.)
[10] For example, G. Lasserre writes: "L'habitude est prise à Libreville de recenser ensemble Togolais et Dahoméens sous l'appellation de 'Popo'." (*Libreville*, Paris, Armand Colin, 1958, p. 207.)
Epstein notes a similar phenomenon in the Northern Rhodesian Copper-belt towns, where one of the major ethnic groups, sanctioned by custom and by census, is the Nyasalanders. Nyasaland is a British-created territorial unit, but people from the Henga, Tonga, Tumbuka, and other tribes are by common consent grouped together as Nyasalanders. (A. L. Epstein, *Politics in an Urban African Community*, Manchester, Manchester University Press, 1958, p. 236.)
[11] By government we mean here the mechanism whereby the norms and goals of the group are defined. There may or may not be an effective, formal structure to enforce these norms.

relationship with traditional chiefs as their *raison d'être*. For example, in the Ivory Coast, Amon d'Aby has described the process as follows:

"L'un des phénomènes les plus curieux enregistrés en Côte d'Ivoire au lendemain de la Libération est la tendance très marquée des élites autochtones vers la création d'associations régionales...

"Ces associations groupent tous les habitants d'un cercle ou de plusieurs cercles réunis. Leur objet est non plus le sport et les récréations de toutes sortes comme les groupements anodins d'avant-guerre, mais le progrès du territoire de leur ressort. Elles ont le but d'apporter la collaboration des jeunes générations instruites aux vieilles générations représentées par les chefs coutumiers accrochés aux conceptions périmés, à une politique surannée."[12]

It should be observed that the administrative units in question (les cercles) are the creation of the colonial government, and have no necessary relationship to traditional groupings. Such ethnic associations, formed around non-traditional administrative units, are found throughout West Africa.[13] A presumably classic example of the significance of tribalism in West African affairs is the role which traditional Yoruba-Ibo rivalry has played in Nigeria politics. Yet, Dr. S. O. Biobaku has pointed out that the very use of the term "Yoruba" to refer to various peoples in Western Nigeria resulted largely from the influence of the Anglican mission in Abeokuta in the 19th century. The standard "Yoruba" language evolved by the mission was the new unifying factor. Hodgkin remarks:

"Everyone recognizes that the notion of 'being a Nigerian' is a new kind of conception. But it would seem that the notion of 'being a Yoruba' is not very much older."[14]

Sometimes, the definition of the ethnic group may even be said to derive from a common occupation—indeed, even dress—rather than

---

[12] F. Amon d'Aby, *La Côte d'Ivoire dans la cité africaine*, Paris, Larose, 1952, p. 36.

[13] Similar phenomena were reported in other areas undergoing rapid social change. Lewis reports the growth in Somalia of a "tribalism founded on territorial ties [in] place of clanship," at least among the southern groups (I. M. Lewis, "Modern Political Movements in Somaliland, I", in *Africa*, XXVIII, July 1958, p. 259). In the South Pacific, Mead observes: "Commentators on native life shook their heads, remarking that these natives were quite incapable of ever organizing beyond the narrowest tribal borders, overlooking the fact that terms like 'Solomons', 'Sepiks' or 'Manus', when applied in Rabaul, blanketed many tribal differences." (M. Mead, *New Lives for Old*, New York, Morrow, 1956, p. 79.) The article by Max Gluckman, which appeared since this paper was delivered, makes the same point for British Central Africa. Cf. "Tribalism in British Central Africa", in *Cahiers d'Études Africaines*, I, janv. 1960, pp. 55-70.

[14] T. Hodgkin, "Letter to Dr. Biobaku", in *Odù*, No. 4, 1957, p. 42.

from a common language or traditional polity. For example, an Accra man often tends to designate all men (or at least all merchants) coming from savannah areas as "Hausamen", although many are not Hausa, as defined in traditional Hausa areas.[15] Similarly, the Abidjan resident may designate these same men as Dioula.[16] Such designations may originate in error, but many individuals from savannah areas take advantage of this confusion to merge themselves into this grouping. They go, for example to live in the *Sabon Zongo* (the Hausa residential area), and even often adopt Islam, to aid the assimilation.[17] They do so because, scorned by the dominant ethnic group of the town, they find security within a relatively stronger group (Hausa in Accra, Dioula in Abidjan, Bambara in Thiès), with whom they feel some broad cultural affinity. Indeed, assimilation to this stronger group may represent considerable advance in the prestige-scale for the individual.[18]

Thus we see that ethnic groups are defined in terms that are not necessarily traditional but are rather a function of the urban social situation. By ethnicity, we mean the feeling of loyalty to this new ethnic group of the towns. Epstein has urged us to distinguish between two senses of what he calls "tribalism": the intratribal, which is the "persistence of, or continued attachment to, tribal custom", and tribalism within the social structure, which is the "persistence of loyalties and values, which stem from a particular form of social organization".[19] This corresponds to the distinction we made above between loyalty to tribal government and loyalty to the tribal community. In using the term ethnicity, we are referring to this latter kind of loyalty. This distinction cannot be rigid. Individuals in West Africa move back and forth between city and rural area. Different loyalties may be activated in different contexts. But more and more, with increasing urbanization, loyalty to the ethnic community is coming to supersede loyalty to the tribal

---

[15] Rouch, *op. cit.*, p. 59.
[16] A. Kobben, "Le planteur noir", in *Études éburnéennes*, V, 1956, p. 154.
[17] The religious conversion is often very temporary. N'Goma observes: "L'Islam résiste mal à la transplantation des familles musulmanes de la ville à la campagne. On a remarqué que le citadin qui retourne à son groupement d'origine revient souvent au culte de la terre et des Esprits ancestraux." (A. N'Goma, "L'Islam noir", in T. Monod, ed., *Le Monde noir*, Présence africaine, No. 8-9, p. 342.) The motive for the original conversion may in part explain this rapid reconversion.
[18] G. Savonnet observes in Thiès, Sénégal: "Le nom de Bambara est employé généralement pour désigner le Soudanais (qu'il soit Khassonké, Sarakollé, ou même Mossi). Ils acceptent d'autant plus volontiers cette dénomination que le Bambara (comme tout à l'heure le Wolof) fait figure de race évoluée par rapport à la leur propre." ("La Ville de Thiès", in *Études sénégalaises*, No. 6, 1955, p. 149.)
[19] Epstein, *op. cit.*, p. 231.

community and government. It is the relationship of this new ethnic loyalty to the emergent nation-state that we intend to explore here.

*
* *

There are four principal ways in which ethnicity serves to aid national integration. First, ethnic groups tend to assume some of the functions of the extended family and hence they diminish the importance of kinship roles; two, ethnic groups serve as a mechanism of resocialization; three, ethnic groups help keep the class structure fluid, and so prevent the emergence of castes; fourth, ethnic groups serve as an outlet for political tensions.

First, in a modern nation-state, loyalties to ethnic groups interfere less with national integration than loyalties to the extended family. It is obvious that particularistic loyalties run counter to the most efficient allocation of occupational and political roles in a state. Such particularistic loyalties cannot be entirely eliminated. Medium-sized groups based on such loyalties perform certain functions —of furnishing social and psychological security—which cannot yet in West Africa by performed either by the government or by the nuclear family. In the towns, the ethnic group is to some extent replacing the extended family in performing these functions.

The role of the ethnic group in providing food and shelter to the unemployed, marriage and burial expenses, assistance in locating a job has been widely noted.[20] West African governments are not yet in a position to offer a really effective network of such services, because of lack of resources and personnel. Yet if these services would not be provided, widespread social unrest could be expected.

It is perhaps even more important that ethnic associations counter the isolation and anomy that uprooted rural immigrants feel in the city. Thus Balandier has noted in Brazzaville the early emergence of ethnic associations tends to indicate a high degree of uprootedness among the ethnic group, which tends to be found particularly in small minorities.[21]

[20] Mercier notes: "Nombreux sont ceux qui, dans l'actuelle crise de chômage, ne peuvent se maintenir en ville que grâce à l'aide de leurs parents. Cela aboutit à une forme spontanée d'assurance contre le chômage." (Op. cit., p. 26.)
See also passim, K. A. Busia, Report on a Social Survey of Sekondi-Takoradi, Accra, Government Printer, 1950; I. Acquah, Accra Survey, London, University of London Press, 1958; O. Dollfus, "Conakry en 1951-1952. Etude humaine et économique", in Études guinéennes, X-XI, 1952, pp. 3-111; J. Lombard, "Cotonou, ville africaine", in Études dahoméennes, X, 1953.
[21] G. Balandier, Sociologie des Brazzavilles noires, Paris, Armand Colin, 1955, p. 122.

But from the point of view of national integration is the ethnic group really more functional than the extended family? In the sense that the ethnic group, by extending the extended family, dilutes it, the answer is yes. The ties are particularistic and diffuse, but less so and less strong than in the case of kinship groups. Furthermore, such a development provides a precedent for the principle of association on a non-kinship basis. It can be seen perhaps as a self-liquidating phase on the road to the emergence of the nuclear family.[22] Thus, it can be said with Parsons, that ethnic groups "constitute a focus of security beyond the family unit which is in some respects less dysfunctional for the society than community solidarity would be."[23]

The second function suggested was that of resocialization. The problem of instructing large numbers of persons in new normative patterns is a key one for nations undergoing rapid social change. There are few institutions which can perform this task. The formal educational system is limited in that it is a long-range process with small impact on the contemporary adult population. In addition, universal free education, though the objective of all West African governments at the present time, is not yet a reality in any of these countries. The occupational system only touches a small proportion of the population, and a certain amount of resocialization is a prerequisite to entry into it. The government is limited in services as well as in access to the individuals involved (short of totalitarian measures). The family is in many ways a bulwark of resistance to change.

The ethnic groups, touching almost all the urban population, can then be said to be a major means of resocialization. They aid this process in three ways. The ethnic group offers the individual a wide network of persons, often of very varying skills and positions, who are under some obligation to retrain him and guide him in the ways of urban life.

By means of ethnic contacts, the individual is recruited into many non-ethnic nationalist groupings. Apter found evidence of this in Ghana, where he observed a remarkable number of classificatory brothers and other relatives working together in the same party, kinship thus providing a "reliable organizational core in the nationalist movement."[24] Birmingham and Jahoda similarly

[22] Forde suggests that "This multiplicity of association, which is characteristic of the Westernisation procedure, is likely to preclude the functional persistence of tribal organisations as autonomous units in the economic or political sphere." (*Op. cit.*, p. 485.)
[23] T. Parsons, *The Social System*, Glencoe, Free Press, 1951, p. 188.
[24] D. Apter, *The Gold Coast in Transition*, Princeton, Princeton University Press, 1955, p. 127.

suggest the hypothesis that kinship (read, ethnic) links mediated Ghana political affiliation.[25]

And lastly, members of the ethnic group seek to raise the status of the whole group, which in turn makes it more possible for the individual members to have the mobility and social contact which will speed the process of resocialization.[26]

The third function is the maintenance of a fluid class system. There is in West Africa, as there has been historically in the United States, some correlation between ethnic groups and social class, particularly at the lower rungs of the social ladder. Certain occupations are often reserved for certain ethnic groups.[27] This occurs very obviously because of the use of ethnic ties to obtain jobs and learn skills.

It would seem then that ethnicity contributes to rigid stratification. But this view neglects the normative context. One of the major values of contemporary West African nations is that of equality. Individuals may feel helpless to try to achieve this goal by their own efforts. Groups are less reticent, and as we mentioned before, its members usually seek to raise the status of the group. The continued expansion of the exchange economy means continued possibility of social mobility. As long as social mobility continues, this combination of belief in equality and the existence of ethnic groups striving to achieve it for themselves works to minimize any tendency towards caste-formation. This is crucial to obtain the allocation of roles within the occupational system on the basis of achievement, which is necessary for a modern economy. Thus, this is a self-reinforcing system wherein occupational mobility contributes to economic expansion, which contributes to urban migration, which contributes to the formation of ethnic associations and then to group upward mobility, which makes possible individual occupational mobility.

The fourth function we suggested was the ethnic groups serve as an outlet for political tensions. The process of creating a nation and legitimating new institutions gives rise to many tensions, especially when leaders cannot fulfill promises made. Gluckman's phrase, the "frailty in authority"[28] is particularly applicable for new nations

---

[25] W. B. Birmingham and G. Jahoda, "A Pre-Election Survey in a Semi-Literate Society", in *Public Opinion Quarterly*, XIX, Summer, 1955, p. 152.
[26] Glick explains the role of Chinese ethnic groups in Chinese assimilation into Hawaiian society in just these terms. (C. Glick, "The Relationship between Position and Status in the Assimilation of Chinese in Hawaii", in *American Journal of Sociology*, XLVII, September, 1952, pp. 667-679.)
[27] P. Mercier, "Aspects des problèmes de stratification sociale dans l'Ouest Africain", in *Cahiers internationaux de sociologie*, XVII, 1954, pp. 47-55; Lombard, *op. cit.*, pp. 57-59.
[28] M. Gluckman, *Custom and Conflict in Africa*, Oxford, Basil Blackwell, 1955, ch. 2.

not yet secure in the loyalty of their citizens.   We observed before that ethnic groups offered social security because the government could not.   Perhaps we might add that this arrangement would be desirable during a transitional period, even were it not necessary. If the state is involved in too large a proportion of the social action of the individual, it will be burdened by concentrated pressure and demands which it may not be able to meet.   It may not yet have the underlying diffuse confidence of the population it would need to survive the non-fulfilment of these demands.[29]   It may therefore be of some benefit to divert expectations from the state to other social groups.

The existence of ethnic groups performing "an important scape-goat function as targets for displaced aggression"[30] may permit individuals to challenge persons rather than the authority of the office these persons occupy.   Complaints about the nationalist party in power are transformed into complaints about the ethnic group or groups presumably in power.   This is a common phenomenon of West African politics, and as Gluckman suggests:

"These rebellions, so far from destroying the established social order [read, new national governments] work so that they even support this order.   They resolve the conflicts which the frailty in authority creates."[31]

Thus, in rejecting the men, they implicitly accept the system. Ethnic rivalries become rivalries for political power in a non-tribal setting.

*
* *

The dysfunctional aspects of ethnicity for national integration are obvious.   They are basically two.   The first is that ethnic groups are still particularistic in their orientation and diffuse in their obligations, even if they are less so than the extended family. The ethnic roles are insufficiently segregated from the occupational and political roles because of the extensiveness of the ethnic group. Hence we have the resulting familiar problems of nepotism and corruption.

The second problem, and one which worries African political leaders more, is separatism, which in various guises is a pervasive

---

[29] Unless, of course, it compensate for lack of legitimation by increase of force as a mechanism of social control, which is the method used in Communist countries.
[30] Parsons, *op. cit.*, p. 188.
[31] Gluckman, *op. cit.*, p. 28.

tendency in West Africa today.[32]   Separatist moves may arise out of a dispute between élite elements over the direction of change. Or they may result from the scarcity of resources which causes the "richer" region to wish to contract out of the nation (e.g., Ashanti in Ghana, the Western Region in Nigeria, the Ivory Coast in the ex-federation of French West Africa).   In either case, but especially the latter, appeals to ethnic sentiment can be made the primary weapon of the separatists.

In assessing the seriousness of ethnicity as dysfunctional, we must remember that ethnic roles are not the only ones West Africans play.   They are increasingly bound up in other institutional networks which cut across ethnic lines.   Furthermore, the situation may vary according to the number and size of ethnic groupings.   A multiplicity of small groups is less worrisome, as Coleman reminds us, than those situations where there is one large, culturally strong group.[33]

The most important mechanism to reduce the conflict between ethnicity and national integration is the nationalist party.   Almost all of the West African countries have seen the emergence of a single party which has led the nationalist struggle, is now in power, and dominates the local political scene.[34]

In the struggle against colonial rule, these parties forged a unity of Africans as Africans.   To the extent that the party structure is well articulated (as, say, in Guinea) and is effective, both in terms of large-scale program and patronage, the party does much to contain separatist tendencies.

Linguistic integration can also contribute, and here European languages are important.   It is significant that one of the Ghana government's first steps after independence was to reduce the number of years in which primary schooling would be in the vernacular.   Instruction in English now begins in the second year. We might mention, too, that Islam and Christianity both play a role in reducing centrifugal tendencies.

Lastly, there is the current attempt to endow pan-Africanism with the emotional aura of anti-colonialism, the attempt to make Unity as much a slogan as Independence.   Even if the objective of

[32] Separatism, of course, arises as a problem only after a concept of a nation is created and at least partially internalized by a large number of the citizens.

[33] J. S. Coleman, "The Character and Viability of African Political Systems", in W. Goldschmidt, ed., *The United States and Africa*, New York, The American Assembly, 1958, pp. 44-46.

[34] There is normally room for only one truly nationalist party in a new nation.   Other parties in West African countries, when they exist, tend to be formed on more particularistic (ethnic, religious, regional) bases.

unity is not realized, it serves as a counterweight to ethnic separatism that may be very effective.

Thus we see that ethnicity plays a complex role in the contemporary West African scene. It illustrates the more general function of intermediate groups intercalated between the individual and the state, long ago discussed by Durkheim.[35] It points at the same time to the difficulties of maintaining both consensus and unity if these intermediate groups exist.[36]

[35] E. Durkheim, *The Division of Labor in Society*, Glencoe, Free Press, 1947, p. 28.
[36] See the discussion of this problem in S. M. Lipset, "Political Sociology", in R. K. Merton, L. Broom, L. S. Cottrell, Jr., eds., *Sociology Today*, New York, Basic Books, 1959.

THE ROOTS OF AFRICAN DESPOTISM:
THE QUESTION OF POLITICAL CULTURE

Ibrahim K. Sundiata

Early in this decade a political observer, looking at one of Africa's least known and most sanguinary states, described Equatorial Guinea as "Cambodia minus ideology" (Pélissier, 1980:13). During the eleven year presidency (1968-1979) of Francisco Macias Nguema, up to half of the population was liquidated or went into exile. Little is known on the internal workings or ideology of the regime. However, just as we can no longer say that there are peoples without histories, we can no longer assume that there are rulers without ideologies. Much statistical and other information on Equatorial Guinea is fragmentary or missing. It is possible, however, to trace the lineaments of the rise and fall of the first post-independent government. It is the purpose of this essay to examine that development. We shall seek an explanation, although it be a partial one, of the ideological and economic conditions which provided the context for the creation of a mass concentration camp in the tropics.

Since the nineteenth century, the materialist/idealist dichotomy has been at the center of much historiographical debate. A sub-theme has been the role of the individual in history. An increasingly wide range of scholars have used material conditions as the basis for their analysis.[1] The individual is not an automous historical force, but rather represents a class and its interests as the class acts to maintain or establish its hegemony. Others, on the contrary, continue to maintain that the individual can, under certain circumstances, mold history to his or her will. It can and has been maintained that the idiosyncratic behavior of a leader can be an important independent variable in history.[2]

Since the era of rapid African decolonization, various writers have brought idealist or materialist analyses, in various guises, to a discussion of the workings of modern African states. This is most interesting on a continent in which many of the Founding Fathers are still national leaders and in which leadership is often linked with national identity. At one end of the spectrum are those who place great emphasis on the role of the leader in the molding of national policy and direction. At the other are those who see African states and their leadership as largely the outcome of internal class development and, more importantly, their relationship to foreign capital and strategic interests. It can be argued that these positions are not ends of a spectrum since analysis can speak of the role of the leader and, at the same time, emphasize his dependence upon exogenous forces. Although this is true, some recent scholarship emphasizes one to the detriment of the other. This is especially the case with regimes which seem to defy utilitarian notions of political rationality.

The problem with certain contemporary studies is that they simplify African reality. Thus far Equatorial Guinea has been explained largely in terms of the pscyhopathology of its first president. Robert Jackson and Carl Rosberg (1982) place Macias Nguema within the group of African leaders they refer to as "Tyrants":

> Tyranny is a residual type of personal regime into which any or all of the other types may deteriorate. In a tyranny not only legal but also all moral constraints on the exercise of power are absent, with the consequence that power is exercised in a completely arbitray fashion according to the impulses of the ruler and his agents. Historically, tyranny has been marked by particularly impulsive, oppressive, and brutal rule that has lacked elementary respect -- and has sometimes shown complete disdain -- not only for the rights of persons and property but also for the very sancity of human life.

Jackson and Rosberg maintain, perhaps more than they would like to, that varieties of personal rule are independent of the material conditions in the rulers' states. "When we inquire," they say "into the relation between a type of personal rule and the underlying socioecomomic environment in African countries, we are struck by a lack of correlation rather than by their interdependence." The "man in history" is central: "The political factors that seem most to affect the type of personal system that emerges are the dispositions, activities, abilities, efforts, and fortunes of the key actors; the system is largely their political handiwork." They conclude that "In sum, whether abusive rule or constructive forms of personal rulership are practiced in a country depends less on underlying social conditions and more on the political actors, who must govern without institutions to assist them."

In the case of Equatorial Guinea, they specifically state that the behavior of Macias Nguema had little to do with underlying economic or sociological causes: "It is quite evident that the tyrannies of Amin in Uganda and Macias in Equatorial Guinea were brought about by the rulers' paranoid fears of the powers of others, but neither Uganda nor Equatorial Guinea had to experience it and their abusive rule for any compelling sociological reason" (Jackson and Rosberg, 1982:76). Furthermore, "Excluding insanity, amorality--contempt for the rights, property, and persons of powerless individuals and a pure power hunger—is the only explanation that can begin to make sense of the unspeakable actions of a Tyrant."

It is true that the reign of terror that was Macias Nguema's rule was not inevitable. On the other hand, to see "pure power hunger" resulting in "unspeakable actions" leaves the most important questions unanswered: If the actions of such leaders simply represent the acting out of individual power lust, by what ledgermain do they induce at least a segment of the population to go along with their utter "contempt for the rights, property, and persons of powerless individuals and a pure power hunger"? If such an explanation is valid, it must ultimately fall back on a adherence to brute force largely divorced from socioeconomic costs and benefits. Taken to its conclusion, it posits a type of collective hysteria.

Ali Mazrui approaches this position when he speaks of the "Warrior Tradition in Africa." He places present-day African tyrants within "a tradition which has at times collapsed in exhaustion under the terrors of white hegemony, but which also had its moments of resurrection." In such a tradition violence "sometimes assumes a disproportionate air of sacredness and mystique. Manhood becomes equated with capacity for ruthlessness, as well as with potential for virility" (Mazrui, 1975b: 84). In this case, the argument comes close to one for African atavism. The explanation for despotic dictatorships in Africa rests on factors of social psychology rooted in the "primordial" conditions of the precolonial past.

African Marxists such as Samir Amin (1974), Mahmud Mamdani, and Wadada Nabudere have attempted to apply class analyis to Africa. Mamdani very rightly acknowledges that the problems of Uganda had "been personalized as the problem of Idi Amin, who is presented as some sort of anthropological oddity" (Mamdani, 1976:vii). He sees the problem of post-independence Uganda as the result of class struggle in which the African "petty bourgeoisie" sought to advance its position after the 1971 coup through collaboration with Amin, who originally seemed to present their interests. Nabudere maintains a similar position and notes that "Bogged down in idealist obscurantism, it [i.e., bourgeois social science] cannot explain the reality" (Nabudere, 1980: i). Like Mamdani, he views the triumph of Amin as the triumph of an internationalized neocolonialism acting in tandem with an indigenous comprador bourgeoisie.

The works of these scholars and others are important antidotes to the tendency to view certain African regimes as personal idiosyncracies write large. At the same time, their use of a limited vocabulary to describe class relations limits their ability to perceive of society and its struggles as a whole. Neither talks in detail about precolonial ideology and both seem to assume that, with the rise of new classes, traditional political ideology withered away. This rather mechanistic approach, too, is fraught with dangers. The Marxist historian Eugene Genovese argues persuasively that "Psychology and ideology are...as much a part of class formation as economic interest." New modes of production, with attendent new relations of production, do not immediately destroy pre-existing ideologies; ideology does not simply reflects material interests, which fluctuate sharply. Therefore "The historical task...is two-fold: to relate satisfactorily the psychological, material, and other aspects of society to each other in such a way as to present reality as an integrated social process; and to avoid a sterile functionalism by uncovering the fundamental pattern of human relationships conditioning both material and spiritual life" (Genovese, 1969: 245).

In his African case, Mamdani acknowledges that he employs class terms derived from elsewhere (e.g., bourgeoisie). He also recognizes that "class formation is a process, and one should not expect to find *pure* forms in reality. Furthermore, *transitional* forms must be analyzed as a moment in a historical process" (Mamdani, 1976: 10). It is perhaps the pace of the process which he and his compeers have overlooked. If classes are changing and not yet changed, it also stands to reason that pre-existing ideologies remain among those in the process of becoming. Materialism devoid of any mention of the non-European political ideology, is bound to fail to explain the ideological variable, which, to some extent, explains African perceptions of enemies and the limits of power.

THE STRUCTURE OF THE COLONIAL ECONOMY

Because class formation is a process and because the changes created by the penetration of capital vary greatly in time, it takes on added importance. Uneven development has characterized the development of many an African state. Stark (1986: 345) observes that "Marxist theorists have been fully aware of the external 'constraints,' and hence they may have been preoccuppied with the penetration by colonialism and imperialism of every corner of the new state, and the effect of these conditions on infrastructure, culture, and the shape of the state itself." In former Spanish Guinea it is the lack of capitalist penetration of "every corner of the new state" which explains much its post-independence history. Equatorial Guinea is an extreme case of unequal development within one polity. In one segment, Biyogo, European capital converted much of the indigenous population into subsidized and fairly prosperous farmers dependent upon Igbo migrant labor. In the other segment, Rio Muni, European capital hardly penetrated at all. It is specious to talk of an articulated bourgeoisie, even a comprador one, coming to power in 1968.

Spanish Guinea could be truly touted as a model of colonial development in the late sixties. Sanford Ungar (1985: 414) observed that the country "was expected to capitalize on its European connections... to make early progress as a nation." Biyogo (then Fernando Po) had one of the highest literacy rates in Black Africa. In 1960, exports from Spanish Guinea (of which Biyogo was the mainstay) totaled more than $33,000,000, the highest level of exports per capita in Africa ($135). Ninety percent of the products of Equatorial Guinea were shipped to Spain. The colony's balance of trade was favorable; in 1962 it reached 823 million pesetas (Spanish Information Service, 1964: 28). The production of high quality cocoa reached a total of about 35,000 tons in 1968 (Legum, 1970: 483). Coffee was the second largest export crop; annual production totalled 20,000 tons in 1968. Biyogo, together with the smaller island of Annobon (now Palagu) had an annual per capita income of between $250 and $280. In 1968 the main island was not only an exporter of cocoa, coffee and bananas, but also possessed some processing industries, such as chocolate and soap factories and palm oil works.

The future seemed bright and three petroleum companies were prospecting for oil offshore. On Biyogo statist economic policies, along with oligopolistic manipulation of cocoa and coffee prices, assured invested Spanish capital a handsome return and transformed the previously marginal Bubi population into a dependent and largely complaisant rural farming group. According to the colonial regime, the subsidies and paternal nurturance given to Spanish Guinea led "to the conclusion that the foreign trade of Fernando Po and Rio Muni depends to a great extent on the rest of Spain, and that any drastic change in the present system of exchange would have serious consequences for both territories" (Spanish Information Service, 1964: 51).

The "model" development of Fernando Po contrasted sharply with the relatively neglected development of more populous mainland Rio Muni. The enclave of 10,039 square miles, had a population of approximately 200,000 in 1968, versus 62,612 on the island. In Rio Muni colonial infrastructure and educational services were rudimentary and Spanish military rule was often brutal. Throughout the colonial period, the indigenous Fang resisted attempts to turn them into plantation laborers, preferring to grow cocoa and coffee on their own small plots. Timber was the mainland's only major export (250,000 tons of okoume wood, used in plywood, in 1968) (*Africa Report*, 1969: 26). Its population of fisherman and peasants had an annual per capita income of $40, compared to between $250 and $280 on Biyogo and Palagu. In the 1960s only 3.4 percent of the total #ainland area was cultivated for cash crops, compared with 24.4 percent of the smaller insular area.

Biyogo, on the other hand, was an example of the extreme proletarianization of migrant labor and, in contrast, the embourgeoisement of the indigenous peasantry. The incorporation of the Bubi into agricultural cooperatives employing foreign labor created a situation the reverse of the peasantization witnessed elsewhere in Africa. The inclusion of the Bubi in the colonial economy was reflected in the fact that in 1964 the per capita income of Fernando Po was $246 per annum, "higher than in 19 provinces of Spain and in many countries" (Spanish Information Service, 1964: 12). This achievement was only possible because of the exiguous nature of the indigenous population and the higher than world prices paid for the colony's produce, a measure designed for the benefit of the European planters and companies.

The prosperity of Spanish Guinea in the years following World War II was was a highly manipulated one. Oligopolistic manipulation, at the expense of the metropolitan consumer, was even less questioned than in a bourgeois democratic regime. By the fifties the economic exploitation of the colony was molded by three groups: resident Spanish fingueros, forestry concessionaires, and metropolitan controlled agrobusiness. By the time of independence the price of cocoa was fixed at approximately 150 percent of the going world price. This price fixing yielded members of a government-backed corporatist body, the Cocoa Syndicate, an extra 393,000,000 pesetas (equal to approximately $5,500,000) (Gard, 1973, 129). Colonial lumber was protected by a duty on foreign lumber, which reached 17 percent in 1967. The tariff assured that wood from Spanish Guinea would have a favored place in Peninsular markets. By 1968 the premium paid on coffee from Spanish Guinea was almost 70 percent of the international market price. This premium gained an extra 240,000,000 pesetas or approximately $3,500,000 for Spanish producers. Spanish Guinea was retained as a highly protected preserve for selected capital and was one of the world's most extreme examples of economic dependence.

In 1960 on Biyogo the number of Europeans was 4,170 out of a total insular population of roughly 63,000. On the narrow east, west and north coasts, up to 2,000 feet were almost entirely devoted to their plantations; in 1964, 600 non-African plantations occupied about 90,000 acres (on the average about 150 acres per plantation) and 40,000 acres were occupied by African farms (averaging thirteen acres per farm) (Church, 1977: 287). The Franco regime boasted of the "trickle-down effect" of colonial prosperity. A 1948 property code did leave a niche for the development of an indigenous class of prosperous farmers. Nonemancipated Africans were, as before, restricted to the ownership of four hectares of land. The law did not recognize automatic native ownership beyond the individual's immediate home and garden, but did recognize collective ownership derived from membership in cooperatives and syndicates (Garcia Dominguez, 1977: 55). The first cooperative was founded near Moka in the late 1930s with the aim of acquiring seeds, fertilizer and tools, and organizing the sale and distribution of harvests. By 1967 the number of cooperatives had grown to twenty-eight units (Gard, 1973: 368)

By the sixties many Bubi were characterized as "quasi-literate well housed cocoa farmers proud of their Spanish citizenship" (Howe, 1966: 48). As in Portuguese Africa, colonial policy differentiated between assimilated and nonassimilated Africans. Colonial land policy, which greatly restricted African property rights, combined with intensive missionary Hispanization to encourage agricultural cooperatives and the quest for *emancipado* status. In the decade of independence, the Bubi were approximately 90 percent literate and active, but subordinate, participants in the export economy. In 1952 the *Delegaciones de Asuntos Indigenas* (Delegations of Native Affairs) was established to oversee lands, the buying and selling of harvests, and the making of loans against native lands. The stated paternalistic aim of the *Delegaciones* was to discourage the renting or alienation of land to Europeans and to encourage Bubi agriculture.

Since the vast majority of cocoa and coffee producing land was already in the hands of Europeans, colonial policy simply stabilized the position of a subordinate African cocoa farming group. The resettlement of the Bubi under missionary auspices and their sparseness made it comparatively easy for Spanish agricultural interests to gain possession of their land. Bubi farmers were often persuaded to exchange their plots for less favorable ones to allow the Spaniards to amalgamate farms into large plantations. In return, the large Spanish firms, combines--the *casas fuertes* -often paid a small annual pension to the Bubi and sometimes provided scholarships for their sons to obtain secondary or higher education in Spain. By the late colonial period almost all of the Bubi agriculturalists were in debt to large Spanish commercial firms (Pélissier, 1968: 37).

The peculiar insular demographic situation militated against the transformation of the Bubi into a labor force for the dominant European plantations. Until the 1940s the Bubi declined because of alcoholism and venereal disease. Biyogo was an agricultural "factory," par excellence. The island's agriculturalists used a migrant wage labor force greater than the European and indigenous population combined. In 1942 an agreement was signed governing the recruitment and treatment of Nigerian laborers. The seasonal nature of employment in Nigeria itself, combined with colonial taxation, made the island a natural vent for Igbo migration. In 1941 there were 10,000 Nigerians already in insular Spanish Guinea. In 1942 there were 17,000 (Osuntokun, 1977, 15). Twenty years later 94 percent of the labor force was imported (Gard, 1973: 872).[3]

As mentioned, whereas Spanish capital converted Biyogo into an agricultural factory, its penetration of the mainland lagged. The territory's low population density and the possibility of out-migration into neighboring colonies militated against the introduction of labor-intensive agriculture. The vacillation of various Spanish governments and the continued resistance of the Fang to European penetration meant that the indigenous population's entrance into the money economy was delayed. In 1960 agriculture employed 83 percent of the wage laborers on Biyogo versus only 25 percent of the wage laborers in Rio Muni (Gard, 1973:871).

The situation in Spanish Guinea was compicated by the fact that the black elite was composed not only of civil servants, company personnel, mission employees, teachers, and small-scale entrepreneurs, but also of members of corporatist inspired cooperatives. Many Bubi had risen to prominence within the artificially maintained prosperity of the colonial agricultural economy and their economic security was tied to the maintenance of a special relationship with Spain. The subordinate but privileged position of the Bubi is also reflected in the distribution of cocoa production. In 1964 and 1965, companies based in the metropole were responsible for 36.5 percent of the cocoa crop, while 42.8 percent was produced on lands controlled by Spanish family concerns or resident farmers (Kobel, 1976: 7; Gard, 1973: 150). The residuum (20.7 percent) was, doubtlessly, largely composed of the harvest from Bubi cooperatives.

Silviculture, the backbone of Rio Muni's economy, was not labor intensive. European economic activity was exogenous, both in terms of capital and labor. If the penetration of capital was slow, the incorporation of the population into the colonial economy was even more so. "If it is assumed that all the non-European public labor force was [Equatorial] Guinea's and that the 100,000 subsistence farmers were Guineans, then by 1962 Spanish colonization had brought jobs to 7.1 percent of the employable Guinean population and had given 81.5 percent of the available jobs to non- Guineans" (Gard, 1973: 872). In the enclave, in forestry, cocoa, and coffee planting, the work force was largely imported. In 1962, 68 percent of the labor force consisted of migrant laborers (6,871 Nigerians and 518 others, mostly Cameroonians and Gabonese). Although Rio Muni had a greater land area than Biyogo (10,039 square miles versus 785), the amount of land devoted to the chief export crops was, proportionately, much less. The output per hectare also varied between the island and the enclave. In 1955, 625 kilograms of cocoa per hectare were produced on the island. On the mainland 350 kilograms per hectare were produced in the same year.

Because of the dependence of Spanish Guinea on the metropole for its "prosperity," the assumption was that an independent Equatorial Guinea would continue to rely heavily on Spain in the economic and cultural spheres.[4] This opting for a neocolonialist solution was only arrived at in the second half of the 1960s. Earlier such a solution was far from a foregone conclusion. Indeed, in 1959 Fernando Po and Rio Muni had been proclaimed overseas provinces of Spain, a move reminiscent of the parallel policy of Salazarist Portugal. In the United Nations demands for the independence of Spanish Guinea peaked in the late sixties and, as elsewhere, "Once colonialism lost its legitimacy, the movement for independence could not stop until all colonies that desired it became self-governing-- including even the tiniest statelets" (Jackson and Rosberg, 1986: 10). The decision to grant independence rested on the assumption that Spain could retain major influence over the new economy.

The African elite was deeply divided over the question of greater autonomy and the possibility of future independence (Ndongo Bidyogo, 1977:89-93). Superficially, the cleavage appeared ethnic (Bubi versus Fang). More fundamentally, it represented differences in positions vis-a-vis the colonial economy. On both Biyogo and in Rio Muni, public sector jobs employed a number of Africans, although they were not proportionately well represented throughout the occupational hierarchy. Thirteen percent of the public sector jobs were held by Europeans and the rest were held by Africans. Interestingly for future developments, 2,097 (or three-fifths) of the public employees worked in Rio Muni, while 1,339 (roughly two-fifths) worked on Fernando Po (Gard, 1973: 872). The bureaucratic elite, drawn from the largest ethnic group, the Fang, while often engaging in patron client relationships with European capital, was increasingly cognizant of the fact that the removal of the political status quo would remove the remaining barriers to their political and economic advancement.

Agriculture rather than the bureaucracy was the linkage between the Bubi agriculturalists and the metropolitan capital. It is also significant that, by the 1960s, one of two blacks sitting on the Spanish cocoa marketing board's committee was Enrique Gori Molubela, one of the chief molders of Bubi political opinion and head of the Fernando Po branch of the Territorial Union of Cooperatives. Organized sentiment against closer union with Rio Muni was much in evidence on Biyogo, where a 1963 autonomy statute with unitary tendencies received only 5,340 "yes" votes, versus 7,150 "no" votes (Garcia, 1977: 71). In August of 1964 a formal separatist campaign began with a meeting of the heads of all the Bubi village councils. The meeting produced a petition asking for administrative separation from Rio Muni, a call which was repeated several times in the following years.

THE NEW ECONOMY

Spanish Guinea became the Republic of Equatorial Guinea in the autumn of 1968. Several political parties were created after the autonomy statute. The mainland based groups—the National Union Movement for Equatorial Guinea (MUNGE), National Liberation Movement of Equatorial Guinea (MONALIGE), and Popular Idea of Equatorial Guinea (IPGE)—favored unitary independence, but differed over the issue of ties with Spain. In 1968, after a stormy constitutional debate in Madrid and a popular referendum, elections were held. The winner, after a runoff, in which more popular Fang leaders largely cancelled each other out, was Francisco Macias Nguema. The former colonial bureaucrat from Rio Muni was originally the candidate favored by outside forces: construction companies and "new" Spanish capital which hoped to break the oligopolies dominant in the preindependence period. The latter was to be of more importance in the long run.

Macias Nguema's economic policy was highly erratic. In early pronouncements it called for a middle path between capitalism and socialism and had mild echoes of the Falangist corporatism. Later, at the rhetorical level at least, it became more self-consciously socialist. Crawford Young's assessment (1982:12) that "the whimsy of petty tyrants such as Macias Nguema..., who occasionally used the Marxist lexicon, need [not] be given credence" is basically correct. His militantly anticolonialist position was a reaction to the rigid structuring of the economy in the Franco period and not a commitment to socialism. His desire to avoid the neocolonial solution envisioned in Spanish decolonization entailed a search for allies beyond the narrow circle of oligopolies dominant in 1968. Frank Stark (1986: 342) notes that in Tanzania John Saul "situates the struggle for development and the state *within* the unformed political class 'X', between those of its members who seek to consolidate the neo-colonial era and those who are moved increasingly to challenge the set-up.[5] This would seem especially true of Equatorial Guinea. By the end of 1969, Macias Nguema had broken with the metropolitan oligopolies and their supporters within the African elite. When an early promise of alternative capital development failed, he increasingly turned to the rhetoric, if not the practice of socialism. In the main, however, kickbacks and payments from foreign entrepreneurs constituted the synapse between the state and outside capital (Gard, 1974).

In the period leading up to independence, Antonio Garcia Trevijano, the chief representative of "new capital" was the Maecenas of several political factions, before settling on Macias Nguema. The new chief of state averred that the developmental aims of the country could "only be achieved with the support of foreign capital....We have no preference for any particular source of capital" (Legum, 1971: B504). To offset the dominance of Spanish capital, however, he and his European advisers sought to encourage the entrance of others. In 1969 Garcia Trevijano advised the new president to establish a national bank with funds derived from a widened market for the country's chief cash crop as a result of the Biafran War (Gard, 1974). Various overtures were made to French capital, but without tremendous success.

By 1978 economic relations with Spain had largely come to a standstill, except for those managed through Garcia Trevijano (Fernandez, 1976: 217-18). Long before, Macias Nguema had taken steps to dismantle the economic structure inherited from colonialism. The continued presence of Spanish interests was only at the sufferance of the President, who was increasingly unimpressed by Spanish efforts to placate him. An abortive 1969 coup attempt convinced the President that entrenched Spanish capital was bent on toppling his government. Also, in the aftermath of independence and in an atmosphere of increasing anti-European violence, an exodus of European planters occurred. Many large Spanish firms closed. At the end of 1969, the Equatorial Guinean Development Institute, an organization with a monopoly on foreign trade, was organized at the suggestion of Garcia Trevijano. The Institute was placed under the directorship of Moses Mba Ada and was intended to take the country out of the Spanish economic sphere. It is significant that it was established with funds derived from the confiscation of the monies of Biyogo's agricultural cooperatives. Its establishment was, thus, a way of replacing the syndicate organization which had characterized the colonial period and of striking at the economic base of the Bubi cooperatives. The Institute collapsed in 1972. In 1975 a company designed to import basic necessities and headed by Garcia Trevijano replaced it.

Force played an important part in curbing the centrifugal forces in a hybrid polity. However, because of the regime's dependence on foreign labor for the production of its chief export crop, state terror was, in the final analysis, economically counterproductive. It aided in keeping the island and the mainland together, but it could not ensure a continued flow of migrant labor. Ultimately, force could not guarantee economic viability, since it could not guarantee the stability of the labor force. In 1974 Nigeria reviewed its labor dealings with Equatorial Guinea and noted that laborers had not been paid for periods longer than six months and that local gendarmerie frequently attacked workers (Osuntokun, 1977: 37). In late 1975 and early 1976 the Nigerian government evacuated thousands of its nationals. The exodus crippled an already desperately ill economy.

The government fell back on the rural population as its base and sought, through the manipulation of traditional kinship imagery and symbols, to appeal to it against the remaining handful of black agriculturalists and functionaries. Disregard for the crumbling economy was accompanied by the claim that it was only neocolonialists who complained about shortages of milk, bread, tomatoes, and sugar "which are not typically African foodstuffs" (Klinteberg, 1978: 25).

As early as 1973, the Macias Nguema party proposed to remedy the labor crisis through the recruitment of 60,000 Equatorial Guineans. The following year the party noted that the requisite workers had not been recruited and urged renewed efforts at production for export. Agriculture continued to run down, especially after of the exodus of Nigerian labor. An African journalist reported that "in the countryside, cash crops have been replaced by fields of indian hemp and opium as the regime's answer to economic paralysis" (*West Africa*, 1975: 1198). In 1976 the President-for-Life decreed compulsory labor for all citizens over age fifteen. A year later the number of unpaid workers was put at 45,000 (including dependents), a figure which represented about one-fifth of the population remaining in the country (Pélissier, 1980:11). These measures did not overcome the desperate downward slide of the economy. As it unravelled, few statistics were kept (most statisticians had fled or fallen afoul of the regime). It is estimated, however, that cocoa production fell from 40,000 tons at independence to approximately 3,000 tons in 1978. Except for coffee (a few hundred tons), the export economy had collapsed by early 1979. The income per capita fell from $170 at the end of 1967 to not more than $70 in 1975 (Liniger-Goumaz, 1979: 18).

Macias Nguema's triumph represented the failure of a black petty bourgeoisie to establish its hegemony in an area of limited capital penetration. This comprador role planned for Macias Nguema by Garcia Trevijano should not lead to the hypostatization of a comprador bourgeoisie. The government, after seeking non-Spanish capital, turned to autarchy rooted in the traditional economy. While some members of the clique around the President sought to enrich themselves through comprador arrangements with foreign capital, the main trend of the regime was away from the embourgeoisement of individuals and groups. It seems to have preferred extortionate relations with foreign businesses. In this it resembled certain African states of the last century.[6] The reassertation of an indigenous bourgeoisie was discouraged, while, at the same time, the power of the center was increased through the use of modern weaponry and foreign troops.

THE STRUCTURE OF THE STATE

The first president of Equatorial Guinea used the instruments of the modern state to mold a new unit appealing to Fang nationalism and disrupting the structures and classes bequeathed by the colonial state (i.e., the metropolitan and resident European bourgeoisies, the black bureacracy, wealthy black cocoa and coffee growers, and the Igbo migrant labor proletariat). He circumvented or cowed traditional rulers and, in the name of African authenticity, replaced them with members of his own clan or subservient members of the marginally employed youth organized in the *Juventud en Marcha con Macias*. The latter proved one of the most important props of the regime. One observer notes that "One of Macias's priorities was the establishment of his own version of the Tontons Macoutes from within the only political party which he allowed to exist" (Sawyer, 1980: 182). The *Juventud* were the most visible agents of the government and they could sustain themselves through the expropriation of goods or persons without official protection. Given the great disparity between the two halves of the Republic, the movement of marginally employed youths to richer areas was both a safety-value and a way of enforcing the will of the President.

In 1970, a year after an abortive coup, the government abolished rival parties and substituted the *Partido Unico Nacional* ("Sole National Party"). Later, the party was rechristened the *Partido Unico Nacional de Trabajadores*, "The Sole National Workers' Party" (PUNT). The 1968 constitution, which had included safeguards for the minorities on Biyogo, fell into desuetude. In 1972 Macias Nguema became President-for-Life and in July of the following year, a new constitution was approved by PUNT and ratified by referendum. A People's National Assembly was to be appointed by PUNT and removed by it at any time. All judges and public prosecutors were nominated by the president. Significantly, those accused of subversion against the state had no rights. Macias was not bound by constitutional considerations under the constitution, although the vice-presidency should have been occupied by an islander. After the fall from grace of Vice-President Edmundo Bosio Dioco, the Bubi was replaced by a Fang from the President's hometown.

Under the dictatorship, there was greater integration in the administration of the island and the enclave. Malabo, as Santa Isabel was renamed in 1973, remained the official capital, but the locus of power shifted to Mongomo, where Macias spent most of his time. Each province was given a "gorci" (*gubernador civil*) and each district was governed by a *delegado gubernativo*. The civilian authority was hemmed in by that of two military officials, one from the National Guard and one from the militia, each of whom commanded detachments of troops. The civilian *delegado* oversaw a subordinate committee composed of the local president of PUNT, the president of the women's section of PUNT, and the president of the youth wing. In theory, the structure was under the control of the party and the military, but responsible to the civilian administration. In reality, the security apparatus was largely autonomous. At the grassroots level, there was increasing domination of traditional structures by Macias' followers; chiefs were replaced by militants selected by Macias (Klinteberg, 1978: 12). *Comités de Base*, composed of the local president of the women's section and the president of the local *Juventud en Marcha con Macias*, existed in every village. One of the committee's chief functions was surveillance and control of movement. Movement was also regulated by checkpoints throughout the country, manned by counterbalanced units of the National Guard and the militia.

THE ROLE OF TERROR

On a rather superficial level, Macias Nguema would seem to bear witness to "the warrior tradition." Such a view would jibe with the frequent analysis of terroristic despotism as the product of the psychopathology. It cannot be denied that he exhibited extremely erratic behavior during his tenure in office. Much of his behavior was capricious. A recognition of this fact does not, however, explain why he was leader of an independent state for more than a decade.

Violence was initially directed at groups who were conspicuously richer and politically dissident, Fang and non-Fang. Liquidations were not based solely on ethnicity, since the President sought to eliminate all Fang politicians who might threaten his leadership.

45

As the regime continued, the circle of repression widened to include greater numbers of all groups beyond the President's coterie. Eventually the circle included intimates from his own terror apparatus.

Political opponents were among the first to feel the vengeance of the regime. In November of 1968 a chief political opponent, Bonifacio Ondo Edu was imprisoned without trial, as were three of his political associates. He was starved and later given the coup de grace in prison. After the abortive putsch of 1969, the ringleader Ndongo Miyone, was killed, as were Saturino Ibongo, Armando Balboa Dougan (member of the legislature and secretary of the National Assembly), Pastor Torao Sikara (president of the National Assembly), and Enrique Gori Molubela (deputy-chairman of the Biyogo provincial council). Many others simply disappeared.

In 1970 the majority of the Bubi politicians on Fernando Po were eliminated. In June of 1974, no less than 118 prisoners were tortured and killed in Bata's central prison. The following year, former Vice-President Edmundo Bosio Dioco committed "suicide" in mysterious circumstances after writing a letter pledging loyalty to "Comrade President-for-Life Francisco Macias" (*West Africa*, 1975: 282). In 1976 the occupation of the Equatorial Guinean embassy in Madrid by exiled students resulted in reprisal killings of their relatives in the Republic. Of the forty-six politicians who attended a Madrid Constitutional Conference in 1967-68, not more than ten were alive at the time of Macias Nguema's fall in 1979. Outside of a few who had died of natural causes, the vast majority had been put to death. The same holds true for the first Legislative Assembly; over two-thirds of its members died violently or disappeared (Artucio, 1980: 44).

Those accused of offenses against the security of the state had no specific rights. The National Guard and the *Juventud* followed no law except the will of the President. Macias Nguema appointed all judges and public prosecutors. Rigid postal censorship, the abolition of passports, and the eventual destruction of canoe traffic from Biyogo reinforced the citizen's isolation. The very vagueness of the often capital charge of being a *descontento* abetted collaboration with the government. State violence was largely extra-constitutional. Since the President-for-Life was the fount of all rewards and sanctions and since no act committed in the President's name could be called into question, the court system was bypassed in favor of a direct system of punishments administered by the security apparatus. Trials were rare. Suspected miscreants were imprisoned without due process.

The President-for-Life headed the security apparatus and controlled its chain of command. This ran through the National Director-General of Security and the provincial governors, down to the district heads of the militia (district representatives of the *Juventud*). At the village level there were local *jefes de sequridad* who often relied on denunciations brought in by village youngsters.

Suspects were arrested and interrogated, often under torture. The Director-General of Security and other officials reviewed the accused's conduct, and, when this process was finished, placed the case before the President-for-Life. There was no trial, no definite sentence, and no defense. Importantly, in Equatorial Guinea, political prisoners fared worse than common criminals. The aim was to destroy political prisoners either physically or morally "since their death was of no account." No jailer "was accountable for dead prisoners and quite often guards were ordered to kill them, for which they were rewarded" (Artucio, 1980: 10).

A psychological profile of the President refers to "his frequent use of drugs (bhang and iboga), his pervasive inferiority complex, his failure as a family man, and his association with cults and witchcraft" (Pélissier, 1980: 11). The Head of State's inability to reproduce has been noted and may be related to general theories of sexual inadequacy and the brutal quest for power. There is sufficient evidence to argue that Macias was "insane." E. V. Walter (1969: 81) notes that the "despot" commanding the state need not be "rational." State terror may exist over fairly long periods of time: "a process of terror may begin with an emotionally disturbed overlord living in the midst of political tensions, who commands his agents to perform acts of violence which induce the fear reaction which in turn yields social effects upon which the political system depends. Some political conditions call forth continuous behavior of the sort encouraging a kind of institutionalized rage...." This may be far from dysfunctional. "The image and definition of the overlord as a dangerous person may enable the power system to function in a set pattern that could not persist in other circumstances....That the consequences may not be intended by the directors or agents of violence is irrelevant." Walter notes: "The 'useful' social effects of irrational violence may or may not be perceived and approved after they emerge from the terror process."

Specific atrocities and the idiosyncrasies of the leader are subsidiary to the question of the structure and function of terror. Obviously, as the history of twentieth century Europe amply demonstrates, terror is not inherently dysfunctional. There are several prerequisites for a functioning terroristic regime: (1) a shared ideology which justifies violence and clearly labels the victims as evildoers; (2) victims whose liquidation will not cause a major dysfunction in the society; (3) disassociation of the agents of violence and the victims from ordinary social life (victims may be defined as "unpersons"). The agents of violence are organized as executioners, alien mercenaries, and secret police; (4) incentives to collaboration; (5) traditional social bonds which survive the terror (or new substituted relationships).

Terror is instrumental--it operates to ensure compliance with the wishes of the individual (the "terroristic despot") directing the state. Terror as a process demands a "source of violence, a victim, and a target." In Walter's "dramaturgic model" of terror, "The victim perishes, but the target reacts to the spectacle or the news of that destruction with some manner of submission or accommodation, that is, by withdrawing his resistance or by inhibiting his potential resistance..." (Walter, 1969: 9). Terror systems create "forced choice" in which "the individuals must choose between two evils, both of which would be rejected in an 'open' situation." Such systems create a situation in which the individual must inform or be informed upon. Avoidance of the noxious alternative puts the individual in collaboration with the system of terror and breaks down solidarity among those outside the terror apparatus. This was specifically characteristic in Equatorial Guinea, where political appointees in the villages received encouragement to bring in denunciations of citizens: "In this system, sympathy becomes weakness, old loyalties [,] betrayal of the Party." The Macias regime made "ruthless and ambitious exposure of potential enemies of the State a matter of personal survival" (Klinteberg, 1978: 33).

THE ROLE OF IDEOLOGY

In the sixties it was common to read lengthy discussions of constitutions and parliamentary systems best suited for emerging African needs.[7] Political arrangements at the local level and the indigenous political environment from which the leadership came were often ignored. Also, the idea of the devolution of power upon an African "elite" probably ignored the fact that in the sixties that elite, which had come to maturity in the period before World War 1I, had expectations and attitudes molded by their early life experiences. In Equatorial Guinea, the President's deepest political beliefs and his ideology did not derive from the hodge-podge of Spanish corporatist beliefs and anticolonial rhetoric to which he was exposed in the 1960s.

Part of the President's ideology or "anti-ideology" can only partially be understood against the backdrop of the previous close collaboration between the church and Francoist colonialism. The twin props of the colonial regime were Catholicism and the Caudillo. African religion was, at best, primitive superstition. In Africa, colonialist propagandists argued that the authoritarian state and its faith would be vindicated. Early on in the Falangist regime, José Cordero Torres (1941: 259) argued that imperial Spain would revive, freed from liberalism, socialism and Freemasonry, and inspired by religion: "There is no *tabu* nor any racial or climatic impossibilty, which, by its existence, would mean our expulsion as a colonizing country." During the Franco years Spanish missionaries worked assiduously for the eradication of African religion and a faith which would insulate the colony from the winds of African nationalism. By independence, Catholicism was, officially, the religion of the majority of the population (Klinteberg, 1978: 50).

Macias Nguema used the party and traditional religion to create an ideology which justified violence against the real or imagined enemies of the regime. Ultimately, he sought not only to disestablish the colonial religious order, but to create a new one centering on himself. Towards the end of his rule, in May of 1978, the government expelled the last Spanish missionaries and the country proclaimed an "atheist state."

The rift between the Church and State had appeared a decade earlier. In April of 1968 Monsignor Raphael Nzue Abuy wrote: "The preocupation of some Catholics about the attitude of the political leaders of Rio Muni have [*sic*] been brought home to us....We...warn you against anti-religious rabble-rousers. He who does not fear God will not respect the laws of Human Rights" (Klinteberg, 1978: 50). Thereafter the clergy were important foci of opposition and subjected to increasing suppression. In 1972 Nzue Abuy was exiled and party officials began emphasizing the slogan "No hay mas Dios que Macias" ("there is no other God than Macias"). A party catechism which stated "God created Equatorial Guinea thanks to Macias. Without Macias Equatorial Guinea would not exist" became obligatory in church services. In 1973 the ruling party said that "The Catholic Church, during its presence in the Republic of Equatorial Guinea, has always been a faithful instrument at the service of colonialism, plotting machinations which apparently were considered religious, and had knowledge of the constant campaign developed clandestinely against the President-for- Life of the Republic" (PUNT, 1973: 4).

In 1974 Macias also de-Europeanized most place names, thus depriving them of both colonial and Catholic connotations (e.g., Santa Isabel became Malabo). He de-Hispanicized his own name and became Masie Nguema Biyogo Ñegue Ndong. The following year a decree ordered priests and pastors to open their sermons with the words "Nothing without Macias, everything for Macias, down with colonialism and the ambitious." In Bata in 1975, the Head of State informed his audience that "false priests" were "thieves, swindlers, exploiters and colonialists" (Artucio, 1980: 12). The populace was warned against contact with Catholic clergy and parochial schools were effectively shut-down by a decree which banned all private education (*West Africa*, 1975:1198).

In Equatorial Guinea the role of religious symbolism in the religious arena was particularly intense. Macias Nguema's anticlericalism cannot simply be explained away as paranoia. Under Francoist colonialism religious diversity existed in neither the metropole or in the minds of its missionaries. Far more than the French, British or Belgians, Spanish colonialism had been identified with a unified and authoritian national church. Before the proclamation of official atheism, the new "Cult of Personality" perpetuated elements of the discredited colonial faith. The Head of State was the "Sole Miracle" of Equatorial Guinea. Church services included sycophantic adulation of the President-for-Life. Political rhetoric evoked the image of the leader as a miraculous figure, eclipsing the discredited roster of Roman Catholic saints: "Slowly like enormous octupi they [i.e., the colonialists] went about slowly enrolling our Nation in their tentacles of death--Equatorial Guinea is lost--in the precise instant in which all appeared lost, there appeared, as in a dream, the Liberator--Father of our constructive revolution" (Ochaga Ngomo, 1970: n.p.).

Besides grafting the "Cult of Personality" onto the existing practice of Christianity, the regime revivified and used traditional religion. Among the Fang, the bwiti movement was both a focus of anticolonial sentiment and a means of interpreting the colonial experience. "Bwiti is contrasted with European religions which use alien ritual elements....This contraaculturative point is frequently extended to a critique of all the material aspects of European life which, it is argued, constitute a threat to the morality and dignity of the Fang way of life" (Fernandez, 1970: 447). The movement, which sought to act as a channel to the ancestors, involved the ritual display of ancestral bones and the taking of a psychoreactive drug, iboga, to obtain visions of the dead. The Spanish had attempted to eradicate the movement in Rio Muni, after accusing it of human sacrifice and anthropophagy (Viladach de Veciana: 1958). The cult had begun to flourish by the First World War and was an important factor in efforts to mobilize pan-Fang sentiment in Gabon after 1945. Indeed, the first president of Gabon, Leon Mba, emphasized Bwiti as a force for national integration (Fernandez, 1982: 348).

In Equatorial Guinea, the President's connection may be similar to Haitian dictator Francois Duvalier's involvement with Vodun--participation in a non-European belief and value system justified the punitive aspects of the regime and had resonance with segments of the unassimilated populace. As in other contexts, "the collective fantasy about the omnipotence of the great destroyer-provider legitimated his violence..." (Walter, 1969: 340). The President's secluded residence in Mongomo in the interior of Rio Muni was more than symbolic, for he increasingly sought to operate within a framework legitimized by traditional political culture.

Much of Macias Nguema's election campaign of 1968 was directed towards members of the Bwiti cult in Rio Muni. He sought a symbiotic relationship with its adherents, one which would, perhaps, overcome his own ambivalences and feelings of inferiority vis à vis European culture--a situation which mirrored larger ambivalences in Fang society. It was widely believed that he was from Gabon where Bwiti was more powerful than in Equatorial Guinea, where it may have been more feared. Macias Nguema, the son of a Bwiti leader, considered the movement a manifestation of African authenticity. The father, Biyogo, known during the Macias years as *Su Santa Padre* ("His Saintly Father"), was renowned for his ritual powers and for his reputed killing of one of his sons.

During the dictatorship, Macias Nguema himself managed to acquire considerable magico-religious power. Rumors that his power had been secured through the effusion of blood heightened his aura of invincibility. Involvement with Bwiti and other religious movements was more complex than a simple manipulation of traditional themes for political ends. Macias Nguema's participation in Bwiti, and in Fang ancestor worship, Bieri, linked him to a powerful precolonial and anticolonial tradition. Propaganda was spread that he had acquired enough countermagic to make him invulnerable. The tiger, "El Tigre" (an animal not found in Africa), became his symbol (Klinteberg, 1978: 53). Macias Nguema, with a flare for the manipulation of symbols, placed his totemic animal on his party's membership card.

Although he eventually violated the covenant between himself and his followers, he attempted to justify certain of his actions by reference to traditional political norms. James Fernandez (1972: 36) has observed, "As we have learned to expect from the value studies of many nonliterate people such as the Fang, the moral code derived from the value system has a situational orientation." Furthermore, "Judgements of behavior by the Fang rest not upon categorical but upon hypothetical imperatives. If one can, indeed, abstract any such thing as a moral code, the question is not (as Malinowski reminded us) how behavior conforms to the code, but how the code is made to fit given situations." Macias Nguema made extensive use of traditional minstrels, *Mvet* singers, in manufacturing and disseminating political propaganda. It is significant that in the 1960s, Gabonese lycèe students, in composing portraits of the ideal Fang leader, often drew upon qualities held by traditional heroes of the *Mvet*: "Be a chief of unapproachable authority. A good chief pardons rarely, but chastises frequently....A chief spits haughtily, he roars and thunders like the storm. He overturns the government of others and provokes calamities" (Fernandez, 1972: 61).[8]

Obviously, different societies have different normative systems. Political culture, as well as consciously propagated political ideology, molds political behavior. Definition and treatment of "in" and "out" groups vary widely. "Amorality" is too vague a term to elucidate political acts in this context. It does not explain why followers follow leaders or if the leaders are divorced from all norms of political behavior. Fernandez (1982: 45) notes an interesting complementarity of attitudes and behaviors between Bwiti and Francoist colonialism: "More than in the French territories, the names and representations of Spanish officials entered into cult life and dances [e.g., the 'Flanco' dance named after Francisco Franco]. Spanish administrators seemed to create more charismatic paternalism in their dealings with Fang." A radical proposition would be that much of the behavior of the leader could, until the middle of the seventies, be rationalized by reference to the norms of both precolonial and colonial authoritarianism.

50

THE ROLE OF ETHNICITY

"Ethnocracy is basically a political system based on kinship, real or presumed." Its persistence is, supposedly, a major characteristic of certain African modern states (Mazrui, 1975a: 66). Criticism of this view points out that "In Africa, the political scientist identified the traditional with the the tribal: tribal society was traditional and primordial, timeless and unchanging." Therefore, "conflict was...explained as tribalism. The *form* of the conflict was presented, *tautologically*, as its own explanation: two tribes fight because they are different tribes" (Mamdani, 1976: 2-3). This point is well made; ethnic conflict proceeds from underlying economic and ideological causes. These are not immutable and they are subject to manipulation by the leadership of ethnic groups. In 1968 the vote on independence appeared split on an ethnic basis: the Bubi of Biyogo versus the Fang of Rio Muni. This division had a clear economic basis. It must also be remembered that a majority of the colonial bureaucracy slated for power in post-independence Equatorial Guinea was Fang. Members of this group staged the abortive coup of 1969 with Spanish connivance. It was this group that, in numerical terms, bore the brunt of the President's liquidations.

Ethnicity was and is important in post-independence Equatorial Guinea, but in a different way. As Jackson and Rosberg (1982: 47) note "ordinarily it is the elite representatives and fiducaries of ethnic groups, more than the general members, who gain privileges or suffer punishments under systems of personal rule." Macias Nguema's victory was the victory of one member of an ethnic group and of one segment of that ethnic group. The dictatorship was not so much a triumph of Fang nationalism, as it was a triumph of the President's hometown coterie. His power base was in the Mongomo district of Rio Muni, especially among members of the Esangui clan. Although the regime attempted to appear populist, its limited base among a segment of the Fang made it highly unrepresentative. The Esangui are among the least numerous of fifty ethnic divisions in Rio Muni. The Mongomo district contained 12,039 inhabitants in 1963, 5.3 percent of the total population and 6.6 percent of Rio Muni's. In the same year, the district's voters (3,441) represented only 2.7 percent of the national electorate. When looked at in terms of ethnicity, the same picture emerges. In 1952 a tenth of the villages in the district were peopled by Esangui and only 11.3 percent of the population belonged to the clan. At independence, some 4,000 Esangui represented hardly 1.5 percent of the total population (Liniger-Goumaz, 1981: 177). Significantly, in the final presidential election of 1968, the Mongomo district voted against Macias Nguema (Liniger-Goumaz, 1979: 46).

Once installed, the President showed a marked tendency towards identifying the regime symbolically with Fang ethnicity, while, at the same time killing off other Fang leaders with a larger popular following. He also demonstrated a tendency towards nepotism and intraethnic exclusivity.[9] In this he differed from the type of despotic ruler who suppresses familial ties in politics and elevates dependent nonconsanguineous subordinates. As the elimination of government officials inherited from the early days of a post-independence coalition proceeded, relatives of the dictator took their places. Teodoro Nguema Obiang Mbasango, the President's nephew and eventual successor, was commander of the National Guard (Liniger-Goumaz, 1982: 58-59).

THE FALL OF MACIAS NGUEMA

The regime maintained itself not only through a system of repression, but also through a system of rewards. In the system established after 1969, the agents of terror (e.g., *Juventud en Marcha con Macias*) were able to both repress insular dissent and plunder the insular economy. Of course, as the economy collapsed, the need for repression increased and the agents of terror began to see diminishing returns. Unlike the Fang of the nineteenth century, the regime was not able to expand the area plundered. Terror was also difficult to delimit. It was on this rock, and not on the application of terror, per se, that the regime ultimately foundered.

Terror exacerbated economic distress. It also exacerbated demographic problems. Critics of the regime charge that the dictatorship had a disastrous effect on the overall population. It has been estimated that the population should have amounted to more than 400,000 at the end of the seventies. However, according to opponents of the regime, the population was no more than 250,000. In 1968 the rate of increase was 1.9 percent per annum. The mortality rate was 7.8 percent in the year of independence (against 27 percent for tropical Africa). According to Liniger-Goumaz (1980: 1), mortality rose to 21 percent per annum in 1978.

By the late 1970s Equatorial Guinea was an economy based on extortion with nothing left to extort. Forced labor affected increasing segments of the population. The 1976 labor decree called for the recruitment of 20,000 workers from Rio Muni (Pélissier, 1980: 11). The recruits' remuneration consisted solely of subsistence (a ration of rice, palm oil, and fish) and made no allowance for the needs of dependents. In addition to a twelve-hour work day, the laborers were subjected to a regimen which included beatings, capricious brutality, and the withholding of food rations. Military personnel and public officials were also made to submit to part-time labor service.

The President-for-Life's rule was increasingly distasteful to friend and foe alike, although neither took action to curb the abuses. Terror within Equatorial Guinea demoralized internal opposition. The country's isolation was acute. This was particularly true of Biyogo, where the confiscation of canoes impeded escape to the mainland. A 1976 invasion attempt at Evinayong in Rio Muni was beaten back and resulted in reprisals in the area of the village. Around the same time, a group of government officials addressed a petition to the President-for-Life, asking for an amelioration of political and economic conditions. Many of the petitioners were executed, leaving only a clique of Mongomo Esangui as the President's intimates.[10] While the dictator's neighbors looked on with more or less neutrality and internal opposition was repressed, various exile groups attempted to launch a campaign against the dictatorship. Groups such as the *Alianza Nacional de la Restauracion Democratica* attacked the regime from abroad, but were themselves subject to factionalism and the divisive activities of Macias Nguema's agents.[11]

As the only Hispanophone state in Africa, Equatorial Guinea was linguistically and culturally isolated from its Francophone and Anglophone neighbors. Also, until the death of Francisco Franco in 1975, Spanish news reports on conditions within the Republic were censured because Madrid hoped to retain entré with its former colony. The potential for exploiting subsoil wealth, as well as the desire to maintain the flow of tropical produce, shielded the regime from scrutiny (Cronjé, 1976).

By the late seventies the regime's terror and mercurial nature provoked increasing scrutiny. The *Federation Internationale des Droits de l'Homme*, the Anti-Slavery Society, Amnesty International, the International University Exchange Fund, and the International Commission of Jurists finally took steps to expose the nature of the regime. In February of 1978, the Secretary General of the United Nations attempted to sound-out the government on the issue of human rights. He received no reply and a working group of the Economic and Social Council (ECOSOC) recommended an examination of the human rights situation in Equatorial Guinea (United Nations Economic and Social Council, 1978: res. 1503, paragraph 6 [a]. In March of 1979 the United Nations Commission on Human Rights decided to name a special rapporteur on the situation. It was further decided that the previously closed discussions of the matter would now become public. Also, in early 1979, a member of the World Labor Conference directing committee asked French President Valery Giscard d'Estaing to break off economic collaboration with Macias. Even friendly regimes appeared to tire of the mercurial behavior of their ally. Cuba had already withdrawn its technical assistance in 1976.

When the regime collapsed, it did not do so because of external pressure. Macias Nguema was overthrown in a palace coup organized by his own subalterns. The system had survived by continuing to provide the coterie around the President-for-Life with benefits. The lower level functionaries in the terror apparatus may have felt a diminution in the rewards falling to them, but Macias Nguema "had all the key positions in the security field in the hands of close relatives, like the traditional Fang leader who handed favor only to his Esengui [*sic*] clansmen and a few trusted or thoroughly compromised people...'" (Pélissier, 1980: 13). Nevertheless, by the spring of 1979 terror in Equatorial Guinea had come to include members of the president's circle itself. He had members of his bodyguard, who were reportedly members of his own clan, executed. In June of 1979 Macias struck at his inner circle by liquidating five military officers, one of whom was the brother of his successor, Lieutenant Colonel Obiang Nguema Mbasango. It may have been evident to Obiang Mbasango, as well as to other members of the president's entourage, that the apparatus of terror was being devoured by its own agents. If the apparatus had been "functional" in 1969, it was definitely dysfunctional ten years later. Those benefitting from the terror had diminished to almost a minority of one.

The President's fall represented the collapse of his own terror apparatus and not a counter thrust by those groups against whom terror was directed. The President-for-Life's actions in 1979 overstepped the limits of terror and called forth a self-protective response from his inner coterie of Esangui clansmen. When questioned as to why they did not strike earlier, they cited fear of his magico-religious power and respect for the legitimacy of his office: "He was the chief, we believed he would become better" (*Le Monde*, 1979: 4). It remained to be seen if the ensuing period would bring any genuine amelioration of either economic or human rights conditions.

The strange career of Macias Nguema in part reflects the different pace of capitalist penetration into the two very unequal halves of Equatorial Guinea. His actions must be seen in light of indigenous resentment at intensive and authoritian Hispanicization during the Franco years, plus devotion to the metropole on the part of a significant segment of the elite on whom power devolved. Up to a certain point, the leaders ruthless suppression of opposition garnered support from elements in Fang society, a society little touched by the economic consequences of Spanish colonial rule. Equatorial Guinea does not defy class analysis; it shows that the classes which colonialism has thrown up elsewhere were still largely embryonic in the last decade before independence.

Stark (1986: 346-47) noted that "A theory of the African state is needed which includes the role of outstanding creative individuals, the work of building institutions and structures, the struggle for dominance between social groups and classes, as well as the constraints on development emanating from the international economic and political systems." Also, we shall have to pay less attention to the idiosyncracies of "tyrants" and more attention to the ethnic, economic, and ideological underpinnings of their rule. This will mean more than merely viewing them as pawns of foreign capital—since this only leaves us with the question of why external capital chose such erratic representatives in the first place. Finally, we shall have to deal with the interdigitation of class and ethnicity. The issue in present-day Africa is in some ways reflective of the older argument over race and class in the African Diaspora. In that situation, the West Indian Marxist C.L.R. James observed that "The race question is subsidiary to the class question in politics....But to neglect the racial factor as merely incidental is an error only less grave than to make it fundamental" (Rodney, 1972: 100). If ethnicity is substituted for race the same holds true for contemporary Africa.

NOTES

1. This tendency has been carried furthest by cultural materialists like Marvin Harris who argues that although it is "aligned...with the teachings of Karl Marx, cultural materialism nonetheless stands apart from the Marx-Engels-Lenin strategy of dialectical materialism." It differs in that "cultural materialists seek to improve Marx's original strategy by dropping the Hegelian notion that all systems evolve through a dialectic of contradictory negations and by adding reproductive pressure and ecological variables to the conjunction of material conditions studied by Marxists Leninists (1980: ix)."

2. For Africa this tendency is exemplified by Kyemba (1977) and Bruckner (1986).

3. For a discussion of the effect of the Second World War on the colony, see G. Clarence Smith (1985).

4. It is very important that public benefit be disentangled from private profit. In the case of Spain and Portugal, imperialism was of little benefit to the metropole as a whole. See Clarence-Smith (1979).

5. Stark cites John Saul, 1976 "The State in Post-Colonial Societies: Tanzania." *The Socialist Register*, p. 351.

6. For a discussion of the varying economic principles of African states in the precolonial period, see Catherine Coquery-Vidrovitch (1976). She believes that ruling groups could extort tribute from subordinate groups without altering the basic mode of production.

7. See Richard Sklar (1983) for an overview of the theories and outcome of the ideas of "democracy" in Africa. For a non-Marxist analysis of class structure in post-colonial Africa, see Sklar (1979).

8. Fernandez (1982: 61) cites as his source on the *Mvet* as Philippe Ndong "Le Mvet," *Réalites Gabonaises*, 3: 3-7. The quote is from the political counsel given the future chief of the Tribe of Flames, Ovang Ndoumou Obame, by his father Ndoumou Obame.

9. Ela Nguema (the President's nephew) served as his aide de camp and Masie Ntutmu (a cousin) was given the Interior Ministry. After the abortive coup of 1969, a cousin Nguema Esono, was appointed Foreign Minister. In 1971 another relative, Eyegue Ntutmu, was appointed governor of Rio Muni. In 1976 Nguema Esono assumed the duties of Vice-President. A nephew, Oyono Ayingono, held three posts simultaneously: Finance Minister, Minister of Industry and Commerce, and Secretary of State for the Presidency. Oyono Ayingono also held the posts of Chief of Protocol and Commissioner of State Enterprises. Feliciano Oyono, a cousin, was permanent secretary of PUNT. The representative to the United Nations was another relative, Evuna Owono Asangono, and the second company of the National Guard was commanded by another cousin, Mba Onana.

10. Liniger Goumaz (1979) reported that Ochaga Ngomo and the chief functionaries of the Ministry of Popular Education, along with Oyono Alogo, Secretary to the Presidency, and Eyegue Ntutumu, the Vice-President, were saved thanks to the intervention of a French forestry concern in Rio Muni. They were, however, discharged.

11. Reportedly, Garcia Trevijano in Spain acted to discredit and create tension between exiled anti-Macias groups. The most well-publicized of the groups, the Alianza Nacional de Restauracion Democratica (ANRD), was formed in 1974. Through its organ, *Voz del Pueblo*, it called for a broad-based struggle against the dictatorship. Citing Amical Cabral, it called for autocriticism and the creation of a new society. This would entail the socialization of the means of production. The collective leadership of the group sought a wide ethnic base; Grey Molay, from Biyogo, was a leading spokesman in international fora, as was C.M. Eya Nchama, who sat on the United Nations Subcommittee for the Prevention of Discrimination amd Protection of Minorities (Liniger-Goumaz, 1982: 52).

REFERENCES

Amin, Samir. 1974. *Neo-Colonialism in West Africa*. New York: Monthly Review Press.

ANRD Position Paper 5. 1975. Geneva: Alianza Nacional de la Restauracion Democratica.

Artucio, A. 1980. *The Trial of Macias in Equatorial Guinea: The Story of a Dictatorship* (Geneva, 1980), 33.

Bruckner, Pascal. 1986. *The Tears of the White Man*. London: Macmillan.

Church, R. J. H. 1977. *Africa and the Islands*. New York: John Wiley and Sons.

Clarence-Smith, G. 1979. *Slaves, Peasants and Capitalists in Southern Angola, 1840-1926*. London: Cambridge University Press

___. 1985. "The Impact of the Second World War on Portuguese and Spanish Africa." *Journal of African History* 26/2: 309-26.

Coquery-Vidrovitch, C. 1976. "The Political Economy of the African Peasantry and Modes of Production," pp. 90-111 in Peter C.W. Gutkind and I. Wallerstein (eds.) *The Political Economy of Contemporary Africa*. Beverly Hills, CA: Sage Publications.

Cordero, Torres, J. 1941. *Tratado Elemental de Derecho Colonial Español*. Madrid: Editora Nacional.

Cronjé S. 1976. *Equatorial Guinea, the Forgotten Dictatorship: Forced Labour and Political Murder in Central Africa*. London: Anti-Slavery Society.

"Equatorial Guinea." 1969. *Africa Report* 14/1: 22-23.

Garcia, Ramon. 1977. *Guinea, Macias, la ley del silencio.* Barcelona:Plaza y Janes.

Fernandez, James. 1970. "The Affirmation of Things Past: Alar Ayong and Bwiti as Movements of Protest in Central and Northern Gabon," pp.427-57 in Robert Rotberg and Ali Mazrui (eds.) *Protest and Power in Black Africa.* New York: Oxford University Press.

___. 1972. "Fang Representations and Acculturation," pp. 3-48 in P. Curtin (ed.) *Africa and the West, Intellectual Responses to European Culture.* Madison, WI: University of Wisconsin Press.

___. 1982. *Bwiti, An Ethnography of the Religious Imagination in Africa.* Princeton, NJ: Princeton University Press.

Fernandez, R. 1976. *Materia Reservada.* Madrid: Sedmay.

Gard, Robert. 1973. "The Colonization and Decolonization of Equatorial Guinea." Unpublished manuscript.

___.1974. *Equatorial Guinea: Machinations in Founding a National Bank.* Pasadena, CA: Munger Africana Library.

Genovese, Eugene D. 1969. "Materialism and Idealism in the History of Negro Slavery in the Americas," pp. 238-55 in Laura Foner and Eugene D. Genovese (eds.) *Slavery in the New World, A Reader in Comparative History.* Englewood Cliffs, NJ: Prentice Hall.

Harris, Marvin. 1980. *Cultural Materialism, The Struggle for a Science of Culture.* New York: Random House.

Howe, R.W. 1966. "Spain's Equatorial Island." *Africa Report* 11/6:48.

Klinteberg, Robert af. 1978. *Equatorial Guinea - Macias Country: the Forgotten Refugees.* Geneva: International University Exhange Fund Field Study.

Kobel, Armin. 1976. "La Republique de Guinée Equatoriale, ses resources potentialles et virtualles. Possibilitiés de développment." Ph.D. dissertation, Université de Neuchatel.

Kyemba, Henry. 1977. *A State of Blood, The Inside Story of Idi Amin.* New York: Ace Books.

Jackson, R. and C. Rosberg. 1982. *Personal Rule in Black Africa, Prince, Autocrat, Prophet, Tyrant.* Los Angeles: University of California Press.

___. 1986. "Sovereignty and Underdevelopment: Juridical Statehood in the African Crisis." *Journal of Modern Africa Studies* 25/2: 1-31.

Legum, C., ed. 1970. *African Contemporary Record 1968-1969.* London: Rex Collings: 483.

___. 1973. *African Contemporary Record. 1971-1972.* London: Rex Collings: B504.

Le Monde. 1975. November 28: 6.

Liniger-Goumaz, M. 1979. "La république de Guinée Equatoriale. Une indépendence à refaire." *Afrique Contemporaine* 105 (September-October): 13.

___. 1980. "La république de Guinée Equatoriale." *Acta Geographica* (Paris), 43, third trimester: 1-21.

___. 1981. "Deux ans de Dictature post-Macias Nguema." reprint, *Genève--Afrique (Journal of the Swiss Society of African Studies)*: 157-80.

___. 1982. *Guinée Equatoriale, De la Dictature des Colons à la Dictature des Colonels.* Geneva: Editions du Temps.

Mamdani, Mahmud. 1976. *Politics and Class Formation in Uganda.* New York: Monthly Review Press.

___. 1984. *Imperialism and Fascism in Uganda.* Trenton, N.J.: Africa World Press.

Mazrui, Ali. 1975a. *Soldiers and Kinsmen in Uganda, the Making of a Military Ethnocracy.* Beverly Hills: Sage Publications.

___. 1975b. "The Resurrection of the Warrior Tradition in African Political Culture." *Journal of Modern African Studies* 13/1: 67-84.

Nabudere, D. W. 1980. *Imperialism and Revolution in Uganda.* London: Onyx Press.

Ndongo Bidyogo, Donato. 1977. *Historia y Tragedia de Guinea Ecuatorial.* Madrid: Cambio 16.

Ochaga Ngomo, B. 1970. "Nacimiento de la libertad de Guinea Ecutorial." *Organo Informativo del Ministerio de Educacion Nacional de Guinea Ecuatorial.* 7: n.pp.

Osuntokun, Jide. 1977. "Nigeria-Fernando Po Relations from the Nineteenth Century to the Present." Sherbrooke, Quebec: Canadian African Studies Association, 26 April-3 May: 37.

___. 1978. *Equatorial Guinea-Nigerian Relations, the Diplomacy of Labor.* Ibadan: Oxford University Press.

Partido Unico Nacional de Trabajadores de la Republica de Guinea Ecuatorial. 1973. "Resoluciones Generales del Tercer Congreso Nacional," Bata.

Pélissier, Réné. 1968. "Uncertainty in Spanish Guinea." *Africa Report* 13/6: 16-38.

___. 1980. "Autopsy of a Miracle." *Africa Report* 25/3: 10-14.

Rodney, Walter. 1974. *How Europe Undeveloped Africa.* Washington, D.C.: Howard University Press.

Saul, John. 1976. "The State in Post-Colonial Societies: Tanzania." *The Socialist Register.*

Sawyer, Roger. 1986. *Slavery in the Twentieth Century.* London: Routledge and Kegan Paul.

Sklar, Richard. 1979. "The Nature of Class Domination in Africa." *Journal of Modern African Studies* 17/4: 531-52.

___. 1983. "Democracy in Africa." *The African Studies Review* 26/3-4: 11-24.

Stark, Frank. 1986. "Theories of Contemporary State Formation in Africa: A Reassessment." *Journal of Modern African Studies* 24/2: 325-47.

Ungar, Sanford. 1985. *Africa, the Peoples and Politics of an Emerging Continent.* New York: Simon and Schuster.

United Nations Economic and Social Council. 1978. Resolution 1503, paragraph 6 [a].

Viladach de Vecina, A. 1958. *La Secta del Bwiti en la Guinea española.* Madrid: Instituto de Estudios Africanos.

Walter, E.V. 1969. *Terror and Resistance: A Study of Political Violence with Some Case Studies of Some Primitive African Communities.* London: Oxford University Press.

West Africa. 1975. 10 March: 285.

West Africa. 1975. 6 October: 1190.

West Africa. 1980. 8 September: 1731.

Young, Crawford. 1982. *Ideology and Development in Africa.* New Haven, CT: Yale University Press.

The Journal of Modern African Studies, 20, 3, 1982, pp. 377–392

In Lieu of Orthodoxy: the Socialist Theories of Nkrumah and Nyerere

by STEVEN METZ*

A QUARTER-CENTURY after its inception, the diversity within 'African socialism' remains astonishing. This category now includes development strategies which range from traditional capitalism with limited sectoral planning to collective forms of national autarky. Although it is generally agreed that none of the forms of African socialism incorporates an 'orthodox' type of Marxism, the tremendous intellectual impact which Marx and Lenin have had on all aspects of social, economic, and political thought means that it is impossible to construct a theory of socialism which is totally outside their shadows. In effect, Marxist orthodoxy inevitably serves as a tool for the evaluation of socialist theory.

But Marx and Lenin would have been the first to admit that the validity of any theory of socialism depends on the historical conditions which form the context for its promulgation and application. As C. L. R. James has written, 'Marxism is a guide to action in a specific system of social relations which takes into account the always changing relationship of forces in an always changing world situation.'[1] Since the contemporary post-colonial situation is so different from early twentieth-century Russia or nineteenth-century western Europe, socialism in Africa has been driven beyond the parameters of Marxist–Leninist orthodoxy.

It is thus imperative to understand African socialism both as an outcome of a specific matrix of historical conditions, and as at least a distant decendent of Marxism. There are three major tenets of the intellectual context of African socialism which are most important for a full understanding of the phenomenon: (1) the ethics of pre-colonial Africa which were based on humanistic values and often on an egalitarian method of production and distribution; (2) the colonial past which challenged the ethics of the pre-colonial system with those of capitalism; and (3) the present, representing a stage of incomplete

* Doctoral Candidate, Department of Political Science, The Johns Hopkins University, Baltimore, and Visiting Instructor, Department of Political Science, Towson State University, Maryland.
[1] C. L. R. James, *Nkrumah and the Ghana Revolution* (London and Westport, 1977 edn.), p. 74.

synthesis, mixing elements of the colonial and pre-colonial past. African socialism is predicted on the belief that the *results* of the capitalist mode of production – the potential to fulfil human needs – can be separated from the ethics of capitalism, which are based on social hierarchy and exploitation. African socialism is thus an attempt to blend what are perceived as the dominant ethics of pre-colonial society with the productive power of modern capitalism.

As Mao Tse-Tung pointed out, every social situation entails a 'principal contradiction'.[1] In the African setting there is a sharp contrast between the useful potential of capitalism and the harmful reality of neo-colonialism which augments human suffering. But contrary to Mao's argument, in this case the solution does not flow with inexorable logic from the contradiction. There are as many theories proposing the synthesis of African ethics with productive efficiency as there are theorists. Because of this, the category 'African socialism' is so heterogeneous, so broad, and so diverse that it can only be thoroughly understood by an examination of the differences and similarities between the leading advocates. It is thus the purpose of this study to compare the theories of two of the 'founding fathers' of African socialism: Kwame Nkrumah and Julius Nyerere.

Like a number of other African politicians, Nkrumah and Nyerere attempted both to explain the need for a socialist transition and to lead this process. Because of this their theories are both abstract explanations containing a social ontology and epistemology, and plans for positive action. It is often impossible to separate the two sides of the issue – the theory and the practice – and both are interrelated in such a manner that one cannot be comprehended without the other. But to truly understand the programmes by which Nkrumah and Nyerere attempted to implement socialism, it is first necessary to examine the theoretical logic which imparted coherence to their strategies; in order to understand socialism as it is, or was, in Ghana and Tanzania, it is first necessary to isolate, analyse, and dissect the theories which motivated these two leaders. Since the implementation of the policies of Nkrumah and Nyerere have been well recorded,[2] this article will focus on the theory underlying their politics.

[1] Mao Tse-Tung, 'On Contradiction', in *Selected Works of Mao Tse-Tung* (Peking, 1977 edn.), p. 331.

[2] Among the better works on this topic are Andrew Coulson, *African Socialism in Practice* (Nottingham, 1979); Goran Hyden, *Beyond Ujamaa in Tanzania: underdevelopment and an uncaptured peasantry* (London and Berkeley, 1980); Bismarck U. Mwansasu and Cranford Pratt (eds.), *Towards Socialism in Tanzania* (Toronto, 1979); James, op. cit.; and Basil Davidson, *Black Star* (London, 1973).

A leitmotif of the study is Marxist orthodoxy. While the degree to which Nkrumah and Nyerere deviated from Marxism will be referred to, the issue of orthodoxy will not be used as a tool of evaluation, but rather as a currency or common language for distinction between the two theories. Although even a perfunctory reading of the two men's work will show that Marxism influenced Nkrumah's work to a much greater degree than that of Nyerere,[1] the use of this criterion of distinction can help to clarify the differences between the two. The measure of Marxist orthodoxy is, as Georg Lukács has pointed out, the use of a particular method and not the application of a specific historical analysis.[2]

Following this point, it will become obvious that while the material conditions faced by Nkrumah and Nyerere were similar, the historical logics which they used differed radically. It will be argued that Nkrumah was the 'more orthodox' of the two, not because he espoused revolution and industrialisation while Nyerere focused on rural socialism, but because he subjected history and political economy to an analysis based on historical materialism. By this use of Marxist orthodoxy as a third variable in the comparison of these two African leaders, it will be possible both to outline the distinctions between their theories more readily, and to place them within the larger context of the intellectual history of political and economic phenomena.

Nkrumah and Nyerere each recognised the deep impact which capitalism had had on their societies, and they realised that socialism was a goal to be sought rather than an extant condition. Thus the essence of their theories is the process of the transition to socialism. But, as Marx and Engels noted, in order to chart a direction of change or a method of transformation, one must begin with the 'real premises' of social conditions.[3]

It is for this reason that the theories of both Nkrumah and Nyerere

---

[1] For instance, according to Cranford Pratt, *The Critical Phase in Tanzania, 1945–1968: Nyerere and the emergence of a socialist strategy* (Cambridge, 1976), p. 63, classical liberalism and Fabianism have influenced Nyerere to a greater degree than Marxism, and in his essay on 'Tanzania's Transition to Socialism: reflections of a democratic socialist', in Mwansasu and Pratt (eds.), op. cit., Pratt categorises Nyerere as a democratic socialist. A. Fenner Brockway, *African Socialism* (Chester Springs, Pa., 1963), places Nkrumah within the category of 'African Marxists' and Nyerere in 'African Pragmatic Socialists'. John S. Saul refers to Nyerere's 'incomprehension of Marxism', in 'African Socialism in One Country: Tanzania', in Giovanni Arrighi and Saul, *Essays on the Political Economy of Africa* (New York and London, 1973), p. 237. Julius Nyerere himself considered Marxism too much the result of specifically European events to be relevant to Africa; see his 'Ujamaa – the Basis of African Socialism', reprinted in *Ujamaa: essays on socialism* (Oxford, 1968), pp. 1–12.

[2] Georg Lukács, *History and Class Consciousness: studies in Marxist dialectics* (Cambridge, Mass., 1971), p. 1. Issa G. Shivji makes the same arguments in *Class Struggles in Tanzania* (New York and London, 1976 edn.), p. 13.

[3] Karl Marx and Friedrich Engels, *The German Ideology* (Moscow, 1976 edn.), pp. 36–7.

concerning the transformation of post-colonial Africa to socialism stem from their evaluations of societies which mix elements of pre-capitalist and capitalist systems with visions of a post-capitalist future. Thus the three key elements of their theories of socialism are: (1) an understanding of the sociology of African states during the post-colonial period of partial transformation; (2) an analysis of the instigative factors and methods of the transition to socialism; and (3) a definition of a socialist society.

THE CONCEPT OF SOCIETY: DIFFERING FOCI

Both Nkrumah and Nyerere believe that socialism is more than simply a form of political economy. But although both would agree with Marx's contention that the 'real foundation' of society is the 'relations of production',[1] they disagree as to exactly what composed the most basic unit for the social organisation of production.

In their analyses of this issue, Nkrumah and later Nyerere made great use of traditional African society. Both often expressed a sort of spiritual longing for a return to some sort of idyllic village life far removed from the pressures of capitalist society. Both argued that, at least in ethical content, the pre-colonial era was far superior to the post-colonial situation. But while both utilised this vision of a bucolic Africa to generate a variation of the Weberian ideal type, the rôle which this played in their theories of socialism differed.

For Nyerere the element of traditional African life which gave his theory what has been called its 'anthropocentric' bent,[2] was the value content of production based on communalism. Nyerere emphasised that in pre-colonial Africa the means of production – especially land – were owned in common.[3] In such a setting, 'everybody was a worker', and there was no social division of labour.[4] Hence the dominant ethic was egalitarian, whereby the social hierarchy was, as in the family, based on wisdom, age, and experience, rather than on economic or class differences. This idea is in accord with Marx's thinking when he wrote:

The first form of property is tribal property... The division of labour is at this

---

[1] Karl Marx, *A Contribution to the Critique of Political Economy* (Moscow, 1977 edn.), p. 20.

[2] James N. Karioki, *Tanzania's Human Revolution* (University Park, Pa., 1979), p. 29.

[3] Nyerere, op. cit. pp. 81–5 and 106–8. See also Julius K. Nyerere, *Freedom and Socialism/Uhuru ua Ujamaa: a selection from writings and speeches, 1965–1967* (Oxford and Dar es Salaam, 1968), pp. 198–9.

[4] Ibid. p. 4.

stage still very elementary and is confined to a further extension of the natural division of labour existing in the family.[1]

Because the ethical content of pre-colonial Africa has been most heavily utilised by Nyerere, critics who focus on the anthropological weakness of his vision of traditional society misunderstand why this ideal type has been emphasised. Although Michael Lofchie, for instance, correctly notes that the purpose of the traditional model in Nyerere's thought is the attempted substitution of moral for material incentives in the Tanzanian economy, his argument that Nyerere's use of this model is doomed to failure because of its historical inaccuracy is less convincing:

Whether Nyerere intended a historical purpose or not, any factual shortcomings in his mythology are a matter of no small importance. For if a political myth of the sort Nyerere espouses is historically inaccurate, its prospects of political success are considerably lessened, since it must inevitably fall short of corresponding to the life experiences of those to whom it is being addressed.[2]

But by definition, a mobilising myth need not correspond exactly to 'the life experiences' of those to whom it is being addressed. In Nyerere's case, these life experiences are those of colonial and post-colonial – or partially transformed – social organisation rather than of traditional life in an unadulterated form. In effect, his use of the egalitarian values of traditional Africa is important because it does *not* correspond to the life experience of Tanzanians; the purposes of the myth of communal Africa for Nyerere are, as John Nellis points out, transcendence and unification, not explanation.[3]

The key difference here – not sufficiently emphasised by either Lofchie or Nellis – is between ideology-as-explanation and ideology-as-transcendental-myth. Nyerere does not use pre-colonial Africa to construct an explanatory ideology, but rather to generate a desire to transcend an unhappy present. The past is essentially motivational. Thus the image of a traditional, ethical Africa plays a similar rôle for Nyerere as the myth of the general strike in the work of Georges Sorel.[4]

[1] Marx and Engels, op. cit. p. 38. For an elaboration of their thinking on this subject, see Karl Marx, *Pre-Capitalist Economic Formations* (New York, 1980 edn.), and Friedrich Engels's more evolutionary and mechanistic approach in *The Origins of the Family, Private Property and the State* (New York, 1978 edn.).

[2] Michael F. Lofchie, 'Agrarian Socialism in the Third World: the Tanzanian case', in *Comparative Politics* (New York), 8, 3 April 1976, pp. 488–9.

[3] John R. Nellis, *A Theory of Ideology: the Tanzanian example* (Oxford, 1972), pp. 101–2. While extremely pessimistic about Nyerere's attempts to use the model of pre-colonial Africa to create a unifying ideology, this is a useful explanation of the mechanics of this process.

[4] See Georges Sorel, *Reflections on Violence* (New York, 1950), especially pp. 123–9.

The use of African pre-history to generate a motivational myth is even more overt in Nkrumah's theory. While Nyerere focused on the interconnectedness of traditional values and the structures which generated them, and thus attempted to modernise some aspects of the traditional method of social organisation, Nkrumah totally jettisoned the institutional format of traditional Africa and concentrated on the emotive and motivational aspects of pre-colonial life. For this reason those who criticise Nkrumah's use of traditional images – for example, Imanuel Geiss, when he argues that Nkrumah's theory represented a 'pronounced oscillation between modern and traditional ideas'[1] – also misunderstand the rôle of myth. But while Nkrumah sought to foster a particular image of pre-colonial Africa which emphasised 'an attitude towards man which can only be described, in its social manifestations, as being socialist',[2] he also argued that 'a return to pre-colonial African society is evidently not worthy of the ingenuity and efforts of our people'.[3] Thus Nkrumah remained aware of the fact that the true value of traditional Africa was its ability to aid in the generation of a motivational myth. This was expressed when we wrote that 'what socialist thought in Africa must recapture is not the structure of "traditional African society" but its spirit.'[4]

Nkrumah was aware that colonialism, and the ensuing partial transformation of the production process, had led to a dominant ideology or myth in Africa which was inconsistent and incomplete[5] – namely, that the continent was largely without a history, intellectually underdeveloped, and naturally subservient to European culture.[6] For Nkrumah the image of traditional African life was to be deliberately altered in order to form the embryo of a new ideology which would transcend the intellectually moribund status of post-colonial Africa. The bases of this new ideology would be the egalitarianism, humanism, and communalism of the pre-colonial ethical system.

But while Nyerere and Nkrumah began with a similar analysis of the status of partially transformed African society, and with related ideas about the rôle of traditional Africa in overcoming this condition, they differed in their assessments of the unit of the social organisation of

---

[1] Imanuel Geiss, *The Pan-African Movement* (New York and London, 1974 edn.), p. 371.

[2] Kwame Nkrumah, *Consciencism: philosophy and ideology for decolonization and development with particular reference to the African Revolution* (New York and London, 1970 edn.), p. 68.

[3] Kwame Nkrumah, *Revolutionary Path* (New York, 1972 edn.), 'African Socialism Revisited', pp. 441. This article was first published in *African Forum* (New York), I, 3, 1966, pp. 3–9.

[4] Ibid. p. 441.

[5] This is the major thesis of *Consciencism*.

[6] While this argument is most vividly and forcefully made by Frantz Fanon, especially in *The Wretched of the Earth* (New York, 1968 edn.), it is also advanced by James, op. cit. pp. 27–40.

production on which the transition to socialism would be centred. For Nyerere, the basic rationale for this transition is ethical; the reason for the existence of socialism is the value system it represents. As Cranford Pratt notes, 'Nyerere's commitment to socialism had at its core a concern with the moral quality of life'.[1] Because of the relationship between this desired ethical condition and production based on the extended family, the basic unit of production in a modern, socialist Tanzania was to be the *ujamaa*. Traditional Africa provided both a motivational myth and some institutional guidelines. Since the ethics of socialism were inseparable from their institutional expression, socialism and *ujamaa* were considered congruent concepts by Nyerere. By the reorganisation of rural production into *ujamaa* units, the ethics of socialism, which had been sublimated but not destroyed, would re-emerge.[2]

For Nkrumah, capitalism was not simply a tide which had flowed in to swamp traditional values and could be made to ebb, thus leaving them uncovered. The effects of colonialism could not be reversed so easily because the changes brought by capitalism were permanent, and the contradictions which accompanied them could only be alleviated dialectically. Nkrumah thus argued that to recreate the ethics of traditional Africa it was not necessary (or possible) to re-establish the institutions which spawned them, but rather that it was essential to build a structure in which 'the principles underlying communalism are given expression in modern circumstances'.[3] The advent of these 'modern circumstances' meant that the traditional method for the social organisation of production – the village – was obsolete; modern production was class production.[4]

Thus both Nyerere and Nkrumah begin with a common premise: the ethical values of traditional communal production. But they differ on the format of production which would best encourage the renaissance of these values. While allowing for some degree of technologically derived change, Nyerere argued that the institutions which first bred

---

[1] Pratt, op. cit. p. 71.

[2] Julius K. Nyerere, *Freedom and Development/Uhuru na Maendeleo: a selection from writings and speeches, 1968–1973* (Oxford and Dar es Salam, 1973), pp. 6–7. Susanne D. Mueller has noted the striking similarities between the *ujamaa* programme in Tanzania and the Narodnik movement in Russia, which was founded on the belief that traditional peasant communalism, based on the *mir*, would form the basis of a truly Russian socialism; see 'Retarded Capitalism in Tanzania', in Ralph Miliband and John Saville (eds.), *The Socialist Register, 1980* (London, 1980), pp. 203–26. Mueller argues that the 'reactionary utopianism' and economic stagnation which result from movements of this type have thwarted the transition to socialism in Tanzania.

[3] Nkrumah, *Revolutionary Path*, p. 444, extracted from Kwame Nkrumah, *Handbook of Revolutionary Warfare* (London, 1968).

[4] See Kwame Nkrumah, *Class Struggle in Africa* (New York, 1979 edn.).

these old values must be recreated. In effect, he felt that changes in the social organisation of production could be *reversed* through will and leadership. Nkrumah, on the other hand, from the perspective of dialectical materialism, believed that change could be encouraged and channelled in a certain direction, but never reversed. While he agreed that the ethics of African communalism remained valid, he felt that they would not re-emerge by copying the structures which originally produced them. For Nkrumah, only 'progressive' changes were real.

Even at this point, their divergence from Marxist orthodoxy begins to appear. In addition to Nyerere's failure to analyse change dialectically, Issa Shivji is convinced that the minor rôle which he assigns to the proletariat in the development of Tanzanian socialism can only lead to rule by a bureaucratic bourgeoisie.[1] In short, Nyerere's sociology has deviated from a Marxist perspective not only in epistomology, by his lack of dialectical analysis, but also in ontology, by the small degree of importance given to the class struggle. Although Nkrumah believed that a true socialist revolution would depend on the growth and radicalisation of the proletariat,[2] he accepted the arguments of Mao that the first stage of this revolution required the establishment of a socialist state by a coalition of the embryonic proletariat, the radical intelligentsia, and the peasantry.[3] This too deviates from the Marxist orthodoxy of Engels and the Russian Mencheviks, which posits a strict morphology of historical development through stages. Indeed, Nkrumah at times seems to have been influenced by Trotsky, such as when he wrote that the creation of a socialist and unified Africa would lead to the destruction of capitalism in the core states.

THE TRANSITION TO SOCIALISM: REVOLUTION VERSUS REFORM

Although Nkrumah and Nyerere agreed that social change was both inevitable and desirable, they held different views about the necessary methods.

For Nyerere, social contradictions could be abated by sublimation.

---

[1] Shivji, op. cit. For a survey of 'left' critiques of Nyerere's theory, see Cranford Pratt, 'Tanzania's Transition to Socialism', loc. cit. pp. 194–207.

[2] Nkrumah, *Class Struggle in Africa*, pp. 64–74.

[3] Nkrumah was unclear as to whether the peasantry in Africa was, in fact, part of the proletariat. For instance, in *Class Struggle in Africa*, p. 79, he writes that 'The countryside is the bastion of the revolution. It is the revolutionary battlefield in which the peasantry *in alliance with* their natural class allies   the proletariat and revolutionary intelligentsia – are the driving force' (my emphasis), while on p. 80 he refers to the proletariat as 'comprising workers and peasants'.

He considered that the desired state of events – the ethical matrix of egalitarian socialism – had been damaged but not destroyed by capitalism. That is, the ethics which determined the form of traditional social relations need only be uncovered; capitalism was so alien to the African psyche that it had not transformed indigenous society in any lasting way.[1] In other words, Nyerere strongly believed that the legacy of capitalism and colonialism could not have destroyed a sense of natural socialism which had developed over centuries. The very artificialness of the ethics of capitalism meant that their removal would proceed almost spontaneously once the structures which bolstered them – colonialism and neo-colonialism – had been destroyed. In effect, the transition to socialism was not to be a revolutionary act of creation, but an evolutionary renaissance of extant but sublimated values.

The key to this line of thought is found in Nyerere's idealism, and in his definition of socialism as 'an attitude of mind'.[2] Unlike Marx, who argued that consciousness was determined by the social organisation of production, Nyerere felt that the relationship between material conditions and consciousness was more bi-directional. While the 'attitude of mind' contention 'did not mean that institutions and organisations are irrelevant',[3] Nyerere felt that a basic incongruity can exist between institutions and ethics. For this reason the transition to socialism would proceed along corollary institutions. All that was needed in Tanzania was to find some way of bringing the institutions of production back into line with the spirit of socialism which had survived the period of colonialism. This idea that the common man possessed an intrinsic moral goodness, which had been dimmed but not extinguished by an unjust system, illustrates the impact of classical political theory on Nyerere's thought.[4]

Nkrumah, on the other hand, appeared to be closer to the orthodox Marxist view that material conditions alone determined consciousness. The 'humanism' of traditional Africa had not been sublimated but drastically altered; the structures which formed the premises of the transition to socialism were not those of the far past, but those of a contradictory, neo-colonial present. That is, Nkrumah always believed that social evolution is a dialectical process, and that the only solution to the contradictions of a partially transformed society was the synthetic creation of a new matrix of social values.[5] Any form of evolutionary socialism, whether the parliamentary type proposed by Eduard

---

[1] See Nyerere, *Ujamaa*, p. 1.   [2] Ibid.   [3] Ibid. pp. 88–9.
[4] This point is made by Pratt, op. cit. pp. 72–7.
[5] Nkrumah, *Consciencism*, pp. 58ff.

Bernstein,[1] or the autarky approach of Nyerere, was impossible. Nkrumah believed that reform does not synthetically alleviate contradiction, but only refines its methods:

The passage from...capitalism to socialism can only lie through revolution: it cannot lie through reform. For in reform, fundamental principles are held constant and the details of their expression modified.[2]

The differing logics incorporated in the theories of Nkrumah and Nyerere become more evident at this point. The Tanzanian leader, who believed that African society was generally homogeneous,[3] felt that when two conditions were contradictory, the solution was to remove or sublimate one. Nkrumah, who believed that capitalism had disintegrated the basic social homogeneity of Africa,[4] argued that, according to the theory of dialectical materialism, when two situations were contradictory, the solution was a synthesis-generating conflict. Thus, for Nyerere the transition to socialism would come through adjustments to the institutions which encouraged the attitudes of capitalism; for Nkrumah it would come through a revolutionary struggle between the force of the future – the proletariat – and the forces of the present, namely bourgeois capitalism and neo-colonialism.

This debate on the method of the transition to socialism – the struggle between reform and revolution – has a long history within Marxism, dating at least from the publication of Bernstein's major work in 1899.[5] Some of the most virulent polemics of those arguing for the necessity of revolutionary change (the 'left' Marxists) have been aimed at those who favoured a non-revolutionary transition to socialism.[6] When Nkrumah writes that reform is never truly progressive because it does not represent the synthetic combination of contradictory elements,[7] he

---

[1] Eduard Bernstein, *Evolutionary Socialism* (London, 1909; republished, New York, 1961).

[2] Nkrumah, *Consciencism*, pp. 73-4.

[3] See, for example, Nyerere, *Ujamaa*, p. 11. Pratt notes, op. cit. p. 77, that 'Nyerere...argued that there were no sharply differentiated economic classes in African society'. For a discussion of the issues concerning the existence or absence of classes in Africa, see Robin Cohen, 'Class in Africa: analytical problems and perspectives', in Ralph Miliband and John Savile (eds.), *The Socialist Register, 1972* (London, 1972), pp. 231–56.

[4] Cf. Nkrumah, *Class Struggle in Africa*, p. 10, 'A fierce class struggle has been raging in Africa'.

[5] Bernstein first developed his ideas on reform and parliamentary socialism in a series of articles between 1896 and 1898 in *Die neue Zeit*. These were expanded and published in book form in 1899 under the title *Die Voraussetzungen des Sozialismus und die Aufgabe der Sozialdemokratie*, from which *Evolutionary Socialism* was drawn. For an explanation of Bernstein's arguments and the criticisms they draw, see David McLellan, *Marxism After Marx* (Boston, 1979), pp. 20–41, and Sidney Hook's introduction to *Evolutionary Socialism*.

[6] The most important and searing criticisms of Bernstein can be found in Lenin's *What Is to Be Done?* and Rosa Luxemburg's *Social Reform or Revolution?* The former has been republished, for example, in Robert C. Tucker, *The Lenin Anthology* (New York, 1975), and the latter in Dick Howard (ed.), *Selected Political Writings of Rosa Luxemburg* (New York and London, 1977).

[7] See, for example, Nkrumah, *Consciencism*, p. 72.

is well within the mainstream of a methodologically-defined Marxist orthodoxy. When he continues one step further and argues that the stifling exploitativeness of neo-colonialism demands violent rectification,[1] he becomes as much the heir of Sorel as of Rosa Luxemburg.

But, as was true with Lenin, Nkrumah's focus on revolutionary violence came after he had exhausted all other avenues for real social change. As Ralph Miliband points out, violent revolution is a strategy dictated by political conditions, and is not the diametric opposite of reform.[2] Thus the difference between Nkrumah and Nyerere on this point is not as simple as that between reform and revolution. Prior to the 1966 *coup d'état*, the Ghanaian leader too was much closer to a reformist than a revolutionary position. The emphasis on the revolutionary potential of reform, whether in Bernstein or in pre-1966 Nkrumah, is obviously a result of incumbency. The key remains with the method: reform for Nyerere was a way of sublimating conflict; for Nkrumah it was, in congruence with orthodox Marxism, a way of continuing 'struggle and more specifically class struggle on many different fronts and at many different levels'.[3] Different logics bred a variety of methods and, equally, various definitions of exactly what socialism was to be.

THE CONCEPT OF SOCIALISM: DIFFERING DEFINITIONS

Both Nkrumah and Nyerere held the almost Platonic notion that the purpose of the state was to create a proper environment for the blossoming of a desired ethical condition. Nkrumah wrote that the goal of the transition to socialism was to reconstruct African society 'in such a manner that the humanism of traditional African life reasserts itself in a modern technical community',[4] while Cranford Pratt points out that Nyerere held a similar view:

[socialism in Tanzania was] a way to utilize modern technology selectively so as to advance the welfare of her people while also building social and economic institutions which will express in modern and national terms the socialist values of traditional African society.[5]

These two leaders also agreed on the most basic feature of the socialist state during this re-flowering of traditional values. According to

---

[1] Cf. Nkrumah, *Class Struggle in Africa*, p. 85, 'But as long as violence continues to be used against the African peoples, the Party cannot achieve its objectives without the use of all forms of political struggle, including armed struggle'.

[2] Ralph Miliband, *Marxism and Politics* (Oxford, 1977), p. 166.

[3] Ibid. p. 161.

[4] Nkrumah, *Revolutionary Path*, p. 439.   [5] Pratt, op. cit. p. 243.

Nkrumah, the first tenet of socialism was 'Common ownership of the means of production, distribution, and exchange. Production is for use and not for profit.'[1] One of the four major points of the Arusha Declaration, which was the most explicit codification of Nyerere's vision of socialism, stated that 'The major means of production and exchange are under the control of the peasants and workers.'[2] But aside from these almost tautological aspects of the two definitions of socialism, the differing logics used by Nyerere and Nkrumah led to a significant divergence of concepts.

Nkrumah's use of dialectical materialism meant that he considered socialism to be merely an historical stage that would itself be transcended once the forces of production in Africa had reached the full potential of their development. The primary problem in Africa during this process resembled that faced by Lenin and the Russian Social Democrats: How can the transitional, socialist phase of the development of society be effected in the most progressive, and, as far as possible, least exploitative way? Or, in other words, How can the development of a classless society be encouraged without the long and tumultuous growth, hegemony, and eventual overthrow of the bourgeoisie?

Nkrumah's answer was virtually the same as Lenin's. This necessary social transformation was to be accomplished by a class-conscious vanguard acting in the name of the proletariat, and promulgating industralisation and the destruction of neo-colonialism.[3] Like Lenin and Trotsky, Nkrumah argued that the only method by which these goals could be attained was through the spread of the revolution to other neo-colonial areas: pan-Africanism, which was seen as a tool for the final destruction of the neo-colonial world economy, was essential.[4] Thus, Nkrumah's definition of a socialist society contained three essential elements: (1) the control of the state by a class-conscious vanguard; (2) industrialisation and the ensuing growth of the proletariat; and (3) pan-Africanism and the destruction of neo-colonial dependency.

According to Nyerere, in what has become one of the most frequently quoted statements of his theory, 'Socialism – like democracy – is essentially an attitude of mind',[5] rather than an institutional structure. This might at first seem to represent a radical departure from a materialist philosophy, and to place the Tanzanian leader more squarely in the

---

[1] Nkrumah, *Revolutionary Path*, p. 466. [2] Nyerere, *Ujamaa*, p. 16.

[3] Within Ghana this vanguard was the Convention People's Party (C.P.P.). Later Nkrumah proposed the formation of an All-African Committee for Political Co-ordination and an All-African People's Revolutionary Army to play this rôle for the continent as a whole. See Book 2, ch. 1, pt. B of *Handbook of Revolutionary Warfare*, extracts of which appear in *Revolutionary Path*.

[4] See, for instance, Kwame Nkrumah, *Africa Must Unite* (London and New York, 1963).

[5] Nyerere, *Ujamaa*, p. 1.

idealist school. This appearance is reinforced by Nyerere's contention that even a millionaire, if in possession of the ideas of socialism, could be a good socialist.[1] If, in fact, he did claim that socialism *equals* socialist consciousness and ethics, then the idealist label would be deserved. However, Nyerere realised that the relationship between socialist organisation and socialist consciousness is dynamic, with each dependent on the other. If socialism was strictly an attitude, and if, as Nyerere argued, this attitude was extant but dormant in Tanzania, all that would have been required for the transition to socialism would be the removal of the neo-colonial restraints on this nascent socialism. But from Nyerere's vigorous efforts to re-organise social production in *ujamaa* units, it is obvious that he felt that the institutional structure of socialism played a major rôle in the growth of the proper consciousness. Thus although it can be argued that Nyerere placed greater emphasis on the mental aspects of socialism than Nkrumah, there is no evidence that he was oblivious to the need for this consciousness to receive institutional encouragement.

This emphasis on consciousness is indicative of the defining element of Nyerere's conception of socialism. What delineates socialism from capitalism is not control of the means of production, but the method of social distribution. A society is socialist when its produce is distributed equitably, and it is capitalist when exploitation is used to fuel personal accumulation.[2]

This focus on the attitudinal aspects of socialism again illustrates the key rôle which the ethical element of social relations played in Nyerere's theory. Socialism for Nyerere was not necessary, as Marx argued, because it was the most efficacious solution to social contradications,[3] but was sought because of the ethical state which it entailed. So in effect, Nyerere considered that the ethics of socialism formed the teleological foundation of the social organisation of production rather than simply a part of the social superstructure.

Because of Nyerere's emphasis on the ethical and psychological elements of socialism, his institutional prescriptions differed from those of Nkrumah. Although the Ghanaian leader remained painfully aware of the essential rôle which economic development played in the overthrow of neo-colonialism and in the creation of the proletariat, he placed tremendous emphasis on industrialisation and mechanisation.[4]

---

[1] Ibid.   [2] Ibid.

[3] This reading of Marx applies, of course, more to the 'late Marx' than the author of the *Economic and Philosophic Manuscripts of 1844*.

[4] For a discussion of the economics of forced industialisation in Ghana, see Emily Card, 'The Political Economy of Ghana', in Richard Harris (ed.), *The Political Economy of Africa* (New York, 1975), pp. 49–92.

Nyerere, on the other hand, focused on the improvement and growth of agricultural production.[1] Since the purpose of socialism for Nyerere was the creation of a certain ethical order rather than the alleviation of contradictions in the social organisation of production, he felt that the use of traditional methods of social organisation would foster at least an acceptable level of economic growth while preserving the humanistic elements of production.[2]

CONCLUSION: DIFFERING LOGICS

Nkrumah and Nyerere began with similar analyses of the primary problems which their nations faced and ended with generally similar notions of what the social organisation of production in a socialist society would look like. Why then, are their paths between premises and conclusions so different? The answer lies with the interpretations of social and historical epistomology and ontology – the logics – employed. Nkrumah utilised a form of dialectical materialism in his analysis. He saw social development as determined not by attitudes or ethics, but by empirical changes in the organisation of production. In an orthodox Marxist vein, Nkrumah felt that this stage of development was defined by the status of class conflict and the forces which this entailed. Contradiction, which was an inevitable result of class society, was alleviated synthetically, through struggle. The only rational strategy for social progress was that which operated within this general framework – the laws of history could be quickened, but not transcended.

For Nyerere there were no fixed stages of development. His theory of history was closer to that of classical European liberals: the way forward can be controlled through effort, rationality, and will. Traditional African life had provided the goal of historical change: an ethical, egalitarian society. The strategy of the political leader entailed the discovery of the paths to this goal and the encouragement of movement

---

[1] Two section headings of the Arusha Declaration, which outlined Nyerere's strategy for the development of socialism in Tanzania, were entitled 'We Have Put Too Much Emphasis on Industries', and 'Agriculture Is the Basis of Development'. For more on the economics of the *ujamaa* programme, see Jonathan Baker, 'The Debate on Rural Socialism in Tanzania', and Jannik Boesen, 'Tanzania: from ujamaa to villagization', both in Mwansasu and Pratt (eds.), op. cit.; also Peter Temu, 'The Ujamaa Experiment', in Kwan S. Kim et al. (eds.), *Papers on the Political Economy of Tanzania* (Nairobi, 1979), pp. 197–2 .

[2] For example, according to Nyerere, *Ujamaa*, p. 92, 'If the pursuit of wealth clashes with things like human dignity and social equality, then the latter will be given priority'. But as Lofchie argues in 'Agrarian Socialism in the Third World', the abysmal economic performance of the *ujamaa* programme has led to its de-emphasis. However, Goran Hyden, op. cit. pp. 194ff., makes a point similar to Nyerere's argument, when he notes that a socialist strategy for development cannot be evaluated on economic performance alone.

towards its achievement. The contradictions faced by African states were not to be solved through internal social struggle, but by eliminating the elements which caused them. Exploitation and capitalism were not to be transcended, but simply removed. While Nkrumah felt that the state could be changed by social relations, Nyerere argued that they could revolutionise the state.

It is possible, at least on a tentative basis, to place Nkrumah and Nyerere within the larger context of socialist thinking. Given the former's emphasis on dialectical materialism and the transformation of society through the leadership of a state controlled by a vanguard party, Nkrumah undoubtedly falls somewhere within what can be called orthodox Marxism–Leninism. However, according to Jitendra Mohan, although 'Nkrumahism...was vaguely seen as the "adaptation" of Marxism to Africa...what the precise adaptations were remained obscure'.[1] By way of contrast, Bethwell A. Ogot suggests that in many ways Nkrumah's adaptation of Marx was just as 'orthodox' as Lenin's was in his time.[2]

Nyerere is even less easy to categorise, although he has been often called a 'populist' or 'democratic' socialist. His theory of history, as noted above, is similar to that of the European liberals. His emphasis on the rôle of pre-capitalist social organisation, on the formation of small, democratic political units, and on 'natural' or traditional forms of social life as justification of socialism, often appear closer to Rousseau than to Marx.[3]

Does the fact that Nkrumah was the 'more orthodox' of the two have more than a passing interest? Perhaps. Nyerere, of course, has been able to retain political power while Nkrumah was removed by a *coup d'état* in 1966. But while Tanzania has moved further and further from the path outlined in Nyerere's theory,[4] Nkrumah's analysis seems vindicated

[1] Jitendra Mohan, 'Nkrumah and Nkrumahism', in Miliband and Savile (eds.), op. cit. *1967*, p. 211.

[2] Bethwell A. Agot, 'Nkrumah Revisits Marx', in *East Africa Journal* (Nairobi), 1, 3, June 1964, p. 30.

[3] The parallels between Nyerere and Rousseau have been noted by Pratt, op. cit. p. 73.

[4] According to Pratt, loc. cit. p. 203, 'Marxist socialists have come to the conclusion that Tanzania can no longer be judged to be in transition to socialism'. Examples and further discussions of these 'left' critiques can be found in Shivji, op. cit.; William Tordoff and Ali A. Mazrui, 'The Left and the Super-Left in Tanzania' in *The Journal of Modern African Studies* (Cambridge), 10, 3, October 1972, pp. 427–45; Christopher Mulei, 'The Predicament of the Left in Tanzania', in *East Africa Journal*, 9, 8, August 1972, p. 32; Susanne D. Mueller, 'Retarded Capitalism in Tanzania'; and Colin Leys, 'The Overdeveloped Post-Colonial State: a re-evaluation', in *Review of African Political Economy* (London), 5, January–April 1976, pp. 39–48.

since he continually argued that the transition to socialism in Africa was impossible so long as the bonds of neo-colonialism were not broken through pan-Africanism. But the 25 years of history which encompass the experiment of African socialism is a tiny slice of time, so while Nyerere's and Nkrumah's theories of socialism can be outlined and contrasted, a complete evaluation must be postponed for the future.

The Journal of Modern African Studies, 20, 1, (1982), pp. 107–126

Ethnicity and Leadership in Africa: the 'Untypical' Case of Tom Mboya

by DAVID GOLDSWORTHY*

THIS article seeks to relate a biographical case-study to some 'liberal' and 'radical' ways of thinking about ethnicity. The Kenyan political leader Tom Mboya, who was active in labour and political affairs from 1951 until his death in 1969, was widely regarded as genuinely non-tribalist in his politics. Yet he exercised successful leadership within a political system characterised very strongly, according to a great many observers and participants, by the play of ethnic forces. His would appear to be a strikingly deviant case, and hence may be seen as a useful point of departure for a reconsideration of ideas about ethnic factors in political leadership.

Lest any liberals or radicals feel that their views are being caricatured in what follows, it should be stressed that particular arguments about ethnicity are not necessarily seen as the exclusive preserve of particular camps. Of course, there is overlap and interpenetration. Not all liberals and not all radicals suffer from paradigmatic tunnel vision, a point which the final part of this article tries specifically to demonstrate. Nevertheless, some arguments are more characteristic of one view than of the other, and the broad labels 'liberal' and 'radical' serve the simple purpose of sign-posting these characteristic features.

The first step is to arm ourselves with a set of descriptive ideas about ethnicity which will be broadly serviceable throughout the discussion.

ETHNICITY

Ethnicity is sometimes conceptualised in terms of objective attributes, or 'badges of identity', such as language and kinship. But it is more generally useful to regard it as a form of consciousness, a *sense* of identity, that is usually associated with the existence of such attributes. Whether

* Reader in Politics, Monash University, Clayton, Victoria, Australia.

this consciousness is 'false' or not may sometimes be at issue between radicals and liberals, but does not matter at this stage; either way, it is consciousness.

In politics, 'ethnicist' – or as it is commonly termed, tribalist[1] – behaviour is action that takes the form it does because this sense of identity exists, or is presumed to exist. There is no doubt that political actors consistently favour their own ethnic 'category' or 'group',[2] and they do so in a variety of ways: by the distribution of jobs, contracts, licences, development grants, etcetera; by the unending competition for these goods, in so far as all concerned are perceived in ethnic terms; and by actions which are designed to exploit or to accommodate other people's sense of ethnic identity. All these are examples of tribalist behaviour, in that they are premised upon the existence of ethnic consciousness. This point is not affected by questions of whether ethnicity is of high or low salience in the actor's *own* consciousness. In practice there is a wide range of possibilities: one actor may feel 'committed' by his ethnicity, another may take a detached and manipulative view.

For ethnicity is a variable, in the full sense of that term. Writers on the subject appear to be in general agreement that ethnicity should be regarded not as a 'constant' form of consciousness, giving rise to fixed loyalties and stimulating predictable actions in all circumstances, but – in Nelson Kasfir's words – as fluid, situational, and intermittent.[3] The sense of ethnic identity is itself mutable; people may shift, in their own and others' perceptions, from one ethnic category to another. Further, ethnicity is only one of many possible identities that can underlie, or be mobilised in, political action, some others being national, racial, religious, and occupational identities. By no means all political situations will evoke an ethnically-defined response, and those that do will evoke it in widely varying degrees of intensity.

[1] Because there are no such words as 'ethnicist' and 'ethnicism' in the lexicon, this discussion will perforce make use of 'tribalist' and 'tribalism'. We are not, however, concerned with 'tribe' in its technical sense, i.e. a consanguineous group under a traditional leader such as a chief, having its own territory and political system.

[2] An ethnic *category* is an aggregation of people who share certain basic cultural attributes, notably language, and claim to have a common ancestry and/or region of origin, but who do not engage in corporate political activities. An ethnic *group* is an aggregation of members of an ethnic category, who are aware of their identity and who actively pursue political, economic, and/or social goals in their presumed collective interest. This usage broadly follows that developed by Abner Cohen, *Custom and Politics in Urban Africa: a study of Hausa migrants in Yoruba towns* (London, 1969).

[3] See, for example, Nelson Kasfir, 'Explaining Ethnic Political Participation', in *World Politics* (Princeton), xxxi, 3, April 1979, especially pp. 369–78; Cohen, op. cit.; and Cynthia H. Enloe, *Ethnic Soldiers: state security in divided societies* (Harmondsworth, 1980), p. 6.

Several writers argue further that ethnicity in the political sphere functions usually as a dependent variable, something which can be directed towards secular ends – political power, material acquisition, etcetera – as and when the situation requires. Walter Barrows, for example, maintains that 'identity ' is mobilised in the cause of 'utility' much more often than vice versa.[1] In a pioneering article, Richard Sklar made a similar point from a radical perspective, suggesting that 'utility' might best be seen in class terms.[2] Both scholars would no doubt accept Robert Melson and Howard Wolpe's general formulation: 'it is probably more accurate to suggest that conflict produces "tribalism" than to argue...that "tribalism" is the cause of conflict'.[3]

It may be said, in short, that radical and liberal writers tend to agree that ethnicity is a form of consciousness that is open to exploitation by politicians. However, they tend to part company on the ideological character of ethnicity, and also on the question of its sources. The divergences on these matters are central to our discussion, and we must now try to pursue them.

THE LIBERAL EMPHASIS ON ETHNIC ENTRAPMENT

If we depart the common ground and enter more thoroughly into the liberal mode of discourse, we will soon encounter certain riders to the preceding account. Generalisations such as those of Barrows and Melson and Wolpe are acceptable; but the qualifiers – 'more often', 'probably' – are important too. To overstress ethnicity's rôle as a dependent variable is to understress its rôle as a psycho-social force having its own undetermined power to shape events. The mobilisation of identity is not always a function of utility; it is perfectly possible, as Abner Cohen argues, that identity may itself determine ways in which utility is both defined and pursued, for the symbols of identity have considerable normative power.[4] Similarly, by no means all manifestations of ethnicity in politics are easily attributable to initiatives taken by leaders. Rather, leaders sometimes appear to be constrained by ethnicity, feeling obliged to recognise its importance in the consciousness

[1] Walter L. Barrows, 'Comparative Grassroots Politics in Africa', in *World Politics*, xxvi, 2, January 1974, p. 284.

[2] Richard L. Sklar, 'Political Science and National Integration – A Radical Approach', in *The Journal of Modern African Studies* (Cambridge), v, 1, May 1967, pp. 1–11, especially p. 6.

[3] Robert Melson and Howard Wolpe, 'Modernization and the Politics of Communalism: a theoretical perspective', in *American Political Science Review* (Menasha), lxiv, 4, December 1970, p. 1123.

[4] Abner Cohen, 'Introduction: the lesson of ethnicity', in Cohen (ed.), *Urban Ethnicity* (London, 1974).

of other people – followers or peers – and to tailor their actions accordingly. Here we are approaching a key idea which may be labelled, for convenience, 'ethnic entrapment'. It reflects, clearly, the notion of ethnicity as an independent variable, and it can be illustrated by culling a few observations from the liberal literature.

Tom Mboya himself wrote of one microcosmic reason for the persistence of ethnic sentiment among African leaders:

They are still to some degree 'communal' because of their background and their relatives remaining tribal, and so they themselves cannot afford to change at the risk of offending and losing their family.[1]

Much broader, however, are the exigencies of creating and maintaining a power base. In the colonial era, remarks Elliott Skinner, 'many an African leader with universalistic values found that he *had to* appeal to group identity based on descent, if he would galvanize his followers to seek political power'.[2] And after independence, as P. H. Gulliver argues,

African politicians *necessarily require* a firm base for their operations in the still unstable, inchoate national arena. What better, in the short run, to ensure support, electoral and other, and to wield a powerful political weapon, than to stand as the representative and spokesman of the tribe?[3]

But what might have been intended for the 'short run' develops very naturally into a political way of life. Politicians based on ethnic constituencies, and tied to them by all manner of reciprocal bonds, will find it extraordinarily difficult to shift to any alternative base. This dependence governs more and more of their decisions and actions. Gulliver writes:

Political leaders can seldom afford to neglect the particularist divisions of their country, the power and support that they derive from one or another of these, and the necessity to satisfy demands of a local or regional kind. The phenomenon of so-called 'ethnic arithmetic' has frequently been noted in the composition of cabinets, committees, boards, secretariats, etc., as particularist interests and loyalties are recognized and catered for.[4]

To some extent these processes constitute both a vicious circle and a self-fulfilling prophecy. On the first of these, Melson and Wolpe observe: 'aspirant politicians make communal appeals and communal

---

[1] Tom Mboya, *Freedom and After* (London, 1963), p. 70.
[2] Elliott Skinner, 'Group Dynamics in the Politics of Changing Societies: the problem of "tribal" politics in Africa', in June Helm (ed.), *Essays on the Problem of Tribe* (Seattle, 1968), p. 183, my emphasis.
[3] P. H. Gulliver, 'Introduction', in Gulliver (ed.), *Tradition and Transition in East Africa: studies of the tribal element in the modern era* (London, 1969), p. 17, my emphasis.
[4] Ibid. p. 19.

demands which exacerbate communal tensions; these tensions, in turn, encourage the recruitment of leaders who will make communal appeals and demands'. And on the second:

the personal fortunes of individuals are generally believed to depend on their communal origins and connections. This being the case, individuals plan and organize accordingly. Thus, the aspirant...politician seeks to mobilize his 'tribal union' behind his candidacy...the common expectation of the primacy of communal criteria produces the self-fulfilling prophecy of communally-oriented competitive strategies.[1]

All these factors combine to weave a net that is very fine-meshed indeed, one which even the most eminent of national leaders have found hard to escape. Thus William Ochieng comments pithily on the dilemma of Jomo Kenyatta in the 1940s: 'He wished to operate as a nationalist leader of Kenya, but the Kikuyu were planning in tribal terms.'[2]

In summation of these various points, we may cite Colin Legum's positing of an essentially reciprocal relationship between leaders and led:

The elitist political leader in the modern system *needs* his 'constituency' – *invariably* a tribe or at best a region – on which to rest his power, just as the tribal or regional constituency needs its loyal representatives to defend and promote their interests in the modern sector.[3]

The idea of entrapment conveyed by such terms as 'needs' and 'invariably' is indeed a strong one. Let us take it that the notion of ethnicity's constraining rôle in politics is sufficiently demonstrated, and look now at a kind of view which, among other things, denies it any such rôle.

THE RADICAL EMPHASIS ON ETHNICITY AS EPIPHENOMENON

To deny ethnicity any political function independent of the machinations of the politicans is not an intrinsically Marxist idea, and there are various non-Marxist formulations of it in the literature.[4] But the Marxist version expresses the idea in its strongest and most distinctive form, perceiving politicians as members of the dominant class and

[1] Melson and Wolpe, loc. cit. pp. 1122 and 1115.
[2] William R. Ochieng, 'Tribalism and National Unity: the Kenyan case', in Aloo Ojuka and Ochieng (eds.), *Politics and Leadership in Africa* (Nairobi, 1975), p. 263.
[3] Colin Legum, 'Tribal Survival in the Modern African Political System', in *Journal of Asian and African Studies* (Leiden), v, 1–2, January-April 1970, p. 112, my emphasis.
[4] See e.g. Elizabeth Colson, 'Contemporary Tribes and the Development of Nationalism', in Helm (ed.), op. cit. pp. 202–3.

regarding the function of tribalism as ideological. Ethnicity serves capitalism by retarding the development of mass class consciousness, which in turn is achieved by the deliberate re-casting of such issues into ethnic terms. Thus politicians seek to secure their class position by constructing intra-tribal patron-client hierarchies, defining social conflicts in terms of ethnic relationships, and so on. According to this argument, although ethnic *categories* have an undoubted objective existence, it does not follow that ethnic *groups* must develop, let alone on a basis of mutual hostility and competition. For that particular trend in contemporary Africa, the agents of capitalism – abetted by bourgeois social scientists – are very largely responsible.

An important statement of this position with regard to Kenya is provided by Colin Leys. Having made no mention of tribalism or ethnicity until well towards the end of his book on Kenyan capitalism, he remarks:

> It is tempting to leave it that way...'tribalism' is in the first instance an ideological phenomenon. Essentially it consists in the fact that people identify other exploited people as the source of their insecurity and frustrations, rather than their common exploiters. Of course this does not happen 'spontaneously'. Colonial regimes have played an important part in fostering tribalism...after independence politicians have often played similar roles.[1]

Leys sees no point, then, in focusing on tribalism, since, being epiphenomenal, it has little explanatory power. Only a materialist analysis can properly explicate political action, which includes the action of political leaders. Leys suggests that 'among Africanists' this point probably no longer needs arguing;[2] and, certainly, there are several other writers who have adopted fairly similar positions.[3]

We have not, be it noted again, sought to argue that the liberal and radical positions are neatly and symmetrically opposed to each other, such that one 'must' be right and the other wrong. Rather, we have tried to indicate some features which these positions have in common, and some which typically differentiate them. It is within this context of ideas that we may now look at ethnicity in Kenya, and the case of Tom Mboya.

---

[1] Colin Leys, *Underdevelopment in Kenya: the political economy of neo-colonialism, 1964–1971* (London, 1975), pp. 198–9.   [2] Ibid. p. 198, fn. 42.

[3] See e.g. Archie Mafeje, 'The Ideology of "Tribalism"', in *The Journal of Modern African Studies*, IX, 2, June 1971, pp. 253–61; Kenneth Good, 'The Static Concept and Changing Reality of Tribe: an aspect of the ideology of underdevelopment', in *Australian and New Zealand Journal of Sociology* (Clayton, Victoria), XI, 3, October 1975, pp. 34–7; and Mahmood Mamdani, *Politics and Class Formation in Uganda* (New York and London, 1976).

ETHNICITY IN KENYA

We remarked at the outset on the perceived strength of ethnicity as a factor in Kenyan politics. Mboya himself wrote that 'Kenya has been afflicted a good deal with negative tribalism'.[1] The most prevalent explanation of this affliction is that the senses of difference among Kenya's ethnic categories developed to an intense degree as a result of the country's specific experience of colonialism. This proposition appears to be common ground for radicals and liberals,[2] in the sense that both are able to interpret it in such a way as to support their positions. Once again, they tend to part company on the question of the precise relationships between ethnicity and class, and on the nature of ethnicity's ideological function. But once that is noted, it can be said that both point to much the same explanatory factors: for example, European settlement and land alienation; the very uneven penetration of western culture and cash economy into different regions; and the administrative practice of divide-and-rule, which in the Emergency of the 1950s was taken to the extreme of forbidding African political organisation, except on a regional basis. Among their other effects, all these factors helped transform Kenya's ethnic categories into fairly exclusivist groups, whose political leaders interacted essentially as ambassadors rather than colleagues.

Most profoundly affected by colonialism were the Kikuyu clans of Central Province. Their powerful grievances and their centrality to the Kenyan system heightened not only their own sense of identity, but also a general sense of difference between Kikuyu and others. Mboya wrote in 1963 of colonial Nairobi, where 'the antagonism between Kikuyu and Luo was such that they fought on sight. They did not even quarrel about anything, they just fought.'[3]

Independence brought a rapid consolidation of the power and prosperity of the better-placed Kikuyu and their political allies, so that senses of difference and feelings of relative deprivation among less-favoured groups reinforced each other to potent effect. Thus the second largest – but generally much poorer – ethnic category, the Luo, had by the late 1960s passed from a brief tactical alliance with the Kikuyu to embittered oppositionism. At the time of his death in 1969, Mboya was the last prominently placed Luo in the Government.

The foregoing are broad brush-strokes indeed, doing little justice to

[1] Mboya, op. cit. pp. 72–3.
[2] See e.g. Leys, op. cit. pp. 200–3; Ochieng, loc. cit., and George Bennett, 'Tribalism in Politics', in Gulliver (ed.), op. cit. pp. 59–87.
[3] Mboya, op. cit. p. 71.

the many complexities and cross-currents of Kenyan politics. Still, they will suffice to convey the background of ethnic tensions against which a closer consideration of Mboya's rôle may now be attempted.[1]

THE CELEBRANT IMAGE: MBOYA AS NON-TRIBALIST

Whatever else may be said about Mboya – and he had many detractors – no one has ever judged him a tribalist. Ochieng's view of him as one of the tiny handful who had transcended 'parochial tribal loyalty', and Cherry Gertzel's judgement that he 'symbolised a commitment to national development [and]...was not an ethnic leader',[2] are entirely typical.

In outline, the conventional picture of Mboya the non-tribalist might be sketched as follows. He was born a Luo in Kikuyu country. He had an unusually travelled childhood, growing up in various parts of Kikuyu, Kamba, and Luo territory, and assimilating the customs and languages of all three. As a youth he learned his trade – that of sanitary inspector – in the multi-tribal environment of the Jeanes School. There he matured into a rational, secular, thoroughly demystified adult. He went on to fashion his whole career in the multi-tribal – though predominantly Kikuyu – milieu of Nairobi. As a labour leader he constructed a pan-tribal trade-union movement, working with and for people who were mainly from ethnic backgrounds other than his own. He then made Nairobi his political base. Alone among Kenyan politicians, Mboya scorned the easy security of an ethnically supportive constituency. Instead, he was elected to the National Assembly three times – 1957, 1961, 1963 – on a multi-tribal vote in the capital city. In the late 1960s he worked zealously to undermine the opposition Kenya Peoples Union, notwithstanding that party's substantially Luo support. No other Kenyan politician before or since has so thoroughly divorced his politics from his own ethnic identity. Mboya thus provided an object lesson in his own declared principles:

That we are born of different tribes we cannot change, but I refuse to believe that because our tribes have different backgrounds, culture and customs, we cannot create an African community or a nation.[3]

The tragic irony is that Mboya was himself a victim of ethnicity. He could never have reached the very top, so it was said, because he

---

[1] The material on which this consideration is based is drawn primarily from David Goldsworthy, *Tom Mboya* (London and Nairobi, 1982).

[2] Ochieng, loc. cit. p. 266; and Cherry Gertzel, 'Development in the Dependent State: the Kenyan case', in *Australian Outlook* (Canberra), xxxii, 1, April 1978, p. 97.

[3] Mboya, op. cit. p. 70.

belonged to the 'wrong' ethnic category; and he was murdered in what appeared to be, in part, an act of Kikuyu political self-interest.

It will be argued here that the image is consonant with the reality only up to a point. This is meant not to belittle Mboya's enormous contribution to national politics in Kenya, but to emphasise the fact that the image, by being a good deal too simple, does disservice both to historical understanding of Mboya's rôle and to a more general apprehension of ethnic factors in politics. That is, it tends to lend credibility to a dichotomistic view: either one is tribalist in one's politics (for whatever reasons), or one is not. The value of a case like Mboya's is that it helps to show that the reality is vastly more complex than that.

To begin developing the point, let us consider Mboya's objective ethnic identity, and what it subjectively meant to him.

MBOYA'S ETHNIC IDENTITY

Tom Mboya was born a 'Suba' Luo. The Suba were by distant origin a Bantu group native to the Mbita-Rusinga area of South Nyanza. In the late eighteenth century the Nilotic Luo migrated into the area from the north, and in due course the Suba came to perceive themselves, and to be perceived by others, as a Luo sub-group. Yet they retain vestiges of their original culture, and are still generally bi-lingual in Suba and Luo.

It is clear that Mboya was conscious of his background and took a definite pride in it. Though he had never lived in South Nyanza, he always spoke of it – and more especially Rusinga Island, where his parents and other kinsfolk lived – as home ('my little island home', he wrote in his memoirs). His marriages were contracted within the Luo community: both his shortlived union under Luo custom in the early 1950s, and his Roman Catholic wedding in 1962. As a young man in Nairobi he chose to live in Kaloleni, the 'Luo' location.[1] He took an active part in the affairs of the Nairobi branch of the Luo Union, serving for a time as its secretary. In 1956–7 he did, it seems, think seriously about standing for Parliment in South Nyanza rather than Nairobi, giving up the idea only because it would have meant forfeiting his established power in trade unionism. Later, he began to deepen his personal stakes in Luoland itself, acquiring a farm in South Nyanza, establishing some small businesses and having a house built in Kisumu, the Luo 'capital'.

[1] Choice was still possible in 1951. After the Emergency began, Mboya was moved by the authorities to Bahati, a mainly Kikuyu location, probably to make surveillance easier by grouping him with the other 'trouble-makers'.

His own views on tribalism were set out at various points in his writings.[1] Mboya distinguished between what he called 'positive' and 'negative' tribalism. The tribalism he condemned in politics was of the latter variety – meaning, essentially, ethnic xenophobia. But he never condemned positive tribalism, by which he meant the communality and generosity of African traditional life, the ethic of 'mutual social responsibility'. This he saw as being of great social and psychic value to masses of people, and he more than once drew comfort from it in his own life.

Mboya was not, then, secular in the sense of lacking particularist loyalty and condemning all things tribal. Rather, his attitude was one of ethnic tolerance blended with a distinct pride in being Luo. And valuing his identity thus, he expected others to do the same.

Such observations may serve as an initial modification of the conventional image. But the key questions are those which arise from the arguments outlined earlier. How far did Mboya, in fact, manipulate ethnicity as a dependent variable in his practical politics? And did even he have to acknowledge the power of the 'ethnic trap', and tailor his politics accordingly?

ETHNIC FACTORS IN MBOYA'S CAREER

1. As Trade Unionist

As General Secretary of the Kenya Federation of Labour from 1953 to 1963, Mboya was clearly non-tribalist in the sense that he showed no obvious favouritism towards Luo colleagues or Luo trade unionists generally. Throughout the years of the Emergency much of his detailed case-work was done on behalf of the Kikuyu workers who were suffering most at the hands of employers and officialdom.

Yet over the years he showed himself well enough aware of the need to accommodate ethnic sensitivities. The trade-union movement was in fact multi-tribal, especially in and around Nairobi where Mboya was based; Kikuyu, Kamba, Luhya, and Luo were all strongly represented. In these circumstances Mboya needed to ensure that the unionists regarded him primarily as their patron rather than as a Luo, for the alternative perception would certainly have limited his effectiveness. Ethnic neutrality was also ethnic rationality. Where, however, a particular union comprised mainly members of one ethnic category, Mboya would not overlook this factor in organising its leadership – a

---

[1] Mboya, op. cit. pp. 67–74; also Tom Mboya, 'Is African Culture Blocking Progress?', in *East Africa Journal* (Nairobi), 1, 10, March 1965, pp. 26–30.

Luo, for example, was sent to run the mainly Luo Dock Workers' Union in Mombasa. And his ethnic neutrality did not prevent him from practising the skills of ethnic arithmetic in constructing 'slates' of candidates for trade-union posts.

This was especially apparent when it came to the crucial business of maintaining the K.F.L.'s power structure and his own position therein. In the late 1950s, for example, several Luhya officials rose to prominence in the Federation. Fairly clearly, Mboya was attempting to build an alliance with the other main ethnic category of West Kenya in order to bolster his position against Kikuyu labour leaders who were beginning to emerge from detention, and who were seeking to re-establish themselves in the labour movement. Subsequently, however, he made a number of significant Kikuyu appointments: Fred Kubai, Jesse Gachago, Babu Kamau, and other militant leaders were all given important posts. This might have seemed to be weakening his own position, since few of these men showed much fondness for Mboya. But to have left the 'new Kikuyu' unrepresented would have been to court an even greater risk of disruption and challenge.

In ways like these, Mboya could be seen as acknowledging the strength of ethnic considerations and acting accordingly. 'Self-fulfilling prophecy', perhaps; but also an example of ethnic manipulation and, arguably, 'entrapment'.

2. As Nairobi Politician

That Mboya was elected three times as a Member of Parliament in Nairobi is often seen as a triumphant vindication of his non-tribal approach to politics. Analysis shows, however, that this is a rather simple view of a complex reality.

His first election in 1957 was achieved in a tiny constituency of some 2,300 voters, mainly Luo, Luhya, and Kamba. Ethnic factors were neutralised in that his major opponent, Clement Argwings-Kodhek, was also a Luo (though Kodhek was not above insinuating to Luo audiences that Mboya, as a Suba, was not a 'true' Luo). Mboya won by no great margin.

During 1957–8 he established a political machine, the Nairobi Peoples Convention Party. As in the K.F.L., he showed due sensitivity to the matter of ethnic arithmetic: the N.P.C.P.'s leadership group in 1958 included three Luo, two Kikuyu, and two Luhya. And again, the return of the Kikuyu in strength around 1960 was well reflected in new appointments to Mboya's organisation.

In fact, between 1957 and 1961 Mboya displayed a consistent and obviously prudential drive to reinforce his position in Nairobi by cultivating links with influential Kikuyu leaders. They included Gikonyo Kiano, Josef Mathenge, Kariuki Njiiri, James Gichuru, Njoroge Mungai, Munyua Waiyaki, and Mwai Kibaki. For various reasons, several of these alliances were fairly short-lived, but that does not alter the point about Mboya's intentions.

The 1961 election was the critical one. Nairobi East, Mboya's constituency, embraced some 40,000 voters of whom about 27,000 were Kikuyu. His major opponent was his erstwhile Kikuyu associate Dr Waiyaki, who was backed by a range of Mboya's powerful foes. Yet Mboya trounced Waiyaki by 31,000 votes to 3,000. How was this achieved?

Gertzel has commented that in the Nairobi of 1961, 'tribe and economics did not obviously run a parallel course'.[1] Her meaning may perhaps be teased out thus. Mboya won because he was, above all, the most effective patron figure in Kenyan African politics. In this period, his was very much a 'politics of utility'. As K.F.L. leader and an M.P., he was a man of established and proven power who got results – whether in negotiating wage rises for workers, securing educational opportunities abroad in the intensely political 'airlifts', or pressuring the British and Kenyan Governments for political freedom. But more specifically, he was a major patron of the Nairobi Kikuyu. For nearly a decade, while many Kikuyu leaders were languishing in detention, he had been effectively representing the interests of Kikuyu workers, detainees, and dispossessed. In this respect his 'non-tribal' work now paid an ethnic political dividend. Once again, it may be said that an ethnically neutral approach in Nairobi was also a rational strategy.

Put differently: Tom Mboya knew very well that if he was to build a career on an ethnically alien base, he would have to follow certain lines of action. It was politically important for him both to forge all the links he could with the Kikuyu leadership, and to become a valued patron of the Kikuyu masses. Once again he was, in short, anything but heedless of the ethnic dimension.

The 1963 election, too, was *sui generis*. This time, in a different and smaller constituency, Mboya's main opponent was an Asian representing a minority party, so that the result was a foregone conclusion.

Later developments in Nairobi politics, however, brought a slide in Mboya's fortunes. In 1968 several of his enemies in the Kenya African National Union, led by certain Kikuyu who seemed affronted by Mboya's continuing tenure of a 'Kikuyu' seat, contrived to seize

---

[1] Cherry Gertzel, *The Politics of Independent Kenya, 1963–8* (London, 1970), p. 11.

control of the Nairobi branch of the party from his lieutenants. In addition, by the late 1960s Mboya had lost much of his local popularity. As a minister he seemed more and more a remote '*Wabenzi*' figure, with little time to spare for grassroots work in his constituency. It is likely that his 1969 re-election campaign – had he lived to fight it – would have been very difficult indeed. Given that a 'politics of identity' was not available to him in Nairobi, he needed his 'politics of utility' to survive; yet by this time he was no longer in a position to engage in such politics.

In this connection it is worth noting certain indications that Mboya was perhaps a good deal more interested in reverting to a 'home' base, where utility and identity converged, than either his admirers or detractors realised.

3. *As Nyanza Politician*

Mboya was always regarded as having no great influence or following in Luoland. The acknowledged and widely popular political leader of the Luo was Oginga Odinga, and within his *fief* Mboya came increasingly to be regarded, it seems, as something of a traitor, a consort of the Kikuyu. One sign of this attitude was that in the 'Little General Election' of 1966, when Mboya was campaigning in Central Nyanza against Odinga's K.P.U., his personal safety was thought to be in jeopardy.

But the view that Mboya lacked a Nyanza following seems, once again, too simple. Odinga's power was unchallengeable only in Central Nyanza. In South Nyanza, Mboya exercised increasing influence during the 1960s, especially in the crucial matters of controlling party branches and tying-up parliamentary nominations in order to reinforce his faction against his opponents in party, parliament, and government. Thus, in both 1961 and 1963, Mboya loyalists won K.A.N.U. endorsement for the key seats in South Nyanza. Leading Mboya associates such as Samuel Ayodo, Otieno Ogingo, and Joseph Odero-Jowi were all based in the region.

No less significant was the manner in which Mboya increasingly acted as a patron or 'big man' in the Rusinga-Mbita area, providing schools, dispensaries, a hospital, a ferry, road lighting, and other coveted services – almost as if he were M.P. for that area, rather than suburban Nairobi. The deepening of his personal business and other interests in the region have already been noted. Collectively, these actions bear the interpretation that he was husbanding his home district against the possible loss of his Nairobi base. And, of course, it might not have been wholly a matter of leadership initiative. It is probable that, as the 1960s progressed, South Nyanza was increasingly demanding such services of Mboya, who was after all the most powerful son of the region in the Government; in other words, that the relationship was reciprocal, and that the phenomenon of ethnic entrapment was part of the picture.

In short, although he was not an active ethnic-regional leader, the links were there, and appeared to be strengthening. And as many have noted, the Luo rage against all things Kikuyu after his murder made him in death what he had not been in life: an ethnic hero.

This brief outline of Mboya's career departs, to some extent, from the conventional picture. He was not so much non-ethnic as ethnically tolerant. He was proud of his ethnic identity, understood ethnicity very well, and explicitly condoned it in certain areas (positive tribalism). Further, he made use of it in politics when it suited him; much more than is generally realised, Mboya resorted to the game of ethnic numbers and to the cultivation of a parochial base. In part, he was being manipulative; in part, he was apparently responding to ethnicity as a constraining factor. But in both instances he was acting essentially in the same cause, that of his own political survival and effectiveness.

Mboya was, in fact, an increasingly vulnerable figure in élite-level Kenyan politics. The reasons for this need not be explored here, but significant among them was the deep hostility of the exclusivist inner clique of Kikuyu leaders towards him. Because of this he had to undertake a long series of defensive measures, several of which entailed the use of the ethnic variable. The preceding account is indicative, but by no means exhaustive; many of these defensive actions were fought inside the Government and the party, as well as inside the labour movement and the constituency.[1]

What this strongly suggests is the danger that lies in perceiving any leader as *either* tribalist *or* non-tribalist, as if this elementary dichotomy covered the possibilities. If Mboya seems on examination to have been 'more' tribalist in his politics than is usually supposed, it is perfectly possible that other leaders may have been 'less' tribalist. In discussing the interactions of identity and utility, to seek simplicity is to be simplistic. Kasfir's terminology – that ethnicity should be seen as fluid, situational, and intermittent – is extremely apposite. Conceiving ethnicity thus, we are confronted with a spectrum of possibilities rather than a dichotomy, and we need feel no surprise at any particular manifestation.

[1] For details, see Goldsworthy, op. cit. especially chs. 14 and 18.

ETHNICITY, CLASS, AND POLITICAL EXPLANATION

The preceding discussion has offered a degree of support to what was characterised earlier as a feature of the liberal view; namely, that ethnicity can function not only as a dependent variable in politics (to be exploited in the interests of the politician), but also as an independent variable (something which limits the politician in his freedom of action). Let us return now to the argument that was earlier described as characteristically radical, and which clearly presents a certain challenge to the liberal view by denying ethnicity not only its potential to operate 'independently' in politics, but also its status as an *explanatory* variable.

According to this argument, ethnicity serves as a convenient ideological weapon in the hands of political leaders. Ethnic categories evolve into mutually hostile ethnic groups largely because leaders deliberately foster this development, in order to mask the true character of exploitative relations within the society. Since ethnicity is, therefore, epiphenomenal, to treat it as an explanatory variable is misdirected effort that merely adds to the general mystification. Only a materialist account can bring out what is important.

Some who subscribe to this view might further argue that to approach the issues by way of political biography is no less a misdirection of effort, on the grounds that biography tends to present individuals, rather than class forces, as shapers of events.[1] Yet, given the basic Marxist position that 'men make their own history, but they do not make it just as they please',[2] the argument that biography is 'irrelevant' cannot logically be sustained. Rather than pursue the point at length here, let us simply note Jean-Paul Sartre's perhaps too didactic remark: 'Valéry is a petit bourgeois intellectual, no doubt about it. But not every petit bourgeois intellectual is Valéry. The heuristic inadequacy of contemporary Marxism is contained in those two sentences'.[3]

Accepting that biography has its uses, there are two ways in which this particular case-study can be related to the general argument. We might ask, first of all, whether there is clear evidence that Mboya, as a political leader in a capitalistic system, made use of ethnicity in the ideological fashion posited. This is obviously a rather narrow and

---

[1] See e.g. Ken Post, 'Individuals and the Dialectic: a Marxist view of political biographies', in W. H. Morris-Jones (ed.), *The Making of Politicians: studies from Asia and Africa* (London, 1976), pp. 17–27.

[1] Karl Marx, 'The Eighteenth Brumaire of Louis Napoleon', in Karl Marx and Friedrich Engels, *Selected Works*, Vol. 1 (Moscow edn. 1962), p. 225. Any liberal biographer would accept Marx's qualifying clause, and the others which follow it in his text.

[3] Jean-Paul Sartre, *Critique de la raison dialectique* (Paris, 1960), quoted by Tony Smith, 'The Underdevelopment of Development Literature: the case of dependency theory', in *World Politics*, XXXI, 2, January 1979, p. 259.

literal-minded question. Nevertheless it permits an answer: from the evidence, no. As we have argued, Mboya used ethnicity more than is usually perceived, but did so chiefly in the interests of maintaining his position against his rivals at élite level, rather than in the cause of altering the consciousness of the masses. Within the given framework of the Kenyan system, his political activities were based on utility rather than identity; he was a man who exhorted all groups to take part in development and who delivered valued goods, such as jobs and education, to recipients who were ethnically alien as well as those who were ethnically kin. We have noted that this approach both reflected his real commitment to the broad national interest, as he conceived it, and represented an ethnically rational strategy in his particular circumstances. But whatever else the ideological consequences of his approach might have been, there is no reason to suppose that they would have included a heightening of the recipients' ethnic consciousness.

Yet this does not take us very far. An apparent exception does not necessarily either prove or disprove a 'rule'. At best it provides an initial minimum ground for scepticism about that rule, and suggests the need for further case-studies to help us establish just how exceptional it actually is.

But in any case, those who take a materialist view could readily argue that Mboya's approach was merely another variant of class strategy pursued with the same general intention; namely, to conceal the class character of exploitation by encouraging clients to look upwards to their patron, rather than laterally, for their salvation.

Arguments around this point can all too easily become circular. To escape the circle we need to confront the second, and much broader, question: namely, the explanatory power, or lack of it, of the ethnic – or, indeed, any other non-class – variable in political analysis. To repeat: the issue is whether such a variable can validly be used to 'explain' aspects of political behaviour, or whether it is indeed epiphenomenal, such that analysis which focuses on it is 'idealist' and misleading.

In the present context, perhaps the most useful way to proceed is to frame the question in a way that puts the onus on the materialist critics to demonstrate their point with reference to a biographical study. Thus: what are the grounds for believing that a materialist approach will suffice to explain a leader's politics?

This is a large question which in turn conjures up far-reaching problems in the sociology of knowledge, the exploration of which lies well beyond the ambition of this article, and which almost certainly cannot be dealt with uncontroversially. What we can do in our brief compass here is to sketch out what a materialist analysis of Mboya's rôle would look like, by contrast with the 'conventional' sketch of Mboya as non-tribalist and the 'revisionist' sketch of Mboya as influenced by ethnicity. Following this, a case will be presented for one possible way of answering the question. It hardly needs pointing out that there are various fairly dogmatic ways in which the issue might be pursued. The argument here, however, will be relativistic and, once again, somewhat sceptical.

So to the sketch. Tom Mboya's politics were determined in the first instance by his growth to maturity within a social and intellectual climate that was premised upon an acceptance of private property relations.[1] He began his rise to power in Kenya's governing class as a salaried spokesman for the wage interests of the so-called 'labour aristocracy'. In pressing for political emancipation, he and the other young politicians of the 1950s were articulating not revolutionary aspirations, but 'the interest of their class – independence as soon as possible, with a minimum of structural change'.[2] Their major goal was to wrest control of the administrative machine from two rival class fractions: the European bureaucrats and the European settler bourgeoisie. With this achieved, thanks in large part to the consent of the imperial metropolis, Mboya became a leading functionary of the post-colonial state. As Minister for Economic Planning and Development he was perhaps not a 'tool' of foreign capital, but was certainly 'collaborating closely with it',[3] and he subscribed strongly to theories of development by way of capital diffusion. It was Mboya who undertook the task of rationalising the state's activities in terms of a petty-bourgeois philosophy described for ideological purposes as African socialism. He was charged, too, with blunting the challenge of the populists and land reformers grouped round Bildad Kaggia and Oginga Odinga.

Like the majority of his colleagues, if to a much lesser degree than most, Mboya used his privileged access to the state apparatus for purposes of private accumulation, securing licences to run a bus company and a beer distribution agency – typically petty-bourgeois forays into the services sector (not the productive sector, which in the 1960s was under fairly monopolistic and largely foreign control). Mboya was, in short, a representative member of his class fraction, one who accepted and encouraged Kenya's integration into the world

[1] Leys, op. cit. p. 60.
[2] Frank Furedi, 'The African Crowd in Nairobi: popular movements and elite politics', in *The Journal of African History* (Cambridge), XIV, 1973, p. 288.
[3] Leys, op. cit. p. 221.

capitalist system, and who reaped personal benefits therefrom. Meanwhile he sought to secure his position by acting as patron to an extensive clientele among the exploited classes. However, this contradiction could not be contained indefinitely; there is evidence that many in grassroots Nairobi eventually came to perceive him as a *Wabenzi* – in other words, as a class enemy.

Such an account of Mboya's rôle is useful for its particular vision. But it is hard to see it as a sufficient account. There are many aspects of his politics which it skirts around, most notably in the matters of getting, keeping, and using power against stiff competition within and beyond the class fraction. These matters are surely central to adequate *political* comprehension; and, in Mboya's case, the ethnic considerations highlighted in the preceding sketch were surely germane.

This is not to maintain that a focus on ethnicity – or any other single variable – would explain more than does a focus on class location. But other approaches do not in general claim a basic determining rôle. And it is at this point that one either does or does not accept the following proposition: every case in political analysis, including every biographical case, has its integrity and specificity, of which only certain facets will be made visible by the use of any one analytical approach; and no approach has sufficient explanatory power as to render others superfluous.

We are here urging the relativity of all political analysis. Were we to seek to develop the case-study further, we could certainly hope to benefit from the insights which a materialist approach can offer. But we would equally maintain that to regard an approach focusing on ethnicity as 'misleading' – rather than, say, 'partial' – is to adopt a blinkered view of reality. As Kasfir puts it, in a comment which has considerable pertinence to Mboya's case, 'where [a man's]...life is in danger on the basis of an ethnic threat, it would be foolish to expect him to ignore ethnic considerations'. Kasfir goes on:

To dismiss all manifestations of politicized ethnicity as irrelevant is to ignore a range of motives many of which will, on empirical examination, turn out to be strongly felt. Even where ethnic symbols are merely the façade for economic grievances, they often structure the political situation and thus affect the outcome.[1]

The case-study supports this line of argument. The very process of describing how so secular-minded a politician as Mboya acknowledged ethnic sentiment in himself, engaged in a degree of ethnic manipulation of others, and was constrained in his choices by ethnic entrapment, is to point up the social vitality of these forces.

[1] Kasfir, loc. cit. p. 369.

Lest too much be seen as riding on one restricted case-study, the argument may here be opened out and related to certain broad concerns in the current literature. The view that the systemic needs of capitalism determine the forms and modes of expression of such a phenomenon as ethnicity is in some conflict with the massive evidence of ethnic (and various other particularist) loyalties and hostilities at work in all historical epochs and all manner of societies. Such a view appears to rest, in fact, less upon empirical observation than upon an *a priori* belief in the global rationality of the capitalist world-system, according to which capitalism becomes, by definition, the dominant mode in all units which it penetrates. Tony Smith has commented with some vigour on this kind of view:

Tribalism as a force in Africa? Colin Leys cannot even bring himself to use the word without putting it in quotation marks...Why? Because the logic of the whole (capitalist colonialism) has found it expedient to work its will in the part (Africa) through creating, virtually *ex nihilo*, the divisive force of 'tribalism'. By such reckoning, all the social structures in history after a certain low level of development in the division of labor could be dissolved – feudal and bureaucratic estates, castes and clans, as well as tribes – in favor of class analysis, the only 'real' social formation.

Because this approach is formulistic and reductionist, it is bad historiography. It is formulistic in the sense that it seeks to specify universal laws or processes in blatant disregard of the singular or the idiosyncratic. By the same token it is reductionist, since it forces the particular case to express its identity solely in the terms provided by the general category...Such writing is tyrannical.[1]

It should be noted that Smith's remarks do not represent an assault on Marxism or neo-Marxism in general, and nor is that the intention here. The target, rather, is 'globally rational' economism, of the kind that produces an insistence on the inevitable hegemony of the capitalist mode of production wherever it interacts with non-capitalist modes in peripheral societies. Just as dependency theory foundered partly on the argument that it attributed an over-determining rôle to external forces, thereby denying internal factors most of their explanatory power, so this kind of economism seems similarly to seek to explain too much with too few variables.

Within the Marxist problematic, there is surely much insight to be found in the approach of those who are prepared to recognise the enduring strength of 'community' in peripheral societies, not as a phenomenon that exists on sufferance, to be co-opted and used by a capitalism that is 'structured in dominance', but as an expression of an alternative (peasant or petty-commodity) mode which retains many

---

[1] Smith, loc. cit. p. 258.

elements of its own vitality and viability. This is a view of the historical process as complex and undetermined; according to which, for example, the peasant mode is not necessarily doomed to suffer a process of articulation, subordination, and ultimate demise, but might even 'outlast' the capitalist mode in the periphery. And it follows, first, that such a phenomenon as ethnicity can have an authentic and enduring social base quite separate from the systemic needs of capitalism; and secondly, that the ways in which ethnicity is used by politicians may similarly derive from imperatives and exigencies not necessarily related to those systemic needs.

We are here touching on some of the larger questions in the sociology of knowledge that were hinted at earlier. The line of thought which underlies the previous paragraph stems from recent studies by Marian Sawer, who demonstrates Marx's own seldom-acknowledged interest in the preservation of 'community' in a non-western context;[1] by Goran Hyden, who looks beyond *ujamaa* in Tanzania with his notion of the 'uncaptured' peasantry;[2] and by Joel Kahn who, with reference to the Indonesian peasantry, rejects both the extreme 'dualist' and the extreme 'global rationality' positions in favour of a qualified and complex dualism.[3] Such works surely open up a fascinating arena for argument; witness the diverse responses which they have already aroused among reviewers.[4]

The implications cannot be pursued further here. But it would seem that there is indeed scope for radical analysis which acknowledges the potentiality of ethnicity to work in undetermined ways. At the very least, it would seem useful to conceptualise both ethnic and class formations, together with their associated forms of consciousness, as variable factors in African politics. They exist and function sometimes in isolation, sometimes contradictorily, sometimes in concert, sometimes with one conditioning, or even determining, the operations of the other. We must then expect these variables to have different degrees of explanatory power in different cases, according to the analytic issues at hand.

[1] Marian Sawer, *Marxism and the Question of the Asiatic Mode of Production* (The Hague, 1977).
[2] Goran Hyden, *Beyond Ujamaa in Tanzania: underdevelopment and an uncaptured peasantry* (London, 1980).
[3] Joel S. Kahn, *Minangkabau Social Formations: Indonesian peasants and the world economy* (Cambridge, 1980).
[4] See e.g. Brian Cooksey's Marxist critique of Hyden, in *Review of African Political Economy* (London), 19, September–December 1980, pp. 100–3, and Kenneth R. Young's sympathetic review article on Kahn's book, 'Non-Capitalist Entrepreneurs in the Modern World System', in *Critique of Anthropology*, forthcoming.

The State of Ambivalence:

Right and Left Options in Ghana

Judith Marshall

Judith Marshall examines the different interests of international
capitalism and the politically powerful groups among the Ghanaian
petty bourgeoisie in Ghana since 1960. She analyzes the conflicting
and complementary relations among them, and compares the
specific policies of successive regimes in Ghana, military and civilian.
She shows that progressive plans for transformation of the neo-
colonial political economy could not succeed without an adequate
class base and mass mobilization. While international capital has been
able to profit from the changing policies of successive regimes it has
been unable to establish stable conditions for its own domination, and
the perpetuation of the privileges of its local partners. The continued
failures of capitalist development strategies sustain the relevance of
radical alternatives, as they did during the Nkrumah period.

Introduction

At the turn of the century, the imperialism of free trade along the
Gold Coast was replaced by the direct colonial management of a peasant export economy, supplemented by the mining of gold and
manganese. By 1931, a small group of foreign trading countries,
themselves dominated by the leading firm, the United Africa
Company, had effectively eliminated smaller competitors, both
expatriate and African. During the war, the Cocoa Marketing Boards
(CMB) were set up to organize the purchase and export of cocoa.
They used their monopoly purchasing powers to accumulate surpluses in Britain. By doing so, they limited farmers' incomes, the
expansion of the consumer market and commercial opportunities
for Ghananian traders. These institutions of the colonial economy
restricted the development of the forces of production. From the
achievement of self-government, economic policies were pursued
which encouraged foreign capital to invest in import-substituting
industries. The direct and indirect costs of this form of industrial

development continued to be financed by the earnings from cocoa, supplemented by mining. Thus capitalism was established in the industrial sector, while peasant and petty commodity production were conserved and subordinated to the requirements of the dominant capitalist mode of production.

The basic contradiction in the Ghanaian economy is the subordination of the cocoa-producing peasantry to international capitalism through the mediation of the Cocoa Marketing Board. The development of the colonial economy created a working class in transport and construction industries, to whom industrial workers were added in the 1960s. However, politics in Ghana has largely been determined by its petty bourgeoisies, engaged in a wide array of commercial and clerical services. On the one hand, the petty bourgeoisie includes self-employed producers, repairers, builders and traders (who are often women). Among them, the most prominent group politically is the commercial petty bourgeoisie, which controls significant sums of money, but whose main objective has been to operate in the interstices of the Ghanaian economy, under the domination of foreign capital. In rural areas, the rich farmer-traders want a strong place within the import-export trade, while city traders want opportunities in the small and intermediate trade which complements the foreign commercial and manufacturing houses. On the other hand, the petty bourgeoisie includes white collar employees, clerks, secretaries, administrators, teachers, community development officers and technicians, many of whom are employed in the state sector. Politically, the leading section of this group is the bureaucratic bourgeoisie. It is intent on consolidating and expanding the position of privilege it inherited in the colonial salary structure. Its senior members have been able to accumulate wealth, to gain access to credit, and to knit personal contracts in the commercial and foreign bourgeoisies which give them an economic and social base for their continuing political power. At different times, a third strategy has been enunciated by progressives from the petty bourgeoisie. Their aim has been to improve the living conditions of farmers and workers, to increase national control over the economy, and overcome the inherent contradictions of the neo-colonial economy.

The process of decolonization was designed to protect the institutions of colonial domination, the state and foreign companies, from any radical challenge, and to bring the commercial and bureaucratic bourgeoisies into alliance with imperialism. The nationalist movement was very quickly deflected from challenging Ghana's links to the world capitalist system. The prewar cocoa hold-up had placed Ghanaian farmers and traders in direct competition with European commercial firms. The immediate postwar period brought an anti-inflation campaign which again agitated against the European firms, United African Company foremost among them. While an end to shortages and high prices of consumer goods was the major demand, there was also great resentment of the continued combination of the firms, which prevented African farmer-traders from competing in produce buying and importing. The 1948 riots with looting and burning of European shops in Accra, Takoradi and Kumasi and the brief general strike of 1950 marked the high point of demands focussed on economic issues. The nationalist movement was skillfully channelled, via the conciliatory posture of the colonial administration, into narrowly political solutions. The right to determination was affirmed, leading to a gradual transfer of power. This kept the key levers of power in British hands as effective bargaining tools against nationalist demands. Everything in the shared power arrangement of 1951-57 militated against any radicalization of the nationalist movement and the genuine decolonization of the state. Imperialism could cede the 'political kingdom' in order to maintain the substance of economic domination.

The ruling Convention People's Party (CPP), the only force that might have rooted itself in the aspirations of the subordinated classes and challenged metropolitan domination, did not do so. It proceeded instead to lose itself in the state. Central leadership became immersed in the day-to-day concerns of government and the morass of electoral politics with its compromises, petty calculations and endless patronage. The middle element of the party, the newly coordinated primary school teachers, 'youth' leaders, officers of farmer-trader organizations, trade union organizers and women's leaders had been vital cadres for early mobilization. Now their energies were dissipated. They were not encouraged to link the central leadership to the masses. The CPP did not develop strong organizations geared to local initiatives, with activists strategically located in all sectors of the society. Instead, a regression to petty opportunism and political hackery ensued.

Where new institutions were introduced during the six years of collaboration, the compromises of shared power became very apparent. Cocoa policy was at the forefront of nationalist agitations, and the CMB had become a key institution for extracting surplus from peasant producers for the metropolitan state. The CPP kept the CMB intact as a source of state revenue. The Gold Coast cocoa surplus continued to accumulate in British banks, on the advice of colonial officials who argued that it created the stability necessary to woo investors. A new institution, the Cocoa Purchasing Company (CPC), was created to purchase cocoa for the CMB, supposedly as a weapon against the expatriate companies. It succeeded mainly in antagonizing the rural privileged, that is the staunch nationalist farmer-traders who had hoped to control purchasing themselves, and the many agents of the companies, now threatened with loss of livelihood. While some poorer farmers genuinely benefited from the accompanying loans scheme and dividends, their potential as a strong rural base of support was unrealized. Like the party itself, the CPC degenerated into a crude vote-buying machine full of personal opportunism. Thus an early policy which could have been an insertion into the rural power structure to challenge the existing economic order, degenerated into a means for petty bourgeois opportunists in the state to compete with other private petty bourgeois interests. The political authority of the CPP began to dwindle even before independence was reached. Left with the alternative of a revolutionary transformation of popular consciousness for real decolonization of the state with all its institutional, cultural and political consequences, the CPP preferred the use of violence, demagogery and mystification.

The Left Option, 1961-66

By 1960 the inadequacies of current policies had become clear. During the 1950s the buoyant world price of cocoa had cushioned Ghana from the full brunt of the contradictions inherent in its peripheral capitalist economy. After the fall in world cocoa prices the continuation of colonial economic and fiscal policies, was no longer possible. The Cocoa Marketing Board continued to appropriate surplus from cocoa farmers to finance the state, there were few import controls, and no effective direction of development strategy. At this point, various social forces began to define their interests more clearly. These ranged from international capitalism's desire to stabilize its domination over a Ghanaian economy more firmly integrated into the international capitalist economy, to halting attempts to move towards socialist strategy.

Both local and international developments encouraged progressive initiatives from among the petty bourgeoisie. Falling cocoa prices and the consequent shortage of foreign exchange clearly exposed the fragility of the neo-colonial economy. The first state delegation to the Soviet Union and China brought home the alternative of a planned economy and a socialist strategy. Ghana had taken the lead in the call for pan-African liberation. In 1961 the All-African People's Conference in Cairo defined and denounced the realities of neo-colonialism. But two particular events were probably decisive. The bitter strike of dockers and railwaymen at Sekondi-Takoradi pitted the demands of the workers against the corrupt old guard in the CPP. Western intervention in the Congo overthrew the progressive and popular leadership of Lumumba to check the process of decolonisation before even engaging the Southern African strongholds of racist domination. Ghanaian progressives came to realize that decolonization was not just a matter of political independence, but required a protracted and many-sided struggle against neo-colonial economic domination.

Progressive organizational and ideological initiatives were taken within the party and the state. State intervention was intended both to break the links of dependency in the export sector, and to initiate industrial development. This was to go beyond the substitution for consumer imports with each factory totally tied to Western sources of raw materials and machinery, and to initiate an integrated and self-sustaining industrial development, based on the development of producer goods and machine-tools industries. At the same time, attempts were made to bring about changes in the ideological and political spheres. Within the mass media and educational system, the continuing hold of cultural imperialism was somewhat demystified. Internationally, Nkrumah initiated a genuinely non-aligned policy and investment, trade and aid relations were for the first time established with the socialist states. Halting steps were taken to check the local privileged, including bureaucratic opportunists and local traders operating under the umbrella of foreign capital.

The failure of the Ghanaian state to carry through its shift to the left raises fundamental issues about the struggle against neo-colonialism. In particular, it raises questions about the relation between the state, and the class forces engendered by the combination of capitalist and non-capitalist modes of production. Progressives acting through the party and the state lacked a class base to sustain and defend their political initiatives.

Foreign capital was keen to prepare for import-substitution industry. It therefore encouraged expansion of ports, roads, power, telecommunications and industrial complexes. Hence projects like Tema Harbour and the Volta River Project had international capitalism's full support. Such projects indeed created demands for machinery, equipment, parts and semi-finished components from Western industry that extended the web of technological-industrial dependency. State expansion of administration and social infrastructure was encouraged, because this increasing public sector was oriented to Western standards in both its private and public consumption. Thus UAC's specialized imports of drugs, medical equipment, business machines and luxury goods for its Kingsway stores all established a small Western-oriented import enclave.

Foreign capital quickly found ways to co-opt the post-1960 sentiments of nationalism and anti-imperialism. In response to plans for state industries to end Ghana's dependent status, international capitalism deftly inserted itself both as opposition and as a willing partner. The corporate world expressed concern at Ghana's leftward trend and spread rumours of economic chaos. At the same time, firms explored joint state-private ventures to co-opt tendencies to more radical economic nationalism. Joint state-private enterprises were established with UAC in beer and textiles. Foreign firms adapted similarly to their exclusion from produce buying and to state control of retail trade. The state marketing boards were established with Cadburys advising about their structure, and the state trading company, GNTC, was set up with a retired UAC manager at its head. Thus international capitalism was extremely resourceful in avoiding confrontations and maintaining a position of strength in the new economic institutions.

The commercial bourgeoisie's interests also began to emerge more clearly. But they were persistently thwarted by progressive measures to gain national control and restructure the economy. The commercial bourgeoisie was prevented from taking control of the trade in staple commodities when the expatriate companies moved on to specialized trade and import-substitution industry. A state buying monopoly, the United Ghana Farmers Council (UGFC) bypassed the farmer-traders in the internal cocoa trade. Exchange controls and restrictions on imports created shortages of trading goods for the aspiring petty bourgeoisie in the retail sector. Shortages of essential components limited opportunities in construction and transport. Later the GNTC, and the People's Trading Shops of 1965 further thwarted their aspirations.

The bureaucratic bourgeoisie was born out of early nationalist desires for Africanization. It had inherited a position of power and privilege. Colonial salary scales and benefits had been established during the shared power period. Now the senior bureaucrats were in a good position to protect themselves from the threats to its position posed both by the general economic situation, and by the intentions of progressives to attack privilege and income disparities. The senior bureaucrats had the capacity to accumulate; they had access to credit, contacts, travel and information about state projects, and used them to establish their economic position. The addition of private business to administrative duties was common throughout the bureaucracy, and furthered the interests of individual civil servants and the web of clients dependent on them. A common form of accumulation was to put a price on the public service under their control ranging from the 10% kickbacks on large state contracts required by senior bureaucrats to the small 'dash' demanded by junior agricultural extension officers in the countryside for issuing fertilizer or hybrid seeds. Public funds were used to accumulate capital for private business interests, large or small. As one farmer said of the Secretary-Receivers of the UGFC: 'Even they do not respect the farmers at all, and even when a very young boy is engaged as Secretary-Receiver for about two years time, you see him riding a very promising car and having mighty buildings with their scanty pay.'

The bureaucratic bourgeoisie's parasitical role suited the desire of international capitalism to establish a new elite. From 1960 the technocratic elite educated in American Unviersities and trained as self-conscious leaders, began to return. They were anti-colonial, but also anti-communist and anti-CPP, highly suspicious of popular mobilization and ideology and convinced of technocratic solutions, ideal intermediaries for international capitalism. More difficult to handle was the crudeness of the operation: unrestricted translation of the economic interests of the newest layers of the privileged to the political process. The destabilizing effect of the blatant corruption that permeated state institutions was as much a constraint on international capitalism's aspirations as it was on the programme of the progressives among the petty bourgeoisie.

At several points, CPP policies ran parallel to the plans of international capitalism—the expansion of infrastructural investments and local control of produce buying and marketing and the retail trade. With all its shortcomings, the industrial programme, which aimed to set up a cluster of light, medium and heavy industrial projects, each producing for one another, impinged on the profitability of metropolitan interests and challenged Ghana's dependency on them. Trade in cocoa, with growing imports, including machinery and technical assistance from socialist countries threatened Western domination. Chana's attempts to transcend African socialism with scientific socialism, and replace populism with a class-based ideology were ultimately too fragmentary and too little related to the concerns of the masses to win popular understanding and support. But they did challenge imperialist ideological hegemony.

The failure of the Cocoa Producers' Alliance in its hold-up against falling prices left Ghana completely vulnerable to the dramatic drop in cocoa prices in 1965. Western financial institutions began to freeze credit supplies. The destabilizing tactics were immediately effective in exacerbating existing difficulties and weaknesses. Nkrumah certainly perceived the situation as one of attack from the West. On 24 August, 1965 he declared to the National Assembly:

Let me state here and now that under no circumstances will we allow those who control and manipulate the world price of cocoa to alter, hamper or curtail our programme of industrial and agricultural development and the expansion of our educational and other social services. The implementation of our Seven Year Development Plan will proceed. Neither the machinations of monopolists in the cocoa trade, nor the obstacles placed in our path by those who seek to control foreign currencies and credits, will cause us to slacken or halt our pace of development. If more sacrifices of luxuries are required, we shall make them. If greater efficiency must be reached in our present production, we shall reach it. But our development goes on.

The mission of the International Monetary Fund (IMF) made explicit the quarrel with Ghana's attempts at autonomy. Further credit was made contingent on dismantling the state industrial sector, established with significant state-to-state aid from socialist countries. The IMF also demanded cutbacks in health, education and social welfare expendigures, which extended well into the rural areas. The tales of economic chaos and megalomania in the Western press prepared both international public opinion and Western-oriented opinion in Ghana for a swing to the right.

Once the army overthrew Nkrumah, other institutions of the state, equally unsympathetic to the aims of the Second Revolution, such as the judiciary and the bureaucracy, as well as the intelligentsia, were quick to support it. The workers and peasants, in whose name the Second Revolution was being promoted, had been passive participants in the process. They experienced the economic dislocations as attacks on their own standard of living, and saw no reason to tighten their belts. Direct military interference from international capitalism was unnecessary in Ghana. The quiet pressures through economic de-stabilization measures and through the cultural imperialism of Western-trained Ghanaians and of Western experts and volunteers sufficiently exacerbated the internal contradictions of the left option as to make a right-wing coup inevitable.

The Right option, 1966-71
Between 1966 and 1971 a very different array of forces was in control of the state. The National Liberation Council (NLC) was right from the start ready to service the interests of international capitalism and to use the state to create the stability necessary for continued domination by foreign capital. It proclaimed its policies to be diametrically opposed to those of the CPP. Vitriolic denunciations of Nkrumah, the CPP and socialism were uttered. All relations with socialist countries were ritualistically purged. Half-completed industrial projects were halted. State industries were sold off to private capital, foreign and Ghanaian. The economy was re-opened to the transnational companies with liberalized import policies and fewer exchange controls. For the first time, the commercial and bureaucratic bourgeoisies were urged to invest legally in private business. There was even a proposal that the foreign trading companies resume their pre-1952 role as produce buyers for the internal cocoa trade, a role which they politely refused. All attempts to decolonize the state came to an abrupt halt. There was real willingness to construct the steady state desired by the international bourgeoisie, right from the resident Harvard economic ivsory team to the Political Committee, made up of old opposition ements like Kofi Busia, who in 1962 had testified before a US

Senate subcommittee that Ghana was the centre of subversive
Communist activities throughout West Africa. The Economic Committee included technocrats from companies like Mobil, freshly
trained at American institutions and ready to do service for international capitalism.

The willingness of the NLC to manage the economy in the interests
of foreign capital was not matched by an ability to create the policies,
institutions and legitimizing apparatus necessary to do so. The NLC
failed completely to organize accumulation and redistribution of
surplus value in a way that could meet the flow of payments to
international capitalism, maintain a high degree of consumption in
the hands of the privileged and at the same time keep up the productivity of a subordinated work force in the forms of production
dominated by the capitalist mode.

The rural areas stagnated. Government-controlled media preached
back to the land, but the reality was abysmally low prices for agricultural produce and minimal supports through feeder roads, storage,
credit, seeds, fertilizer and transport. Middlemen profiteering and
'market queens' with monopoly control of local produce markets
exacerbated the situation. The rational choice for peasants was to
produce little for the market. The dramatic increase in cocoa prices
during the spring of 1966 was a major factor ensuing in the initial
economic viability of the NLC. The balance of payments crisis was
temporarily averted and consumption privileges were returned to the
elite, with shops again full of imported commodities. The retail trade
network functioned actively. Any illusion of general economic well-
being was belied by the strike actions of urban workers. Between
1963 and 1968 the cost-of-living index had risen by 85%. Measured
in real terms, the 1968 minimum wage was 65% of the 1939 minimum. Massive retrenchment from state projects in industry, construction, infrastructure and state farms drastically cut back employment opportunities. It is estimated that some 63,000 workers were
laid off over a two year period. While strikes were officially illegal
there were in fact some 200 strikes and lockouts during the 3½ years
of military rule. These were generally cloaked from the public eye
and were handled with varying mixtures of paternalism and harshness,
including dismissals and even police action which killed three striking
mineworkers at Obuasi in March 1969.

In August 1969 came the much-heralded return to civilian rule which
put Busia's Progress Party in control of the state. It was a rather contrived electoral process. Busia had a year's head start in campaigning
through his position in the Civic Education Centre. CPP tendencies
were eliminated by law when political parties were legalized and most
ex-CPP politicians were disqualified. The Progress Party's willingness
to manage the state for the transnationals was clear. Its ability to
bring any cohesion amidst the contradictions of the Ghanaian political
economy was minimal.

More than a quarter of the registered labour force, some 600,000, were
unemployed in 1970. By 1971, cocoa prices were again falling and
debt-repayment and foreign exchange crises were seemingly a

permanent feature of the economy. There were cutbacks on social services and a freeze on wages. The cost of living in April 1971 was up 100% from March 1963 with a 4.7% increase from March to April alone. Even the privileged became disenchanted at the PP's inability to guarantee its consumption style. America's devaluation sent shock waves reverberating through Third World economies. Ghana, heavily dependent on its cocoa sales to the American market was particularly vulnerable. Handling of class relations was inept. An arrogant and school-teacherish Busia, combined with a PP machine reminiscent of the worst excesses of the CPP, all in a climate of tremendous economic difficulties, made for a convergence of grievances. Senior bureaucrats were uneasy at Busia's purge of more than 500 civil servants, based in many cases on personal vendettas of PP members and expedited without right of appeal. Highly unpopular foreign policy measures linked Ghana with Ivory Coast in its willingness to enter a 'dialogue' with South Africa. The subordinated classes, the peasants, workers and lower levels of the petty bourgeoisie, were subjected to a drastic economic squeeze. Rural areas were affected not only by inflation, but by the disappearance of aliens from neighbouring West African countries forced to leave under the highly unpopular Aliens Compliance Order, which affected rural petty commodity production and trade as well as cocoa labour. Not only the economic but also the social and political questions were ineptly handled. The PP was generally identified as an Akan government, exacerbating the sentiments of tribalism, rooted in colonialism's heritage of regional disparities divided along tribal lines. The rural response was one of low productivity and general stagnation.

Events between March and September 1971 brought workers and the state to the confrontation point. In March, three striking workers were killed at UAC's timber operation at Samreboi. In July, the Railway Engineman's Union staged a major strike, backing salary demands with sabotage on the railway lines. From January 1970 to June 1971 alone, there were 102 strike actions with 172,997 man days lost. The austerity budget of August 1971 spelled the end of the Busia regime's capacity to maintain the state. It brought in import surcharges, restrictions on luxury goods and a development levy on salaries and wages. This prompted strike threats, particularly against the levy, and a demand for a raise in minimum wages to 75 pesewas (roughly 75 cents) per day. The state went into action with a new Industrial Relations Act in September, rushed through with a certificate of urgency, which effectively smashed the Trades Union Congress (TUC). It claimed the TUC was an illegal organization created by the CPP which had been maintained after the coup only by oversight, and revived the tired accusation of Communist infiltration of the trade unions. By October, there were rumours of a general strike to overthrow the PP.

In December 1971, the cocoa price plummeted to £194 per ton, the lowest level since 1965. A massive 44% devaluation was instituted. This amounted to a virtual collapse of the state with the economy in chaos, repression increasing, and dwindling support even from the privileged sectors. Once again the military intervened, this time offering an alternative in a situation of growing worker militancy and economic collapse, with a new attempt to stabilize the situation once again in the interests of national and international capital.

International capitalism's assessment of the 1970-71 period was clear from the Unilever Annual Report. It suggested that despite the increased difficulties over debt repayments and foreign exchange leading to the drastic devaluation of December 1971 and the coup of January 1972, there was only a slight drop in profits in UAC operations from the very high level of 1970. While textiles, timber and shipping were reported to have had some difficulties, motors and earth moving equipment had an outstanding year, chemists, food operations and general trading ventures all did very well. There was much new building including new factories and extensions of existing ventures. Clearly UAC found the succession of military and civilian governments an arrangement quite compatible with extension of its interests. But, while international capital was able to expand its interests, it was not able to achieve the stable climate to guarantee a steady outflow from Ghana to cheap produce and payments for imports, debt repayments, patents and licenses. The economic contradictions created by wildly fluctuating cocoa prices on world markets, import-substitution industry and inflation did not permit stable domination.

The National Redemption Council (NRC) 1971-1975
Yet another military regime, the National Redemption Council, has managed the state for the past four years. Has this been merely a restabilization exercise, a change of government but continuity with the NLC-PP strategy? Or does the more populist style and language of revolution of the NRC indicate potential for more radical actions and use of the state to implement more progressive policies?

Given the economic chaos inherited from the Busia regime, the NRC's first hurdle was a restoration of some measure of economic stability, with a more viable pattern of accumulation and distribution of surplus value. Many of the measures were precisely those of the CPP after 1961. The increase in cocoa prices and higher prices on world markets for gold and timber after 1971 gave some initial leeway. A rigorous curtailment of imports and campaigns to popularize locally produced goods, a revaluation of the cedi, and repudiation of some debts and a rescheduling of others were all carried out to stabilize the economy. The major new policy was Operation Feed Yourself (OFY). An array of material and moral incentives were offered, ranging from guaranteed minimum prices to a Food Production Corporation, state farms and technical inputs such as seeds, fertilizers, tractors and combine harvesters. Rice production increased from 11,000 tons in 1971 to 61,000 in 1973. Maize production made a phenomenal jump from 53,000 tons in 1971 to 430,000 tons in 1973. As a policy to ease foreign exchange pressures, OFY had some success, although the dramatic leaps in oil prices more than matched the savings from decreased food imports. In 1972, oil imports amounted to 28 million cedis. By 1974, they were estimated at 130 million cedis. OFY tended to create an array of economic dislocations. Those benefitting from the guaranteed prices and government-subsidized inputs were not primarily Ghanaian villagers whose lives were rooted in the land. Rich farmers, civil servants, businessmen and military officers responded with great alacrity to the new opportunities. There were few controls over middleman activities or transport bottlenecks caused by high-priced oil and spare parts shortages. Those farming on sufficient scale and with independent transport could benefit from higher prices at regional depots. Poorer farmers saw price gains disappear in local transport increases or middleman extractions. Produce rotted in remoter areas for lack of transport. Wages were increased first to C1.29 per day and later to C2 per day, but still lagged far behind inflation. The local food price index in August 1972 had climbed to 253 from its March 1963 base of 100. By August 1973, it was up to 344. Nor were savings in foreign exchange unambiguous. An interchange in 1973 at the UAC-owned Crocodile Matchet Factory, producing Ghana's basic agricultural tool typifies the dilemma of dependent industrialization. The visiting Commissioner for Agriculture commented that Ghana could not afford to import all agricultural machinery and needed to rely on traditional inputs to increase production. The UAC manager replied that the factory could readily produce more 'made in Ghana' matchets if the government would only grant the import licenses for more steel! Similarly, increased demand for oil and spare parts for the transport sector exacerbated foreign exchange problems. But there was little interest in replacing motor transport with water and bicycle transport. Thus attempts to tackle foreign exchange problems at one point simply raise them at another without a more fundamental strategy of transformation based on self-reliance and local initiative and innovation.

Rather than transforming agriculture in Ghana, OFY created a parallel production and marketing structure. The increased food produced on state farms and the farms of bureaucrats and businessmen was channeled into a state marketing structure which supplied institutions and the privileged classes through supply depots close to the government ministries. This alternative structure with its controlled prices was inaccessible to peasants, petty commodity producers and urban workers, who remained tied to the web of patron-client and debtor-creditor relations with local traders and transporters.

The NRC has fared somewhat better than the Busia regime in attempting to balance off the interests of all classes including the international bourgeoisie. The style of vigorous pragmatism and distrust of political rhetoric gained a degree of popular support initially, particularly in combination with the populist approach, eg the concern expressed via the media for the common worker and his housing problems, or the illusion of simple solutions which called on student volunteers to get sugar cane harvested for cane factories with a long history of supply and labour problems. Relations with wage workers have been designed to appease the antagonisms of the Busia period. Trade union legislation was promised soon after the coup and the TUC almost immediately reinstated. Workers fired for strike action regained their jobs and the Dawn Broadcast of January 1974 brought promises of salary increases for workers of 3½% over cost of living index. In the context of a much improved balance of payments position and a trade surplus, such concessions were not difficult. Still, within months, striking dockworkers defied anti-strike laws to press for higher wages and by August 1974, a wage increase of 2 cedis per day was announced. With the cost of living soaring, this still meant little gain for the average worker.

The state's management of relations with classes subordinated to the capitalist mode, the peasantry and petty commodity producers, combined the rhetoric of energetic problem-solving with the reality of continued impoverishment. Prices offered to cocoa farmers by the CMB were so low as to provide little incentive for increased production, and even when world prices rose to £700 per ton, the CMB paid only £290 to local producers. The remainder was redistributed via the state. By 1975, it had become necessary to create a Ministry of Cocoa Affairs to attempt revitalization of the cocoa industry. As in food production, OFY tended to benefit mainly the rich peasants. The government also began to establish capitalist agriculture, and increasingly urged foreign companies to invest in agriculture. Land concessions, refused to expatriates by the colonial government, were now offered by the post-colonial state for production of both food and agricultural raw materials. UAC interests expanded to include participation in a Cotton Production Company jointly with the National Investment Bank, the Agricultural Development Bank and the three UAC-controlled textile operations. Valco is proposing to get involved in rice production.

Petty commodity producers continued to experience very directly the dislocations of the economy. Restrictions on imports and high cost of transport placed severe constraints on the array of small-scale economic activities in Accra in everything from shortages of plastics for shoe-makers to transport slowdowns for lack of spare parts. NRC plans announced in 1975 to make improvements may well aim to pre-empt political unrest from this sector. The NRC has proved a steady ally of international capitalism, with its needs for a cheap labour force and an institutional framework for continued penetration and domination. The early repudiation of debts and the hard line on rescheduling caused a minor flurry in the West. This proved to be a classic state function, checking some capitalists in order to restabilize the system as a whole. Subsequent policies have readily accommodated international capitalism. Moves in 1975 to take majority ownership in extractive industries such as minerals and timber came when these were by no means the fastest growing or most profitable of foreign interests. The manner of take-over from the transnationals challenged neither continued Western access to these resources nor continued high profits from them. As Col. Acheampong said on taking a 55% share in several timber companies:

Apart from the demoralizing political consequences, one only has to examine the inflow of foreign investment against the outflow resulting from the demands for transfers of capital, to realize how inimical has been the effect of foreign domination on the Ghanaian economy. I came to a firm and positive conclusion that our perennial balance of payments problems could never find lasting solutions, nor could we hope to achieve any reasonable growth unless action was taken to replace foreign domination. (*West Africa,* January 8, 1973.)

Yet he went on to say that foreign participation was to be welcomed; only foreign domination was to be constrained. There was seemingly no concern about the technical and management contracts remaining with the 45% shareholders. With transfer pricing and an array of book-keeping mechanisms in their world-wide operations at their disposal, this ensured for the transnationals continued control with the added security of state participation. The current array of project possibilities, such as Krupp in iron, an American-Japanese consortium including Kaiser in bauxite mining, Mitsubishi and Nippon in another aluminium smelter shows that the transnationals are clearly ready for such 'participation'.

The Ghanaian state is the entry point for these 'development' projects. They gain attractiveness for the transnationals basically by offering higher returns on capital than investment elsewhere, with low return to labour as a basic feature of that profitability. The state plays an important ideological role in cloaking such investment with a rich rhetoric about needs for aid and technical assistance based on short-ages of capital and lack of technology. Each issue of the *Ghanaian Times* or *Graphic* portrays NRC leaders energetically in control of economic development, opening projects, welcoming delegations of investors, signing contracts, discussing aid programmes. Yet at the same time, debate is stifled about more genuine options for transformation. The *Legon Observer,* one of the few publications to raise critical questions about such policies as OFY and slum resettlement, found itself rather abruptly terminated in mid-1975.

Since Nkrumah's death, there has been a readiness on the part of the NRC to associate itself with Nkrumah's programmes for Ghana's development. Yet clearly none of the negative lessons of the CPP years have been learned. The centralization of powers, his presidentialism and commandism isolated Nkrumah from popular aspirations and support. This ultimately separated him from the only real basis for an alternative to continued foreign domination, a state based in a mobil-ized and conscious people. The lack of popular participation, of structures for meaningful local initiatives, ultimately doomed to failure all schemes emanating from the President's office. The NRC in no way learned this lesson. The militarization of politics has meant a structuring of political life on military lines with few representative institutions. There is little indication of any politicization of the mili-tary, which might lead to mobilization based on education and popular persuasion as an alternative to moral exhortations and chain-of-command leadership.

It would be a mistake, however, to construe the Ghana situation as static. The NRC are open to being influenced by the particular histori-cal conjuncture as were the petty-bourgeois progressives of the CPP. It is still possible for a fraction of the military to articulate an alterna-tive, progressive strategy. The capacity of the military to identify downward is reinforced by its concrete experiences with Ghanaian realities. This comes through its own petty bourgeois class background reinforced by the extended family system, and also by the origins of many in the military in the less developed areas of Ghana, such as the north. The potential for identification with the masses comes from military postings to border points and underdeveloped regions, from anti-smuggling programmes which revealed clearly the workings of the cocoa economy, from anti-cholera campaigns revealing rural health conditions, and from flood relief programmes revealing rural poverty.

Some NRC members have begun to ask more fundamental questions arising from their experiences as managers of the Ghanaian state. Some may be moving towards solutions that go beyond populism to questions of imperialism and class struggle. Thus far, a form of state capitalism with increasing joint state-private ventures seems to have accommodated the forces seeking less direct foreign control. So long as high prices for exports prevail and imports are controlled, the technological-industrial dependency has some viability. The recent trends of falling cocoa and rising oil prices bring the old contradictions again into full play.

Bureaucratic and commercial petty bourgeois fractions have thus far been unable to consolidate their positions in a substantial enough fashion to guarantee any long-term cohesion and stability. This stems in large part from the extreme vulnerability of the Ghana economy to externally precipitated crises. It stems also from a history of struggle in Ghana. The Nkrumah years and the attempts to articulate a left option are an important component of Ghana's recent history. Despite the failure of the left option, it provides an important reference point, a remainder of the possibility of an anti-imperialist programme for genuine self-reliance and equality. Worker and student unrest comes readily to the surface when the many suffering economic hardships are confronted with the flaunted privileges of the few. It becomes increasingly more difficult to manage class relations and to contain popular aspirations by demagogy, mystification and repression.

MILITARY VIOLENCE AGAINST CIVILIANS: THE CASE OF THE CONGOLESE AND ZAIREAN MILITARY IN THE PEDICLE 1890—1988

By Mwelwa C. Musambachime

> Violence is not power but [it is] an instrument of power.
> — Hannah Arendt

> The deciding factor in every social relation of power is, in the last resort, the superiority of physical force.
> — Wilhelm Liebknecht

> In studying political organization, we have to deal with the maintenance of social order, within a territorial framework by organized exercise of coercive authority through the use, or the possibility of use, of physical force ... the policy and the army are instruments by which coercion is exercised.
> — A.R. Radcliffe-Brown[1]

These quotations underline the focus of our study: the use of violence as an instrument of power. Max Weber's famous definition of power that "one actor [or a number of actors] within a social relationship will be in a position to carry out his [or her] own will despite resistance" helps to focus on the repressive or manipulative processes of power and the conditions within which obedient wills are created through the threat of the use of force.[2] Force, as we shall see in this paper, is a crucial element in a particular transformation or disposition, not merely in the keeping of order among the citizens.[3]

　　Violence as an instrument of power is exercised by the army—one of the most efficient instruments for establishing a ruler's influence. In his analysis of patrimonial authority, Weber gives special attention to the structure and social organization of the military forces. In doing so he identifies four basic types of military organizations used in these particular situations. The first consists of peasants, slaves, serfs, or other subordinates who are given land in exchange for their services. This, he notes, is highly unstable, for once the dependents are settled on the land, their involvement in agricultural work lessens their

---

[1] Hannah Arendt, *On Violence* (New York, 1970) 35; Wilhelm Liebknecht, *Karl Marx: Biographical Memoirs* (translated by Ernest Untermann) (Chicago, 1908) 301; M. Fortes and E. E. Evans-Pritchard, eds., *African Political Systems* (London, 1969), xiv.

[2] Max Weber, *The Theory of Social and Economic Organization* (Glencoe, 1947) 152; Max Weber, "Politics as a Vocation" in H. H. Gerth and C. Wright Mills, *From Max Weber: Essay in Sociology* (London, 1951), 55-61.

[3] Frantz Fanon, *The Wretched of the Earth* (Hammondsworth, 1969), 27-84; B. Marie Perinbam, "Violence, Morality, and History in the Colonial Syndrome: Frantz Fanon's Perspectives," *Journal of Southern African Affairs*, 3, 1 (January 1978), 7-34.

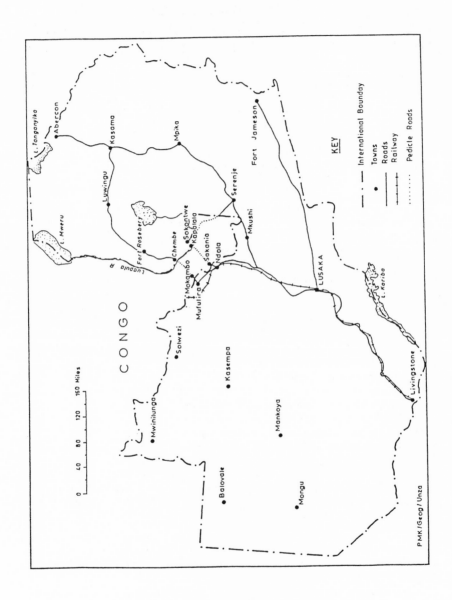

Map 1

POSITION OF THE CONGO PEDICLE

effectiveness as fighters. Consequently, a ruler has to organize a military force to protect his interests consisting of former slaves who are not involved in agriculture and are cut off from the local society. Such an army is held together by adequate and regular pay, without which it cannot function as a disciplined force. Third is the recruitment of mercenaries, composed of foreigners having no real contact with the subject population. And fourth is the formation of a personal army recruited from the less privileged social strata, which is transformed into a national army to protect the interests of the ruler.[4]

Weber's typology provides a useful starting point in our study of the use of violence by the military against civilians with reference to the Belgian Congo (now Zaire)—particularly in the area known as the Pedicle. Here, the Belgian administrators were referred to as "Bula Matare" ("Breaker of rocks") by the Africans to describe the brutality of their administration and maltreatment of the colonized Africans. The Belgians proudly used this name to refer to their administration.[5] During the colonial period, the Congolese military closely approximated the second and third types in Weber's typology while the post-colonial military resembles the fourth. The Congolese military, as various studies show, exercised brutal force and violence on the population—a legacy which continues today.[6]

Crawford Young, who has made an extensive study of political processes in the former Belgian Congo, advises that "no summary of the Congolese [or for that matter the Zairean] political scene can ignore the instrument of force" and violence associated with the army. The Congolese spoke the "language of pure force," accompanied by violence and force.[7] In this, the Congolese army were not alone. Other armies and police forces in other parts of Africa, were products of violent systems, as Allen and Barbara Isaacman, John MacCracken, and Phyllis Martin have shown. In maintaining law and order, enforcing authority, and protecting the interests of the colonial powers, the soldiers and policemen employed intimidation, undisguised coercion, and violence to support their

---

[4]Quoted in C. Wright Mills, *The Power Elite* (New York, 1956), 171.

[5]According to Vellut, Mbula Matari or Boula Matari was an image of "a 'colonial hero' who wanted to be feared for his strength and admired for his wealth." Jean-Luc Vellut, "Mining in Belgian Congo," in David Birmingham and Phyllis Martin, eds., *History of Central Africa*, II (London, 1983), 162; see also his "Materiaux pour reconstituer l'image du blanc au Congo Belge 1900-1960," in J. L. Vellut, ed., *Stereotypes nationaux prejuge's raciaux xixeme et xxeme slecles* (Louvain à la Neuve, 1982), 91-116; See also J. Crockaert, *Bula Matari ou le Congo Belge* (Brussels, 1929); M. Crawford Young, *The Politics of the Congo: Decolonization and Independence* (Princeton, 1965), 98; Guy Burrows, *The Curse of Central Africa* (London, 1903), 83.

[6]E. D. Morel, *Red Rubber* (London, 1907), see also his *King Leopold's Rule in Africa* (London, 1904); L. H. Gann and Peter Duignan, *The Rulers of Belgian Africa* (Princeton, 1979); Crawford Young and Thomas Turner, *The Rise and Decline of the Zairean State* (Madison, 1985), 4-5; Bryant Shaw, "Fore Publique: Force Unique. The Military in the Belgian Congo 1914-1939" (Ph.D. thesis, University of Wisconsin, 1984).

[7]Young, *The Politics of the Congo*, 438.

predatory inclinations.[8] What differentiates the Congolese army from these other examples is the degree of violence. The use of force in the Belgian Congo which had few parallels in Africa, and has been studied by a number of scholars. In addition, there are a number of commentaries by visitors from the early 1900s.[9]

Origins

The beginning of the Belgian Congo as a colonial state began in 1876 when King Leopold I of Belgium founded the International African State. In 1885, the name was changed to Congo Free State. It had very flexible boundaries, which were later legalized by treaties with Portugal, Britain, and Germany. The treaty to formalize the boundary between North-East Rhodesia, North-West Rhodesia, and the Congo Free State was signed on 12 May 1894 by Belgium and Great Britain. The boundary as delimited covered the southern section of the Congo Free State, which stretched from the southern shore of Lake Tanganyika to Lake Mweru, then along the Luapula River to Lake Mweru, then along the Mpanta Meridian (Latitude 11 41' S. Longitude 29 49' E) to the Congo-Zambezi watershed, then along it to Longitude 24 E, which formed a tripartite boundary point separating Angola, Congo Free State, and North-West Rhodesia.[10] As so defined, the boundary created a narrow piece of land known as the Pedicle, which jutted between North-East and North-West Rhodesia, almost separating the two (see map). The presence of the Pedicle created transportation difficulties between North-East and North-West- Rhodesia, prompting the British South African Company (or BSAC), the ʻadministering power to appeal to the British government for a readjustment of the boundary with Belgium.[11] The BSAC made several proposals which included exchange of land either along the northern boundary between Lakes Mweru and Tanganyika or west of the Kafue River in what is today the Zambian Copperbelt for the southern portion of the Pedicle, which would allow the administration to establish its communication lines between North-East and North-West Rhodesia on "firm ground." The Belgians rejected all these proposals.[12]

The Congo Free State, as created by Leopold, fitted the Weberian definition of a state "founded on the use of force," with the right to use it

---

[8]John MacCracken, "Coercion and Control in Nyasaland: Aspects of the History of a Colonial Force", *Journal of African History*, 27, 1 (1986), 127-47; Allen Isaacman and Barbara Isaacman, *Mozambique: From Colonialism to Revolution* (Boulder, 1983), 29-31, 34, 37, 42; Phyllis Martin, "The Violence of Empire," in David Birmingham and Phyllis M. Martin, eds., *History of Central Africa* II (London, 1983), 20-21.

[9]Ilunga Kabongo, "Ethnicity, Social Classes and the State in the Congo 1900-1965: The Case of the Baluba" (Ph.D. Dissertation, University of California–Berkeley, 1973), 202-03; J.M. Moubray, *In South Central Africa* (London, 1912), 127-9; Reports by correspondents of the *Livingstone Mail*, 27 July 1912 and 4 January 1913.

[10]A. Castlein, *The Congo State* (New York, 1907), 23-26; P. Jentgen, *Les frontières du Congo Belge* (Brussels, 1962), 12; E. Hertslett, *The Map of Africa by Treaty, II* (London, 1967), 553; A. A. Keith, *The Belgian Congo and the Berlin Act* (London, 1962), 6.

[11]Mwelwa C. Musambachime, "How the Kaputa Border Row Flared Up," *Sunday Times*, 15 July 1984, 5.

[12]Raymond L. Buell, *The Native Problem in Africa*, II (London, 1965), 497.

whenever it pleased those in power.[13] Force and violence were freely used to cow the African population and drive them into the collection of rubber and ivory, which went to enrich Leopold's account. To ensure that there was no interruption in the flow of these goods and to maintain law and "order and . . . enforce its command," the Congo Free State established the *Force Publique* in 1885, which performed both military and police functions. Initially all the recruits in the Force Publique were foreign Africans from East Africa (Zanzibar, Somalia, and Ethiopia) and West Africa (Nigeria, Gold Coast, Dahomey, and Sierra Leone), who were commonly referred to as Hausa. They were labor migrants as well as mercenaries similar to those employed by East African traders who operated in the parts of the Congo before the establishment of the colonial state.[14]

In 1885, recruitment of the Congolese into the Force Publique began. At first it was voluntary but due to the low pay being offered—30 centimes a day (amounting to 9 francs) for first enlistment and 55 centimes per day (amounting to 16 francs, 50 centimes) per month, only one-third of what was paid to government and railway employees—few volunteers offered themselves.[15] To augment the number of volunteers, the government resorted to conscription. Chiefs were asked to send conscripts, and usually slaves, impoverished people, prisoners, criminals, the chronically ill, and mentally disturbed in the community were sent.[16] This state of affairs continued throughout the colonial period. The annual report on the army for 1954 noted that "many recruits from urban centers were assigned to the army because of their undesirable traits. The Territorial administration often recruited them in the Force rather than send them back to the villages."[17] The Commission for the Protection of Natives in 1919 stated that when the administration recruited directly, "the hunt for men throws terror into the villages, provokes rebellions, and arouses towards the Administration a state of surly defiance and hostility."[18] The Force Publique was unpopular among the Congolese, as statistics given by Raymond Buell indicated.[19]

Initially, a large portion of recruits in the Force Publique came from the Azande, Batetela, and Bangala groups from the North-east part of the Congo, regarded by the Belgians as the most aggressive and warlike of the Congolese ethnic groups.[20] According to one source, the Belgians hoped to turn to a "loftier cause the enthusiasm [these groups showed] in their domestic struggles."[21] After

---

[13]Gann and Duignan, *The Rulers of Belgian Africa*, 73; 225; Buell, *The Native Problem*, II, 496.

[14]Gann and Duignan, *The Rulers of Belgian Africa*, 73.

[15]Buell, *The Native Problem*, II, 497.

[16]*Ibid.*, 497; Gann and Duignan, *The Rulers of Belgian Africa*, 76-77.

[17]Belgian Congo, *Rapport sur l'administration de la Colonie* (Brussels, 1954), 49.

[18]Belgian Congo, *Bulletin Official du Congo Belge* 1920, 647, quoted in Buell, *Native Problem*, II, 497.

[19]Raymond Buell gives the breakdown of the Camp at Elisabethville which had about 565 soldiers: 363 were conscripts (64 percent); 66 volunteers (11.1 percent); 86 enlisted (15 percent)—50 of whom had served 16 years or more and 36 had served more than seven years. Buell, *Native Problem*, II, 497.

[20]Gann and Duignan, *The Rulers of Belgian Africa*, 76; Young, *The Politics of the Congo*, 438.

[21]Anonymous, "Mutiniere au Congo," in *Bulletin Militaire* (March, 1947), 21.

the mutiny in the Batetela groups in Luluaborg in 1896, enlistment spread to other ethnic groups in the Congo.[22] And using a policy of social distance which was also widely used in Mozambique, the Rhodesias and South Africa, the recruits in the Force Publique were "deliberately posted away from their own area [of origin] lest they [would] be swayed by local sympathies."[23] In short the soldiers became foreigners among the Congolese people.

The Force Publique soldiers performed the same functions as soldiers and policemen in other parts of Africa. Writing about the Nyasaland police, John MacCracken has observed that they served as

> as frontline troops in the struggle to uphold the authority of government, the police played a crucial role in sustaining imperial control at the cheapest possible cost. Through their employment, the state was able to ensure that hut tax was paid, labour was coerced, workers discipline and European property protected.[24]

Apart from these responsibilities, the Force Publique soldiers also supervised the building of government posts and construction of roads. Above all, they preserved the entity of the colonial state.[25]

In employing social distance, the Belgians also saw to it that the Force Publique was alienated from the Congolese masses. This was strongly enforced by the Belgian officers who sought to instill in the troops an *esprit de corps* based on loyalty to the state. They encouraged the use of Lingala, a *lingua franca* used by traders trading in the Upper Congo and along the Congo River to enhance the pride of the troops and create a sense of belonging to a military elite.[26] An article in the 1954 *Bulletin Militaire* stressed this element:

> the best remedy for subversion and corruption in the army is the isolation of troops by inculcating a positive zealotry towards their craft and mobility of military ideals [by teaching them] to despise the masses who lack military discipline.[27]

This point was later touched on, in 1974, by General Molongya Mayikusa, then chief of cabinet in the Ministry of Defence who observed that the Force Publique

> used to resemble an army of mercenaries who lived removed from the population at large. This is reflected in the fact that the soldier considered himself an elite, while viewing civilians as nothing but "savages." The soldier [was] a person without

[22]Gann and Duignan, *The Rulers of Belgian Africa*, 76-77.

[23]Martin, "The Violence of the Empire," 16-17.

[24]MacCracken, "Coercion and Control," 127.

[25]Buell, *Native Problem*, II, 496.

[26]Anon., "Mutinerie au Congo," 21.

faith or soul, torturers of the civil population, and furthermore ignorant. The antagonism was exploited to a point where the military and the civil populations, though united by blood, thoroughly and profoundly detested one another. . . .[28]

The Congolese soldiers drank excessively, beat up civilians, stole their valuables, set fire to villages, and raped women at will. They also supplemented their low wages by extorting food, chickens, livestock, fish and beer from the local people. Others made false arrests as a prelude to extorting bribes.[29] They disregarded with impunity, the authority of chiefs and headmen while carrying out their duties. Their uniform was associated with terror. The method used did not bother the officials as long as the quotas were met. Some soldiers, according to Buell's and Moubray's accounts, became "tyrants," levying rubber and ivory on their own account as well as their masters'.[30] No action was taken against them. A report in the *Livingstone Mail* gives an example of the policemen:

> [The] Native policemen do as they like—preying on other natives. . . . This sort of thing occurs openly even in the presence of Europeans who are not anxious to parade their altruism, but take pains to conceal their disgust. If such conditions obtain in towns, what must be the state of things outside where these tyrants are not even under such ineffective restraint as their inexperienced officers care to exercise.[31]

The answer is that they were worse. To meet quotas and have a surplus for themselves, the soldiers employed various methods: holding chiefs, women, and children for ransom, burning villages as a form of warning or punishment, and flogging. The Force Publique attained a notorious reputation for indiscipline and violence.[32] Dugald Campbell, a missionary in charge at Johnston Falls—

---

[27] Young and Turner, *The Rise*, 363, 449.

[28] Quoted in Young and Turner, *The Rise and Decline*, 263.

[29] According to Buell, the Force Publique were paid 30 centimes a day (about 9 francs per month), on first enlistment. On the second it rose to 55 centimes (16-50 francs per month). These wages were a third of what government paid. The low salaries were supplemented by payments of four yards of blue cloth to the soldier and another four to the wife. The cost of one man in the Force Publique was estimated by Buell to be about £21 per year, while in Uganda it was £36. Buell, *Native Problem*, II, 496, 498.

[30] *Ibid.*, 498; Moubray, *In South Central Africa*, 127-28; *Livingstone Mail*, 27 July 1912, 4 January 1913.

[31] *Livingstone Mail*, 27 July 1912. In a report to the high commissioner for South Africa, the resident commissioner recalled after a tour of Katanga that "I was told the conduct of the native police leaves much to be desired and that in their dealings with the native they are inadequately controlled by their officers. Such defects as may exist in the administration of the native would seem however as a rule to be due to ineffectiveness rather than any 'mauvaise volonté' on the part of the Europeans." National Archives of Zambia (NAZ), BS 3/405: Resident Commissioner Salisbury to High Commissioner, 29 September 1917; Moubray, *In South Central Africa*, 128.

[32] Buell, *Native Problem*, 497.

Mambilima on the lower Luapula has left a graphic account of the state of affairs:

> I have made a journey myself [to several parts of Katanga] and found the [soldiers] everywhere living like kings, plundering, killing and burning villages in the name of the State. . . . Every time I made representations they were declared impossible or the answer was "I shall ask my head sentry to make inquiries," the head sentries being one of the worst blackguards in the country. Nothing was ever proved. He could not believe that his soldiers could be guilty of such misconduct or "well, they must have carte blanche or the natives would not respect the State." Sometimes "Might is Right" would be the curt reply.[33]

With officials giving the soldiers *carte blanche* to act as they pleased, the pillaging and plunder in the countryside reached such proportions that administrative officials and soldiers and administrative stations were shunned.[34] A number of villages living along the boundary quickly moved to North-East Rhodesia. "The wholesale exodus," reported Campbell, "is due to Belgian raiding and maltreatment of natives."[35] These atrocities only stopped after the issue of "red rubber" was given wide publicity in Europe by Morel and others. Although the Belgian officers deplored their behavior, they appeared incapable of enforcing discipline. As a ʰresult, the Force Publique attained a notorious reputation for indiscipline and violence.

The Force Publique were also deployed in the Pedicle. Here they held senior positions commanding troops drawn from the local ethnic groups (Yeke, Sanga, Nyamwezi, and Lunda) who enlisted for three years. These troops were, according to one source, a more "well trained . . . efficient and reliable force than what the British had in North West Rhodesia or North East Rhodesia." In the Pedicle they were stationed at Kalonga and Sakania.[36]

Military Violence along the Sokontwe-Serenje Road

The presence of the Congo Pedicle created an immediate problem for the British South Africa Company: that of communication between Fort Rosebery and Ndola and between Fort Rosebery and Serenje. The area between Serenje and Sokontwe, which lay in North-East Rhodesia, was covered by the Bangweulu Swamps making it impossible to have road communication linking the two administrative stations. In spite of this difficulty, Harrington, the native commissioner at Fort Rosebery constructed a road between Fort Rosebery and

---

[33] Quoted in E. D. Morel, *Red Rubber* (London, 1919), 45.

[34] Dugald Campbell, in the *Echoes of Service* (September, 1898), 92.

[35] See example, *Red Rubber* and *King Leopolds*.

[36] NAZ/BS1/83 Vol. I: J. E. Stephenson, Ndola, to Administrator (North-East Rhodesia), 23 August 1903; NAZ/B S1/85 Vol. II: H. Harrington to, Fort Rosebery to Administrator 13 July 1903.

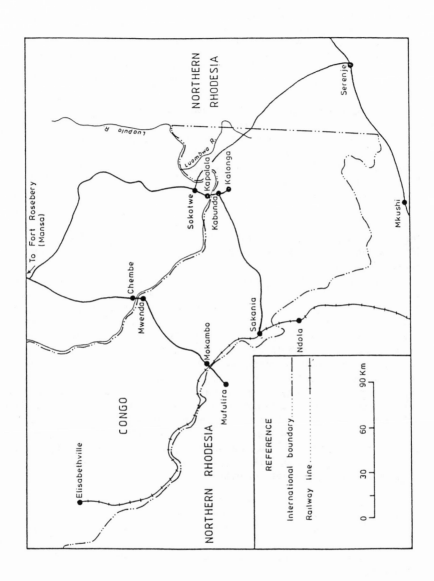

Map 2

THE CONGO (ZAIRE) PEDICLE

Sokontwe on the upper Luapula in 1901.[37] And Hector Croad constructed another road linking Serenje to the Luombwa, where it crosses the Mpanta Meridian. This point and Sokontwe were separated by a distance of 40 miles (about 64 kilometers), which lay in the Pedicle.[38] The use of this stretch required permission from the Belgian authorities. The alternative route was to go from Serenje to Mpika, Kasama, and Luena (a forerunner to Luwingu) before reaching Fort Rosebery—a distance of nearly 1,000 kilometers, which took three to four weeks as opposed to five to six days between Fort Rosebery and Serenje via Sokontwe.[39] Permission was granted on a number of conditions requiring those using the road to be in possession of a pass issued by the native commissioner's office, and not to carry a gun or recruit labor in the Pedicle. The route was opened in January 1902 and was largely used by mail runners employed by the BSAC administration, porters employed by the African Lakes Corporation to transport merchandise from Fort Jameson to Fort Rosebery for distribution in their shops in Mweru-Luapula, and by large caravans of porters engaged by the Tanganyika Concessions Limited to transport goods from the port of Chinde on the Indian Ocean and from Karonga on the northern part of Lake Nyasa to Kambove in Katanga, where the company was involved in prospecting for copper and other minerals.[40]

Although porters, mail runners, and caravans observed the conditions laid down by Major Weyns who was in charge of the operations of the Comite' Spe'cial du Katanga (CSK), their security was not assured at all. Almost immediately after the opening of the route, reports started reaching the native commissioner at Fort Rosebery that mail runners and caravans were being attacked, beaten, and robbed by Congolese soldiers. Mail bags were seized and scattered while loads of merchandise were impounded. Some mail runners and porters were mutilated and in some cases murdered.[41] According to Robert Wright, a trader operating in the Sokintwe area, these soldiers "roamed about uncontrolled" committing atrocities. They "instilled fear [in the local people] who were terrified in dread of their visits."[42] European traders were not spared either. Several were attacked and beaten, and their goods stolen; two were known to have been murdered.[43] In 1903, the frequency of attacks increased. In June, another attack occurred. H. T. Harrington, native commissioner for Luapula, filed a report with the administrator as follows:

---

[37]NAZ/KDF 3/1: Mweru-Luapula District Note Book (MLDN), Vol. 1, p. 496; Vol. III, p. 496; Vol II, p. 498.

[38]H. C. Dann, *The Romance of Posts of Rhodesia, British Central Africa and Nyasaland* (London, 1940), 63-64, 90.

[39]NAZ/BS1/83 Vol I; Administrator to Secretary (BSAC), 7 July 1902.

[40]NAZ/KDF 3/1: MLDNB Vol. I, p. 496.

[41]NAZ/BS1/83 Vol II: Harrington to Administrator, 13 July 1903.

[42]Robert Wright, "Trading on the Luapula 1900-1904 Part I," *Northern Rhodesia Journal*, 5, 2 (1962), 268; 489-90.

[43]NAZ/BS3/85: Administrator to Secretary, BSAC, 7 July 1902: J. Wills, to Civil Commissioner, 18 July 1902; Wright, "Trading," 489-90.

> I had to go to the Belgian station at Kalonga. There has been trouble again on the mail road again, our mail carriers were knocked down, their uniform torn off and mail bags carried off.... It was [on the] orders of the Belgian Police.[44]

On 13 July, he filed another report on the

> assault by the Belgian Police on two British South African Company mail carriers on the road between sokontwi (sic) and the Luwombo (sic) River. The mail carriers started off from Sokontwi with the Fort Jameson mail on the morning of 20th of June, they were supplied with a pass as was required by the Belgians. At Paula's Village, 10 miles along the road they were met by men of Bula Matar [chef de poste, Kalonga] who asked what they were doing. They answered that they were Sokontwi mail carriers. They were knocked down, their uniforms torn off, the mail taken from them also they were beaten and tied up and kept there til about 4:00 p.m. ... when they were to go on their way ... by Kalonga Police out of uniform and they had a gun.[45]

Harrington went to see the *chef de poste*, who regretted the incidence and apologized. He also assured that such incidences would not occur. This of course was of little value because "he seemed to have little control over his askari [soldiers] who seem to do much as they please and were none too respectful towards me."[46] The attacks continued. On one occasion, in August 1903, Robert Wright had to fire on the Congolese soldiers attacking a caravan to scare them off. As a result of his action, the road was closed, disrupting traffic between Serenje and Sokontwe.[47] It was reopened soon after some negotiations. This became a pattern which was a forerunner to what was to happen frequently after 1960.

The beating of porters and mail runners and the frequent closures of the road did not please the North-East Rhodesia administrators. On 7 July 1903, the administrator wrote to the secretary of the BSAC requesting him to ask the Foreign Office to "obtain from the Congo Government, either an admission of our right of way or a definite and permanent arrangement which will enable us to maintain communication across the Pedicle." He went on to add that

> Free and uninterrupted communication between Sokontwe and Serenje is most desirable for both administrative and commercial reasons and I do not think the Congo Government can refuse to accede to such a reasonable and necessary arrangement, especially in view of the fact that passage of travellers and merchandise and mail from the

---

[44]NAZ/BS1/83 Vol. II: Harrington to Administrator, 27, 1902.

[45]NAZ/BS1/83 Vol. II: Harrington to Administrator, 13 July 1902.

[46]NAZ/BS1/83 Vol. II: Harrington to Administrator, 13 July 1903.

Congo Free State through North East Rhodesia endured many
years absolutely free and unrestricted.[48]

Although the Rhodesian officials knew that the Congo Free State officials were
"determined to make things as unpleasant as possible" for them, they did not wish
to retaliate in kind by stopping the transit of mails and good from Karonga to
Kambove.[49] They continued to plead with the Belgian officials to keep the road
open. The road continued to operate in a state of insecurity until September 1910.
Caravans were regularly stopped, with traders beaten and robbed. When the
Rhodesian authorities brought too many complaints to the Belgian authorities,
the latter's response was to close the road without prior warning and reopen it
whenever it suited them. The Rhodesian authorities were completely helpless to
do anything.[50]

Between 1904 and 1910, the road assumed an additional importance in that
it was now being used by recruited and voluntary labor to travel to Broken Hill
(now Kabwe) Mine, Southern Rhodesia, and South Africa to work either in the
mines or on the farms. Mining and agriculture required an abundant supply of
cheap labor. To tap this labor, the Rhodesia Native Labour Bureau was formed in
1904 and in the same year, started recruiting labor for Southern Rhodesia from
both North-East and North-West Rhodesia. Labor recruited from the area lying
between Sokontwe and Lake Mweru used the Sokontwe-Serenje road. Returning
migrants carried boxes "weighing 50 to 60 lbs containing the usual collection of
clothes . . [and] the usual . ! . household utensils and very often a sewing machine
or bicycle."[51] Some of these were ambushed by the Congolese soldiers who
arrested them on trivial charges, and intimidated, harassed, and beat them up
before stealing their goods.[52] Numerous complaints were made to the Rhodesian
officials on the insecurity of the road. As a solution to the problem, a proposal
was made to construct the Serenje-Sokontwe road within North-East Rhodesia.
Surveys were conducted and estimates made; however, the lack of sufficient
funds made it impossible to construct the road.[53] It had to wait for independent
Zambia, using Chinese aid, to finally construct the road which now links Serenje
with Mansa.[54] The outbreak of sleeping sickness in 1908/09 along the upper

---

[47]Wright, "Trading," 489-90.

[48]NAZ/BS1/83 Vol. II: Administrator to Secretary BSAC, 7 July 1903.

[49]NAZ/KDF 3/1: MLDNB Vol. III, p. 16.

[50]NAZ/MLDNB, Vol. III, 496; Dugald Campbell's letter to the Board of Directors of the Plymouth
Brethren, published in the *Echoes of Service*, (1904), 317.

[51]Archives of the Council of World Missions: London Missionary Society: Central Africa
(ACWM/LMS/CA: H.C. Nutter, Annual Report for Mbereshi Mission from 1919: Interview: Safeli Chibwe,
Mansa, 27 March 1975.

[52]Interview: Mwansa Nsakanya, Chisembe, 19 April 1975.

[53]Mwelwa C. Musambachime "Origins of the Samya-Serenje Road" unpublished paper, 10-14: NAZ/KSK
3/1: Serenje District Notebook, Vol. I, p. 72.

[54]The road took over ten years to complete; it was opened in 1983.

Luapula River forced the administration to look for an alternative route to link North-East and North-West Rhodesia.[55]

Kapalala—Sakania Road

The problems faced by labor migrants on the Sokontwe-Serenje road forced many to look for an alternate route. They found one linking Kapalala with Sakania and Sakania with Ndola. It was merely a footpath but it reduced the number of days taken to reach Ndola via Serenje from fourteen to only three or four days.[56] By 1908, the Native Labour Bureau and other recruiting agents for Bwana Mkubwa were using the path to ferry their labor to employment centers.[57] In 1909 when the railway line reached Ndola and made it into a terminus for Mweru-Luapula, the route assumed additional importance. Goods destined for Fort Rosebery, Kawambwa Chienge, and Luwingu were left at Ndola to be transported to Fort Rosebery and other destinations by porters across the Pedicle. This was further enhanced during the First World War when it became an important transit route for ferrying war materials to the front. In 1916, the Northern Rhodesia administration sought and got permission from the governor general of the Belgian Congo to upgrade the route to an all-weather gravel road to allow motorized transport to move faster in carrying food and material between Ndola and Kabunda.[58] In addition, a large number of recruits to and from employment centers in Ndola, Broken Hill, Southern Rhodesia and South Africa used the route. The pattern of incidents occurring along the Serenje-Sokontwe road were duplicated. Soldiers deployed at Sakania and Kabunda often waylaid caravans and returning migrants. In 1911, the *Livingstone Mail* carried an article stating that "small parties of one or two [migrant workers] returning home ran the [risk of arrest by the Askaris]. The Native Police conduct their inquiries with fixed bayonets at the ready and their white soldiers with loaded revolvers in either hand."[59] In such circumstances, migrant workers who continued the practice of carrying boxes or huge loads were asked to unload their goods and produce receipts for each item. Those which could not be authenticated were confiscated. Customs duty was paid on sewing machines and bicycles. Unlucky migrants were beaten and robbed of their money and goods—even if they had passes authorizing them to pass through the Pedicle.[60] Those found without passes were arrested on the spot and jailed for a month. They were then deployed

---

[55]On the impact of sleeping sickness, see Mwelwa C. Musambachime, "Social and Economic Effects of Sleeping Sickness," *African Economic History*, 10, (1981).

[56]Nsakanya.

[57]Interview: Joseph Pardon Mansa, 26 April 1975; NAZ/KDF 3/1 MLDNB, Vol. III, 496.

[58]Nsakanya; Pardon; Chambala Kafutu, Mansa, 21 April 1975.

[59]*Livingstone Mail*, 9 December 1911.

[60]H. C. Marshall, "Water Transport in the Bangweulu Swamps," *Northern Rhodesia Journal*, 3, 3 (1956), 189; NAZ/ZA1/9/18/38: E. H. Goodall, Provincial Commissioner (PC), Ndola, to Secretary of Native Affairs (SNA), Livingstone, 12 November 1930; This, and other abuses to which Northern Rhodesians were subjected is graphically portrayed in a fictional novel by U. C. Chishimba, *Namweleu: The Story of the Legendary African Lion*, (Lusaka, 1988), 109-17.

either on public projects, collecting firewood for the soldiers and European officials, or cleaning the surroundings of Sakania, Kalonga, and Kabunda.[61] There was no avenue for appeal. On release, complaints were made to Northern Rhodesian officials at Fort Rosebery.[62] To avoid these experiences, many labor migrants wanting to pass through the Pedicle were, according to the general manager of Bwana Mkubwa Mine, forced to "travel by night because they were afraid of Congo Police who arrest them and are said to ill-treat them."[63] Some were caught by lions and leopards.[64]

The harassment of Northern Rhodesians was not only a preserve for the Force Publique soldiers. In a number of cases villagers living in villages along the route often posed as soldiers in order to steal from the transiting migrants. Some of these villagers became "professional thieves" who made a living by robbing Northern Rhodesians. In 1914 the district commissioner for Mweru-Luapula made the following report:

> Complaints have been received from time to time of thefts of loads on the Ndola—Fort Rosebery Road. These crimes appear to be the work of a gang of professional thieves who live partly in Congo territory and partly in Sokontwe's country . . . who carry on their operations on that portion of the road which passes through Congo territory between Sakania and [Kabunda]. In some cases these thieves have to resort to personal violence. Fort Rosebery traders have suffered from these thefts, also native repatriates returning from Southern Rhodesia and Elisabethville. The highway robberies and thefts are by no means new, but have been in existence—off and on—for the past eight or nine years.[65]

The complaints increased in number during the period of the First World War, as many Northern Rhodesians elected to seek wage labor rather than be conscripted as war porters. Others who served as war porters did not want to be recalled because conditions were very poor. They left their villages to seek wage labor along the line of rail or in Southern Rhodesia. The flow of labor migrants across the Pedicle increased with the beginning of mining activities on the Copperbelt in 1926.[66] The number of complaints received was on the increase.[67]

---

[61]NAZ/ZA1/9/18/38: PC to SNA, 22 September 1930. 111-17. Nsakanya. This according to Buell, was what all prisoners were expected to do. Buell, *Native Problem*, II, 498.

[62]Nsakanya; Interview Mwape Chanda, Mansa, 7 August 1979.

[63]NAZ/ZA1/9/18/38: J. A. Andrews, Compound Manager, Bwana Mkumbwa Mining Company, to Manager, Ndola, 7 November 1930. This was confirmed by oral sources.

[64]NAZ/ZA1/19/18/38: Lieutenant Payson, BSAC Polic, Report on the Ndola Fort Rosebery Route, September, 1915.

[65]NAZ/ZA7/3/4: Quarterly Report for the period 1 July to 30 September 1914 for Fort Rosebery Sub District.

[66]Nsakanya; Pardon; Chanda.

For the Northern Rhodesian officials, the problem was compounded by a very high turnover of Belgian officers sent to Kalonga. The native commissioner at Fort Rosebery worked extremely hard to establish personal contact with the chef de poste at Kalonga and to draw his attention to some of the complaints so that they could be investigated. In a number of cases, the two officials even worked out measures to ensure the safety of the migrants. In some cases it worked, in others it did not. The native commissioner's frustration is reflected in this report for January 1926:

> I again visited the Chef du Poste at Kalonga on 12 January. I found that the official with whom I had reached an agreement in October had been replaced by another, M. Sobet, who stated that he could not observe the agreement to accept passes signed by chiefs. He said that passes even issued by me, were insufficient proof of identity.[68]

The frustrations of the Northern Rhodesia administrative officials were summed up by the provincial commissioner who noted that it was "extremely hard to deal with such variable people as Belgians; every official seems to be a law into himself. The Belgians, I suppose, dislike our people [transiting the Pedicle]."[69] The numerous complaints passed on to him drew this conclusion:

> Some of the complaints emanate from the dislike of a failure to obey by the Northern Rhodesian natives of some more strict Congo regulations. Our people are not subject to many restrictions . . . and they do not appreciate that certain restrictions have to be complied with when [transiting the Congo Pedicle].[70]

In 1930, following the outbreak of Foot and Mouth Disease in Southern Province and Bulozi and venereal diseases in Elisabethville, a cordon was placed on the movement of people and goods across the Pedicle. Africans travelling to and from the Copperbelt were required to carry in addition to the identity certificate (*chitupa*) and a pass (*laissez passer*), medical certificates certifying them free from venereal and other contagious diseases. These documents had to be checked and validated at either Sakania or Kalonga border posts. Due to poor publicity, these requirements were not known by many Northern Rhodesian travellers. The result was that those who did not "have Congo medical certificates stamped on their Registration certificates were detained and imprisoned for

---

[67]For example, in 1926, the magistrate at Fort Rosebery, reported that "the Belgian Representative at Kabunda [actually the administrative centre was Kalonga] has a reputation for treating carriers very harshly." NAZ/ZA1/5/1: Magistrate, Fort Rosebery to Secretary for Native Affairs, (SNA), 18 August 1926.

[68]NAZ/ZA1/5/: NC, Fort Rosebery to SNA, 9 October 1926.

[69]NAZ/ZA7/3/26/8: Annual Report for Fort Rosebery District for the Year ending 32 March 1927.

[70]ZA7/3/26/8: D. C., Fort Rosebery to SNA, 28 October 1926.

evading" the regulations.[71] Commenting on the situation, the provincial commissioner for Mweru-Luapula observed that the

> Belgian authorities adhere very strictly to the regulations imposed by them and in the case of [Northern Rhodesian] natives whether innocently or otherwise caught in any act of evasion, the punishment . . . is severe, usually two months in gaol.[72]

The magistrate for Fort Rosebery District collected a number of complaints from those arrested, which have left a graphic description of the suffering the Northern Rhodesians experienced at the hands of the Congolese officials. Let us begin with Katungi Kamulema, a Henga from Karonga District in what is today Northern Malawi, who reported that:

> The Belgian Askare [police] arrest larger numbers of travellers who cross the Congo strip to come to the Copperbelt [without the medical certificates]. They are put in the gaol and are forced to work. They are guarded by armed Askari. They are forced to work for two months and then let go. They do all sorts of work, road repairing, gardening, carrying of wood and water, etc. They (sic) are many Rhodesian natives at Belgian Bomas [at Sakania and Kalonga].[73]

And Kafwanda, a Lunda from Kawambwa reported that:

> I went to Ndola for work last rains [1929]. . . . On my return, I got to Sakania. On arrival at Kabunda the Belgian Officials . . . sentenced us to 15 days' imprisonment and a fine of 15 francs each drawing water, cutting firewood, hoeing, etc. We completed a month and were then released. . . . I lost my box which contained 3 pairs of shorts (khaki), 3 women cloths, 2 shirts, 1 pair trousers, 2 vests, 1 sweater, 2 hats, 2 children's dresses, 2 colored handkerchiefs and 10 pieces of soap. I value these articles at £3 4s 6.[74]

And others had this to say:

> We were in the Congo not far from the border . . . [when] two Askari accompanied by a Belgian official arrested us. We had our necks tied together with a rope to prevent us from escaping and marched to Sakania under escort. On arrival . . . we were put in the gaol. . . . The Belgian official told us our

---

[71]NAZ/ZA1/9/18/38: Andrews to Manager, Bwana Mkubwa, 7 November 1930.

[72]NAZ/ZA1/9/18/38: PC, Fort Rosebery to SNA, 22 September 1930.

[73]NAZ/ZA1/9/18/38: Depositions by the NC, Fort Rosebery, 14 September 1930.

passes ought to have been signed by a doctor. We were put in
neck-chains [and] worked on the road . . . drawing water, and
wood cutting—all kinds of work. We were fined 7s each in
English money, then let go.[75]

And Lameck Sichone of Isoka, who was in a group of twenty men and
women arrested in the Pedicle, had this to say:

We were on a native path. We met a native orderly and
messenger [who] demanded [the] production of our "fitupas"
[registration certificates] as we were on our way to Ndola.
They said you must come along to the Boma to have your
fitupa stamped. They tied us in twos and threes and we went
to the Boma at Kabunda. . . . The official told the police to
take us to the gaol and put neck irons on us. . . . We were sent
to work on building, hoeing, drawing water. . . . we worked as
convicts for two weeks.[76]

Similarly, Northern Rhodesians who attempted to transport fish to Ndola
were arrested and jailed. Here is a testimony of what Kunda of Fort Rosebery
experienced:

I and three others from my village decided to come to Ndola
to sell dried fish. . . . we crossed the border [into] Congo Belge.
. . . We were arrested by Belgian Askari. . . . They did not tell
us why they were arresting us. They beat us with their hands,
but we managed to escape to Serenje District. We sold our fish
there. . . . I do not know why we were ill-treated by the
Belgian Askari. We had done no harm and carried our tax
receipts to show (sic) who we were.[77]

In a number of cases, the beating received by the Northern Rhodesians
were very severe, and some people died.[78] To avoid these experiences many
Northern Rhodesians decided to sell their fish to European traders operating on
the Congo side of the border very cheaply—less than one penny per pound
instead of four pence.[79]

In 1940, the district commissioner for Fort Rosebery noted, after a tour of
Sokontwe area that:

---

[74]NAZ/ZA1/9/18/38: Deposition . . . 14 September 1930.

[75]NAZ/ZA1/9/18/38: Deposition . . . 12 December 1930.

[76]NAZ/ZA1/9/18/30: Deposition . . . 17 November 1930.

[77]NAZ/ZA1/9/18/30: PC, Fort Rosebery, to SNA 22 September 1930; Deposition . . . 10 October 1930.

[78]NAZ/1/9/8/30: Deposition . . . 16 October 1930.

[79]T.R. Mvusi, "The Creation of Unemployment in Northern Rhodesia 1899-1936" (Ph.D. thesis, Northwestern University, 1984), 190.

> More complaints were made to me on the trip by the natives who stated that on entering the Congo, they were liable to arrest and imprisonment even if they had passes ... signed by the Native Authority. One man produced a Congo Government receipt for 42 francs which he said he had paid as an alternative to imprisonment. He had both a pass and identity certificate.[80]

The Northern Rhodesian officials did not know how to solve the problem. They complained to the Belgian officials from time to time. Except in one case where two Congolese policemen were jailed for their excesses, they had no positive results from their complaints.[81] The provincial commissioner for Mweru-Luapula complained that "there was no remedy open ... which would have the effect of easing the situation with regard to the attitude adopted towards [the Northern Rhodesian] natives by the Belgian officials."[82] In short, the Northern Rhodesians passing through the Pedicle were at the mercy of the Congolese soldiers.[83] The plight of the Northern Rhodesians transiting the Pedicle was brought to the attention of the Western Province Regional Council on 17 July 1944 by Dauti Yamba, representing Luanshya. In the motion he tabled, he informed the members that he had been

> asked by many people on the Copperbelt to bring to the notice of the council the difficulties Africans were experiencing by having to pass through Congo territory to and from their districts in Western Province. ... people travelling between the Copperbelt and these districts (east of the Luapula) have many troubles crossing Congo territory. ... At present people were being detained by Customs Authorities at Sakania and having their goods confiscated, being required to produce evidence that they were examined by a doctor, and were subjected to much abuse and rough treatment.[84]

Yamba asked the administration to make representations to the Belgian government to "allow transit across the Pedicle without let or hindrance." He suggested that the government explore the possibility of acquiring the Pedicle from the Congo or to arrange an "exchange" of territory so as to do away with the awkward "foot" jutting into Northern Rhodesia. The motion was supported by all the members. The government promised to look into the matter but nothing

---

[80]NAZ/SEC 2/872: Tour Report of Sokontwe area 15 March 1940.

[81]NAZ/ZA1/18/38: SNA to Chief Secretary, 30 May 1931.

[82]NAZ/ZA1/9/18/38: PC to SNA, 22 December 1930.

[83]This is gleaned from a statement by one source "Because we had to cross the Pedicle to go to the Copperbelt or Fort Rosebery, we were at the mercy of *Bakaboke*" (local name for the Congolese soldiers). Nsakanya.

[84]Northern Rhodesia Government, *Report of the Second Meeting of the Northern Rhodesia Western Province Regional Council*, July 1944, 18-19, Nsakanya.

happened. A year later, the issue was debated again at the third meeting of the Council.[85] In November 1946, the issue was discussed at the first meeting of the Northern Rhodesia African Representative Council in a motion tabled by Chief Kopa. The chief called on the government to "protect Northern Rhodesian Africans who cross the Belgian Congo." He went on to echo Yamba's earlier suggestion to consider the possibility of acquiring "the Congo Pedicle." Edward Sampa, who seconded the motion, was more explicit when he stated that:

> It is a sad thing to go through the Congo. When going through the area we meet with many difficulties. If you go through the Congo and you happen to meet a policeman of the territory, the first thing he does is to try and beat you and rob you of your belongings, even though you have done nothing wrong.[86]

Again, the members urged the government to act but nothing came out of their pleas.

The Fort Rosebery—Chembe—Mokambo—Mufulira Road

Although the Northern Rhodesia government continued to use the Fort Rosebery—Kapalala—Sakania—Ndola road, they had a number of misgivings about it. First was the insecurity posed by the Congolese soldiers. Second, the road was generally "impassable to motor traffic" during the rainy season, as bridges on a number of rivers and large sections of the road between Kapalala and Fort Rosebery were swept away.[87] Further, the road was regarded by the administration and the African population in general as being too "indirect" and long (as it was about 300km to reach Ndola) for the people living along the Luapula River and the shores of Lake Mweru where a flourishing fishing industry existed, exploited mostly by Greek traders to feed the workers in the Katangan mines and urban centers. As a result of this, many fish traders who would have wanted to take their fish to the Copperbelt took their fish to Katanga.[88] And third, the administration were of the view that "the customs and immigration formalities required by the Belgian authorities in connection with travelling through the Pedicle are both irksome and a cause of unnecessary

---

[85]Northern Rhodesia Government, *Report of the Third Meeting of the Western Province Regional Council*, July 1945, 15, 16.

[86]Northern Rhodesia Government, *Proceedings of the African Representative Council*, November 1946, Col. 102; Stewart Gore Browne, "The Anglo-Belgian Boundary Commission in 1911-1914," *Northern Rhodesia Journal*, 5, 4 (1964), 316.

[87]Northern Rhodesia Government Notice Number 157 of 1936; NAZ/SEC 2/198: Northern Province Newsletter, 31 March 1940; Interview Thom Kashimbaya, Mufulira, 17 July 1979.

[88]NAZ/SEC2/227: Minutes of the First Meeting of the Northern Province (Western Areas), Regional Council held at Fort Rosebery 23-24 May 1944; Interview, Mwape Songolo, Mansa, 8 September 1985. On the fishing industry see M. C. Musambachime, "Development and Growth of the Fishing Industry in Mweru-Luapula 1920-1964" (Ph.D. thesis, University of Wisconsin, 1981), esp. Chs. 3 and 8.

delays."[89]   As a result of the desire to cut out these delays and smooth communication between Fort Rosebery and the Copperbelt, and to capture and redirect some of the lucrative fish trade to the Copperbelt, the administration proposed in 1930 the construction of a shorter road between Fort Rosebery and Mufulira via Mokambo (a distance of about 170km). By 1930, a foot path existed between Fort Rosebery and Mufulira which was heavily used by workers to and from the Copperbelt in order to avoid the indirect Ndola–Sakania–Kapalala–Fort Rosebery route.[90] A proposal for the construction of a road linking Fort Rosebery with Chembe on the Luapula River was discussed and accepted by the Northern Province Provincial Council in 1938. A sum of £5,000 was also committed.   Construction could not begin, however, because there was "no definite understanding . . . from the Belgian Government that they would construct that section of the road lying between Luapula and Mokambo to complete the through road from Fort Rosebery to the Copperbelt."[91] To try and expedite things, the Northern Rhodesia administration informed the Belgian administration of Katanga that they were "prepared" to construct the road and "bear the full cost," which in 1942, rose to £7,000.[92] The Belgians refused to accept the offer and instead proposed shelving the project "for the time being."[93] After intensive negotiations the project was revived in 1944 and the Northern Rhodesia government committed £7,600 to the construction of the road and £4,300 (760,000 francs) for the construction of a pontoon.[94] The road became operational in July 1947. Within a month, it proved very popular, providing service to 5,135 Africans, 530 bicycles, 131 motor vehicles, and 180,000 pounds of merchandise. Within two months most of the traffic between the Copperbelt and Fort Rosebery was directed to this route.[95] It also gave a boost to the fishing industry in Lakes Mweru and Bangweulu, allowing fishermen and traders to move their loads of fish to the Copperbelt.[96]

As soon as the road became operational, the same stories of beatings, robberies, arbitrary arrests, and imprisonment began to be reported. Trivial offenses committed while at the border post, such as allowing a child to cry,

---

[89]NAZ/SEC 3/149: Senior PC, Ndola to Administrative Secretary, Lusaka, 27 August 1947; Kashimbaya, Interview, Jameson, Mwenso, Mulundu, 18 April 1975.

[90]NAZ/SEC 3/149: Telegram, Chief Secretary to Chef du Secretariat, Elisabethville, 9 May 1930; Mwape Songolo; Kashimbaya; Mwanso.

[91]NAZ/SEC 2/10: Minutes of the Third Meeting of the Provincial Council, Northern Province, 1938, p. 4; Minutes of the Fourth Provincial Council, Northern Province, 1939.

[92]NAZ/SEC 3/149: Chief Secretary to Chef du Secretariat, 7 November, 1939, see also other letter dated 24 November 1941 and 7 July 1942.

[93]NAZ/SEC 3/149: Director, Public Works Department (PWD), to Chief Secretary, Lusaka, 6 March 1942; Chef du Secretariat Provincial, Elisabethville to Chief Secretary, Lusaka, 26 June 1941.

[94]NAZ/SEC 3/149: Director, PWD, to Chief Secretary, 9 August 1947.

[95]At the opening of the road, the PC hoped that the new road would be "of the greatest value in opening one of the most valuable rural producing areas."

NAZ/SEC 2/198: Northern Province Newsletter, 1 July 1947.

[96]Mwape Songolo; Interview, S. J. Musango, Twapia, Ndola, 19 July 1979.

spitting of saliva, throwing away a banana skin, or wearing a hat in presence of a soldier earned the offender a stiff fine or detention or both. The brutality inflicted on the Northern Rhodesians created fear and uncertainty for those passing through the Pedicle. They only relaxed after reaching the Northern Rhodesian side.[97]

The situation worsened after independence of the Congo in June 1960, and the secession of Katanga from the rest of the Congo. Travellers were frequently beaten, robbed, and killed. There were levies for being fat, bald-headed, smart, wearing a hat when passing through the immigration office (*Bureau d'immigration*), having a wrist watch, bicycle, camera, radio, sewing machine, or anything else of value. There were unnecessary delays to force the victims to part with their money or valuable items. No receipts were given. Truck and bus drivers as well as fish traders were made to part with a substantial amount of money to grease the hands of the soldiers. Those who failed to pay had their vehicles impounded.[98] The situation became progressively worse after Zambia's independence in 1964. Hardly a month passed without the report of some misfortune befalling a Zambian traveller or with the border being closed. Nobody was spared: party and government officials and members of Parliament suffered the same fate as ordinary passengers. The situation worsened with the decline in the wages paid to the military personnel in Zaire. As payment of wages was irregular, many soldiers resorted to using force and violence against the Zambian passengers passing through the Pedicle.[99]

Violence against Northern Rhodesians (now Zambians) is a colonial legacy that was condoned by the Belgian administration. It instilled fear—not respect—for the Congolese and later Zairean soldier by the Northern Rhodesians. This was well exploited by the soldiers to get what they wanted from the travellers. Although these activities were known to the administration they were not widely reported and neither did the government protest in strong terms to the Belgian Congo. With the coming of independence, this changed. These incidents are now given wide coverage and the Zambian government has protested to the Zairean government from time to time.[100] The harassment of Zambian travellers in the Pedicle has become a thorn in the relations between Zambia and Zaire.[101] Although there have been several meetings of the Zambia-Zaire Joint Permanent Commission, formed in 1974, little has been achieved.[102] The Pedicle remains an ever-present problem which has chilled relations between

---

[97] Kashimbaya, Mwenso.

[98] Mwenso; Kashimbaya.

[99] Musango; Kashimbaya; Pardon.

[100] Kashimbaya was a regular victim.

[101] Pardon, Nsakanya, Kashimbaya.

[102] For a detailed discussion see Bartha H. Zimba, "Zambian Policy Towards Zaire 1964-1978" (M.A. thesis, Carleton University, 1979), 145; Rajah Kunda, "The African Boundary Problem with Special Reference to the border dispute between Zambia and Zaire (LLB Obligatory Essay, School of Law, University of Zambia, 1981), 37; R. H. Nketani, "Boundary Problems in International Law with Special Reference to African Boundary Disputes and their Settlement" (LLB Obligatory Essay, School of Law, 1980), *Africa Contemporary Record*, 1973/74, BB334.

Zambia and Zaire. Zambians are now encouraged by the government to use the newly constructed Samfya-Serenje road which bypasses the Pedicle and ensures security for the Zambians.[103]

Conclusion

In 1918, at the signing of the Treaty of Brest Litovsk between Germany and Soviet Russia, Trotsky is reported to have remarked that "every state [was] founded on force."[104] Max Weber argued later that a "state had the monopoly to claim the legitimate use of force."[105] And extending this argument further, McIver stated that "coercive power is a criterion of the state, but not its essence. . . . It is true that there is no state where there is no overwhelming force. . . . But the exercise of force does not make a state."[106] The task of this paper was to show how in the Belgian Congo and later in Zaire, force and violence have been freely used as instruments of authority. The Force Publique were left free to use force and violence not only against the Congolese but also against Northern Rhodesians transiting through the Pedicle. The actions of the Force Publique reflect the observations made by Bertrand de Jouvenel who argued that "a man feels himself more of a man when he is imposing himself and making others the instrument of his will," which, he added, "gives him incomparable pleasure."[107] Apart from pleasure, there was in the case of the Force Publique and other violent military forces elsewhere, the element of domination which bred fear among the victims, in this case, Northern Rhodesians. The cultivation of this fear created an advantage which was well utilized by the Force Publique in dealing with their victims who were either beaten, robbed, jailed or even killed. This state of affairs was partly due to indiscipline and partly to the fact that the soldiers received poor wages, forcing them to supplement their income by exhortation, brutality, terror, and violence. Beyond supplementation, a desire to accumulate became their primary object. Bribery and corruption became an accepted way of life. Where these could not be employed, violence and force were readily used to induce submission and reduce the chances of resistance.

---

[103]Kunda, "The African Boundary Problem," 37; *Africa Contemporary Record*, 1974-75, B 333-4.

[104]Arendt, *On Violence*, 37.

[105]Max Weber, *The Theory*, 152.

[106]R. M. McIver, *The Modern State* (London, 1926), 222.

[107]Bertrand de Jouvenel, *Power: The Natural History of its Growth* (London, 1952), 110.

Revue canadienne des études africaines / Canadian Journal of African Studies
Volume VIII, n° 1, 1974, 3-23

The Social Origins of Ugandan Presidents:
from King to Peasant Warrior *

ALI A. MAZRUI **

RÉSUMÉ – L'origine sociale des présidents ougandais:
du roi au soldat paysan

Il faut distinguer la démocratie électorale de la démocratie structurelle. Tandis que la première implique l'exercice du vote et un affranchissement élargi, la seconde se traduit par le recrutement d'élites dans des secteurs sous-privilégiés de la société. Le premier président de l'Ouganda, Sir Edward Mutesa, était roi, élu par le Parlement à la présidence. D'un point de vue électoral, sa présidence était la plus démocratique qui soit. Le troisième président de l'Ouganda, Idi Amin, est un soldat paysan tiré du monde rural. D'un point de vue structurel, c'est sa présidence à lui qui est la plus démocratique. Entre Amin et Mutesa se situe le règne du président Obote, éduqué à Makerere, descendant de chef et issu fondamentalement de la classe moyenne.

À son tour, la démocratie structurelle comporte trois dimensions. Selon la première, les privilèges héréditaires s'effacent devant la concurrence des qualifications; ainsi, Mutesa obtint la présidence en partie grâce à ses privilèges royaux héréditaires, alors que Amin acquit celle-ci par ses dons militaires et politiques. La deuxième dimension concerne l'éducation; Mutesa était diplômé de Cambridge, tandis qu'Amin n'a même pas son certificat d'école primaire. La troisième dimension est d'ordre géoethnique: Mutesa provenait de la tribu la plus importante et prospère au cœur du pays; Amin est d'un groupe ethnique périphérique aux frontières du Zaïre et du Soudan. Tout comme Néguib en Égypte, Grunitzki au Togo, Napoléon en France et Hitler en Allemagne, Amin a pris le pouvoir comme individu marginal. Milton Obote marque le stade intermédiaire entre la pompe de Mutesa et la rusticité d'Amin.

L'avenir de l'Ouganda demande la réconciliation entre démocraties électorale et structurelle, lorsque les soldats réintégreront leurs casernes et que l'électorat décidera si les chefs traditionnels auront à nouveau leur mot à dire dans le système politique du pays.

* * *

The first president of Uganda, Sir Edward Mutesa, was a king. The third president, General Idi Amin, was a common man from the womb of the countryside. In between these two was President A. Milton Obote, descended from a chiefly family in Lango, educated at Makerere, and basically a member of the middle class. In the history of the presidency in Uganda so far we have, therefore, a process of structural democratization, starting with a king-president, then a president drawn from the

---

* This essay originated as a public lecture delivered in Jinja Town Hall, Uganda, in April 1971.

** Hoover Institution, Stanford University, and University of Michigan, Ann Arbor.

middle classes and a chiefly house in Lango, and finally a president drawn from more humble origins.

We might here distinguish two forms of democratization – electoral democracy and structural democracy. Electoral democracy, as its name implies, entails the exercise of the vote, and an expanding franchise. Sir Edward Mutesa was the first elected head of state in the history of Uganda, and so far the only one freely elected. He was, of course, elected by Parliament, rather than directly by the population. Nevertheless, this was the only presidency which emerged out of a real interplay of political forces, competing for the highest office, and culminating in the choice of Mutesa as head of state. Before him was the governor-general, representative of the Queen and by definition, in this context, in non-elective office. After Mutesa was Obote, initially self-appointed as president following the Daudi Ocheng parliamentary motion of February 1966, but later confirmed by his hold over what remained of the Uganda Peoples' Congress, and by the support he enjoyed at the time within the armed forces. We shall return to the Ocheng motion.

General Amin's presidency was born out of a military *coup*, and therefore was again non-elective. If we define democracy by the yardstick of the electoral process we must, for the time being, regard the presidency of Mutesa as the most democratic in Uganda's history so far.

And yet we are faced with the paradox that this was the presidency of a king, descended from a line of kings of the Baganda, acquiring power and influence through hereditary privilege. Was the electoral process an adequate system of democratizing the presidency of Uganda? Should not the top man in the country be more typical of the population as a whole?

Here, then, we have two senses of being representative of the people. One sense is again the electoral sense, whereby someone is chosen by the people and acquires his representativeness from the declared will of the people, either directly, or through the elected representatives. In the case of Mutesa it was the elected representatives in Parliament who voted for him as president. This is the electoral sense of "representativeness."

But there is a structural sense of representativeness – not in the sense of a man elected by the people but in the sense of a man more typical of the rest of his country. This is what I call the structural sense of representativeness. The criteria are based on the structural composition of the society as a whole, and the leadership is considered representative if it reflects that structural composition.

Nikita Khrushchev, in a campaign speech in a Soviet election in 1958, applied the structural criteria to the composition of the Congress of the United States, and thereby managed to reveal that the composition was not democratic in the structural sense, even if it was highly democratic in the electoral sense. This is what Khrushchev said:

> Take the present composition of the United States Congress. Of the 531 Congressmen, more than half are lawyers and one quarter are employers and bankers. All of them are representatives of Big Business. How many workers are members of the United States Congress? There are no real workers in the American Congress. Or let us see how many ordinary farmers are members of the American Congress. There are no farmers either. Seventeen and a half million Negroes or ten point four per cent of the country's entire population, are citizens of the United States. How many Negroes have been elected to Congress? According to American sources, there are three Negroes in the United States Congress, or 0.56% of the total number of Congressmen. Or let us see how many women

are members of the United States Congress. In all, seventeen women have been elected to Congress, or only 3%. [1]

What Khrushchev was saying was that the American Congress was not really representative of the composition of the American people. From a structural point of view, the composition of the American Congress needed to be really democratized.

If we now turn our eyes towards Uganda we find that the history of the presidency consists of a transition from electoral democracy to structural democracy. The transition has not been a conscious design, but the structural transformation is nevertheless real.

What should be remembered is that democratization in a structural sense has in turn been along three dimensions. One dimension concerns a change from ascription and hereditary succession to secular and competitive credentials for power. Mutesa became president of Uganda partly because he had inherited the throne of Buganda. He was elected by Parliament as president from a number of candidates, all of whom were traditional or neo-traditional rulers. As king of the Baganda, Mutesa's qualifications for the headship of state were therefore in part ascriptive and hereditary. Amin, on the other hand, became president of Uganda through a triumphant manipulation of military and political skills. The structural change in the presidency was from mystical credentials to naked cunning.

Another level of structural democratization involved a change from an educated president to a semi-literate one. Mutesa was a product of Cambridge university; Amin had hardly completed primary education. Mutesa was suave, sophisticated and cosmopolitan, Amin came from the ranks of the barely literate.

The third level of structural democratization was *geo-ethnic*. Mutesa came from the heartland tribe of Uganda, the largest and most prosperous community; Amin came from a peripheral ethnic group on the outer borders with the Sudan and Zaire.

By a curious destiny, it was the military profession which narrowed the cultural gap between these two historically significant Ugandans. Let us therefore first turn briefly to their historical backgrounds before relating those backgrounds to the wider issues of social change in Uganda.

I - HISTORY IN UNIFORM

The first president of Uganda, Sir Edward Mutesa, was a soldier by honorary affiliation, by training and by romantic aspiration. The third president of Uganda, General Idi Amin, is a soldier by training, experience and life-long profession.

It was in 1939 that Mutesa went through the initial ceremonies of coronation upon his father's death. When he later returned to Budo he had a new possession – the first rifle he ever owned. It was presented to him by the British resident, Tom Cox. Mutesa kept it in working order until the fateful year of 1966 in Uganda.

Mutesa's father was a captain under the British monarch – Captain Sir Daudi Chwa II. Amin's father is also reported to have had a military background. He was apparently a member of the King's African Rifles for a while, and rose quite high during those difficult days. It was at about the age of twenty that Idi Amin himself

---

1. Khrushchev, "Speech at Meeting of Electors of Kalinin Constituency, Moscow, March 14, 1958," in N. S. Khrushchev, *For Victory in the Peaceful Competition with Capitalism* (Moscow, Foreign Languages Publishing House, 1959), pp. 155–158.

joined the King's African Rifles as a private, with little formal education behind him. But he had qualities of leadership, and sheer physical presence, great enough to win him rapid promotion to lance-corporal, then to corporal and then to sergeant.

In 1959 Idi Amin was promoted from sergeant-major to *effendi*, a rank which had been resurrected to provide new promotion opportunities for outstanding African soldiers.

Amin was then commissioned second-lieutenant in 1961, on the eve of Uganda's independence. With Independence he became captain.

Captain was also a title which Mutesa acquired, but through a different career. Mutesa's finest military skill was his marksmanship. He was not using the rifle for military purposes, but he was acquiring proficiency in handling it. It was in 1945 that he left Makerere to go to Cambridge in England. His greatest success at Magdalene was, in fact, with the rifle. In his second year at the College he won the shooting cup for Magdalene with the best individual score.

He joined the Cambridge Officers' Corps soon after arrival at the University, and became an officer. His enthusiasm for shooting practice was tested in the severe winter of 1946–47. Mutesa insisted on going to practice at the range, and won a revolver shooting competition.

He then formally applied to join the army, specifying the Grenadier Guards as his first choice. He was interviewed ferociously by a lieutenant-colonel and then was accepted. It was King George VI who, as a personal gesture of good-will, suggested that Mutesa be made a captain. Mutesa went to Buckingham Palace for the ceremony.

> Though I had been kindly given my rank, I had now to earn it. This I proceeded to do at the Victoria Barracks, at Windsor, and at Caterham and at Warminster. My liking for uniforms and pleasure in being smartly turned out were an asset. My unpunctuality was, temporarily, cured. At Windsor we were on parade at 8 a.m., when we were drilled. Then it was our turn to shout orders, which is harder work still. If your voice did not reach what the drill sergeant considered sufficient volume, he would tell your squad to carry on even if they were heading for a brick wall and therefore total chaos. The rest of this course, which was specially designed for training young officers, consisted mainly of weapon training and a knowledge of such things as first-aid. [2]

While Amin had later claimed service experience in Burma, Mutesa seriously considered the possibility of going to Malaya with the 3rd Battalion of the Grenadier Guards. But Mutesa's commanding officer summoned him and told him that the choice was between Mutesa returning home to his people or electing there and then to remain in the army. Of course, although Mutesa later spent many years unwillingly away from his people, there was no question of actually electing a military career instead of the Kabakaship. Nevertheless, Mutesa did sometimes wish it were otherwise. As he came to put it twenty years later:

> If it had been possible, I think I should have been a soldier. Certainly I had enjoyed these months as much as any. [3]

The outbreak of World War II took place in the same year as the coronation of Mutesa. But before he died, Sir Daudi Chwa had issued a proclamation allowing the

---

2. The Kabaka of Buganda, *Desecration of My Kingdom* (Constable, 1967), pp. 98–99.
3. Ibid., p. 101.

Baganda to volunteer for war service. Other Ugandans also participated. Mutesa was himself keen to join up, but his Regents and the Governor would not entertain the possibility. A division of the King's African Rifles was sent to Burma. Was Idi Amin among them? Certainly, Lincoln Nddaula, the Kabaka's brother, was. [4]

Two decades later Uganda was independent, and by 1963 Mutesa was commander in chief of the Armed Forces of independent Uganda. This was the year that Idi Amin was promoted to the rank of major. The following year witnessed the mutinies in East Africa, followed by the replacement of British officers which thus accelerated promotions for Ugandans. Idi Amin became Colonel Amin, and held the post of deputy-commander. Then began the rather uncanny series of "25th Januarys" in the history of independent Uganda.

It was on 25th January, 1964, that British troops disarmed the mutineers at the Jinja armoury, and restored civilian supremacy in Uganda. It was on the 25th January, 1966, that Daudi Ocheng began to elaborate on his charges of corruption against members of the Uganda government, implicating Idi Amin, and later Obote, and Ministers Onama and Nekyon. The UPC Parliamentary group met on January 31st, and decided to reject Ocheng's motion, recommending the suspension of Idi Amin pending an investigation. The fateful motion, which later encompassed the Head of Government himself, did not come before Parliament until February 4th, 1966. But what needs to be noted here for the time being is the simple fact that the 25th January 1966 fell within the stream of accusations, which culminated in the Ocheng charges in Parliament accusing Amin and Obote of corruption and misappropriation for personal use of gold and ivory from Zaire (then the Congo). This in turn precipitated the entire Uganda crisis of 1966.

Then came 25th January, 1970, when Brigadier Ocoya was murdered in Gulu, together with his wife. He was the second highest ranking officer after Amin, by that time.

Finally came 25th January, 1971, when the armed forces of Uganda at last terminated the rule of Milton Obote, and established a military government in Uganda, with a technocratic cabinet.

It was, of course, the 1966 crisis which led to the detention of the former commander of the army, Brigadier Opolot, and the assumption of the army command by Amin. Until then Amin had been deputy-commander. As deputy-commander he had comparatively limited contact with President Mutesa. Mutesa himself believed that Obote had specifically asked Amin never to approach Mutesa, although the latter was, in fact, his commander in chief. If a meeting was necessary between Colonel Amin and President Mutesa, only Prime Minister Obote could determine that necessity. Amin, in other words, was to have no dealings with Mutesa without the express permission of Obote.

On the lighter side of their relationship, Amin had made an impact on Mutesa when he had been to the Palace informally, and Mutesa had watched him box. Way back in his Cambridge days in the 1940's Mutesa had himself boxed for his college, Magdalene. Amin's interests in other sports also appealed to the aristocratic instincts of Mutesa. Amin was an accomplished rugby player, a game of great significance in the history of British public schools and in its effect on the British ruling elite. In his youthful days in England Mutesa had found that games were his

---

4. Ibid., p. 88. There is disagreement about whether Amin served in Burma.

first source of friends. His interest in boxing, shooting and riding prepared him to appreciate the sporty side of Amin; in Mutesa's own words:

> Amin was a comparatively simple, tough character. He had been to the Palace, and I had watched him box, which he did efficiently.[5]

Already the difference between the king and the boxing champion was a difference between hereditary status and acquired rank. But then came 1966, and the ultimate confrontation at the Palace between Obote's forces and the Kabaka's guards. Did Amin command the attack on the Palace? Mutesa's answer went thus:

> I did not see Colonel Amin, but I expect he was in command. Obote remained well away from the scene.[6]

What Mutesa was suggesting was that Obote, having ordered Amin to attack the Palace, then allowed himself to enjoy the relative security of distance from the battle-ground. Mutesa conceded that Amin as a soldier under civilian authority had to obey commands. He was in the same position as those soldiers in Kenya during the Mau-Mau insurrection who obeyed the command of the colonial authorities to control or suppress the rebellion in Kikuyuland.

If Mutesa himself had been allowed to go to Malaya as a soldier after the end of World War II, he might have had to shoot Malay communists. What did a Muganda have to do with a left-wing insurrection in Malaya? Very little – except that he who joins an army accepts to carry out the orders of his superior officers as far as is honourably possible. There is no doubt that the third president of Uganda had participated in the ouster of the first.

But even those who continued to feel that Amin should not have participated in the attack on King Mutesa's palace, the Lubiri, had to bear in mind that nation-building required a capacity to be selective in what one remembered. It was the French philosopher Ernest Renan who, in 1882, wrote an essay entitled "What is a Nation?", and then proceeded to observe that one essential factor in the making of a nation is "To get one's history wrong." In an exaggerated way Renan was making a basic point not only about successful nationhood, but also about successful marriage. The secret of successful marriage over a long span of time is to know what to forget.

Such considerations are indeed at play in nation-building, and in relations between groups generally. Accord between those groups necessitates a cultivated ability to emphasize the positive aspects of their relationship, and try to control and underplay the negative aspects.

There are a number of things in Buganda's relations with her neighbours which need to be forgotten. There is a history of arrogance, and cruelty by the Baganda and among the Baganda. There is also a history of aggression and cruelty against the Baganda. It can indeed be argued persuasively that Uganda is an impossible country to govern with the support of the Baganda, but it is also impossible to govern effectively without the support of the Baganda. There are, in other words, seeds of profound discord between Buganda and some of her neighbours. And yet the process of nation-building in Uganda cannot really start without recognizing the importance of this central cleavage. The first major destination in the process of national

5. Ibid., p. 185.
6. Ibid., p. 192.

integration in Uganda must, therefore, be a struggle to make it no longer true that Uganda is ungovernable with or without the Baganda.

So far the military regime which has come into being since January 25th, 1971, has attempted to keep the balance between, on the one hand, conciliating the Baganda and, on the other, stopping short of giving them their greatest desire of all. Although now no longer publicly discussed, the biggest ambition among the Baganda is probably still the restoration of the monarchy, and the military government has continued to resist pressures in that direction. There are clear dangers of alienating other parts of the country if this particular wish of the Baganda were to be, too hastily, granted. The military government would, by such a restoration, ensure that it had the support of the Baganda, but at the serious risk of losing support elsewhere. On the other hand, Uganda is equally ungovernable without the Baganda, and so any denial of passionate requests from the Baganda has to be done in a conciliatory move. Concessions of a significant kind have to be given. Sometimes the concessions may be little more than granting certain ceremonial rights to the Baganda. But even more dramatic was Amin's concession to bring the body of Sir Edward Mutesa back to Uganda from its burial place in England.

History very often has its surprises. The life history of Sir Edward was itself a game in surprises. After the attack on his palace in 1966, many thought he had died. *The Daily Express* in London carried the headline "King Freddie is dead." As Mutesa himself was struggling through the bushes to safety before he left Buganda, he was often afraid of being mistaken for a ghost by his own supporters, leading to screams which might have resulted in his being discovered.

In 1966 when they expected him to have died, Mutesa had lived. In 1969 when they expected him to live, he had died.

Mutesa died in London after making plans for the celebration of his birthday, the following day. His sense of order was again striking. It was on 22nd November, 1939, that the Katikiro of Buganda announced:

> The fire of Buganda is extinguished. Our beloved Kabaka, His Highness, Sir Daudi Chwa, released his hold on the shield at seven o'clock this morning.

Exactly thirty years later to the day, November 22nd, 1969, Mutesa symbolically released his own hold on the shield in England. That uncanny habit of Uganda's historical dates of playing games of coincidence was once again at work.

Yet the every place of his death was symbolic when seen in the total circumstances of Mutesa's life. Mutesa came to have one funeral in London and another in Kampala and Mengo. Two funerals for one man. Between England and Buganda, Mutesa had shared his life. And then between England and Uganda he came to share his death.

This duality of Mutesa's cultural affiliation brings us to the second dimension of structural democratization in Uganda – the transition from a suave and highly westernized president, on the one hand, and, on the other, a semi-literate head of state.

II – CULTURAL DUALISM
AND HISTORICAL CONTINUITIES

In Mutesa we had a trans-cultural man, a figure of cultural continuity. He represented the forging of two national cultures in one person. In this case the man is symbolic of

Africa's predicament, in the sense of intermingling between indigenous traditions and the imported British heritage.

There is no doubt that Mutesa was a man of two worlds in this sense. Even his eligibility for the Kabakaship presupposed his being sufficiently Anglicized to be able to talk in terms of equality with the British and protect the autonomy of Buganda. The choice of the Kabaka was to be made by the Lukiiko. We know that the Kabaka did not need to be the eldest son of the king he succeeded. Certainly Mutesa was not. Nor did the Kabaka need to be a legitimate son of his father's, though Mutesa was indeed legitimate. The father's own preference before his death did count for a lot, and Mutesa's father had indicated his preference for Mutesa. But an English education, either given locally in Uganda or administered in England, was deemed, by the time of Mutesa's succession, to be an important precondition for the effective discharge of the Kabaka's duties. Mutesa himself in his book *Desecration of My Kingdom* assures us that, important as an English education was, it was not "conclusive."

> During his life a Kabaka may hint as subtly or blatantly as he wishes as to whom he personally favours, and such hints may well carry weight, but he cannot will the Kabakaship as you will a possession. I think my father did drop such hints, and it is true that I had an English tutor, as he had done, but this was by no means conclusive – my eldest brother, for example, was educated in England. [7]

In an important sense the Kabakaship had already become an Anglo-African institution, and the English language as a precondition for effective Kabakaship was an important element in this trend towards biculturalism.

The English language became important also for membership of the Ugandan parliament as independence approached, and was in any case a major factor in the political culture of Uganda as a whole. Milton Obote lamented when he was president about the impact of the English language on Uganda as a society, pointing out that it tended to stratify society into those who spoke the language well and therefore had access to certain advantages, and those who did not speak it well and were thereby handicapped. Mastery of the English language had become a basis for a new form of aristocratic privilege – until the army *coup* of January 25, 1971. English will remain important in independent Uganda both in politics and outside politics. But one of the consequences of the army *coup* lay in destroying the myth that a high political position could not be effectively held without the command of a foreign language. There are other qualities for leadership apart from linguistic versatility, and very often those others might be much more important.

Both in Uganda and elsewhere in East Africa, Muslims have lagged behind in education. One of the major reasons was simply the massive role which Christian missionaries played in education in East Africa. Many Muslim parents were afraid of sending their children to missionary schools, out of understandable fears that the ultimate purpose of Christian missionary activity was to Christianize Africans. The Kakwa as a tribe have large numbers of Muslims, like my own Swahili people in Mombasa. All African Muslims had been profoundly suspicious of missionary schools, and their educational and linguistic qualifications have been affected by that.

In Buganda Mutesa had also noticed this lag, and had become aware that there were fewer Muslims with a good command of the metropolitan language than either

---

7. Ibid., p. 76.

Protestants or Catholics. It was against the background of this simple fact that the King and I first met.

It was early in the 1950s that the late Kabaka Mutesa II of Buganda paid a visit to the Mombasa Institute of Muslim Education in Kenya. He arrived there after sunset with his entourage, but without notice to the institution. No special arrangements had been made to receive him and his group. I received a phone call from his host in town indicating that the group was coming to the Institute. The Institute, built in Arabian style in the immediate suburbs of Mombasa, constituted at the time one of the show places of the town. My own position in it then was that of boarding supervisor, a position somewhat comparable to that of a warden in a hall of residence. I was, therefore, available at night when the Kabaka and his group came to visit the Institute. I showed them round some of the major sections of the educational institution, and then tried to entertain them to some non-alcoholic Muslim refreshments in my modest apartment.

Many years later I discovered that one of the things which had impressed the Kabaka's group was the phenomenon of a young Muslim speaking English so "fluently." Apparently the Kabaka on his return to Buganda recounted the episode. More than ten years after the event I was myself a resident in Uganda and was introduced to one of the Muslim members of the Buganda royal house. This was Prince Badru Kakungulu, a leader of the Muslim community and an uncle of Mutesa. When it was explained to the Prince who I was, complete with my family background, his eyes brightened up. He remembered so late in the day the comments made by the Kabaka and his group about a young Muslim in Mombasa who spoke English fairly fluently. The Prince himself had been a member of that group at the Mombasa Institute of Muslim Education. [8]

But it was not, of course, merely the command of the English language which made Mutesa a trans-national figure, otherwise large numbers of educated Africans might have to be fitted into that category. Mutesa did not simply have a command of the English language; he was in addition profoundly anglicized. The special tutoring he had in English ways, the long contacts with members of the British upper class, even the additional attention he received at King's College, Budo, and at Makerere College, all contributed towards the foundation of Mutesa's deep acculturation.

Both his education and his political career came to add further dimensions to his trans-nationality. His education at Makerere was interrupted to make it possible for him to go to Cambridge. This decision was taken partly by Oxford Englishmen – the Governor, Sir John Hall, and George Turner, the Principal of Makerere College at the time. The British old-boy network played its part.

> Ernest Haddon, a friend of my father's and a lifelong friend of mine, was returning to live at Cambridge, as he still does, and George Turner had a brother who was a don at Magdalene and subsequently my tutor. These were, I think, the deciding factors [behind the choice of Cambridge]. [9]

---

8. This incident is discussed in a related context in my paper "Islam and the English language in East and West Africa," chapter ix, *Language Use and Social Change*, edited by W. H. Whiteley, (London: Oxford University Press, on behalf of the International African Institute, 1971), pp. 181–186. For a more detailed account of the incident and its sociological significance consult also "The King, the King's English and I," *Transition*, no. 38, 1971.

9. *Desecration of My Kingdom, op. cit.*, p. 91.

Again the continued contacts with the British upper classes deepened this exposure further. A particularly memorable occasion for him was when George VI suggested to the Grenadier Guards that Mutesa be made a captain of the Guards. Mutesa went along to Buckingham Palace for the ceremony. Mutesa was a little nervous but he had been well briefed. He held his cap properly under his arm, saluted the King at the right moment and,

> a nice point of etiquette in which I had been instructed, when we were talking afterwards I accepted a cigarette the King offered me. To refuse, I had been told, might seem hypocritical, as I was a known smoker. I almost finished it when he recalled his own visit to Uganda as Duke of York and memories of my father. [10]

But it was not merely his education, including an exposure to some military training, which linked Mutesa to England. Politics also came to play their part. He was exiled twice to England, first in 1953 in a confrontation with the British Governor, Sir Andrew Cohen. The confrontation was, in part, connected with questions of Buganda's autonomy in relation to the British, and also Uganda's autonomy in relation to Kenya settlers. The precipitating factor had been a speech by the Colonial Secretary which seemed to suggest the formation of an East African federation which, in the circumstances of the day, would have meant greater settler say in Ugandan affairs. Buganda reacted sharply to this speech, and before long there was a fusion between the issue of Buganda's rights as against the Governor, and Uganda's rights as against white settler dreams of an East African federation.

Sir Andrew Cohen sent him into exile, ostensibly for ever. Mutesa lived in England, partly in comfortable respite and partly in continuing agitation for his return to his people. His first year was very miserable, but it was also deepening his love for England. By the time he was being recalled to return to his people, he knew what he would miss. He recalled:

> It can never be pleasant to be an exile. My first year was miserable, though I was living a life that must have looked easy and luxurious from a distance. As the certainty that I should return grew, however, my love for England was able to struggle with my pain at being forced away from Uganda. [11]

It was also partly because of this experience that he began to feel very much like a "liaison" between England and Uganda, as he called himself.

The capacity of the Baganda to be deeply Anglicized and at the same time profoundly traditionalist remains one of the fascinating aspects of these people. Sometimes it is the Africans who have completely abandoned their roots who become particularly hostile to foreign influences and western ways. Their own abandonment of their roots creates a sense of insecurity, and a struggle starts to recapture a little of the mystique of the past. Some of us turn to a dress which is clearly less western in trying to reassure ourselves that we are indeed different and more than black Europeans. Others use alternative gimmicks, like libation in Ghana at a ceremony which is otherwise western, or an extra-mural lecturer denounces western cultural imperialism. Many of these elements, ranging from the wearing of *kitenge* shirts to writing *Song of Lawino* are indications of a cultural complex – westernized African intellectuals not yet completely at peace with themselves.

---

10. Ibid., p. 98.
11. Ibid., p. 139.

But many Baganda have been different. They have shown no great evidence of anglophobia, nor ritualistic rejection of British ways. On the contrary, their taste in dress is sometimes singularly British. The Kabaka or King wore a *kanzu* at times, the Nabagareka or Queen wore a *basuti* at times. They could wear their own national dress with elegance, while they were also capable of wearing western dress with striking fastidiousness. It was Professor Lloyd A. Fallers, former director of the East African Institute of Social Research and now Professor at the University of Chicago, who once wrote:

> One of the striking characteristics of the Baganda is their ability to wear western clothing with a real feeling for style. Over much of Africa, western clothing is worn like an uncomfortable ill-fitting uniform, but Baganda men and women have penetrated sufficiently into the inner recesses of western style that many of them can wear western clothes with real taste...The Kabaka himself is an elegantly-tailored, Cambridge-educated young gentleman who speaks flawless English. [12]

What should be remembered is that westernization differentiated Amin not only from Mutesa but also from Obote. It is to this stage in the democratization process that we must now turn.

III – THE COMING OF THE COMMON MAN

The voice which most consistently sang the song of the common man was the voice of Apolo Milton Obote, the middle class President from a chiefly family in Lango District. Contrary to certain assumptions, Obote did not start speaking about the common man on the eve of his Move to the Left. He was using the imagery of structural democracy from his earliest days in parliament. In the initial phases he thought electoral democracy could result in structural democracy, that by giving the vote to the common man one could produce the kind of government that was democratic in terms of being typical of the people. In March 1960, while Obote was aiming for universal adult franchise, he betrayed this unconscious equation between electoral democracy and structural democracy. He said in Parliament:

> Mr. Speaker, whatever we may be in life, whatever we may be in Government, however proud we may be of being Ministers in Central Government, however much we may feel proud of being Members of Legislative Council, the man who is important is the common man. [13]

There were interruptions in the course of Obote's delivery, but he then proceeded to make his point more explicit. He rejected criteria of education as the basis of political power and influence; he rejected the criteria of wealth.

> ...we cannot be bullied about that because somebody has got a university degree, therefore he is much more important. He is not important in Uganda. We cannot be bullied that, because someone has got thousands of pounds in his pocket, therefore he is considered important enough for an extended franchise. He is not important. The man who is important is the common man who must have a vote. [14]

---

12. Fallers, "Ideology and Culture in Uganda Nationalism," *American Anthropologist*, vol. 63 (1961), pp. 677–686.

13. Debate on the Constitutional Committee Report, *Parliamentary Debates*, 40th Session, 7th March, 1960, *Hansard*, pp. 374ff.

14. Ibid.

Obote himself had passed through Makerere College as a student. His intellectual orientation included literary anglophilia. He adopted the first name "Milton" in honour of the author of *Paradise Lost*. And while a student at Makerere, Milton Obote had prophetically played Caesar in a college production of Shakespeare's *Julius Caesar*. Yet Obote did show egalitarian leanings from quite early.

Later in life much of Obote's utilisation of the concept of the common man was connected with his opposition to aristocratic privilege, and connected further with his republicanism. He did indeed form an alliance of convenience with Kabaka Yekka, which he broke later. He also cooperated in facilitating Mutesa's election to the Presidency of Uganda. But there did remain in Obote a hankering for structural democracy, both in the sense of having some kind of tribal representativeness in positions of authority and fair distribution of power among the different parts of Uganda, and also in the Leftist sense of giving the ordinary man a greater say in the affairs of the nation. Obote's republicanism may also have been connected with his Lango origins. Though descended from a chiefly family, Obote knew that he belonged to a relatively egalitarian culture. Privilege among the Lango was far less hierarchical than among the Baganda.

But Obote was not consistent in his policies, nor was he tough enough with his ministers. His own ascent to the presidency was in the direction of greater structural democratization, at least to the extent that he was not a king. But the nature of his ascent, including his blatant endeavour to save his political career in February 1966 regardless of the consequences, was seriously anti-democratic in the electoral and constitutional sense.

Then in 1968 he started talking about a move to the Left, and finally in 1969 he emerged with the *Common Man's Charter*. The same concept which he had used in that parliamentary speech in the Legislative Council in 1960, when he was asking for universal adult franchise, now became the cornerstone of his socialistic creed. In 1960 the idea of the common man was still very much in the liberal tradition in Obote's mind, implying electoral power universally extended. But, by 1969, his ideas were getting more purely structural, in the sense of wanting power to devolve to those who were really typical of the composition of society.

Obote declared in the *Common Man's Charter* an opposition not only to a division of society between the rich and the poor, but also to a division between the educated and the uneducated. He was all too aware that formal education, and the English language as a political and economic asset, conferred on those who had received them certain privileges. Parliament itself was inaccessible to those who did not have an adequate command of the English language. The *Common Man's Charter* denounced those who were "educated, African in appearance but mentally foreign."

And then, on January 25, 1971 a voice was heard on Radio Uganda. The voice had a Lugbara accent, speaking halting English, seemingly educated only modestly. In a fundamental sense it was a voice from the hinterland of Uganda, the voice of a common man in the sense which Obote himself would, in different circumstances, have emphatically conceded. That modestly educated Lugbara voice on Radio Uganda enumerated eighteen points against Milton Obote, the author of the *Common Man's Charter*. Before long we knew that our new President was Major-General Idi Amin, with less than full formal primary education, though self-educated in other spheres. He was not the son of a chiefly family, as Obote had been. He was not a product of Makerere College, as Obote had been. He was not an intellectual, as Obote had been.

Colin Legum, a friend of Obote's and Commonwealth correspondent of *The Observer*, was deeply distressed by the *coup*. His initial reports in *The Observer* indicated a complete acceptance of Obote's version not only of the causes of the *coup* but also of what was happening in Uganda. It was almost as if Colin Legum had suspended his better judgment, in instinctive revulsion against the overthrow of Obote.

But what is significant from the point of view of this analysis is what Legum had to say about Idi Amin, in an article written for the British socialist publication *Venture*. One would have thought that in such an egalitarian publication, committed to some of the oldest values of the Fabian Society, the significance of Amin's commonality would have occurred to Legum. He denounces Amin "this rough-hewn, self-made soldier" – and then proceeds to castigate Amin for "having always preferred the company of his non-commissioned officers to his modern corps of officers." Legum sees this as further evidence of an inner antagonism in Amin to educated and sophisticated people. The article was published after Amin had already shown his readiness to appoint a carefully selected council of ministers, with a wealth of administrative and organisational experience, including among them no less an educated person than a university professor. The council of ministers reflected the continuing participation of the educated middle class in policy-making, but the top man in Uganda was no longer necessarily drawn from that class. The structural democratization of the commanding heights of the polity had at last come full circle. [15]

IV – ON REVOLUTION AND THE MARGINAL MAN

The third dimension of structural democratization is the *geo-ethnic* one. This involves the role of the marginal man in history. The first *coup* in post-colonial Africa was the overthrow of King Farouk in Egypt in 1952. To lend respectability to the *coup*, and reassure the population of the rationality behind it, the soldiers entrusted leadership to General Mohammed Naguib. In ancestry General Naguib was a trans-national man, in the sense that his mother's side originated in the Sudan while his father's was Egyptian. In this sense he was a marginal man.

The first military *coup* south of the Sahara in Africa took place a decade later. This was the *coup* which started with the assassination of Togo's President Sylvanus Olympio. In order to lend respectability to the *coup*, and reassure the population that the country was in responsible hands, the soldiers formed a provisional government, and entrusted the presidency to Mr. Nicolas Grunitzky. Mr. Grunitzky was a marginal trans-national figure in almost the same sense as General Naguib. Mr. Grunitzky was born of a Polish father and a Togolese mother in the town of Atakpame in Western Togo in 1913.

The first social revolution which took place in anglophone East Africa was the Zanzibar revolution of January 1964. The leader of the Zanzibar revolution was a marginal figure in a different sense from either Naguib or Grunitzky. John Okello was a trans-national figure in the sense that he was a Ugandan who had led a revolution in

---

15. Legum's conception of Idi Amin in the terms quoted above occurs in his article "Uganda after Obote," *Venture*, vol. 23, no. 3, March 1971, p. 20.

Zanzibar. He was someone drawn from another society but cast in the role of initiator of fundamental change in a country of later adoption. "Field-Marshal" John Okello was later eased out of power, and was succeeded in Zanzibar by the towering figure of Sheikh Abeid Karume.

Sheikh Karume too was a trans-national marginal figure. His father was from Nyasaland (now Malawi), and some accounts of his life place his own entry into Zanzibar at the age of ten. Prior to one of the elections of pre-revolutionary Zanzibar Abeid Karume's citizenship was challenged in a court of law. Did he have a right to lead a political party in Zanzibar? Did he have a right to stand for election in a Zanzibari legislature? It was the Nationalist party, later overthrown by the Zanzibar revolution, which was challenging Abeid Karume's credentials for political leadership in Zanzibar. Karume won the case. He was, after all, a citizen, even if he had previously been of Nyasaland extraction. Nevertheless, from the point of view of our analysis in this essay, Karume was yet another instance of the trans-national marginal man in major movements of change in Africa.

The Zanzibar revolution was a revolution, primarily arising out of popular discontent and the challenge of armed civilians, rather than from any professional army. The Zanzibar experience cannot therefore be described as a military *coup*.

The first military *coup* in anglophone East Africa must therefore be deemed to be the Ugandan *coup* of January, 1971. The soldiers handed over power to Major-General Idi Amin. Major-General Idi Amin was a marginal figure in a third sense, different both from the category of Naguib and Grunitzky and the category of Okello and Karume. In General Amin we have a trans-national figure connected with a more fundamental aspect of the African scene. This is the aspect concerned with the division of ethnic communities across official territorial boundaries. Amin's father was born in what is now the Sudan. The border with Uganda was transferred to the jurisdiction of the Khartoum government. It might, therefore, be said that Amin's father was born a Ugandan, but the borders of Uganda have contracted since then.

In any case the Kakwa tribe continues to be divided between Uganda and the Sudan, with some Kakwa also in the Congo (now Zaire).

Thus the marginality of Amin is an ethnic marginality rather than a personal one. He belongs to a small community which extends over more than one territorial entity. The marginality of Naguib and Grunitzky, on the other hand, was a personal trans-nationality. They themselves were of mixed parentage, trans-national in dimension.

The marginality of John Okello and Abeid Karume is also basically personal, in the sense that it was they themselves who were previously of foreign ancestry and yet came to play a leading role in a country of adoption.

The question which arises is what elucidation does this throws on the role of the marginal man in major movements of transformation in Africa. Obviously certain distinctions would need to be made. In the case of Naguib and Grunitzky the trans-national figures did not themselves symbolise great revolutionary fervour. On the contrary, they were chosen because of the air of solidity and calm respectability which their names would lend to the *coups* which had taken place in their countries. Their personal careers had a good deal to do with the air of respectability that they had acquired. But even in their case it might be said that they derived part of their capacity to inspire confidence from their status as marginal men. There are occasions when distance from the major contending families in a particular country, or from the heart of the web of kinship in relation to political power, could itself be a worthy qualification in moments which need national reconciliation. It is like looking for somebody from a small tribe, as a way of averting rivalries between big tribes.

Comparable considerations are sometimes at play in African countries when a vice-president has to be chosen. In a country with, say, two major tribes, when the president is drawn from one of them, is it safe that the vice-president should be from the second? Would this create certain temptations in the political process? Would the problem of succession be compounded precisely by the ethnic balance which had sought to manifest itself too immediately in a kind of institutional balance? Kenya had to confront this situation when the time came to choose a vice-president, especially after the fall of Oginga Odinga. In terms of sheer political dynamism, and in terms of his record during the colonial struggle for liberation, Tom Mboya was, in many ways, an obvious man to be second in command to Jomo Kenyatta. But precisely because Mboya had such charismatic claims to be heir presumptive to the presidency, and also because he came from the second biggest tribe in Kenya, a tribe which was now increasingly competitive, Mboya was not in the running for the vice-presidency. The choice for the new vice-president in Kenya's history fell on a trans-national figure in almost Grunitzky's sense. This was Joseph Murumbi, the son of a Masai mother and a Goan father. There was an element of marginality in Murumbi's background which made him suitable to be both a major figure in politics and yet not too serious a complication to issues of balance of power between sizeable contenders. [16]

In the case of John Okello, his role in the Zanzibari convulsion was not in lending respectability to it, but in actually initiating it. John Okello and his band of fighters captured the armoury at Ziwani in Zanzibar, distributed the new weapons to those raw political challengers, and inaugurated the most convulsive revolution in the region.

Why was a Ugandan successful in launching a revolution outside his own country? In terms of roots on the island, John Okello was more of a foreigner in Zanzibar than the Sultan he overthrew. The Sultan was born a Zanzibari, so was his father, his grandfather, and his grandfather's father. Sultan Jamshid was indubitably much more Zanzibari than John Okello; but he was definitely less African than John Okello. In terms of nationality John Okello was a marginal man, coming from Lango to initiate a violent eruption in Zanzibar. But in terms of ethnic identity it was the Sultan who was the marginal man, part-Arab, part-African, more fully Zanzibari than the man who overthrew him but less purely African than his enemies.

For a delirious few weeks John Okello might indeed have derived his mystique from his distance. The local Africans in Zanzibar had inter-penetrated with the Arabs, either culturally, religiously, or biologically. Islam was the religion of the great majority of Africans, as well as of the Arabs. Swahili was the language of both groups, and Swahili as a culture, born of both Arab and African traditions, was dominant in the population as a whole. There was no doubt that the local Africans shared a large number of attributes with the Arabs that they were now challenging.

But precisely because the challenge was against the Arabs, it made sense that its chief articulator in the initial stages should be distant enough to symbolize the purity of the African challenge. The bonds in this case were not the bonds of culture, or of religion, or even of inter-marriage. In many ways the majority of Zanzibari Africans

---

16. On his resignation to enter a business career Murumbi was succeeded as Vice-President by Daniel Arap Moi, drawn from minority tribes of Kenya.

had more in common with the majority of Zanzibari Arabs than they had with this Langi revolutionary from Uganda. But what was at stake in that revolution was racial sovereignty rather than national sovereignty. By the tenets of national sovereignty, as I have indicated, Sheikh Ali Muhsin the leader of the Zanzibari Nationalist party which was overthrown, as well as the Sultan himself, were more Zanzibari than John Okello. But by the criteria of racial sovereignty, it was the fact John Okello was an African in a purer sense than either Muhsin or the Sultan which really mattered. And a Langi on the Isle of Cloves was a symbol of pure Africanity.

As we indicated, John Okello, having served his purpose and being basically an unpredictable if charismatic personality, was eased out of office. And Abeid Karume another trans-national man assumed supreme authority.

In the April of the same year of the revolution, Zanzibar and Tanganyika were united to form what came to be known as the United Republic of Tanzania. Revolutionary leadership in Tanzania came to be firmly held by Julius Nyerere. But the first major challenge to the stability of Nyerere and even to his status as a revolutionary came to be articulated by yet another trans-national man.

This time it was Oscar Kambona who was born in 1928, the son of a Nyasaland Anglican priest who had crossed the border to live and serve in southern Tanganyika. Kambona himself insists that this is a misinterpretation of his family background. Certainly it is defensible to see his case as very similar to that of General Idi Amin, a trans-national figure because the community to which he belonged defied artificial territorial definitions. And yet, in a sense, the situation was enough to give Nyerere's government an excuse to withdraw Kambona's citizenship. Kambona heard of this withdrawal from an official of the Tanzanian High Commission in London. The grounds were ostensibly connected with his alleged extra-Tanzanian origins. In many ways Kambona is much more of a Tanganyikan than Abeid Karume is a Zanzibari, since Oscar Kambona was at least born in Tanganyika and his community had branches across both sides of the border between Tanganyika and Malawi. Karume's community, on the other hand, is not really trans-national in that sense. Karume's father was decidedly an immigrant, and so was Karume himself.

The tradition of trans-national figures playing dominant roles in great movements of change is by no means peculiar to Africa. Napoleon from Corsica and even Hitler from Austria spring to mind. Nor is the tradition in Africa peculiar to this century. We started by mentioning Naguib in Egypt. But in fact the great initiator of modernization in Egypt was Mahomet Ali, the modernizing Ottoman ruler of nineteenth century Egypt. That Kakwa boy from Uganda's border with the Sudan, Idi Amin, lies in a tradition at once old and momentous.

It is partly this peripheral background of Amin which brings us back firmly to the issue of structural democracy. Was Amin's assumption of power an instance of the periphery taking over the centre? Was it a case of the countryside taking over the capital city? Was it a case of the common man assuming supreme authority?

If Amin is placed once again alongside Mutesa, the evolution towards this structural democracy becomes clearer. Mutesa was a king, Protestant, and privileged. Amin was a commoner, Muslim and poor. Mutesa came from the region of the capital city, in the full glare of national centrality. Amin came from the periphery of the country, descended from a small tribe. Mutesa was Cambridge-educated, a friend of African and British upper classes, a host as well as a guest of kings and princes. Amin was a rough and ready soldier, sometimes accused by his critics like Colin

Legum of preferring "the company of his non-commissioned officers to his modern corps of officers." In short, Mutesa was a king; Amin was a peasant warrior.

Yet these two figures were destined to share a moment of national reconciliation. The rough boxer from Arua became suddenly a commanding figure of presidential dignity in 1971, showing signs of warmth and magnanimity. General Idi Amin might well emerge as the first really charismatic national leader that Uganda has had. He seems to have a certain personal magnetism, which Mutesa found only because he was Kabaka with all the mystique of kingship, and which Obote never found. And this peasant boy from the borders of Uganda and the Sudan, descended from a tribe which was not uniquely Ugandan but split across the frontier, became the instrument for ensuring that the king of the heartland tribe of Uganda, the Baganda, did in fact fulfill in death what he had promised in life – "In the end I shall return to the land of my fathers and to my people." [17]

V – WESTERNISM AND THE MILITARY

In the final analysis it was the military profession which helped to breech the cultural gap between General Amin and Sir Edward Mutesa. Mutesa, by being the king of the heartland tribe, was geographically central in Uganda. But by being Anglicized to the extent that he was, Mutesa was culturally marginal in Uganda.

Amin, on the other hand, was the exact reverse. By being a member of a tribe on the very borders of Uganda, Amin was geographically marginal. But by being drawn from the womb of the countryside, and by being highly indigenous and non-westernized in many of his inclinations, Amin was culturally central.

But the military profession was the bridge between the cultural world of Edward Mutesa and that of Idi Amin. In its own specialized way, a military career in the Ugandan army was a semi-westernizing process for Amin. The rituals of the military in Uganda, from the drill to the ceremonial music, are overwhelmingly British derived.

A member of the British delegation to the funeral of Sir Edward Mutesa exclaimed to me in private how British Uganda had appeared to him in the five days he spent there. I told him that although the British influence was still significant in Uganda, the particular five days of his stay had been especially anglo-centric. I argued that there were three reasons why the entire atmosphere of the funeral had included this heavy British dimension. The first reason concerned the fact that the funeral was designed to be with full military honours. And military honours, and all military ceremonies, in all the armies of English-speaking Africa, remained firmly within the British tradition. There had been less inclination to change the rituals of the military than there had been with regard to the Westminister model of political arrangements. The music, therefore, which accompanied the coffin at the Kololo airstrip had a singularly Britannic tone.

The second reason why the five days were so anglo-centric concerned the simple fact that the funeral had to have important Christian rites. Among African countries, Uganda is particularly religious. Religion in Uganda has tended to affect politics much more than it has done in most other parts of the African continent. Moreover, the cleavage between Catholics and Protestants has, in part, resulted in a purist

---

17. *Desecration of My Kingdom, op. cit.*, p. 194.

approach to ritual and ceremony in both denominations. There were, therefore, fewer changes in Ugandan Christianity at large, when compared with its European counterparts, than might have been the case without this tendency towards purity. The ceremony at Namirembe Cathedral, very moving in its simplicity, was nevertheless something indistinguishable from similar ceremonies in that other St. Paul's Cathedral four thousand miles away.

The third reason why those days of Mutesa's funeral were so anglo-centric would bring us back to the Baganda and their own capacity to imbibe so much which was British, and at the same time remain so deeply African in their traditions. Again few people have put it better than Lloyd Fallers in his introduction to the symposium entitled *The King's Men.* Fallers has this to say:

> Baganda are, in many ways, extremely "acculturated" and the leading members of society are the most acculturated of all. There are here no culturally conservative, traditional chiefs pitted against a group of young, western educated commoner politicans. Baganda do not see or practice politics in these terms, as so many African peoples do, rather, Ganda society has acculturated, as it were, from the top down, and hence the new culture tends to have universal legitimacy. Indeed, from the point of view of the Baganda, this new culture, which includes many Western ideas of government, Western education, Anglican and Roman Catholic Christianity, the motivations appropriate to a money economy – all this has been *their* culture in a fundamental way. They have so to say, "naturalized" the foreign elements and thus kept a sense of cultural integrity and "wholeness' through a period of radical change.[18]

It is the convergence of these three factors – Anglicized military rituals, anglicized Christianity, and Anglicized Ganda styles – which gave those five days of the funeral of Sir Edward Mutesa that highly anglo-centric personality.

As they sounded the last post at the ancestral quadrangle of the Kasubi tombs, and President Amin stood to attention under the blazing sun of Kampala, in the full splendour of a Britannic military tradition, the two soldier presidents of Uganda were suddenly culturally close.

There had been a last post in the first burial of Mutesa in London in 1969. On that occasion the military component of the burial was handled by the British Grenadier Guards. Now the Grenadier Guards were only part of the ceremony. The bulk of the military component was the Ugandan army. And yet the universe of discourse between that trumpet in London in 1969 and the trumpet at the Kasubi tombs in Uganda in 1971 was indeed a shared universe.

Two funerals for one man. Yes, between England and Uganda, Mutesa had shared his life. Yes, between England and Uganda, he had come to share his death.

The peasant warrior from West Nile, now head of state, lay a wreath at the coffin in a concluding farewell gesture. Then the remains of the late Sir Edward Mutesa received a final presidential salute. The coffin was handed over by the Uganda army to the Baganda elders. And five hundred years of African history came to an end.

Or did it? Were peasant warriors to be forever supreme from now on? Was the principle of kingship in Uganda forever dead?

---

18. L. A. Fallers (editor), *The King's Men: Leadership and Status in Buganda on the Eve of Independence,* (London: Oxford University Press, 1964), p. 9.

VI - TOWARDS THE FUTURE

What of the future? The future must be a quest for some meeting point between structural democracy and electoral democracy in Uganda. There has to be a return to civilian politics, to resurrect electoral democracy, and there have to be policies which increase social mobility and expand opportunities for that mysterious individual about whom Obote sang so much – the Common Man of Uganda.

In the issue of marrying structural democracy with electoral democracy the issue of kingship itself comes into play. My own position on the matter has been clear. As I indicated to an interviewer of the *Sunday Nation* (Kenya), in February 1971, I am not a "republican fanatic." I do not believe that kingship is wrong in its own right, nor do I share the automatic aversion to feudalism that some of my colleagues and friends have. If someone had asked me in 1966 whether the kingships in Uganda should be abolished, my answer would have been no.

But now that they have been abolished, and Uganda has been without them for a number of years, my own feeling is that a restoration would be dangerous. My arguments again are not identical with those of people who see the kingdoms as divisive elements.

I have never been convinced that in February 1966 the system of government in Uganda as such had failed. On the contrary, my view has been that in February 1966 it was not the whole survival of Uganda as a nation which was at stake; it was the survival of Milton Obote as Head of Government. The Daudi Ocheng motion in Parliament, and the kind of massive support it received, with only one dissenting voice from John Kakonge, implied that it was possible to ease Obote out of office through new realignments of political forces in Uganda. It had, by then, dawned upon the Baganda that they could not hope to have an effective share in national affairs without seeking allies beyond their own regional borders. The Daudi Ocheng motion signified such a quest for alliances. And all politics is, in some fundamental sense, a persistent realignment of forces in pursuit of changing aims and interests. The Ocheng motion was the nearest thing to a vote of no confidence that Obote as Head of Government had ever had to face. The appointment of a commission of enquiry by parliament in the full awareness that Obote was not in favour of such an enquiry was again a dramatic assertion that it might be possible to ease Obote out of power without resorting to extra-constitutional means. Some extra-constitutional means were indeed envisaged, including some by people such as Mutesa himself. But the parliamentary vote indicated that the aim of changing the leadership of the U.P.C. could, in fact, be realized short of a resort to extra-constitutionality.

But Obote returned from his trip to the north, suspended the constitution, relieved Mutesa of the Presidency, declared himself executive President, and put in detention five of his Cabinet colleagues. What Obote had done in *February* must, therefore, be regarded as a case of political self-preservation, rather than national self-preservation. What Obote had to do in *May* 1966 was more clearly a national endeavour, as the wrangles which his own action in February had released were now endangering the integrity of the country itself.

Were the kingships fundamentally divisive? We ought not to look at 1966 for the evidence, for the evidence is not really there. What we had at the beginning of that year was a situation where a major king in the country, the Kabaka, was being forced to establish new alignments with others, in order to achieve the ouster of his political opponents. This is a classical political game, inevitable in any society which permits politics, and is no indication whatsoever of the viability of the nation concerned.

But although I would not have been in favour of the abolition of kings in 1966, I am more uneasy about their restoration later. Too many people outside Buganda have, by now, assumed that the disappearance of the kings was itself an indication that the different regions of Uganda had now achieved equality. The kings of Uganda were not a sign of disunity, as many have argued; but they could have been symbols of inequality. The Baganda especially had, because of the peculiar circumstances of the colonial period and the privileged status they enjoyed, evolved into something like a caste. The Baganda were the Brahmins of Uganda in a loose sense. And part of the lustre and glitter of being a Brahmin at that time was connected with the monarchy in Buganda. Many Ugandans outside Buganda were sometimes tempted to imitate certain elements of Buganda political culture. Even Ganda administrative institutions were objects of emulation. Yes, the Baganda were the Brahmins of Uganda – and the Kabakaship symbolised their status.

Then Obote, in a confrontation of power, succeeded in doing certain things which were unhealthy for the country; but at the same time accomplished the task of cutting down the Baganda to size. He, at any rate, made it easier for future governments of Uganda to establish parity of esteem and equality of treatment between the Baganda and the other regions.

But need the restoration of the monarchy imply a privileged status reactivated? After all, the other kings in Uganda were not as powerful as the Kabaka, and did not in reality imply greater privilege for the regions concerned. This is true. Yet equality sometimes must not only be accomplished; it must also be seen to have been accomplished. Restoration of the monarchy could imply, wrongly or correctly, a restoration of the privileged Brahminism of the Baganda.

And yet finally there is one argument which the Baganda might be forgiven for advancing. The issue of whether there should be kings or no kings in Uganda should, in the opinion of some of the more sophisticated Baganda, be a matter to be decided in the normal electoral and political process; rather than a matter for a decree. Amin is justified in saying that he has no intention of restoring the kings; after all, a military government should be no more than a caretaker government. Should not the issue of restoring kingship be left to the processes of civilian politics when these are restored? If the Baganda can convince the rest of their countrymen in Uganda that there is a case for resurrecting some of the traditional institutions, without the power they enjoyed, would not the kingships then have been restored through democratic means?

I have not myself fully resolved the ethics of this position. It is true that questions of this kind are at the heart of constitutional problems; and the kind of constitution which Uganda is to have one day should be a matter to be resolved when civilian politics are restored. Why should not the issue of kingship be resolved as part of the total constitutional arrangements?

It may well be that the Baganda would fail to convince the rest of Ugandans that kings need to be restored. If that is the case, then the Baganda would have to accept the verdict of the nation as a whole. The issue would have been postponed for resolution in the free political battlefield of a free country. If the Baganda lost in their bid to persuade their compatriots that kingships should be restored, electoral democracy would itself have pronounced a verdict in favour of structural democracy. That would be the highest point of fusion between the liberty which is yielded by the electoral process and the parity which emerges out of structural democratization. Let a national vote of Uganda decide whether any particular part of the country is to have a constitutional monarch. And, if the national vote decides negatively, parity and liberty in Uganda might at last find a point of symbolic integration.

The presidency itself, while remaining accessible to a peasant warrior, would no longer be available for a royal contender. Such an electoral verdict could be another major stage in the history of Uganda as a plural society.

In the sense of renunciation of hereditary leadership, democratization would be consolidated. In the sense of partial demotion of the educated class, democratization would be enhanced. And in the sense of expanding opportunities for previously peripheral tribes and regions, democratization would at last be truly under way.

UGANDA BEFORE, DURING, AND AFTER AMIN

Bert N. Adams

University of Wisconsin-Madison

"Every African government knows that its first problem is how to hold the country together when it is threatened by wide disintegration" (Wallerstein 1961, p. 88). Immanuel Wallerstein's comment at the beginning of the 1960s is most appropriate to those sub-Saharan African nations which incorporate within their boundaries societies formerly competitive with or antagonistic to each other. Uganda is one of these. The Kenya-Uganda border separates peoples, such as the Pokot, who should be together, and the excolonial boundary brings together peoples who perhaps should be apart. Besides ethnic/boundary difficulties, Uganda lived through eight years of leadership by Idi Amin and is now trying to reconstruct an economy which has always thrived on agricultural self-sufficiency. Let us examine Uganda's recent history.

UGANDA BEFORE 1971

Central to understanding the integration problem in the modern nation of Uganda is the historic antagonism between the Nilotic peoples of the north, particularly the Acholi and Langi, and the Bantu peoples of the south, especially the Baganda, and the subconflict between ethnic groups within these categories, such as Banyoro and Baganda. First colonially and now nationally, these former rivals find themselves drawn together under a single government, whose major problem has been to balance the Nilotic-Bantu antagonisms and at the same time to keep both the Baganda and the other peoples of the nation moderately satisfied. Writing in the mid-1960s, Elizabeth Hopkins described the struggle between the Baganda and other ethnic groups in Uganda during the first few years of independence as follows: "Each tribe, whether from north, east, or west, assessed its position, not in terms of the alien communities (i.e., Europeans and Asians), but in terms of the relative degree of privileges *vis-à-vis* the Baganda that it was able to secure from the central administration. The parochial focus on the Baganda was also an important factor inhibiting any serious anti-colonial hostility on a national level, for potential political unrest outside Baganda tended to polarize around issues such as perceived areas of discrimination or the acquisition of concessions previously extended to Buganda" (Hopkins 1966, p. 129).[1]

NOTE: This is a revised version of a paper presented at the 23rd Annual Meeting of the African Studies Association, Philadelphia, Pennsylvania, 1980 October 16. Bert N. Adams, Department of Sociology, University of Wisconsin, was on the faculty of Makerere University, Kampala, when Amin came to power in 1971, and for one and one-half years after that, and he returned to Uganda for briefer visits in 1979 and 1980.

Rural Africana, 11 (Fall 1981) 15

At the granting of independence in 1962, Mazrui points out, those who had been "foreigners" became part of the "self" in a self-governing Uganda. Lango, Bunyoro, Buganda, and other separate societies were now part of the new nation-state called Uganda (Mazrui 1967, p. 5). The attempt was made to balance the old antagonisms by granting several of the southern ethnic groups, most importantly the Baganda, federal status, so that they were in many ways semiautonomous kingdoms. Furthermore, the King or Kabaka of Buganda was made President of Uganda, while a Western-educated leader from Lango, A. Milton Obote, became Prime Minister. Such an arrangement, though tenuously balanced, avoided any design for separatism on the part of the Baganda. Geographically, economically, and in terms of national power, it was not feasible for the rest of the country to allow Buganda to go it alone, and federal and kingship privileges seemed to satisfy their desires during the early years of independence. However, the tensions between Baganda and others, and between Kabaka and Prime Minister, were never laid to rest. By 1965 a shift had begun to occur in the party alignments of Catholics and Protestants, and Obote saw his party coalition disintegrating. The seat of government was in Buganda territory, and Obote saw the Baganda maneuvering into a postion where they might make Uganda into a Buganda empire. Acting with swiftness in 1966, he quelled a Baganda uprising, drove the Kabaka into exile, abolished the kingdom status of the Baganda and others, and imprisoned Baganda leaders. Thus, Baganda dominance was broken. With Baganda leaders "detained" and their king in exile, a one-party system was effected under Obote, and increasing numbers of Obote loyalists from the north—especially Acholi—were recruited into the army.

The capital city of Kampala, however, is in Buganda territory. The hatred of the Baganda and other southern groups for Obote's regime smoldered underground, spreading quietly and waiting for its opportunity. In addition, Obote's "move to the left" during 1970 alienated other groups, most specifically the army.[2] The opportunity for Obote's opponents arose while the Prime Minister was attending a Commonwealth Conference in Singapore. Moving against northern Members of Parliament and army personnel, General Idi Amin carried out an army takeover of the Ugandan government on January 25, 1971. The public portion of the army coup was completed in a matter of hours; the purges within the army continued for several months.[3] Parliament and politics were abolished, and effective opposition was silenced. Idi Amin was in power.

AMIN AND THE MEANS OF REGIME PERPETUATION

The attempts of President Amin's military government to gain some form of social support and national integration had to surmount both the old secessionist or separatist inclinations of ethnic groups such as the Baganda and Karamojong, and lack of acceptance by the northerners, especially Langi and Acholi, who had been the prime bases of former President Milton Obote's strength. What were the means at this disposal, how did he use them, and what went wrong?

(1) *The symbolic leadership of President Amin and the army* derived from several sources. First, Amin was originally from the Uganda-Sudan border area, and while this did not give him a strong built-in basis for ethnic support, it likewise avoided traditional ethnic group opposition. That is, because he did not represent the Acholi, Langi, Teso, Baganda, or one of the other powerful Ugandan ethnic groups, he was not immediately defined as "one of them" by any provincial group. This in itself helped at the outset to soften polarization along the old lines. Also, he released the Baganda leaders from detention and installed several of them in his newly constituted government. This, of course, strengthened his support among the Baganda, who were already in sympathy with his takeover due to their hatred of Obote's regime. In fact, much of his early support came from the Baganda, who looked to a reinstatement of many of the privileges which had been theirs prior to 1966. He and the army were ubiquitous in the Ugandan press, and were depicted as embodying the essence of Uganda's strength and security. Following the government takeover of the Kampala newspaper *Voice of Uganda*,[4] hardly a day passed without Amin's picture appearing on the front page. (2) The press was also used for *populist propaganda,* indicating the broadness of Ugandan support for Amin's regime. Frequently during 1971-72 one could pick up the morning paper and read of some show of support for the military government. It might be the Ankole elders bringing long-horned Ankole cattle to give to the President or Acholi dancers coming to Kampala to dance for him or people from Mubende or Masaka pledging their allegiance by marching through Kampala to the Parliament building. Such demonstrations indicated mass support and, from the government's perspective, were seen as possible forerunners of greater support. Even Amin's dreams, so maligned by the Western press, were a form of populist propaganda. When Amin "dreamed" he should expel the Asians, many village Ugandans identified with and understood their leader. This is why some writers of this time described Amin as the nearest to a "truly African leader."

(3) *Direct promises* to the people were a major part of Amin's early policy. Irrigation in Karamoja, a branch university in Gulu, a tarmac road to Kitjum, removal of people from overcrowded Kigezi perhaps to Karamoja, new schools in many places, new job and business opportunities for Ugandans, movement away from government ownership of large corporations, release of those in detention: all these and other promises were made in the first few months of the Amin administration. Some, such as the last two, were effected almost immediately, while many of the others were rallying points for popular support for several years in anticipation of their fulfillment.

Two factors which operated as opposite sides of the same coin were Amin's (4) *accessibility* and his (5) *control of media.* Closely related to his symbolic leadership and to the integration of the masses and their leaders, President Amin made known upon his assumption of power that he would be available to all the people. "You must come to me with your problems" was the theme incessantly repeated. Nor did he wait for them to come. There was seldom a week during 1971-72 when the President did not appear before a group somewhere in Uganda to talk and listen. It might be the Baganda elders or the townspeople of Soroti or the Makerere University faculty or the Asian leaders, but he was truly available to the people. This, of course, was meant to be evidence both of his trust in the people and his interest in them as individuals. Much of his early travel was to the northern provinces, where the response to his administration was lukewarm at best. Such accessibility had both the positive aspect alluded to and a preventive aspect. The latter is predicated upon the fact that he not only wanted people to come to him with their problems but he wanted them to go *nowhere else*. A disgruntled elder or teacher was not to write a local newspaper, such as the *Voice* with his complaints, but was to contact the President's office. Every question and criticism was to be brought to him first. This, then, gave his office control over the dissemination of information through the news media, so that the picture presented to the public could be one of unified support rather than dissension. Such controlled unity had in itself a considerable propaganda value in the perpetuating of Amin's regime.[5]

Control of the media brings us to a further mechanism which Amin used both systematically and selectively: (6) *force and control*. The army purged many of its northern members, and other Obote sympathizers were either killed or fled into exile. In addition, Parliament and politics were abolished, so that no dissenting voice had organized expression. Many of the intelligentsia of Uganda fled the country, and Amin continued with periodic purges—of the army, various ethnic group leaders (including some of the Baganda he had released from detention), and Christian leaders—whenever "confusing voices" of criticism arose. We shall return to the issue of force in the discussion of his downfall.

The final three survival means used by the government of the Second Republic involved what might be called "selected enemies." (7) *The past government was one enemy*. Right after a change of rulers it is quite possible to "buy time" by blaming the ills of the nation on its former regime. Unquestionably, some of Obote's policies, such as the Nakivubo Pronouncements, giving the government majority control of large corporations, were less than successful in stimulating the Ugandan economy. Likewise, there had been some diversion of government funds to private interests during Obote's time. Obote was, in many ways, a private capitalist and a public socialist. It was, therefore, possible for Amin to trace many politico-economic problems to the previous regime's policies and activities. In this way, support could be maximized while the new government "straightened out the mess." "Let's unite to rectify these problems" was a useful rallying cry during the early months of the Second Republic.

(8) *A second enemy was the external:* Tanzania strongly supported Obote

during and after the coup and was slow in recognizing Amin's government. Thus, conflict with Tanzania was used to increase the sense of common cause within Uganda. Even purges within the Ugandan army were blamed on Tanzania, a handy external scapegoat. From time to time tension between Uganda and Kenya, including the Irsaeli raid on Entebbe, was a rallying point for national sentiment in Uganda. Finally, the government had (9) *internal alien enemies* at hand. First, it was the eight hundred Israelis, who in March of 1972 were defined as saboteurs and given three days to leave the county. This expulsion resolved Uganda's debt to Israel and brought Libyan oil money flowing in. However, the great internal scapegoat for Uganda's economic troubles was the fifty thousand Asians, with their control over much of the business sector and their generally assumed nonpatriotism. An alien and successful internal minority, such as the Asians, was a perfect target for national animosity, and thereby a source of national unity. It was not incidental that the order expelling non-citizen Asians from Uganda and announcing Uganda's "economic war" was read in all parts of the country by members of Amin's government. For this move had a propaganda and integrative value far surpassing any other single move made by Amin. With the departure of the Asians, Amin had to look for other internal enemies; and he found them in the British, the Kenyans, the Rwandaise, and others living in Uganda.

The actions of Idi Amin, especially in the early years of his regime, become understandable when viewed in the context of such mechanisms for national integration and regime survival. He acted decisively, especially against the Western powers, and this decisiveness made him a major thorn in the flesh of those powers—which tried continuously to discredit him. Yet, as one of the few African leaders who risked "thumbing his nose" at the Western world, he gained more than a little admiration—though often hidden from Western eyes and ears—from the leaders of Africa and from his own people. As Rollow noted in 1974, there are hardships in Uganda, but they seldom affect the shambas, and Amin created a Ugandan middle class. He still had at the time, according to Rollow, deep-rooted mass support (1974, p. 42). At greater length "M'Biru," a Ugandan, stated the following in 1973: "By all means let us condemn Amin's excesses, especially against his political opponents in Uganda, and sometimes silly utterances, but let us not allow those to blind us to the fact that he has changed the African image in the world in a very positive way, and shown him-self to be closer to thinking of the African masses than most of his brother presidents....he has roused African youth to think aloud, and made the world conscious of African intentions. More importantly, he has shattered the myth that African leaders only bark but never bite" (*Africa* 1973, p. 25).

So Amin is understandable in terms of the classic political mechanisms of integration-survival. So he was, at least in 1973-74, more popular than the Western press would admit. What, then, happened to Amin's regime?

As the years passed, the former Obote regime became decreasingly available as a scapegoat for Uganda's problems; the Second Republic had to stand on its own record. Likewise, internal alien enemies became more and more difficult to discover. The major tools of integration and regime persistence that remained viable were the propaganda of symbolic leadership and mass identification with the nation, control of opposition and of the media, territorial integration by forces, and the keeping of promises, including economic populism. But these were not sufficient in Uganda. For one thing, symbolism and national identification are only partially successful at best in nations such as Uganda; the masses do not yet find their major identity in being Ugandans but in their continuing ethnic-regional ties. For another thing, internal alien enemies gave way to internal enemies who were *not* alien. As the President turned upon the Baganda intelligentsia and Uganda's Christian leaders, it became apparent that, to Amin, "the enemy is us." Though this regime could ill afford it, Amin increasingly used force against all those who would criticize or even advise him. Furthermore, the spoils of the "economic war" fell primarily into the hands of the Army and other Nubians of Amin's ethnic group. Finally, Amin failed to keep many of his promises to the people. The use of force and symbolic identification must be accompanied by the satisfaction of people's needs and expectations. It was not enough to be a "big man in Africa"; Amin did not meet his people's needs and apparently had no plans for Uganda development. His expediency and fear caused his base of support to diminish greatly between 1975 and 1979, giving the exiles and Tanzanian soldiers the opportunity to move against him.

UGANDA AFTER AMIN[6]

Amin, president for eight years, was overthrown in April 1979 by an invasion force of Tanzanian soldiers and Ugandan exiles. Westerners and Ugandans alike believed that Amin's removal would solve the country's problems. Whether one is optimistic or pessimistic about Uganda's future, several points are apparent. First, the overthrow of Amin was not a panacea for Uganda's ills. Second, old ethnic animosities, new factions, and the split between exiles and nonexiles have emerged with the removal of the common focal point—Amin. Third, it will require both decisive and conciliatory action by any Ugandan government to solve the country's factionalism and crisis of confidence. Let us examine some of the current factions and problems.

Within months after the fall of Amin, there were several clear-cut factions in Uganda. Amin retained some supporters, especially in the far northwest and northeast parts of the country. Loyal Amin soldiers have roamed the semi-arid towns of Karamoja district and have abortively invaded West Nile. Furthermore, villagers who identified with Amin's Africanization of Uganda and his "African" style of leadership can still be found.

Yusuf Lule, former Vice-Chancellor of Makerere University, was chosen

President following the overthrow of Amin. The Uganda Consultative Council (UCC), consisting of some thirty former exiles who fled during Amin's regime, saw Lule as an elder statesman and possible conciliator, and he was enthusiastically supported by the Baganda. Yet Lule suggested that the Tanzanian liberation troops be replaced by Israeli, British, and American soldiers; and the rumor spread that he planned to bring in the son of the former Baganda King as his second-in-command. These and other excuses were used by the "young Turks" of the UCC to label Lule a reactionary and to replace him with Godfrey Binaisa. With this change, the new government lost the support of the Baganda, who recalled the days when Binaisa had strongly backed Obote. Yet Lule continued to have much support from the Baganda, who wanted a president to represent their interests.

Binaisa, many Ugandans felt, came into power to run a "holding operation" in Uganda for Obote. At the propitious time, Obote would be brought back from Tanzania to take over. Binaisa, himself, however, represented Uganda in Cuba at the meeting of the heads of nonaligned nations and began to develop a sense of satisfaction at being Uganda's President. Yet he came to be at odds with the army and was demoted, with a military commission headed by Paulo Muwanga assuming power alongside the UCC.

There were those who still supported then exiled ex-President Obote, and wanted to see his firm hand in control of Uganda once again. One of his chief friends was President Julius Nyerere of Tanzania, and Tanzanian influence included thousands of Tanzanian troops then on Ugandan soil, as well as Ministers and members of the UCC who returned to Uganda from Tanzania. Obote has, of course, since returned to Uganda and assumed the presidency after a disputed election.

Besides the traditional ethnic divisions and the current factions, there is one further division within Uganda. Those who remained in Uganda during Amin's regime see those who left as having "abandoned ship," as having shirked their responsibility at a time when Uganda needed them. Those who left accuse those who remained in Uganda of having been collaborators, of having "played ball" with Amin in order to survive. Both criticisms are correct: to survive, some had to leave; and to survive within the country, the rest had at least tacitly to collaborate. The UCC was established as a council of exiles, and those who remained were unrepresented immediately after Amin's overthrow. In addition, the latter feel that they understand Uganda and its current needs and problems better than those who left.

In the 1980 election campaign, the two major parties were the Uganda People's Congress of Obote, backed by the military, which represents Lango, Teso, and Acholi in the North, with support in Ankole and parts of the south as well, and the Democratic Party (D. P.) of Lule and the Baganda. Two smaller parties are the Uganda Patriotic Movement (UPM) of Museveni, Mushanga, and

Bidandi Ssali, which is supported by some Basoga and Westerners, and the Conservative Party. The conservatives want to bring back the federal system, only this time for all the districts, not just the four southern ones which had federal privileges in the early 1960s.

During my visit to Uganda in September 1980, I heard the following predictions about the elections: (1) they will never take place; (2) the outcome will be rigged; (3) they will take place but change nothing; (4) there will be a coup right before the elections; (5) there will be a coup right after the election, if the "wrong" party wins; (6) there will be a fair election, and it will begin to change things for the better in Uganda. The least prevalent opinion, I might add, is the last.

In the course of the election campaign, Kisamba of the D. P. was shot and his car stolen, Mushanga of the UPM was threatened, and Obote was shot at. No party was immune. An insight expressed by one observer in Uganda is that many of the current leaders and politicians have lived in exile and know they could do it again. Thus, they won't compromise and are not really committed to the country, feeling that "if I don't get what I want, I will simply leave again." Thus, there is ambition without commitment.

The capable leaders are overworked, attempting to run for office while continuing to carry out their functions. "We are making progress" was the feeling of Kabwagyere, the Minister of Transportation, "but everyone wants everything solved at once. Also," he adds, "people come to me about flat tires, or their car being stuck in the mud. (After all, I am the Minister of Transportation). But how can I ignore them? If I ignore such small needs, they will lose faith in us even more."

Most of Uganda is quiet, and life goes on normally. The major danger seems to be in Karamoja, West Nile, and in the capital city of Kampala and its surrounding area. The war to overthrow Amin seriously affected only the southern towns, which were Amin's strongholds or were identified with his people: Mbarara, Masaka, Entebbe, Kampala, and Bombo. By the time the war reached Kampala, Amin was on the run. Shelling was limited to certain key buildings, such as the government printing office, with Parliament and the Ministries untouched. In the wake of any war, security is a problem. In Uganda, it has combined with a lack of trust to result in discouragement bordering on despondency in the capital city. Some gunfire occurs nearly every night, despite a curfew. There are several explanations of the shooting. First, some argue that the retreat of Amin's army left many arms for civilians to claim and that it is civilians who are shooting other civilians and taking what they want at night. The recent finding of a homemade bullet in a victim lends some credence to this view. Second, some believe that the underpaid Tanzanian soldiers, who guard Kampala by day, are robbing by night. Third, others feel that it is not random but organized terrorism. In particular, Baganda terrorists or revolutionaries are believed to be trying to undermine the current government. Fourth, an interesting theory during the fall of 1979 was that certain members of the UCC itself were behind the shooting, for the purpose of undermining the government in order to justify returning Obote to office. The majority opinion seems to be that soldiers and terrorists account for most of the shooting. More important, however, is the very existence of so many explanations and so many factions and divisions in the capital. Furthermore, the shooting itself, whatever its source, keeps security the number-one issue facing the new government. As one Ugandan expressed it: "Under Amin, we knew that if we did not have a profitable retail business, stayed away from the army's women, and said nothing political, we were safe. Now, danger is everywhere." The perception is, of course, considerably greater than the actual danger.

This comment introduces a further problem confronting Ugandans: their own discouragement and despair. The focus is, once again, in the city of Kampala, where factionalism is most evident and where economic inflation is rampant. Many Ugandans still do not think in terms of the nation but in terms of their own ethnic group: Baganda, Acholi, Banyankole, and so forth. Thus, with the defeat of Amin, each group expected its needs and desires to be fulfilled. The factionalism, which had been submerged by Amin's despotism, reemerged with a vengeance. This, coupled with the insecurity of life in the capital, has caused some to speak favorably of Amin's regime. In addition, the removal of Lule, however necessary some see it to have been, caused Western nations, such as Britain and the United States, to withhold aid until Uganda could get its own house in order. The withholding of aid has, of course, had the effect of impeding reconstruction even further, with the result that many Ugandans themselves doubt increasingly the ability of the current government to solve the country's multiple problems.

This mass discouragement likewise affects the dealings of individuals with each other. Joseph Kamisi, a school teacher, said that he is afraid to leave his car for repairs but must spend the day in the garage for fear that parts will be removed instead. Again, what matters is not whether his fear is totally grounded in fact but the fear itself. This crisis of confidence and trust is the interpersonal side of the coin of national insecurity.

A problem discussed at some length in other parts of this journal concerns the Ugandan economy. Inflation is rampant and the *magendo*, or black market, is ubiquitous and open. A bar of soap is Sh 45/; one egg is 11-12/; sugar can go as high as Sh 200/; toilet paper is 35-40/; and if one wants to buy furniture at a recently reopened shop in Kampala, it will cost Sh 20,000/ for a dining table with six chairs, 18,000/ for a couch and two chairs, or Sh 21,000/ for a large bedstead and mattress. More shops are open in downtown Kampala than a year ago, but prices are extremely high with respect to local salaries. There are shortages—some real, some fabricated by hoarding—and the *magendo* complicates everything. The exchange rate is still a Uganda shilling to a Kenya shilling officially, but on the black market one can get ten or more Uganda shillings for one. The devaluing of the currency to the black market rate has been proposed as a partial solution to this, but no one in power wants to take this unpopular step. Though some rural Ugandans are involved in *magendo*, it is, of course, primarily the urban poor who suffer from the inflation, since those with monetary connections outside the country can play *magendo*, while those in the rural areas can still (with exception of Karamoja) live off the land.

The Madhvanis and Mehtas, the two Asian industrial families that left the country in 1972, have returned, on the basis of joint ownership with the government of their industries. They are, however, finding it extremely difficult to get started, due to shortages of parts and machinery. As in parts of the economy, reconstruction moves slowly if at all. Even a reconstruction project like the rebuilding of the northern portion of Kampala road is viewed negatively by some, who see it as taking much too long and as financial exploitation by the Ugandans who have the contract to build the road.

A final problem of reconstruction concerns much of the infrastructure of urban life. The water supply has been down for long periods, making necessary the delivery of water in tank trucks, for a price. Electricity is off from time to time, roads need work, and the clean-up of garbage is being done with too few trucks. Here, as elsewhere, it sometimes seems as if a step forward is accompanied by two steps backward.

The Ugandan peoples have been known as achievers and problem-solvers, and this bodes well for the long-term future. Yet in the current situation they need leaders who are more concerned about the people and the nation than to "get what they can while they can." Those of us who have lived there look back with fondness at Uganda's recent past and continue to look for signs of hope for the immediate future. Currently, Uganda's signs are mixed. There is agricultural capability and traditional optimism, but at present these are overlain with factionalism, *magendo* and fiscal weakness, and urban insecurity.

NOTES

[1] For more on the history of Uganda prior to 1961 and the particular role of the Baganda in that history, see Apter 1967.

[2] Much of Obote's "move to the left" can be found in two 1970 documents: *The Common Man's Charter* and *The Nakivubo Pronouncements*.

[3] For an interesting interpretation of the coup as class based, rather than regionally or ethnically based, see Lofchie 1972, pp. 19-35. Another interpretation is found in Mittlemen 1971, pp. 184-202.

[4] *The Voice of Uganda* was previously called the *Uganda Argus*.

[5] Later, as Amin's support lessened, a favorite theme and basis for suppression were the "confusing voices" of dissent.

[6]Portions of this discussion are adapted for Adams 1979.

REFERENCES CITED

Adams, Bert. "After Idi Amin, Turmoil Persists." *Christian Science Monitor* (December 11, 1979): pp. 12-13.

Africa. "A Ugandan's Viewpoint." 27 (November 1973): 16-25.

Apter, David E. *The Political Kingdom in Uganda*. Princeton: Princeton University Press, 1967.

Hopkins, Elizabeth. "Racial Minorities in British East Africa." In Stanley Diamond and Fred G. Burke, eds., *The Transformation of East Africa*, pp. 83-153. New York: Basic Books, 1966.

Lofchie, Michael F. "The Uganda Coup—Class Action by the Military." *Journal of Modern African Societies* (10 May 1972): pp. 19-35.

Mazrui, Ali A. *Toward a Pax Africana*. Chicago: University of Chicago Press, 1967.

Mittleman, James H. "The Anatomy of a Coup: Uganda, 1971." *Africa Quarterly*, 10, 3 (October-December 1971): 184-202.

Rollow, Jonathan. "Uganda's Amin Economic Revolution." *Africa Report*, 19, 3 (May-June 1974): 36-38, 42.

Wallerstein, Immanuel. *Africa: The Politics of Independence*. New York: Vintage Books, 1961.

The Movements of National Liberation

Basil Davidson

Up till the early 1960s, these colonies that the Portuguese called 'provinces of Portugal' had all existed behind 'walls of silence' built by Portugal since the 1880s, and raised higher by the Salazar dictatorship of the *Estado Novo*. Little could be learned, outside those walls, about the African populations enclosed within them. The few critics who came from Portugal were banned or imprisoned. Other foreign visitors were businessmen or political supporters of the *Estado Novo*; a few exceptions, honest journalists or other investigators, were hounded by the colonial police as soon as their attitudes were known or even guessed.

Then, quite suddenly in 1974, as it seemed to people in the world outside, the walls were thrown down, the prisons opened, the light of day was let in, and the Portuguese colonial system removed from the scene. Following that overthrow of the *Estado Novo* and its fascist administration, all these peoples rapidly won their independence: first, Guinea-Bissau, then Mozambique and Cape Verde and São Tomé, and at last, after repelling a South African invasion, Angola. Practically from one year to the next, the strategic balance in crucial regions of the continent, especially in relation to the white racist regimes of the south, was changed in favour of all those trends that are identified with African emancipation.

Yet the change marked by this collapse of Portuguese colonialism was not really as rapid as it seemed to the world outside, nor was it at all sudden except in its last dramatic phases. It was the fruit of a long historical process. Many years were required to ripen that fruit, and then there had to be more than a decade of warfare against a most determined enemy. The outside world began to hear a little about that warfare late in the 1960s; but the warfare was only the 'outward and visible' sign of the process of ripening nationalism.

Developed in movements of national liberation—in Angola the Movimento de Libertação de Angola (MPLA), in Guinea-Bissau and Cape Verde the Partido Africano de Independência de Guiné e Cabo Verde (PAIGC), in Mozambique the Frente de Libertação de Moçambique (FRELIMO), and, after these, in São Tomé and Principe the Movimento de Libertação de São Tomé e Principe (MLSTP)—this process in Portugal's African colonies became an integral part of the flowering of nationalism in the whole continent.

But it became a part with special features of its own. These features are what give the movements in these countries their importance in modern African history. For they can be said to open a new chapter, point in a new direction, and mark a new approach to the problems of independence. They have been defined as the features of a revolutionary nationalism.

Why and how did this happen? What are we to understand, historically, by this move from one type of nationalism to another? Where does its lasting significance probably lie? This article discusses questions such as these.

5

Origins

In their beginnings, the nationalist movements here had no great difference in their hopes and calculations from nationalist movements in other colonies. If they were launched a little later than most nationalist movements in Africa, this was only because Portuguese colonial repression, Portuguese refusal to make even the smallest concessions to African demands, was stiffer than elsewhere, even much stiffer. News of what was happening in Ghana, Nigeria and some other colonies certainly slipped through the 'walls of silence' during the 1950s; but the Portuguese authorities heard it too, and responded by strengthening their police and filling their gaols.

Obliged to act illegally, the men and women who launched these movements still hoped that they could organise forms of pressure—illegal strikes, illegal demonstrations, illegal demands for political change—which could extract concessions, or, at least, could gradually reform some of the worst aspects of the Portuguese colonial system: aspects such as forced labour, the forced growing of export crops, the denial of all civic rights, and so on. At the same time they hoped that democratic world opinion would come to their aid in pressurising the Portuguese to move with the times. In all this, except in their total illegality, these movements acted at the start like most nationalist movements elsewhere, and with much the same objectives. They acted, in other words, to secure a *reform* of the colonial system, so that, little by little, their peoples could advance to political equality and therefore to self-rule by agreement with the colonial power.

But it didn't work. To each illegal strike, demonstration or political demand the Portuguese dictatorship replied with a greater repression than before. In doing so, of course, it reflected the fascist mentality of the *Estado Novo* which denied all democratic rights to the people of Portugal itself. But we should note that its stubbornness also reflected the condition of Portugal itself: above all, Portugal's social backwardness and poverty.

As early as the eighteenth century, Portugal had become a 'half colony' of much stronger imperialist powers, especially of Britain, and had in fact received its share in the colonial partition of Africa only thanks to British protection at the Berlin Congress of 1884–5. So Portuguese imperialism, as it developed through the late nineteenth and twentieth centuries, was really a 'sub-imperialism'. This was the central fact that steered Salazar's refusal to reform the Portuguese colonial system. He saw that Britain and France, even Belgium, might be strong enough to make political concessions and still retain great influence in their former colonies. But he argued that Portugal could not do this. If Portugal began to make concessions, then Portugal would be swept from the scene and its influence displaced by that of stronger powers. Putting this another way, 'sub-imperialist' Portugal could envisage nothing like a 'neo-colonial' solution. It had, Salazar believed, to keep all or lose all; and in trying to keep all, Salazar then discovered, Portugal's patrons in Western Europe and North America were in fact willing to give him their full support.

This conviction of Salazar's, and of those who ruled with him, did not come as a surprise to the men and women who pioneered the work of colonial liberation: notably Agostinho Neto, Lucio Lara and Mario de Andrade in Angola; Amílcar

6

1.1. The late Agostinho Neto (left), photographed in a guerrilla zone of eastern Angola in
1970

1.2. Aristides Pereira, secretary general of PAIGC (right) and Luiz Cabral (deputy secretary-
general), now Presidents respectively of Cape Verde and Guinea-Bissau

7

1.3. The late Amilcar Cabral (left) and his brother Luiz

Cabral, Aristides Pereira and Luiz Cabral in Guinea-Bissau; Eduardo Mondlane, Marcelino dos Santos and Samora Moises Machel in Mozambique; and their close companions in these territories, including women of distinction such as Déolinda de Almeida, Carmen Pereira and Jozina Machel. They had wanted to give every chance to peaceful forms of pressure; but they were not taken unawares when these all failed, and when protesters were met, increasingly, by the bullets of the colonial police.

They drew two conclusions from Portuguese colonial violence. Recalling these conclusions in 1969, Mondlane put them in this way:

> (We saw that) first, Portugal would not admit the principle of self-determination and independence, or allow for any extension of democracy under her own rule. . . . Secondly, moderate political action such as strikes, demonstrations and petitions, would result only in the destruction of those who took part in them. We were, therefore, left with these alternatives: to continue indefinitely living under a repressive imperial rule, or to find a means of using force against Portugal which would be effective enough to hurt Portugal without resulting in our own ruin.

It was the PAIGC that led the way in finding the answer to this problem: the means to use effective force against an unbending dictatorship. In August 1959 an illegal strike of dockers (but all strikes were illegal) organised by the PAIGC in Bissau, the capital of Portuguese Guinea as it was then called, was shot back to work with more than fifty dockers killed and many wounded. This was the last attempt by the PAIGC to operate a policy of peaceful pressure; any further attempts of that kind would result, all too obviously, only in the ruin of those who made them. A few weeks later, at a clandestine meeting in Bissau, the PAIGC leadership decided upon armed struggle as the only effective way ahead.

8

1.4. The late Eduardo Mondlane speaking at a FRELIMO Congress in 1968. His successor, Samora Machel, now President of Mozambique, can be seen seated right

The MPLA followed in 1961, and FRELIMO soon after its formation in 1962. With this, the challenge to colonial rule was clearly stated. But the question remained: how was the challenge to be met?

Development

Deciding to fight the colonial system by open warfare was one thing: doing it with success had to be quite another. Much courage and tenacity, they saw, would be required for that; but it was just as obvious to the pioneers that

9

1.5. Carmen Pereira, leading organiser of the Guinea-Bissau women's movement

courage and tenacity would never be enough. Other African peoples had abundantly displayed those qualities in wars of anti-colonial resistance; and the tale of their defeats was a long one. As well as courage and tenacity there would have to be an effective theory and practice: a policy and political programme, that is, capable of winning their peoples for an *active participation* in the struggle for liberation. There would have to be, in short, a politics of liberation capable of using warfare as a means of progress.

10

The movements evolved this politics of liberation. They evolved it gradually, making many mistakes, learning painfully from experience. They had to work out new ideas, invent new methods, practise new attitudes. In their guerrilla warfare they practised the techniques that were already known and possible: ambush, rapid movement, successive concentration and dispersal of fighting units, and the rest. In all this there was little or nothing that was new or original. What was new and original was their politics of liberation. It was above all their politics, not their warfare, which explains their eventually great success. This politics may be said to form their central contribution to continental history.

In the space we have here, let us briefly look at this politics in the case of the PAIGC. The politics practised by the MPLA and FRELIMO were in all essentials just the same.

When Amílcar Cabral launched the PAIGC in 1956, he had five companions upon whom he could entirely rely, and only five. For three years these worked at winning new members in Bissau and other small towns, and they had a little success. Yet they were still very few when they decided in 1959 to prepare for an armed struggle. Having decided that, they saw that all success would have to come from winning adherents in the countryside, where more than nine-tenths of the whole population lived. Yet the people of the countryside were at that time not in the least concerned with ideas about winning independence or building a nation. Those ideas meant nothing to them. They were concerned with quite other matters: how to get rid of local Portuguese officials, traders, tax-collectors; how to get better prices for their produce, and cheaper goods to buy; how to end forced labour and the forced growing of crops for Portuguese export companies. Cabral put it in this way when leading his followers into the work of persuading rural people that independence alone could start to solve their problems:

> Keep always in your mind that the people are not fighting for ideas, for the things in anyone's head. They are fighting to win material benefits, to live better and in peace, to see their lives go forward, to guarantee the future of their children.

And therefore the men and women of the PAIGC, the pioneers who began the work, must

> practise revolutionary democracy ... hold frequent meetings ... hide nothing from the masses of our people .. tell no lies ... claim no easy victories ...

All this was obviously going to be difficult; and yet it proved possible, it worked. Cabral taught his followers to make their way into the villages, find out what people in this or that village really thought and wanted, and explain just why the struggle for liberation could help them. And the young militants of the PAIGC, few of whom were over twenty-five and many younger, found that gradually they could win a hearing. They worked clandestinely in the villages. Otherwise they lived in the bush; and they lived hard, always in danger of arrest and death. They learned how to show that local grievances or demands were only part of a whole colonial situation, and that to change this situation it would

11

be necessary to work and fight, unitedly, to get rid of the system which had imposed it. In this way, the 'little words' about local grievances could gradually be joined to the 'big words' about independence and nationalism.

There came a time, around 1962, when the support and sympathy of village people began to develop into a readiness for active participation in the struggle. From this point onwards the movement began to acquire real substance. The armed struggle could be launched, in January 1963, with the assurance that wide masses of rural people would not only support it, or sympathise with it, but would also join it. And this participation, with the political work of explanation and persuasion continuing all the time, meant that the armed struggle could now begin and could eventually succeed.

Each of the movements had to fight a big colonial army raised by the Portuguese dictatorship and sent to Africa. Towards the end, when the dictatorship had mobilised everyone it could, these colonial armies became relatively enormous. If calculated on the basis of metropolitan populations, they were more than seven times' bigger than the biggest American army sent to Vietnam; and Portugal was having to spend about 45 per cent of its national budget on these wars they were fighting in Africa. This was where Portugal's allies came in. Only the continuous military and financial support of these allies in Western Europe and North America made it possible for Portugal to go on with this huge military effort. All the major Western powers and some of the minor ones in the North Atlantic Treaty Organisation (NATO) provided military aid, whether in arms, ammunition, equipment, bombing and fighter planes, napalm and defoliants.

On their side the liberation movements where helped by some African countries, by the Swedish Government and unofficial support groups in the Western countries, and above all by the USSR, Cuba and several other communist countries. But none of this aid could match the arms and equipment given to Portugal by its allies except, towards the end, in the matter of Soviet ground-to-air missiles to bring down bombing or fighter planes. These missiles were made available to the PAIGC only at the beginning of 1973, and then to the movements in Mozambique and Angola.

Yet the movements had one superiority which the Portuguese proved quite unable to match. This was their superiority in political thought and practice. Right to the end the Portuguese generals maintained a racist attitude to the Africans they were fighting, refusing to believe that such 'savages' could out-think as well as out-manoeuvre them. In this they followed not only their fascist mentality, but also the declared belief and policy of the Salazarist state. According to these, in the words of Salazar's right-hand man and brief successor, Marcelo Caetano, when lecturing at the University of Lisbon in 1954, 'the Africans are incapable of developing on their own the countries they have inhabited for thousands of years': because, Caetano continued, 'the Africans have never invented any useful technology, nor conquered anything for the benefit of mankind', so that 'the Africans must be treated as productive elements who are organised, or have to be organised, in an economy governed by whites'. Unable to practise the arts of peace, the Africans were therefore unable to practise those of war; and it only remained for Salazar's generals to prove it.

12

1.6. Part of an unexploded napalm canister dropped by the Portuguese on Guinea-Bissau and photographed the day afterwards

They failed to prove it. The Africans made rings round them. Applying their politics of liberation to the problems of armed struggle, the liberation movements worked out tactics and strategies which could enable them to win, even though the process of winning had to be long and painful. Starting out with small

13

guerrilla groups in favourable zones of bush or forest, they were able to build their forces to the point where large units could be formed: large units but also non-localised units, available for rapid movement over long distances, and capable of fighting wherever they were sent.

Assured of rural support and active help in the countryside, these mobile units grew in size and strength, learned the use of weapons requiring the measurement of range (even though nearly all the fighters were illiterate), and fought ever more effectively in combination with each other. In this way the guerrilla armies grew from a few hundred fighters to many thousands; but as they grew, so also did their political understanding, and, with that, their readiness to accept a tight discipline as well as the political and social programmes of their movements.

At this point, around the middle and late 1960s, each of the guerrilla armies was able to practise a strategy of rapid concentration and dispersal. Cabral explained it in this way:

> In order to dominate a given zone, the enemy is obliged to disperse his forces. In dispersing his forces, he weakens himself and we can defeat him. Then in order to defend himself against us, he has to concentrate his forces. When he does that, we can occupy the zones that he leaves free and work in them politically so as to hinder his return there.

And the Salazarist generals fell into the trap thus set for them. They used their very large armies to garrison a very large number of villages and small towns, as well as to drive very large numbers of rural people into 'protected camps', called *aldeamentos*, where, it was hoped, these people would be kept 'free from guerrilla infection'. This proved a vain hope. But only towards the end, in 1972 and later, did Salazar's generals turn to other tactics. They raised African commando units, highly trained and paid at privileged rates so as to buy their mercenary loyalty, and sent these commandos out in helicopters to raid the zones controlled by the movements. But these new tactics, though by no means ineffective, came too late to save Salazar's generals from defeat.

By the end of the 1960s a clear pattern had emerged. Though the Portuguese could hold the towns and certain adjacent areas, they could not clear the freedom fighters from the countryside. There the movements built large zones free from Portuguese control or influence. And in these zones, which they called 'liberated zones', the movements set about the further development of their politics of liberation. They made these zones the 'laboratories' in which they could test their theory and practice, and prepare for the time when the wars should be won.

Here it was, in the liberated zones, that the movements could begin to produce the first material benefits of liberation, and thereby enlarge the active participation of the rural masses. What were these benefits? They were of two kinds: negative and positive. On the side of negative benefits, the movements expelled all colonial officials and traders. They ended all colonial taxes and exactions. They abolished forced labour and the forced growing of crops. On the side of positive benefits, they set up a public trading system of their own, bringing in goods given them by their foreign friends and exchanging these for rural

14

produce. They founded bush schools and clinics where none had ever existed before, and staffed these with teachers and nurses drawn from trained men and women in their own ranks: trained, often, in Europe or in Cuba. Still more important for the future, they set about launching a democracy in the liberated zones. Village people were called on to elect representative committees, to which the movements assigned the responsibilities of local government.

So it came about that the independent states of the future were founded and were shaped in the liberated zones even while the wars continued. Peoples who had long governed themselves before the colonial period, and had then lost that right, now began to govern themselves again. Their history could begin once more: but a history launched now in a new direction suitable to living in the modern world. The structures of traditional forms of democracy were displaced by modern forms, embodied in representative committees at the 'grass roots' of society.

Achievements
When independence came in 1974–75, the movements were seen to have chalked up three major achievements.

First, on the military field, they had fought the armies of fascist Portugal to a standstill. Here and there they had defeated those armies outright: the PAIGC, for example, practically destroyed the Portuguese air force in Guinea-Bissau after they got the use of ground-to-air missiles. General Costa Gomes, the Portuguese Chief of Staff, summed it up in May 1974. Speaking in Mozambique, he

1.7. Aristides Pereira, secretary-general of the PAIGC, declaring Guinea-Bissau's independence in September 1973, a year before the war with Portugal ended

15

said that: 'Our armed forces have reached the limits of neuro-psychological exhaustion.' More bluntly, the fascist armies had had enough.

Secondly, on the political field, the influence of the ideas of liberation had thrust their way through the fortifications of the Portuguese, and begun to work on the hearts and minds of the men in the Portuguese armed forces, winning a sufficient number of these to the cause of overthrowing the Salazar regime. Under the slogan of 'Decolonisation and Democratisation', this overthrow was carried out in April 1974 by young officers of a semi-secret organisation called the Armed Forces Movement (AFM). Many had fought in Africa, where they had come under the influence of the ideas of liberation. Just how far this was the case may be seen in a striking example which I will quote here. On 29 July 1974, the officers' assembly of the AFM in Guinea-Bissau met in the central barracks of Bissau, and issued the following statement, passed unanimously:

> The colonised peoples and the people of Portugal are allies. The struggle for national liberation has contributed powerfully to the overthrow of fascism, and, in large degree, has laid at the base of the Armed Forces Movement, whose officers have learned in Africa the horrors of a fruitless war, and have therefore come to understand the roots of the evils which afflict the society of Portugal . . ..

So the 'savages' despised by Salazar's generals had turned the tables on their oppressors in a double sense. They had defeated those oppressors in Africa. But they had defeated them in Europe as well.

Thirdly, and again on the political field, the movements had used their warfare as the servant of their politics: and in such a way, as we have seen above, that democratic states were able to come to birth even while the wars continued. And here we reach another aspect of this story, an aspect of increasing interest since the wars ended. It is the aspect which I have referred to, at the beginning of this article, as marking a new approach to the problems of independence: the aspect which they themselves define as revolutionary nationalism.

Faced with Portugal's refusal to make any concessions to equality or progress, the movements had been obliged to go to war. Having gone to war, they could win only on one condition. This was that they first of all won the participation of the rural masses. But to win that participation they had to prove to the rural masses that the struggle for liberation—for independence, for national identity—was really worth the sacrifices it called for. We have seen how they set about doing that: by their courage and tenacity but also, and even more, by their politics of liberation: by ensuring both negative and positive gains for the populations of the liberated zones.

New states began to take shape in the liberated zones. But these embryonic states were entirely different from the states of the colonial system. They were democratic in structure, egalitarian in concept, and constructed so as to hinder the re-emergence of self-appointed ruling groups of 'privileged elites'. They were not modifications of the colonial state brought about by reform: on the contrary, they were the product of a revolutionary destruction of the colonial state. Nothing less in their circumstances could have led to success. The rural masses

16

1.8. FRELIMO leader Samora Machel addressing village people in Tete province

rallied to the movements because the politics of liberation gave power and primacy to the rural masses. That was the secret of these victories.

But once they had won their victories, the movements could have no intention of going into reverse. On the contrary, their task as they saw it when the wars were over was to continue in peacetime what they had begun in war. The problems would be different. In many ways the problems would be more difficult. But the solutions, essentially at least, would be the same. Power and primacy should continue to pass to the masses of ordinary people. These should continue to be helped to master the problems of power by extending and improving their structures of representation. Old or new forms of personal exploitation should continue to be fought against and steadily removed. New systems of economic life should be raised against all forms of collective or public exploitation. Democratic networks of education should be built. Public health services should concentrate on preventive rather than curative medicine. Dignity and an independent self-respect should rule the day. There should be happiness.

Such are the policies and attitudes of mind with which these movements have carried their peoples out of the colonial system. They could not avoid the bitterness of war. But they have not allowed that bitterness to cloud the peace they have won. They have put that bitterness behind them. And this, we may agree, is another of their achievements: and not perhaps the least.

17

For further reading

The following is a short list of introductory works in English or French; most have extensive bibliographies. They refer chiefly to the main colonial period and the struggles for liberation.

General

BOXER, C. R., *Race Relations in the Portuguese Colonial Empire, 1415–1825*, Clarendon, Oxford, 1963.

DUFFY, JAMES, *Portuguese Africa*, Harvard, 1959.

— — *Portugal in Africa*, Penguin, London 1962.

FERREIRA, E. DE S., *Portuguese Colonialism in Africa*, UNESCO, 1974.

Angola and São Tomé

BENDER, GERALD J., *Angola Under The Portuguese*, Heinemann, London, 1978.

DAVIDSON, BASIL, *In the Eye of The Storm: Angola's People*, Longman, 1972; Penguin, London 1975.

HEIMER F.-W. (ed.), *Social Change in Angola*, Weltforum, Munich, 1973 (in English).

PÉLISSIER, R., *Les Guerres Grises: Résistance et Révoltes en Angola (1845–1941)*, Pélissier, Montamets (France), 1977.

— — *La Colonie du Minotaur: Nationalismes et Révoltes en Angola (1926–1961)*, Pélissier, Montamets (France), 1977.

WHEELER, D. L. and PÉLISSIER, R., *Angola*, Pall Mall, London, 1971.

Cape Verde

CABRAL, AMILCAR, *Unity and Struggle* (Collected Writings), Heinemann, London, 1979.

CARREIRA, A., *Migrations from the Cape Verde Islands*, trans. and ed. C. Fyfe, forthcoming.

Guinea-Bissau

CABRAL, AMILCAR, *Unity and Struggle* (Collected Writings), Heinemann, London, 1979.

DAVIDSON, BASIL, *The Liberation of Guiné*, Penguin, London, 1969; new and enlarged edition, Zed, London, 1980.

RUDEBECK, LARS, *Guinea-Bissau*, Scandinavian Inst. of African Studies, Uppsala, 1974 (in English).

Mozambique

ISAACMAN, ALLEN F., *Mozambique*, Madison, 1972.

— — *The Tradition of Resistance in Mozambique*, Heinemann, London 1974.

MONDLANE, EDUARDO, *The Struggle for Mozambique*, Penguin, London, 1969.

18

MACHEL, SAMORA, *Mozambique: Sowing the Seeds of Revolution*, Mozambique Information Office, 34 Percy Street, London WC1, 1974.
— *Establishing People's Power*, Tanzania Publishing House, Dar es Salaam, 1977.
SPENCE, C. F., *Moçambique*, Bailey and Simpson, London, 1963.
For recent information, see *People's Power*, the quarterly journal of the Mozambique Angola Guinea Information Centre, 34 Percy Street, London, WC1.

19

Note de Recherche / Research Note

The Revolution in Portugal's African Colonies :
A Review Essay*

John S. SAUL**

INTRODUCTION

The coup in Portugal and the subsequent movement towards the independence of that country's three erstwhile colonies has served finally to underscore for all, what more knowledgeable observers have understood for some years – that the black challenge to white minority rule in Southern Africa is of great depth and seriousness and that, ultimately, it can and will succeed. Perhaps, in consequence, we will see less in future of the kind of academic superciliousness which has dictated that the bland and mis-leading – but "objective" – analyses of conservative writers be granted greater credence in Africanist circles than the writings of committed and activist – hence "non-objective" – writers ! For as several of the books to be examined here demonstrate, much was known about "Portuguese Africa" – long before last year's dramatic coup – which "informed opinion" in western countries (including Canada) chose, quite simply, to ignore. Nor have books such as those by Minter, Davidson and Cornwall, even though written prior to the coup, been altogether outstripped by events. There remain lessons to be learned from a careful examination of the struggle which has taken place in Guinea-Bissau, Mozambique and Angola – lessons relevant not only to the future of these three societies as they move to chart their post-colonial futures, but lessons which are also relevant to the continuing struggle for liberation which now escalates in Zimbabwe/Rhodesia, in Namibia and in South Africa itself. To some of these lessons we shall turn in this essay.

I

In an admirably clear, if somewhat abbreviated form William Minter's *Portuguese Africa and the West* provides an exemplary overview of the situation which made Portuguese Africa a forcing-house for revolution. The three major sets of actors are

---

* William Minter, *Portuguese Africa and the West* (Penguin, Harmondsworth, 1972) ; new edition, with a fresh postscript entitled "The Nixon Doctrine : What Rôle for Portugal," published by Monthly Review Press. New York, 1974 ; Basil Davidson, *In the Eye of the Storm* (Doubleday, New York, 1972) ; Barbara Cornwall, *The Bush Rebels* (Holt, Rinehart and Winston, New York, 1972) ; Richard Gibson, *African Liberation Movements* (Oxford University Press, London and New York, 1972).

** Atkinson College, York University. Toronto.

present and well accounted for in his volume : Portugal itself, those western interests, state and corporate, which became its allies in empire, and the African people of the colonies – seen, primarily, as they came to organize themselves for successful struggle within their own liberation movement. For present-day purposes it is perhaps fortunate that Minter's major emphasis is on the western – and especially American – interests which have been implicated in Portugal's African wars. Since these interests are very far from having disappeared from the scene in post-coup Southern Africa, the continuing relevance of the book is underscored. But Minter also provides a thumb-nail sketch of Portuguese "ultra-colonialism, " a phenomenon which is even now of more than historical interest if only because of the nature of the African opposition – profoundly more radical than that which emerged elsewhere in colonial Africa – to which it has given rise. As we shall see, the pattern of development of the several impressive popular movements which have liberated the Portuguese colonies cannot be understood outside an analysis of the peculiarly intransigeant colonialism they were forced to confront. In addition, there is a second reason of almost equal importance for our continuing interest : it is precisely the blighted legacy of the colonial experience – Portugal's warping of the Guinean, Mozambican and Angolan economies in particular – which now defines the enormous challenges confronting these same liberation movements as they come to power. Consequently, it seems appropriate to say something further about Portugal in Africa here.

For the Portuguese record was a particularly grisly one, even when measured against the flagrant racism and blunt exploitation which has marked other colonialisms on the African continent. Its history stretches back to the fifteenth century when Portuguese ships first began to touch the African coastline and forward, through the brutalities of the slave trade, to a twentieth century pattern of forced labour and entrenched hostility to African demands for self-determination even at a time when other colonial powers were granting formal independence to their own African colonies. It was Perry Anderson who first described this record as being one of "ultra-colonialism" – "at once the most *primitive* and the most *extreme* form of colonialism" – and traced its roots to the peculiar character of Portugal's own status as an imperial power. [1] For Portugal itself is a poor, underdeveloped country, and for centuries has been as much a colony of stronger countries, most notably Britain, as it has been a colonizer in its own right. More recently, it was to become the associate of others – of the United States, of West Germany and of South Africa – and one of the chief merits of Minter's account is to trace in great detail the nature of these links. But Portugal's own record, its refusal to yield for so long to the tide of recent history and to the just demands of the peoples under its colonial sway, remains worthy of careful analysis.

It is true that the Portuguese first came to Africa as early as the fifteenth century, but for a very long time their presence was mainly confined to the coastline, with occasional sallies into the interior to bolster trading network or to set one tribe against another in the interest of strengthening their own hand – a policy of "divide-and-rule" which the Portuguese pursued, though with diminishing success, to the 1970s. For much of this period the economic key was the slave-trade which continued within the Portuguese empire until 1869. It has been estimated that the Congo-Angolan states lost over 7 000 000 people during four and a half centuries to this cruel traffic, including most of the 3 600 000 who wound up in Brazil. The record of this trade,

---

1. Perry Anderson, "Portugal and the End of Ultra-Colonialism," *New Left Review*, nos. 15–17 (1962), Part II, p. 97.

which was only marginally less horrific in Mozambique on the east coast, should itself have been sufficient to undermine Portugal's claims to a "civilizing mission" in Africa. But Portuguese exploitation of their African wards did not end with the conclusion of the slave trade.

Instead, the framework of further exploitation was to be provided by outright occupation and the institutions of formal colonialism. Thus it was not until the latter part of the 19th century that Portugal finally moved to consolidate its grip in Africa, and then under the threat of its eclipse as a colonial power by other, even more active and effective, imperialisms. Then, while Africa was being carved up by Britain, Germany, France and the rest, the territorial boundaries which now demarcate Angola, Mozambique and Guinea were blocked out. At that time, too, Portugal finally began to bring the African population to heel in all corners of these territories – with characteristic ruthlessness and against bitter resistance. Indeed, it was only in 1913 in Angola, the 1920s in Mozambique and 1936 in Guinea that African resistance can be said to have been at last crushed, a fact conveniently forgotten by recent apologists for Portugal who have spoken of that country's 500 year "presence" in Africa. Moreover, by these late dates there were already stirring those territorial-wide nationalisms which came to present an even more effective challenge to Portuguese hegemony than such early, dramatic, but often localized resistance to the imposition of colonial rule. It is the liberation movements which, in giving effective expression to this new nationalist consciousness, have now brought to a close the Portuguese chapter in Africa.

We shall return to a discussion of the rise of African nationalism and of the liberation movements. Here we must note that even as Portuguese colonial rule was being thus established at bayonet point, the particular character of Portuguese domination was reaffirmed : "Portuguese colonial policy to this day has been moulded by the early patterns of slavery, trade and pacification." [2] As noted, this policy in turn owed a great deal to Portugal's own poverty and underdevelopment. From a very early point in the modern era, Portugal had developed a relationship with the rest of Europe whereby it supplied raw materials to advanced countries, and imported manufactured goods. Typical of this pattern was the Treaty of Methuen which, in 1703, granted Portugal entry for its wine into the British market while Britain, in return, received privileged entry for its textiles. Through such a network of relationships, surpluses reaped in the colonies, including gold from Brazil, merely passed through Portugal and were, in effect, accumulated and put to productive use in Britain and other parts of Western Europe. While these latter countries then experienced industrial revolutions, Portugal remained under the domination of an old-fashioned landed oligarchy, linked to the Church and the military, and hostile to the emergence of an independent and effective capitalist class. The country became a stagnant, quasi-feudal backwater.

This meant that the form of liberal democracy whose development accompanied the further evolution of capitalism in many parts of Western Europe and North America did not take root in Portugal. Evidence for this is provided by the convulsive and short-lived history of the Portuguese republic, in existence only between 1910 and 1926. Fascism was more successful : in 1925 the military overthrew the Republic and, shortly thereafter, dictator Antonio Salazar came to power. His *Estado Novo* – New State – was a corporate state, setting itself firmly against "modernism" and democratic trends. In its broad outlines the Salazarist system remained entrenched under Salazar's successor, Marcelo Caetano right up to the day of the coup. Accordingly,

---

2. Ruth First, *Portugal's Wars in Africa* (International Defense and Aid, London, 1971), p. 2.

elections are rigidly controlled and carefully orchestrated, trade unions are government sponsored and most forms of dissent are ruthlessly crushed by a highly developed network of political police. The liberation movements in Africa were never to lose sight of the fact that in Portugal itself most Portuguese also suffered under an oppressive, dictatorial regime and the support which they were eventually to receive from popular forces within Portugal in the wake of the 1974 coup amply demonstrated the wisdom of this perception.

However, it was in the colonies that the logic of oppression worked itself out most relentlessly. All colonialisms have used some measure of constraint to pitch-fork Africans into the labour force, particularly during the initial stages of colonial rule. But the impact of dynamic economies like those of Britain and France was dramatic. In their colonies, pre-capitalists patterns were eroded, and soon the lure of economic incentives began to replace this initial application of force in providing the colonialists with necessary manpower. Not so with Portugal. As Anderson has noted,

> the most notorious single feature of the Portuguese African colonies is their systematic use of forced labour. It is this which immediately identifies the Portuguese variant of colonialism as against all others.

The infamous decree of 1875, defining labour policy, was little more than an attempts to guarantee retention of the master-slave relationship despite the formal abolition of slavery. And this attempt has lain at the heart of Portuguese practice to the present-day. A decree of 1899 captures the characteristic tone of Portuguese legislation on the subject :

> all natives of Portuguese overseas provinces are subject to the obligation, moral and legal, of attempting to obtain through work the means that they lack to subsist and to better their social condition.

Over the years an entire range of techniques were found to accomplish these ends : correctional and obligatory labour, contract labour and, of course, "voluntary labour," the latter entered into under the threat of punishment if an able-bodied man were found to be "idle." Even when Africans were left on the land, as in the cotton-growing areas of Northern Mozambique, enforced cultivation has been the rule rather than the exception ; in these cases, the price structure also was manipulated against the African cultivator, enabling the colonial government to skim off most of the proceeds from such production. Small wonder that in 1954 Marcelo Caetano could summarize the philosophy underlying Portuguese colonial practice in the following succinct manner :

> the natives of Africa must be directed and organized by Europeans but are indispensable as auxiliaries. The blacks must be seen as productive elements organized, or to be organized, in an economy directed by whites.

To be sure, some marginal adjustments were made in this system in recent years : slightly higher wages, the removal of some of the most glaringly anomalous legal compulsions from the statute books. But the essential nature of the colonial economy is clear. The overall system worked to press Africans into the economic service of the Portuguese, of the South Africans (who draw labour from Mozambique in particular) and of those multinational corporations which operated in the colonies. Moreover

> the violence it (forced labour) introduces into the society is a contagion... it settles on everything and deforms it. In the end, violence tends to coincide with the very notion of social relations themselves. [3]

---

3. Anderson, *op. cit.*

All colonialisms exploit African labour, Portugal's more than most ; this in itself provided sufficient reason for militant resistance to the continuance of foreign rule. But there has been a second, equally fundamental, aspect of the colonial impact which must be discussed. For all colonialisms also warp the African economies which they touch in another way, by imposing upon these economies a subservient position in the world economy. From this position of dependence springs economic activity which serves first and foremost the needs and interests of the colonizer, rather than meeting the long-term requirements of the colonized territory for its own sustained transformation. Colonial economies are forced to produce raw materials for the "mother-country," with their lines of communication all directed outwards to the sea instead of facilitating the kind of internal economic links which might trigger off real development. Under such circumstances, too, capital is accumulated primarily in the metropolitan centre and full-fledged industrialization is facilitated only there.

In recent years, of course, radical economists have come to see this continuing pattern of dependence and subordination, rather than merely the shortfalls of technology and capital emphasized by more conventional economic theories, as being the major constraint upon economic transformation in the "Third World". It is this pattern, in fact, which Andre Gunder Frank and others have spoken of as guaranteeing only the further "development of underdevelopment." The liberation movements are themselves well aware of this reality ; just such an insight has been one of the elements which has lent urgency to their demands and which has given them an increasingly revolutionary character. Amilcar Cabral, leader of the struggle in Guinea-Bissau until his untimely assassination at the hands of Portuguese agents, summarized this point succinctly :

> we therefore see that both in colonialism and in neo-colonialism the essential charac-
> teristics of imperalist domination remain the same : the negation of the historical
> process of the dominated people by means of violent usurpation of the freedom of
> development of the national productive forces.

The conclusion which he drew from this analysis is equally significant :
> if we accept that national liberation demands a profound mutation in the process of
> development of the productive forces, we see that this phenomenon of *national
> liberation* necessarily corresponds to a *revolution.* [4]

At stake, quite literally, was the right of Africans in "Portuguese Africa" *to make their own history* – politically, culturally, economically.

In the meantime, the "development of underdevelopment" in Portugal''s African colonies continued, a pattern most evident in Mozambique where the two main sources of territorial revenue continue to be the remittances of Mozambicans recruited to work on the mines elsewhere in Southern Africa (particularly in South Africa itself, through the Vitwatersrand Native Labour Association), and revenues from the carrying-trade between South Africa and Rhodesia and the sea. In addition, Mozambique's exports are all agricultural : cashew nuts, sugar, tea, sisal. There has been little chance that a balanced and self-sustaining development effort could arise from such a situation. Angola, forced into a similar mould was even more lucrative for the Portuguese, its trade providing much of the revenue which financed the Portuguese war machine. Coffee was crucial, the major earner from Portugal's African colonies, but minerals became increasingly important, diamonds joined by iron ore and, especially, oil. Finally, in Guinea it was the trade, carefully controlled and milked by the Portuguese,

---

4. Amilcar Cabral, "The Weapon of Theory," in *Revolution in Guinea* (London, 1969).

in groundnuts, palm kernels and vegetable oils which built similar distortions into that economy – though in the Guinea case this pattern began to be undermined some years ago by the liberation of a large proportion of the territory and its coming under the soon-to-be proclaimed Republic of Guinea-Bissau.

Sometimes this colonial pattern serviced Portuguese industrialization at the expense of the colonies ; thus cotton from Mozambique and Angola was processed by Portugal's textile industry, and returned (like some other Portuguese manufactures) to a protected market in Africa. But more often the effective economic links have been with more advanced capitalist centres, Portugal reaping its benefits – foreign exchange earnings from coffee sales abroad, for example – by playing a virtual middle-man's rôle in the outside world. If anything, this pattern intensified in recent years, the stepping up of expropriation by foreign firms of non-replenishable resources (the iron ore and oil just mentioned) represented not only a virtual theft from the African population of their birthright but also another way for the Portuguese to gain a middle-man's profit – this time from capital inflows and from royalties, profits tax and rents. The huge hydro-electric schemes at Cunene in Angola and Cabora Bassa in Mozambique were equally directed outward, representing once again a "violent usurpation of the freedom of development of the national productive forces." For these schemes were designed primarily to service the emergy needs of South Africa and Rhodesia, and involved vast commitments of resources by the Portuguese to a particular pattern of economic policy and economic change for the future which in all probability would not have chosen by the Africans themselves.

This was the underlying economic reality. Caetano's statement, quoted earlier, demonstrated the Portuguese long-time rationale for the existence of such a relationship between Portuguese and African in the colonies. However, this was not a particularly attractive rationale. More often the Portuguese tried to tell a different story, saying that, unlike other colonialisms, they are working toward the unified and multi-racial society of the future. In fact, this became a part of the whole myth of imperial destiny which played so prominent a part in Portuguese rhetoric ; it also informed the doctrine of "luso-tropicality" developed to prove that the Portuguese had a peculiar vocation for "working with" different races in other corners of the world. Yet, even if it were true that the fanatical extremism on the race question which marks South Africa's ideology of *apartheid* was not quite so prominent in "Portuguese Africa," the Portuguese approach was actually no less insidious. It constituted an ugly paternalism which looked only to the "assimilation" into the Portuguese community of those few Africans who could become as much like the Portuguese as possible.

Prior to the 1960s this approach was actually enshrined in law. An African could become an "assimilado" by passing the requisite language examination, earning a certain income, paying a fee (even though no such barriers to citizenship were placed before the often-illiterate Portuguese settlers coming to Africa). Needless to say, the vast mass of the African population were to be classified instead as "indigenatos" – natives. In the glare of world opinion in the sixties, this distinction was quietly dropped, but the underlying premises remained the African population was by definition "un-civilized," their cultures worthless, there aspirations, insofar as they deviated from the desire to become "honorary whites" (in the phrase of FRELIMO's late president, Dr. Eduardo Mondlane), to be considered aberrant. Moreover, even if one were to overlook, for the moment, the racist premises underlying the very notion of assimilation, certain figures were revealing : by the 1950s the *assimilado* category encompassed only 30 000 of the African population in Angola and in Mozambique 5 000, or .007%

186

of the African population ! Thus Portuguese colonialism, poverty-stricken as it was, neither would nor could provide the amount of education necessary to realize even its professed aims of assimilation – let alone provide the level of literacy and range of skills which would allow the African population to develop itself. So much for the myth of multi-racialism. So much, too, for those other adjustments of the 50s and 60s by means of which the colonies were even more directly linked to Portugal as "overseas provinces," becoming an integral part, it was argued, of the Portuguese state. Manipulative formulae all, continuing evidence of the doomed Portuguese attempt to have their presence in Africa both ways – privileged exploiter and helpmate to the African. A much more accurate indication of their true position *vis-à-vis* the African population was, of course, their violent and contemptuous rejection of those African demands for self-determination which came to the fore during this same period.

We return by this route, to an earlier question : why did Portugal, alone of the traditional colonial powers in Africa and unlike Britain, France, Belgium and even Spain, grimly hang on to its colonies against the seeming tide of history and the mounting demands of the people in those colonies ? Our analysis suggests an answer to this query, albeit a complex one. Most important, perhaps, was Portugal's continued economic weakness. Other imperial countries could hope to maintain their powerful voice in the affairs of their former colonies even after the granting of formal political independence. This is the so-called "neo-colonial solution" and is best exemplified by the fate of the former French colonies, most of which France continues to dominate to the present day more than ten years after independence. But, as Minter states,

> such influence depends on economic power : the ability to provide aid ; to control enterprises through technicians as well as investment ; to maintain good trade relationships by pressure on susceptible governments ; to support with open or covert action the removal of governments that prove troublesome.

In contrast, it was only its direct hold on the lever of power in the colonies – upon the colonial state – that enabled Portugal to profit from the economic exploitation of Angola, Mozambique and Guinea – by claimed a percentage of the action, as it were. Even were a "false decolonization" to produce a very pliant and subservient African government in any of these territories, such a gouvernment would most likely deal directly with the strongest of economic powers – with South Africa, with the United States, with West Germany, and the like – rather than with Portugal. Under such circumstances, Portugal would be deprived of even those benefits attendant upon the middle-man's rôle which it has claimed for itself. In consequence, the granting of independence seemed a much more costly option to Portugal's rulers than it did for other colonial powers.

In addition, there are other, non-economic, factors which can be mentioned, the political realities of Portugal for example. That country was, of course, an overtly authoritarian society. In consequence, not only was it difficult to theorize a logic of freedom for the colonies in Black Africa, but also potentially dangerous to consider establishing a democratic precedent there. The Portuguese people might then have been encouraged to intensify their parallel demands for self-determination in Portugal itself ! There was also a third, cultural-ideological, factor. Authoritarian regimes are particularly in need of myths to legitimize their continuing usurpation of power both to themselves and to others. History decreed that Portugal's myth should be that of empire, "luso-tropicality" and mission. The constant reiteration of such slogans suggests the extent to which they provided a certain glue for the system ; they could not, for that very reason, be readily re-evaluated by the powers-that-be. It is even possible that some of the rulers had come to believe them themselves.

Of course, the coup in Portugal has since demonstrated the importance of these latter points : the retreat from colonialism did indeed involve a complete overthrow of the Portuguese system domestically. But for a very long time there was little reason to anticipate any such denouement. As the liberation movements developed their critique of colonialism they saw that the mould of Portuguese colonialism was not about to crack from within in any significant respect. Despite some real costs, the ugly and anachronistic use of systematic violence to shore up racism and colonialism continued in Portugal's African colonies and, from the African perspective, seemed likely to do so until the perpetrators of that violence were forceably driven from the field. This in turn was the task that the liberation movements in Angola, Mozambique and Guinea-Bissau, reluctantly but resolutely, set for themselves.

Unfortunately, it was equally apparent that the liberation movements would have to fight not merely Portugal but also that country's powerful allies. At first, at the outset of the liberation struggles, the pattern was not quite so clear-cut. Thus there were early indications that western governments, perhaps even South Africa itself, could have swallowed the notion of black governments coming to power in an independent Angola or Mozambique. Indeed the United States, particularly in the very earliest days of the Kennedy Administration, seemed to be actively pressing for decolonization of Portugal's African colonies (this on the then current assumption that quite moderate and pliable black governments would inherit power, of course). But the intransigeance of the Portuguese, analyzed earlier, made any such smooth transition to neo-colonialism impossible. It became necessary for the Kennedy team and subsequent administrations to accommodate themselves to Portugal's position and even to cultivate an active partnership with that country. And his arrangement in turn became all the more attractive as the liberation movements themselves were radicalized and developed into much less certain guarantors of some future "false decolonization."

As Minter makes quite clear, the twin pillars of such western support for Portugal were the existing networks of western defense, notably the NATO alliance, without which Portugal could not have sustained its expensive military effort on three fronts, *and* the prevailing pattern of trade and investment. The economic link, in particular, merits some further comment here. As noted above, Portugal's position in the imperial hierarchy had granted it the status of a mere "middle-man" with respect to Angola, Mozambique and Guinea. Indeed, the threatened loss of this status was one of the most important reasons for Portugal's reluctance to seek a "neo-colonial" solution and to begin the dismantling of the structure of formal colonialism. In so characterizing Portugal as an "imperial middle-man" we refer not merely to its ability to earn from the export of African primary products (and African labour) to the outside world. Portugal has also forged a historical partnership with other western interests in carrying out colonial designs right inside the African territoires themselves. This is not surprising when one remembers that foreign capital has dominated a large proportion of the productive sectors of Portugal's own domestic economy. Similarly, from a early date, Portugal "contracted out" a range of colonial economic activities, including numerous large estates in Mozambique – the British-owned Sena Sugar Estate, for example – and Angolan enterprises like the Benguela Railway and the Angolan Diamond Company (Diamang).

To be sure, under Salazar's "New State" Portuguese policy reflected an uneasiness with such a state of affairs ; the government actually mounted a vigorous effort to counter these trends by sealing Africa off for Portuguese enterprise, restricting foreign investment (other than that from Portugal !) in the colonies and placing highly restrictive tariffs upon foreign imports. But this attempt did not survive the rise of the African challenge to colonialism. Reversing its position in the early 60s, Portugal encouraged the flow of foreign capital into the African colonies, intending not only to reap economic benefits from the fresh supply of capital and revenues, but also to tie these large foreign companies, and ultimately their home governments, into an even more vigorous defense of the Portuguese position in Africa.

> Today the foreign firm is given guarantees... better than the potential investor from Portugal itself, such as guarantees for the repatriation of capital, profits and dividends, and customs exemptions on plant and raw materials. [5]

To a very late date this tactic worked well. To take but a single example, it was precisely in such realities as the active rôle of Germany's Krupp empire in the exploitation of Angola's Cassinga iron deposits that one will find the roots of Chancellor Willy Brandt's tortuous pre-coup formulation (trotted out when countering the excessive zeal for liberation expressed by some officials in his own Social Democratic Party) :

> The Federal Government can not back the Portuguese point of view that Angola and Mozambique are one indivisible entity with Portugal. However, this is an internal problem of our ally Portugal, a problem which we must not interfere with !

In agriculture, in mineral extraction, and in the light industrialization of the colonies one soon saw busily at work a full range of corporations from western countries, from Japan, and, of course, from Rhodesia and South Africa (the latter country also being deeply involved in those aforementioned huge and menacing hydro-electric projects – Cunene and Cabora Bassa in Angola and Mozambique respectively). Most ominous of all, perhaps, was the growing economic involvement of the United States, dramatically exemplified in the absolutely crucial rôle played by the Gulf Oil Company which by 1973 was draining off almost 150 000 barrels of oil per day from Cabinda in Angola. Not only were the Portuguese thus furnished with vital revenues, but the white Southern African redoubt as a whole was being given a safe source of potential oil supply for facing down any further sanctions or oil blockade. Moreover, as Minter demonstrates, the involvement of American corporations stretched beyond gulf to companies such as Bethlehem Steel, which was, at one point, developing concessions right within the battle areas of Mozambique.

It seemed clear that the activities of these corporations provide particularly important reasons why United States' backing for Portugal intensified in recent years. In fact Richard Barnett, citing this and other evidence of growing American military and economic support for Portugal in a 1972 survey of American policy towards Southern Africa, could conclude that

> ...the United States (under the rhetoric of containing violence and preventing war) now appears ready to step up its assistance to the minority racist and colonial governments in beating back challenges to their rule. [6]

This is also a reality which Minter explores with great care in the post-script to the second edition of *Portuguese Africa and the West*.

Needless to say, it is now clear that this entire structure of domination was much less stable than it sometimes appeared. Minter presents its major weakness clearly

---

5. First, *op. cit.*, p. 26.
6. Richard Barnett, "Nixon's Plan to Save the World," *New York Review of Books*, November 16, 1972.

– the fact that the liberation movements were too strong to be defeated militarily. This was an insight which General Antonio de Spinola – sometime military governor of Guinea-Bissau (where he master-minded the assassination of Amilcar Cabral) and ultimately an important actor in the post-coup drama in Portugal – came to share, as witnessed in his book, *Portugal and His Future*. In that volume, published early in 1974, Spinola brought out into the open the military weakness of the Portuguese position, counselling instead a political solution – one which would judiciously Africanize colonialism and manipulate federal formulae to a point where a line against genuine liberation might more easily be held.

It was also apparent that, in so arguing, he spoke for a broader constituency. Perhaps it is here – with, to be sure, the benefit of hindsight – that Minter's book can be most easily faulted. For he gives too little sense of the growing contradictions within Portugal itself. There a measure of economic development found many important Portuguese trusts increasingly orienting themselves towards Europe and the E.E.C., while also regretting the costs to "economic rationality" of an anachronistic fascist system at home and those wasting colonial wars abroad. Not for nothing had Spinola been a director of the powerful Champalimaud group! Simultaneously, social and economic change and a continuing state of war (involving massive conscription) had also undermined the acceptance of their lot by broader masses of the people – one important manifestation of this dissatisfaction being the large-scale migration of workers to neighbouring European countries. In these and other ways crucial props for the Portuguese system were being eaten away. When younger officers than Spinola pushed the regime it came toppling down.

Of course, no one could have predicted what was to follow. Spinola, now brought into the junta in order to legitimate the April coup as well as provide a symbol of moderation for Portuguese trusts and western interests alike, sought to contain the situation. Until his unceremonious departure from power in September he worked not only to slow down the pace of events at home but also to find the key to a neo-colonial solution for Portugal in the colonies. Unfortunately for Spinola, however, a combination of developments – including the further revelation of a radical vocation on the part of the Armed Forces Movement (which had spear-headed the coup) and a release of popular energies beyond anything expected by even the most sanguine observers confounded these aspirations. None of which is to argue that the situation has permanently clarified itself in Portugal. There a struggle is certainly on-going. What does seem to have happened, however, is that breathing-space has been created by progressive forces sufficient to lift the dead-hand of Portugal from Africa once and for all. As a result, in September (1974) Guinea's independence was recognized – *by the Portuguese* – and plans were soon afoot to facilitate the transfer of power in the Cape Verde Islands as well. That same months, Mozambique under the *Frenté da Libertacao de Moçambique* (FRELIMO) began the transition to its own promised independence on June 25, 1975. More recently, a settlement has been reached in Angola, with November 11, 1975 named as the date for the final transfer of power. *Sic transit* Portugal.

Not so Portugal's erstwhile allies! The NATO powers, the multinational corporations, South Africa (all so well described by Minter) – these continue to hover close to the scene. It can be assumed that the extreme nature of the denouement of the Portuguese coup – an unpredictable and accelerated pattern of change domestically, a remarkably unequivocal decolonization in Africa – has caught all of them off-guard. Dramatic departures emerged so quickly and from such unpredictable quarters – from within the army, for example – that there was at first relatively little that could be done to affect the direction of events. Instead these western sponsors and Southern African allies would have to like with the changes and, as the dust settled, attempt to tame them. Moreover, in so doing they could have some degree of confidence. It is only necessary to remind ourselves of Portugal's rôle as imperial middle-man. With Portugal out of the game, such forces will merely bring their undoubted power to bear more directly, if still quite subtly. Portugal, in the person of General Spinola, has been denied a neo-colonial solution ; that country's former sponsors will now try their hand.

The key to such an attempt is also clear from our earlier discussion. It is precisely the crippling imprint of Portugal's bankrupt colonialism upon the economies and social structures of the former colonies which now threatens to impede the logical extension of those colonies' revolution-in-the-making. For example, Pretoria can hope that the "spontaneous" tendencies of a Mozambican economy warped, as we have seen, by the Portuguese to service South Africa's needs will lock the new country into a position of subservience. [7] Similarly, the multinationals (and such sub-imperial potentates – General Mobutu for example – as they have also created in the area) will seek to use their powerful purchase on the Angolan economy to bend any post-colonial government to their will. [8] Undoubtedly the ground for such results has been well-prepared by five hundred years of "ultra-colonialism." Nonetheless, this is not the whole story by any means. "Ultra-colonialism" has had a second legacy, already hinted at : the creation of *strong, popular, ideologically-advanced* liberation movements, movements which have defeated the Portuguese and which alone provide some firm prospect of pre-empting a neo-colonial anti-climax in "Portugal's African colonies." It is to these movements that we must now turn our attention.

II

The history of African resistance to the imposition of Portuguese rule is as old as the history of that rule itself. We have already cited the fierce initial resistence offered by the African population in many parts of the three colonies and noted just how recently it is that Portugal can be said to have "pacified" all the peoples involved. As Minter observes in his book :

> the history of the wars of resistance... is hardly more than two generations removed from the present liberation movements, and the memories are alive today.

---

7. Of course, there have been other, even more immediate costs to Mozambique of the Portuguese presence which bear noting. Thus, at the time of writing, the transitional government is faced with something approximating a famine in parts of Cabo Delgado province precisely where Portugal's retaliatory raids and strategic hamlet programmes had been most intense during the war years

8. Significantly, these realities are not lost on Portugal's new leaders. In an interview in December, 1974, Portugal's Minister of Foreign Affairs, Mario Soares noted that "in small countries like ours, which are still in the beginning of development, the multinationals tend to be a model of economic colonialism. We have dissociated ourselves from colonialism ; we absolutely do not want to contribute in any way to the creation of other forms of colonialism and abuse. In fact we were a colonial power that in turn was colonized by the multinationals operating predominantly in the Portuguese overseas territories. The fruits of the immense riches of Angola and Mozambique were not for Portugal, but served to enlarge the profits of the multinationals, which had an interest in the existence of colonial rule." (*La Stampa*, December 3, 1974, translated in *Facts and Reports*, V. 4, # 26, December 21, 1974).

Yet these exemplary struggles in the past did remain localized, defining themselves primarily in regional or tribal terms. The significance of contemporary liberation movements has been the new sense of territory-wide nationalism which they represent.

The immediate protagonists of this new nationalism were men and women of the cities, employed nearer the centre of the colonial system and often possessing some minimal formal education (yielded, albeit grudgingly, by colonialism). In this situation they were better able to perceive the overall nature of that system and to understand the means necessary for challenging it. At first their mode of challenge tended to be cultural, vaguely reformist, even elitist, only gradually taking on a more effective and broadly political expression as the pace of change in the rest of the continent picked up and as the full meaning of colonialism was more clearly grasped. But demands for reform were scotched by the Portuguese much more ruthlessly than by other colonial powers. Moreover, when pressure for change from the broad mass of the population also began to surface the Portuguese response was even more brutal. In Guinea, at Pijiguiti in 1959, fifty striking dock-workers were shot down by the Portuguese ; at Mueda, in northern Mozambique in 1960, 600 Africans were killed while peacefully protesting Portuguese handling of agricultural matters ; the same year in Angola, at the village of Catete, 200 were killed or wounded while demonstrating peacefully against the arrest, public flogging and imprisonment of Dr. Agostino Neto, the prominent nationalist leader. This was precisely the point in the history of other colonialisms when the imperial power usually chose to negotiate with the spokesmen of nationalism – gambling, in part, on the elitism of these same spokesmen to restrain any radicalization of nationalism and intending to co-opt them into a smoothly functioning system of continuing economic dependence. However, we have seen that the possibility of such a response was not open to the Portuguese. Turning a deaf ear to peaceful protest, the Portuguese chose instead to perpetuate and intensify the violence of their colonial presence. They thus forced the Africans to take up arms to bring that presence to an end.

Here Basil Davidson's brilliant account (in his *In the Eye of the Storm : Angola's People*) of the emergence of such a struggle in Angola – an account which blends in its writing profound historical depth with on-the-spot immediacy – is required reading. He recounts clearly the manner in which this festering colonial condition first exploded in Angola. The *Popular Movement for the Liberation of Angola* (MPLA) had been organized as a nationalist movement in 1956, but was driven underground by general harassment and by the actions of PIDE, the Portuguese political police. However, in early 1961 a series of dramatic events brought the Angolan struggle to the attention of the world. Resistence to enforced cotton growing in Kasanje led to "Maria's War" – overt action by peasants in the area. At about the same time, MPLA attempted to free political prisoners being held in Luanda, the capital. The Portuguese response to the February initiatives, and to a rebellion in northern Angola launched by the *Unioa de Populacoes de Angola* (UPA) a month later, was particularly ruthless. It has been estimated that some 30 000 to 50 000 Africans died in the savage Portuguese "pacification" programme which followed these events. Yet at this stage, as in the past, the African challenge was still largely spontaneous and localized. The mounting of co-ordinated and effective guerilla warfare was to take more time and face real set-backs.

At first the UPA, soon to form a government-in-exile (GRAE) and ultimately to change its own name (to FNLA), seemed the most active agent of Angolan nationalism and continued for a time to have a marginal guerilla presence in the north.

But, as Davidson shows, its strength was sapped by the opportunistic leadership of Holden Roberto, by too close ties to Mobutu's Congo (and hence, it would seem, to American influence) and too narrow an identification with a particular ethnic base, the Bakongo people. The *Uniao para la Independencia Total de Angola* (UNITA), a third movement which emerged with Jonas Savimbi's splitting away from UPA in 1964, professed readiness to launch a struggle in Eastern Angola which would be more closely linked to popular aspirations and popular participation. The extent of its actual success to date remains a matter of controversy, although, Davidson's conclusion that, at best, it had remained very small and has been effectively stalemated up to the time of the coup seems a sound one. However, both movements lingered on – to become much more active and salient protagonists in the complicated post-coup situation.

Of far greater significance was MPLA itself which finally did begin to regroup itself and demonstrate renewed strength. At first it concentrated its activities on the small enclave of Cabinda because of the difficulties of linking up, via an unfriendly Congo, with those of its units which continued to operate in the Dembos forest north of Luanda or, clandestinely, in Luanda itself. Logistically, therefore, Zambia's independence in 1964 was a key development and meant both that preliminary political mobilization of the people could begin in the eastern regions of the country and that fully effective guerilla warfare could be launched in Moxica district in 1966. From there the struggle was to be pushed into ten of Angola's fifteen districts, with MPLA managing to withstand general offensives launched by the Portuguese in 1968 and subsequently. As a result, Basil Davidson could conclude in 1970 that while

> the guerillas have formidable problems still ahead : in military reorganization, in logistics across huge but widening distances, in building mass support in the central and western districts... yet they are moving on. Steadily, if slowly, they are "marching to the Atlantic." Already... they are west of the Cuanza river, pushing deeply into the "colonial heartlands" of the Portuguese. [9]

It is true, as we shall see, that even after 1970 difficulties continued to plague MPLA, and determined that its advances be less dramatic than those achieved in Guinea-Bissau and in Mozambique. Nonetheless, despite the Portuguese deployment of some 60 000 troops a significant proportion of the country had been liberated prior to the coup – and the struggle was advancing.

The *Partido Africano da Independencia da Guiné e Cabo Verdé* (PAIGC), organized in 1956 under the brilliant leadership of Amilcar Cabral, a Cape Verdean trained as an agronomist in Lisbon, and drawing on the support of urban workers and assimilados in Bissau (the capital), also learned its lesson from the results of peaceful protest – at Pijiguiti and elsewhere – and moved towards armed struggle. Profiting from the Angolan experience, the PAIGC chose to prepare carefully for military action by first developing an efficient organization, mobilizing popular support through clandestine political work and establishing firm international contacts. When guerilla action began in 1963 with the opening up of fronts in the south and the north, the situation was ripe ; by 1965 half of Guinea could be considered part of the liberated area. In 1966, despite the increase in Portuguese troops from 10 000 to 25 000 (to rise to 85 000 in the 1970s), a third front was opened in the east. Even within earshot of the capital armed attacks began to occur, and by 1973 the guerillas had obtained control of *80% of the territory.*

---

9. Basil Davidson, "Angola," in *The Spokesman* (London), December, 1970, p. 17.

The Portuguese continued for some time to command the air with often devastating effect and could maintain fortified towns and bases. In the last years of the war, however, even this began to change as the military capability of PAIGC was strengthened further through the introduction of more autonomous regional commands, the promotion of many junior officers and the acquisition of important new weapons. During a period of six months in 1973 PAIGC shot down more than 25 planes. With local peasant militias (FAL) established to defend the liberated areas, the regular army (FARP) was able to tighten its ring around many of the fortified bases (bases which had served in the past as launching pads for counter-insurgency patrols and as overseers of *aldeamentos* – strategic hamlets), and to occupy such large centres as Guiledje, abandoned by the Portuguese in May 1973, after a long siege and the ambush of supply convoys. By then, PAIGC could itself move more freely, with heavy vehicles in some cases, and even attack the towns still held by the Portuguese. Thus, when Guinea-Bissau declared its national independence on September 24, 1973, it did so from a position of considerable, and growing, military strength. Here, certainly, was one very important nail in the coffin of the Portuguese.

The FRELIMO grew from the same social roots as the other movements and represented at its foundation in 1962 a coming together of a number of nationalist organizations primarily operating in exile in neighbouring African countries. FRELIMO, under the leadership of Dr. Eduardo Mondlane, a Mozambican who has worked at the United Nations and as a Professor of Anthropology in the United States before returning to Africa, requested the Portugues to grant independence. Predictably the Portuguese response was to crack down on African activities, especially in the urban areas. The absolute necessity of military action became perfectly clear, and FRELIMO prepared for this carefully, beginning the fighting on September 25, 1964. Progress in the two northern provinces of Cabo Delgado and Niassa was sufficiently marked by 1968 that FRELIMO was able to launch armed struggle in a third key province, Tete, where once again the Portuguese were slowly but surely driven back.

Thus, by 1972, Cabo Delgado and Niassa were liberated areas, except for a few posts, towns and concentrations of strategic hamlets. The same was true for much of Tete, where FRELIMO soon breached the natural barrier of the Zambezi River, previously a major factor in Portuguese strategic thinking, and where guerillas began to harass effectively transportation into the area of the Cabora Bassa dam site. 1972 and 1973 provided even more dramatic evidence of progress. For in mid-1972 FRELIMO announced the opening of a front in the strategic and densely-populated province of Manica e Sofala in the very heart of Mozambique. Soon the war hovered close to the important port of Beira and brought successful assaults upon Rhodesia's road and rail links to the sea ; there were also attacks on the pylons and transmission lines designed to carry Cabora Bassa power to the south.

Equally impressive, and parallelling the Guinean situation, was the increased ability of FRELIMO to carry the fighting directly to the Portuguese in their fortified bases. Mid-September 1972 saw a raid, involving use of 122 mm rockets, on Mueda airstrip which destroyed 19 planes and also saw a growing number of direct attacks on military posts in Cabo Delgado province and elsewhere. In Tete province, Chingozi airbase near Tete town suffered a similar attack, 17 aircraft being destroyed. And in June 1973, only weeks after General Kaulza da Arriaga (then Commander-in-Chief for Mozambique) had assured his men that the Cabora Bassa zone was impenetrable, FRELIMO attacked Chitima, the command centre for Portuguese forces guarding Cabora Bassa. In desperation during this period the Portuguese turned, as also in

Guinea-Bissau and Angola, to strategic hamlet campaigns, to fruitless "great offensives" (involving the use of massive bombing, napalm, herbicides and other artifacts of counter-insurgency) and, concomitantly, to the grossest kind of intimidation of the African population. Witness the massacre at Wiriyamu in December, 1972 – the essentials of the story so brazenly queried by much of the North American press at the time but now admitted to by the Portuguese themselves. Yet all such attempts failed. Fully one-quarter of the country could be said to have been effectively liberated by the time of the coup. Moreover, it was FRELIMO's dramatic drive further south from 1972 which, above all other factors, sapped the will of the Portuguese soldiers to continue their wars.

In sum, the military picture became one of an increasingly successful challenge or Portuguese military rule. However, it would be misleading to leave the discussion of the liberation movements at this point ; developments in the political and socio-economic spheres were at least equal importance, and in fact help furnish an explanation for the degree of military success which could be achieved. Though this is a complex story, it is nonetheless one which must be sketched out here, however superficially, in order that the nature of the revolutions which have been taking place in Portugal's African colonies be better understood. [10]

Politically, an instructive point of departure is a comparison with the pattern which has emerged in much of independent Africa. As President Nyerere of Tanzania, the most insightful of post-independence leaders, has argued, the nationalism which won independence in Africa in the fifties and sixties was in some senses a superficial accomplishment. In its aftermath, the leaders too easily entrenched themselves as a new privileged class, and the masses of Africans too easily lapsed back into apathy and cynicism. To obtain "real freedom" in all spheres of life, and to claim control over the productive forces (in Cabral's phrase), some form of "'socialism" is required ; at the very least, "to build... real freedom" there must be "a positive understanding and positive actions, not simply a rejection of colonialism and a willingness to cooperate in non-cooperation." [11] In Nyerere's Tanzania this kind of self-criticism had led to a real attempt in the post-colonial period to move beyond a superficial kind of nationalism to a more revolutionary version of it, a version which emphasizes genuine "self-reliance" and attempts to express and to meet the real needs of the vast majority of the population. The striking feature of the kind of struggle which the people were forced to fight in Angola, Mozambique and Guinea was that such a struggle had already begun to reshape the conventional pattern of African nationalism, dictating, *in the nationalist phase itself*, an attempt to restructure social, economic and political relationships in a fundamental way.

Inevitably, some of the nationalists who emerged in Angola, Mozambique and Guinea favoured the familiar pattern. Conservatively, they were prepared to pursue

10. The following argument draws upon the more detailed presentation in my essay, "FRELIMO and the Mozambique Revolution," in *Monthly Review* (March, 1973) and reprinted in my *Canada and Mozambique* (TCLPAC 121 Avenue Road, Toronto, 1974).

11. Julius Nyerere, "Introduction" to his *Freedom and Socialism* (Oxford University Press, London, New York, Dar es Salaam, 1968), p. 29. Of related interest is the distinction between "revolutionary nationalism" and conventional nationalism developed by FRELIMO Vice-President Marcellino dos Santos in an interview entitled "FRELIMO Faces the Future," in *The African Communist*, # 55, 1973 ; see also the speeches of Samora Machel, FRELIMO's President, collected in Samora Machel, *Mozambique : Sewing the Seeds of Liberation* (London, 1974).

their own privileges as actively as they pursued independence, and to play down the importance of mass involvement, using vague appeals which asked no basic questions about the nature of the society which was to be brought into being. Unfortunately for them, in the context of a genuine liberation struggle this kind of nationalism *did not work* as it had for African leadership groups elsewhere on the continent. For a successful liberation struggle required that the energies of all the people be released in a new way. For example, the freedom fighters have had to rely on the peasants as active partners in the struggle – to protect them, to help in carriage and supply of produce, and to serve as a popular militia. Obviously, these duties have required more from the people than "a rejection of colonialism, and a willingness to cooperate in non-cooperation." Instead, they demand "a positive understanding and positive actions," a level of popular consciousness and commitment which is unlikely to emerge unless the leadership has forged a closer, more effective, link with the broad mass of the people fighting for their liberation.

For these reasons, genuinely democratic methods of political work were necessary to close any possible gap between leaders and people. The entirely new programmes and institutions in the spheres of health, education, production and trade which developed in the liberated areas to service the people's needs and aspirations may also be cited in this connection. In launching such novel activities crucial choices were being forced upon the movement, choices which ultimately came to feed the further democratization and radicalization of their struggles. Thus new patterns of education had to be developed which attack elitism and preempt privilege as effectively as they communicate skills ; similarly, the collective practices which are emphasized increasingly in the economic sphere – marketing, distribution, production – serve not merely to pool popular energies but also to combat any temptation towards entrepreneurial aggrandizement on the part of the leadership. Nor is it accidental that within this overall process many of the hard problems of liberating women from the bonds forged by tradition and by colonialism were being confronted in a striking manner. And that concerted and quite self-conscious efforts to transform other aspects of traditional cultures were also in train in order to meet the requirements of a new society without, however, entirely denaturing those cultures.

Here it is essential to stress that these emphases were very far from being mere theorizing : the concrete record of accomplishment on the ground was an extraordinarily impressive one. Though a number of other first hand accounts might also be cited, it is with respect to these realities that Barbara Cornwall's book, *Bush Rebels*, makes its greatest contribution. Writing in a highly personal vein she does capture something important, too, about the impressive quality of the FRELIMO and PAIGC cadres who are leading that transformation. Certainly her account of visits to the liberated areas of Mozambique and Guinea-Bissau at a relatively early date (1968) square well with my own experience of a similar trip to the liberated areas of Tete Province, Mozambique, with FRELIMO in 1972. [12] Perhaps the book hovers a bit uneasily between being a memoir and being an analytical account, but the sense of new societies building institutions responsive. for the first time in many generations, to the needs and desires of the people themselves in nicely communicated.

In addition, as I had occasion to note during my own trip, the continuing confrontation also meant that the leadership as well as the people had a greater

---

12. An account of my trip was published in *Monthly Review* (September, 1974) and reprinted in *Canada and Mozambique (op. cit.)*.

opportunity to become aware of the complicated network of external forces which locked Portuguese hegemony into place ; the crystallization of a much more meaningful anti-imperialist ideology was a result. This gain, like the others mentioned above, is significant. In these varied ways, in fact, the knot of neo-colonialism and under-development was being untied at a very early stage in "Portugal's African colonies." Consequently, it was not merely a fight for independence that was underway there, but a genuine revolution, a revolution full of great promise for post-liberation society in the ex-Portuguese territories.

Such a pattern of development had one tremendously important corollary : the creation of some degree of tension within the African nationalist camp itself. Davidson summarizes this point succinctly in his book :

> There is a general rule by which all movements of resistance produce and deepen conflicts within themselves as the reformists draw back from the revolutionaries and, in drawing back, fall victim to the game of the enemy regime.

Thus movements like PAIGC, FRELIMO and MPLA were, in reality, two entities for much of the early period of their existence : a conventional nationalist movement unable to secure an easy transition to power, and a revolutionary movement, struggling to be born. Concretely, this dichotomy found its expression in a struggle within the leadership – with those prepared and those not prepared to make the transition to revolutionary practice increasingly pitted against one another. As the struggle developed the broader mass of the people also came to be arbiters of this conflict, in defense of their own interests and in the interests of genuine change. It was, in fact, this "logic" of the struggle in Portugal's African colonies which could be seen to be working itself out and making the process of radicalization a cumulative one.

The result of this process in Guinea was the success of the PAIGC and the crystallization of a revolutionary line of development. Cabral's assassination by Portu-guese-sponsored infiltrators of the movement did demonstrate some of the dangers which continue to plague a guerilla force during the transition period and under pressure from the colonial power. However, it was the smooth transition to a new leadership – Aristide Pereira as Secretary-General of PAIGC and, more recently, Luis Cabral as President of the new Council of State – and the continuing strength of the post-Cabral PAIGC which became its most striking feature, a fact confirmed by the aforementioned proclamation of an independent Guinea in September, 1973. We have noted the military basis of this proclamation ; its political basis is of at least equal importance. Thus, twelve years of patient work by PAIGC in the rural areas of the country organizing village and sector committees to manage local affairs had resulted in the emergence of a viable nation-wide system of popularly-elected Regional Assem-bly. In 1972, PAIGC sector committees registered about 58 000 voters, and the series of elections which followed produced the popular representatives to the National Assembly. It was these representatives, sitting in the Assembly alongside a minority of members nominated directly by PAIGC, which then adopted a constitution, elected a Council of State, and proceeded to declare Guinea-Bissau an independent and sovereign Republic. The fact that this Republic was soon recognized by over eighty other countries was an indication of the importance of this development, and in retrospect can be seen as a crucial step forward in the further isolation of Portugal.

Guinea-Bissau, independent on this basis and under the leadership of PAIGC, is obviously no ready candidate to partake of a "neo-colonial solution." The same is true of FRELIMO in Mozambique, though the latter movement has come to such a position of strength and clarity with somewhat more difficulty. Thus some unsympathetic observers – like Richard Gibson in his tendentious and misleading volume *African Liberation Movements* – saw signs of weakness in the fierce infighting within FRELIMO in the period both before and after Eduardo Mondlane's assassination by the Portuguese (in 1969). In fact, this was precisely the period when the most progressive of the FRELIMO leadership consolidated their position, finding their base in the new reality of the liberated areas and in their ability to move with the radicalizing logic of a genuinely popular struggle. The were opportunist elements in FRELIMO (like the movement's one-time Vice-President, Uriah Simango) who harboured elitist or entrepreneurial ambitions, who feared the people and who manipulated regional, tribal and racial slogans to advance their own interests. But they found themselves isolated, soon to drop away from active struggle or even to pass over to the side of the Portuguese. As a result, subsequent meetings of the movement's central committee and other bodies were able to devote their full attention to the more positive tasks of laying down plans for the future with significance both for the quality of life in the liberated areas and now for the shape of a free Mozambique. It is readily apparent that FRELIMO under the leadership of its new President, Samora Machel had developed in practice a most revolutionary form of nationalism. [13]

As noted, it was precisely the kinds of tension attendant upon the transition to revolutionary nationalism which Richard Gibson has chosen to concentrate upon in his book – and willfully to misinterpret. For his picture of FRELIMO is an entirely fabricated one, made up of "feuding, restive troops," of "exaggerated war claims," of justifiably "irate students" (Gibson here ignoring Father Gwenjere's crude attempts to manipulate racist and elitist sentiments at the Mozambique Institute during the period of FRELIMO's crisis) and of an "incredible tendency to settle inner-party squabbles in blood" (Gibson here relying almost exclusively for "evidence" on the desperate accusations of that arch-reactionary Uriah Simango at the time of the latter's expulsion from the movement). One gets little sense of the realities which would eventually find Gwenjere and Simango surfacing in Mozambique to support the abortive white-led counter-revolutionary coup in September 1974, a coup designed to reverse the granting of Mozambican independence. Yet such a denouement for these men's careers was fully predictable from their opportunistic actions at the time of the struggles within FRELIMO, important struggles the significance of which Gibson entirely fails to document or to explain.

In a similar vein, COREMO (a virtually non-existent Mozambican "liberation movement") is propped up – like other similarly shadowy movements in other territories – for the reader by Gibson as some vague kind of alternative to FRELIMO, while hints are dropped from time to time that the latter movement is, in any case, merely a subservient wing of the African National Congress of South Africa – and hence of Moscow ! Worse yet, Gibson's chapter on FRELIMO is of a piece with his misleading accounts of liberation movements elsewhere in Africa. Throughout, a pseudo-Maoist perspective is adopted in order to legitimate the presentation of scurrilous rumour after scurrilous rumour, all serving to *denigrate* the African side of the struggles in Southern Africa. After all, academics might ask, would a "Maoist" purposely attempt to make the liberation movements look bad ? *Ergo*, his charges must be true – the more outrageous the better. But why continue ? It would be tedious to

---

13. My own detailed account of this period of FRELIMO's development, written, it would seem, only shortly after Gibson's, appears in the article cited in footnote 10, above.

document the case against Gidson further. One might better query why one bothers at all with such a book – even if it does bear the imprint of Oxford University Press. Perhaps it is because many Africanists – who should know better – continue to treat the volume as a reputable source.

Building his analysis on such flimsy foundations, Gibson could conclude his account of the Mozambican situation at the end of 1971 by stating that

> as 1971 passed, COREMO was unable to repeat this success, and with the continuing debility of FRELIMO, it was nevertheless obvious there existed no more constant or immediate threats to the Portuguese than those created by their own contradictions !

No benefit of hindsight is necessary here ; any close and honest observer of the Southern African scene would have known, at the time, that such a conclusion was laughable. Subsequent events have only made it seem the more so. We have mentioned the fact that FRELIMO's continued and growing strength helped bring about the coup in Portugal. It must also be stressed that the irresistible force of FRELIMO – and of PAIGC in Guinea-Bissau – were equally crucial factors in the post-coup period. For the Spinola faction within the Portuguese junta worked vigorously to facilitate that "'false decolonization" conceptualized in the general's famous book. Soon various compromise formulae were being offered to the movements – Portuguese-supervised elections, various forms of cooperative coalitions and the like. Yet the liberation movements never lost sight of the fact that they were now playing from strength : with a base for further military operations, if necessary, in the liberated areas, and with obvious manifestations of popular support breaking out everywhere in the country, including in the larger towns and cities. Their demand : unequivocal recognition of their independence. Their principled position was a particularly crucial challenge to Spinola ; he had no real answer to the colonial question. The continued pressure of the liberation movement thus combined with factors mentioned earlier –, with the further radicalization of the Armed Forces Movement and with the dramatic release of popular energies in Portugal, to sweep the general aside. The way was then open for genuine negotiations, for Mozambique's political independence – and, eventually, for carrying out the further revolutionary task of reshaping those cruelly twisted socio-economic structures which are Portugal's chief legacy in Africa.

Unfortunately, as hinted earlier, the Angolan picture has been much more complicated, marred by a degree of factionalism and intrigue on the African side vastly more disruptive than in Mozambique and Guinea. Nor does Gibson, for all his fascination with any hint of divisiveness, shed much light on this phenomenon where, in Angola, it has surfaced significantly ; he is much too preoccupied with explaining away MPLA as some mere expression of Moscovite manoeuvrings and with validating UNITA's slender claim (based, it would seem, on an occasional rhetorical flourish) to Maoist orthodoxy. At the same time, it is precisely here that one must also express certain misgivings about Davidson's own account of Angolan developments. He does, of course, trace in an exemplary manner the early struggles – even more harrowing than those which racked FRELIMO in Mozambique – to forge a revolutionary direction for MPLA and dates the "Conference of Cadres" held by the movement in 1964 as the point at which President Agostino Neto began to point the way forward to the consolidation and radicalization of the movement and of the new Angola which has since begun to take shape in the liberated areas. He is also determined not a gloss over many of the difficulties which have since confronted MPLA, particularly the problem of gaining military access to the economically strategic and populous northern and central regions of Angola, via Zaire ; as already noted,

Zaire's President Mobutu has chosen to favour Holden Roberto's FNLA, a conservative and militarily passive movement which has often played upon ethnic tensions to retain even a semblance of support. This much is clear. However, the ground is less adequately prepared by Davidson for understanding the divisions which *reemerged* to disrupt MPLA itself in 1973 and 1974 when, most notably, Daniel Chipenda, military leader and second-in-command, made a damaging bid for power attempting in his turn to manipulate tribal (Ovimbunda) consciousness as a building block for his own aggrandizement. It is apparent, at least in retrospect, that MPLA – operating, admittedly, in a harsher geographical and socio-economic setting than its counterparts in Guinea-Bissau and Mozambique – had not altogether succeeded in finding the political keys to revolutionary success.

Davidson's overall emphasis is sound, nonetheless. MPLA, having fended off Chipenda's challenge and continuing under the leadership of Dr. Neto, remains the only real vector for comprehensive and meaningful change in Angola. Certainly General Spinola was under no misapprehensions in this regard and as long as he remained a significant factor in the post-coup decolonization equation he worked to isolate MPLA and advance its rival movements. This was a reality presented clearly by no less respectable as source than London's *Sunday Times* when it summarized Angolan developments – including an important secret meeting between Mobutu and Spinola held on the island of Sal shortly before the latter's fall from office – as follows :

> When Roberto announced his ceasefire on Tuesday from Kinshasa... the Portuguese governor's offices in Luanda applauded the news... He added that everything now favoured the opening of official missions by the various liberation movements in Luanda – with the exception of the MPLA and "in particular its Agostinho Neto faction."
>
> Nobody will be more pleased by this outcome than the western oil executives who are beginning to see the prospects of huge profits from Angola. So long as MPLA had a chance of becoming the dominant liberation movement, the oil companies had good reason to be worried. In February MPLA had warned them that when Angola became independent "all these companies will be chased from our national territory and all their equipment and assets seized."
>
> Spinola's elaborate courtship with Mobutu, Roberto and Savimbi has made Angola safe for capitalism – for the moment. And the new Lisbon junta has not allowed its more left-wing domestic policies to stand in the way of the "spirit of Sal." [14]

In the event, further radicalization in Portugal did work, ultimately, to change the Portuguese input. With the temporary appointment of Admiral Rosa Coutinho – the "Red Admiral" – to replace the above-mentioned governor in Angola, MPLA was brought firmly back into the picture, if only as one movement among three co-equals. Interestingly, Coutinho in a recent interview has presented a particularly clear picture of what is at stake in the inevitable jockeying for position which must follow from such a situation. [15] For him, FNLA can be seen to be a movement of the right and the one with the closest ties to large-scale international capital. UNITA, closer to the centre of the spectrum, is the movement with closest ties to local, especially Portuguese-settler, capital (a very large and politically active settler population being another distortion in the social structure left behind by the Portuguese). And MPLA, with its

---

14. "Angola : The Carve-up of Africa's El Dorado," in *Sunday Times* (London), October 20, 1974.

15. Interview with Rosa Coutinho in *El Moudjahid* (Algiers), December 17, 1974.

progressive ideas and working-class base, Coutinho sees to be very much the party of the left. Note the emphasis : here factionalism is interpreted without illusion – as being in large measure the manifestation of external interests introduced by colonialism and now anxious to divide-and-rule in order to reduce the lowest common denominator of post-colonial politics to a very manageable minimum.

Reinforcing this general pattern are other closely related and cumulatively damaging effects which spring from the existence of FNLA and UNITA – the politicization of ethnicity, for example. Thus FNLA will certainly continue to fan the flames of Bakongo ethnic consciousness, while Savimbi seems already to have made great headway in post-coup politics by presenting himself as the champion of the Ovimbunda. [16] Of course, it remains true that these and other problems have not forestalled the recent forging of an alliance between the three movements, an alliance which has proven sufficient to facilitate negotiations with the Portuguese and to guarantee the creation of a transitional government united as least until the time of elections immediatly prior to independence day (November 11). Yet the fact remains that not far beneath the surface of this alliance lurk many of the features of a classic neo-colonial syndrome. In consequence, concerned observers will want to watch the further evolution of the Angolan situation with great care. It remains to be seen whether MPLA – in a political context very different from the forcing-house of guerilla struggle – can move to reactivate the Angolan revolution and thus fulfill the broader promise of its anti-colonial struggle. In Angola, especially, *a luta continua* – the struggle continues.

*   *   *

This, then, is the essential backdrop to the current conjuncture in Portugal's former colonies : a revolutionary nationalism which has broken through the barrier of Portuguese "ultra-colonialism" now stands poised to confront the more subtle dangers of a threatened neo-colonialism. In Guinea-Bissau and Mozambique the strength and sense of direction of PAIGC and FRELIMO greatly enhance the prospects of those countries' carrying the struggle forward with success into the post-colonial era, while in Angola the situation is much more hazardous, the continued "negation of the historical process of the dominated peoples" by imperialism (in Cabral's phrase) representing a very real danger which cannot be ignored. To attempt any more precise predictions at this point would, of course, be fool-hardy. But something of the drama of the continuing struggles in soon-to-be-independent "Portuguese Africa" may be grasped by so posing the issues involved.

Very specific predictions are unlikely to be much more rewarding with reference to the rest of white-ruled Southern Africa. Nonetheless, here too a few general comments may be in order. Lenin once remarked that there are places and periods where history seems to move forward with seven-league boots. Clearly, the breakthrough in Portuguese Africa exemplifies the existence of just such a period in Southern Africa. First to feel the true magnitude of the change is Zimbabwe/Rhodesia. Having

---

16. There are even some additional "movements" which have surfaced in the post-coup period in Angola and which may yet cause damage, FLEC, a seperatist movement in the oil-rich Cabinda enclave, for example. Rumoured to be working in collusion with Gulf Oil and possibly General Mobutu this group has been demobilized, at least for the time being, by MPLA and the Portuguese. And Chipenda himself has surfaced with a handful of followers, first, in Zaire, under the protection of Mobutu and, more recently, in Luanda.

faced, over the past few years, its first really damaging military challenge from the African population and now much more uncategorically vulnerable with a free and unfriendly Mozambique along its flank, the illegal Smith regime has come to seem an increasingly bad bet even to its South African supporters. Recent events suggest that the latter are prepared to pull the rug out from under Smith and company – to attempt to buy time by making a deal with Black Africa at the expense of the Rhodesian settlers. Yet it will be difficult for the South Africans to draw the line there. Its own illegal hold upon Namibia is also coming under increasingly effective fire from within that territory and in the international arena. And even at home there have been more signs of ferment in the past few years – among workers, among students, in the Bantustans – than for some time previously. A revolution has come not merely to Portuguese Africa but to all of Southern Africa.

Let us return by this route to our introductory paragraph. Perhaps, in the wake of the dramatic developments which have been traced in the essay, it will be more difficult for Canadian "Africanists" to patronize and to ignore the Davidsons, the Minters and the Cornwalls who will continue to chronicle this on-going revolution. Perhaps we will see fewer reviews like that by one singularly misinformed Canadian Africanist who once praised Gibson's volume (in *African Affairs*) as a "timely and lucid monograph" and who then proceeded to take at face value such Gibsonesque propositions as the "fact" that conflicts within the movements "explain the protracted nature of the liberation struggle" or that movements like GRAE and COREMO (by name) are to be considered "more radical and self-reliant transnational groupings" than MPLA and FRELIMO ! At the same time, it should not be considered adequate merely to *understand* the situation more clearly. The struggles in Southern Africa deserve *active support* in their own right. Moreover, Canada's record in that part of the world leaves much to be desired, our occasional pious pronouncements being completely undercut by our economic, military and diplomatic links to the side of the white regime ; such a situation calls for *active resistence*. [17] But how many Africanists – all of whom, the present writer included, have carved lucrative careers for themselves out of Africa like so many latter-day Henry Morton Stanleys – can be expected to so engage themselves in significant action in support of African freedom ? Past experience suggests that, initially, their number will be small. Even in Canada, however, the struggle continues.

17. For an introduction to the theme of Canadian complicity in Southern Africa, see *Canada and Mozambique* (*op. cit.*), chapter 1 and the Afterword, or contact the Toronto Committee for the Liberation of Southern Africa (TCLSAC), 121 Avenue Rd., Toronto. See also Cranford Pratt, "Canadian Attitudes Towards Southern Africa : A Commentary," in *International Perspectives* (November/December, 1974), p. 38.

The Journal of Modern African Studies, 26, 1 (1988), pp. 51–70

The Nationalist Revolution in Eritrea

by JOHN MARKAKIS*

Now in its third decade, the nationalist revolution in Eritrea is Africa's longest conflict, and one whose nature is often misunderstood by friend and foe alike. Its supporters see it as an anti-colonial campaign, the same as that waged by people elsewhere for independence. Certainly, colonialism has something to do with it, since Eritrea itself was its creation. However, Eritrean nationalism did not emerge as a reaction to the colonial situation. It made its appearance after the collapse of Italian rule, when the fate of the former colony hung in the balance. The issue that proved the catalyst was Ethiopia's determination to absorb Eritrea, as she was soon to do with the collaboration of many of the inhabitants. These peculiar origins have been cited as good reasons for dismissing Eritrean nationalism as a sham, even though the events of the last 25 years offer ample proof to the contrary.[1] This article offers a summary view of the conflict's history, and makes an attempt to distil the essence of the movement which is still fighting Ethiopia.[2]

ORIGINS

It is worth recalling that the struggle for independence in most parts of Africa had two, often contradictory, dimensions, one of which pitted the colonial subjects against their alien rulers. A parallel encounter, equally intense but less publicised, was fought among ethnic groups and regions, and the parties representing them, for control of the colonial state and the spoils of independence. Many of them did not hesitate to seek support from the metropolitan power, and some went as far as to seek to delay independence. More often, the weaker sought protection in federal schemes, and not a few African states attained independence in that form, although this proved to be a passing fashion.

* Professor of African Studies, University of Crete, Rethymno.

[1] On this debate, see Okbazghi Yohannes, 'The Eritrean Question: a colonial case?', in *The Journal of Modern African Studies* (Cambridge), 25, 4, December 1987, pp. 643–68.

[2] See also John Markakis, *National and Class Conflict in the Horn of Africa* (Cambridge, 1987).

In Eritrea, Italian rule came to an end with the British invasion in 1941, and the country remained under British administration until 1952. During that period, an intense and sometimes bloody struggle took place over the future of the former colony. Given the prior demise of colonial rule, the contest was fought among Eritreans, and it was this internecine aspect that became the hallmark of an incipient nationalism. The conflict was precipitated and exacerbated by Ethiopia's claim to annex Eritrea, and almost immediately became tainted with religious passion, when the Christian clergy hastened to rally their flock to Ethiopia's side. Opposition to union with Ethiopia and support for Eritrean independence came initially from the Muslim community.

Religious enmity between the two communities of almost equal size was nothing new, nor was religion the real bone of contention now. Muslim pastoralists on the lowlands and Christian peasants on the plateau had never been good neighbours, but the reason was a perennial competition for land, not the difference in faith. Indeed, their adherence to rival religions probably was the ideological expression of this material antagonism. The large Muslim trader community had reasons of its own for choosing its political ground. Dominant in the Red Sea ports, it had a stranglehold on trade with the Eritrean plateau and Ethiopia, a fact that did not endear its members to the Christians who ruled there. Muslims also controlled trade in Ethiopia itself, where they were segregated, denied the right to own land, and excluded from state office. Understandably, most Muslims were alarmed by Ethiopia's claim to Eritrea, and opted for independence instead.

On the other hand, most Christians saw a link with Ethiopia, a country ruled by their Abyssinian kinsmen, as the guarantee of their own dominance in Eritrea. They were led by a small group which had acquired a modicum of education under the Italians, whom they had served. Now unemployed, they saw a chance to make a bid for control of the local administration under Ethiopian auspices. They had the militant support of the Abyssinian church in Eritrea, whose land and other privileges had been taken away by the Italians and had not been restored by the British. Similar losses were sustained by the Abyssinian aristocracy in Eritrea under Italian rule and, like the clergy, they were hoping to recover lost fortunes under Ethiopian suzerainty. Together they rallied the peasantry to the movement of union.

However, the communal fronts were not solid. There were significant defections from the Christian camp, but the most telling split was in the Muslim ranks and this followed class lines. The leadership of the Muslim League, the principal organisation for independence, supported the abolition of serfdom among the pastoralists, and thus earned the enmity of tribal chiefs and dispossessed owners of serfs. Consequently, as the four-power commission that was sent to investigate the situation in 1947 reported, 'a considerable number of representatives of the aristocratic classes are in favour of union with Ethiopia, although some of them admitted that they left the Muslim League because it had promised their serfs more rights.[1] Other splits involved Muslim dignitaries in Massawa and western Eritrea who, for reasons of their own, opted for Ethiopia. Finally, hoping to recover lost wages and pensions, former soldiers supported the restoration of Italian rule, an option advocated by the frankly named New Eritrean Pro-Italy Party.

Obviously, the political choices made by the main social groups were not unrelated to their own material interests, as they perceived them at the time. The promotion of these interests hinged upon the state created by colonialism and made it the focal point of conflict. The common goal was to secure maximum access to the power of the state and the resources it commands. The Muslims saw independence as the most promising setting for the achievement of that goal, especially since any link with Ethiopia was for them a grievous political disability. Conversely, Christians believed that such a link guaranteed their political supremacy in Eritrea. It may not have seemed so at the time, as they clamoured for union with Ethiopia, and they were no doubt labouring under a grave misapprehension concerning Addis Ababa's intentions. The truth became clear later, but it was predicted at the time by G. Treyaskis, a British official, who wrote: 'undue Ethiopian interference in Eritrean affairs might provoke a dangerous, if not immediate, reaction on the part of Eritrean Abyssinians'.[2]

Through a United Nations-sponsored compromise, Eritrea became self-governed in 1952 within a federal union with Ethiopia. Though short of a majority, the Unionists won the larger number of seats, and were able to form a government with the support of their Muslim allies. Their opponents declared themselves willing to co-operate and were well represented in the Eritrean Parliament. It was an auspicious start, complete with a model constitution, elections, a free press, and a budding trade-union movement; all in stark contrast to the feudal régime across the border in Ethiopia.

[1] Composed of representatives from the United States, U.S.S.R., Britain, and France, the Commission visited Libya and Somalia as well.
[2] G. Trevaskis, *Eritrea: a colony in transition* (London, 1960), p. 130.

Ethiopian interference, the end result of which was to destroy the federation and to frustrate Eritrean expectations of self-rule, was not long in coming. It did not only drive the earlier advocates of independence to rebellion but, as Trevaskis foresaw, alienated the former Unionists also to the point where they gradually defected to join the movement for Eritrean independence. The first to feel Addis Ababa's heavy hand were the former leaders of the pro-independence movement, most of whom had to flee abroad for their lives. They congregated in Cairo, where they began to plan the revolution. Unionist leaders who were committed to self-rule were soon discarded and replaced by others willing to implement Ethiopian plans. Tedla Bairu, the foremost Unionist leader and first head of the Eritrean Government, was dismissed in 1955 and some years later joined the nationalist movement.

Eritrea's experiment with self-rule and democracy was short lived. The first elections, held in 1952, were also the last free exercise of its kind. Soon afterwards, opposition parties were intimidated into inaction, the press was muzzled, trade unions were crippled and, by the mid-1950s, Eritrea was well on its way to becoming another province of Ethiopia. For Muslims, loss of self-rule meant essentially relegation to second-class citizenship and, not surprisingly, they were the first to react. The smashing of the labour movement alienated a sizeable working class, whose majority were Christians, and which was already hard hit by the deflation of the local economy after a wartime boom had fostered rapid urbanisation (about one-fifth of the population) and record employment levels. Thousands of Eritreans were compelled to migrate to Ethiopia and the states of the Arab Gulf to find jobs. Later they responded to the appeal of the nationalist movement, and their financial contributions helped to sustain the armed struggle.

A group that was to play a key rôle later in the evolution of the nationalist movement was the budding Eritrean intelligentsia, Christian in its majority, whose members were gaining their secondary education in the late 1950s and 1960s. They reacted militantly to the dismantling of the Federation, beginning with a major demonstration against the raising of the Ethiopian flag in their schools in 1957. From then on, they joined every manifestation against Addis Ababa, and in the second half of the 1960s they swelled the ranks of the Eritrean liberation fronts with dramatic results for the nationalist cause.[1]

---

[1] For a review of the bibliography relevant to this period, see John Markakis, 'No Longer a Hidden War: recent writings on the Eritrean nationalist struggle', in *The Journal of Modern African Studies*, 19, 2, June 1981, pp. 362–6.

THE ERITREAN LIBERATION MOVEMENT

The launching of the movement was a Muslim initiative, and it preceded the abrogation of the Federation and the official annexation of Eritrea in 1962. The pioneers were a group of young Eritreans living across the border in Port Sudan, who were inspired by the Sudanese nationalist victory in 1956. Their leader, Mohammed Said Nawid, had gained some political experience as a youthful member of the Sudanese Communist Party. In 1958, he and a few others formed the Eritrean Liberation Movement (E.L.M.), known among Muslims as *Harekat* ('Movement' in Arabic), whose statutes declared: 'Muslims and Christians are brothers and their unity makes Eritrea one [nation]'.[1] The E.L.M. spread to the towns of Eritrea, where it became known among Christians as the *Mahaber Sowate* (Association of Seven) because its members were organised in underground cells of seven. The youthful founders of the first Eritrean liberation movement had no clear programme of action, only the wish to prepare for the inevitable confrontation with Ethiopia. The closest they came to a choice of strategy was their intention to infiltrate the Eritrean police force and carry out a *coup d'etat* from within.

The appearance of this organisation was greeted with hostility from the exiled Eritrean political leadership in Cairo.[2] They refused an invitation to join the E.L.M., and moved to block its progress instead. Idris Mohammed Adam, a former president of the Eritrean Assembly, who was in the process of forming the Eritrean Liberation Front (E.L.F.), launched a campaign of denounciation, claiming that the E.L.M. was being promoted by Communists and probable Ethiopian agents. A war of words ensued, alerting Ethiopian security, which then began a series of arrests that netted most leaders of the organisation and unravelled its cell structure, so that the E.L.M. was unable to react when Ethiopia finally annexed Eritrea in November 1962.

An incident that occurred earlier has since acquired great symbolic significance as the herald of the Eritrean revolution, though neither the E.L.M. nor the E.L.F. had anything to do with it. The hero was Hamid Idris Awate, a veteran outlaw who had gained notoriety in nomad tribal clashes in the western lowlands during the 1940s. When the Ethiopians started rounding up potential trouble-makers at the turn of

---

[1] 'Statutes of the Eritrean Liberation Movement', 1982, in Arabic. A copy of this two-page mimeographed document is in the author's possession.

[2] Wolde Ab Wolde Mariam, the foremost Christian spokesman for independence, was an exception. He agreed to become the E.L.M. representative in Cairo.

the decade, Idris took to the bush with a handful of followers. He clashed with pursuing police on a hilltop in the Barka region in September 1961, and gained lasting, if not quite deserved, fame for having launched the armed struggle, because both the E.L.M. and the E.L.F. claimed him as their own. Although Awate died in his sleep a few months later, for several years the E.L.F. cultivated the impression that he was its field commander.

THE ERITREAN LIBERATION FRONT

Awate's companions remained in the area, and were joined by other Eritreans who defected from the Sudanese army and the Eritrean police, and they formed the nucleus of what became a sizeable guerrilla force under the E.L.F. Idris Mohammed Adam's second-in-command was Idris Osman Galadewos, a law graduate of Cairo University, and they were soon joined by Osman Saleh Sabbe, a school-teacher, to form the leadership of the nationalist movement for a decade.

Weapons were acquired first from Syria, after the rise to power there of General Amin el-Hafiz in March 1963. Iraq was the second country to offer arms and training to the E.L.F. guerrillas, whose numbers reached about 1,000 in 1965. The régimes in Syria and Iraq were strongly influenced by the Baathists, whose pan-Arab vision seems to include Eritrea. They were also willing to discomfit the Ethiopian imperial régime, a client of both the United States and Israel, and to compete with Egypt for regional influence. While extending hospitality and moral support, however, Egypt did not offer material aid to the Eritrean nationalists. In 1965, the E.L.M. also managed to acquire some weapons in the Sudanese market and made an ill-fated attempt to establish an armed presence in northern Eritrea. A unit of 50 men sent to the Sahel was attacked and disbanded by the E.L.F. with the loss of six lives. This was the first bloodshed in a long history of internecine violence that was to mark the course of the Eritrean revolution.

Until now, the E.L.F. force was concentrated in the western lowlands, the homeland of most of its members, where it posed no threat to Ethiopian control of the densely populated and economically important highland region of Eritrea. As the size of the force increased, dispersal became necessary for strategic reasons as well. A re-organisation took place in 1965, based on the territorial model of the Algerian *Front de liberation national*, whose eight-year long struggle had succeeded in 1962. The E.L.F. field structure was divided into four geographical zones that covered all Eritrea. A revolutionary command was established in Kassala, inside the Sudan, whose envisaged rôle was to centralise administrative and military control, and to link the zones with the leaders in Cairo who acted in the name of a supreme council, though no such body was ever formally constituted.

The territorial system had inherent flaws, and these soon became apparent. With a political leadership residing permanently abroad, the four zones developed into autonomous fiefs, with their commands acting on their own authority with little reference to the revolutionary command in Kassala or the supreme council in Cairo. Worse, each zone became identified with the dominant ethnic group in its territory, and inter-zone relations came to reflect old ethnic and sectional rivalries. The trio of leaders in Cairo encouraged this tendency, each becoming the patron of the zone in his native region and using it as a personal power-base. The revolutionary command in Kassala was ignored and never lived up to its name, watching ineffectually as the contradictions inherent in the territorial division produced the first major crisis in 1967, the result of Christian participation in the struggle.

There were hardly any Christians in the E.L.F. until 1965. Apart from the fact that few lived in the lowlands where the Front first became established, their participation was inhibited for some time by the Muslim make-up of the E.L.F., and the Arab posturing of its leadership. Most E.L.F. members saw it at the time as a Muslim movement, and its leaders could not resist the flattery of seeing Eritrea portrayed as part of the Arab world. Arabic is not the language of any group living in Eritrea, save the tiny Rashaida nomad tribe, but it is the *lingua franca* of educated Muslims and those who worked in the Middle East, and it became the official language of the Front. Its leader, Idris Mohammed Adam, held outspokenly hostile views about the Christians, because earlier they had supported union with Ethiopia.

Christian political attitudes, however, had changed radically by the mid-1960s. The annexation of their country and the harshness of imperial rule had cooled the feelings of Christian Eritreans towards their Abyssinian kinsmen. Economic stagnation was a further reason, and there were others. For example, while the position of Muslims was made worse by the proscription of Arabic from the education system – an injury to which the Ethiopian Government added insult by printing the *Quran* in Amharigna – Tigrigna, the language of Christian Eritreans, came under the same ban. This meant that Eritrean students had to master Amharigna, as well as English, in order to complete secondary school and compete for entry to the University of Addis Ababa. Those who managed this feat faced the demoralising prospect of a career in the service of a régime where, as John Spencer notes, to be an Eritrean was 'a chink in his armor'.[1]

Not surprisingly, students and young graduates were the main source of recruitment for the nationalist movement in the late 1960s, and they brought with them the Marxist convictions and radical political attitudes prevalent in student circles at the time. A new zone under a Christian commander, the fifth, was created to accommodate them. Encompassing Hamasien province, which includes Asmara and holds some 25 per cent of Eritrea's population, this was conceivably the most important zone. However, it had no time to fulfil its potential before the first Ethiopian offensive came in 1967.

Until then, the Ethiopian régime had made little use of its military might: an army of some 40,000, equipped and trained by the Americans. The burden of the fight against the guerrillas had been borne by paramilitary units trained by the Israelis. The creation of the fifth zone, immediately dubbed the 'Christian zone', changed the complexity of what was regarded until now as just another uprising among Muslim nomads in the lowlands. An entire army division was thrown into a campaign of pacification, wreaking havoc among the populace and producing the first wave of Eritrean refugees to reach the Sudan. E.L.F. resistance was unco-ordinated, with the force in each zone looking out for itself, mostly by taking cover and leaving the civilians to their fate. The defects of the territorial system, and the ineffectiveness of the leadership were made painfully obvious.

An incident that occurred in the aftermath of the offensive highlighted another crucial flaw: the Front's failure to integrate the recent intake of Christian recruits. While the commander of the fifth zone was absent in Kassala, his Muslim deputy accused 27 Christians of failing to perform their duty during the offensive, and summarily executed them. Shaken, the zone commander defected to the Ethiopians, taking with him 19 more of his co-religionists. This episode had profound repercussions, because it showed how vulnerable Christians were in a movement structured on ethnic lines and infused with sectarian passions.

The Christians were a small minority in the E.L.F., but they were not the only ones who were dismayed with the existing state of affairs. The poor showing of the guerrilla army during the Ethiopian attack

---

[1] John H. Spencer, *Ethiopia at Bay: a personal account of the Haile Sellassie years* (Algonac, Michigan, 1984), p. 123fn.

frustrated many of the young, educated and politically sophisticated cadres, and a process of inquiry began which became known as the *Eslah* (Reform) movement. Criticism was directed initially against the zonal fragmentation of the army, but soon came to focus on the ineffectiveness of the unrepresentative and absent leaders. Ironically, this was a time when they were making progress abroad. They had secured recognition and support from several more states, including Saudi Arabia, which gave funds to buy a small ship, and South Yemen, which allowed Aden to become a trans-shipment port for supplies destined for Eritrea. China gave a load of rifles in 1966, and also trained a few guerrillas, as did Cuba in 1967.

The movement for reform acquired momentum and a degree of co-ordination after the return of those trained abroad. The first group of five who came back from China were appointed political commissars in the five zones, and they were among those who engineered a meeting in June 1968 to discuss the Front's problems and propose reforms. Without reference to Kassala or Cairo, they resolved to dismantle the territorial system and to unite the army. Implementation was delayed for more than a year due to the opposition of the political leadership abroad, but finally a meeting held in August 1968 abolished the zones, as well as the revolutionary command in Kassala. The latter was replaced by an elected general command based inside Eritrea. The supreme council was dismissed shortly afterwards, in a bold act that plunged the E.L.F. into a long period of factional strife. Osman Saleh Sabbe created a rival organisation, the Peoples Liberation Forces (P.L.F.), while conservative elements from the western lowlands formed another breakaway faction named Obel, after a river in their homeland.

Another group to leave the E.L.F. at this time comprised Christians who felt that the movement's defects had not been removed by the recent reforms. A tragedy that helped to drive them out was the massacre of Christian workers who had recently joined the Front: as many as 300 were accused of being Ethiopian agents, were tortured under interrogation and shot. About the same time, two Christian cadres prominent in the reform movement were killed in Kassala by E.L.F. officials. The new leadership did little to exculpate itself of responsibility, and the impression persisted that it was unwilling to accept large numbers of Christians for fear of losing control of the movement.

Some Christians joined Sabbe in the P.L.F., while others lost heart and gave up the struggle. A few gathered on a mountainous spot near

Asmara determined to fight on. They were joined by other defectors from the E.L.F., as well as by newcomers to the field from the towns. In August 1971, they elected a five-man leadership, in which Isayas Afeworq was the principal figure, and shortly afterwards drafted a manifesto entitled 'We and Our Objectives'.[1] Condemning the use of sectarianism as a political strategy, and rejecting the Arab language and pose adopted by the E.L.F., the authors of this document did not conceal the fact that they were Christians. Faced with a choice between death at the hands of Muslim fanatics and surrender to the Ethiopians, they declared, they had chosen to fight on in a separate organisation.

It was imperative for the splinter groups to combine, if they were to survive, and this was done in January 1972 when a united front was formed, called E.L.F.–P.L.F. A few weeks later they were attacked by E.L.F. forces, and a civil war began that was to continue intermittently for a decade. The first round lasted two years, and was fought in the Sahel province in the north, where the Ethiopians were barely present. Although the E.L.F.–P.L.F. had only about 400 men initially, it managed to survive and establish a secure foothold in that region, doubling its strength by the end of 1974. With Osman Saleh Sabbe as its representative abroad, it made up for the loss of Syrian and Iraqi aid by winning the favour of Colonel Muammar Gadafy of Libya. More importantly, the young radicals who led the E.L.F.–P.L.F. force in the field were able to hammer out a political consensus that ultimately united them. In September 1973, a mostly Muslim contingent led by Ramadan Mohammed Nur and the Christians under Isayas Afeworq merged to form the core of what was to become later the Eritrean Peoples Liberation Front (E.P.L.F.).[2] The leaders of Obel refused to join the radicals in this merger, and were later to follow Sabbe when he also parted company with the latter in 1975.

A similar effort to forge political cohesion on ideological grounds was made in the older Front by the so-called Labour Party, a group formed in 1968 'to secure power in the E.L.F. for the revolutionary forces' and ultimately 'establish a socialist state in Eritrea'.[3] A clandestine organisation whose existence was a well-known secret, the Labour Party acquired widespread influence and a following of nearly 500 in the E.L.F. during the 1970s. Nevertheless, although many of those elected to leadership positions by the first national congress of the

[1] The son of a minor functionary, Isayas abandoned university study in 1966 to join the E.L.F.

[2] Ramadan and Isayas were in the first group trained in China.

[3] These goals are listed in a document entitled 'Principles of the Eritrean Democratic Working Peoples Party: its purpose and strategy', in Arabic, dated 1 January 1980.

E.L.F. in 1971 were members of the Labour Party, they failed to overcome the manifold centrifugal forces – sectarian, sectional, ethnic – warring inside the Front. These were reflected in the large and fractious leading organs of the E.L.F., where every ethnic, regional, and religious group fought to secure representation in order to protect their position in the nationalist movement and their future interests in independent Eritrea.[1] The leading members of the Labour Party were not immune to such factionalism, and were never able to work as a team. Consequently, as one of its founders put it, 'instead of becoming a leading vanguard, the Party became an advisory body'.

THE RISING TIDE

Even as the nationalist movement was undergoing a major internal crisis, some spectacular actions brought the E.L.F. its first international publicity. Guerrilla activity in Barka, Sahel, and Keren provinces reached a level that forced the Ethiopian Government to put them under martial law in September 1970. In November of the same year, a train was destroyed on the Asmara-Keren line, then a motorised convoy was ambushed, and the Ethiopian military commander in Eritrea was killed. Abroad, E.L.F. saboteurs destroyed Ethiopian Airlines planes on the ground in Rome, Frankfurt, and Karachi, and hijacked another in flight.

The death throes of the imperial régime in 1974 were punctuated by a series of military mutinies, and among the first to rebel was the hard-pressed second division in Eritrea. This signalled a long period of military disarray which paralleled the enfeeblement of the Ethiopian state during the first years of the military junta known as the *Dergue* (Committee). This was illustrated by the five changes of commander of the second division during the first two years of the new régime. At the same time, the collapse of the *ancien régime* emboldened Eritreans in all walks of life to voice support for the nationalists. Even the Eritrean members of the Ethiopian Parliament were moved to resign *en masse* in August 1974, because Eritrean nationalists were not included in the amnesty granted to political prisoners. Defections from the Eritrean police and para-military units became commonplace, and a veritable flood of young Eritreans poured into the areas controlled by the nationalists. The strength of the E.L.F. and the E.L.F.-P.L.F. multiplied several times within a couple of years, until each had as

[1] Idris Mohammed Adam, for example, retained enough support among his Beni Amer kinsmen, to gain election as chairman of the 19-member revolutionary council in 1971.

many as 20,000 active members. Since most of the newcomers were Christians, both organisations acquired a solid Christian base which sealed the adherence of this community to the nationalists cause. By this time, one can reasonably argue, an Eritrean national consciousness, forged in the struggle, had emerged.

The collapse of the *ancien régime* marked the dawn of a new era in Ethiopia. Fundamental economic and social reforms were decreed by the *Dergue*, which proclaimed its conversion to Marxism soon after taking power. One thing did not change, however, namely the resistance of the Ethiopian state to the structural reforms demanded by many dissident groups. The new leaders proved as obdurate as Haile Sellassie on this point, as made plain with their initial slogan 'Ethiopia First'. The *Dergue* sought to outflank the rebels by choosing a man of Eritrean parentage, General Aman Andom, as Head of State, and sent him to Eritrea to persuade the inhabitants that their demand for independence was no longer relevant because the revolution that overthrew the imperial régime had freed all Ethiopians from oppression. A diplomatic mission was dispatched to the Arab states at the same time to persuade them to stop supporting the nationalists in Eritrea. South Yemen and Libya complied, and extended a helping hand to Addis Ababa instead. Cuba did likewise. China's initial benevolence towards the Eritreans was intended to force Ethiopia to recognise Peking and cease its opposition to China's admission to the United Nations. When these aims were attained in 1970, Peking had immediately rejected further applications for aid from the Eritreans.

The upheaval in Ethiopia found the nationalists locked in civil war and unable to formulate a joint response. Nevertheless, they took the opportunity offered by the enemy's weakness to push their forces towards Asmara, by-passing and encircling the smaller towns, and by September 1974 were camped within sight of Eritrea's capital city. The following month, a clash between them provoked a spontaneous reaction on the part of the people in Asmara and surrounding villages, who came out in thousands to impose a truce and demand an end to internecine strife. Under such pressure, the rivals began a process of intermittent negotiations for unity, which proved long drawn and ultimately fruitless. However, it did prevent major clashes between them for several years, and at the end of January 1975 they collaborated in a spectacular attack on Asmara. A couple of weeks later they opened the gates of two prisons and freed nearly 2,000 political prisoners.

The E.L.F. held its second national congress in May 1975, and finally got rid of Idris Mohammed Adam, who was replaced as chairman of the revolutionary council by Ahmed Nassir, a younger man trained in Syria and a member of the Labour Party. By now a significant proportion of the E.L.F. rank-and-file were Christians, and they also occupied about a quarter of the posts filled by the congress. Despite the Labour Party's ascendancy, the E.L.F.'s outsized, democratically elected leadership was a mixed bag still, comprising traditionalists beholden to sectional and ethnic group interests, and radicals of diverse backgrounds who proved unable to work as a group. Consequently, the E.L.F. remained bereft of cohesiveness and unity of purpose at the top, a defect that was to prove its undoing.

In 1976, Sabbe, acting on his own, concluded a unity agreement with the E.L.F. on behalf of the E.L.F.–P.L.F. This was rejected by the leadership in the field, and following a long period of recriminations, Sabbe and his followers abroad, joined by the Obel faction inside Eritrea, went their separate ways, retaining the name E.L.F.–P.L.F. Delighted with this turn of events, the E.L.F. allowed Sabbe to set up camp in a small enclave in the west, in order to keep him as a factor to be manipulated in the contest with its main rival, the Eritrean Peoples Liberation Front (E.P.L.F.), the name adopted by the bulk of the former E.L.F.–P.L.F. force.

By this time, the *Dergue* had opted for a military solution. Reinforcements had been sent to Eritrea, and General Aman Andom, who opposed the move, had been killed. The conflict escalated rapidly, absorbing increasingly more manpower and resources from a régime in Addis Ababa that was struggling against several other foes as well. A critical moment was reached when the United States began to distance itself from Ethiopia by cutting off military aid. Although this was to prove a temporary setback, since the Soviet Union soon came to the *Dergue*'s rescue, the Eritreans were encouraged to move against the besieged towns. Their offensive began early in January 1977 with the fall of Karora, an outpost on the northern border, to the E.P.L.F., which went on to capture the towns in the Sahel and Keren provinces, while the E.L.F. took the towns in the western lowlands, save Barentu. Both Fronts then moved their forces to the central highlands and, by September, only Asmara and the ports of Massawa and Asab remained in Ethiopian hands. The E.P.L.F. scored the greater gains and took control of the central plateau, as well as Sahel and Keren, while the E.L.F. retained a highland corridor connecting the areas it controlled on the eastern seaboard with its stronghold in the western lowlands.

The E.P.L.F. held its first congress in January 1977. The long-awaited affair was carefully planned by the cohesive leadership of the

Front, which presented detailed political proposals and a finely balanced list of candidates for election. The programme envisaged an independent Eritrean state where the economy would be largely state-owned and centrally planned. Tigre and Tigrigna, spoken by the former serfs and the Christian highlanders respectively, became the official languages of the E.P.L.F. Religion was disassociated from education, and this, along with the rejection of Arabic, was in sharp cultural contrast with the E.L.F. programme, which remained sketchy and ambiguous.

The congress elected a central committee of 30 men as well as a politbureau of 13, both evenly balanced between Christians and Muslims – evidence of the care with which the leadership sought to secure sectarian equity in the Front's leading organs. Even so, the Muslims were mainly from the Red Sea coast, with only a token representation from the western lowlands, the stronghold of the E.L.F. The central committee comprised mostly young, educated men who had joined the E.L.F.–P.L.F. in the 1970s. The politbureau, on the other hand, had a majority of veterans who had joined the E.L.F. in the second half of the 1960s, and had been trained abroad. The founders of the movement remained at the helm, with Ramadan Mohammed Nur becoming secretary-general and Isayas Afeworq his deputy. Real power lay in the hands of this group, whose cohesiveness contrasted sharply with the fractiousness that characterised the leading organs of the E.L.F. Having survived a serious challenge to their position in 1973–4 from a group of ultra-radicals dubbed *Menka* (Bat), they laid heavy emphasis on political education and internal security, which made the E.P.L.F. the most disciplined and effective movement in the Horn of Africa. Freed from the ill-matched alliance with Sabbe and the Obel groups, the leadership of this Front displayed unusual cohesion and unity of purpose, attributes that have served the E.P.L.F. well.

The E.P.L.F. was soon to gain a numerical advantage over the E.L.F. by attracting more recruits from the densely populated central plateau. The political appeal of the E.L.F. in this region suffered a heavy blow in 1977 by the defection of the faction known as *Falool* (Anarchist), most of whom were Christians. Dissatisfied with the moderate political posture of the older Front, and suspecting it had no real desire to resolve the conflict with the E.P.L.F., they organised what they called the Democratic Movement and tried unsuccessfully to challenge the leadership. The outcome was the defection of some 2,000 fighters, many of whom joined the E.P.L.F. The loss to the E.L.F. was more serious than the number of defectors, because the echo of this incident helped to turn the flow of recruits from the highlands towards the E.P.L.F., which soon outstripped its rival in size.

By early 1978, the rival movements controlled the whole of Eritrea, save for the four towns mentioned above, having set up their own separate administrations and mobilised the population in mass organisations. The E.P.L.F. excelled in this because it assigned high priority to political and organisational tasks, maintaining that the class struggle is co-ordinate with the struggle for national liberation, and making a bold attempt to promote social transformation in the midst of the war against Ethiopia. The E.L.F. deemed this combination of tasks reckless, because it ran the risk of dividing Eritrean ranks along class lines and weakening the momentum of the nationalist revolution.

Spurred on by the 1975 land reform in Ethiopia, the E.P.L.F. carried out its own reform in the areas it controlled. Steps were also taken to promote female emancipation, no mean a task given the weight of tradition, especially among Muslims. Women were urged to join the mass organisations in the liberated areas, and recruitment picked up into the Front, mainly among Christian females. Eventually, women came to represent about 30 per cent of its strength. They were involved in all its activities, including combat, and lived on equal terms with, and among, the men. In 1977, the E.P.L.F. decreed a marriage law banning polygamy, child betrothal, concubinage, and dowry, and gave women and children equal rights with men.

STEMMING THE TIDE

Seemingly, the lowest point in the fortunes of the junta in Addis Ababa was reached in mid-1977, when the Somali army invaded the Ogaden and drove Ethiopian forces back to Harar. The invasion was a boon for the *Dergue*, enabling it to raise a patriotic crusade against its assorted enemies, and also provided the Soviet Union with the justification for intervention in the form of massive military assistance. The régime was able to equip several new divisions, which were trained by Cubans. In March 1978 the Somali army was driven out of the Ogaden by an Ethiopian counter-attack spearheaded by Cuban combat units.

It was Eritrea's turn next. Neither their recent successes, nor the impending Ethiopian onslaught, had moved the rival Fronts closer to unity. To make certain that they remained divided, the *Dergue* sowed new suspicion between them by opening talks with the E.P.L.F. in East Berlin, while an E.L.F. delegation was being received in Moscow.

Divided, the nationalists had no hope of defending their recent gains against an Ethiopian force of 100,000, backed by vastly superior weaponry and complete control of the air. The E.L.F. was the first to be mauled when it made an attempt to resist, and was quickly forced to withdraw to the western lowlands. The E.P.L.F. carried out what it called a 'strategic withdrawal', taking everything useful that could be carried off, before retreating to the Sahel hills.

In mid-1978, all the towns were lost, save Nacfa in the Sahel, and the bulk of Eritrea's population were under Ethiopian rule once more. It was a serious reversal for the nationalists, indicating that the prospect of attaining their goal through force of arms was remote.[1] On the other hand, Ethiopian failure to eliminate the guerrillas altogether kept nationalist hopes alive, and a steady stream of recruits continued to reinforce the Fronts. Of the two, the E.P.L.F. maintained a higher profile by holding on to the Sahel redoubt, an ideal guerrilla terrain from which it could not be dislodged by the Ethiopians, and to the town of Nacfa, now a lifeless ruin, which became the symbol of nationalist resolve.

For the Ethiopians, Nacfa became the target of successive major military operations of the type never seen before in this part of Africa. The forces at the disposal of the régime in Addis Ababa expanded prodigiously. No less than 20 divisions were added to the original four, and universal conscription was introduced in 1983 to maintain what had become by far the largest military establishment in the continent. The Soviet Union provided the hardware, and endorsed Addis Ababa's ideological rationale for the war, claiming that by opposing a progressive régime the Eritrean nationalists objectively were siding with counter-revolution. Yet, the Russians kept out of direct involvement, as did the Cubans. On its own, the Ethiopian army proved unable to breach the nationalist defences in the Sahel. Here the lightly armed Eritrean fighters – most of them battle-scarred teenagers – held their ground, taking a heavy toll among the Ethiopians, particularly the hastily trained and unenthusiastic mass of peasants forced into the militia divisions.

In January 1980, the E.P.L.F. counter-attacked to spoil the preparations for another offensive, and rolled the Ethiopian force back from Nacfa. Worried about the possibility of an Ethiopian collapse, the Soviet Union made a diversionary move in February by inviting the

---

[1] To some it indicated that the Eritreans have no prospects at all of ever reaching their goal. Such a view is put forth in Hagai Erlich, *The Struggle Over Eritrea, 1962–1978* (Stanford, 1982).

E.L.F. to Moscow for talks.[1] The ploy worked, the E.P.L.F. accused its rival of treason, and a new round began in the Eritrean civil war. It was to be the last for the E.L.F., whose strength had been sapped by the reversal in 1978. It no longer attracted as many recruits, and by the end of the decade its active strength was put at about one quarter of the E.P.L.F.'s estimated 40,000.[2]

The defeat of the E.L.F. was assisted by the Tigray Peoples Liberation Front. Founded in 1975 to wrest self-rule for the province adjacent to Eritrea, the T.P.L.F. became an effective guerrilla movement with the help of the E.P.L.F., and in return harassed the Ethiopians on the main routes to Eritrea which cross Tigrai. It eventually joined its mentor in an all-out attack against the E.L.F. with whom it had never had good relations.[3]

In August 1981, the last E.L.F. units were pushed into the Sudan where they were disarmed by the Sudanese army. Political disarray followed the military collapse. Abdallah Idris, the E.L.F. military commander, arrested other leaders and installed himself at the head of the Front. Splinter groups proliferated, each claiming to speak for the E.L.F. and blaming the others for its disintegration. Thus, after two decades of struggle, the oldest Eritrean nationalist organisation was torn apart by factionalism.

The E.P.L.F. now gained control of the western lowlands for the first time, and faced the challenge of winning the allegiance of groups which had been the oldest and most steadfast supporters of the E.L.F. Among them were nomad pastoralists like the Beni Amer, for whom Islam is the essence of nationalism. The E.P.L.F., by contrast, considers religion irrelevant, if not a hindrance, to its mission and is unwilling to accommodate its claims, whether Muslim or Christian. Theoretically correct, nevertheless, this attitude has political shortcomings. In the Eritrean context, religion does have a significant political dimension that is difficult to ignore; although, let it be said again, this has little to do with faith itself. The historical evidence shows how religion defines cultural attributes, and hence identity. In certain circumstances, because it represents tangible interests, this identity determines political

[1] The talks were mainly of an academic nature, as the Russians tried to convince the Eritreans that since capitalism had not developed in Eritrea, it was impossible to speak of nationalism. When the visitors declared that Eritreans were engaged in an anti-colonial struggle, their hosts replied that since capitalism had not developed in Ethiopia either, that country could not be considered a colonial power.

[2] Neither Front ever disclosed information about its strength. The numbers cited here are interpolations of varied estimates.

[3] The story of the T.P.L.F. appears in Markakis, op. cit. ch. 9.

attitudes. During the 1940s, Muslims and Christians, by and large, were moved by perceptions of their respective interests to join opposed camps, thereby playing into Ethiopia's hands.

Although this original schism was largely transcended by the 1970s, the nationalist movement remained deeply divided and weakened. To a certain extent, this stemmed from the insecurity of sectarian and ethnic groups, 'which are trying at an early stage to secure their position in future Eritrea', as an E.L.F. publication put it. Such striving led to a relentless struggle for power within the movement. Ideological discord was another significant divisive factor at one stage, when the younger radical generation clashed with the conservative founders of the movement. To make matters worse, the division correlated to some extent with sectarian and ethnic cleavages, and resulted in the violent fracturing of the E.L.F. Subsequently, after the young radicals displaced the older generation from power in both Fronts, it became difficult to see significant ideological differences between them that would justify continuing debilitating discord. Personal ambitions and hatreds, often blamed for this situation, no doubt were a contributing factor but hardly a primary cause.

Much more important have been the different perceptions that the main rivals have of the future for which they are fighting. One scenario is of a society and culture based on Islamic values and the Arab language, and closely linked to the Arab world which has consistently supported the Eritrean revolution. This was the perception of the E.L.F., and it reflects a deeply-felt need of Eritrean Muslims, especially the intelligentsia, to identify with a literate culture of historical importance and a renascent Arab world whose economic and political support would be essential for the maintenance of Eritrean independence in the shadow of Ethiopia. By contrast, the E.P.L.F. rejects the Arab language and regards the Arab connection as artificial, even dangerous, because it highlights religion and cultivates links of dependence with conservative Arab régimes in the Gulf. Instead, a close relationship with a reformed Ethiopia is considered indispensable to the future peace and prosperity of Eritrea. Each side suspects the other would rely on outside support – Arab or Ethiopian – to impose its own conception of the Eritrean identity. More than anything else, it is these conflicting perceptions of the future that are the main obstacle to Eritrean unity.

The military stalemate that continued since 1978 was broken in 1984 when the E.P.L.F. went on the offensive. In January, it captured Tessenei near the Sudan border, and two months later its units descended on the northern coastal plains to clear the Ethiopians from that region. When the guerrillas captured Barentu, a prize that had always evaded them, in July 1985, it seemed that the tide of the revolution was rising again. However, without defence against heavy armour and air attacks, the Eritreans were no match for the Ethiopian army in positional warfare, and it was not long before the town was lost with heavy casualties for the guerrillas.[1]

The inconclusiveness of this action was symbolic of the war itself which, after a quarter of a century's fighting, was no nearer to resolution. A military solution has not seemed a realistic prospect in the best circumstances, let alone during the grim 1980s. Drought and famine, frequent visitors to the region, returned in 1983 before the inhabitants had time to recover from their sufferings in the mid-1970s. Distracted by the manifold violent confrontations it was engaged in, the military régime in Addis Ababa had done little in the meantime to prevent a recurrence of the disaster. Instead, it busied itself erecting a political façade, complete with a constitution, party, and elections. In 1984, the Dergue celebrated the political achievements of ten years in power, while a famine ten times worse than previous disasters hit the northern part of Ethiopia. An unprecedented international relief effort was launched to save those it could reach. Others perished in unknown numbers.

Eritrea and Tigray were among the worst hit areas. The plight of the people there was exacerbated because neither the Ethiopian régime nor its opponents were willing to make the concessions required for an efficient relief system to operate. The former would not allow supplies to be forwarded to areas it did not control, while the latter claimed the right to control the distribution in areas under their mastery. As a result, many thousands of Eritreans and Tigrayans were compelled to trek to the Sudan to find relief. The international organisations involved were unable to break the *impasse*, and a few of them, Canadian and American, began to co-operate with the E.P.L.F. and T.P.L.F. by forwarding supplies through the Sudan to their areas.

Drought and the spectre of famine reappeared in 1987. Although by this time Ethiopia had become a ward of international charity, the *Dergue* continued to hamper the supply of food to rebel-held areas. It also persisted with a policy of forced resettlement of impoverished

---

[1] Among the casualties probably were two key members of the leadership, whose deaths were revealed during the 1987 congress. They were Ibrahim Aafa and Mesfin Hagos, both members of the politbureau and its military committee. The former, a one-time sailor in the Ethiopian navy, was the E.P.L.F.'s foremost military strategist.

peasants from Tigray and elsewhere, which its enemies regarded as an attempt to depopulate dissident provinces. The attitude of the rebels themselves hardened. Both the Eritreans and the Tigrayans attacked relief convoys and destroyed provisions in September/October 1987, to drive home the point that political imperatives remained paramount. The luckless people in the affected areas were left to find salvation on their own.

In mid-March 1987, the E.P.L.F. held its second congress during which it celebrated its unification with the fragment calling itself the E.L.F.-Central Leadership. A change in the hierarchy made official the acknowledged primacy of Isayas Afeworq, who became secretary-general, replacing Ramadan Mohammed Nur. The latter remained a member of the politbureau reduced in size (from 13 to 9), and in power, because its members were no longer heading major departments. On the other hand, the central committee more than doubled in size (from 30 to 71), and a woman was elected to it for the first time.

The view of the future expressed by the 1987 congress was sombre. The E.P.L.F. hopes for a transformed Ethiopia under a democratic régime that will accept and co-operate with an independent Eritrea. To that end, it urges other dissident movements – there are at least half a dozen – not to split the country, but to fight for a reformed and united Ethiopia. Understandably, that prescription is not to everyone's taste, especially those who profess to be fighting for national self-determination, and it alienated the T.P.L.F., which claims the right to determine for itself whether or not Tigray will remain within Ethiopia. Given the unlikelihood that the declared goal of the E.P.L.F. can be achieved by the efforts of such variegated opposition, the congress forlornly called on the army in Ethiopia to overthrow the régime.

THE DEATH OF CHAMINUKA: SPIRIT MEDIUMS, NATIONALISM AND THE GUERILLA WAR IN ZIMBABWE

TERENCE RANGER

The death of Chaminuka, 1883

Throughout southern, central and eastern Africa there are myths of martyred prophets. Only very rarely, however, is there any written documentation to help date and situate the prophets so central to oral tradition. The case of Pasipamire, medium of the spirit Chaminuka, is very different. For Pasipamire's death we have concrete written evidence as well as a rich growth of myth.

The famous hunter, F. C. Selous, first told the world about Pasipamire in 1881, with the publication of his book, *A hunter's wanderings in Africa*.[1] Selous recounted that in August 1878 he heard from white elephant hunters of 'a very powerful "Umlimo" or god', who lived at Chitungwiza, near present-day Beatrice. This was Pasipamire, medium of Chaminuka. Pasipamire was regarded as owner of the land; hunters had to seek his permission to 'kill the elephants nicely' and to donate gifts of ivory and cloth. Shona supplicants came from 'distant' kraals; Lobengula, king of the Ndebele, sent Pasipamire 'presents of cattle, young girls, etc'. Other Shona chiefs, wrote Selous, 'are the victims of continual depredation', but Pasipamire had accumulated 'a considerable store' of cattle and ivory.

There was not much here of the resistance hero of later oral traditions. But in his *Travel and adventure in south east Africa*, published in 1893, Selous gave an account of Pasipamire's death at the hands of the Ndebele early in 1883.[2] According to Selous's informant, Lobengula had sent presents to Pasipamire together with a request that he come to visit the king of Bulawayo. Accordingly the medium set out with a small party. At the Shangani river they were met by 'the greater part of the (Ndebele) fighting men from the eastern side' of Matabeleland.

Selous's account of Pasipamire's death still makes no mention of the predictions which figure so largely in oral versions, but there is certainly an atmosphere of heroic dignity:

As they advanced Bavea said to her aged husband, 'They are going to kill you; I know the Matabili. Run! run! I see blood in their eyes; run! run!' But

Terence Ranger is professor of modern history at Manchester University and last year he revisited Zimbabwe.

1. F. C. Selous, *A hunter's wanderings in Africa*, Richard Bentley, London, 1881, p. 331.
2. F. C. Selous, *Travel and adventure in south east Africa*, Rowland Ward, London, 1893.

349

the old man answered, 'Child, I am too old to run.   If his day has come, Chameluga does not fear to die, but bid my son, who is young and swift of foot, creep away in the bushes whilst there is yet time, and carry the news to my people.'[3]

The Ndebele then surrounded Pasipamire and killed him, in what Selous inaccurately called 'one more of those tragedies . . . which are so common in the interior of Africa that they excite but little attention'.   Pasipamire's son managed to get back home and to warn the people of Chitungwiza; when the Ndebele arrived they found the village abandoned.

The rise of the Chaminuka myth

Whether or not Selous's account, based on the story of Bavea, Pasipamire's wife, was factually accurate, he was certainly wrong to imagine that the medium's death would excite little further attention.   There rapidly grew up around the dead 'Chaminuka' that cluster of myths which were available to Central African peoples to mark out an event as profoundly significant.   It was said that the Ndebele had been unable to kill the medium with guns or with spears and that he had in the end to show them how the job could be done—by a boy under the age of puberty.   It was said that before he died Pasipamire predicted the coming of the whites and the downfall of Lobengula.   In a period of rapid and traumatic change, these stories proclaimed that the Shona prophet had not been overthrown and overcome but that even in his death, and by means of it, he comprehended events and controlled them.

Before long these stories came to the attention of whites.   In many versions they did not seem to threaten white interests: Pasipamire, after all, had predicted the downfall of the Ndebele at white hands.   There was nothing proto-nationalist about the version of the stories published by F. W. T. Posselt in 1926.[4]   But in 1928 the radical missionary Arthur Shearly Cripps published his *Chaminuka: The Man Whom God Taught.*   Cripps's version *was* proto-nationalist and it had an enduring influence on Christian educated Africans. 'Any nation would be poor indeed', wrote Cripps, 'if it had no real hero of its own'.   Fortunately, the Shona had Pasipamire.   Nor was Pasipamire merely a hero; he was a prophetic fore-runner of an African Christianity.   So old Murambwa, whom Cripps claimed as an informant, had once been a disciple of Pasipamire; now he was a Christian.   Murambwa 'believed in God's Son; also he honoured God's prophets. . . .   One of these prophets was Chaminuka, the hero of his own people, and of (his) own youth.'   Moreover, Cripps saw Pasipamire as a hero for the future as well as for the past:

Are not the people and the land ill-content and wistful, as a flock scattered and a fold that wants its own shepherd?   When will a hero and a wise man once

3.   Ibid., p. 114.
4.   F. W. T. Posselt, 'Chaminuka the wizard', *NADA*, **4**, 1926.

more move among the tribesmen of that African east country?   When will the
rumour run through the villages that Chaminuka is come again? Mashonaland
has not gone out of mourning for Chaminuka yet: earth and sky
and folk alike have a look of brooding expectancy.[5]

Chaminuka mediums and the administration

There was a real sense in which Cripps gave the myth of Pasipamire
Chaminuka to the men who came to lead the first articulate indigenous political
associations and made it possible for these rather self-consciously 'progressive'
and Christian men to turn a spirit medium into a hero.   Meanwhile, however,
the Chaminuka spirit was still finding mediums and the idea of Chaminuka was
working itself out in other very different intellectual environments.

So far as we know there was no medium of the Chaminuka spirit involved in
the 1896 risings.   Still, those risings had made the administration wary of spirit
mediums.   When in 1903 a woman claimed to be possessed by the Chaminuka
spirit and summoned chiefs to her kraal, the administration was careful to ensure
that spies attending the meeting.   According to them the medium said while in
trance:

I am Chaminuka.   I know everything.   I am all powerful.   I caused the
downfall of the Barozwi and the Matabele and I will cause the white man to
leave the country.   Nothing is impossible to me.[6]

The medium was at once arrested and interrogated but she committed suicide
before she could be put on trial.[7]

Nearly thirty years later, another female medium of Chaminuka attracted the
attention of the administration.   She was Reresayi of Gutu district; she was
'very intelligent, clear of speech and an expert at repartee . . . under the delusion
that Chaminuka's spirit has entered her and her only desire is to assist and do
good among her fellow beings.'[8]   A less favourable report asserted that she was
claiming to be 'the Government in charge of rain' and saying that tribute should
be paid to Chaminuka rather than to the administration because 'Government is
stealing the natives' money'.[9]

Then in 1934 a young man claimed to be possessed by the Chaminuka
spirit.   He was Muchetera Mujuru of the Chiduku Reserve in Makoni
district.   With Muchetera the literary and the oral histories of Chaminuka came
together.

5.   A. S. Cripps, *Chaminuka. The Man Whom God Taught*, The Sheldon Press, London, 1928.
6.   Assistant N.C., Salisbury to Chief Native Commissioner, 2 April 1900, N 3/1/18, National Archives, Salisbury.
7.   NC, Marandellas, to CNC, 12 December 1903, A 11/2/12/11, National Archives, Salisbury.
8.   NC, The Range, to CNC, 28 July 1931, s. 138.22.1930–31, National Archives, Salisbury.
9.   Assistant NC, Buhera, to CNC, 3 March 1931, s. 138.22.1930–31, National Archives, Salisbury.

Muchetera Mujuru and the Shona cultural revival

Underlying the nationalist upsurge of the 1960s was a discovery of the splendours of the Shona past, of Shona religion and of Shona music. These splendours were given important endorsement by the work of white scholars; by Michael Gelfand, with his books on Shona religion; by Donald Abraham, with his work on the Shona empires; and by Paul Berliner, with his account of Shona *mbira* music. The key informant of all three of these scholars was Muchetera Mujuru, who claimed to be possessed by Chaminuka.

When Michael Gelfand's book, *Shona Ritual with Special Reference to the Chaminuka Cult*, appeared in 1959 it was greeted with delight by most of those interested in the African past of Zimbabwe. It offered the first coherent account of Shona religion which it took very seriously. As became plain with his later books, Gelfand himself worked mainly as a recorder; the coherence in *Shona Ritual* came mostly from Muchetera, who offered a centralized, hierarchical model of Shona religion, with the Chaminuka spirit and its medium at the top; who offered also a centralized imperial version of the Shona past, with the Chaminuka spirit crucially involved; and who offered, finally, a triumphalist account of his own dominant influence in Makoni district and throughout Mashonaland. On a re-reading of the book Muchetera's own self-interest in providing such accounts is very clear: but in 1959 they fed straight into the rather different interests of the cultural nationalists.

Gelfand's account of Shona religion runs:

> The Mashona do not know Mwari (God) or approach Him directly, but only through Chaminuka the great messenger, the link between God and the people. No one dare show disrespect to Chaminuka for when he is annoyed there is no rain. . . .

> At the head of the tribal spirits is Chaminuka and under him are a variable yet large number of tribal spirits . . . who care for large regions or provinces. . . .- The leser *mhondoro* are intended merely to carry messages or news of events to the greater ones, who in their turn report to Chaminuka. . . . It is believed that all the spirits receive instructions from Chaminuka.[10]

Carrying out later researches in other areas and with other informants, Gelfand discovered that this was much too over-simplified a picture. But its very simplicity and assertion of one overall Shona religious system proved powerfully attractive.

Muchetera provided a similarly simple and attractive notion of Shona political history. The spirit of Chaminuka had first spoken from the air at Great Zimbabwe 'among the Varozvi'. The spirit sent messages to the people, interpreted to them by one Mutota; then Mutota's daughter became pregnant of the

10. Michael Gelfand, *Shona Ritual, With Special Reference to the Chaminuka Cult*, Juta, Cape Town, 1959, pp. 13–14.

Chaminuka spirit and bore a son. Mutota became the first medium of Chaminuka and his son, Chikara, became the first chief of the Rozvi. So the Chaminuka spirit founded the spiritual and political order of the Shona 'empires'.

Moreover, all other Shona chieftancies had to seek legitimation from the Rozvi and from Chaminuka:

> After the death of a chief his people used to take a hoe with them and go to consult the chief tribal spirit of the district to ask who was to be the next chief. The spirit would tell them his name, and they would then go to Zimbabwe where the VaRozvi lived. On arrival they were told that the chief guardian spirit would choose their new chief. On reaching the home of Chaminuka they clapped their hands. . . . Chaminuka was satisfied and the VaRozvi agreed that all was now in order.[11]

Eventually there was a quarrel between the Rozvi and the Chaminuka spirit; 'the *mhondoro* was angry. It told them that . . . the Varozvi would be overcome by the Matabele and that they would become a subject race. . . . With their spirit now lost the Varozvi were soon conquered by the Matabele.' Once the Chaminuka medium was established at Chitungwiza 'all the different Shona chiefs brought cattle in honour of Chaminuka'.[12]

Muchetera's version of the death of Pasipamire was suitably dramatic. The Ndebele 'were angered that the spirit had deserted them for the . . . Shona tribes'; 'Chaminuka prophesied that his medium . . . would be killed. Pasipamire informed the Madzviti that he knew of their plans but was fully prepared to meet them in battle.' He was captured, however, and his Shona adherents did not fight for him: he was at last killed by a little boy: 'a patch of grass as large as his head appeared on the ground where he fell forward', 'Then the voice of Chaminuka was heard by all gathered, telling them that Lobengula would be defeated by another race who would come from the east'.[13]

After all this, it was hardly surprising that Muchetera claimed remarkable powers for himself as medium of Chaminuka. He had triumphed over numerous rival claimants and imposters; various people had tried to kill him but found him invulnerable—as Muchetera said to one of them, 'If any of you think of harming me you will kill yourself instead because it is not Muchetera whom you wish to kill, but the tribal spirit. Chaminuka can read your thoughts and informs Muchetera'. The other great spirit mediums recognized his superiority; so did the local chiefs. Muchetera's account ended with chief Makoni and the other chiefs attending the rain ceremony of February 1949 at Muchetera's village, and with chief Makoni promising to report to him 'any omissions on the part of his people so that they could be remedied'.[14]

11. Ibid., p. 205.
12. Ibid., pp. 31–32.
13. Ibid., p. 32.
14. Ibid., pp. 34–39.

All this had a great effect in placing Chaminuka at the centre of the new vision of the Shona past. Even more influential—because it came from a more formally qualified historian than Gelfand—was Donald Abraham's 'The Roles of "Chaminuka" and the Mhondoro cults in Shona Political History', a lecture given in 1963 and published in 1966.[15]   In previously published work on the Mutapa empire Abraham had made no mention of Chaminuka and had depended on the medium of the Mutota spirit as his major informant.[16]   But by 1963 he had discovered Muchetera, who was overwhelmingly the most important source for his 1963 paper.

Abraham admitted that 'the historical identity of Chaminuka is uncertain' and that 'there are apparently no Portuguese documents relating to the *mhondoro*-cults of the Rozwi'.   But he drew on Muchetera and allied mediums to produce an impressive picture of Chaminuka's ancient centrality.   Chaminuka was possibly an ancestor of the NeMbire founders of the 'centralized polity' which became 'firmly established with headquarters in the locality of what developed into Great Zimbabwe'; the Rozwi monarchy there was 'called into being either by Mwari or by the Chaminuka Spirit in association with him'.   A concept of 'a pyramidal, graded spirit-structure, with Mwari . . . at the top—Chaminuka . . . immediately beneath him—and the tribal spirits, also beneath Chaminuka, in the lowest grade, seems already to have crystallized in its essentials by the earlier 17th century'.

Abraham, who was far from being sympathetic to African nationalism in its 1960s manifestations, nevertheless freely used the language of nation.   'The main, moral cement at the national political level derived from Mwari and his lieutenant, Chaminuka'.   Chaminuka possessed 'unimpaired sanction to preserve the structural continuity of the Rozwi state; and when subsequently periods of interregnum occurred, it was to the Chaminuka spirit that application was made for confirmation of successors to the subject tribal chieftancies'.   After the downfall of the Rozwi state, 'the Chaminuka cult did survive until 1883 as a focal point of Shona national resistance to the Ndebele'; it 'now operates in the Chiduku Reserve, Makoni District'.[17]

The third major work of scholarship which under-girds the Shona cultural revival is Paul Berliner's *The Soul of Mbira. Music and Traditions of the Shona People of Zimbabwe*, published in 1978 and based on research carried out over the period 1971 to 1975.   By this time Muchetera was an old man; nevertheless it is Muchetera and his family together with the descendants of Pasipamire who dominate Berliner's book.   Berliner's main associates were Cosmas Magaya and Luken Pasipamire, members of the Pasipamire family, and Ephat Mujuru,

15.   D. P. Abraham, 'The Roles of "Chaminuka" and the Mhondoro Cults in Shona Political History', *The Zambesian Past. Studies in Central African History*, eds., E. T. Stokes and R. Brown, Manchester University Press, 1966, pp. 28–46.
16.   For example, D. P. Abraham, 'The Early Political History of the Kingdom of Mwene Mutapa, 850–1589', *Historians in Tropical Africa*, eds. E. T. Stokes and R. Brown, Salisbury, 1962, pp. 61–90.
17.   D. P. Abraham, 'The Roles of "Chaminuka" and the Mhondoro Cults'.

grandson of Muchetera, who had learnt his *mbira* playing in his grandfather's village.   But Muchetera himself played for Berliner; his performance of 'Nyamaropa yeVana Vava Mushonga', recorded in 1971, is included in *The Soul of Mbira* record album; the Shona text of this song, with English translation is published in the book as an appendix; and Muchetera is cited several times as an informant.

Muchetera's testimony all went to emphasize the association of *mbira* music with Shona religion and especially with Chaminuka.   Muchetera's own set of *mbira dzavadzimu* 'are said to have been played at the nineteenth century court of Chitungwiza for Chaminuka'; 'according to [Muchetera] Mujuru, in the court of Chitungwiza a man named Dandara was Pasipamire's acolyte and Zhanje, Mpawose and Muchaonwa were among the most important mbira players.   In the accounts of Mujuru and Pasipamire's descendants, a group of mbira players accompanied the great medium on his journey to meet Lobengula.   In the confrontation with the Ndebele, Pasipamire's mbira players performed the music which enabled Pasipamire to become possessed by Chaminuka and thereby to elude his assailants.'   Muchetera also gave a characteristic account of the origins of the *mbira*:

According to Mujuru, the mbira first came from a place white men had never seen ... located north of Rusape.... At first the mbira mysteriously sounded from inside a large rock near a circular stone house with no door.   People gathered whenever they heard the mbira's music emanating from the rock.   The people believed that the voice was that of Chaminuka. ...   Later Chaminuka took possession of a man named Nyadate, through whom he told the people to make mbira.   Nyadate showed the people how to make mbira, which they learned to play by listening at the rock.[18]

Chaminuka was the founder, not only of Shona religion and politics but also of Shona culture.

Muchetera was clearly a virtuoso informant.   With his *mbira* playing also on record and his performance of rituals the subject of several ethnographic films, it is hard to deny him the title of the single greatest influence on the Shona cultural revival.[19]

Chaminuka in the mass nationalist movement

This scholarly material flowed into nationalist use of the Chaminuka myth.   Nathan Shamuyarira tells us that in the 1950s 'Mashona reaction looked to the past for comfort and took as tribal hero the tall bearded prophet

18.   P. F. Berliner, *The Soul of Mbira. Music and Traditions of the Shona People of Zimbabwe,* University of California Press, Berkely, 1978, pp. 36, 45, 47.
19.   P. F. Berliner, *op. cit.,* p. 270 for list of films.

Chaminuka . . . a great prophet and symbol of . . . resistance . . . a binding factor in resisting the settlers.'[20]   George Nyandoro, in particular, made great play with the memory of Chaminuka in his speeches at nationalist rallies.   In 1958 Herbert Chitepo's allegorical poem, *Soko Risina Musoro*, which portrayed the need to recover tradition, introduced Chaminuka into his account of a declining kingdom in Manicaland—even though it seems unlikely that the Chaminuka spirit was venerated in Manicaland in the past:

Their land is filled with sickness and dry weather,
Chaminuka has feet no longer,
The wealth of the earth has vanished into its belly.[21]

The death of Pasipamire became a central theme of Shona novels and poems.   In 1972 Lawrence Vambe gave an extraordinary nationalist elaboration of Selous's bare account.   Lobengula made an 'all-out bid to bring the whole of Zimbabwe under his control' by 'the extraordinary measure of attacking Chitungwiza . . . the Mecca of Shona religious pilgrimage and national aspiration'.   Lobengula was convinced that if he killed Pasipamire 'he would eliminate the Shona spirit of resistance and independence'.   Indeed, says Vambe, Pasipamire *was* 'the source of all Shona strength'.   In Vambe's narration, the attack on Chitungwiza becomes a great battle.   The village was 'defended by an army of picked regiments from most of the main tribes in both free and occupied Zimbabwe', so that the Ndebele were 'compelled to beat a hasty retreat', even though they carried off Pasipamire.   Lobengula offered Pasipamire 'all the honours he wished to employ all his spiritual gifts . . . in the service of the Ndebele nation', but Pasipamire would 'on no account . . . be the instrument of slavery by the Ndebele or anyone else'.[22]

Vambe was not ranked among the most militant of nationalists, but Chaminuka's memory was appealed to by those who were.   In 1972 guerrillas named one of the new war-zones in the north-east after him.   Young men going over the border to join the guerrillas from Muchetera's own Makoni district came back into the coutnry bearing the 'Chimurenga name' of Comrade Chaminuka.[23]   Poets of the liberation struggle invoked his name:

Atop twin breasted mountains
Yet our guardians writhe.
Nehanda, Chaminuka.
No sleep they have till our chains snap. Then
Grim-faced warriors with crimson on foreheads
March across the land. . . .

20.   Nathan Shamuyarira, *Crisis in Rhodesia*, Andre Deutsch, London, 1965, p. 29.
21.   Herbert Chitepo, *Soko Risina Musoro*, OUP, London, 1958.
22.   Lawrence Vambe, *An Ill-Fated People*, Heinemann, London, 1972, pp. 67–70.
23.   I myself met two 'Comrade Chaminukas' while researching in Makoni district in early 1981.

And with the guerilla victory, the poet sees:

Chaminuka bristling in manly pride.
Ninety dread years have passed.[24]

Muchetera incorporated into the struggle

Muchetera not only made a major contribution to Shona cultural nationalism and to the centrality of Chaminuka: in 1978 two publications linked him and his circle directly with the resistance struggle. One was Berliner's book. Berliner showed the close connection of *mbira* traditions with the Chaminuka mediums and with the family clusters of Pasipamire and Muchetera. He showed how these *mbira* players had been discriminated against by missionaries and other whites. And he showed the connection between Chaminuka, the *mbira* and nationalist resistance:

A statement that seems to be a straightforward historical reference to Chitungwiza can have a powerful political meaning as well: Chaminuka has become a powerful political symbol among the Shona in recent years.[25]

According to Muchetera, the *mbira* players of Pasipamire had given him his invulnerability. Now the *mbira* would offer protection once again:

One young impassioned musician, prophesying with bravado the inevitable revolution of Zimbabwe's Africans against their European oppressors, envisioned that day: 'When European soldiers come to surround my house, firing guns, I will play the ancient songs for the mbira and when the spirit comes to me, I will walk through their bullets without harm'.[26]

Moreover, Berliner argued that the *mbira* players had already suffered in the struggle:

The mbira renaissance in the contemporary Zimbabwe . . . is a testimony to the courage of past and present generations of mbira players who have refused to submit to the hostile colonialist pressures against their art. Because of the support that African nationalist guerillas have received in recent years from important traditional religious figures in certain parts of Zimbabwe, some mbira players are said to have been victims of harassment for their association with these figures. . . . As early as 1973, I received unconfirmed reports of

24. Godfrey Ndhlala, 'Night at Noon', *And Now the Poets Speak*, eds, Mudereri Kadhani and Musaemura Zimunya, Mambo, Gwelo, pp. 126–127.
25. Berliner, *op. cit.*, p. 178.
26. Berliner, *op. cit.*, p. 49.

performers in northern Zimbabwe who were fined or arrested for their performance of mbira music.[27]

The apotheosis of Muchetera as resistance hero came in Stanlake Samkange's novel, *Year of the Uprising,* also published in 1978. It did not seem fitting to Samkange that the Chaminuka spirit was absent from the historical record of the 1896 risings—which had come to be seen as the first instalment of the liberation struggle. So Samkange in his novel had the woman, Mponga, who *does* appear in the historical record, possessed by the Chaminuka spirit. In the sixth chapter Mponga's claim to such possession is tested by the priests of Mwari. She proves the legitimacy of her possession by reciting the history of Chaminuka and his mediums, 'matters on which she was known to know next to nothing'. Samkange puts into Mponga's mouth, word for word, the story which Muchetera gave to Gelfand and which was published in *Shona Ritual.* More than that: he has Mponga carry on with her story—which is supposed to be an account of the nineteenth century mediums who preceded her—right up to the mediumship of Muchetera himself. Mponga—who in Samkange's novel becomes the major ideological influence on the 1896 rising—ends her validating narrative with the words:

It is not Muchetera whom you wish to kill but the tribal spirit. Chaminuka can read your thoughts and informs Muchetera.[28]

Muchetera's resistance credentials could hardly have been more strongly stated.

The death of 'Chaminuka', 1977
Muchetera's song, as translated in Berliner's book, runs:

Here we face death, Nhandare . . .
Death has come to us, Nhandare . . .
Father! It comes openly, Nhandare.
My death means perishing for ever . . .
At my death bury me by the wayside.[29]

I do not know if this song will come to be thought prophetic but at any rate by the time it was published—and by the time Samkange's book appeared—Muchetera was dead.

On the evening of 31 January 1977 a group of armed men came to Muchetera's kraal at Dambatsoko in Nedewedzo headmanship in Chiduku Tribal Trust Land. 'They called at his home', recalls an eye-witness, 'and shot him dead.

27. Berliner, *op. cit.*, p. 245.
28. Stanlake Samkange, *Year of the Uprising*, Heinemann, London, 1978, pp. 43–49.
29. Muchetera Mujuru, 'Nyamaropa ye Vana Vava Mushonga', Appendix 1, Berliner, *op. cit.*, pp. 260–61.

His *banya* (spirit-hut) was blasted. The men ordered that the surrounding people go about their normal duties as usual until after seven days when they were to bury the deceased's bones unceremoniously'.[30]

Who were these men who killed the asserted medium of the great Chaminuka spirit, the spirit in whose name the guerilla war was being waged? They were not members of the Security forces nor of Bishop Muzorewa's Auxiliaries. They were not even—as in 1883—Ndebele. In fact they were Shona-speaking guerillas belonging to ZANU-PF.

How are we to account for this? Certainly not in terms of any repudiation by these guerillas of the *idea* of Chaminuka or the idea of the importance of the spirits in the fight against the whites. The link between Chaminuka—as an idea—and the fight against the whites was as close in Makoni district as anywhere else. In 1962/3 militant nationalist youth there 'began to say that Africans should return to the worship of Chaminuka'; as we have seen young men from the district took Comrade Chaminuka as a 'Chimurenga name'; the very guerilla group which shot Muchetera called the people together and told them: 'We are fighting a war which is supported by the spirit mediums. We want you to be on our side.'[31] The explanation must lie elsewhere and it lies, I think, in a re-examination of Muchetera's career in the religious politics of Makoni district.

Muchetera's 'loyalist' alliance with the whites

The fact of the matter was that Muchetera's own motive in building up the importance of the Chaminuka spirit to white investigators such as Gelfand, Abraham and Berliner was significantly different from the motives of African nationalists in making the use they did of his material. Muchetera was mainly concerned to impress upon *whites* how important Chaminuka had been and how important consequently he, as Chaminuka's medium, also was. Muchetera needed to do this because his relationship with the chiefs and mediums of Makoni district was not at all as he described it to Gelfand. Muchetera was not accepted by the chiefs of Makoni district and he needed white recognition and patronage to build up his position there.

In this strategy Muchetera was eventually successful. By the time he died he had come to be recognized by the white administration as a very important person; he was much used by them and generously rewarded. I need now to document both these assertions in turn.

Muchetera told Gelfand that chief Makoni recognized his spiritual supremacy. It is very doubtful whether this had ever been true and it was certainly not true in 1959, when the book was published. All the available evidence shows that the Makoni chiefs did not propitiate any of the claimed mediums of Chaminuka in the twentieth century. In 1903, for example, when

30. Interview between P. M. Chakanyuka and Mandironda Beatrice, 1 February 1981. Peter Chakanyuka worked as my research assistant; my debt to him in this article will be obvious.
31. N. E. Thomas, 'Christianity, Politics and the Manyika', doctoral thesis, Boston, 1968, p. 114; interview with P. M. Chakanyuka, 28 March 1981.

the woman medium of Chaminuka summoned all the Shona chiefs to her kraal, chief Ndafunya Makoni did not go himself, but sent a detective to investigate. Ndafunya had become chief as a result of his support of the whites against the rebel chief Chingaira Makoni; Chingaira had been executed in 1896 and Ndafunya put in his place.   He did not go to wait upon Chaminuka, but several of 'the chief Headmen, being those who are hostile to the present Makoni' did, prominent among them the Rozwi chiefs who lived in Makoni's area.[32]

Nor was this episode merely the atypical caution of a stooge chief.   As the twentieth century wore on and one member of the Ndafunya family followed another as chief Makoni, so the house began to achieve its own legitimacy and a set of interests distinct from those of the administration.   This led them to work closely with spirit mediums—but *not* with the mediums of Chaminuka.

In 1930, for example, the Native Commissioner, Rusape, told the Chief Native Commissioner about Rozwi delegations from Makoni district going to make gifts to a powerful medium of the Chaminuka 'connection', Goronga. 'This is an annual occasion', he wrote, 'and the visit is made to a rain-maker in the Lomagundi district with a report about the weather and to enquire about the prospects of rain.'   In the past a representative of chief Makoni also used to make the pilgrimage, 'but the latter discontinued the practice some years ago having his own rain-makers in the persons of Sakureba and Chendambuya'.[33] At the time of Reresayi's claim to be medium of Chaminuka, in 1931, a number of mediums arose in Chiduku Reserve, claiming to be 'sons' of Goronga: the administration believed this to be connected with the re-emergence of the Chaminuka spirit.   But 'Makoni has not sent a representative to attend any seance in the Reserve'.[34]

This was the situation, then, when Muchetera claimed to be possessed of the Chaminuka spirit in 1934 and came to set up his spiritual head-quarters in Chiduku.   Oral testimony is clear that in these early days hundreds of suppliants flocked to his kraal: but it is clear also that the people of chief Makoni were not among them.   The Makoni chiefs turned to mediums who incarnated dead Makoni royals—the medium of the Chendambuya spirit, who lived in the north of the district, and in particular the medium of the Sakureba spirit who lived in Makoni Reserve, close to the burial hill of the Makonis.   In fact, the Ndafunya line of chiefs had compensated for the circumstances of Ndafunya's accession by living at the ritual centre of the chiefdom and paying scrupulous respect to their spiritual obligations to the ancestral dead.   The Makoni chiefs also looked with much suspicion on the Rozwi leaders in their district: in the nineteenth century chief Makoni had been paramount over all the district and the Rozwi chiefs Tandi and Chiduku had done them homage, but in the twentieth century the

32. NC, Makoni, to Acting CNC, 30 November 1903, A 11/2/12/11, National Archives, Salisbury.
33. NC, Rusape, to CNC, 29 December 1930, s. 138.22. 1931–33, National Archives, Salisbury.
34. Acting NC, Rusape, to CNC, 4 August 1931, s. 138.22.1930–31; Acting NC, Rusape to CNC, 22 and 30 September 1931, s. 138.22. 1931–33, National Archives, Salisbury.

colonial administration showed a dangerous tendency to recognize Tandi and Chiduku as chiefs in their own right. Muchetera's claim to speak for Chaminuka, great spirit of the Rozwi, and his demand that the Makoni chiefs recognize his supremacy was hardly likely to meet with much favour. And from Muchetera's point of view the problem was that his kraal in Nedewedzo lay in an area directly controlled by chief Makoni.[35]

In 1952 the Ndafunya family monopoly of the Makoni chiefship came to an end. The new chief was Zambe, surviving son of that Chingaira who had been executed by the British in 1896. Zambe refused to go to live at the ritual centre of the chiefship in Makoni Reserve and continued to reside at his home in Chiduku. Zambe determined to break the mould of the Ndafunya family tribal system; since the main Makoni spirit mediums had worked so closely with the Ndafunyas he resolved not to use them, and he looked around for other sources of ideological legitimacy.[36] It might have seemed an opportunity for Muchetera.

It was, in fact, very much the reverse. Zambe found his alternative ideological support in Chatambudza Samukange, also resident in Chiduku Reserve, who was held to be medium of the Mabvakure spirit, 'the original founding ancestor' of the Makoni line.[37] He ignored government recognition of other chiefs and headmen and allocated land freely in their areas. He signed himself as 'paramount', despite administrative rebuke. And he made it plain that he would brook no opposition and no claims to an influence greater than his own.

By the time Gelfand came to Makoni district to talk with Muchetera the medium was already at daggers drawn with Zambe Makoni. The old chief refused to accept that Muchetera was the authentic medium of Chaminuka. For his part Muchetera claimed superiority over every chief in Zimbabwe. In 1962 their hostility came to a head. In the words of the deputy Secretary, Administration:

> Chaminuka is a famous ancestral spirit but various persons have claimed to be the living host of the spirit and it is very difficult to determine how legitimate their claims to possession are. Certainly Africans are divided in their beliefs as to who the genuine Chaminuka is and Chief Makoni has for a long time been one of those who considered Muchetera's claims to be quite bogus.

35. For the interactions of spirit mediums and the Makoni chiefs I have drawn upon the following files held at the District Commissioner's office, Rusape: 'Weya: Chendambuya'; 'Old Papers on Chief Makoni'; 'Makoni'; 'Makoni: Headman Rugoyi'. For the Rozwi chiefs in the district and their relations with mediums I have drawn on files 'Chiduku: Chief Tandi' and 'Chief Chiduku: Chiduku'.
36. This point is developed in Terence Ranger, 'Tradition and Travesty: Chiefs in the Makoni District, 1960–1980', *Africa*, forthcoming.
37. DC, Rusape, to Member in Charge, Special Branch 7 March 1966, file 'Chiduku: Headman Masvosva'; DO, Rusape, to DC, Rusape, 12 March 1971; DC, Rusape to PC, 18 March 1971, file 'Makoni', District commissioner's office, Rusape.

As to the facts of this case, the Native Commissioner advises that dissension in a particular kraal led Chief Makoni to split the kraal and allocate new lands. Muchetera was one of those involved in the land argument before the Chief and it must be assumed that in the course of the proceedings the old bitter controversy over the Chaminuka spirit erupted. The Chief choked off Muchetera for his pretensions and ordered him and his companions to remain at at the Chief's kraal while he further investigated the problem of the spirit.

Muchetera and his acolytes were held for ten days: they were made to share 'in the tasks of the kraal', though Muchetera himself was exempted 'as a possible spirit medium'.[38]

Roland Hatendi, the Native Commissioner's main African assistant, was present at the kraal when the confrontation between Muchetera and Zambe Makoni began:

> They talked for hours and I only listened to the beginning. Zambe asked Muchetera why he claimed to be so great. Muchetera said that he was possessed by the great spirit, Chaminuka, and that he only could make rain. Zambe replied: 'I have my own men who are rain-makers who pay their respects to me as well. You don't pay your respects to me. I am not interested in you and I do not accept you as a medium.'[39]

Plainly Muchetera could expect little so long as Zambe remained chief. Zambe died in August 1970, after a long and autocratic reign. He was replaced by Muzanenamo, son of Ndafunya. Muzanenamo reversed some of Zambe's practices: he based himself at the ritual centre of the chiefdom and worked closely with the medium of the Sakureba spirit and other ritual officers. But he showed himself no more tolerant of Muchetera and no more ready to accept the pretensions of the Rozwi chiefs.

Muchetera's response was to try to get the Nedewedzo area taken out of chief Makoni's jurisdiction. In 1973 there was a dispute over the succession to the Nedewedzo headmanship. Muchetera argued that control of the area and the power to nominate the headman really belonged to chief Chipunza: 'The spirits tell me that we all belong to Gunguwo... who came from Chipunza'.[40] Muchetera pressed the matter vigorously in the first months of 1974, coming into Rusape in his full ritual regalia to lobby the District Commissioner. The DC sent Muchetera and the other pro-Chipunza delegates on to chief Muzanenamo Makoni, who responded with fury:

> If these people keep on fighting against me I shall have to let them move from Dewedzo their beloved Chief Chipunza.... I re-warned and advised

38. Depute Secretary, Administration, to Minister of Internal Affairs, 24 November 1962, file 'Makoni', DC's office, Rusape.
39. Interview with Roland Hatendi, Tandi, 21 February 1981.
40. Notes of a meeting, 16 July 1973, file 'Chiduku: Headman Nedewedzo', DC's office, Rusape.

Muchetera to move from my district if he keeps on fighting against me.   I'm really angry about them.[41]

In May 1974 Muzanenamo gave notice that he had chosen a man to become headman Nedewedzo and that he was summoning 'that man Muchetera . . . so that he will not cause trouble on the day of installation'.[42]

It is clear, in short, that on this question at least Muchetera comprehensively misled Gelfand.   It is also clear that Muchetera's strategy was to compensate for the hostility of successive Makoni chiefs by seeking to gain white patronage. One of the oddities in the rise of cultural nationalism was the fact that Gelfand and Abraham, whose work gave it so powerful a stimulus, were themselves out of sympathy with the nationalist movement.   Gelfand's argument—and apparently also Muchetera's—was rather that African 'traditions' constituted the best guarantee of loyalty and order:

It is remarkable (wrote Gelfand in *Shona Ritual*) how well behaved the rural Africans who practice their religion are at religious ceremonies and how law-abiding, polite, kind and considerate they often are in ordinary life.[43]

Muchetera himself adapted the traditions of Pasipamire's predictions so as to give the same message: 'Europeans will enter the country and bring peace. They will not interfere with your customs and will respect your property.   Even poor people will be able to possess cattle without any interference'.   Provincial Commissioner Woollacott, to whom this version of the prophecy was given, found it 'uncanny' in its 'accuracy'![44]

Roland Hatendi recalls that 'Muchetera himself was a really good supporter of the Government.   He used to tell the DC when he was in that area, "Don't worry.   Chaminuka will stand by the Government and see that their orders are carried out".'[45]   During the open nationalist period Muchetera started a branch of the ruling United Federal Party at his kraal.   When he was arrested by Zambe in 1962, Muchetera appealed for aid to the UFP member of parliament, Chad Chipunza: Chad complained that in molesting Muchetera, 'a stout opponent of the banned ZAPU' and member of the UFP, Zambe was showing himself sympathetic to nationalism.[46]

Peter Moda Chakanyuka, a member of a family resident near to Muchetera's

41.   Chief Muzanenamo Makoni to DC, Rusape, 18 April 1974, file 'Chiduku: Headman Nedewedzo', DC's office, Rusape.
42.   Delegation to the District Commissioner led to Muzanenamo Makoni, 7 May 1974, file 'Chiduku: Headman Nedewedzo', DC's office, Rusape.
43.   M. Gelfand, *Shona Ritual*, p. 7.
44.   R. C. Woollacott, 'Pasipamire—Spirit Medium of Chaminuka, the "Wizard" of Chitungwiza', *NADA*, 9, 2, 1975, p. 157.
45.   Interview with Roland Hatendi, Tandi, 21 February 1981.
46.   Interview with Chad Chipunza, Salisbury, 2 April 1981; Deputy Secretary, Administration, to Minister of Internal Affairs, 24 November 1962, file 'Makoni', DC's office Rusape.

kraal and a family stoutly committed to the nationalist movement since the late 1950s, describes their reaction to Muchetera:

When Muchetera first claimed to be possessed by Chaminuka very many believed in him and came to his kraal. But when it came to the idea of nationalism he used to associate with the District Commissioner, had pictures of Europeans in his *banya* (spirit hut), stopped eating *sadza* (meal porridge) and depended on tea. He always wore his hair uncut and plaited, his black robe, to show he was a regional spirit medium, but he used to come into our family eating house every day to eat buns and tea. He had ceased to be African. He rode a bike and never walked. He acted on the principle that if a person was well known to whites he would gain their support.

Muchetera wanted to gain the chiefship of Dewedzo for his family and backed Chipunza against Makoni. In 1961 or 1962, when Dewedzo was fully ZAPU, even the children, my uncle threw him out of our eating house. He caught him by the throat and shouted: 'You think that this country can be led by the whites'. He threw him out. Muchetera had to cycle all the way to Dowa Purchase Area to get his bread and tea.[47]

After the banning of the nationalist movements in 1964, Muchetera built up a circle of 'loyalist' mediums. One of these, Mbuya Chigutiro, told the Anglican pastor, Salathiel Madziyire, in the early 1970s how she travelled from her home to Marandellas district three times a year to attend the ceremonies at Muchetera's:

She says that there were false mediums who frightened the public with wild claims and she blamed the failure of the rains on these people. But her own organization coincided in many ways with the customs of the Church.... They were different from the spirit of Mbuya in Nyandoro who had caused the failure of the rains. She believes that in the early days of the current political strife, a man appeared at Chitungwiza, where the great Chaminuka medium was killed by the Ndebele in the nineteenth century. He falsely claimed to be Chaminuka. But neither he, nor any other false spirit, can stand against the true power of Chaminuka. Chaminuka [Muchetera] will overcome false prophets.

'All this is quite different', remarked Madziyire, from the 'many other "gods" and spirits ... introduced recently as a result of the political crisis in Rhodesia'.[48]

47. Interview with P. M. Chakanyuka, Salisbury, 28 March 1981.
48. S. K. Madziyire, 'Heathen Practices in the Urban and Rural Parts of Marandellas Area', *Themes in the Christian History of Central Africa*, eds., T. O. Ranger and J. Weller, Heinemann, London, 1975, pp. 78–90. See also footnote 60, page 369.

The administration in Makoni district and Muchetera

It took some time for the administration to make full use of Muchetera and his 'loyalist' circle of mediums.   Undoubtedly the work of Gelfand and Abraham, so much based on Muchetera's evidence, contributed greatly to a revival of interest in spirit mediums on the part of government.   The District Commissioners who were delineating 'communities' in the mid 1960s were told in their general instructions that hitherto the great importance of the mediums had been over-looked; they were asked to pay special attention to their role.   But the delineation exercise was aimed at producing workable communities at the headman level; there was little for a medium of Chaminuka to do in such a context, though Muchetera did show a lively interest in the 'community development' structures erected in Nedewedzo.

In the 1970s there was a great development of administrative 'tradition', as District Commissioners searched for ways of making chiefs fully legitimate.[49]

In Makoni district this did lead to an administrative attempt to find a genuine medium of the Goronga spirit in order to instal an authentic chief Chiduku, but that was as close as the exercise got to the Chaminuka circle.   It was naturally the mediums of the Makoni chiefdom itself who were the objects of most administrative interest and research.

So Muchetera enjoyed administrative good-will and protection against the anger of successive chief Makonis, but for a long time no more.   The change came with the success of the guerilla war from 1972 onwards.   The guerillas campaigned in the name of the spirits and of Chaminuka in particular.   It was high time for the administration to play their own Chaminuka card.

The guerilla group who killed Muchetera in January 1977 took very good care to explain why they had done so.   As Peter Chakanyuka recalls:

After Muchetera's death they called a meeting to explain why he had been killed.   They said that while they were still in Mozambique and trying to infiltrate into the north-east he went up in a helicopter to drop leaflets against them, saying 'I Chaminuka condemn the terrorists'.[50]

In February 1977 an African Catholic woman, curious to know about the motives and attitudes of the guerillas, visited the group which had just killed Muchetera.   In her report to the Catholic Justice and Peace and Commission, she recorded their reply to her questions on the killing:

The group admitted responsibility and said that the man was killed because he had accused them of destroying the country by their fighting. . . .   He had travelled to protected villages in the Chiweshe area telling the African people there that unless they stopped helping the 'Terrorists' there would be no

49.   See footnote 36.
50.   Interview with P. M. Chakanyuka, 28 March 1981.

rain.... Muchetera had been paid by the government ... he appeared to have plenty of money at the time.[51]

All this made Muchetera a prime target. He had constantly stressed his invulnerability; now he had to be killed to show that he was not the true Chaminuka:

They shot him in the chest and they rocketed his *banya*.[52]

The guerillas and spirit mediums

It must be clear now why Muchetera was shot in 1977, the year before Berliner and Samkange linked him so firmly to the liberationist tradition. But Muchetera's death did *not* mean that the guerillas ceased to make use of spirit mediums in Makoni district or elsewhere. What it *did* mean was that they made no use of 'supra-tribal' mediums in Makoni; instead they turned to the mediums of the spirits of dead chiefs and headmen, spirits who had a particular claim to particular areas of land.

Peter Chakanyuka tells us that the group which shot Muchetera:

worked with Murwira, a female medium, in Dewedzo. Murwira was the spirit of chief Chipunza's deputy in Dewedzo and he could give them protection in this area. Comrades used to gather for every ritual at his place. In every difficulty they went to consult him. Today we have no chief but the medium is very influential.[53]

George Bhongoghozo, intelligence officer for the guerilla groups in Makoni during the war, describes how the ritual officers of the Makoni chiefship worked with them:

The mediums lived near Matotwe, the burial hill for the Makoni chiefs. They carried out special ceremonies there so that we could enter the caves and they showed us where to go so as not to alienate the spirits. The Chief approved of our use of the place. These mediums used to foresee and warn us of enemy attacks.... The masses used to believe that we moved supernaturally and not on our own feet. They did not know that we had been warned to escape an attack by the mediums of Matotwe.[54]

The great majority of the guerillas in Makoni district were 'strangers' born in

51. 'The Testimony of Mrs O. M. . . . who visited the "Vakomana" in the Marandellas Area, February 1977', file 'Guerilla Reports', Justice and Peace Commission archives, Salisbury.
52. Interview with Father Peter Turner, Umtali, 14 March 1981; interview with P. M. Chakanyuka, 28 March 1981.
53. Interview with P. M. Chakanyuka, 28 March 1981.
54. Interview with George Bhongoghozo, Rusape, 16 February 1981.

other districts. This was a matter of policy so that they were not involved emotionally when it came to taking action against 'sell-outs'. But it posed some problems of legitimacy for them, especially as they attacked and killed chiefs and headmen who worked with and for the administration. Mediums, speaking for dead chiefs and headmen, could give this legitimacy, as well as a secure relationship with the land. From the point of view of the people in general, a relationship between the guerillas and a medium was one way of ensuring that the actions of the fighting men observed some local rules. From this point of view of the mediums—many of whom had very sensibly shied away from all overtures from the administration—an alliance with the guerillas ensured that they would be given proper respect.

In February 1981 I spoke with the medium of the Akuchekwa spirit, senior spirit of the Tandi chiefship. He told me that he 'used to see the "boys" in my own person in 1979. I know they came to consult the spirit'; but of course since this consultation took place while he was in a possession trance, he did not know what had been said. An acolyte supplied these details:

> Akuchekwa told the boys he would protect them but that they must not do the things which the spirits disliked. The spirits refused to accept the shedding of innocent blood. If 'sell-outs' went to the boys and said 'This one is a witch', 'this one is an informer', they were not just to kill them. The boys obeyed the spirits. Things were quite perfect then. And the spirits protected the boys.[55]

The medium himself recounted that 'one of the boys came in possessed by an alien spirit but he was chased away by the spirits of the land. Before the war a lot of people were Christians but now they are believing in the spirits.'[56]

Amon Shonge, leader of a co-operative farming project in Weya Tribal Trust Land, in the north of Makoni district, and member of the newly elected Maungwe District Council, sums up the role of mediums in the war:

> There are many spirit mediums in Weya. Some of them were also consulted by the Security Forces and some were actually killed for this by the comrades.... The main medium the comrades used was the chief medium of headman Mwendaziya, Mukuwamombe, the greatest spirit of them all. The medium had been living in Tanda but the comrades brought him into Weya. They wanted him here because he was supposed to be the one who could make the land safe. This use of mediums was the same everywhere. The comrades had to contact the spirit medium first to introduce themselves. Then they would be told what to do. They were told which were the holy places and given some sort of by-laws to guide them. They were

55. Interview with an alcolyte of Akuchekwa, Tandi, 27 Februar, 1981.
56. Interview with Robert Tinarwo, medium of Akuchekwa, Tandi, 27 February 1981.

told that they must not kill innocent people.   Nearly everyone then started to feel that the mediums were very important people.   The mediums felt that they had been forgotten but now they were remembered.[57]

Conclusion

The story of the death of Muchetera reveals some of the ambiguities in the rise of Shona cultural nationalism.   It has not, of course, brought the development of the Chaminuka history itself to a halt.   That history continues, both at the incarnational and the literary level.

Aeneas Chigwedere, in his remarkable *From Mutapa to Rhodes*, tells us that in December 1975 a group of mediums, including a medium of the Goronga spirit, gathered secretly on top of mount Wedza, singing 'Chaminuka is the King'; a man was possessed by a spirit which would not reveal its identity.   On 23 August 1976—four months only before the death of Muchetera—once again on mount Wedza, the spirit revealed that it was Chaminuka:

He was quick to add that nobody should reveal this and threatened to kill anybody who did so.   The reason was that the political situation was dangerous.   If he was known to have come home, his children from the bush . . . would immediately want to make use of him and his medium would be killed by the Rhodesian troops.[58]

In Chigwedere's eyes Muchetera had been nothing but an imposter: at his death there remained the true Chaminuka medium, who has still not yet fully revealed himself.

Meanwhile, liberationist poets have hailed the election victory of ZANU/PF in 1980 and the independence celebrations in April in terms reminiscent of Cripps's story of Pasipamire's Easter-time martyrdom:

> And so on that misty morning . . .
> That awesome Easter tide morn
> That terrible mist
> That forever hung heavy on the land
> Began to lift . . .
>
> And as the dying spirit
> Faded from the glades
> They came down from the mountain
> Bearing arms on their shoulders
> And palm branches in their hands,
> The symbol of the new order. . . .

57.   Interview with Amon Shonge, Weya, 25 March 1981.
58.   Aeneas Chigwedere, *From Mutapa to Rhodes*, Macmillan, Salisbury, 1980, pp. 74–75.

But before the mist
Was swallowed into the virgin light
A fearsome sight
We beheld
Of still bodies
And broken guns,
High
On the mountain slopes

'These are them
That have died
A ransom
For Zimbabwe.
Broken they lie
On the mountain side
Yet not in death they lie
But in immortal love of Nehanda,
Anointed of Chaminuka,
Priest primordial;

And though their names
Be not on cathedral marble writ
Yet with throngs
Of living warriors forgotten
They shall forever live.'

CHORUS:
Et lux perpetua
Luceat eis,
Quia pius es.[59]

Acknowledgement

The research on which this article is based was carried out on a grant from the SSRC.

59. Chris Magadza, 'The Return', *And Now the Poets Speak*, eds., M. Khadani and M. Zimunya, Mambo, Gwelo, 1981, pp. 154–155.
60. (See p. 364) Peter Fry in his *Spirits of Protest*, London, 1976, describes a contestation between Muchetera and the 'Wild Man of Chitungwiza' who also claimed to be Chaminuka (pp. 43–44). Fry himself met Muchetera in the DC's office at Marandellas; Muchetera 'announced that he was the medium of Chaminuka. By way of proof, he motioned forward one of his acolytes who was bearing a carefully tended copy of *Shona Ritual*' (p. 127).

Journal of Southern African Studies, Vol. 14, No. 2, January 1988

The Zimbabwean War of Liberation:
Struggles Within the Struggle

NORMA KRIGER*

Peasant Consciousness and Guerrilla War in Zimbabwe by Terence Ranger addresses recent research interests in informal, invisible, everyday resistance (for example, tax evasion) in the context of peasant colonial history. [1] For the war period, he combines a study of peasant consciousness with more established research interests in peasant organisation, mobilisation and ideology during a revolution. [2] By showing how 'everyday' peasants' resistance underpinned their more dramatic revolutionary input during the guerrilla war, Ranger moves us away from the deeply ingrained image of passive peasants who occasionally burst into violent revolt in a crisis situation provided outside leadership is available. [3] Ranger's work will be of immense interest to those interested in rural class relations, national liberation movements, and Zimbabwean agrarian history.

Our research concerns intersect for the guerrilla war period, where we both examine peasant mobilisation and participation in the guerrilla war, as well as intra-societal relationships. [4] We worked in different Shona-speaking districts – Ranger in Makoni, myself in Mutoko – and approach the war period emphasising different features of the past. Ranger sees peasant participation in the war as sharing important continuities with a history of 'everyday' peasant resistance; I focus on the continuities of obstacles to organised collective action between the open nationalist

---

* My thanks to: the organisers and participants at the Conference; Terence Ranger whose work inspired me; Dick Werbner, Michael Schatzberg, and Toby Ditz for helpful comments; the Political Science Department at The Johns Hopkins University for making it possible to attend the Conference; my dissertation chairman, Lucian Pye and advisors – Suzanne Berger, Sara Berry, Myron Weiner – and the many Zimbabweans whom I cannot name here but who made this research possible.

[1] Terence Ranger, *Peasant Consciousness and Guerrilla War in Zimbabwe. A Comparative Study* (London, 1985).

[2] For example, the works of Barrington Moore, Jr., *Social Origins of Dictatorship and Democracy. Lord and Peasant in the Making of the Modern World* (Boston, 1967); James C. Scott, *The Moral Economy of the Peasant. Rebellion and Subsistence in Southeast Asia* (New Haven, 1976); Samuel L. Popkin, *The Rational Peasant* (Berkeley, California, 1979); Joel S. Migdal, *Peasants, Politics and Revolution* (Princeton, New Jersey, 1974).

[3] James C. Scott, *Weapons of the Weak. Everyday Forms of Peasant Resistance* (New Haven, 1985), p. xvi, 32-5. Scott discusses the shift in research focus from formal organisations to everyday resistance, and suggests reasons for it.

[4] Norma Kriger, 'Struggles for Independence: Rural Conflicts in Zimbabwe's War of Liberation' (Ph.D., Massachusetts Institute of Technology, 1985). I am revising this, so my arguments may depart somewhat from the dissertation. The revision chiefly affects the emphasis I give to class conflicts during the war, and I am indebted to Ranger's work for helping me to rethink their significance.

phase and the guerrilla war. For all these overarching differences, we produce remarkably similar descriptive material on the war period. Nevertheless we go on to offer different interpretations. I will argue that these may be traced to our different central concepts and methodological approaches. Before doing so, I present a synopsis of Ranger's work.

Synopsis

At the core of the book is the concept of peasant consciousness, its relationship to rural differentiation, and its historical 'stages' of growth or 'levels'. Peasant consciousness refers to the peasants' understanding of their grievances as a class. [5] Their grievances relate to how white farmers and the state undermine their commitment to agricultural production and to defend this 'peasant option' 'as best they could'. [6] The peasantry is internally differentiated and this is reflected in a differentiated consciousness. [7] This internally differentiated class consciousness or peasant consciousness that is shaped by what happens in production has an ideological expression in peasant religions. [8]

Peasant consciousness is a teleological concept. It moves through inevitable stages until it reaches maturity in a peasant radical nationalism. [9] What propels it from stage to stage is the growing intensity of peasant grievance as the 'peasant option' is steadily undermined. [10] The first level of consciousness was acquired in the struggle to become peasants in the aftermath of colonial conquest and the alienation of land; it was a struggle to resist working for whites. [11] The 1930s introduced a higher level or another stage of consciousness among Shona-speakers: '. . .peasants of all sorts became much more aware of the role of the *state*, where in the period before 1930 they had been more aware of the emnity (sic) of white farmers'. [12] But urban-based political organisations failed to address rural issues, and the rural elite did not provide leadership for organised resistance. [13] The next stage of peasant consciousness – peasant radical nationalism – required that

(T)he peasant option had to be not only restricted and impeded but really threatened with 'destruction'; government intervention in peasant cultivation had to reach a peak of coercive intensity which was still only foreshadowed by the developments of the 1930s; peasants had to encounter political movements which spoke directly to rural grievance and held out some sort of hope of alleviating it. [14]

This occurred in the 1950s and '(A)t its highest stage of development this fusion of Shona cultural nationalism and peasant radicalism proved potent enough to allow the spread of ZANLA's guerrilla action. . .' [15]

[5] Ranger, *Consciousness*, p. 48, 84.
[6] Ranger, *Consciousness*, p. 15, 42.
[7] Ranger, *Consciousness*, pp. 43-4.
[8] Ranger, *Consciousness*, for example, p. 43, 88, 90, 185-6, 256.
[9] Ranger, *Consciousness*, p. 84, 88.
[10] Ranger, *Consciousness*, p. 90.
[11] Ranger, *Consciousness*, p. 21, 29, 31.
[12] Ranger, *Consciousness*, p. 84.
[13] Ranger, *Consciousness*, p. 81-3.
[14] Ranger, *Consciousness*, p. 90; see also p. 137.
[15] Ranger, *Consciousness*, p. 137.

Ranger argues that the 'existence, extent and intensity of the nationalist peasant consciousness produced a different balance between peasants, nationalist activities and ultimately guerrillas in Zimbabwe than that which developed in Lusophone Africa'.[16] In the 1970s, peasant radical nationalist consciousness 'was highly conducive to mobilisation for guerrilla war. . .', and consequently, there was less 'necessity for political education' by guerrillas than there had been in Mozambique.[17] Compared with Mozambique, radical peasant consciousness allowed for a 'more direct input by the peasantry into the ideology and programme of the war'.[18] The resulting ideology incorporated a belief in mediums and support for a ZANU-PF government that would return their expropriated lands and 'would no longer interfere in peasant production but would content itself with ensuring high prices, good marketing facilities, supplies of cheap fertiliser and so on.[19] It made possible the collective action of peasants and guerrillas.[20] Especially after the internal settlement in 1978, rural class conflicts assumed growing importance but they never culminated in rural class warfare or civil war.[21]

The concluding chapter focuses on the changing relationship between the state and the peasantry in the first years of independence. Initially, peasants had advantages vis-a-vis the state unusual to African peasantries. In the first year after the 1980 independence elections, 'a self-conscious and even organised peasantry' confronted 'an enfeebled, transitional and rudimentary state apparatus'.[22] Ranger anticipated a shift in the balance of power between the state and the peasantry 'as the new administrative system stabilises and as the negative peasant achievement of ending agrarian coercion and the positive peasant achievement of exerting pressure for land redistribution came to their natural term. . .'[23]

Let me identify what I consider to be two major areas in which Ranger and I disagree, before illustrating why I think our differences are rooted in distinct conceptual and methodological approaches. I found that the ZANU-PF organizations set up by the guerrillas required guerrilla violence and force to function. Consequently, I reject the concept of sustained popular support or voluntary cooperation between guerrillas and peasants or local elites. My primary emphasis is on how guerrilla inability to establish 'liberated zones' made it inevitable that mobilisation would require ongoing violence. As a corollary, I disagree with Ranger's emphasis on the effectiveness of peasant-guerrilla ideology, and in particular the role of spirit mediums, in peasant mobilisation.

Looking at how the guerrilla war affected rural society, I found gender, generation and lineage tensions to be at least of equal importance to class tensions within rural society. Additionally, I maintain that these local level struggles preoccupied peasants. Even peasant attacks on white farms and rural administration were

[16] Ranger, *Consciousness*, p. 14.
[17] Ranger, *Consciousness*, pp. 24-25.
[18] Ranger, *Consciousness*, p. 14.
[19] Ranger, *Consciousness*, p. 177; see also pp. 182-3, 189-90, 192.
[20] Ranger, *Consciousness*, p. 180.
[21] Ranger, *Consciousness*, p. 264-5, 269.
[22] Ranger, *Consciousness*, p. 291.
[23] Ranger, *Consciousness*, p. 319.

understood by peasants in terms of their local interests. This leads me to challenge Ranger's concept of peasant radical nationalism. Because of the importance which I attribute to local struggles, and the considerable civilian and guerrilla violence and force that were employed by contestants, I am willing to talk of civil war, while recognizing that none of the participants were government loyalists or had government protection. What I am describing is a revolution within a revolution.

Conceptual and Methodological Issues

Nowhere in Ranger's book is there a definition of peasants. He appears to employ two different definitions. For the earlier colonial period, his peasant category includes mixed-subsistence farmers and migrant labourers, small peasant producers, rural entrepreneurial producers — Reserves entrepreneurs until centralisation in the 1930s eliminated them, and then master farmers in the Reserves and Purchase Area farmers — and, until their eviction, 'squatters' on European farms and unoccupied Crown Land allocated for Europeans. Later, Ranger very clearly distinguishes peasants from teachers, storekeepers and other businesspeople whom he now refers to as 'petty bourgeois' or 'rural middle class'. [24] He also separates out Purchase Area farmers, master farmers and other 'progressives' from his peasant concept.

In the ideal 'pure peasant option' in the early colonial period, a defining feature of peasants is their commitment to agricultural production and resistance to migrant labour: they do not want to work for whites or the state because wage labour will adversely interfere with their production. [25] However, by the 1960s, '. . .the peasant option had become viable almost everywhere only on the basis of male family members having access to extra-agricultural wages'. [26]

One problem with the 'full peasant solution' is that it requires peasants to resist migrant labour, because it can only make them worse off. Yet many peasants voluntarily engage in migrant labour and it sometimes actually promotes agricultural prosperity. Many of Ranger's Reserves entrepreneurs and Purchase Area farmers got their cash to invest in farming from working for the government as police, teachers, clerks and sometimes 'boss-boys' on European farms and mines. Ranger is clearly aware of the value that migrant labour can have as a strategy for accumulating capital for investment in farming. [27] Yet conceptually, up until the open nationalist period, migrant labour is universally antithetical to peasant production. Ian Phimister succinctly states the relationship between migrant labour and production. In his view, neither state offensives (fiscal) nor eviction notices by farmers and companies especially after 1907 and up to the 1920s 'succeeded in transforming *all Africans* into labour migrants when they were not subsistence cultivators and into subsistence cultivators when they were not labour migrants'. [28]

---

[24] Ranger. *Consciousness*, p. 254, 275.

[25] Ranger. *Consciousness*, p. 15, 25, 27.

[26] Ranger. *Consciousness*, p. 311; see also pp. 331-2, footnote 77, p. 292.

[27] Ranger. *Consciousness*, p. 27, 54, 62, 64-5, 77.

[28] Ian Phimister, 'Peasant Production and Underdevelopment in Southern Rhodesia', *African Affairs*, 13 (1974), p. 251; see also p. 244.

A second problem with his peasant concept is that it permits no voluntary change in commitment to agricultural production. For example, when he describes the growth of small businessmen in Makoni in the 1930s, he notes that 'some store-owners were ex-Reserve entrepreneurs who turned to commerce when they lost opportunities to produce maize; others were returning labour migrants who were unable even to get a footing as a small peasant in the reserves'.[29] Once again, though, the evidence in his text suggests otherwise. He seems to accept a district commissioner's observation that ' ''(E)nlightened natives are most keen on entering business on their account'' ',[30] and his description of how 'a pioneering Reserves entrepreneur' became 'a pioneering businessman' underlines the element of choice that individual was exercising.[31] Up until the open nationalist phase, even when people develop other commitments that might override their interest in farming, they still remain peasants.

Another problem with the 'pure peasant option' is that it seems entirely hypothetical. Ranger describes Makoni District as atypical because of the extent to which 'the peasant option could be (so) successfully developed',[32] and chooses it partly for this reason: 'it seems most logical to consider those areas where an attempt was being made to resist demands for labour altogether and to opt for a full peasant solution'.[33] Yet even in Makoni District migrant labour had been a fact of life from the early colonial period. There was the quite extensive experience of forced labour in the 1890s that Ranger records.[34] Ranger supports that Makoni 'became one of the districts notoriously least productive of migrant labourers'[35] with a quote from the district commissioner who claimed that in 1908 at most one-third of Makoni men had worked for Europeans during that year.[36] This seems to underscore how extensive migrant labour was even in the ideal case. Even if these migrants perceive themselves as peasants — and we do not know that — their wage labour experience is so intertwined with their agricultural production experience that 'peasant consciousness' does not seem a useful concept.

Ranger offers two different justifications — one theoretical, another personal — for focusing on peasant consciousness rather than migrant consciousness. Ranger argues that 'the Zimbabwean peasantry cannot be regarded as merely a class in transition to being proletarian. The Zimbabwean peasantry, diversified as it is, must . . . be regarded as a class in itself'.[37] Between viewing the peasantry as a transitory class and as a 'class in itself', there is the possibility of a stable migrant labour system. Ranger acknowledges this in his second and different justification for looking at peasant consciousness:

there is no way in which peasant experience and peasant consciousness can be separated from worker experience and worker consciousness in a labour migrancy system like that of Zimbabwe. . . . . .I can justify myself partly on the grounds that . . . .it is very difficult indeed

[29] Ranger, *Consciousness*, p. 240.
[30] Ranger, *Consciousness*, p. 238.
[31] Ranger, *Consciousness*, p. 240-1.
[32] Ranger, *Consciousness*, p. 45.
[33] Ranger, *Consciousness*, p. 27.
[34] Ranger, *Consciousness*, pp. 29-30.
[35] Ranger, *Consciousness*, p. 30.
[36] Ranger, *Consciousness*, p. 35.
[37] Ranger, *Consciousness*, p. 289.

to find out much about the history of the African peasantry, at any rate after the work of Robin Palmer runs out in the early 1930s. Perhaps a stronger and truer reason is that I so greatly enjoyed my interactions with the peasantry of Makoni and so much valued their readiness to entrust to me their sense of the meaning of their experiences.[38]

The almost one-to-one correspondence that Ranger posits between growing peasant consciousness and the progressive undermining of the 'peasant option' means that changes in consciousness can be inferred from changes in peasants' objective situation. This absolves him of the need to find out what peasants consider to be central issues in their lives and how they feel about them. In Ranger's book we rarely hear directly from the peasants themselves. For the period before open nationalism, he relies on mission and, more especially, state archives. The state, primarily concerned that Africans not disrupt 'law and order', is an attentive recorder of African grievances against its policies that have any potential for creating disturbance. Otherwise, as James Scott notes for state archives generally, 'the peasantry appear(ed) only as anonymous contributors to statistics on conscription, crop production, taxes, and so forth'.[39] Ranger's concept of a peasant consciousness that is shaped by experiences in agricultural production meshes well with the official historical record, as does his focus on African sentiments towards state policies and white farmers as opposed to intra-African relations. For the open nationalist period and the guerrilla war, Ranger draws again on the official record and mission archives, autobiographical accounts of leading participants, Clutton-Brock's correspondence[40] with leading nationalists in Makoni, and on interviews. Only about one-third of his interviewees were peasants, and just over half of these actually appear in the text. (See Table 1.) His key informants for this period are nationalist politicians, teachers, storekeepers, and church-related people. (See Table 2.) The Africans in this group include some unusually dedicated and irrepressible nationalists who chose to confront the coercive power of the state when many others were unwilling to do so. These men were fortunate to be linked to the inspiring Clutton-Brock, based at St. Faith's Mission. Ranger pays tribute to him and others there: 'One of the reasons why Makoni became a leading Congress district was that the influence of the ideas from St. Faith's radiated out from it to the primary school teachers of the neighbouring Reserves.'[41]

Even if one believes, along with Ranger, that the most critical variable influencing peasant consciousness is exploitation/discrimination/oppression in the sphere of agricultural production, one may argue that there is a gap between objective exploitation (or discrimination or oppression) and peasant experience of it.[42] This

[38] Ranger, *Consciousness*, p. 16.

[39] James C. Scott, *Weapons of the Weak*, p. xv.

[40] Guy Clutton-Brock is a Welsh missionary who came to St. Faith's Mission in the 1950s. He tried to find means of establishing racial cooperation and initiated the Cold Comfort Farm Society outside Salisbury where cooperative farming was practised. He was deported from Rhodesia but retained contact with leading nationalists in Makoni.

[41] Ranger, *Consciousness*, p. 154.

[42] Ranger speaks of grievances rather than exploitation. For different conceptions of the relationship between exploitation and consciousness, see James C. Scott, *Weapons of the Weak* (New Haven, 1985); Quinton Hoare and Geoffrey Nowell Smith (eds. and translators), *Selections from the Prison Notebooks of Antonio Gramsci* (London, 1971).

makes it imperative to talk to peasants to find out how they give meaning to their acts and those of others. Similarly, if you suspect that peasant behaviour and consciousness are not correlated, speaking to them is indispensable. For example, peasants could be passive and not even engage in 'everyday' kinds of resistance and still be amenable to mobilisation because of their quietly held and unde-monstrated values and beliefs.[43] Ranger's data are almost exclusively about peasant behaviour, reported through non-peasants. In short, his concept of peasant con-sciousness and his methodology are logically consistent, but in my view, respectively too narrow and indirect. These conceptual and methodological approaches provide a springboard from which to discuss and explain our inter-pretive differences.

Interpretive differences

Ranger accords primary explanatory power to the peasant-guerrilla ideology for effective peasant mobilisation in at least the two-thirds of Shona-speaking Zim-babwe.[44] In my work, I focus on guerrilla violence as the chief influence on mobilisation, and the problems posed for mobilisation by the omnipresent Rhode-sian Security Forces. Ranger does refer to 'the fearsome military power' of the Rhodesian Security Forces, but the peasants 'showed that it *was* possible after all to endure it. Peasant support for the guerrillas did not flag'.[45] I do not think that Ranger ever explicitly discusses guerrilla violence. He does note that especially in the late 1970s, peasants withdrew their support when they sometimes perceived guerrillas 'to be acting arbitrarily and without respect for the moral economy of the war'.[46] Correspondence that he cites, however, documents how the petty bourgeoi-sie saw itself trapped between the violence and demands of the Security Forces and the guerrillas.[47] Ranger comments on their plight: 'By 1979 the rural middle class did not know . . . who had brought them into their present situation; by contrast with the clarity of radical peasant ideology, they did not know even what to hope for, except for an end to the war.'[48]

Why the neglect of the effect of guerrilla and Security Force violence on peasant consciousness and hence on mobilisation? Ranger's concept of peasant conscious-ness is so narrowly conceived that there is no scope for violence. Focused on resistance to white farmers and state interference in agricultural production, there is no room for the influence of violence on peasant consciousness, independent of its effect on production. But Ranger is well aware of the dimensions of guerrilla violence and its effect on peasant support, and has written interestingly on the subject in 'Bandits and guerrillas: the case of Zimbabwe'.[49]

---

[43] James C. Scott, *Weapons of the Weak*, pp. 38-45.
[44] Ranger, *Consciousness*, for example, pp. 206-8, 212, 216.
[45] Ranger, *Consciousness*, p. 181.
[46] Ranger, *Consciousness*, p. 212.
[47] Ranger, *Consciousness*, p. 274-5.
[48] Ranger, *Consciousness*, p. 275.
[49] Terence Ranger, 'Bandits and guerrillas: the case of Zimbabwe', in Donald Crummey (ed.), *Banditry, Rebellion and Social Protest in Africa* (London, 1986), pp. 373-96.

At the outset of the essay, he relegates the importance of guerrilla violence for mobilisation, noting that the process by which the guerrillas established their legitimacy with the peasants 'remains by far the most important thing to discuss'. [50] Guerrilla legitimacy rested on their strict adherence to certain principles of conduct, laid down by mediums: no drinking, no drugs, thorough investigations before killing 'sell-outs', no sex, etc. [51] Before 1978, cases of particular guerrilla groups misbehaving were isolated. Only in 1978 and 1979 did most groups' behaviour deteriorate and pose a general 'crisis of guerrilla legitimacy'. [52] How did peasants respond? The random, isolated breaches of conduct before 1978 made no dent on peasant support. Peasants had their own reasons for supporting the guerrilla war, so 'even if particular guerrilla bands behaved brutally and in breach of the rules of conduct, peasants continued to back guerrilla war in principle'. [53] This undermines a central argument in the book about the important function of guerrillas as political educators responsible for intensifying peasant grievances and mobilising them. It also raises questions about how influential the mediums and their rules were vis-a-vis guerrillas.

What about peasant response during the crisis of legitimacy in 1978 and 1979? Here we are informed that 'observers both within and outside the guerrilla movements began to fear a wholesale collapse of rural support'. [54] Ranger reproduces a complaint to the Catholic Commission of Justice and Peace from a local elite in which the latter describes guerrilla oppression of the people. The writer warns that people have 'become disillusioned and would gladly return to their old way of life even if they were deprived of land and they had to get rid of their cattle'. Ranger comments dismissively: 'It is clear that this conclusion underestimated peasant determination and that the report as a whole depended too heavily on the evidence of local elites.' [55] Ranger's low regard for the ability of local elites to speak on behalf of peasants is to the point, in my view, but surprising because in his book we learn about peasant consciousness during the war chiefly through the voice of local elites or guerrillas. Ranger does cite a peasant informant on her fear and terror of the guerrillas, after witnessing the deaths of alleged 'sell-outs' and witches by guerrillas at a 'morari' (meeting), only to explain it away again. [56]

In assessing the impact of experiences like this, one has to bear in mind two considerations. One is that the 'Security Forces' were constantly exposing peasants to much more arbitrary and terrible sufferings. . . . The other was that peasants often excused guerrillas of responsibility for unjust punishments or extortionate demands, blaming these on the young boys and girls (the mujibas) who acted as go-betweens. [57]

By discounting their experience, he does not have to reconsider his thesis on the effectiveness of guerrilla-peasant ideology in mobilising peasants.

[50] Ranger, 'Bandits', p. 381.
[51] Ranger, 'Bandits', p. 381.
[52] Ranger, 'Bandits', p. 386.
[53] Ranger, 'Bandits', p. 386.
[54] Ranger, 'Bandits', p. 386.
[55] Ranger, 'Bandits', p. 389.
[56] Ranger, 'Bandits', p. 385.
[57] Ranger, 'Bandits', p. 385.

Guerrilla mobilisation *was* effective and produced ZANU-PF support committees that were responsible for providing logistical support for the guerrillas: food, clothing, money and information. But mobilisation was achieved through guerrilla coercion rather than guerrilla ideology. In selected villages in four wards in Mutoko district, I systematically interviewed men and women who had served on these committees about their war experience. Amidst the extraordinarily diverse organisational arrangements, some common themes emerged. Sometimes people were appointed by the guerrillas; sometimes they were elected. Elections cannot be described as 'voluntary'. If people did not elect committees, the guerrillas would appoint people and resisting villagers would pay the penalty associated with being identified as 'people who did not support the war'. Committee members saw their elections as undesirable: a task pushed onto them by others. Many went to great lengths to find an 'exit option'.[58] Such strategies included being out of the district on business on the day of the election, feigning sickness, and so on – behaviour that fits the pattern of 'everyday' resistance to state interference. The rapid rate of turnover of committee members was phenomenal; interviewing a war-time village committee often meant an introduction to virtually all resident adults. Sometimes people agreed to rotate responsibility for committee work; otherwise people devised strategies to limit their length of service – again, those 'everyday' patterns of resistance. When adults spoke of executing their committee duties, they spoke of a host of fears and anxieties. For example, the person who used the money collected by the village to buy shoes for the guerrillas could easily be caught with twenty pairs by the Security Forces. The risks of being caught were always high. To get to a bus stop entailed a good walk and the prospects of running into soldiers. The buses were almost always stopped and searched. If the items were not delivered on time, the guerrillas might be angry and 'not understanding'. It is important to remember that whereas committee members had special responsibilities, all rural residents were obligated to contribute food and money to the guerrillas, whose numbers continued to multiply. All adults had to attend 'moraris' or morale boosting sessions at which the guerrillas would lead in political songs and slogans, sometimes try 'sell-outs', and discuss other problems with the people. Ranger bypasses this crucial arena of collective peasant action: 'The peasants did not merely provide food and shelter and information; they also *acted* in the war', helping the guerrillas to attack the civil administration and white farming activities.[59]

To talk of support – active or symbolic – in such an environment is wrongheaded.[60] To infer peasant attitudes to the guerrillas from their behaviour is bound to conceal their feelings. One has to solicit their ideas about their experiences. Enduring guerrilla violence and sustained popular support cannot coexist, although guerrilla violence and mobilisation (at least in the short-term) apparently can. In

---

[58] Albert O. Hirschman, *Exit, Voice and Loyalty* (Cambridge, Massachusetts, 1970).

[59] Ranger, *Consciousness*, p. 180.

[60] Tom Lodge, *Black Politics in South Africa Since 1945* (Johannesburg, 1983), p. 126. He distinguishes between active and symbolic support. Active support includes 'voluntary' tax collections, elections, membership in an organisation, voluntary attendance at meetings. Presumably he would mean voluntary elections, and voluntary membership. See also David Easton, 'A Re-assessment of the Concept of Political Support', *British Journal of Political Science*, 5 (1975), pp. 435-457.

circumstances of coercion, compliance mixed with 'everyday' peasant resistance strategies against the guerrillas are the more likely responses. My difference with Ranger, then, is over the relative influence of guerrilla-peasant ideology and guerrilla violence in the mobilisation process. Its roots are in his peasant consciousness concept which excludes the potential impact of guerrilla violence and Security Force violence on peasants. My own argument is that in a situation where the guerrillas are unable to establish liberated zones, as in the Zimbabwean case, guerrilla violence rather than guerrilla ideology will be the dominant mode of mobilisation. [61] Peasants are unlikely to be enthusiastic supporters over an extended period. They may be jubilant for a short while, but then a horrible incident with either the guerrillas or the Security Forces will take its toll.

The second part of my critique is about the way in which Ranger deals with relationships within rural society during the war. Ranger focuses on the radical nationalist consciousness that binds peasants together and does not regard the petty bourgeois-peasant tensions as an important war-time conflict. I perceive peasant energies to be absorbed in gender, lineage, generation and intra- as well as inter-class conflicts. It is not that Ranger ignores completely these conflicts, but they are not integrated into his concept of peasant consciousness and remain a minor sideshow in his argument.

Of all conflicts during the war, Ranger gives centre stage to rural class warfare. Interestingly, his discussion focuses on whether the guerrillas identified any group as class enemies, and only in passing on intra-rural class conflicts. Both kinds of conflict were contained. Especially after the Internal Settlement in 1978 rural class warfare seemed likely. It was averted because 'the presumed petty bourgeois supporters of Muzorewa in the rural areas' who came under guerrilla attack after 1978 'did not come under the protection of the new regime'. [62] Also, if other members of the bourgeoisie 'were prepared to co-operate with the guerrillas, . . . they were regarded as invaluable allies'. [63] Class tensions were also apparent between peasants and Purchase Area farmers, rural businessmen and foreign migrants. But they 'have been a minor theme by comparison with peasant participation in the attack on white farm and ranchland during the war . . .'. [64] Class conflicts complicated guerrilla mobilisation and diverted peasant and guerrilla attentions from the main arena of the war against the whites and the state, but never overshadowed it.

Ranger does allude to the gender and generational tensions that the young guerrillas initially provoked.

. . . there were some substantial discontinuities also which made it difficult for there to be immediate or total collaboration between the peasant elders and the young guerrillas. To begin with the guerrillas *were* young and they were closer to the teenagers of Makoni District than

[61] *Weekly Mail* (Johannesburg, South Africa), May 15-May 21, 1987, p. 7. Speaking to the first conference of the Institute for a Democratic Alternative for South Africa, the acting Publicity Secretary of the United Democratic Front spoke of the difficulties of 'organising democratically at gunpoint'. He said that 'the need for tight security and secrecy obviously puts a strain on the development of a mass-based democratic practice'.

[62] Ranger, *Consciousness*, p. 269; see also pp. 264-5.

[63] Ranger, *Consciousness*, p. 272.

[64] Ranger, *Consciousness*, p. 287; see also pp. 284-6.

they were to the resident elders. Men in their fifties, who had hitherto dominated Makoni peasant radicalism and who were used to controlling a flock of dependent women — wives, daughters, daughters-in-law — now found that the initiative had passed to young men with guns. These young men called upon the unmarried women of Makoni to act as their cooks, informants and messengers and in these latter two roles teenage girls were able to exercise a good deal of power, for the first time in Makoni's history. [65]

After the war, Ranger found 'a good deal of remembered resentment among elders and parents directed against the power exercised by the *mujibas* during the war'. [66] According to an informant, 'most of the people who are said to have been killed by the guerrillas are the direct victims of the mujibas. These sometimes robbed civilians, abused the populace at beer parties, and in most cases misrepresented the comrades' aims and commitments'. [67] Another arena of tension surrounded the role of chiefs and headmen. On the one hand, Ranger states that 'the administration was totally wrong to suppose that chiefs and headmen did or could command such (peasant) support'. [68] On the other hand, guerrilla attacks on the 'tribal authorities', like the gender and generational tensions generated by the arrival of the young guerrillas, were also unsettling. [69] With these references to tensions in rural society, Ranger proceeds with his chief concern: the cooperative relationship between peasants and guerrillas. 'All in all, some means was urgently required to give the guerrillas legitimacy in terms of Makoni's own past and to give the peasants some way of controlling the young men with guns. The spirit mediums provided just such a means.' [70] They 'most effectively' laid down 'norms of conduct' for the guerrillas. [71] 'With this kind of endorsement there was no danger that the guerrillas would be repudiated by the peasant elders.' [72]

Apart from the conceptual and methodological problems in overstating the unifying force of peasant nationalism, the evidence for peasant cultural nationalism is unconvincing. In the period of open mass nationalism, mediums are an indicator of peasant radicalism and nationalism in that they contribute to a common cultural identity. [73] In the 1970s, mediums become increasingly relevant to 'peasant resentment over land alienation and the enforcement of agricultural rules'. [74] At Triashill mission, the original Catholic foundation in Makoni in 1890, intensive farming 'opened up the peasant option' for the first time in the 1960s. [75] Although the rise in the influence of mediums is generally associated with the decline of the peasant option, here their influence expanded despite its opening up. Intensive agriculture brought greater agricultural prosperity, and even though coercion was

[65] Ranger, *Consciousness*, pp. 206-7.
[66] Ranger, *Consciousness*, p. 292.
[67] Ranger, *Consciousness*, p. 292.
[68] Ranger, *Consciousness*, p. 253.
[69] Ranger, *Consciousness*, p. 208.
[70] Ranger, *Consciousness*, p. 208.
[71] Ranger, *Consciousness*, pp. 211-12.
[72] Ranger, *Consciousness*, p. 211.
[73] Ranger, *Consciousness*, p. 189, 13-14, 215-16.
[74] Ranger, *Consciousness*, p. 190.
[75] Ranger, *Consciousness*, p. 193; see also Terence Ranger, 'Holy Men and Rural Communities in Zimbabwe, 1970-1980', in W.J. Sheils (ed.), *The Church and War*, in *Studies in Church History*, vol. 20 (London, 1983), pp. 443-461.

not used, the new rules associated with this kind of farming aroused peasant resentment, and also led to a rise in the mediums' influence.[76] I do not want to quibble over the breakdown in the posited central relationship between declining agricultural prosperity, coercive state intervention and the rise of the mediums as a symbol of radical nationalist peasant consciousness, of which Ranger is aware, nor the contradictory evidence that when other parts of the district were experiencing nationalist activity in the early 1960s, the Triashill fathers 'gave thanks for the relative tranquility of their peasant flock in the open nationalist period'.[77] Rather, I wish to raise questions about the evidence for the rise in medium worship an indication of cultural nationalism.

Ranger's informants stress that the Triashill peasants were both practising Catholics and medium worshippers.[78] This is reaffirmed by Norman Thomas' study that describes how in 1966 the Triashill Catholics asked the church for its *official* approval of the worship of ancestors and tribal spirits.[79] What is interesting about Triashill mission is that even though the peasants were radical nationalists in the 1960s, the mediums' influence did not continue to grow, as we might have anticipated from Ranger's posited relationship between the influence of mediums and intensifying peasant radical nationalism. Even though Triashill peasants continued to be radical nationalists and supported the war, Catholic priests rather than mediums gave the guerrillas' legitimacy.[80] Some explanation is required for the failure of the mediums' influence to continue to rise.

The problem, it seems, arises from inferring beliefs and attitudes from behaviour. The fact of greater ritual observance is not a measure of the rise in mediums' influence. When Triashill peasants sought *official* church approval to do publicly what they had been doing unofficially before and openly requested permission from the mediums not to have to observe one of the two rest days,[81] they may have been making a public gesture to nationalist pressures to revive ancestor and medium worship. What matters − if guerrilla ideology which draws so heavily on mediums is to be an effective mobiliser − is the *strength of belief* in medium worship. Further evidence suggests that the influence of mediums might even have been declining in Manicaland in the 1960s. Thomas reports that most Africans rejected the traditional link of religious and political authority, and that urban residents were more favourable in their attitudes to mediums on this issue than rural people.[82] In a society where settler and missionary influence has been so pervasive, it would be surprising

[76] Ranger, *Consciousness*, pp. 191-2.

[77] Ranger, *Consciousness*, p. 242. The evidence on the rise of medium worship is also contradictory. First we are told that mediums played an increasing role in Weya in the 1960s (p. 194); but in 1981 an informant remarked that until the war 'mediums felt that they had been forgotten. . .' (p. 212).

[78] Ranger, *Consciousness*, p. 191-2.

[79] Norman Ernest Thomas, 'Christianity, Politics, and the Manyika: A Study of the Influence of Religious Attitudes and Loyalties on Political Values and Activities of Africans in Rhodesia' (Boston University Graduate School, Ph.D., 1968, Religion).

[80] Ranger, *Consciousness*, p. 215.

[81] Ranger, *Consciousness*, p. 193.

[82] Thomas, 'Christianity', p. 179.

for the strength of precolonial peasant values, no matter how adaptable to a changing environment, to survive colonial conquest and rule. [83]

The importance of differentiating commitments to beliefs is underlined in Ranger's discussion of their relationship to nationalism. While he cites Thomas' work that relates 'differential commitment to religious belief and practice' and nationalism, [84] he fails to make the distinction between high and low church attenders that Thomas does, and thereby conceals the great deal of variation in attitudes to political group participation within denominations. Ranger says that the Methodists, like the Apostolics, 'largely abstained from nationalist politics in the early 1960s'. [85] Actually, Thomas' point was that in the older churches, high church attenders 'have no time for politics. Members and adherents outside the church nucleus, however, have rejected the church as the sole arbiter of their conduct. It is from this segment that the nationalist political groups draw the bulk of their membership and leadership'. [86] In fact, since 1960 Methodists ranked alongside Roman Catholics as the strongest participants in nationalist parties in the rural area, with respectively 35.6% and 41.8% adults reporting membership in a political party. [87] Only Methodist high church attenders abstained from nationalist politics, as was the case in the other older churches.

Ranger endorses the view that 'the story of the nationalist struggle in Zimbabwe is not just the tale of the African National Congress and the National Democratic Party, of the ZAPU-ZANU split . . .', [88] and notes that his book is 'an account of consciousness at the grass-roots so that national events and national associations enter the book as they entered the rural areas – intermittently and from outside'. [89] I am in full agreement that much of what is most interesting in politics may occur outside formal organisations, yet there is the danger that we miss important differences between those who participate in organisational politics and those who do not. Thomas has some interesting data that differentiate the attitudes of political group members from non-members in Manicaland in the 1960s. He poses the question: 'Is widespread resistance to European rule (therefore) imminent in Manicaland?' His answer is sobering. 'Our data does not support this conclusion. Most respondents have the habit of law-abidingness. Only about one in ten displayed that strong rejection of existing civil authority which leads them into political groups which advocate civil disobedience.' [90] There were also significant differences in attitude between party and non-party members in responses to questions such as who should vote. 73% of political party members favoured universal suffrage compared with just over 59% of non-party members. [91] If we differentiate attitudes among a general population, party membership turns out to be important.

[83] For an argument in support of the survival of peasant values, see James Scott, and Albert Memmi on the specific issue of the survival intact of the belief in spirit mediums.

[84] Ranger, *Consciousness*, pp. 255-6.

[85] Ranger, *Consciousness*, p. 256; see also p. 263.

[86] Thomas, 'Christianity', p. 328.

[87] Thomas, 'Christianity', p. 218, 220.

[88] Ranger, *Consciousness*, p. ix.

[89] Ranger, *Consciousness*, p. xi.

[90] Thomas, 'Christianity', pp. 308-9. He notes that a majority of respondents accepted the principle that they *should* disobey laws which they consider unjust. (p. 309)

[91] Thomas, 'Christianity', p. 185.

In addition to the strength of Shona cultural nationalism, to which belief in mediums is an important contributor, Ranger characterises peasants as nationalists partly on the basis of their anti-state posture. That they 'desired a transformed state'[92] does not make them nationalists; nor does their opposition to local administrative bodies with taxing authority necessarily imply a rejection 'on nationalist grounds'.[93]

Lastly, Ranger argues that even the banning of the nationalist parties in 1964 did not result 'in a cowed and passive peasantry'.[94] In Makoni, peasants continued to resist local administrative interference as they had always done, and ZAPU meetings continued to be held.[95] Ranger may be correct for Makoni district, although his evidence for parts of it, as he says, is 'more scattered' than for one corner of the district.[96] One measure of peasant resistance might be the number of prosecutions under security laws and the number of detention and restriction orders. Between 1964 and 1971, these figures show a steep decline.[97] They suggest that the administration was not alarmed by the rather isolated instances of peasant resistance that were being recorded for Makoni in district files.

Apart from the problems of evidence that raise questions about Ranger's characterisation of peasants as radical nationalists from the late 1950s, the primary problem is his narrow conception of peasant consciousness and the reinforcement it receives from his methodological approach. Ranger does provide for the internally differentiated peasantry to have a differentiated peasant consciousness, reflected in peasant religion. Scattered throughout the history of the pre-war period, there are references to intra-peasant conflicts, but they are subordinate to peasant class consciousness.[98] Inter-class conflicts are a minor theme, because embedded in the peasant consciousness concept is the assumption that the state and white farmers are at the centre of their grievances. Similarly, the peasant consciousness concept excludes the possibility of gender, generation and lineage conflicts, except as they relate to agricultural production. Even then, it is the state that is the target of peasant resentment. With the emphasis on the effective cooperative effort between guerrillas and peasants, Ranger's study masks the extent to which local people used the guerrillas for their own non-nationalist, locally-centred interests that figured so prominently in my research, to which I now return.

A universal feature in an extremely diverse set of organisational arrangements from village to village was that teachers, agricultural demonstrators, storekeepers and Purchase Area farmers were not part of the committee structure. While different logistical reasons justified this arrangement, it was also preferred by both the peasants and the local elite and expressed a symbolic class distance and lack of trust. Teachers, for instance, often responded that being integrated in the committees

[92] Ranger, *Consciousness*, p. 177.
[93] Ranger, *Consciousness*, p. 296.
[94] Ranger, *Consciousness*, p. 160.
[95] Ranger, *Consciousness*, p. 160.
[96] Ranger, *Consciousness*, p. 169.
[97] Claire Palley, 'Law and the Unequal Society: Discriminatory Legislation in Rhodesia under the Rhodesian Front from 1963 to 1969'. Part 2, *Race*, XII, 2 (1970), pp. 163-4.
[98] Ranger, *Consciousness*, p. 48, 87, 80-84, 107.

would have made them vulnerable to the hostilities of the peasants, exposing them to the risks of being labelled a 'sell-out'. Many went to live in their home areas when schools closed because 'it was better to be among people whom you knew'. This suggests an insider-outsider tension too. From the peasants' point of view, teachers had many opportunities to inform on their activities: each month they went to the district administration office to collect their salaries, and their schools drew frequent visits from the Security Forces who knew guerrillas were visiting them. The security problem, related to the absence of liberated zones, created an opportunity for peasants and their children to express these class (and insider-outsider) tensions. Allegations that elite members were government informers were always credible in the tight security context, with Security Forces torturing and beating to extract information. These meshed with guerrilla suspicions about the loyalty of the petty bourgeoisie.

Chiefs and headmen were in a similar situation. On the one hand, they received pay from the government for maintaining 'law and order'; at the same time they were supposed to represent their people. In many areas, but not all, guerrillas soon abandoned trying to mobilise around 'traditional leaders' because either they chose to inform on them, or else Security Force pressures resulted in them breaking down and giving information. Either way, they were unreliable. Guerrillas were correctly suspicious and killed many chiefs and headmen. Locals who were hostile to the 'traditional leaders' took advantage of the security situation to label them informers and draw a response from the guerrillas.

One of the more interesting results of interviewing committee members was that in two out of the four wards a pattern emerged of all committee positions being held by members of the non-ruling lineages, and very occasionally members of the ruling lineage but not of chiefly families. Commoners and families belonging to the ruling lineage but not the chiefly families articulated deep resentment against the ruling families' monopoly of powers in land allocation and local judicial functions, and their abuse of them to favour their own friends and close kin.[99] Chiefs and headmen stayed aloof from the committees, consoling themselves that the war was an interlude after which the status quo would return, and seeing in the guerrilla practice of offering prayers to the tribal spirits some reassurance that they were still important and respected. In the eyes of the commoners, the 'tribal authorities' were not interested in what they perceived to be demanding and risky work, and followed what had long been their practice of letting commoners do the 'dirty work' of organising logistical support for the guerrillas. Nor did they, the commoners, want the 'traditional leaders' to have committee positions because they perceived them as 'sell-outs'. With the many chiefs and headmen killed by guerrillas or under suspicion, the war presented a marvellous opportunity for commoners − a majority in one ward, a minority in the other − to monopolise the committee positions. In their view, they were replacing an hereditary leadership that had abused its monopoly powers, discriminating against commoners. I am aware of the ethnographic literature that maintains that the distinction between royal and commoner

[99] For similar grievances expressed in the 1950's, see Barry Neal Floyd, 'Changing Patterns of African Land Use in Southern Rhodesia' (Ph.D., Syracuse University, 1959), pp. 118-19.

lineages does not imply a political or social significance in Shona society.[100] What I am suggesting is that the war created an unusual moment for commoners to organise on the basis of their status as members of non-ruling lineages in order to effect an internal political revolution.

Youths are in a structurally disadvantaged position in Shona society. They saw in the arrival of the guerrillas possible allies. Youths formed a separate wing of the local ZANU-PF support organisation, indicating the generational distance perceived between the married adults who participated in the committees and their children. Youths spent much more time with the guerrillas and were often their peers, enabling them to establish a closer relationship with them than was possible for most adult committee members, who were additionally disadvantaged by their high rate of turnover. As one of Ranger's informants noted, many elders resented the youths for their brutal behaviour during the war. (Also, I should add, parents had high regard for the valuable role that the youths played during the war, frequently applauding their bravery even though they were usually unarmed and comparing it favourably with the performance of the armed guerrillas.) The youths are held responsible for much unnecessary killing of alleged 'informers'. They often beat their elders when they refused to immediately obey guerrilla orders to attend a 'morari', move their homes from the streets where the soldiers had too easy access to them, not travel on roads they had landmined, and so forth. Included in the potpourri of motives behind youths' behaviour was a desire to impress their new masters and peers with their zeal and to assert themselves over their elders. But there was also fear of guerrilla punishment if they failed to carry out orders. When elders or other youths complained to the guerrillas of youths' misbehaviour, the guerrillas usually beat them publicly. A good deal of youths' behaviour fits the broad category of 'everyday' resistance, against the guerrillas and the 'parents', as the elders were called.

Shona society also structurally disadvantages women, creating gender tensions. Many women claimed to have established their own committees to assert their independence of the men. Again, there were logistical reasons for the way in which women were incorporated into the committee structure. In areas where the guerrillas had easier access than the Security Forces, women were most likely to have their own committees. When security conditions were very tight, women were integrated with men into committees and often were assigned the tasks of going to buy items because they aroused less immediate Security Force attention than did men or young boys. Many women used the guerrillas to try to bolster their influence vis-a-vis their husbands. They called on the guerrillas to get their husbands to stop beating them or divorcing them, and the guerrillas desperate for local supporters, often intervened on their behalf, sometimes publicly beating errant husbands.

For all these reasons, I argue that rural society experienced not a civil war in the sense that the two sides were composed of loyalists and regime opponents, but an internal social and political revolution, with much of its attendant violence. By maintaining the 'traditional' offices of the Shona tribal system in the Tribal Trust Lands, and prohibiting African political participation outside this system, European

[100] Hilda Kuper, 'The Shona' in Daryll Forde (ed.), *Ethnographic Survey of Africa. Southern Africa. Part IV* (London, 1955), p. 28.

rule ensured that the lineage organisation of precolonial society — with its associated gender and generational features — would continue to have relevance in local politics. While preserving the form of precolonial politics in the Tribal Trust Lands, successive colonial governments closed off many of the precolonial mechanisms for resolving them, and through socioeconomic policies such as migrant labour, actually exacerbated them. Colonial policies transformed and froze rural society, resulting in its political underdevelopment.[101] The war was an opportunity for many oppressed groups to challenge their oppressors. Whites and the state were not the only oppressors; nor were they always the most vulnerable and accessible. The viciousness of the local struggles underscores their importance. To accuse people of not supporting the war became a nationalist disguise for a host of social and political struggles, and many simply petty personal rivalries.

Conclusion

Ranger's treatment of peasant consciousness, on his understanding of the term, is skilful and makes prominent the neglected issue of invisible, informal everyday peasant resistance through Zimbabwean history. By drawing chiefly on his own evidence and my work on Zimbabwe, I have tried to show that his peasant consciousness concept is too limited to issues of class resistance against state intervention in agricultural production. Consequently, he omits from his *central argument*, the influence of kin, inter- and intra-class relations, gender and gener-ation, guerrilla and state violence. Despite this limitation, Ranger's work is a landmark study that opens for debate and further research an exciting topic.

Table 1 — *Interviewees*

This table is based on all those interviewees whose material is used in the text, as well as those for whom occupational data were available. A caveat: a few individuals could have been placed in more than one occupational category but this does not affect the peasant category. I follow Ranger's narrower peasant category that he uses in the latter part of his book.

National politicians from Makoni (3 MPs, a Deputy Minister, an ex-MP from the 1960s)	5
District Administration (an ex-District Commissioner (DC), an assistant DC, a District Administrator, the secretary of Makoni Rural District Council)	4
Guerrillas	8
Teachers (one was also an auxiliary priest, most were active nationalists with official party positions)	5
Church (seven fathers, a bishop, an archdeacon, a Church of God group, a sister)	9
Businessmen/storekeeper/lorry driver	4

[101] Richard M.G. Mtetwa, 'The Political and Economic History of the Duma People of South-Eastern Rhodesia From the Early Eighteenth Century to 1945' (Ph.D., University of Rhodesia, 1976), p. 554. Mtetwa applies the concept of political underdevelopment to the Duma. See also Albert Memmi, *The Coloniser and the Colonised* (Boston, 1967), pp. 90-103; Frantz Fanon, *Black Skin, White Masks* (New York, 1967); *Selections from the Prison Notebooks of Antonio Gramsci.*

Farmworker	1
(wife of foreigner, moved to Tribal Trust Land in the war)	
ex-Selous Scouts	1
Purchase Area Farmer	1
Peasants	14
(a master farmer, a chief, a chief and councillors, a headman, a medium. Eight are not quoted in the text)	
TOTAL	52

Two ZANU-PF committees — at village and district level — were interviewed, as well as a UANC provincial organiser. There is only information for two of the District Committee members: the chair had been a teacher before becoming a builder; the secretary had been a policeman until the war changed his life. [102]

Table 2 — *Elite Informants*

The following fourteen people are admittedly among the most distinguished whom Ranger relies on for oral and sometimes written evidence.

Solomon Chavanduka	an agricultural demonstrator for ten years, became a farm owner at Dowa Purchase Area, Makoni. He is the father of a well-known Zimbabwean sociologist, Gordon. [103]
Chad Chipunza	a United Federal Party MP and parliamentary secretary for the Federal Ministry of Home Affairs in 1962. [104]
Roland Hatendi	a local historian, former teacher and headmaster of the first school in Dowa Purchase Area until 1943. Joined the Native Department in 1945 as the district commissioner's assistant. [105]
Father Kenny	stayed on Triashill mission station and St. Barbara's throughout the war. This was unusual — most missionaries left during the war and went to live in town — and reflects the good relations he established with the local population. [106]
Moven Mahachi	leader at Cold Comfort Farm, became manager at Nyafaru Cooperative when Cold Comfort was banned in 1971. After independence was appointed Deputy Minister of Lands, Resettlement and Development. [107]
Columbus Makoni	a friend and business associate of Basil Nyabadza, detained in 1959. Became MP for Makoni after independence. [108]
Stephen Matewa	headmaster at Toriro, Chiduku Tribal Trust Land. Had been associated with cooperative farming ventures at St. Faith's and Nyafaru. A member of ZANU from 1963. During the war he was an auxiliary priest and looked after refugees and local schoolchildren, and his congregation. Matewa emerges as an extremely brave man, well-connected even overseas and able to use his connections to get supplies for the guerrillas and people of Toriro. Through the Anglican hierarchy, he got the

[102] Ranger, *Consciousness*, pp. 327-8, footnote 23.
[103] Ranger, *Consciousness*, p. 234, 236.
[104] Terence Ranger, 'The Death of Chaminuka: Spirit Mediums, Nationalism and the Guerrilla War in Zimbabwe', *African Affairs*, 81, 234 (July 1982), pp. 349-369; Reg Shay and Chris Vermaak, *The Silent War* (Rhodesia, 1971), p. 13.
[105] Ranger, *Consciousness*, pp. 241-2, 157-8.
[106] Ranger, 'Holy Men'.
[107] Patricia Chater, *Caught in the Cross-fire* (Harare, 1984), pp. 100-1.
[108] Chater, *Cross-fire*.

Toriro area declared a zone where military action would not occur. Toriro became a resupply area for the guerrillas. [109]

Didymus Mutasa
grew up at St. Faith's where he was deeply influenced by Guy Clutton-Brock, a Welsh missionary. (see fn. 38) Went to secondary school, helped run adult education courses on weekends at St. Faith's, and became chairman of a cooperative Cold Comfort Farm Society initiated by Clutton-Brock. In 1966 he was appointed a director of Nyafaru Cooperative. The cooperative at Cold Comfort was banned in 1971 when members were correctly suspected of being in touch with exiled nationalists. Along with others, he was detained. In 1973 he was released provided that he left immediately for England for education. After independence he became Speaker of the Legislative Assembly and also MP for Makoni. [110]

John Mutasa
older brother of Didymus. A member of Makoni Student Association, founded in the 1950s by secondary school students. Farm manager of the cooperative farm scheme started by the Clutton-Brocks at St. Faith's. Arrested in 1959 for three months during the state of emergency. When St. Faith's was given a new priest who froze the bank account of the cooperative and appointed a white manager over John, he resigned. Arrested again in 1975 for helping the guerrillas. [111]

Maurice Nyagumbo
a migrant labourer in South Africa until 1955 when he returned to Makoni and bought a grocery store. Detained in 1959 along with other Congress leaders from Makoni – John Mutasa, Columbus Makoni. Rearrested in 1975, along with cousin Basil Nyabadza (in charge of an unusual community at St. Francis Church and a successful businessman), John Mutasa and Nyabadza's nephew for helping with the guerrilla effort. Nyagumbo received a fifteen year prison sentence with five years suspended. He started to study for A levels, and later a degree course. After independence, he became Minister of Mines and MP for Makoni. [112]

Mhondiwa Remus Rungodo
worked in South African hotels, returned to Makoni to help run a bakery in Chiduku Reserve. Joined ZAPU, detained when it was banned in 1964. [113]

Amon Shonge
from Weya Tribal Trust Land in Makoni district, worked as labour migrant for a while. Became a member of ZAPU, and also of Cold Comfort Farm Society. Arrested and detained in 1971 when the Society was banned. Returned to Weya that year and with his wife founded at their own home the Mukute Farm Society, modelled on Cold Comfort Farm Society. Some of his correspondence with Clutton-Brock during the war is used in Ranger's text. Became a district councillor after the war. [114]

Father Turner
stationed at St. Therasa's, Chiduku Tribal Trust Land from 1977 to 1979. [115]

Father Vernon
stayed on throughout the war at St. Killian's in Makoni Tribal Trust Land. From St. Barbara's to St. Killian's were granite hills which made for good guerrilla bases, leading the Rhodesian government forces to more or less withdraw from here in 1977. The area came close to being a liberated zone, and guerrillas could be seen ploughing. Here church attendance actually increased during the war. [116]

---

[109] Ranger, 'Holy Men'.
[110] Chater, Cross-fire, pp. 15-16.
[111] Ranger, Consciousness, p. 246; Chater, Cross-fire, pp. 7-8, 15, 114-15.
[112] Ranger, Consciousness, p. 242; Chater, Cross-fire, p. 7, 114-15.
[113] Ranger, Consciousness, pp. 241-2, 157-8.
[114] Ranger, Consciousness, p. 163, 178, 321; Ranger, 'The Death of Chaminuka', p. 367.
[115] Ranger, 'Holy Men', pp. 448-9.
[116] Ranger, 'Holy Men', p. 449.

The Journal of Modern African Studies, 11, 2 (1973), pp. 267–303

Obstacles to Guerrilla Warfare – a South African Case Study

by SHERIDAN JOHNS*

MORE than ten years after the turn from non-violence to organised violence by the African opposition in South Africa the white Nationalist régime remains firmly entrenched in power. Its security forces have successfully suppressed sabotage campaigns initiated in the early 1960s, unco-ordinated terrorist attacks mounted during the same period, and incipient guerrilla action in South-West Africa in 1966. At the call of the authorities in Salisbury they joined their northern neighbours to defeat armed incursions in Rhodesia during 1967–8, and more recently they have contained sporadic attacks in the Caprivi Strip along the Zambian border. The South African Government appears confident that its forces can continue to thwart any future attempts at domestic insurgency.

Despite the record of Nationalist success and heightened preparations for counter-insurgency, African opponents of the régime remain dedicated to their original goal – the overthrow of white minority rule in South Africa. Although the African National Congress (A.N.C.), the oldest African nationalist organisation of South Africa, presently shows few signs of overt activity within the Republic, it remains committed to an armed struggle against the powerful forces of *apartheid*. The frustrations and failures to date of the A.N.C.'s efforts at forging an effective armed challenge to white power illustrate the awesome obstacles confronting any non-white opponent of the Nationalist régime.

THE ERA OF MASS PROTEST

The difficulties encountered by the A.N.C. in shifting to an armed struggle can only be fully understood by reference to its experiences in the first 12 years of Nationalist rule.[1] The advent of the Nationalist Government in mid-1948 coincided with a shift in the balance of

---

* Associate Professor of Political Science, Duke University, Durham, North Carolina.

[1] For general accounts of the A.N.C. in the 1950s, see Mary Benson, *South Africa: the struggle for a birthright* (London, 1966); Edward Feit, *South Africa: the dynamics of the African National Congress* (London, 1962), and his *Urban Revolt in South Africa, 1960–1964: a case study* (Evanston, 1971), pp. 14–48. An analysis of the A.N.C. in the context of South African liberalism is found in Janet Robertson, *Liberalism in South Africa, 1948–1963* (Oxford, 1971).

forces within the A.N.C., and strengthened the determination of the Africanist-oriented leaders of the Congress Youth League to push the A.N.C. towards a more aggressive strategy. At the annual meeting of the A.N.C. in December 1949 the Youth Leaguers successfully elected their supporters to key positions; they also secured the endorsement of their own *Programme of Action*, which demanded direct representation for Africans in government bodies, and committed the A.N.C. to the use of the strike and the boycott in expanded passive resistance campaigns to further its goals.

In reaction to the relentless tightening of segregation for all non-whites and further restrictions on opposition political activity, the new Youth League representatives in the leadership of the A.N.C. reversed their opposition to joint work with non-Africans. In co-operation with the South African Indian Congress, the South African Coloured People's Congress, and sympathetic whites organised into the Congress of Democrats, the A.N.C. embarked upon a series of campaigns in the 1950s within the framework of the *Programme of Action*.

In the first major effort, the Defiance Campaign of 1952, more than 8,500 selected volunteers from the A.N.C. and its associated bodies deliberately contravened segregatory laws until outbreaks of violence and harsh government reaction led to the demise of the campaign.[1] The energies of the A.N.C. and its allies were then channelled into a nationwide effort to bring together representatives of all South African racial groups and political bodies in a 'Congress of the People' to formulate a programme for a non-racial, majority-ruled South Africa. The culmination of the campaign was a meeting in Kliptown, Johannesburg, in June 1955, at which several thousand delegates formalised the multi-racial Congress Alliance and endorsed the Freedom Charter, a document which demanded an end to *apartheid* in all spheres of South African life, a non-racial democracy on the basis of universal suffrage, large-scale social and economic reforms designed to improve the lot of non-whites, and government ownership of banks, mines, and large industries.

Subsequently the A.N.C., with the support of its allies, undertook a series of campaigns to challenge specific *apartheid* measures as they were implemented. Already during 1954–5 the A.N.C. persuaded residents in Johannesburg to refuse to move to new housing in a government-designated African area; and African parents throughout

[1] For a detailed study of the Defiance Campaign, see Leo Kuper, *Passive Resistance in South Africa* (New Haven, 1957).

South Africa were urged to boycott schools operated according to the Bantu Education Act.[1] In the latter years of the 1950s the A.N.C. organised several national stay-at-home strikes of short duration, usually timed to coincide with an important white political event. Support was given to the four-month Alexandra bus boycott in Johannesburg in 1957, and attempts were made to organise similar acts of solidarity in other South African cities. Campaigns were also mounted for the boycott of specific goods produced by Afrikaner Nationalist businessmen. In localities throughout the country local A.N.C. branches led protest demonstrations against government regulations and the establishment of new *apartheid* practices.

The common features of these A.N.C. campaigns were growing involvement in political activity by the African masses, a consolidation of links with their non-African partners in the Congress Alliance, and an unchanging commitment to non-violent and disciplined action. Although the campaigns of the 1950s marked a new era of sustained militancy by the A.N.C., they could also be viewed as a continuation on a higher plane of the strategy employed by the movement since its inception in 1912.

In the anti-pass demonstrations after World War I, and in protest meetings during and after World War II, the A.N.C. had invited mass participation to demonstrate its potential strength. The campaigns of the 1950s systematised the involvement of A.N.C. members and supporters by organising them into trained volunteer groups in the Defiance Campaign, and then subsequently attempted to mobilise all Africans for participation in A.N.C.-sponsored strikes and boycotts.

In the decades before 1948, important figures in the A.N.C. leadership had looked to white liberals for encouragement and support. In the late 1920s and again in the 1940s, the A.N.C. had also accepted help from the multi-racial Communist Party, including African communists who joined fully in A.N.C. activities. In the 1950s, the A.N.C. took pains to strengthen its organisational ties with Indian and Coloured bodies. It also invited aid from sympathetic whites, although most liberals rejected unconditional support for the A.N.C., preferring the *ad hoc* arrangements of the past. In consequence the Congress of Democrats, the white component of the Congress Alliance, was dominated by more radical democrats, many of whom were associated with the underground South African Communist Party

[1] An analysis of the two campaigns focusing upon organisational performance is available in Edward Feit, *African Opposition in South Africa: the failure of passive resistance* (Stanford 1967).

which had been reconstituted in 1953 after the dissolution and banning in 1950 of its predecessor, the Communist Party of South Africa. In this fashion the traditional links with white liberalism were supplanted by close associations at the upper level with white communists.

In the past, often with endorsement from white liberals, the A.N.C. had concentrated upon petitions and deputations to white authorities; in the 1950s the A.N.C. did not abandon these techniques, but its emphasis shifted sharply to organised civil disobedience, strikes, and boycotts. In its campaigns of passive resistance the A.N.C. meticulously adhered to non-violent tactics. Overseas support was also sought, not only from liberal sympathisers in Western Europe and North America as in the past, but also from the Afro-Asian bloc, the Communist states, and the United Nations. The A.N.C. leaders seemed to rest their hopes in ever more extensive peaceful demonstrations as a means of bringing white South Africa to a reconsideration of its policies, either through respect for the new assertiveness of Africans and their supporters in the Congress Alliance, or through prods to the Christian or humanitarian conscience of a segment of the white population. It was also hoped that overseas condemnation of *apartheid* would induce additional pressure upon the Nationalist Government to shift its policies.

The hopes of the A.N.C. were consistently frustrated by the Government, which met each attempted challenge with harsher law-enforcement, heightened surveillance, stricter restrictions on political activity, and unflagging determination to extend *apartheid*.[1] Although plans were made in the early 1950s for an underground organisation to complement the existing A.N.C. structure, the scheme was never implemented fully in practice. The A.N.C. remained a highly visible organisation, its leaders at all levels known to the police. It continued to utilise South African legal institutions to the ability of its limited resources to resist government attacks on its activities and programmes. Both the extent of government harassment and the A.N.C.'s tenacious employment of legal devices were symbolised in the five-year Treason Trial of 156 leaders of the Congress Alliance during 1956–61.

It is impossible to estimate accurately the extent of support for the A.N.C. among the African population, but it is unquestioned that the Defiance Campaign attracted thousands of new members and sympathisers. While subsequent events may have alienated some who feared

---

[1] Perhaps the best survey of this process is to be found in Muriel Horrell, *Action, Reaction, and Counteraction: a review of non-white opposition to the apartheid policy, counter-measures by the Government, and the eruption of new waves of unrest* (Johannesburg, 1963).

further government persecution, or who faulted the A.N.C. for its failure to block the Government, the activities of the A.N.C. and its allies continued to provide a focal point for group solidarity and symbolic resistance to the Nationalist régime for thousands of Africans.

At the same time the tactics of the A.N.C. provoked controversy within the ranks of the organisation over the rôle of non-Africans at the leadership level, the nature of communist involvement and participation, and the continued adherence to passive resistance. Invoking the Africanist orientation of the Congress Youth League of the mid-1940s, groups of generally younger A.N.C. members accused their leaders of submitting to non-African domination in the multi-racial Congress Alliance. They argued that alien communist ideology had intruded to dilute and divert the force of African nationalism. Impatient with the lack of success of the A.N.C. and its non-African allies, the critics urged an ill-defined new strategy of more direct confrontation with the machinery of *apartheid*. In 1958 the dissident Africanists broke with the A.N.C. and in 1959 they launched the rival Pan-African Congress (P.A.C.). With a platform emphasising that African freedom should be sought by Africans alone upon a platform of African nationalism, the P.A.C. announced its intention to challenge the A.N.C. for African support and to mobilise Africans for confrontation with the Government.

The P.A.C. chose the hated 'passes' as the object of its first nation-wide campaign, and urged all Africans, not merely selected volunteers, to refuse to carry passes and invite arrest by the police. Explicitly eschewing violence, the leaders of the P.A.C. apparently hoped that the arrest of many thousands of African demonstrators would clog the jails, disrupt the machinery of state, and provoke a collapse of governmental authority. On 21 March 1960, the opening day of the P.A.C. campaign, panicky police fired into a crowd of Africans demonstrating before the police station at Sharpeville, killing 69 and wounding hundreds. In reaction to this tragedy, and demonstrations elsewhere in the country, the Government invoked emergency regulations, arrested hundreds of political leaders, and hurried the enactment of the Unlawful Organisations Act, under which both the P.A.C. and the A.N.C. were declared illegal.

The initial response of the fragmented A.N.C. leadership, now forced to operate in secrecy, and liable to prosecution merely if apprehended while engaged in A.N.C. activities, was threefold. Tentative steps were taken to establish an underground organisation to carry on political work in the radically changed situation, and Oliver

Tambo, Deputy President-General, was sent out of the country to set up an external mission. At the same time A.N.C. leaders joined with other prominent Africans of all political persuasions (including the P.A.C.) at a Consultative Conference on 17 December 1960, in Orlando, Johannesburg, to plan for further political action. The fragile unity established here was subsequently broken when the representatives of the P.A.C. and the Liberal Party withdrew from the Continuation Committee established to plan an 'All-In Conference', charging that the A.N.C. and its allies were attempting to utilise the new machinery to advance their own partisan ends. Despite attacks from P.A.C. supporters and Liberals, the All-In Conference was held on 25–26 March 1961; Nelson Mandela and other A.N.C. leaders not banned at the time dominated the proceedings. In line with the established practices of the preceding decade, plans were made for a three-day stay-at-home strike on 29–31 May to coincide with the declaration of the Republic of South Africa. Despite pockets of strong support in the face of government intimidation, the strike was unsuccessful. Its failure was a final harsh demonstration to the leaders of the A.N.C. of the futility of the tactics of the past.

THE TURN TO VIOLENCE

In the reassessment which followed, voices were raised for a further exploration of the tactics of non-violence, but the weight of opinion was that the A.N.C. had no alternative but to shift to violence. Joined by willing communists of all races, selected A.N.C. leaders formed a new body, *Umkhonto we Sizwe* (Spear of the Nation), to organise violent action against the Government.[1] The strategy adopted, and the structure devised to implement it, envisaged a long-term, multi-stage campaign of disciplined violence in which a hard core of trained militants, supported by mass-based political activity and crucial external aid, would confront state power with the ultimate goal of seizing it.

From the inception of *Umkhonto* its joint A.N.C./Communist Party leadership emphasised the necessity for 'properly controlled violence'. Aware that segments of the population were demanding immediate action, and yet fearful of the consequences of a full-scale civil war

[1] Using evidence from the reports of subsequent trials, Feit's *Urban Revolt* contains the most extensive analysis of this first period of underground activity by the A.N.C. and its allies. The statement of Nelson Mandela at the 'Rivonia Trial' presents an explanation of the origins of *Umkhonto* and its activities by the first leader of the underground A.N.C.; see his *No Easy Walk to Freedom* (London, 1965), pp. 162–89.

on racial lines between the powerful white state and its non-white opponents, *Umkhonto* gave first priority to a campaign of sabotage against power and communication facilities and government buildings; every effort was to be made to avoid the loss of life. According to Nelson Mandela, it was hoped that the disruption of these vital facilities would disrupt the South African economy and intimidate potential foreign investors, thus leading white voters to reconsider the policies of *apartheid*. The destruction of government property was viewed as a series of symbolic acts to buoy African spirits and to pre-empt attempts at spontaneous unorganised violence.[1]

In the remote expectation that the 'demonstration effect' of successful widespread sabotage without loss of life would prod white South Africa to shift its policies, *Umkhonto* retained elements of the strategy of the 1950s. Yet shortly after the commencement of the sabotage campaign in December 1961, if not before, the leaders of *Umkhonto* were preparing for a possible shift to guerrilla warfare in the event of their failure to change Nationalist policy. Thus, Nelson Mandela travelled secretly to independent African countries and Europe in early 1962, to seek material support and training facilities for prospective A.N.C. cadres to be smuggled out of South Africa. His efforts to secure external support were continued and expanded by the external mission of the A.N.C. and its Congress allies. The leaders of *Umkhonto*, including Mandela before his arrest in August 1962, considered plans for guerrilla warfare to be undertaken by the trained cadres upon their return to South Africa. It was anticipated that the mere initiation of such warfare would quickly rally new recruits to swell the ranks of the insurgent forces. From expanded bases in the countryside the growing guerrilla groups would move to more direct and extensive confrontation of government forces.

The planning and execution of the ambitious schemes of *Umkhonto* were placed in the hands of a small 'National High Command', comprised primarily of Africans, Indians, and whites who had been prominent in activities of the Congress Alliance. From secret headquarters in Rivonia, an outlying suburb of Johannesburg, the National High Command supervised efforts to create a tightly knit hierarchical underground organisation which would recruit members for training in sabotage techniques, organise an 'underground railroad' to spirit additional recruits northwards to independent Africa and friendly socialist countries for military training, and carry out a carefully orchestrated campaign of sabotage as a prelude to the eventual

[1] Ibid. pp. 170–71.

initiation of guerrilla warfare. From the membership of the A.N.C., its Congress allies, and the Communist Party, individuals were co-opted into *Umkhonto* and trained for participation in sabotage or other activities. The new organisation was deliberately kept separate from the underground A.N.C., which was regarded as an inappropriate vehicle for the conduct of a necessarily conspiratorial campaign. Inevitably the lines between the two underground bodies became blurred, but *Umkhonto* retained its autonomy as the nerve centre for the projected sabotage.

Constrained by the exigencies of underground operation in a hostile environment fraught with government-devised obstacles, and further hobbled, as Edward Feit has argued, by failures of co-ordination, technical bungles during sabotage attempts, frictions within the organisation, and ultimately by the very nature of the conspiratorial cell system,[1] *Umkhonto* nevertheless forged sufficiently effective machinery to commit over 150 acts of sabotage in a campaign which caught public attention and concern, both within and outside South Africa. The reaction of the Nationalist Government was even more determined than its response to the earlier non-violent campaigns. Instead of wavering the Government unhesitatingly introduced a panoply of laws which made sabotage a capital crime, vastly expanded the powers of the police to conduct investigations, and authorised additional stringent restrictions upon suspected political activists. Police officers, some of whom were sent to Algeria and Angola for anti-guerrilla training, were given the full support of the Government to suppress the activities of *Umkhonto,* and all other organisations or individuals which were considered a threat to the state.

With the arrest of the National High Command at Rivonia in July 1963, and their subsequent conviction and imprisonment in 1964, the leadership of *Umkhonto* was decapitated. In a series of related police actions, facilitated by a network of informers and by the willingness of the police to use harsh methods of interrogation, the state apprehended the second echelon of leaders and apparently most of the rank-and-file saboteurs. A few important members evaded the police net and escaped into exile, but the bulk of the *Umkhonto* activists were sentenced to prison, often for lengthy terms. Simultaneously the police moved against the underground A.N.C., particularly in the Eastern Cape, where it had been most strongly established. In this fashion thousands of past members and possible future recruits were imprisoned. Through wide-ranging new legislation and vigorous action

[1] Feit, *Urban Revolt*, pp. 202–10 and 257–77.

the government security forces successfully smashed *Umkhonto* and rendered the A.N.C. underground ineffectual by the mid-1960s.

In retrospect the exiled leaders have acknowledged that they gravely underestimated the ruthless determination of the Nationalist Government to crush the underground A.N.C. and *Umkhonto*. It is conceded that the cadres of both were unprepared for the situation of illegality in which they were forced to operate after 1960:

Still suffering from the habit of semi-legal days prior to the banning of the movement, we had not yet devised a tight conspiratorial method of work which made it extremely difficult for people to know more than they were entitled to. The looseness in the machinery of the organization made betrayal by the weak and the provocateurs easy. Those who broke down were able to betray many units and individuals. Notorious traitors emerged who enthusiastically betrayed their former comrades. The most serious blow was the discovery of the headquarters of the High Command of M.K. [Umkhonto] in Rivonia. The enemy was thus able to smash the very heart of the organization and this was a very serious setback.[1]

The burden for the preparation of any further challenge was thus immediately shifted to the exiled representatives of the A.N.C. and its allies, and to the *Umkhonto* recruits who had successfully escaped abroad for military training.

THE BURDENS OF EXILE

In his perceptive essay on the exile condition of the Southern African liberation movements, John Marcum delineated three clusters of problems with which the leaders and members must deal in turn: environmental, existential, and technical.[2] The external mission of the A.N.C. faced distinctive problems in establishing an effective base outside the country by virtue of its past patterns of overseas connections, the nature of its alliances with non-African opposition groups, and its close ties with the multi-racial Communist Party. The ability of the A.N.C. to maintain its effectiveness and momentum were complicated over time as its links with South Africa became attenuated, and as its leaders and members became preoccupied with the problems of maintaining themselves and their organisation in exile. Intertwined were the questions posed by the changing requirements of the central *raison d'être* of the external organisation – the initiation and direction of armed struggle within South Africa.

[1] *Sechaba* (London), 5/6, December 1971/January 1972, p. 14.

[2] John Marcum, 'The Exile Condition and Revolutionary Effectiveness: Southern African liberation movements', in Christian P. Potholm and Richard Dale (eds.), *Southern Africa in Perspective: essays in regional politics* (New York, 1972), pp. 262-75.

Unlike the Zimbabwean nationalist groups which had earlier focused hopes upon British intervention in Rhodesian politics to advance their cause,[1] the A.N.C. had centred its efforts upon domestic activity. Yet throughout the 1950s it had welcomed support from sympathisers in America and Western Europe, particularly Britain, as well as gestures of solidarity from socialist countries; since the start of the Defiance Campaign in 1952 it had also encouraged the annual debates upon *apartheid* at the United Nations which led to progressively stronger moral condemnation of the Nationalist Government. More belatedly it moved to make connections with the African nationalist movements which were coming to power with the end of British and French colonial rule.

When the A.N.C. in 1960 hurriedly established an external mission headed by Oliver Tambo, it found an international environment which initially seemed congenial to the claims of those whose plight had been dramatised throughout the world by Sharpeville and its aftermath. At the United Nations even the western powers joined strong condemnations of *apartheid*. Although they refused to endorse the economic sanctions against South Africa voted overwhelmingly by the General Assembly in 1963, the western powers, with the exception of France, supported a ban on the sale of weapons. In Western Europe and North America, A.N.C. emissaries received wide sympathy in liberal circles and polite receptions from leading political figures. Communist countries orchestrated new campaigns of solidarity, backed by offers of scholarships and other material aid. Additional moral support came from Afro-Asian solidarity conferences and other Third-World organisations.

On the African continent the prospects for the A.N.C. also seemed promising. To many Africans (and observers outside Africa as well) it looked as if the tide of independence was sweeping inexorably southwards, driving the remaining white-dominated régimes before it. Although the connections between the A.N.C. and African nationalist movements elsewhere on the continent were weak (with the exception of those in neighbouring territories), the A.N.C. was seen as a representative of the wave of the future in Southern Africa. When Nelson Mandela travelled northwards in early 1962, he was received by African leaders in East, West, and North Africa, facilities for training were obtained in Ethiopia and Algeria, and funds were pledged for

[1] The details of the international campaign of the Zimbabwean nationalists are to be found in John Day, *International Nationalism: the extra-territorial relations of Southern Rhodesian African nationalists* (London, 1967).

the coffers of *Umkhonto*. Yet the process of transforming the first foot-holds in independent Africa into a solid base for effective operation proved diverting and time-consuming.

In the eyes of some Africans the multi-racial nature of the Congress Alliance, and the links of the A.N.C. with South African communists, compromised the nationalist credentials of the A.N.C. It is reported that certain African governments refused to accept non-African military trainees, and that the A.N.C. attempted to underplay the participation of communists in its ranks.[1] In Ghana, a magnet for African revo-lutionaries in the early 1960s, the A.N.C. encountered scepticism and hostility from Nkrumah's lieutenants, who inclined towards the rival P.A.C. with its explicit pan-African ideology.[2] Elsewhere A.N.C. representatives also found themselves in competition with P.A.C. exiles for the favour of host governments; in the mid-1960s the rivalry became three-way with the appearance of exiled representatives of the Unity Movement of South Africa. With the establishment in 1963 of the Organisation of African Unity, and its more specialised Liberation Committee as the co-ordinator of pan-African endorsement of, and aid to, African liberation movements, the A.N.C. was forced to contend with its rivals in additional crucial arenas.

Within the larger councils of the O.A.U. the A.N.C. has had to lobby regularly, not only to get general resolutions of opposition to *apartheid* translated into more concrete commitments of support, but also to attempt to ensure that the composition and mandate of the Liberation Committee are congenial to A.N.C. interests.[3] Perhaps even greater efforts have been consumed in direct negotiations with the Liberation Committee regarding the terms of its support and the allocation of funds. The returns have been uneven, but the effort to keep the question of white-ruled Southern Africa at the top of the O.A.U. agenda cannot be neglected.[4] In its quest for reliable support

[1] Feit, *Urban Revolt*, pp. 232–33.

[2] An indication of the unhappiness of the A.N.C.'s communist ally with the situation in Ghana can be found in *The African Communist* (London), 9, April/May 1962, pp. 11–12.

[3] The nature of some of the anxieties regarding the O.A.U. Liberation Committee have been articulated publicly by spokesmen for the Communist Party; ibid. 36, First Quarter 1969, pp. 16–17.

[4] The extent of the disappointment of the A.N.C. with the O.A.U. Liberation Committee can be inferred from reports that in the first six months of 1967–1968 the A.N.C. was promised $80,000, but received only $3,940; *The Sunday Telegraph* (London), 4 May 1969. The National Executive Committee of the A.N.C. has also criticised the O.A.U. Liberation Committee for its support of the P.A.C.; *The African Communist*, 38, Third Quarter 1969, p. 27. For a general analysis, see Yashpal Tandon, 'The Organization of African Unity and the Liberation of Southern Africa', in Potholm and Dale (eds.), *Southern Africa*, pp. 245–61.

within independent Africa, the A.N.C., like most liberation movements, has found direct arrangements with particular states of most use; it has singled out Zambia, Tanzania, the United Arab Republic, and Algeria as its most steadfast backers.[1] Yet the establishment and maintenance of close relations with these states inevitably has meant lengthy and delicate negotiations with their Governments in order to define the terms under which the A.N.C. could import arms, train cadres, conduct military exercises, and organise its resources for a return to South Africa. Thus, the necessities of intra-African diplomacy have placed great demands upon A.N.C. personnel and resources.

Relationships with communist countries have also posed problems for the exiled leaders of the A.N.C. The longtime ties between the A.N.C. and the South African Communist Party were drawn tighter through their underground co-operation in *Umkhonto*; financial support for the organisation was obtained outside South Africa and channelled back through local communist channels.[2] In the conditions of exile the distinctions between the two groups were even further blurred, and the South African Communist Party has continued to give strong support to the A.N.C. and the Congress Alliance. Undoubtedly the presence of prominent communists within the A.N.C., and their heavy representation among the exiled leadership of the non-African components of the Congress Alliance, facilitated further access to communist capitals. In the early 1960s the A.N.C. procured training facilities, arms, and other supplies from both China and the Soviet Union, as well as from Cuba and East European countries.

Yet the very intimacy which opened doors for the A.N.C. within the communist world also embroiled it in the dispute between the Soviet Union and China. The A.N.C.'s South African communist allies adopted an unswerving pro-Soviet position,[3] and when Sino-Soviet rivalry surfaced at international conferences attended by members of the external mission of the A.N.C., their delegation generally supported the Soviet view. The P.A.C., in contrast, was drawn to the Chinese position, and in response found warm encouragement for its strong antagonism to South African communists and the non-white thrust of its ideology. Peking's support for the A.N.C. was terminated and the P.A.C. replaced it in the mid-1960s as the legitimate South African

[1] *Sechaba*, 3, July 1969, p. 8.   [2] Feit, *Urban Revolt*, pp. 296-7.
[3] See, for example, the statement of the Central Committee of the South African Communist Party in *The African Communist*, 29, Second Quarter 1967, pp. 15-17, and the speech of J. B. Marks, Chairman of the South African Communist Party, at the International Meeting of Communist and Workers Parties in Moscow in June 1969; ibid. 38, Third Quarter 1969, Special Supplement, pp. 49-56.

liberation movement.[1] The tendency of the A.N.C. to look primarily to the Soviet Union and its communist allies was thus reinforced. While the expanded links with the Soviet Union and its East European supporters have sustained a flow of vital material support from the most affluent section of the Communist bloc, they also continued to provoke contention within the ranks of the A.N.C. and to provide a target for opponents in the ongoing struggle to maintain support.

In the Communist bloc and Africa the primary concerns of the A.N.C. were operating facilities and material aid. Elsewhere the A.N.C. concentrated upon strengthening opposition to the South African Government and broadening its international condemnation. A.N.C. leaders frequently made presentations at the United Nations where they had the satisfaction of noting progressively harsher condemnation of South Africa each year. A.N.C. representatives also regularly appeared on the anti-imperialist conference circuit, where unanimous resolutions were passed in opposition to *apartheid*. In Western Europe, the United States, and the 'white' Commonwealth, the A.N.C. continued to find prominent individuals and organisations to attack the actions of the Nationalist Government. Yet the rising chorus of world-wide indignation did not translate itself into appreciable pressure upon South Africa's major economic partners, nor did it move the western governments, which continued to maintain correct relations with a régime whose racial policies they professed to abhor. Although the A.N.C. could demonstrate that it had supporters and sympathisers throughout the world, it could find little evidence that their moral stance against *apartheid* had moved South Africa's rulers.

While the difficulties of coping with an unfamiliar external environment, and generating effective pressure upon Pretoria, brought uneven success, the problems of maintaining cohesion in exile and organising for a return to salient activity within South Africa proved far more intractable. The A.N.C. (and its rivals) face a determined foe which commands the most powerful state apparatus, and the strongest and most sophisticated economy on the African continent. Its determination is immeasurably stiffened by the fact that for the majority of white South Africans there is no 'mother country' to which they could flee; the southern tip of Africa is their only home. These disadvantages, which have always confronted the African opposition in South Africa, have been compounded by distinctive features of the exile situation in which the A.N.C. was forced to operate. Unlike all other Southern

---

[1] For a more general discussion of the impact of the Sino-Soviet dispute upon the Southern African liberation movements, see Marcum, loc. cit. pp. 266–8.

African liberation movements, the A.N.C. has no convenient potential sanctuary in a friendly independent state contiguous to its own country. South Africa is buffered by sympathetic white-ruled territories (Angola, Mozambique, and Rhodesia), and by independent, but economically beholden black-ruled states (Botswana and Swaziland) which refuse to permit organised political activity directed against their powerful neighbour. Pretoria's position was vastly enhanced by its success in apprehending the top echelon of the internal *Umkhonto* and A.N.C. leadership. Its action snapped the lengthy and tenuous communication lines between headquarters at 'home' and the exiled A.N.C. representatives. Yet more significantly it suddenly forced the external mission of the A.N.C., which had primarily been conceived as a public relations office, to become a full-time strategy and command headquarters. Since it had always been intended that the centre of gravity of A.N.C. and *Umkhonto* activity would remain in South Africa, the A.N.C. external mission found itself with responsibilities for which it was ill-prepared organisationally or otherwise.

A STRATEGY FOR GUERRILLA WARFARE

The onerous new burdens imposed upon the exiled A.N.C. leaders coincided with the start of the flow into A.N.C. camps in Tanzania of trained *Umkhonto* recruits. Their return brought into sharp focus two vital questions of long-term import: what was to be the nature of the relationship between the political structure of the A.N.C. and the military organisation of *Umkhonto*, and what strategy of armed struggle was to be adopted? No matter what answers were given, the A.N.C. leaders also faced logistical questions of how the *Umkhonto* cadres and their supplies would return to South Africa across intervening inhospitable territories. In the interim, the more mundane problems of coping with the tedium of day-to-day existence could not be ignored. It is impossible to detail the internal debates within the A.N.C. for lack of extensive information, but it is possible to discern some of the lines of argument and policies adopted on the basis of comments by A.N.C. leaders and their allies, and reports from other sources.

The problem of the relationship between the political leaders and the military cadres very probably posed itself in quite specific forms, but it also was an issue which was intertwined with broader strategic questions concerning the nature of the armed struggle to be organised. For military cadres 'itching for action and physical confrontation with the enemy', confinement in the camps in Tanzania must have been extremely frustrating.[1] At a time when the mystiques of guerrilla wars in China, Vietnam, Algeria, and Latin America were being exalted in revolutionary circles of all persuasions, it is almost certain that the *Umkhonto* trainees vigorously debated the applicability of various successful models to the South African struggle. For some, the formula propounded by Che Guevara (and Régis Debray) must have been particularly alluring, with its contention that the key to a successful revolution was the initiation of guerrilla action by a determined military *foco* operating in isolation from, and freed from the constraints of, an overly cautious political body. Even if this conception of guerrilla warfare was not being debated in the *Umkhonto* camps, several fashionable theories were under discussion in the upper echelon of the exiled leadership of the A.N.C. and its allies. Joe Matthews, editor of the A.N.C. monthly magazine published in London, expressed his concern:

We must arm the people not only with modern weapons but with revolutionary skill and ideas. Above all South African revolutionaries must master the problems posed by the South African revolution. The tendency to draw relevantly and irrelevantly from other struggles by analogy should not be encouraged. True, we must be ready to learn from the revolutionary experience all over the world. But in the end the creative thinking of our own revolutionaries is required to be applied to the South African revolution.[2]

Matthews' warnings were echoed in an analysis of guerrilla warfare presented to a conference at Oxford by Joe Slovo, a longtime communist and activist in the Congress Alliance who had lived in London since his escape from South Africa in 1963.[3] While endorsing (as had Matthews) the idea that military action should be initiated before the full maturation of a classical revolutionary situation, and that it would meet with growing support from the African masses, Slovo specifically criticised Debray's conception of the *foco*. In a subsequent article in *The African Communist* (which, in turn, was reprinted as a separate pamphlet by that journal), Slovo expanded upon his critical analysis of Debray's theory, stressing the incorrectness both of the latter's view of the military *foco* as the sole factor in creating victory, and of his contention that this should not be responsible to a superior political authority, but should itself assume political leadership.[4] Slovo's stance

[1] *Sechaba*, 5/6, December 1971/January 1972, p. 15.

[2] Joe Matthews, 'Forward to a People's Democratic Republic of South Africa', ibid. 1, September 1967, p. 11.

[3] Joe Slovo, 'The Armed Struggle Spreads', ibid. 2, May 1968, pp. 2–6.

[4] Joe Slovo, 'Latin America and the Ideas of Régis Debray', in *The African Communist*, 33, Second Quarter 1968, pp. 37–54. For a further elaboration of these views, see his 'Che in Bolivia', ibid. 38, Third Quarter 1969, pp. 46–61.

was echoed in the authoritative statement of strategy enunciated in 1969 at the Third Consultative Conference of the A.N.C. in Morogoro, Tanzania:

We reject the approach which sees as the catalyst for revolutionary transformation only the short-cut of isolated confrontations and the creation of armed resistance centers.

...our movement must reject all manifestations of militarism which separates armed people's struggle from its political context...[T]he primacy of the political leadership is unchallenged and supreme and all revolutionary formations and levels (whether armed or not) are subordinate to this leadership.[1]

Yet the A.N.C. leaders by no means rejected all elements of the Guevara–Debray model, or for that matter certain precepts of Mao Tse-tung, in devising the approach to guerrilla warfare which they regarded as appropriate. In successive pronouncements by its leaders and in the statement, 'Strategy and Tactics of the African National Congress', adopted at the Morogoro Conference, the A.N.C. reiterated its belief that the long history of African resistance to white domination, the political experience gained in the mass struggles of the 1950s, and the intensified repression of the 1960s, made the moment ripe for the commencement of guerrilla warfare as the first stage in a protracted struggle for the seizure of power. In the view of the A.N.C. the primary theatre of guerrilla warfare would be shifting bases in the countryside, but actions 'of a special sort' in urban areas would be an important auxiliary. Yet final success would only be achieved as a result of patient and long-term organised political participation of the majority under the firm direction of the A.N.C.

Accordingly, the guerrilla struggle was to be grounded in the 'maximum mobilization of the African people as a dispossessed and racially oppressed nation'. Explicitly the A.N.C. argued that 'the main content of the present stage of the South African revolution is the national liberation of the largest and most oppressed group – the African people'. Simultaneously it was recognised that Indians and Coloureds as oppressed groups also had a vital rôle to play as 'an integral part of the social forces ranged against White supremacy'; but whites, 'apart from a small group of revolutionary Whites who have an honoured place as comrades in the struggle', were regarded as supporters of the existing *status quo*. Thus, the A.N.C. envisaged a confrontation initially along the lines of colour, which, it emphasised, was 'not of our choosing; it is of the enemy's making'. In keeping

[1] *Sechaba*, 3, July 1969, pp. 18–19.

with the classical canons of guerrilla warfare, the A.N.C. expressed confidence that in the long run the initial weaknesses of the non-white majority – in relation to the power of the white South African state – could be converted into factors of strength, paving the way for the achievement of majority rule.[1]

Having reaffirmed its commitment to the commencement of guerrilla struggle and enunciated its assessment of the nature of that struggle, the A.N.C. still faced the problem of how to translate its aspirations into reality. In the early 1960s unarmed recruits had attempted to filter back into South Africa individually and in small groups, but many were apprehended and imprisoned by the Rhodesian and South African authorities.[2] Access through Botswana, which had been uncertain under British strictures on political activity by South African exiles, became more difficult after the granting of independence in October 1966 to a Government which understandably feared to risk antagonising such a powerful neighbour. Confronted with the failure of its efforts to infiltrate potential guerrillas back into South Africa, the A.N.C., 'after long and frank discussions' in which *Umkhonto* cadres participated, resolved to shift its tactics to attempt armed infiltration through Rhodesia.[3] For this purpose it entered into an alliance with the Zimbabwe African People's Union (Z.A.P.U.), the larger and better financed of the two national liberation movements, which in the mid-1960s had begun to send guerrilla cadres back to Rhodesia from bases in Zambia.

In August 1967, and again in the first half of 1968, joint A.N.C./ Z.A.P.U. guerrilla bands crossed into Rhodesia. While still in the northern part of the country they were engaged by Rhodesian troops who immediately called for, and received, reinforcements from the South African Police. In a series of sharp encounters these forces broke up the irregular columns, although not without suffering losses of men and equipment. The A.N.C. (and Z.A.P.U.) guerrillas not killed or captured in Rhodesia escaped into Botswana where they were imprisoned and subsequently deported to Zambia, or they made their way directly back to Zambia. Although the joint expeditions of 1967–68 failed signally to move *Umkhonto* activists into South Africa, the A.N.C. initially continued to place its faith in the potential of the

---

[1] See ibid. pp. 16–23 for the full text of the statement on the 'Strategy and Tactics of the African National Congress'.

[2] In 1965 the Minister of Justice reported that 85 persons had been arrested returning to South Africa after military training outside the country; *House of Assembly Debates* (Cape Town), 11 June 1965, col. 7918.

[3] *Sechaba*, 5/6, December 1971/January 1972, p. 15.

alliance with Z.A.P.U. as a means to return its trained cadres 'home' where they could establish guerrilla bases on South African soil. In underground leaflets distributed in South Africa, and in external statements, the A.N.C. heralded the encounters in Rhodesia as the opening battles in a war which would soon spread southwards.[1]

Behind the front lines, however, the A.N.C. was apparently encountering problems among some of its future troops. In 1968 a substantial group of *Umkhonto* cadres fled from A.N.C. camps in Tanzania to Kenya where they sought political asylum. Spokesmen for the dissidents charged that the camp commandants were living extravagantly at the expense of the rank and file, that tribal favouritism was practised, that no challenges of pro-Soviet positions were allowed, and that the first incursion into Rhodesia had been a suicide mission staged merely to eliminate dissenters and to demonstrate to potential suppliers of material aid that the A.N.C. was actively engaged in armed struggle.[2] It is certainly possible that the statements of the defectors were deliberately exaggerated to justify their action, and spokesmen of the A.N.C. vigorously denied their accusations. Yet the top leadership had recognised that it had come under substantial criticism, and that a deep-rooted malaise was impairing the effectiveness of the organisation. In this spirit the leading representatives of the A.N.C. and its non-African allies were summoned to the Third Consultative Conference at Morogoro, Tanzania, in late April 1969.[3]

AN OCCASION FOR REAPPRAISAL

In pre-conference discussions among the members of the A.N.C. and their allies within South Africa, in friendly African countries, in India, and in East and West Europe, 19 discussion documents were prepared and an additional 34 were submitted by individual supporters. For seven days in Morogoro over 70 delegates from sections of the A.N.C., from the *Umkhonto* training camps, and exiled leaders from the South African Indian Congress, the South African Coloured People's Congress, the South African Trade Union Congress, and the

---

[1] See, for example, the New Year's message of Oliver Tambo, 'Call to Revolution', ibid. 2, January 1968, pp. 2–5; and the text of a leaflet distributed within South Africa, ibid. 2, February 1968.

[2] See 'An African's Story of a Terrorist Training Camp', in *Intelligence Digest* (Cheltenham), 368, July 1969, pp. 17–18; and Richard Gibson, *African Liberation Movements: contemporary struggles against white minority rule* (New York, 1972), pp. 70–2.

[3] For overlapping, but significantly different reports of the conference, see *Mayibuye* (Lusaka), 10, May 1969; *Sechaba*, 3, July 1969; and *The African Communist*, 38, Third Quarter 1969, pp. 15–30.

South African Communist Party debated the future course of the A.N.C. This was the first time that non-African delegates from outside the A.N.C. had participated fully in a formal A.N.C. decision-making meeting. Apparently younger men from the *Umkhonto* camps sharply challenged past practices and demanded radical changes:

[I]t was their presence, their mood of revolutionary urgency, their voice and their demands which prevailed at Morogoro; their insistence on priority for the armed struggle and the mobilization of all revolutionaries at home and abroad, their demand for changed structures to meet the needs of the new phase of the revolution, for new and higher standards of political and personal conduct of all in the movement.[1]

Considerable differences were very likely present at the opening of the conference, but as debate progressed 'in an atmosphere of complete frankness' the delegates were able to reconcile their positions.[2]

In the view of the leaders of the A.N.C. the root of their difficulties were organisational, and could be traced directly to their sudden and unexpected assumption of command outside South Africa in 1963:

The External Mission had, however, been sent out to undertake certain specific tasks, vital but supplementary to the internal struggle. The total command of the people's army and the prosecution of the armed struggle was not, initially, one of these tasks. The leadership vacuum resulting from the destruction of the internal military structure saddled the External Mission with this additional task. In the course of time and by an accumulation of experience it became clear that the External Mission as then constituted was not organizationally geared to undertake the urgent task of undertaking the People's War. As the External Mission attempted to play this vital role many weaknesses began revealing themselves, weaknesses inherent in the contradiction between organization and method of struggle. Gradually these weaknesses became magnified and harmful, affecting discipline and morale; unhealthy tendencies crept into the Congress.[3]

The analysis of the A.N.C.'s communist allies also made it clear that internal organisation was shattered, grass-roots activity was limited, communication links were broken, and a gap was evident between the leadership and the rank and file.[4] Thus, the first priority of the conference was to make the organisation of the A.N.C. appropriate to the tasks and situation which would confront it in the 1970s.

Reorganisation was not, however, merely a matter of rearranging command structures and reallocating authority. It cut directly to

[1] *The African Communist*, 38, Third Quarter 1969, p. 16.
[2] *Sechaba*, 3, July 1969, p. 2. 'If there were factions at the beginning these rapidly dissolved themselves in the course of the conference', *Mayibuye*, 10, May 1969, p. 3. Reports in *The African Communist* also emphasised the open and self-critical nature of these discussions.
[3] *Mayibuye*, 10, May 1969, p. 2.
[4] *The African Communist*, 38, Third Quarter 1969, p. 18.

central questions concerning the relationship of the A.N.C. with its non-African allies, the proper balance between internal and external work, and the potential effectiveness of the armed cadres in the struggle against white power.

In what might be considered, in part, a reaction to longstanding charges made by the P.A.C. and others that the A.N.C. was controlled by non-Africans, the conference made it explicit that the primary concern of the A.N.C. was the national liberation of the African majority, and that this was to be reflected in the organisation. Thus, there apparently was no attempt made by any participants to retain the structure of the Congress Alliance, but proposals were made to establish a national liberation front analogous to that utilised in Algeria and Vietnam. The conference rejected these proposals on the grounds that in South Africa the revolutionary opposition was already united behind the Freedom Charter. The solution adopted was to provide for the 'participation in full of members of the national groups, working class and revolutionary organisations which support the armed struggle'.[1] Under this formula Indians and Coloureds, trade unionists of all races, and communists of all races 'who show themselves ready to make common cause with our aspirations [were to] be integrated on the basis of individual equality' into the A.N.C.[2] Nevertheless this was to remain a primarily African organisation by virtue of the numerical majority of the Africans among the oppressed of South Africa. The new formula was reflected in the election by the conference of a new National Executive Committee of nine Africans, and the establishment of a Revolutionary Council to include also individual Coloureds, Indians, and whites.

In the opening address Oliver Tambo, who was subsequently re-affirmed as Acting President-General, had urged all members of the A.N.C. 'to cast their eyes southward, to prepare to go home'. He stated that in the past too great emphasis had been placed in international solidarity work by the external mission, and henceforth it should be placed in proper perspective.[3] The conference subsequently emphasised that centrally directed illegal machinery was needed to organise 'the revolutionary forces in our country',[4] and this suggests that the delegates were anxious to attempt to shift the balance back towards work within South Africa, and to re-establish a centre and

[1] *Mayibuye*, 10, May 1969, p. 10. The only mention of the abortive proposal for a national liberation front appeared in this journal.
[2] *Sechaba*, 3, July 1969, p. 22.
[3] *Mayibuye*, 10, May 1969, p. 8.
[4] Ibid. p. 10. No reference to this decision appeared in *Sechaba* and *The African Communist*.

network of the sort destroyed by the Rivonia raid and its sequels. The more specific means by which this goal was to be achieved and the relationship which any internal centre was to enjoy with the external mission were not, understandably, elaborated in public.

From the published reports of the conference, however, it is evident that the new organisational structure was designed to divide responsibilities in a fashion which it was hoped would avoid the confusion of the past. The trimming of the size of the National Executive Committee from 23 to nine members was designed to facilitate decision-making. The creation of a special Revolutionary Council seems to have been an expression of the hope that greater effectiveness could be achieved if the direction and oversight of the armed struggle were made the responsibility of a specialised body free from other tasks. In an effort to prevent tensions of the type which provoked the flight of dissidents to Kenya in 1968, the incoming National Executive Committee was urged to spell out a code and oath to be adhered to by all members, and to create an ombudsman or commission 'to receive, investigate and act upon any complaints and receive grievances in all sectors of the movement'.[1] In a parallel move suggesting awareness of the dangers of a 'generation gap' the conference noted that inadequate attention had been paid to the problems of youth and students, and that personnel must be specifically devoted to their organisation. Similar concern was expressed about the neglect of special work among women. By the range of its actions and the sweeping nature of its declared intentions, the conference underlined its contention that a thorough organisational overhaul was essential to stem the debilitating consequences of the A.N.C.'s enforced exile.

The 1969 Morogoro conference also made explicit a general line of strategy for guerrilla warfare towards which the A.N.C. had already been moving. In determining the focal point for their political activity those present dealt directly with a contentious question which had long engaged the African opposition and its supporters – was the mainspring of the revolution to be nationalism or class action? It was the unequivocal view of the conference that the first priority of the A.N.C. was the mobilisation of the African majority as a nation, including the 'stimulation and deepening of national confidence, national pride and national assertiveness'. In the distinctive situation of South Africa the special rôle of the large and growing working class was recognised as a force whose 'militancy and political consciousness as a revolutionary class will play no small part in our victory',

[1] *Mayibuye*, 10, May 1969, p. 14.

yet it was to be subsidiary to the potential revolutionary power of the aroused African nation. In the eyes of the conference 'to blunt [the latter] in the interests of abstract concepts of internationalism is, in the long run, doing neither a service to revolution nor to inter-nationalism'.[1] With this formulation the A.N.C. perhaps was rejecting positions advanced by some of its communist supporters, but more significantly it moved to strengthen its image as a pre-eminently African organisation, and thus to disarm critics who might have questioned its full authenticity as a nationalist movement.

One of the other central strategic questions was the A.N.C./Z.A.P.U. alliance. The failure of the joint columns in Rhodesia had fuelled dissension within the *Umkhonto* camps, and had given ammunition to the African nationalist opponents of both the A.N.C. and Z.A.P.U. The conference acknowledged that 'some legitimate questions can be asked as to the scale, the scope of the alliance, and whether it could lead to a lack of attention to that which is specific and different in the situations of the two countries'. Its answer was an assurance that the questions had been considered fully by the leaders of the two allied organisations, and that the alliance with Z.A.P.U. should be not only continued, but strengthened. Furthermore, the conference asserted that there was an 'urgent need (long overdue) of establishing a properly organised alliance between ANC/ZAPU/FRELIMO/MPLA and SWAPO'.[2] Thus, the response of the A.N.C. to its critics and to the expanding 'Unholy Alliance' between South Africa, Rhodesia, and Portugal was a call for a counter-alliance to co-ordinate guerrilla pressures upon the rulers of the white bastion.

In its evaluation of sources of support outside Southern Africa the conference exhibited a new selectivity which portended a further refinement of efforts to obtain external support. No longer was the possibility of pressure from the western powers on South Africa remotely entertained; instead they were castigated as incorrigible imperialists and the main prop of the white régimes of Southern Africa. It was also hinted that the A.N.C. considered support from independent Africa less than complete. Amidst general praise for the rôle of the O.A.U., and particular reference to aid from Zambia, Tanzania, the United Arab Republic, and Algeria, the conference report noted: 'this is not to say that there are no weaknesses in the O.A.U. or in some of the states composing this great organization'.[3] In more specific terms the A.N.C. welcomed the aid which it had received from the O.A.U. Liberation Committee while simultaneously castigating it for its

[1] *Sechaba*, 3, July 1969, pp. 22–3.   [2] Ibid. p. 10.   [3] Ibid. p. 8.

recognition of the P.A.C. The conference also curtly noted: 'We have received much support from China in our struggle. Recently, through no fault of the ANC this support has been withheld.'[1] Thinly veiled references to 'reckless and disruptive activities' within international anti-imperialist organisations suggested further unhappiness with Chinese actions.[2] The A.N.C. clearly indicated the sources which it regarded as reliable by characterising the 'pillars of the anti-imperialist movement' as:

the Soviet Union, the Socialist states in alliance with the progressive states of Africa, Asia and Latin America, the revolutionary liberation movements in countries which are still under colonial or white minority rule, and democratic forces in the imperialist countries themselves.[3]

The outline of the more discriminating strategy of the A.N.C. with regard to external support had been presaged at the International Conference of Solidarity with the Peoples of Southern Africa and the Portuguese Colonies held in Khartoum in January 1969. Sponsored by the Soviet-oriented World Peace Council and the Afro-Asian People's Solidarity Organisation, this gathering was dominated by delegations from the A.N.C., Z.A.P.U., South-West African People's Organisation (S.W.A.P.O.), *Frente de Libertação de Moçambique* (Frelimo), *Movimento Popular de Libertação de Angola* (M.P.L.A.), and *Partido Africano da Independência de Guiné e Cabo Verde* (P.A.I.G.C.) – all of which maintained cordial relations with Moscow – and representatives from the Soviet Union, East European states, and pro-Soviet communist parties. Noticeably absent were spokesmen from almost all the independent African states.[4] Delegations were excluded from nationalist movements inclined towards Peking – the P.A.C., Zimbabwe African National Union (Z.A.N.U.), *Comité Revolucionário de Moçambique* (Coremo), and *União Nacional para a Independência Total de Angola* (U.N.I.T.A.).

The Khartoum conference endorsed detailed resolutions articulating an accelerated international solidarity campaign. Yet in a departure from past pronouncements they urged governments to recognise the six participating nationalist movements as the 'sole official and legitimate authorities of [their] respective countries'.[5] Simultaneously the

---

[1] *The African Communist*, 38, Third Quarter 1969, p. 28.

[2] *Sechaba*, 3, July 1969, p. 8.

[3] Ibid. p. 6.

[4] See *The African Communist*, 37, Second Quarter 1969, p. 21.

[5] *Sechaba*, 3, April 1969, p. 3. For selected speeches and messages of support, see ibid. 3, March 1969, pp. 4–10. An appraisal of the conference from another perspective appeared in *The African Communist*, 37, Second Quarter 1969, pp. 13–22.

resolutions emphasised the need to concentrate upon the procurement of material support from all potentially sympathetic sources. In the eyes of Richard Gibson the Khartoum conference should be viewed as an attempt to by-pass the O.A.U. Liberation Committee.[1]

At Morogoro the A.N.C. did not repeat the implied suggestion that it would seek recognition as a government-in-exile, nor did it move explicitly to distance itself from the O.A.U. Liberation Committee (to which it directed specific thanks for help in facilitating the conference). But it did give broad endorsement to the strategy for an international solidarity campaign enunciated at Khartoum. Pointedly it reiterated:

On the international front our object, apart from rallying the forces of progress into the solidarity movement, is the more urgent task of getting all democrats drawn into direct commitment to the ANC and our armed struggle.[2]

In this fashion the A.N.C. gave notice that henceforth its primary concern was no longer merely verbal condemnation of *apartheid* but concrete support from committed sources.

ADDITIONAL BARRIERS TO SUCCESS

Events after the 1969 Morogoro conference forced the A.N.C. to rethink its hopes of forging alliances with other national liberation movements, and to focus its diplomatic energies towards blunting the unexpectedly widespread favourable response in Africa to Pretoria's call for dialogue between white and black Africa. Outside Africa the A.N.C. could claim the first tangible rewards of its campaign for new sources of material support, but the prospects of substantial additional funds remained limited. Developments within South Africa highlighted the apparent estrangement of the exiled A.N.C. from new currents of challenge to the Nationalists, and underlined the organisational weaknesses of the A.N.C. 'at home'.

The most serious blow to the A.N.C. was the rapid collapse of its Z.A.P.U. ally. During 1969 dissension among rank-and-file guerrillas, disputes between leaders and ethnic rivalries hardened into factionalism which blocked effective action. The A.N.C. was powerless to halt the disintegration of Z.A.P.U., which culminated in fighting between members of rival ethnic groups, and an open break in the leadership in early 1970. Subsequent efforts to effect a reconciliation failed, and

[1] Gibson, *African Liberation Movements*, p. 66.
[2] *Sechaba*, 3, July 1969, p. 3.

elements of Z.A.P.U. broke away to join dissidents from Z.A.N.U. to form a third Zimbabwean national liberation group, the Front for the Liberation of Zimbabwe (Frolizi).[1] In consequence the A.N.C. quietly dropped its insistence upon the correctness and necessity of the A.N.C./Z.A.P.U. alliance, and shifted its attention to other means for the return of its exiled trainees to South African soil.[2] In retrospect it has been argued by a communist supporter of the A.N.C. that the Zimbabwean campaign revealed that 'without internal organization, mass mobilization and mass support, armed activity becomes strangulated'.[3]

Outside of Southern Africa the A.N.C. faced a different set of challenges centred around South African attempts to leapfrog northwards into black-ruled Africa. Malawi's receptivity to Pretoria's hand of friendship had long antagonised the A.N.C., but it was only when the leaders of Ghana, the Ivory Coast, and other francophone states began in 1969 and 1970 to endorse efforts to seek accommodation with South Africa that the A.N.C. felt threatened that its lukewarm support from many O.A.U. members might be converted into a neutralism which could only benefit Pretoria. Tanzania, Zambia, Algeria, and other supporters of the A.N.C. spearheaded opposition to the pro-dialogue trend, and a substantial majority at the O.A.U. summit meeting of June 1971 was mustered against the attempt of the Ivory Coast to discuss proposals for a summit meeting with the South African Government. Subsequently the campaign for dialogue suffered further setbacks (particularly with the overthrow of the régime of President Tsirinana of Madagascar in May 1972, and the cooling of relations between Lesotho and South Africa), but the readiness with which many governments had initially responded to Pretoria's blandishments exposed further the fragile underpinning of A.N.C.

---

[1] For a discussion of the dissension within Z.A.P.U. and the subsequent formation of Frolizi, see Gibson, op. cit. pp. 169–74 and 183–4.

[2] In December 1970, James April, a Coloured veteran of the first A.N.C./Z.A.P.U. campaign in Rhodesia, who had subsequently returned to Zambia after a prison sentence in Botswana, flew back to South Africa on a regular commercial flight, carrying forged identification papers. He sent messages to England in invisible ink, while attempting to establish links among the Indian community of Durban, but was apprehended in early 1971, tried, and sentenced to 15 years imprisonment. A report of his trial in a South African newspaper was republished in *Sechaba*, 5, August 1971, pp. 4–5.

Throughout the 1960s South African authorities have also alleged that the A.N.C. was making plans to return its trainees to isolated points along the coast. In 1969 eleven A.N.C. supporters were convicted upon charges which, *inter alia*, accused them of searching for suitable submarine landing sites; Muriel Horrell, *A Survey of Race Relations in South Africa, 1969* (Johannesburg, 1970), p. 64.

[3] *The African Communist*, 47, Fourth Quarter 1971, p. 30.

support on a continent, where verbal condemnation of *apartheid* was almost universal. Although the O.A.U. and other regional gatherings of African leaders have recently reaffirmed their support for armed struggle in Southern Africa, the A.N.C. still undoubtedly must spend much time and energy to assure regular material support from sources in independent Africa.

In the short term, prospects for support from liberal and socialist circles in Western Europe appear promising. The campaign for material commitments to supplement moral condemnations scored its first major breakthrough with the decision of the World Council of Churches in September 1970 to allocate funds to liberation movements in Southern Africa, including the A.N.C., for 'non-military purposes'.[1] Elsewhere in Western Europe and the United States, various political groups and private organisations have also made financial commitments to Southern African liberation movements.[2] While the sums contributed have helped the A.N.C., it is doubtful that they have provided the resources for a radical escalation of activity. Their value remains primarily symbolic. Substantial expenditure of the already over-extended external resources of the A.N.C. will still be required to ensure and enlarge future contributions.

Yet the central problem confronting the A.N.C. is not the mobilisation of support from outside South Africa, but the establishment of an effective base inside. Government security forces continue to utilise the full range of resources at their command to harass, restrict, and imprison the still visible leaders of the A.N.C. and its allies, and to destroy any underground organisation.[3] Although the accelerated implementation of *apartheid* has brought new misery to thousands of non-whites (principally Africans) forced into makeshift resettlement camps and rising levels of resentment – noted by both white and African observers – among the urban African population there is little evidence that any A.N.C. underground organisations have been able to capitalise upon these events to organise protests against government

---

[1] Brief reports on the action of the World Council of Churches and its repercussions in South Africa are to be found in Muriel Horrell, *A Survey of Race Relations in South Africa, 1970* (Johannesburg, 1971), pp. 15–18, and *A Survey of Race Relations in South Africa, 1971* (Johannesburg, 1972), pp. 51–3.

[2] A partial list of supporters is available in ibid. p. 94.

[3] The most regular and comprehensive summaries of the actions of the Government are to be found in the annual *Survey* compiled by Muriel Horrell for the South African Institute of Race Relations; see especially her section, 'Detention and Trial under the Security Laws'. A.N.C. publications tend primarily to note actions taken against their members and supporters; see, for example, *Sechaba*, 5, May 1971, pp. 8–9, and 6, February 1972, pp. 3–4.

actions. Increasingly opposition within South Africa to official moves is being articulated by new political actors, drawn either from among those participating in government-sponsored institutions of separate development (e.g. Chief Buthelezi of the KwaZulu Territorial Authority or Sonny Leon of the minority Labour Party in the Coloured Persons' Representative Council), or from younger Africans, Coloureds, and Indians in the South African Student Organisation and the 'Black Consciousness Movement'.

The inability of the A.N.C. to take full advantage of the changed circumstances within South Africa has been implicitly recognised by their exiled leaders. At a meeting of the National Executive Committee in Lusaka in August 1971, the new evidence of growing discontent and the wider articulation of protest was welcomed, but the A.N.C. hinted at its isolation from the process.[1] It called for an end to the 'leadership vacuum', which it suggested had prevailed since the arrest of the National High Command at Rivonia eight years before. While the commitment of the A.N.C. to armed struggle was reaffirmed, and the particular importance of work among the non-white working class was reiterated, the leaders paid particular attention to the new voices of protest. They explicitly recognised that the students, churchmen, and teachers in the 'Black Consciousness Movement' were a 'very important group of people, capable of providing leadership and consequently requiring our closest attention and guidance'.[2] Subsequently appeals by A.N.C. leaders emphasised the importance of mobilising 'our black power', and stressed the identity of interests between the 'Black Consciousness Movement' and the A.N.C. in exile.[3] While the Bantustan leaders have not been conceded the same importance, the A.N.C. and its allies have recognised that it might be possible to utilise limited aspects of the machinery of separate development for the achievement of their goals.[4] In response to events within South

---

[1] 'In a word, these "new" militant demands from our people, echoed from all corners of the country, are in fact the same demands which the African National Congress has been making on behalf of our people for years, i.e. the demands for higher wages, for the abolition of job reservation, proper education, the expropriation of all our land from the Whites, etc.' *Sechaba*, 5/6, December 1971/January 1972, p. 20.   [2] Ibid. p. 21.

[3] See, for example, Oliver Tambo, 'Mobilize Our Black Power', ibid. 6, February 1972, pp. 4–5; and 'Black Consciousness', ibid. 6, May 1972, pp. 18–20.

[4] See, for example, the report of a discussion on the Bantustans by members of an A.N.C. youth and student school; ibid. 5, November 1971, p. 13. A commentator from the communist perspective has warned against too close an identification with even selected Bantustan leaders, but has recognised 'that some members and supporters of the revolutionary movement may even find it expedient to make use of apartheid institutions to be able better to destroy them'. Sol Dubula [pseud.], 'Trends in "Bantustan" Politics', in *The African Communist*, 48, First Quarter 1972, p. 61.

Africa the A.N.C. has sought to link itself with the signs of new black assertiveness lest the direction of protest slip further away from its hands.

The continuing odyssey of the A.N.C. shows no signs of coming to a successful conclusion. In a spate of recent analyses on the difficulties and prospects of revolutionary change in Southern Africa by a student of guerrilla warfare (J. Bowyer Bell),[1] American and European academics of various political persuasions (Lewis H. Gann, Kenneth W. Grundy, John Marcum, Edward Feit, Heribert Adam),[2] a former South African policeman (Michael Morris),[3] an Indian South African sociologist (Fatima Meer),[4] and a black American journalist (Richard Gibson),[5] there is virtually unanimous agreement that early efforts to mount armed struggle in South Africa were doomed to failure, and that future efforts have little chance of success in the short, if not in the long, run.

For Bell and Gann, who examined the difficulties of the A.N.C. in the context of a broader analysis of violent revolutionary change and guerrilla warfare, the most salient shortcomings have been the absence in South Africa of the very specialised conditions in which armed revolutions have succeeded elsewhere, and the 'malpractice' of revolutionary theory by would-be guerrillas. For Grundy, who also examined the A.N.C. as part of a wider study of guerrilla warfare in Africa, the primary difficulty for the A.N.C. has been its inability to free itself from the miasma of the exile condition; his analysis dovetails fully with the more extensive arguments of Marcum. In the view of Morris the frustrations of exile are also important, but the key element in explaining the failure of the guerrilla bands is the lack of support that they received from the indigenous target population within Rhodesia. In a different context, that of the activities of the A.N.C. and *Umkhonto* from 1960 to 1964, Feit agrees but places greatest importance upon organisational factors: the intrinsic strength of an established political

[1] J. Bowyer Bell, *The Myth of the Guerrilla: revolutionary theory and malpractice* (New York, 1971); and 'The Future of Guerrilla Revolution in Southern Africa', in *Africa Today* (Denver), 19, Winter 1972, pp. 7–15.

[2] Lewis H. Gann, 'No Hope for Violent Liberation: a strategic assessment', in *Africa Report* (Washington), 17, February 1972, pp. 15–19; Kenneth W. Grundy, *Guerrilla Struggle in Africa: an analysis and preview* (New York, 1971); John Marcum, loc. cit.; Edward Feit, *Urban Revolt*; and Heribert Adam, *Modernizing Racial Domination: South Africa's political dynamics* (Berkeley, 1971).

[3] Michael Morris, *Terrorism: the first full account in detail of terrorism and insurgency in Southern Africa* (Cape Town, 1971).

[4] Fatima Meer, 'Africa Nationalism – Some Inhibiting Factors', in Heribert Adam (ed.), *South Africa: sociological perspectives* (London, 1971), pp. 121–57.

[5] Richard Gibson, *African Liberation Movements*.

system dominated by a privileged minority, and the inherent weakness of the hierarchical underground cell structure upon which the A.N.C. and its allies sought to base their operations.

For Adam the central question is less one of organisation, but rather of the dynamics of power; in his estimation, like most academic analysts of South Africa, the A.N.C. failed to recognise the essential tenacity and adaptability of the 'modernizing racial oligarchy' which has ruled South Africa since 1948. From Meer's perspective of closer involvement with the radical South African opposition, the barriers to success in armed struggle were primarily psychological: the temperamental incapability of Africans to use violence and their lack of sufficient motivation. In the committed analysis by Gibson, which focuses almost exclusively on African resistance and not on the workings of the white régimes, the blame for the failure of the A.N.C. rests with the willingness of its leaders to choose 'Soviet hegemony' over 'pan-Africanism', and its consequent inability to 'Africanize Marxism–Leninism' in a fashion analogous to Mao Tse-tung's adaptations for China.[1]

Although the foci of the analyses vary, all nine observers emphasise that the overwhelming military and economic superiority of the Nationalist Government, the extensive legal and police machinery at its disposal, the ruthless willingness with which it has been used, and the unity within the white *laager* have been crucial factors in the success of the ongoing Nationalist counter-insurgency campaign. The corresponding material weakness of the A.N.C., its lack of effective organisation, its underestimation of the determination of its foe, and the imperfect cohesion in its ranks, are also given substantial weight in explaining the failure of the A.N.C. (and its rivals) to mount a serious challenge to Nationalist power. There is also broad agreement that the configuration of power in the external environment is weighted in favour of the South African Government, and that in the foreseeable future it is unlikely to shift.

THE A.N.C. IN COMPARATIVE PERSPECTIVE

The recent upsurge in military activities by guerrilla movements in Mozambique and Rhodesia testifies to an intensification of pressure along South Africa's northern marches. Nevertheless, the short-run perspective before the A.N.C. remains unpromising, particularly when contrasted with the visible evidence of the decade-long armed struggles

[1] Ibid. pp. 64 and 75.

in Angola, Mozambique and Guiné-Bissau. An analysis of the comparative strengths and weaknesses of the Portuguese, Rhodesian, and South African régimes, the relevance of the 'domino theory' to Southern Africa, and the possibility of shifts within the international environment are beyond the scope of this article.[1] But consideration of features of the experiences of the nationalist movements in the other white-ruled territories of Southern Africa (and Guiné-Bissau) will deepen our understanding of the dilemmas facing the A.N.C.

In the Portuguese colonies, the 'reformist option', as Basil Davidson has characterised it, never existed for the African nationalist movements.[2] Although this option ultimately proved a chimera for the A.N.C., its influence was profound. Illusory hopes for the 'Cape Liberal' tradition, underpinned by the Christian mission background of many African leaders, persisted long past the point in time when a decision to shift from non-violent struggle might have stood a remote chance of possible success.[3] Even after the turn to violence in 1961, hope persisted that in some fashion the 'demonstration effect' of sabotage would be sufficient to move white South Africans to make concessions to African opinion. In South-West Africa and Rhodesia the Namibian and Zimbabwean leaders were also initially sustained by the hopes that their goals could be achieved through the *deus ex machina* of external intervention by the United Nations or Great Britain respectively. In the Portuguese territories,[4] where the low overall rate of

[1] Two provocative scenarios of the future in Southern Africa are given by Grundy, op. cit. pp. 153–88, and Christian Potholm, 'Toward the Millennium', in Potholm and Dale (eds.), *Southern Africa*, pp. 321–31.

[2] Basil Davidson, 'In the Portuguese Context', in Christopher Allen and R. W. Johnson (eds.), *African Perspectives: papers in the history, politics, and economics of Africa presented to Thomas Hodgkin* (Cambridge, 1970), p. 330.

[3] Bell doubts in *The Myth of the Guerrilla*, p. 155, that armed struggle by the African majority could ever have been successful in South Africa in the face of white might and determination; in any case, he argues, when the decision was taken in 1961 the option was no longer valid.

[4] Useful sources on the background of the nationalist movements in the Portuguese colonies include the following: Ronald Chilcote, *Portuguese Africa* (Englewood Cliffs, 1967); John Marcum, 'Three Revolutions', in *Africa Report*, 12, November 1967, pp. 9–17, and 'Liberation Movements of Portuguese Africa', written for the United Nations Association of the United States of America, Inc., 1 June 1970; and Michael A. Samuels, 'The Nationalist Parties', in David M. Abshire and Samuels (eds.), *Portuguese Africa, A Handbook* (New York, 1969), pp. 389–405. For more extensive general treatments of the nationalist movements in particular colonies, see John Marcum, *The Angolan Revolution*, vol. 1 (Cambridge, Mass., 1969); Douglas L. Wheeler and René Pélissier, *Angola* (New York, 1971); Gérard Chaliand, *Armed Struggle in Africa: with the guerrillas in 'Portuguese' Guinea* (New York, 1969); Basil Davidson, *The Liberation of Guiné: aspects of an African revolution* (Harmondsworth and Baltimore, 1969); Ronald Chilcote, 'Mozambique: the African nationalist response to Portuguese imperialism and underdevelopment', in Potholm and Dale (eds.), *Southern Africa*, pp. 183–95; and Eduardo Mondlane, *The Struggle for Mozambique* (Harmondsworth and Baltimore, 1969).

development had in any case produced a far smaller western-educated élite, the nationalist leaders who emerged in the post-war period soon abandoned any hope for peaceful constitutional reform in the face of the intransigence of the Portuguese colonial administration, and in the absence of any prospect of an influential liberal constituency within Portugal itself. Their decision to organise for violence was made consequently without the necessity of shedding the longheld hopes and illusions of a tradition of non-violence.

The absence of a 'reformist option' also had significant implications for the organisational potential of the anti-Portuguese nationalist groups. From their inception P.A.I.G.C., Frelimo, Coremo, M.P.L.A., U.N.I.T.A., and the *União das Populacoes de Angola* (U.P.A.) were illegal underground bodies. Their form of organisation did not make them immune from the determined campaign of the Portuguese security police (P.I.D.E.) to destroy them, but they did not suffer the trauma and confusions of a forced shift to illegality. By virtue of their mode of operation their leaders and cadres were not so easily known to the Portuguese authorities. Although P.I.D.E. enjoyed considerable success periodically in penetrating the internal organisations of the nationalist groups (e.g. the wave of arrests of M.P.L.A. supporters in 1959–60, the apprehension of P.A.I.G.C. leaders in 1959, and the round-up of the Frelimo underground network in southern Mozambique during 1964–5), its task was very probably more difficult than that of the South African and Rhodesian authorities who had the benefit of knowledge gained during the semi-legal phase of African nationalism in South Africa, South-West Africa, and Rhodesia.

The majority of the anti-Portuguese movements either were formed in exile (Frelimo, Coremo, or U.P.A.), or not long after their creation took the decision to shift their headquarters to an exile base. In the case of P.A.I.G.C., the particularly small leadership core of the organisation has been apparently able to maintain an unusual degree of cohesion in its new external environment. The other movements (M.P.L.A., U.P.A., Frelimo, and Coremo) have been plagued by problems within the syndrome of the 'exile condition' delineated by John Marcum; but they have not been faced with the difficulties suddenly put before the external mission of the A.N.C. in 1963 when it was forced to function as a command centre for the organisation of armed struggle – albeit originally conceived as a public relations office and relay station subordinate to internally-based headquarters. The Zimbabwean and Namibian nationalist movements in exile have faced problems similar to those of the A.N.C. In contrast, from the beginning the exiled headquarters of the anti-Portuguese movements were established as the planning headquarters for guerrilla warfare, and the recognised centre of authority within the movement. (With the successful establishment of secure liberated areas within Guiné-Bissau, Mozambique, and Angola, new problems concerning the relationship between headquarters and the commanders in the field have arisen, but this situation is not relevant to the A.N.C. in its present situation, although it could be so in the future.)

Although the leaderships of the A.N.C. and its chosen allies (Frelimo, M.P.L.A., P.A.I.G.C., Z.A.P.U., and S.W.A.P.O.) have been characterised as élites 'with some exposure to, if not a sophisticated grasp of, Marxist–Leninist ideology',[1] only the A.N.C. and the M.P.L.A. have been directly involved with formally organised communist parties. Within Mozambique and Guiné-Bissau there may have been individual members of the illegal Portuguese Communist Party who were active in the nationalist organisations. In Rhodesia and South-West Africa individuals linked with the South African Communist Party, either as members or sympathisers, have very possibly participated in the nationalist movements. In Angola in the late 1950s a branch of the underground Portuguese Communist Party played an important rôle in the establishment of the M.P.L.A., and a number of its members who escaped the P.I.D.E. arrests in 1959–60 have continued to participate in the M.P.L.A.[2] These individuals, possibly joined by others converted to communism while in exile, may maintain cohesion as organised and separate cells within their respective nationalist organisations. Yet there is little overt evidence to date in these territories of separate communist parties *per se* conceiving for themselves an autonomous rôle within the nationalist organisation. In contrast, the members of the South African Communist Party (and its legal predecessor, the Communist Party of South Africa), have always regarded themselves as belonging to an independent Marxist–Leninist body with a distinctive rôle to play in addition to their support of, and participation in, the national liberation movement against the white-minority régime of South Africa.[3]

[1] Marcum, 'The Exile Condition', loc. cit. p. 267.

[2] Marcum, *The Angolan Revolution*, vol. 1, pp. 27–30.

[3] For a detailed treatment of the Communist Party of South Africa and its relationship to non-white politics, see Sheridan W. Johns, III, 'Marxism–Leninism in a Multi-Racial Environment: origins and early history of the Communist Party of South Africa, 1914–1932', Ph.D. dissertation, Harvard University, 1965; Edward Roux, *Time Longer Than Rope: a history of the Black Man's struggle for freedom in South Africa* (London, 1948; 2nd edn. Madison, 1964). A discussion of the relationship between communism and the A.N.C. focusing upon the post-1950 period is to be found in Feit, *Urban Revolt*, pp. 278–300. For an official survey

Since its emergence into semi-public view in the late 1950s through the issuance of separate underground publications, the South African Communist Party has openly asserted its rôle as a vital element in the A.N.C., the Congress Alliance, and *Umkhonto*. In addition, through the pages of *The African Communist*, its quarterly journal published in exile, the Party has also provided a platform for other African communist parties and the Soviet point of view within the international communist movement. The question of whether or not the Party has obtained 'control' of the A.N.C. is not relevant to this analysis, but it has continued to participate as a separately organised group within the ranks of the A.N.C. The reorganisation of the A.N.C. to include non-African supporters directly within its ranks has now eliminated the formal distinctions which in the past placed non-African communists outside the organisation; in consequence, leading non-African communists (e.g. Dr Yusef Dadoo and Joe Slovo) now participate as recognised members of the A.N.C. within the highest councils of the organisation. The change from the looser alliance to a single integrated body does not by any means necessarily eliminate the lines of cleavage between Africans and non-Africans, between communists and non-communists. The presence of a Marxist 'caucus' continues to have consequences for both the internal and external affairs of the A.N.C.

Within the A.N.C. the communists, by nature of their commitment to the Party and their belief in its inevitable mission, can be expected to maintain a cohesiveness probably greater than that of the non-communists of various persuasions. In A.N.C. activities and councils this might give them a weight out of proportion to their numbers. It remains possible that, as in the past, the presence of the communists within the A.N.C. might provoke dissension among the membership. As long as the main leaders of the A.N.C. and the major part of its activities remain centred in exile, the potential for an increase of communist members within the A.N.C. will be considerable, particularly as the A.N.C. is likely to retain, if not strengthen, its links to the Soviet Union and its allies – among its most steady sources of moral and material support in the past. This continuing association gives the A.N.C. an important prop which at the least would probably prevent it from disintegration in exile from lack of means of subsistence.[1]

by a member of the South African Communist Party, see A. Lerumo [pseud.], *Fifty Fighting Years: the South African Communist Party, 1921–1971* (London, 1971).

[1] The viewpoint of the A.N.C. leaders on communism has been most explicitly articulated by the late Chief Albert Luthuli, President-General of the A.N.C., in *Let My People Go: an autobiography* (London, 1962), pp. 153–5; and by Nelson Mandela, in *No Easy Walk*, pp. 178–84.

Although particular African states might object to the close relations between the A.N.C. and both the South African Communist Party and extra-continental Communist governments, the majority seem willing to tolerate, if not welcome, such support in the common struggles against *apartheid*.

From its side the Communist Party of South Africa shows no indication of deviating from its enthusiastic support of the A.N.C. Yet it has also given no signs of abandoning its own separate identity, viewpoint, and organisation. The augmented Central Committee decided in 1970:

> to direct its main efforts to the reconstruction of the Party at home as an organization of professional revolutionaries, closely in contact with the working class and peasantry and able to carry on the propaganda and organization of the Party.[1]

This is a reaffirmation that it intends to remain an autonomous, but fully involved, component of the underground political life of the revolutionary South African opposition. For the A.N.C., then, the nature of its relationship to Marxism–Leninism will continue to be shaped by the fact that it has within its ranks, and yet also as an external ally, an organised communist party with its own long history and distinctive vision of a socialist South Africa.

The longstanding participation of communists in the A.N.C. did not mean, however, that they were any more prepared for, or attuned to, the harsh realities of organising an armed struggle in post-1960 South Africa. Although the communists contributed much of the structural skeleton and financial sinews of the initial internal *Umkhonto* organisation, their vulnerability was exposed equally with that of their A.N.C. partners by the arrest of the National High Command at Rivonia, and by subsequent actions of the security police during the mid-1960s culminating in the apprehension and imprisonment of Bram Fischer and other party leaders. By the Party's own admission important officials have been imprisoned for life or long terms, its internal organisation has incurred 'serious setbacks', and its cadres are widely scattered;[2] like the A.N.C. the Party is directed from exile and the reconstruction of its internal structures is only now being given the highest priority. The experience of the Party in the 1960s illustrated that commitment to the 'more revolutionary' ideology of

---

[1] *The African Communist*, 43, Fourth Quarter 1970, p. 54. Earlier the Central Committee had asserted that 'the strengthening of the independent organization of the Party itself is a vital and indispensable task of every member'; ibid. 29, Second Quarter 1967, p. 13.

[2] Ibid. 43, Fourth Quarter 1970, pp. 51–2.

Marxism–Leninism and an illegal organisation were insufficient to protect it from the same fate that befell the A.N.C. at the hands of the South African security forces. Like the A.N.C. the Communist Party suffered disastrously from the visibility of its leaders, its devotion to the habits of the past, its overly optimistic prognosis of the imminence of the outbreak of revolution, and its underestimation of the resolution and resourcefulness of the Government.

The experience of the P.A.I.G.C. in its struggle in Portugal's smallest, least profitable, and climatically least hospitable colony might not seem particularly relevant to the A.N.C. facing the juggernaut of Afrikaner white power in Africa's richest and most developed country. Yet upon closer examination it throws the problem of revolution in South Africa into high relief. Fortunately the evolution of the policies of the P.A.I.G.C. of Guiné-Bissau can be examined in detail by virtue of the easy availability of the writings of the late Amilcar Cabral, Secretary-General of P.A.I.G.C.,[1] and detailed reports on Guiné-Bissau by several sympathetic European journalists and scholars.[2]

The P.A.I.G.C. was founded in 1956 by six men of petty bourgeois origin dedicated to end Portuguese rule through the instrumentality of an underground political party operating within a broadly Marxist framework. In its original formulation the P.A.I.G.C. counted on the working class to be the social base for the advance of its revolutionary ends, but soon realised the limited potential of the tiny local proletariat. When a strike in 1959 led to the massacre of over 50 workers by Portuguese troops, the P.A.I.G.C. pulled back from the tactics of confrontation in Bissau. Shortly thereafter, the city-based underground P.A.I.G.C. shifted its strategy, and moved its headquarters out of the country. It resolved to undertake all means of struggle, including armed action, and henceforth determined that the peasantry were to be the main force for the achievement of national liberation. The P.A.I.G.C. had a unique asset for its new strategy, because Cabral had intimate acquaintance with the rural areas gained by a country-wide agricultural survey which he had conducted for the Portuguese Government during 1952–54.

Yet initially the P.A.I.G.C. lacked direct links with the peasants, and pragmatically looked for promising manpower to be trained for

[1] Amilcar Cabral, *Revolution in Guinea: an African people's struggle* (London, 1969); and 'National Liberation and Culture', Syracuse University, Program of Eastern African Studies, Occasional Paper No. 57, 1970.

[2] Notably Chaliand, *Armed Struggle in Africa*; Davidson, *The Liberation of Guiné*; and Lars Rudebeck, 'Political Mobilisation for Development in Guinea-Bissau', in *The Journal of Modern African Studies* (Cambridge), x, 1, May 1972, pp. 1–18.

this purpose. It found that the most appropriate group was neither the peasants still resident in the rural areas, nor the urban petty bourgeois or established workers, but the 'rootless' young recent migrants from the countryside. A small number of carefully selected recruits were then trained in a party school established in neighbouring Guinea, from where they filtered back to the P.A.I.G.C. To their initial surprise they found the peasants suspicious and uninterested in their call to prepare for armed revolution. After a period of trial and error, during which the cadres learned to tailor their appeal to the specific features of the district in which they were operating, and to avoid approaches couched in the abstract terminology of anti-imperialist rhetoric, the P.A.I.G.C. was able to establish footholds within rural Guiné-Bissau. But it was only in 1963 that the P.A.I.G.C. felt strong enough to begin limited guerrilla action. In the ensuing period the rate of recruitment increased steadily, and the P.A.I.G.C. was able to claim in 1966 that it controlled half of the territory.

Yet in the process of extending its liberated zones the P.A.I.G.C. encountered further problems of ethnic friction, and reluctance among the militants of one region to participate in armed units in another region. Further tactical adaptations were required. To secure additional support, and to accelerate the process of nation-building while the guerrilla struggle was still in progress, the P.A.I.G.C. established a political infrastructure, created essential economic institutions, and organised rudimentary social services in liberated zones.

In Guiné-Bissau many of the ingredients for an ultimately successful revolutionary guerrilla war seem to be present. From its inception the P.A.I.G.C. has been led by a small, self-selected band of men dedicated to the goals of national liberation and social revolution. The P.A.I.G.C. has never had to contend with a 'reformist' past, nor has it had to cope with long-established divisions among widely diverse political persuasions and groups within its own ranks. Although committed to a particular theoretical framework, the closely knit leadership of the P.A.I.G.C. has shown an eclectic flexibility in revising theory to conform to changing perceptions of the local reality, and consistent sophistication in adapting tactics to particular situations. On the whole it has shown a keen awareness of the nature of its Portuguese opponent, it has been realistic in estimating its own strength, and has been sensitive to its own weaknesses. Furthermore, the P.A.I.G.C. operates in a West African setting where geography, tropical climate, lack of colonial penetration, and limited metropolitan economic stakes favoured the initiation and expansion of guerrilla warfare by Africans against a white colonial administration. In carefully planned stages, usually preceded by patient political mobilisation of key elements of the local population, the P.A.I.G.C. has consolidated its liberated zones to cover most of rural Guiné-Bissau. Nevertheless, even with these multiple reinforcing advantages, the P.A.I.G.C. after almost a decade of armed struggle has been unable to dislodge the Portuguese from the capital and major towns of the colony. To date Portugal, sustained ultimately, in the eyes of the P.A.I.G.C., by her N.A.T.O. allies, has not wavered in her determination to retain at least armed enclaves in Guiné-Bissau despite the constantly rising high cost of doing so.

That the P.A.I.G.C. with so many factors in its favour has not been able to oust the Portuguese highlights the magnitude of the task before the African National Congress. It is evident that the painstaking, step-by-step advance of the sort achieved by the P.A.I.G.C. in Guiné-Bissau has at best barely commenced in South Africa. The conduct of the P.A.I.G.C. suggests food for 'creative thinking' of the type advocated by Joe Matthews for South African revolutionaries.

By the very nature of their commitment to armed struggle, and the exposed nature of their situation, the A.N.C. and its allies do not publicise many details of their thinking upon strategy and tactics. The report of the meeting of the National Executive Committee in August 1971 suggests that a process of further re-evaluation is continuing. Whereas, in statements in the late 1960s, A.N.C. leaders expressed belief that revolution would come to South Africa 'sooner than many people think',[1] the National Executive Committee now merely noted cautiously that 'conditions are maturing in our country, which correctly exploited, could raise our struggle to new revolutionary heights'.[2] The A.N.C. neither can, nor does it wish to, abandon its commitment to armed struggle as the *sine qua non* of any transfer of power from white to black in South Africa, but its timetable for success has clearly been lengthened into the more indefinite future.

---

[1] *Sechaba*, 1, September 1967, p. 11.
[2] Ibid. 5/6, December 1971/January 1972, p. 21.

SOCIAL DYNAMICS 9(1) 50-66 1983

RETHINKING THE 'RACE-CLASS DEBATE' IN SOUTH AFRICAN HISTORIOGRAPHY

DEBORAH POSEL Nuffield College, Oxford.

This article argues that revisionist historiography has constituted a debate with its liberal opponents which has an 'either-or' form: either class or race has analytic primacy, and either segregation/apartheid is functional or dysfunctional to capitalist growth. This has led revisionists into reductionism and functionalism, despite frequent disclaimers to the contrary. Failure to conceptualise and address the relative independence of social factors has, as a corollary, a functionalist rendition of their relationship to capitalist interests and development. By way of illustration an article by Wolpe and a book by Saul and Gelb are criticised for analytical shortcomings. Finally revised conceptualisations of the relationships between race and class and between capitalist development and racial policies are proposed.

A theory is as deep and wide-ranging as the kinds of problems it addresses. The way a problem is formulated previews the variables, and their interrelationships and effects which are thought to require investigation. Thus the questions which we ask of history act like probes, on the front end of our inquiry, delineating its ground and directing the depth and range of its focus.

The major contribution of the so-called 'race-class debate' was to have put a new sort of question onto the agenda of South African historiography, which inaugurated a more wide-ranging and penetrating theoretical approach than had informed studies of South African history until then. Challenging liberal historians who saw apartheid (or segregation, before it) as wholly independent of, and at odds with, the logic of economic growth, revisionists such as H. Wolpe, M. Legassick and F. Johnstone stressed the functional compatibility and dependency between South Africa's political and economic systems. The central questions which this 'race-class debate' thus launched were: how did segregationist, and now apartheid policies *reproduce* and *promote* capitalist interests? And how has the course of capitalist development in South Africa *determined* the shape of its racial policies?

However, as we shall see, at least as regards those revisionists who situated and defined their work within the theoretical framework of this debate,[1,2] the very terms of their disagreement with liberals often led them to address these questions almost exclusively. Thus, in many cases, what began as an *emphasis* on the class functions and determinants of apartheid and segregation, expanded and solidified into a theoretical and methodological approach, or

problematic,[3] which imposed a functionalist and reductionist perspective on the study of South African history. Within such academic circles, the South African 'social formation' has been treated as if a functionally integrated whole, its racist political and ideological superstructure wholly serving the interests of the capitalist base which determines it. As a result, having opened up a new ground for historical inquiry, such revisionist theory has also tended to close it off to further expansion. For, the price paid for this approach is a foreclosing of inquiry into other sorts of questions concerning the tensions and contradictions in the relationship between racial policy and capitalism, on the one hand, and the irreducible importance of political and ideological factors, on the other.

Arguably, these are exactly the sorts of questions which economic and political developments during the 1970s, and the state's current 'reform' initiatives bring into sharp relief. The striking degree of compatibility between economic growth and political repression in South Africa during the 1960s provided the historical backdrop and vindication for the early stages of the 'race-class debate'. But it is the stresses and strains in this relationship during the 1970s and into the 1980s, which now demand our attention and explanation, and which can lead us into a new stage in the debate between liberals and revisionists.

This paper is an attempt to develop this argument, in the following way:

1. I will first briefly survey the terms and form of the 'race-class debate', as it originated in the early 1970s.
2. I then suggest how, given the 'either-or' quality of this debate, the very questions which

expanded our theoretical and methodological horizons also came to impose constraints of their own. These take the form of a reductionist and functionalist problematic, which has seeped into much revisionist historiography, despite frequent disclaimers to the contrary.

3. Next, the sorts of explanatory difficulties and limitations which this problematic generates, and which confirm its latent presence, will be illustrated by a brief assessment of two influential revisionist studies, one by Harold Wolpe, and the other by John Saul and Stephen Gelb. My aim is to show that revisionist historiography has often been stuck with needlessly restrictive and inept theoretical resources for dealing with its own historical material.

4. This critique of the reductionism and functionalism inherent in Wolpe's, and Saul and Gelb's positions, leads us into a reconstruction of both the terms of the debate between liberals and revisionists, and the nature of the most convincing revisionist case.

The Terms of the 'Race-Class Debate'

It would be a mistake to impute complete unity or homogeneity to the liberal position. However, since our present focus is on the development of certain revisionist theory in and through the 'race-class debate', rather than on the theoretical perspective of both contending parties, we can safely sidestep a study of variations within the liberal camp at this point. We need only consider the revisionist version of the liberal position, since this is the object of the revisionist critique, which is in turn the mainspring of the alternative theoretical and methodological approach declared by a large number of revisionists.

In the revisionists' eyes, the nub of the liberals' case consists in their stand on two related issues:

i) The general analytic relationship between the concepts of race, racial policy and ideology, on one hand, and those of class interests, relations and struggle, on the other.

ii) In particular, the relationship between policies of racial discrimination and capitalist development, from the late nineteenth century onwards.

With respect to the first, revisionist protagonists in the debate interpret liberals as treating racial prejudice, rather than class struggle, as the heart of the conflicts and inequities within South African society. Liberals, on this view,

thus regard the dynamics of racial discrimination as the prime mover of the country's history. 'Race' is therefore taken as the primary variable in liberal analysis, in which class relations are seen to be treated as secondary to, even derivative of, racial conflict.[4]

Secondly, revisionists understand liberals to be arguing that apartheid policies have imposed irrational and unnecessary constraints on the vigour of capitalist growth in South Africa. Liberals, they say, see racism in South Africa as wholly at odds with renewed economic growth, the force of the latter being sufficient finally to erode its racial fetters. On this view, industrialisation and capitalist development produce not merely an economic interest in liberal reforms, but an ultimately irresistible pressure issuing inevitably in evolutionary change in that direction. In Frederick Johnstone's words,

According to this approach, the system of racial domination in modern South Africa is seen and explained as a 'dysfunctional' intrusion upon the capitalist economic system, stemming from non-material factors outside it such as prejudice, racism, nationalism, and 'social and cultural pluralism', but doomed over the long term to destruction by the inexorable imperatives of rational industrialism and 'colour-blind' capitalism. (Johnstone, 1976: 1-2).

The liberal position is thus characterised as a declaration of the analytic primacy of variables of race *over* those of class, and of the complete dysfunctionality, *rather than* functionality, of segregation and then apartheid for capitalism in South Africa.

When defined in antithesis to this liberal stance, revisionism amounts to a simple reversal of the purportedly liberal priorities: class now has primacy over race, and segregation and apartheid are seen as functional, rather than dysfunctional, to the development of South African capitalism. Such revisionists thus cast themselves as the opposition to the liberal protagonists in a debate which has a tacitly 'either-or' form: either class *or* race has analytic primacy, and either segregation/apartheid is function *or* dysfunctional to capitalist growth. That both issues are set up in 'either-or' terms is reflected in the form taken by typical revisionist rejoinders to the liberals. For example, Frederick Johnstone, in his pioneering study of racial policies within the gold mining industry, explains that his

... general thesis is that this racial system may

be most adequately explained as a class system — as a system of class instruments . . . generated, and determined in its specific nature and functions, by the specific system of production and class structure of which it formed a part; and that these historical developments may most adequately be explained in terms of this explanation, and tend to confirm, as historical manifestations, the class nature of this system and thus the validity of this explanation. (Johnstone, 1976: 4).

In explaining racial policy in terms of class factors, without *posing* the question of their interdependence or historically variable relationship, Johnstone thus accepts and reproduces the terms of the debate as having an 'either-or' form.[5] 'Class' and 'race' are presumed to be analytically independent categories, ranked hierarchically and invariably, with 'class' as the more fundamental variable, accounting for the development and functions of racial policies. The very terms in which the 'race-class' debate is set up thus preclude a different mode of inquiry, oriented by a different question, which does not seek a uniform ranking of one variable over another, but rather their concrete interrelationships, in the ways in which racial cleavages and practices themselves structure class relations. This would make the concept of 'race' analytically inseparable from our understanding and very conceptualisation of existing class relations in any particular conjuncture.

A similar form of argument characterises revisionist views of the relationship between segregation/apartheid, and capitalism. As if forced to choose between regarding apartheid (or segregation) as always functional *or* dysfunctional to capitalist interests, many revisionists have set out to show all the various ways in which apartheid has functioned to advance economic growth in South Africa. Not surprisingly then, questions about the contradictions or tensions between the two are not typically incorporated into the theoretical premises and framework of this historiography. Martin Legassick's formulation of his problem in 'South Africa: Capital Accumulation and Violence' typifies this approach:
   . . . this essay seeks to show that the specific structures of labour control which have been developed in post-war South Africa are increasingly functional to capital: though the particular combination of class forces which instituted them and have maintained them may be debated, nevertheless they serve the

interests of capitalist growth in the South African situation. (Legassick, 1974: 269).

Of course, the questions which preoccupied the early revisionists have been important and pioneering ones, especially pertinent against the backdrop of the 1960s during which economic growth in South Africa flourished (second only to Japan's) at the same time as state repression continued to intensify. Certainly, the early stages of the 'race-class debate' were conducted in the wake of one of the starkest demonstrations of a largely successful partnership between capitalist growth and racially discriminatory policies. Nor were the capitalist benefits of racism confined to the '60s: the continued expansion of the South African economy testifies prima facie to a persistent, if historically variable, compatability between the country's political and economic systems. Furthermore, the early articles by Johnstone, Wolpe and Legassick, for example, which exhibited this collusion, opened up a new and rich agenda for historical inquiry: studies of the relationship between the state and white working class, the class bases of Afrikaner nationalism, intra-capitalist conflicts, and forms of African working class resistance, were all made possible by the original revisionist breakthrough.

Nevertheless, while probing and innovative, the 'race-class debate' has also led many revisionists into a reductionist and functionalist approach to the study of South African history, one which is needlessly rigid and inhibiting. The following discussion looks firstly, at the source and nature of this approach, and secondly, at some of its analytic constraints.

The Drift Into Reductionism and Functionalism

I have argued above that having situated their perspective within the context of an 'either-or' type of debate with liberal scholars, revisionists have thus tended to limit their theoretical and methodological options, to a choice of class over race as their primary variable, and to viewing apartheid and segregation as functional rather than dysfunctional to South African capitalism. Now in this way, an initial enthusiasm for, and concentration on, questions about the economic determinants and functions of segregation and apartheid often became an exclusive and limited preoccupation with these issues alone. Unfortunately, given the way the terms of the 'race-class debate' were originally cast, questions about the dysfunction of racial policies and about the irreducible importance of racial factors, have largely been confined to the liberal camp.

We should look now at the theoretical and methodological legacy of this repetition of and preoccupation with a limited set of questions.

Firstly, the systematic ranking of 'class' as a variable more important than 'race' has tended to sponsor a base-superstructure model for the explanation of South African society and history. Even if the terms 'base' and 'superstructure' are not used explicitly, the intention of the model is realised in the treatment of 'class' as uniformly more fundamental than, and analytically separable from, variables of 'race', such that class relations and capitalist growth are seen to determine and account for racial policies, which function to reproduce this economic base. (See Johnstone, 1970; Davies, 1979b; O'Meara, 1975).

Secondly, given the theoretical and methodological constraints engendered by the terms of the 'race-class debate', it is often a highly reductionist and functionalist version of the base-superstructure model which underpins the writings of Johnstone (in his early writings), Wolpe, Legassick, O'Meara and Davies, for example, notwithstanding many disclaimers to the contrary. Consider the slide into a reductionist problematic first. Although declaring a serious respect for the 'relative autonomy' of racial practices and ideology, Dan O'Meara for example, still stipulates that

... variations in racial policy must be seen as flowing from changes in the structure of production and the alignment of class forces in the social formation. (O'Meara, 1975).

Here, an inquiry into the reciprocally determining and relatively independent dynamic of racial policy seems to be precluded by methodological fiat. To go about explaining "variations in racial policy . . . as flowing from changes in the structure of production . . . and class forces" is to set up the inquiry in terms which foreclose an interest in, and treatment of, the possibly autonomous or irreducible role of racial policy in shaping the "structure of production and the alignment of class forces" themselves. The terms in which any question is posed offer a way of discovering some things and ignoring others. O'Meara's approach addresses questions concerning the dependency of South African racial policy on capitalist processes only. This in turn leads him (knowingly or unknowingly) to treat this dependency as *sufficient* to explain the development of the country's racial policies. Hence the tacit reductionism inherent in the

form of his inquiry and ensuing explanations.

Robert Davies too, neglects his own reminders about the need to take questions of race seriously. In introducing the broad outlines of his approach in *Capital, State and White Labour in South Africa: 1900-1960,* Davies unwittingly illustrates how an apparent interest in racial factors as forces (in part) in their own right, is no sooner uttered than it is suppressed by the terms in which he formulates the goals of his class analysis.

Contrary to the assertions of certain critics, the purpose of this analysis is not to deny the importance of racist ideology and racial prejudice, but rather to see these as phenomena arising in the class struggle and therefore themselves requiring analysis and explanation, instead of, as in the liberal problematic, the 'self-evident' starting point of all 'analysis' and 'explanation'. (Davies, 1979a: 3).

Davies thus sets out to explain how class struggles account for racial ideology and prejudice, again in terms which prejudge the uniform, unidirectional primacy of the former over the latter. The very way in which Davies formulates and orients his inquiry silences any question about the ways in which class struggle itself "requires analysis and explanation" in the light of the possible reciprocal effects and impact of irreducibly racial factors.

Notice therefore, that my point is not that many revisionist thinkers have explicitly denied, or deliberately excluded, the salience of racial factors as contributing in part to an explanation of capitalist development and class struggles themselves. Rather, any declared interest in these questions is involuntarily rendered mute and impotent by the terms in which the relationship between capitalist production and racial factors is examined and evaluated. It is this foreclosing of inquiry that produces reductionistic explanations, and which evidences the presence of a perhaps unintentionally reductionist problematic.

The corollary of failures to conceptualise and address the relative independence of racial factors, is a functionalist rendition of their relationship to capitalist interests and development. Consider for example, Johnstone's stance in his early and seminal paper, *White Prosperity and White Supremacy in South Africa:*

... far from undermining White supremacy, economic development is constantly reinforcing it. Its power structure is continually strengthened by its own output. In a circular process, the African workers produce the wealth and power which enable the Whites to go on strengthening this structure of production which goes on producing the power which goes on strengthening the structure and so on. It is precisely the function of apartheid to render this process as effective as possible. (Johnstone, 1970: 136).

In this paper, he explains the nature and development of apartheid wholly in terms of the functions which it performs in "strengthening . . . the structure of production".

Martin Legassick too, explains the "specific structures of labour control . . . in post-war South Africa" in terms of the functions which they performed in serving the "interests of capitalist growth in the South African situation", (Legassick, 1974: 269) on the underlying assumption that this produces a complete explanation of the said structures of labour control.

Again, I am not accusing any revisionists of expressly precluding the possibility of conflicts of interests having emerged between segregation and then apartheid, and capitalist development in South Africa. Rather, I am pointing to the ways in which the terms of their original questions and the resultant closing off of important areas of inquiry, has involuntarily produced functionalist moulds for the forms of explanation given in answer to these questions.[6] Those revisionist writers who channelled their inquiry into a study of the functions of apartheid/segregation, in terms which ipso facto excluded a simultaneous grasp of its possible dysfunctions, thereby denied themselves the opportunity of conceptualising the effects of apartheid as a specific (and historically variable) *combination* of functions and dysfunctions.[7] Posing the question in this way would entail a shift onto a different theoretical and methodological terrain which, freed from the constraints of the original 'race-class debate', could articulate the contradictions or tensions between South Africa's political and economic systems without thereby crossing over into the liberal camp.

We must look now at some of the costs and limitations of this functionalist and reductionist perspective on South African history. For, my criticism of such revisionists is not the mere fact that a particular problematic or paradigm has accreted through the repetition of certain questions to the exclusion of others; this is an epistemological feature of any historiography. Rather, my contention is that given the needlessly restrictive character of their original questions, these revisionists have ended up with an inhibiting and uninteresting problematic, ill-equipped to deal with their own historical insights.

Analytic Shortcomings

I will deal with this problem as exemplified firstly in Harold Wolpe's seminal paper, *Capitalism and Cheap Labour-Power in South Africa: From Segregation To Apartheid,* and secondly, in Saul and Gelb's recent book, *The Crisis in South Africa.* Both these writings exemplify the sorts of explanatory limits produced by a reductionist and functionalist problematic, and at the same time, illustrate the curious disjuncture between the kinds of historical insights and commentary which revisionist historiography contains, together with its *implicit* theoretical underpinnings, and the *explicit* theoretical labels and conclusions brought to bear upon them.

Wolpe's paper can be read to contain two hypotheses, one explicit and theoretically articulated; the other, implicit and theoretically anonymous. The first, which Wolpe expressly set out to argue, accounted for the difference in kind between segregation and apartheid policies, and the transition from the one to the other, in terms of the different economic conditions which determined them. Thus, the abstract of the article states:

> In this article, substantial differences between Apartheid and Segregation are identified and explained by reference to the changing relations of capitalist and African precapitalist modes of production. In these conditions Segregation gives way to Apartheid which provides the specific mechanism for maintaining labour power cheap through the elaboration of the entire system of domination and control and the transformation of the function of pre-capitalist societies. (Wolpe, 1972: 425).

Wolpe argued that during the Segregation period, the state could still rely on agriculture, subsistence production in the reserves to supplement migrants' wages, thus contributing to the maintenance of cheap African labour. The Apartheid state however, confronted a situation in which pre-capitalist production in the reserves had disintegrated, so as to diminish its contribution to the wages of migrant labourers. Thus,

> Whereas Segregation provided the political structure appropriate to the earlier period, Apartheid represented the attempt to maintain the rate of surplus value and accumula-

tion in the face of the disintegration of the pre-capitalist economy. Or, to put it in another way, Apartheid, including separate development, can be best understood as the mechanism specific to South Africa in the period of secondary industrialisation, of maintaining a high rate of capitalist exploitation through a system which guarantees a cheap and controlled labour force under circumstances in which the conditions of reproduction (the redistributive African economy in the Reserves) of that labour force is rapidly disintegrating. (Wolpe, 1972: 430-431).

Apartheid represented a combination of attempts to guarantee cheap labour power in the face of the ailing capacity of the reserves to fulfil this function by contributing to migrant workers' subsistence. For example, industrial decentralisation policies facilitated the employment of African labour at low wages, even in semi-skilled or skilled positions.[8] Also, the Apartheid state's intensified control over the allocation of African labour was designed to ensure that Africans were forced into accepting such terms of employment. Finally, the Apartheid state's policy of separate development involved the commitment to revitalising and entrenching tribal authority, customs, and methods of production, as means for the "political, social, economic and ideological enforcement of low levels of subsistence", (Wolpe, 1972: 451) which further abetted the imposition of low wages on the African migrant labour force.

Each facet of apartheid policy was thus seen by Wolpe as a "function of the economic changes in the Reserves, which generate(d) a threat to the cheapness of labour power" (Wolpe, 1972: 447). In this way, Wolpe presented and interpreted his argument as an illustration of the primacy of capitalist development and class interests in determining the forms which racial policy took, and the functions which it performed.

However, this apparently simple connection of explanatory sufficiency between the development and interests of capitalist production, and shifts in South African racial policy, was belied by Wolpe's own historical commentary towards the end of the very same article. This discussion in fact implicitly sponsored a non-functionalist and non-reductionist explanation of Apartheid policy, but these theoretical and methodological leanings were never made explicit and elaborated. Here, Wolpe showed, firstly, that declin-

ing agricultural production in the reserves, together with the ensuing rural and urban poverty and unrest, were prominent problems on the White political agenda during the 1940s; but, secondly, that different possible solutions to these problems were favoured by different alliances of class interests. For example, English manufacturing capital, represented in the party political sphere by the United Party, supported labour policies which reduced dependency on migrant labour, at least as far as the urban-based manufacturing sector was concerned. Strong enough to pay higher wages and eager to boost the industry's productivity, manufacturing capitalists favoured strategies to stabilise urban African labour, allowing wages, standards of living and levels of skill to rise accordingly. (Wolpe, 1972: 445). The priority of agricultural capital however, was still cheap, unskilled labour, which is why it endorsed the Nationalist Party's labour policies mentioned earlier (viz. decentralisation of industry, intensified influx control etc.). Theirs was an interest in enhanced and extended state control over the movements and organisation of the African labour force (which also coincided with the interests of White workers, by protecting their privileged position as a "labour aristocracy"). (Wolpe 1972: 446).

This historical account thus showed that in 1948, both the United Party and the Nationalist Party proposed policies which represented attempts to address the problems produced by the serious decline in the reserves and ensuing urbanisation (i.e. problems of urban and rural poverty; growing unrest in the form of strikes and riots). Furthermore, both policies would have promoted the interests of capital, albeit in significantly different ways, by following divergent routes towards renewed capitalist development in South Africa. On this account, therefore, Nationalist Party policy — apartheid — was clearly neither a necessary nor an inevitable outcome of capitalist processes and interests at the time. The transition from segregation to apartheid can no longer be explained in terms of changed conditions of the reproduction of labour-power alone, since this would simply restate the problem of why apartheid, and not the United Party's reformism, succeeded segregation. Thus, while these economic conditions and their effects might have been necessary conditions for the transition from segregation to apartheid, they cannot be sufficient to explain this transition, and to account for the "substantial differences" (Wolpe, 1972: 425) between the two. Wolpe's theoretically explicit hypothesis was reductionist in having set up the issue to be explored in terms which tacitly attributed explanatory sufficiency to an account of these merely *necessary* conditions. Furthermore, this reductionist bent steered him away from formalising and explicitly incorporating the non-reductionist theoretical implications of his own historical account, as examined above. In short, therefore, Wolpe's explicit hypothesis was theoretically contrived and inappropriate, while his implicit hypothesis remained theoretically inarticulate.

John Saul and Stephen Gelb's discussion of purported "crises" during the 1940s and 1970s in South Africa, involuntarily inherited the functionalist legacy of the 'race-class debate', which finally disabled their conception of "crisis" itself. Furthermore, as in Wolpe's case, Saul and Gelb's formal theoretical categories and perspective are at odds with some of their historical, theoretically anonymous (but not theoretically neutral or presuppositionless) commentaries.[10]

Saul and Gelb collude with the picture of twentieth century South African history which seems to have become dominant, and perhaps unquestioned, within many[11] revisionist circles. The history of the South African state post-1910 is cast in terms of a functional alliance between segregation, then apartheid policy, and capitalist growth, which was disturbed only by the eruption of two major "crises", in the 1940s and 1970s respectively.[12] By reviewing Saul and Gelb's discussion of the said "crisis" of the 1940s, I hope to illustrate some of the ways in which this depiction of recent South African history is itself symptomatic of a revisionist failure to escape a functionalist perspective. The ambiguity and inapplicability of Saul and Gelb's concept of "crisis" are exactly a measure of the limitations and distortions which a functionalist problematic imposes.

Saul and Gelb's account of the 1940s-"crisis" is already so short and compressed that it is worth simply quoting it in full:

A number of trends coincided, most important the rapid escalation of Black resistance to the exploitive racial capitalist system. This, in turn, was directly related to the continuing evolution of South African capitalism. There were two main features here. First, the overcrowded reserves had entered into precipitous economic decline, and could no longer play quite the same role they had in subsidising wages. Full, rather than quali-

fied proletarianisation was afoot, meaning that Africans in larger numbers than ever before were being pushed to the towns and held there. Moreover, this coincided with a second process. In the wake of the protectionist policies established between the wars and of a boom — begun when South Africa abandoned the gold standard in 1933, but reinforced by the economic opportunities provided by the war — rapid economic growth highlighted by secondary industrialisation was taking place. The fresh demands for African labour including that of the semi-skilled and therefore more stabilised variety, meant that an active pull was also being exerted by the towns and by emergent industrial capital. It was these trends, then, which produced not only a vast — and ultimately irreversible — growth[13] in the urbanised African population, but also a dramatic escalation of trade union organisation and working class militancy. When the latter process advanced so far as even to include migrant workers, and culminated in the extraordinary African mine-workers strike of 1946, South African ruling circles were shaken to the core. (Saul and Gelb: 13-14).

But have Saul and Gelb really described and accounted for a state of "crisis"? What *is* a "crisis", and how was it determined and manifest in this case of South Africa during the late 1940s? Saul and Gelb describe the crisis as a point at which a number of trends "come together",[14] as if this coincidence differentiates the "crisis" from preceding periods. However, the interrelationships and reciprocally exacerbating effects of these trends, described in the quote above, surely characterised them from their inception. What then makes their conjuncture in the 1940s sufficiently singular and profound as to warrant the designation "crisis"? Saul and Gelb do not formulate, let alone address, the question. They do not attempt to differentiate the hallmarks of a "crisis" as a recognisably distinctive threshold in an otherwise ongoing "coincidence" of these escalating trends. Instead, they locate the presence of the "crisis" in the mere existence of these trends, and the fact of their interrelationship. The result is a failure to distinguish the critical features of the 1940s, as compared with preceding or subsequent decades. As we shall see, the concept of "crisis" is left barren, and its application to the 1940s analytically superfluous. Consider each of these trends, the alleged sources of the "crisis", in turn.

Firstly, the decline of the reserves had set in by the late 1920s already,[15] so that their role in subsidising black wages had been diminishing steadily long before the 1940s. Nor did this trend cease after 1948,[16] the beginning of what Saul and Gelb see as the Nationalist Party's strategies to "manage" the crisis. Arguably, agricultural production in the reserves (later, the bantustans) has never enjoyed a permanent or wholesale recovery[17] since the early part of this century — long before, and after, the said "crisis". At what point then, and why, did this *ongoing* decline reach crisis proportions?

A similar point can be made about the increasing rate of African urbanisation, the second crisis-producing trend. "Full proletarianisation" (i.e. complete reliance on wage labour) was already "afoot" during the 1920s.[18] Furthermore, the rate of increase of the urban African population was already dramatic and rising by then.[19] Also, growing proletarianisation has persisted long after 1948, when the process of "crisis-management" allegedly began. Again therefore, what Saul and Gelb offer as an "index" of an "organic crisis" in the 1940s was an endemic and constant phenomenon. Yet they fail to distinguish the onset of the "crisis" according to a particular — specified — *degree* or mode of development of these structural tensions.

The prevalence of militant black resistance is also endemic to the system of South African capitalism. Certainly after World War I, the country saw a wave of strikes which never wholly abated up to, and beyond, the 1940s "crisis". Nor were popular uprisings, boycotts and riots unique to this period. Furthermore, obversely, Saul and Geld have not established convincingly that popular resistance during the 1940s ascended to "critical" proportions. Or, at least, if the level of resistance reached during the 1940s coincides with what they understand to be a "critical" threat to the very survival of the state, then their meaning of the term is suspect. They describe the 1940s as a period in which black resistance, culminating in the 1946 African miners' strike, was sufficient to shake "South Africa's ruling circles . . . to the core". But on what grounds is this assertion based? Certainly the state's response to the 1946 strike was swift and unwavering; the strike was quickly and effectively crushed. At no point was the stability of the White state seriously endangered. In what sense, therefore, was the very "core" of White hegemony besieged? Again, Saul and Gelb do not acknowledge or confront

the question.

Finally therefore, the only evidence which Saul and Gelb adduce for the presence of an "organic crisis" during the 1940s is the manifestation of certain endemic tensions and stresses in the system. The fact that these have been ever-intensifying and -receding means that the existence of a "crisis" would have to be distinguished according to a particular *degree* or moment of their intensification — namely, that point at which the quantitative escalation of these systemic stresses became *qualitatively* singular and important, in bringing the South African state to a critical threshold. Yet the problem of identifying this qualitative discontinuity is one which Saul and Gelb never confront.

Why is it, then, that Saul and Gelb fail to pose the very question on which the viability of their thesis concerning the presence of a "crisis", be it in the 1940s or 1970s, must depend? Why do they investigate the "crisis" in terms which premise its purportedly singular and rare existence on the mere presence of economic and political trends which became endemic to the development of South African capitalism long before, and outlasted, each of the said "crises"? The ways in which Saul and Gelb do and do not go about investigating the "crises" illustrate the strictures of their latent functionalist problematic. For, it is only by starting off within a broadly functionalist perspective, in terms of which a social system is 'normally' functionally integrated, that one is led to treat the mere manifestation of dysfunction as 'abnormal', the index of a "crisis". Surely the fact that Saul and Gelb are content to identify the indices of the 1940s crisis according to the manifest stresses and strains within South African society, without differentiating between their 'normal' ups and downs, and the critical threshold, testifies to their failure to escape a functionalist perspective on the problem? That their use of the term 'crisis' finally does not mean anything more than 'a period of intensified threat' simply reflects the inappropriateness of this perspective, and its mismatch with the nature of South African historical development.[20]

Ironically, the way out of a functionalist perspective on the 1940s, as well as a functionalist conception of a "crisis", is latent within Saul and Gelb's own historical account. Their "crisis theory" can be seen as an attempt to expose the historical limits and failures of the functional alliance between South Africa's racial policy and capitalist system, but one which is still caught up within a functionalist problematic. This is why the functional alliance in question is seen to break down in periods of "crisis" only. To steer clear of a functionalist perspective on the South African state, with its vacuous notion of "crisis",[21] we must recognise that the historical relationship between racial policy and capitalist development in South Africa has *continuously* exhibited a *combination* of functional and dysfunctional features. The functionalist treatment of the mere manifestation of dysfunction as 'abnormal' is wholly inappropriate and misleading. Furthermore, in fact, this alternative perspective on the history of the South African state makes better sense of Saul and Gelb's own historical narrative. For, each of the "trends" which they single out as the source and hallmark of the "crisis" of the 1940s (i.e. the decline of the reserves; ineluctable growth of African urbanization; growing African mass militancy) exemplifies exactly the *endemically dysfunctional* aspects of the relationship between South Africa's racial policies and capitalist system.

Firstly, declining reserve production was the price paid for efforts to concentrate large sections of the African population in the reserves, and their exploitation as migrant labourers with mere "temporary sojourner" status in the 'white' urban areas of South Africa — a strategy which was in evidence, albeit unevenly, from the early 1920s. Dependent on the existence of the reserves, the migrant labour system represented, in part, an attempt by the state to keep wages low, urban African numbers down, and to legitimise the denial of political rights and adequate social services to those who did become urban residents. However, the migrant labour system increasingly overburdened its own foundation, namely, the capacity of the reserves to absorb these large numbers of people. The continual decline of the reserves, in part, exacerbated the urban influx, one of the very factors which the migrant labour policy was intended to control.

Secondly, the trend towards "full proletarianisation" in the urban areas of South Africa, influx control measures notwithstanding, also displays the systemic tension between the economic pressures of capitalist development and the racial policies contemporaneous with it. In the interests of White economic and political supremacy, the practitioners of both segregation and then apartheid sought to curb the numbers of urban Africans, in part to contain the visible and ongoing threat to the regime from within these urban communities (the

larger ones in particular). However, the growth of urban-based secondary industry since the 1920s, and especially during and after the boom of the 1930s, was accompanied by growing demands for semi-skilled and skilled workers, "stabilised" and permanently settled in these urban areas.

The apartheid period has continued to reproduce this tension between these economic and political interests. The result has been an ever-growing African influx into the urban areas, despite increasingly repressive influx control measures. This has been coupled with a permanent (if variable) housing shortage in these areas, a deficiency of social services, urban poverty, disease and dissatisfaction — in short, the very conditions which have, in part, nurtured the urban African threat to White hegemony which apartheid policies have long since sought to contain.

Lastly, Saul and Gelb's third "critical" trend, the permanent militant mass African opposition to the system of racial capitalism, has reflected the costs borne by the South African state for having avoided policies which would have incorporated the African population into the institutions of parliamentary democracy in South Africa, political parties and trade unions in particular. For, having been denied a legitimate, institutionalised platform for the expression and resolution of grievances, and largely opposed to the racist regime, the African population has presented a constant threat to the state, wielded in illegal forms. Yet, the functional alliance between capitalism and racially discriminatory policies has run on exactly this exclusion of the African majority from the sorts of institutions which would have increased their legitimate economic and political bargaining power. The very strengths of the relationship between racial policy and capitalist growth in South Africa, have also been the sources of its weaknesses.

In short, therefore, the very trends which Saul and Gelb singled out as the hallmarks of such a serious abnormality as an "organic crisis" (one of only two in the country's recent history), are thus more fruitfully conceptualised as the endemic 'dysfunctions' in the relationship between economic development and racial policy in South Africa, since the 1920s at least. These 'dysfunctional' trends have vacillated in degree and prominence, depending on the period in question. Saul and Gelb are certainly correct in describing the 1940s as a period in which the tensions between racial policy and economic interests had rapidly intensified, particularly after the war, and had won a conspicuous and important place on the White political agenda (as Wolpe showed). However, this should not of itself entitle us to see the decade as one of "organic crisis". Indeed, the term remained analytically superfluous and empty throughout Saul and Gelb's account. Instead, we have now only reformulated the *question* of how to distinguish a threat to the state as profound as a "crisis": a "crisis" must be recognised and specified as a *qualititative* singular degree or threshold in quantitatively ongoing trends of opposition and structural tension. (An investigation of this problem is beyond the scope of this paper, however).

Wolpe's, and Saul and Gelb's arguments have shown up the sorts of explanatory blinkers which are imposed by a reductionist or functionalist problematic. Indeed, the very presence of the blind spots in each of their explicit hypotheses testifies to the effective, if involuntary, presence of these limiting perspectives on their respective problems. Furthermore, while purportedly arguing in defence of their declared hypotheses, each presents a historical account which is better conceptualised in different — non-reductionist and non-functionalist — ways. In exposing the analytic shortcomings of these writings, we were thus led in the direction of non-reductionist, non-functionalist positions on the key issues in the 'race-class debate' viz. firstly, the general analytic relationship between variables of 'race' and 'class', and secondly, the relationship between segregation/apartheid and capitalism. It is worth briefly recapping the course of this argument, before reconstructing the terms of the 'race-class debate' and the revisionist position within it.

Both Wolpe's, and Saul and Gelb's writings on the 1940s have shown that an understanding of South Africa's capitalist history must start from the premise that there is no single road to capitalist development. Capitalist interests in general neither functionally necessitate nor wholly determine any one particular set of economic and political structures and policies. Wolpe's account demonstrated that two different capitalist scenarios were both on the political agenda, each favoured by different class alliances represented politically by the National and United Parties respectively. (Viz. agricultural capital, together with the Afrikaner petty bourgeoisie, parts of the White working class, and growing pockets of Afrikaner commercial capital, supporting the National Party's

racially discriminatory and labour-repressive policies, on the one hand; and English manufacturing capital, elements of mining capital and the remainder of the White working class, preferring the United Party's liberalisation of the capitalist system, on the other.) Both possible avenues for capitalist growth represented attempts to grapple with the salient economic and political problems of the time, discussed by Wolpe. Both can be described, and indeed in part explained, according to the different class alliances which endorsed them. Yet an account of these problems and class interests adduces at most the *necessary conditions* for the particular route of development followed; but it is *not sufficient* to explain this course fully. Economic and class variables set limits on party political and ideological forces, but there comes a point at which an explanation of the transition to apartheid devolves on the simple fact that the National Party had a surprise and slim election victory in 1948. Well-organised, ideologically assertive and uncompromising, the National Party capitalised on the United Party's ideological and political disarray and the collapse of the Labour Party,[22] drawing a large vote from the White mine-workers to clinch the election. Saul and Gelb's account shows, moreover, that the victorious National Party policy was not consistently functional towards the interests of capital in the country. The system of racial capitalism was shown to exhibit inherent contradictions, its very strengths the source of instability.

Clearly therefore, with respect to the first issue in the 'race-class debate', racial policy in South Africa cannot be *reduced* to the simple reflex of class forces. Political and ideological factors which explain the capacity of a particular party and class alliance to win political power, also thereby contribute to an explanation of the very structure and history of capitalist production in the country. As regards the second issue, functionalist explanations of segregation and apartheid policies fly in the face of historical accounts of their development. Neither was wholly functional for capitalism in the country. Thus their political implementation cannot be explained by the functions alone, in the manner characteristic of a functionalist analysis.

Rethinking the 'Race-Class Debate'

We are now in a position to redefine the terms of opposition between liberal and revisionist historiography, to make for a more apt and interesting debate between them. It is time to supercede the original 'either-or' options regarding, firstly, the general analytic relationship between variables of 'race' and 'class'; and secondly, the relationship between capitalist development and racial policy. Let us consider each of these issues in turn.

1) The Relationship Between Variables of 'Race' and 'Class':

The original terms of debate pit the least interesting and convincing versions of both the liberal and revisionist cases against each other. I hinted earlier in this paper that revisionists tended to take on the crudest liberal position, in terms of which variables of 'race' alone explained the structure and history of South African society. Their more sophisticated liberal opponents however, have also recognised economic forces at work in the shaping of South African racist policies. S. Herbert Frankel, for example, writing in 1928, claimed that

... there is no purely 'native' problem at all, and . . . the really pressing problem is one of National Production and the economic status of the Union. (Frankel, 1928: 15)

He interpreted the segregation into locations of Africans living outside the Reserves, as having been a policy "designed to meet two fears", one of which was "that if the natives were all placed in a compact area of their own, a sufficient labour supply would no longer be available." (Frankel, 1928: 15)

More recently, Francis Wilson, writing in the *Oxford History of South Africa,* alleged that

the political pressure for the passing of the Natives' Land Act (in 1913) came, almost entirely it seems, from those who wished to ensure a cheap supply of labour. (Wilson, 1971: 129)

Also, Ralph Horwitz has contended that "the Native Labour Regulation Act of 1911 was designed to force Africans off the land at less than market cost to capitalist employers." (Wright, 1980: 46)

Still, even on the most generous interpretation, the liberal understanding of the economic underpinnings of South Africa's political system is confined within a methodologically individualist problematic; that is, the economic determinants of racial policy are characterised in terms of the intentions and volition of particular individuals or groups thereof. Class forces, on this view, represent merely the arithmetic sum of the power and influence of such

groups. For, the concept of 'class', if invoked at all, here refers to an aggregate equal simply to the sum of its parts. 'Class', in other words, does not designate an objective structural phenomenon which analytically precedes an account of the interests and intentions of particular individual members, either singly or collectively. However sophisticated an interpretation we give of the liberal position, it still stops short of an understanding of the role of objective class forces which both constrain and enable individual intentions and actions, and which are not fully subject to conscious individual or group control.

Revisionism, on the other hand, operates with an historical materialist conception of class, as a set of social relations, structurally specified[23] according to the position of members vis-à-vis the means of production. Classes are divided according to their differential access to ownership and control of the means of production.[24] Now the historical materialist notion of 'class' is, of course, notoriously controversial, and subject to constant rethinking and updating. This is not the time to explore the complexities of such issues. Still, it is important to indicate some of the analytic contributions of the concept, which are lost to the liberal historian.

There is nothing mysterious or metaphysical in a structural[25] conception of 'class'. It refers simply to a series of relations of production, which *constitute* the role and position of individual members. Membership of the working class, for example, is defined according to the common lack of either ownership or control of the means of production, and the necessity to sell labour-power in exchange for a wage. On this view, the perpetuation of economic inequality between working class and bourgeoisie is thus not simply a reflection of personal failings or wholly political constraints on workers, but illustrates the objective economic constraints on the possibilities for their acquiring and accumulating capital, individual effort and determination notwithstanding. Liberal historians however, explain economic inequality in South Africa in terms of individual limitations or institutionalised racial discrimination alone, without incorporating an analysis of the structural constraints on the majority of Africans *qua members of the working class.* Then, since institutionalised racism is taken as the only systemic determinant of the inequality of resources, opportunity and income in the country, the removal of apartheid is seen to be sufficient to restore at least equality of opportunity and resources to the population as a whole. The naivete of this expectation derives directly from liberals' failure to take the *combination* of racial policy and objective class forces into account.

A methodological individualism is similarly inept in its analysis of the power of the African working class. In methodologically individualist terms, the power of a class *qua class* is explained as the arithmetic sum of the power of individual members. So, class power increases as a function of the number of class members. Moreover, there is no difference in *kind* — only in degree — between the power of an individual class member and the power of the class as a whole. In terms of this approach then, the threat to White supremacy posed by the African workforce derives first and foremost from its numerical majority. However, this sort of analysis surely fails to grasp the nature and significance of the working class' power to withold its labour in any capitalist society, including the South African case. Any single worker can in principle always refuse to work, and be sacked as a consequence, with no cost to anyone but himself or herself. However, when a mass of workers withdraws its labour in a strike, capitalist interests are threatened as the source of profit is temporarily frozen. The power of the working class here derives from its structural position in the process of production, which is not reducible to a simple sum of the individual powers of its members. Their power qua class is qualitatively distinct from that of a merely arithmetic aggregate of individuals. In the South African case therefore, the relationship between the state and African work-force should be grasped within the framework of a class analysis. For example, the National Party's original attempts to control African workers by outlawing their unions and banning their union leaders, cannot be seen as simply the product of racist policy. It is also motivated by an interest in control over the African working class *qua class*.

This revisionist case against liberal historiography should not, and need not, depend on the kind of reductionist class analysis which many revisionists have advanced. The sort of class analysis which my paper has been advocating is non-reductionist in two sorts of ways. Firstly, as we have seen, an account of class relations is necessary, but not sufficient, for an understanding of the South African state and its preferred path towards renewed economic growth. The *political power* of one class alliance over another requires in part, its electoral majority,

at least, which is in turn affected by such variables as ideological and political control, individual leadership, ethnic cleavages and nationalistic sentiment, and historical contingencies such as wars or droughts. In particular, an explanation of any popular action — or inaction — must allow for the role which ethnic and ideological affiliations might have played as forces in their own right. As Adam and Giliomee ask rhetorically, "why should the independent role of beliefs not be granted, even in shaping an economic environment?" (Adam and Giliomee, 1979: 47)

Furthermore, the relative priority and particular impact of any of these variables vis-à-vis class determinants is historically variable, and therefore not amenable to general, a priori theoretical specification. Class analysis does not involve the application of a complete, ready-made general theory of class relations to particular historical cases; rather, the very nature and significance of class relations is in part historically specific and variable.

Secondly, in addition to its avoidance of the pretence of having provided complete or sufficient explanations, the sort of class analysis of South African society which I have defended, is also non-reductionist in acknowledging the interpenetration of class and racial cleavages as a *single* reality. Class relations in South Africa have been constituted in part along racial lines; that is, access to ownership and control of the means of production in the country has itself been a racial issue. Thus, the formation of an African bourgeoisie, for example, has been *structurally distinct* from that of the White bourgeoisie, given the presence of manifold politico-legal barriers on the acquisition and accumulation of capital by Africans within South Africa. Likewise, we cannot fully make sense of the structural (ie. objective relational) position of the African working class *qua class* without also taking account of their race, as the basis of what some revisionists such as Frederick Johnstone have called the "ultra-exploitability" (Johnstone, 1976: 20-22) of African workers, that is, the use of extra-economic coercive measures to facilitate a supply of 'ultra-cheap labour" (Johnstone, 1976: 20) for White capitalist enterprise. As Johnstone explains,

... the white property owners ... developed their system of class domination as one of racial domination, which, by restricting the property ownership and property rights of non-whites, and by restricting the political rights of non-whites to various forms of extra-economic compulsion and domination, served specifically to perpetuate the economic dependence of the non-white population and to secure the ultra-exploitability of their labour. (Johnstone, 1976: 23)

It is methodologically sterile, therefore, to insist on a variant of class analysis of South African society which depends on hierarchically ranking 'class' *over* 'race', as the fundamental variable which accounts for all others but which is itself self-explanatory. Racial cleavages contribute to an explanation of class differentiation itself. Thus, what is fundamental and distinctive about the South African case is the *unity* of class and race as the source of structural differentiation in the society.[26]

2) The Relationship Between Capitalist Development and Racial Policy:

I have argued in this paper that the original terms of the 'race-class debate' tended to reserve the acknowledgement of "contradiction between economy and polity" (Wolpe, 1970: 151) in South Africa for the liberal camp. Yet, albeit under the banner of their "crisis" theory, Saul and Gelb for example, *did* expose the *duality* of South African racial policy this century, as simultaneously functional and dysfunctional vis-à-vis capitalist production there. Although they failed to formally conceptualise it as such, their historical account revealed both segregation and apartheid as a contradictory combination of policies which have simultaneously both promoted and undermined the cornerstones of the social formation.

Indeed, other revisionists too, such as Stan Greenberg, Rob Davies, Dan O'Meara and Alex Callinicos, have dealt with the state's patent instabilities and problems during the 1970s by focusing exactly on the conflicting economic and political imperatives of the system of racial capitalism in the country — but through a functionalist lens, which produces the image of a "crisis", rather than of of endemic contradictions. In his paper, *Capital Restructuring And The Modification of the Racial Division of Labour In South Africa,* Rob Davies for example, has argued that

the continued reproduction of a racist, hierarchical division of labour, at least in its present form, no longer accords with the interests of the bourgeoisie or indeed of any significant fraction thereof. (Davies, 1979b: 182)

Clearly Davies acknowledges the current contradiction between the racist division of labour and the "economic imperatives of capital accumulation in the South African social formation". (Davies, 1979b: 182) However, he omits to mention that job reservation has consistently been opposed by certain sectors of the bourgeoisie, notably, amongst English manufacturing capitalists — an omission which confirms my suspicion of the latent functionalist problematic underlying his analysis, which only takes account of 'dysfunctions' in the system via the notion of "crisis".

A more fruitful, non-functionalist, revisionist appraisal of the relationship between capitalism and racial policy in South Africa should take full account of the long-standing, internal contradictions within capitalist interests themselves. While mining, agriculture and manufacturing capital have all shown their overall compatibility with the country's racially discriminatory policies and institutions, these have arguably inhibited the optimal development of at least certain sections of the manufacturing sector. The shortage of skilled and semi-skilled labour, together with the restriction of domestic markets, has constrained the productivity of branches of manufacturing industry. David Yudelman makes this sort of point in criticising revisionists for having failed to repudiate convincingly the liberal thesis that

. . . as an industry later develops new demands on its labour, . . . it generally make(s) *economic* sense to educate that labour, stabilize and pay it better. (Yudelman, 1975: 92)

Now perhaps Yudelman is wrong in stating the point generally, for all sectors and on all occasions. The revisionists influenced by Nicos Poulantzas have ably demonstrated the need to disaggregate the idea of capitalist interests,[27] so as to recognise 'fractional' differences. Still, Yudelman's point is in fact conceded by revisionists such as Saul and Gelb, Davies, Callinicos and others, with respect to the manufacturing sector at least.

Once the revisionist position is reformulated in a non-functionalist way, the motion for debate with liberals concerning the relationship between racial policy and continued economic growth, must be revised accordingly. Clearly, the versions of the liberal and revisionist positions now under consideration *concur* in acknowledging "contradiction between the economy and polity"[28] in South Africa. Indeed, both liberals and revisionists have drawn attention to the ways in which the pressures of capitalist development do seem to be wearing down its racial fetters.[29] Both schools of thought, when confronted by the contemporary South African state, are agreed that the important and interesting question to be asking is: can the country keep to its present racially restricted course of economic growth, or are the costs (such as the shortage of skills; restricted domestic markets and African purchasing power; a narrowing power-base of White hegemony; escalating militant opposition amongst African communities, trade unions etc.) becoming too great?

This degree of unanimity between liberals and revisionists does not obliterate their differences, however. Firstly, liberals are still liable to the revisionist charge of having ignored or underplayed the functions which racially discriminatory practices *have* performed in promoting capitalist enterprise in the country. As Martin Legassick has said, contrary to liberal opinion,

    . . . far from being archaic, the economic policies of the Nationalist government were equally (ie. like those of the United Party, issuing from the Fagan Commission) directed in the interests of capitalist rationalisation, including the securing of foreign capital, loans and technical know-how. (Legassick, 1974: 10)

Like many revisionists, most liberals too fail to start from the premise that "there is no single road to industrialization", (Trapido, 1971: 309) and instead regard the development of liberal democracy as functionally necessary for the pursuit of economic growth in South Africa. Our reconstructed revisionist position however, interprets the relationship between racial policy and economic growth in the country as both functional and dysfunctional, and thus inherently contradictory. Different periods in the country's history can be distinguished according to which of the antithetical faces of this relationship is uppermost. Thus, for example, during the 1920s, 40s and 70s, the stresses and strains of the system of racial capitalism were visibly exacerbated; whereas the 1930s, 1960s were periods in which the functional alignment between the booming economy and racially discriminatory policies was noteworthy. The particular degree of stability which characterises the South African state during a given period depends primarily on the relative strength of opposing forces, both within the capitalist class and between capitalist and working classes.

Thus the course of South Africa history is conceived as one of *continual, but oscillating* struggle between conflicting class and other factions, rather than as long periods of stability and repression of conflict, interrupted occasionally by the finally irrepressible eruption of "structural" or "organic" crises.

Secondly, while both the liberal and reconstructed revisionist positions recognise manifest contradictions between South Africa's political and economic systems, they diverge in their analyses of the state's response to these problems, and in their prognoses for the course of change in the country. Liberals remain confident that the country's injustices and inequities can be eradicated by liberal reforms of existing political and economic institutions, enacted by the state, finally cognisant of the irrationality of racially discriminatory policies. The elimination of the contradiction between economy and polity is treated as a matter for incremental reform from above, in response to the inescapable pressures of economic 'realities'. For revisionists on the other hand, liberals still underestimate the degree of endemic functional compatibility between apartheid and capitalism in the country, and thus also the resilience of existing political institutions against genuinely liberal reform. Current reform strategies are interpreted as adaptive, rather than liberalising. Furthermore, the class underpinnings of racial injustices in South Africa are such as to mitigate the possibility of a just distribution of resources by the changeover to liberal democratic institutions alone.

To conclude, if one of the goals of revisionist analysis is to inform the process of change in South Africa, then it is important that the 'race-class debate' be engaged anew in these revised terms. The analytic limitations of a functionalist approach can produce politically naive expectations of change as structurally inevitable. For, the idea of a "structural crisis" developed from a functionalist perspective on the last decade in South Africa gives the misleading impression that irresistible structural pressures will do the work of exacting fundamental change in the country. It is true that structural strains weaken, and could at some unspecified future time break, the edifice of White supremacy. But the eradication of economic and political inequities in South Africa is still, as it always was, a matter for ongoing and fluctuating struggle. Furthermore, the composition and course of this struggle should be perceived in non-reductionistic terms. For, firstly, it would be politically shortsighted to underestimate the importance of political and ideological affiliations as forces in their own right, with respect to both the defenders of the status quo and their radical opposition. Secondly, an understanding of the complex interplay of economic, political and ideological forces in the country illumines the need for, and forms of, multifaceted strategies for change, which do not see opposition to White supremacy as being mobilised along class lines alone.

Revising the terms of the 'race-class debate' not only expands further the scope and agenda of revisionist inquiry into South Africa's past; it is especially pertinent to a realistic assessment of the contemporary period.

NOTES

1. For example, many of the writings of Harold Wolpe, Martin Legassick, Rob Davies, Dan O'Meara, Alex Callinicos, John Saul and Stephen Gelb, Frederick Johnstone (he shifts towards a methodological pluralism by 1978 — see *The Labour History of the Witwatersrand*, Social Dynamics, Vol. 4 no. 2 Dec 1978) Marion Lacey, Mike Morris, and others. Obviously however, there are many revisionists who do not fit into this category; my case is not a blanket critique of all revisionism, but is directed only against those revisionist writings which have, voluntarily or involuntarily, been set within a reductionist or functionalist problematic.

2. Cf. many other revisionist writings which implicitly or explicitly exemplify a non-reductionist, non-functionalist approach eg. by W. Beinart, P. Delius, S. Marks, S. Trapido, C. Van Onselen, and others.

3. By the term 'problematic' I mean a set of categories and a priori assumptions and premises, which together imply a particular way of posing problems and articulating their solutions. A 'problematic' is thus an epistemological concept, referring collectively to the means whereby the object of inquiry is conceptualised and investigated.

4. The writings of P. Van den Berghe and I.D. Macrone are typically cited as exemplary of this liberal stance.

5. By 1978 however, his position had changed. See footnote 1 above.

6. The same sort of argument has been levelled by marxists against liberals, criticising them not for deliberately suppressing questions of class, but for being unable to appreciate the significance of class determinants from within the confines of their individualist problematic. See eg. Davies: 1979a: 2

7. A number of revisionist historians have pointed to these 'dysfunctions' in various concrete cases; indeed, I later argue that this is exactly what emerges from Saul and Gelb's account of the growth of racial policy in their book (Saul and Gelb, 1981). My point here is rather about the limits of the revisionist problematic on a declared theoretical and methodological front, which affects the ways in which questions, premises and conclusions are explicitly conceptualised and articulated.

One of the points which I make later in the paper concerns the curious mismatch between this explicit theoretical and methodological perspective, and some of the historical material purportedly marshalled in confirmation of it.

8. These industries were not subject to the Industrial Conciliation Act or Wage Act, and were therefore not hampered by job reservation laws which kept skilled and semi-skilled positions for whites, paying them higher wages than could have been the case had white and black labour been able to compete for the same positions.

9. He claims, for example, that the Fagan Commission, on which the United Party based its electoral platform in 1948, had been "appointed in 1946 by the United Party government precisely in response to the changing nature of African political struggle," (Wolpe 1972: p. 445) and thus by implication, also the changing economic conditions accounting for this struggle.

10. These commentaries are theoretically anonymous, but not theoretically neutral. I am not arguing in empiricist fashion that historical accounts can be presuppositionless. My point is rather that the presuppositions which *do* inform these revisionist historical commentaries are evident in content but not by name, lacking formal, declared theoretical status.

11. In addition to the works already cited in the text and footnotes of this paper, see also B. Bozzoli: 1978, S. Greenberg: 1980.

12. Rob Davies, for example, also sees a "crisis" in the early 1920s. But Saul and Gelb finally settle on taking the 1920s as a period of near, but not complete, crisis.

13. Was it ever reversible? Certainly the statistics show an ever-increasing growth rate from the 1920s, which was always irreversible in the sense that the urban pull was irreversible, as the manufacturing sector grew.

14. A state of crisis is commonly depicted as a point at which things 'come to a head', as if this concentration of tensions explains and differentiates the crisis. (See, eg. B. Bozzoli: 1978: 48) But the idea of things coming to a head is simply a metaphorical synonym for, rather than a solution to the problem of, identifying a crisis.

15. This was noted by the Native Economic Commission of 1932, for example.

16. According to D. Hindson, the GDP per head of the de facto African homeland population fell between 1946 and 1960, and attained a level in 1970 which was probably little different from that in 1946. (Hindson, 1977)

17. Of course, this is not to deny regional variations in the degree of agricultural productivity, nor its dependence on income or class.

18. For example, the Economic and Wage Commission of 1926 drew attention to the plight of "detribalized natives" who had severed all connections with the reserves. (UG 14/1926: 198)

19. Between 1904 and 1921, the number of urban Africans (including temporary residents) rose by 71,4% (Paul Rich, 1978: 180)

20. Saul and Gelb claim to be using the concept of "organic crisis" in its Gramscian sense, but fail to explicate the concept fully. Their case about the applicability of a Gramscian approach to the understanding of "crisis" to the South African case is wholly unargued. Indeed, as I have explained in another paper, *Theories of "Cri-*

sis" and The Crisis of Theory, Gramsci's notion of "organic crisis" rests on assumptions which do *not* apply in the South African case so that it cannot be appropriated unreflexively and en bloc, in analyses of South African state. Thus, recourse to Gramsci's concept of crisis does not address or answer any of the problems which I have been discussing in Saul and Gelb's account of the "crisis" of the 1940s.

21. I am not arguing that *all* concepts of "crisis" are vacuous, only the ones which issue from a functionalist problematic unable to conceptualise systemic dysfunctions in any other way.

22. See R. Davies, 1979a: chapter 7 for a more detailed discussion of these developments.

23. By 'structure' I mean a set of relations which constitute and define the place of individual members as bearers of these relations. This is not meant to entail that individual identity is exhaustively determined by its structural nexus; structures are necessary but not sufficient conditions of individual agency. Individuals are bearers of structural relations in this limited sense only.

24. 'Ownership' and 'control' of the means of production are difficult notions to specify precisely. But the point I wish to make does not necessitate exploring these complexities, although it does presuppose the assumption on my part that the difficulties involved are not in principle insuperable.

25. Note that there is an important distinction between a structural and structuralist conception of class. On a structural version of the concept, objective social relations constituting a class are seen as necessary conditions of, and partial constraints upon, the agency of their individual bearers. Structuralism however, regards an analysis of such objective relations as *sufficient* to account for individual agency, at least as far as is relevant to the social scientist. The structuralist takes agency as the explanandum, but never part of the explanans.

26. This does not imply that variables of race are exhaustively dealt with at this level, only that the fundamental structural impact of racial cleavages must be understood in conjunction with class divisions.

27. Of course, recognition of important intra-capitalist differences and tensions is not restricted to a Marxist structuralism. The point can be made without necessarily carrying along with it the entire structuralist position.

28. Wolpe characterised the liberal position thus, *in contradistinction to* his revisionist alternative.

29. The point is made especially with regard to the fate of the racist hierarchical division of labour. Always used in accordance with economic need, job reservation policy has completely eroded in response to a serious skills shortage.

30. This perspective is not original to this paper, of course. It is explicitly stated by Martin Plaut and Duncan Innes, for example, in Plaut and Innes, 1976 and implicit in the works of G. Van Onselen, Trapido, Beinart and others.

REFERENCES

Adam, Heribert and Giliomee, Hermann
1979   Ethnic Power Mobilized: Can South Africa Change? New Haven: Yale University Press.

Bozzoli, Belinda
1978   'Capital and the State in South Africa', Review of African Political Economy, 11.
1981   The Political Nature of a Ruling Class. London.

Davies, R.
1979a Capital, State and White Labour in South Africa, 1900-1960 London: Harvester Press.
1979b 'Capital Restructuring and the Modification of the Racial Division of Labour', Journal of Southern African Studies 5 (2).

Frankel, S.H.
1928   'The Position of the Native as a Factor in the Economic Welfare of the European Population in South Africa', Journal of the Economic Society of South Africa 2 (1).

Greenberg, Stanley
1980   Race and State in Capitalist Development. New Haven: Yale University Press.

Hindson, D.C.
1977   'Conditions of Labour Supply and Employment for African Workers in Urban-based Industries in South Africa, 1946-1975', unpublished seminar paper.

Johnstone, F.
1970   'White Supremacy and White Prosperity in South Africa', African Affairs 69 (275).
1976   Class, Race and Gold. London: Routledge and Kegan Paul.

Kaplan, D., Morris, M. and O'Meara, D.
1976   "Class Struggle and the Periodisation of the State in South Africa', Review of African Political Economy 7.

Legassick, Martin
1974   'South Africa: Capital Accumulation and Violence', Economy and Society 3 (3).

O'Meara, Dan
1975   The 1946 African Mineworkers' Strike and the Political Economy of South Africa', Journal of Commonwealth and Comparative Politics 13 (2).

Plaut, Martin and Innes, Duncan
1976   'Class Struggle and the State', Review of African Political Economy 7.

Rich, Paul
1978   'Ministering to the White Man's Needs', African Affairs 57 (2).

Saul, John and Gelb, Stephen
1981   The Crisis in South Africa: class defence, class revolution. New York: Monthly Review Press.

Trapido, Stanley
1971   'South Africa in a Comparative Study of Industrialisation', Journal of Development Studies 7.

Wilson, Francis
1971   'Farming'. In Monica Wilson and Leonard Thompson (eds.), Oxford History of South Africa. Volume II Oxford: Clarendon Press.

Wolpe, Harold
1970   'Industrialisation and Race in South Africa'. In S. Zubaida (ed.), Industrialism and Race in South Africa. London.
1972   'Capitalism and Cheap Labour Power in South Africa: From Segregation to Apartheid', Economy and Society 1 (4).

Wright, Harrison
1980   The Burden of the Present. Cape Town: David Philip, Third Impression.

Yudelman, David
1975   'Industrialisation, Race Relations and Change in South Africa', African Affairs 74 (294).

Journal of Southern African Studies, Vol. 13, No. 3, April 1987

Street Sociology and Pavement Politics: Aspects of Youth and Student Resistance in Cape Town, 1985

COLIN BUNDY

Introduction

Thousands of young South Africans were detained, whipped, teargassed, and fired upon in 1985. Even larger numbers were mobilised at rallies, in organisations, and behind street barricades. There has been widespread recognition of the distinctive contribution made by the youth within a broader political struggle. As one commentator put it:

They are very frustrated and very angry. In a critical moment of our history, these passionate, dedicated, immature, politically untutored students have taken over. Now they are getting their political education very quickly.

In a repressive political context, where other forms of mobilisation and organisation are proscribed or harassed, social institutions like schools become important recruiting grounds for the teenage 'shock troops of a nation-wide political insurrection'.[1] Consider the political career of B— in this respect. His school, although designed to inculcate respect for the regime, instead

served as a way station on the road to revolutionary politics, the school's rigid discipline apparently provoking widespread defiance of authority. In the lower grades, student dissidence took innocuous forms. . . But by the time B— entered the upper grades. . . student dissent had become more sophisticated. He became a member of a radical student group that organised discussion circles and circulated illegal literature. . . [At this time] social unrest and open protest. . . deepened and spread. . . at 16 B— was already a leading member of the student movement. . . The feverish disorders of that year drew B— and a generation of like-minded schoolboys into the arena of serious revolutionary politics. . . At seventeen, B— thus became. . . a full-time activist.

The political education of school or college students is often spectacularly rapid. Initial involvement over local issues translates into activism that links up with

(Where necessary I have used the terms African, coloured, and white to distinguish between 'racial' categories enforced by the state. Such usage does not indicate any acceptance of such categories. I use the term 'black' to refer to all who are not classified as 'white'. DET (Department of Education and Training) schools are for African pupils and DEC (Department of Education and Culture) are for coloured pupils.)

[1] *City Press*, 20 April 1986, quoted in L. Chisholm, 'From Revolt to a Search for Alternatives', *Work In Progress*, no. 42 (1986), p. 15.

broader, non-educational movements. Of particular importance in this shift are 'alternative' educational activities, through which students not only become exposed to critical thought, but also challenge in their everyday practice the most immediate hierarchies that confront them. A participant in such activities recalled:

It was a period of permanent assemblies and sit-ins against repression. The claims were for a democratic student union and for general freedoms. . . These freedoms were established in the [schools] which became 'liberated territories', and we had to defend them day by day. Support from the students quickly increased through the struggle. There was a fantastic life. . . with plays, films, exhibitions, conferences and lectures, posters, wall magazines which were now openly anti-regime, denouncing repression and the dictatorship.

The observations in the preceding three paragraphs will seem thoroughly familiar to any who have observed popular resistance in South Africa since June 1976. As it happens, the quotations illustrating each paragraph are drawn, respectively, from the Indonesian anti-colonial revolution, from Tsarist Russia in 1905, and from student opposition in the twilight days of Franco's Spain. [2]

Such comparisons prompt certain questions. What general explanations for youth-based resistance are available? What explanatory force do they possess for the South African case? Are there instances that offer a structural, rather than superficial, basis for comparison? Some tentative answers to these queries are proposed in Section 1 below.

Section 2 attempts to provide a South African context for the Western Cape study. It characterises the structural crisis confronting the South African state, and suggests how the 'crisis in the schools' is related to the wider phenomenon. It asks, in other words, whether it is possible to isolate a 'youth' component in popular resistance, analytically distinct from the broader struggle. It seeks to identify the specific material/demographic/social base on which school and youth resistance politics is constructed − and in doing so draws upon some of the theoretical and comparative data visited earlier.

In Section 3 the wide-angled lens is replaced by one focused more narrowly, and in relative close-up. Its subject is the educational boycott and other youth-based political activities in greater Cape Town in 1985. It poses a number of local, specific, and fairly immediate questions: what were some of the key characteristics of youth politics in Cape Town during 1985? How did these resemble, and differ from, earlier moments of activism − especially the 1980 schools boycott? What strengths and weaknesses can be identified in Cape Town's youth-based politics? What forms and patterns of consciousness are discernible − and what relevance might they have for the future?

(1) Some Theoretical and Comparative Perspectives

There are several theoretical explanations of radicalism in 'youth politics'. They stemmed initially from Mannheim's characterisation of generations in sociological

[2] J.R.W. Smail, *Bandung in the Early Revolution, 1945-6* (Ithaca, New York, 1964), quoted in H. Moller, 'Youth as a Force in the Modern World', *Comparative Studies in History and Society*, 10 (1967-8), 237-60, p. 248; S.F. Cohen, *Bukharin and the Bolshevik Revolution* (Oxford, 1980, pp. 8-11; J. Maravall, *Dictatorship and Political Dissent: Workers and Students in Franco's Spain* (London, 1978), p. 113.

rather than in merely biological or chronological terms; and were greatly stimulated by attempts to explain student revolt in advanced capitalist societies in the 1960s. The dense growth of these latter analyses was to some extent cross-fertilised with studies emphasising the salience of youth-based resistance in nationalist and anti-colonial movements (such as Turkey, China, Egypt, Indonesia, the Gold Coast, etc.) In the classic Marxist texts, there was exploration of the class identity and character of the intelligentsia; Lenin wrote suggestively about contradictory elements within student movements; and Gramsci's concern with the relationship between revolutionary politics, intellectuals and the state is central to his writings.

What follows is not a systematic review of this literature, but a consideration of key themes and concepts which may sharpen and clarify analysis of recent South African youth/student resistance. While many accounts of post-Soweto popular struggles acknowledge the leading role played by youth militants, there is little theoretical or comparative commentary.

The best developed of the theoretical models of youth radicalism are various versions of generational conflict. All are intellectually descended from Mannheim's notion of a 'social generation'. Its members do not merely co-exist in time and space: they become a social generation when they 'participate in the common destiny of that historical and social unit.'[3] By grappling with a distinct set of social and historical problems they develop an awareness and common identity – a generational consciousness, analagous to class consciousness and national consciousness.

More recently, Abrams has revisited the 'problem of generations', and in an illuminating passage argues that the speed and intensity with which such consciousness is created can vary greatly. The more complex, ambiguous and diversified are the 'possibilities of adulthood', the more rapidly and forcefully are 'new social generations forged out of the entry of youth into adult life.' Societal turbulence lends an edge to generational consciousness: 'structural differentiation makes for faster history.' In particular, historical experience of 'war, revolution, crisis or liberation' is singularly important for the configuration of society as a whole: 'an age group located at such a moment in history can create a whole new social generation.'[4]

Less concerned with the identity of social generations as historical creations – yet in effect demonstrating their importance – are approaches stressing population growth and patterns of age distribution as the demographic bases of youth politics. Moller, for instance, describes the period since the beginning of the nineteenth century as 'the age of the "population explosion"', and argues that within the phenomenon of rapid population growth the demographic variable of age distribution carries particular implications. A relative increase in the ratio of youth to total population, especially if the society is also undergoing disruptive economic and social change, directly increases the likelihood of cultural and political change.[5]

[3] K. Mannheim, *Essays on the Sociology of Knowledge* (London, 1952, originally 1928), pp. 286-320; quotation p. 303. See also M. Rintala, 'Political Generation', *International Encyclopaedia of the Social Sciences*, vol. VI (New York, 1968), p. 92.

[4] P. Abrams, *Historical Sociology* (London, 1982), 240-66; quotations at pp. 255, 256.

[5] Moller, 'Youth as a Force in the Modern World', p. 254.

After surveying a number of twentieth century risings and revolutions, Moller finds that 'young people provide the driving force and often, to a great extent the intellectual and organisational leadership.'[6]

But what is the nature of the link between student rebels and intellectual leadership? This is effectively a sub-head in a broader issue that has long concerned Marxism: the historical and political role of intellectuals, and their relations with working class movements. Marx and Engels devoted three paragraphs of the *Communist Manifesto* to answering the question 'How does the proletarian movement acquire educated elements?' Partly — they said — through impersonal pressures on sections of the middle class intelligentsia, precipitating them into the ranks of the working class; but also partly through conscious political choice. When class struggle reaches critical dimensions the 'process of dissolution' in the old society 'assumes such a violent, glaring character that a small section of the ruling class cuts itself adrift, and joins the revolutionary class.'[7]

In their later writings, Marx and Engels viewed bourgeois intellectuals ambivalently: on the one hand as ideologists for the ruling class, but on the other hand as potential recruits to the struggle for socialism. Both authors delivered diatribes against the self-importance, irresolution and non-revolutionary philosophising of intellectuals in nineteenth century socialist movements. They said little specifically about students; what they did remark was frequently caustic (Engels: 'How awful for the world. . . that there are 40,000 revolutionary students in Russia, without a proletariat or even a Russian peasantry behind them. . . all of them officer candidates without an army.')[8] Bourgeois intellectuals, concludes Draper, can tend to be 'more volatile, erratic and unstable than most workers. . . This pattern may reach a peak with students, who are after all apprentice intellectuals.'[9]

Lenin — writing during decades of student activism in Russia — paid considerably more attention than Marx or Engels to youth and students. Some of the writings collected in *On Youth*[10] are essentially hortatory; a number are devoted to the role of the young as the builders and inheritors of a new society. In the more analytical passages, two themes emerge: a genuine enthusiasm for the revolutionary energies of students and young workers; and an insistence on certain objective limitations to their revolutionary capacities. Broadly speaking, there is a shift over time in Lenin's perceptions from the first, more positive, position to the second, more sceptical.

Thus, in 1903 Lenin wrote warmly of students:

They are the most responsive section of the intelligentsia, and the intelligentsia are so called just because they most consciously, most resolutely and most accurately reflect and express the development of class interests and political groupings in society as a whole.[11]

---

[6] *Ibid.*, p. 256.

[7] Quoted in H. Draper, *Karl Marx's Theory of Revolution*, Vol. II, *The Politics of Social Classes* (New York, 1978), p. 509.

[8] See *ibid.*, pp. 502-45; Engels is quoted in L.S. Feuer, *The Conflict of Generations: The Character and Significance of Student Movements* (New York, 1969), p. 163.

[9] Draper, *Politics of Social Classes*, p. 519.

[10] V.I. Lenin, *On Youth* (Moscow, 1970).

[11] *Ibid.*, p. 89.

In October 1905 (against a backdrop of unprecedented student/worker alliances in Russia) he wrote that 'The students are guided by a sound revolutionary instinct, enhanced by their contact with the proletariat.' In the same month he exuberantly urged the Combat Committee of the St Petersburg Bolsheviks:

Go to the youth, gentlemen! That is the only remedy! Otherwise − I give you my word for it − you will be too late. . . and will be left with 'learned' memoranda, plans, charts, schemes, and magnificent recipes, but without an organisation, without a living cause. Go to the youth.

But the student 'strikes' of 1908 were greeted with reservations and criticism. Even the 'most active elements' of the students still clung 'to pure academic aims' and reformist goals; they were bound by 'thousands and millions of threads' to their class origins − 'the middle and lower bourgeoisie, the petty officials, certain groups of the peasantry, the clergy, etc.' Then, and subsequently, Lenin upbraided students for characteristically youthful errors. He warned against infection by 'the itch of revolutionary phrase-making' − that is, 'superb, alluring, intoxicating' slogans without objective content. He called for vigilance against youthful ultra-leftism; chided immature rigidity and impatience; and scoffed at inexperienced or romantic revolutionism. [12]

Gramsci, in a sense, returned to the original query of the *Communist Manifesto* when he asked 'Does every social group have its own particular specialised category of intellectuals?' And like Lenin, Gramsci was convinced of the contribution of intellectuals to working class politics: 'in order to organise itself as a class, the proletariat needs intellectuals, in other words, leaders.' [13] But his approach involved a significant departure from classical Marxist thought, above all in the meaning he gave to the notion 'intellectual'. An intellectual was not defined in terms of mental labour, but instead in terms of performing particular functions in society.

His concept of organic intellectuals − 'organic' to a social class, giving that class 'homogeneity, and an awareness of its own function' − is elaborate and subtle, and has been widely discussed and criticised. [14] Here, it is necessary only to note Gramsci's capsule definition of an organic intellectual as an active participant in political life, 'constructor, organiser, and permanent persuader' of a class; and to remember that the existence of such intellectuals, as a 'left tendency', is facilitated by 'a break of an organic kind within the mass of [traditional] intellectuals'. [15] Such a fission is more likely to happen when a society is gripped by an organic crisis: a concept applied to contemporary South Africa in Section 2 below.

Writing as the events of May 1968 still reverberated, Hobsbawm delineated one axis along which such an 'organic break' could occur; a revolutionary shift by a

---

[12] *Ibid.*, pp. 104, 131, 110-11; and see V. Desyaterik and A. Latyshev, *Lenin: Youth and the Future* (Moscow, 1977), pp. 137-39.

[13] C. Buci-Glucksmann, *Gramsci and the State* (London, 1980), p. 27.

[14] See, e.g. *Ibid.*, pp. 3-46; R. Simon, *Gramsci's Political Thought* (London, 1982), pp. 93-101; G. Vacca, 'Intellectuals and the Marxist Theory of the State', in A. Showstack-Sassoon (ed.), *Approaches to Gramsci* (London, 1982); P. Anderson, *Considerations of Western Marxism* (London, 1979).

[15] A. Gramsci, *Selections from the Prison Notebooks*, ed. Q. Hoare and G. Nowell Smith (London, 1971), p. 10.

generation of young intellectuals.[16] Starting with the observation that 'the characteristic revolutionary person today is a student or (generally young) intellectual', he asks *why* intellectuals become revolutionaries. Conscious revolutionism arises when people confront the apparent failure of all alternative ways of realising their objectives, 'the closing of all doors against them.' Locked out of our metaphorical house − he suggests − we opt to break down the door: 'even so we are unlikely to batter in the door unless we feel that it will give way. Becoming a revolutionary implies not only a measure of despair, but also some hope.' This optimistic desperation occurs, typically, in societies 'incapable of satisfying the demands of most of their people', societies 'in whose future few believe.'[17]

The radicalism of the late 1960s and early 1970s (Hobsbawm argues) sprang from a renewed 'period of general crisis for capitalism'. This crisis, moreover, bore acutely upon intellectuals, their numbers greatly swollen by the growth of scientific technology and tertiary education. An unprecedented expansion of higher education had three consequences: an acute strain on educational institutions; a multiplication of first-generation students; and 'speaking economically, a potential overproduction of intellectuals.' Student unrest, under these circumstances, is almost inevitable. 'A large body of students facing either unemployment or a much less desirable employment than they have been led to expect. . . are likely to form a permanent discontented mass' and feed into radical movements.[18] This analysis − it will be argued in Section 2 − is directly applicable to South Africa.

The concepts and perspectives discussed above recur in some of the case studies of youth movements elsewhere. If comparative insights are available from a voluminous literature, where might they be sought? Studies of highly advanced capitalist society, clearly, have less correspondence with the South African case than instances of late and unevenly developing capitalist economies. Moreover, if recognisably equivalent economic features were also accompanied by political authoritarianism, then the comparative exercise is potentially more useful.

Latin American case studies, accordingly, provided some suggestive pointers. In many countries, between the 1930s and 1950s, in the context of depression and dictatorships, student protests became 'the earliest and most significant bases of opposition to authoritarian governments'. At the same time, student revolutionaries learned that without allies elsewhere in society they could not topple regimes: 'they could articulate issues, assume vanguard positions, and take great risks, but in order to overthrow authoritarian governments. . . coalitions were necessary.'[19] In a number of cases, not only university students but also high school students became caught up in oppositional politics.

The Mexican student rising, brutally repressed in the glare of world-wide publicity during the 1968 Olympic Games, has a number of similarities with events in South Africa in 1976 − and 1985. Mexico, like South Africa, is a peripheral

[16] E.J. Hobsbawm, 'Intellectuals and the Class Struggle' in *Revolutionaries* (London, 1973) pp. 245-66.
[17] *Ibid.*, pp. 245, 248.
[18] *Ibid.*, pp. 252, 254, 263.
[19] A. Liebman, K. Walker and M. Glazer, *Latin American University Students: A six nation study* (Cambridge, Mass., 1972), p. 25.

economy that has attained a measure of independent capitalist growth. GNP increased by over 300% between 1940 and the mid-1960s: an assessment at the time held that Mexico was 'one of the handful of so-called underdeveloped nations to effect the transition to sustained, more or less self-generating economic expansion.'[20] (If such a judgement rings hollow in the mid-1980s — as an increasingly embattled regime grapples with unemployment, inflation, a fall in oil revenue, and a huge foreign debt — this may offer further congruencies with the South African case!)

The student revolt began in 1966 on the campus of the main university in Mexico City — but in July 1968 it broadened and deepened. A fracas between teenage high school students was broken up by riot police — and when students marched to protest against state violence, this was also brutally dispersed.

Enraged, the students barricaded themselves in nearby preparatory schools, using commandeered public buses for their barricades. . . Other schools were occupied by the army and police to prevent their use by student demonstrators. . . Strikes spread throughout Mexico City's schools, supported by students and teachers alike.

After several months during which it sought to contain and defuse student militancy, in October the state opted for all-out repression, and soldiers opened fire on demonstrating students. 'The Mexican student movement ended with. . . several hundred deaths, several hundred student activists and some professors in jail, and scores of others in exile.' The rising quelled, the state responded with a mixture of reforms (the voting age was lowered from 21 to 18, certain political prisoners were released) and repression (a new penal code defined more sweepingly sedition, sabotage and 'conspiracy against the nation').[21]

A second case study also resounds with resemblances: the substantial role played by student militants in the closing years of the Franco regime in Spain. Students and workers were 'the two crucial political movements working against the dictatorship' — and at one point a trade union leader saluted the young in these words: 'Today the students are the vanguard of all revolutionary struggles. In the last twenty years they have become part of the vanguard of the working class movement.'[22] So significant are some of the parallels between the Spanish and the South African case, that it may be useful for an analysis of the latter to outline the former, by drawing on an excellent study by Maravall.

He characterises Spanish fascism as a 'specific historical product in the context of a capitalist economy and a system of capitalist class domination. . . and where systematic labour-repressive policies are consistent with sharp class divisions.' Between 1955 and 1975, the relative stagnation and economic autarchy of the post Civil War period was replaced by Spanish participation in the international capitalist boom. Between 1951 and 1958, the GNP per capita grew at 4.45% p.a. (only Italy and Germany achieved higher rates in Europe) — and between 1960 and 1965 the annual growth rate of the GNP was a phenomenal 9.2%. Rapid industrialisation

---

[20] W. Glade and C. Anderson, *The Political Economy of Mexico* (Madison, Wisc., 1963), p. 3 — quoted in Liebman et al., *Latin American University Students*, p. 168.
[21] Liebman et al., *Latin American University Students*, pp. 186-200; quotations at pp. 187, 189.
[22] Maravall, *Dictatorship and Political Dissent*, pp. 11, 12.

promoted social changes: Maravall singles out internal migrations and urbanisation as especially important. This provided the context for the resurgence of working class dissent in Spain.

Student opposition surfaced in 1956, (preceded by the emotional funerals of Ortega y Gasset and Baroja: 'funerals were in those years a safety valve for political expression', recalled an activist) but was stepped up in the mid-1960s. An embryonic democratic students' movement was created; students established links with the working class movement, holding demonstrations in solidarity with industrial strikes. By 1968, notes Maravall, activism had also become more radical:

Limited demands for legalisation of the SDE, for a democratic university, were articulated in a global attack against the regime and this was in its turn integrated within a socialist alternative against monopoly capitalism.

One of the factors stimulating student opposition was — for the first time in a generation — the fairly widely available Marxist literature in Spain between 1967 and 1975. Maravall calls this a 'tolerance at the ideological level' by the regime which was not matched 'at the level of organisational politics'. The target of severe repression in 1969, student militancy re-emerged in 1973, in a more underground, more revolutionary form.[23] Maravall's analysis of student/worker alliances — and the factors that enabled them — is taken up in a subsequent section.

(2) The South African Context

How do the theoretical and comparative approaches outlined above inform one's understanding of South African realities? Firstly, the notion of a self-conscious 'generation unit', with its implications for concerted social and political action, is directly relevant. The youthful militants of the ICU,[24] the radicals who formed the Independent ANC,[25] and the young intellectuals of the ANC Youth League all chafed against the restraint and moderation of their elders; they were the precursors of the Black Consciousness ideologues, the *enragés* of 1976, and the township comrades of the 1980s. Studies of the Soweto risings, in particular, show clearly how a self-aware age-group sought generational unity, distanced themselves from their parents, and spoke for 'we, the youth of South Africa.'[26]

Secondly, the demographic factor is obviously of real importance in South Africa. The 1980 Census returns demonstrated an age distribution typical of a society in a phase of accelerated population growth. Half the population is under the age of 21. Over 43 per cent of the African population is under the age of 15 (corresponding figures for coloureds and whites are 39.75 and 28 per cent). Simply on the basis of the large contingents of children and young adults, one might predict social and

[23] *Ibid.*, pp. 2, 25, 102-3, 114, 9.

[24] See H. Bradford, *A Taste of Freedom: The ICU in the South African Countryside* (forthcoming).

[25] See W. Hofmeyr, 'Agricultural Crisis and Rural Organisation in the Cape: 1929-1933' (M.A. thesis, UCT, 1985).

[26] See, e.g., A. Brooks and J. Brickhill, *Whirlwind Before the Storm* (London, 1980), p. 81; J. Kane-Berman, *South Africa: The Method in the Madness* (London, 1979), pp. 125-36.

political pressures. To move beyond mere arithmetic argument, and to endow demographic data with socio-historic dimensions, it is necessary to consider economic, educational, and employment trends as well.

Doing so leads to a third general finding. The 'potential overproduction of intellectuals' noted by Hobsbawm, with its attendant student unrest, presents itself in South Africa in a form that is at once chronic and acute. Underlying and shaping the youth component of the political confrontations of the past decade (as distinct from the broader pattern of exploitation and oppression that generates black opposition) have been three inter-related factors. These are (i) the glaring defects of black education; (ii) the very substantial expansion of black schooling over the past couple of decades; and (iii) the issue of unemployment amongst black school-leavers.

It scarcely wants reiterating that the inequities and disparities within the segregated educational system both reflect and reproduce broader relations of exploitation and dominance within the society. Nor is there any need here to rehearse the depressing set of statistics and lived realities of gutter education as they affect black (and most acutely African) children. Grossly crowded classrooms are taught by ill-qualified teachers in authoritarian schools; pupils who survive monumentally high drop-out and failure rates are forced into deadening reliance on rote learning of heavily ideological syllabi. [27]

And not surprisingly, the short-term or immediate demands of student movements — from SASO and SASM through to COSAS — have addressed themselves directly to the manifest shortcomings of the education system. Highly specific demands about textbooks, school equipment, corporal punishment and sexual harassment have been joined by calls for elected Student Representative Councils, for the scrapping of the age restrictions that disqualify older (and frequently politically active) students, and for the non-victimisation of student leaders. From these demands it is a short step to the argument that true educational reform can be achieved only in a unitary system of free and compulsory schooling — and that such a system can only be won in South Africa through fundamental political transformation.

As important as the defects of black education, but less frequently mentioned, is the huge expansion of high school and tertiary education that has taken place over the past twenty years. The bare outline of the story is conveyed in the following table: [28]

Expansion of African Education Since 1960

Year	Secondary School	Matriculants	University
1960	45,598	717	1,871
1965	66,568	1,606	1,880
1970	122,489	2,938	4,578
1975	318,568	9,009	7,845
1980	577,584	31,071	10,564
1984	1,001,249	86,873	36,604

[27] See the Bibliography 'The Education of Black South Africans' by P. and J. Kallaway, in P. Kallaway (ed.), *Education and Apartheid* (Johannesburg, 1984).

[28] The table is constructed from statistics in the annual Surveys of the South African Institute of Race Relations.

Between 1960 and 1975 the numbers of Africans in high schools increased seven fold; in the next decade, they trebled again. The numbers proceeding to matriculation have increased even more startlingly: between 1960 and 1984 there was more than a hundred-fold increase. Senior secondary education for Africans in 1960 was still the prerogative of an elite; by the 1980s it had become a mass phenomenon. (Within sharp limits: only some 35% of the 15-19 year age group was enrolled in high schools in 1980. This compared with a ratio of 77% for Coloured and 86.4% for white children in the same age group.)[29] The totals for Coloured education show a similar 'massification': there was a total high school enrolment in 1960 of about 25,000; in 1970 of 57,420 and in 1984 of 158,000.

This spectacular growth in black schooling stems from two distinct causes. On the one hand, there has been an explicit attempt since Soweto to upgrade education so as to stave off school-based rebellion. On the other hand, black schooling was already showing mass growth before Soweto – and the impetus was mainly economic. The growth of the economy through the 1960s, a perceived skills shortage, and pressure from employers all shaped policy. Both these aspects – the place of education within the wider reformist strategies of the state, and the structural demands of a rapidly growing economy – have been discussed elsewhere.[30]

Even had the South African economy remained stable through the seventies and into the eighties, it is likely that the growth in black student numbers would have stretched the educational institutions uncomfortably. In the event, the protracted economic crisis of the past twelve years, assuaged only by the temporary benisons of rising gold prices, has seen the overall quality of black education fall. An inadequately financed system has strained to accommodate a ballooning school population. This combination of numerical growth and deteriorating conditions was inflammable enough; combustibility was ensured by the irregular but persistent recession. Overall, the economic crisis has sapped the living standards of the black working class; of central importance to the argument here has been the mounting unemployment – particularly youth unemployment.

There are no official statistics for the total number of unemployed workers in South Africa; estimates by academics, state officials and trade unionists vary widely; but the overall profile is clear enough. Ever since the late 1960s, a reserve army of unemployed has grown. In 1985, somewhere between 15% and 30% of the work force was unemployed. Within this huge total, high school leavers have fared particularly badly. They have been thrust onto the labour market at precisely the moment that it is contracting; many are too highly educated for cheap or unskilled labour; and white collar openings are increasingly the preserve of those who manage to attain tertiary education. Almost two of every three unemployed blacks are under the age of 30.[31] ('What good is matric to get a job? Much better have a driver's licence' commented an unemployed youth in Cape Town in 1985.)

[29] E. Dostal and T. Vergnani, *Future Perspectives in South African Education* (University of Stellenbosch, Institute for Future Research, 1985), table 2, p. 8.

[30] See, e.g., the chapters in Part IV of P. Kallaway, *Apartheid and Education*.

[31] South African Institute of Race Relations, *Survey of Race Relations in South Africa, 1982* (Johannesburg, 1983), p. 72.

The impact of unemployment, and indeed unemployability for many, has undoubtedly been a spur to radicalism among black school students and school leavers. Its stimulus was added to an already highly charged circuit. By any stretch of the sociological imagination, the recipe for marginalising and alienating a generational unit is comprehensive enough. Take politically rightless, socially subordinate, economically vulnerable youths; educate them in numbers beyond their parents' wildest dreams, but in grotesquely inadequate institutions; ensure that their awareness is shaped by punitive social practices in the world beyond the schoolyard − and then dump them in large numbers on the economic scrap-heap.

To conclude this section, it remains briefly to relate the 'crisis in education' to the broader, structural dilemmas confronting the South African state. Gramsci's concept of an organic crisis has been fruitfully applied to contemporary South Africa; its contours and fault lines have been charted. [32] In baldly summary form, one can identify the major components of an endemic and manifold instability.

At its heart is a crisis of capital accumulation. The halcyon years of growth and boom that shaped the 1950s and 1960s have stuttered into decline and contraction. The business pages of the South African press read like a litany of distress. Inflation, unemployment, and bankruptcies rise; fixed investments, domestic savings, and profits fall. These are integrally related to South Africa's status as a relatively backward capitalist power. Increasingly monopolised, national capital inextricably conjoined with foreign capital, the domestic economy sneezes convulsively when international capitalism catches cold. The prophylactic vagaries of a buoyant gold price can stifle the symptoms, but not cure them. When its remedial virtues wane, economic distemper is rife − in the form of balance of payments deficits, mounting foreign indebtedness, and a shrunken Rand.

Economic malfunctions do not occur in a socio-political vacuum. On the contrary, they aggravate and are aggravated by social and political conflicts. South Africa's historical birthmark − distinguishing it from other middle-ranking capitalist powers − is the non-incorporation of the majority of its working class into its social and political institutions. The historical development of racial capitalism has created a series of antagonistic social divides: between possessors and dispossessed, between employers and workers, between black and white. So acute are these antinomies, that merely to regulate and preserve existing social relations the state has no option but to resort to authoritarian weapons and practices. Coercion, not consensus, is the social cement of the state edifice.

The principal contradiction − between large capitalist concerns and an exploited, oppressed and concentrated black working class − is no theoretical abstraction. It is the central feature of South Africa's recent history. In the 1970s, industrial conflict and mass political challenges served notice on capital and the state that the quiescence of the 1960s was ended. Political opposition moved rapidly through several phases. Reinvigoration and mobilisation under Black Consciousness was followed by the eruption of 1976/7. This in turn was succeeded by a phase (c.1979-83) in which a decentralised, localised, radicalised community-based

[32] J. Saul and S. Gelb, *The Crisis in South Africa* (New York, 1981); articles in *South African Review Three* (Johannesburg, 1986).

politics took root.[33] In mid-1983, the formation of the National Forum and the United Democratic Front provided national umbrella structures for the new community politics. Since July/September 1984, political struggle has been extended and further radicalised in a number of ways.

These aspects of the organic crisis – profound problems of capital accumulation and of class rule – have also intensified a rupture at the ideological level. Positing a 'crisis of legitimacy', Posel and Greenberg both stress the ideological reformulations that have occurred in the course of the state's reform project(s) of the past eight years.[34] This flux and confusion in the ideological domain creates a number of contradictions. In their analysis of the 'predominantly coercive state' in contemporary Latin America, Lowy and Sader identify an important aspect of 'a profound crisis of hegemony':

> The ideological apparatuses [are] incapable of skilfully performing their functions as genera-tors of consensus. . . Schools, universities, the church, and political parties have experienced an increasingly intense crisis and encountered increasing difficulties in propagating the ideology of the established order.[35]

The 'established order' in South Africa has faced a precisely similar problem. This tendency of the ideological apparatus to buckle has ensured the pre-eminence of educational institutions as a site of struggle in recent years.

(3) Student/Youth Politics in Cape Town in 1985

Several accounts already exist of the sequence of events during the 1985 schools boycott in Cape Town.[36] They show that in the first half of the year the Cape peninsula was relatively unaffected by political and educational struggles being waged elsewhere in the country. The declaration of a State of Emergency over parts of the country in July provided a major impetus to organised youth-based politics: within a week scores of thousands of students were participating in a boycott of classes and a new co-ordinating body was created. From July until November, youth-based resistance – including the schools boycotts, the rallies and meetings, alternative education projects, direct action to harry and thwart security force movements – was the most dynamic element in local politics. It provided the 'inspiration and framework for other forms of community action' such as the consumer boycotts, the Pollsmoor marches, and the September stay-away.[37]

---

[33] M. Matiwana and S. Walters, *The Struggle for Democracy: A Study of Community Organisations in Greater Cape Town from the 1960s to 1985* (Cape Town, 1986), pp. 24-31.

[34] D. Posel, 'State Ideology and Legitimation', conference paper, New York, September 1982; S. Greenberg, *Legitimating the Illegitimate* (forthcoming).

[35] M. Lowy and E. Sader, 'The Militarization of the State in Latin America', *Latin American Perspectives*, vol. 12, no. 4 (Fall 1985), p. 10.

[36] M. Hall, 'Resistance and Revolt in Greater Cape Town', paper for the conference on the Western Cape, UCT, July 1986; R. Jordi, 'Parents, Workers, Unite with our Children': An analysis of the character of resistance in Greater Cape Town in 1985' (unpublished typescript): I am grateful to Richard Jordi for letting me read and use his typescript before it has been submitted for publication; SAIRR Regional Topic Paper 86/2, 'The Political Crisis as it affected educational institutions under the DEC' (Cape Town, 1986).

[37] Jordi, 'Parents, Workers, Unite with our Children'.

While mobilising and organisational efforts of student activists − of which more below − played a part, beyond any doubt the major factor in ratcheting up student/youth militancy in Cape Town between July and December was the state's heavy-handed coercive measures. The rapid transition within a school, from peaceful rally through 'planks and hankies' preparedness[38] to confrontation with soldiers and police behind fiery barricades, was repeated time and again. Invasions of schools by police, the massive show of force on the day of the proposed march on Pollsmoor, the banning of COSAS, Carter Ebrahim's closure of the schools, the Thornton Road 'trojan horse' shootings: each of these, and many other incidents, provided the student movement with new grievances, with first-hand experience of the state's repressive capacities, and with heightened militancy.

Hall, the SAIRR, and Jordi provide full chronologies and a wealth of detail: here, a skeletal summary of dates and developments may be useful for what follows.

Cape Town 1985: Chronological Outline

Mar	5	UWC students boycott for one day in solidarity with students elsewhere in SA
	28	3,500 attend commemoration service for Langa (Uitenhague) victims at UWC
May	1	More than 30,000 students at DEC high schools boycott classes in protest against events in Transvaal and Eastern Cape
Jul	19	1,500 students at Guguletu service for Cradock Four dispersed with teargas and gunshot
	20	State of Emergency declared in 36 districts
	23	4,000 students at UWC come out on boycott
	25	Students at 29 DEC schools join boycott
	26	WECSAC, representing 45 schools & colleges, formed
	29	DET schools embark on boycott
Aug	1-23	Numerous rallies, police reprisals
	20	Call for W. Cape consumer boycott
	28	Attempted march on Pollsmoor; massive security operation; COSAS banned
	29 to	
	Sep 5	Mounting youth/security forces clashes
Sep	6	Carter Ebrahim closes 464 schools and colleges
	10/11	Stayaway
	17	Schools 'reoccupied'
Oct	1	Official re-opening of DET and DEC schools
	15	Thornton Road shooting
	16-31	'Apogee of the rebellion in W. Cape' (Hall)
	26	State of Emergency in W. Cape
Nov/Dec		DEC examinations
Dec	28/9	SPCC National Conference

Very briefly, the content and course of youth/student struggles in 1985 can be summarised, before various aspects are examined in more detail. By the end of July, DET schools had joined UWC and DEC schools and colleges on a boycott of classes. Initially, DET school students and the Parent Action Committees of Langa, Guguletu and Nyanga focused mainly on school grievances. The leaflet *Meet Our*

---

[38] 'Half an hour later, two Casspirs arrived containing about fifteen heavily armed policemen. This resulted in the students becoming extremely agitated. They armed themselves with planks from the back of their desks, tied hankies around their faces for the teargas and got ready, naively, to defend themselves. . .' − from 'Inside Boycotts − a Teacher's Story', *Deduct* (UCT Education Faculty, October 1985), p. 15.

Demands Now issued by the Joint SRCs and PAC in late July or August dealt mainly with age restrictions, SRC recognition, examination fees, school bus fares, shortage of classrooms, and the range of subjects taught. (These were preceded by calls for the ending of the State of Emergency and the withdrawal of troops from the townships.)

The focus of the DEC boycott, in July/August, was more broadly political. It expressed solidarity with students boycotting elsewhere; it protested against the State of Emergency; it invoked opposition to tricameralism and 'dummy MPs'; it included general educational demands like democratic SRCs with local issues such as the reinstatement of a dismissed teacher.[39] The closure of the schools by the state to some extent realigned the main agitational thrust of the boycotters. Student/youth demands increasingly meshed with those of community organisations in the call for popular control over the schools. The new Parent/Teacher/Student Associations (PTSAs) formed in DEC schools called for democratic local control as the first step towards a free, compulsory, unitary educational system.

'How many of us will find jobs?'

The unfolding of resistance in Cape Town should also be related to some of the variables identified in previous sections as having a bearing on youth-based politics. Age distribution and school-leaver unemployment both merit attention. As far as the proportion of young people in the overall population is concerned, it should be mentioned that for the African population in Greater Cape Town (GCT) the ratio is lower than in the country as a whole — because of tight restrictions on normal family life, the number of migrant workers, the high masculinity ratio, etc.

For those classified as 'Coloured', the age distribution exhibits the large youthful contingent discussed earlier. Almost 36% of the coloured population of GCT is in the age group 0-14 years (comparative figures for whites and Africans are 23.3% and 27.3%) and the 1980 Census revealed that 60% of the coloured population is under the age of 25 years. A particularly high concentration of young adults is the demographic legacy of a 'baby boom' between 1960 and 1965.[40] The rapid population growth has outrun employment opportunities. If the 1980s 'are confronting youth in many countries with a concrete, structural crisis of chronic economic uncertainty and even deprivation',[41] this is well illustrated in GCT.

Examination of trends since 1980 reveal that 'unemployment has risen substantially for all age groups and shows a marked upward trend.'[42] Its brunt has been placed on what is still a relatively poorly educated 16-25 year old age bracket. Sixty-five per cent of unemployed coloureds in GCT are in this group. Moreover, unemployment showed a particularly sharp rise in 1985. Youth unemployment (which remained a fairly constant percentage of rising total unemployment) was

[39] *Cape Times*, 1 August 1985.

[40] D. Pinnock, *The Brotherhoods: street gangs and state control in Cape Town* (Cape Town, 1984), p. 56.

[41] V. McMenamin, '"Coloured" Youth Unemployment in Cape Town' (B.Soc.Sci., Hons. dissertation, UCT, 1986), p. 7.

[42] *Ibid.*, p. 30.

particularly affected. In the following table, the figures are those of the Department of Manpower — and reflect *registered unemployment statistics*. These figures under-represent the total of youth unemployed in several respects.[43] Nonetheless, even if the *scale* of the phenomenon is being minimised, the *trend* emerges clearly:

Coloured Unemployment by Age Group: Average Monthly Figures[44]

	under 21	21-35 yrs
1981	197	1056
1982	242	1478
1983	310	2821
1984	245	2082
1985	516	5445

Awareness of an acute unemployment problem for school-leavers is undoubtedly widespread in DEC schools, and is explicit in a number of the pamphlets and leaflets distributed before and during the 1985 school boycotts. 'Millions of young people are unemployed in our country. For months we struggle to find a job after we leave school, whether in Std 5 or 10' ran one.[45] A pamphlet issued in September or October 1985 pointed out that 'The reality is that there is no work and that the majority of students will be *forced* into cheap labour. . . or form part of the 6 million unemployed.'[46] Local conditions were sometimes highlighted: 'Every fourth person in Mitchells Plain, every second person in Atlantis, is unemployed.' A Groenvlei matric pupil spoke bitterly during the boycott: 'even if we pass', he asked, 'how many of us will find jobs? The reality is that there are no jobs for us; white pupils with Std 8 certificates get jobs before those of us with matric certificates.'[47]

Unemployment could also feed very directly into political involvement. A recent school-leaver being interviewed explained rather engagingly that 'In 1985 I was unemployed and just an activist.' Nationally, the youth congresses which have proliferated since 1982 have their base in the urban unemployed; they have 'infused a deeper, sometimes more desperate, militancy into student and community politics.'[48]

If these demographic and economic features arguably predisposed school students and young coloured adults towards oppositional politics, it is now necessary to look at other, more specific aspects of youth consciousness and political behaviour in 1985. These include: youth self-awareness; the search for unity with community and other political groupings; alternative education and 'awareness programmes';

[43] An extremely narrow definition of 'unemployment' is used; moreover, many unemployed youths will not have worked previously, and are therefore not entitled to UIF. (See McMenamin, '''Coloured'' Youth Unemployment', pp. 8-9, 28-9.)

[44] Table derived from figure 18, pp. 56-7, in McMenamin, '''Coloured'' Youth Unemployment'.

[45] Cape Youth Congress, 1984 pamphlet.

[46] Athlone Students Action Committee, Sep/Oct 1985.

[47] Joint SRC townships/BISKO/LOGSAC/MITSAC/MAC/HSAC/ASAC pamphlet, October 1985; *Cape Times*, 9 October 1985.

[48] Chisholm, 'From a Revolt to a Search', p. 17.

militancy and activism; political precocity − and immaturity; observable political strengths and weaknesses exhibited by youth/students in 1985; and the question of student/worker alliances.

'Almal is saam in die struggle'?

Generational consciousness amongst politically active youth was as evident in Cape Town as elsewhere in South Africa. The point could be demonstrated with any number of student publications and statements, but is illustrated here with a single emphatic example. A first year college student makes substantial claims for the contribution to the struggle by his generation:

I mean there is no doubt about that, that the whole struggle in South Africa is dominated by the students. The students are in the forefront of the struggle. This is not a familiar thing if we look at the history of other countries [like Zimbabwe, Angola and Mozambique] where it was a question of guerrillas. South Africa takes a very different dimension, totally, we the students being in the forefront. The students organising and − you know − shaping the history of the country; and hence it is the students who forced apartheid to introduce so-called reforms. It is the students that have made different organisations the world over, like financial organi-sations, to threaten to cut their loans or whatever to South Africa.

Yet, very often, this kind of perception is tempered by recognition of the limits of 'student power'. The same student quoted above continued:

The students are in the forefront, but it is not the students alone − it is the students with the back − the backbone of the whole thing is the workers. You know, even if the students can go on with whatever they do, but as long as the workers continue to support apartheid, there will hardly be any change. . . but as long as the students together with the workers and all the progressive people of South Africa work together they are going to [win their struggle].[49]

The topic of student/worker alliances is discussed separately below. A number of other linkages are suggested in the phrase 'all the progressive people' − and many of these were explored by youth/student politicians in Cape Town.

The question of cooperation across generations was an ever-present one in 1985 − and the formation of Parent/Teacher/Student Associations (PTSAs) was an impor-tant attempt to answer it. Time and again, student/youth groups stressed to their members the desirability of making common political cause with their parents. 'We must build representative student organisations to work through our problems with our parents and progressive teachers', urged the Students of Young Azania (SOYA) in August. Young people were called on to recognise the sacrifices their parents had made, and the hardships they suffered. Even so, an implicit criticism of the older generation's political position ran through this discourse. An April pamphlet explained: 'Students have an important role to play in explaining to our parents why the [consumer] boycott is important.'[50]

Partly overlapping with youth/parent relations, was another linkage widely discussed in youth/student circles: the relationship of their struggles to those of 'the community'. (This is not the place to review the problematic nature of the concept.)

---

[49] Interview.
[50] NUSAS/COSAS/AZASO pamphlet, April 1985.

This relationship was seen in various ways. At times, it was perceived as a difficulty whose solution must be sought: one of the five aims and objectives of the Cape Youth Congress (formed in 1983) is 'to normalise the relationship between youth and parents'. In the second half of 1985, the need for community-wide unity became more urgent. A pamphlet issued in August argued:

It is important that we build strong student, youth and community organisations because a well-organised community can never be defeated. It is important that we form student-teacher-parent bodies so that we can stand united in this time of intense repression. Some schools have already taken such steps. The struggles in the classrooms must be taken to the community and the struggles in the community must be taken to the classrooms.

Such sentiments did not remain only at the level of rhetoric. Student and youth movements consciously sought ways of linking with other organisations and other campaigns. At the end of the first week of boycotts, UWC students began a mass meeting by hearing reports from groups of students liaising with community organisations.[51] Student Action Committees (SACs) worked together with existing youth and civic organisations. On a number of occasions, students sought and won extensive public backing for their stand on boycotts, the return to the schools, and examinations. Ironically, perhaps the most effective agent of such unity was the state. Indiscriminate violence against protesting scholars won them sympathy – and the closure of schools, more than any other single action, outraged both middle class and working class coloured parents. The formation of PTSAs not only made concrete the terms of youth/community unity, but also posed a radically alternative conception of how schools should be administered.

The mass action by pupils and teachers, children and parents, on 17 September, in a symbolic re-occupation of the closed schools, was the highwater mark of this development. It also provided a dramatic cameo of community militancy: At Alexander Sinton High School a 'citizen cordon' of commandeered vehicles six blocks deep effectively kept police under siege for two hours in the school (which they entered to arrest 173 people). Indeed, a number of reports from GCT during 1985 noted instances of communal solidarity translated into practical politics: in Athlone, for example, doors stood open whenever word filtered down the street of police or army movements; 'That way' (explained a housewife) 'the kids can run into any house they see for safety.'[52] Graphically, the *Weekly Mail* reported:

Pressmen have seen youths being egged on by adults. Parents have been seen directing children in dragging old fridges and mattresses out of houses to be piled on to the barricades, and throwing their household benzine into the flames.

And:

As soon as the police and army arrive, the streets are suddenly filled with private cars going nowhere in particular, making progress down the main thoroughfares a slow process for the ponderous Buffels and Caspirs.[53]

[51] *Argus*, 31 July 1985.
[52] *Cape Times*, 12 November 1985.
[53] *Weekly Mail*, 25-31 October 1985; 14 November 1985.

At times, indeed, the words of a ditty sung at the rallies sounded almost literally true: 'Al die mamas en die papas, die boeties en die sussies, die oumas en die oupas, die hondjies en die katjies — almal is saam in die struggle.'

Education for Liberation?

In his study of the 1980 DEC school boycotts, Molteno paid close attention to the political dynamics of the school and even the classroom. He argues that hierarchic and coercive structures and practices of these schools were directly challenged. The element of control 'was most consistently and completely overturned in the boycott'. While recognising certain limitations to student actions and perceptions, he concludes that they did 'albeit temporarily — transform certain social relations fundamental to schooling as currently constituted'. Molteno and other commentators also discussed critical attention directed towards syllabi and the content of education in 1980. [54]

In 1985, too, 'alternative education' and 'awareness programmes' bulked large during the boycotts of formal classes. Students found larger numbers of teachers and principals supporting (or at least not obstructing) them: a tendency which found organisational expression in the formation of WECTU. Only days after the boycott had begun, a DEC liaison officer admitted that 'at some schools pupils held awareness programmes instead of classes.' [55] The main current of alternative education flowed in similar channels to those of 1980: debates, discussions, invited speakers, plays, poetry readings, films and songs. Prescribed textbooks were critically dissected; the daily press was read 'politically'. In one school, a teacher recounted, discussions were arranged on such topics as the State of Emergency, the cancelled All Blacks tour, education in South Africa, the consumer boycott, and the history of black resistance. The same observer described the SRC at his school in admiring tones:

They can, and did, draw up and implement awareness programmes. . . and were in a position to call for stayaways (which were a hundred per cent effective). . . It became increasingly obvious that the real power lay in the hands of the students. [56]

Two features are worth remarking. First, these sessions of informal education undoubtedly play an important part in forming and sharpening youth consciousness. A DEC teacher was struck by 'the depth of the discussion in these classes', and concluded that 'much informal debate had already taken place on the street or in the playgrounds.' He also commented on the 'self-discipline exercised at our normally

---

[54] F. Molteno, 'Reflections on Resistance: Aspects of the 1980 Students Revolt' in Kenton-in-the-stadt, Education Conference Papers (1983), pp. 36, 57, 40-45; the piece is drawn from his 'The Schooling of Black South Africans and the 1980 Cape Town Students Boycott' (M.Soc.Sci., thesis, UCT, 1983). See also C.J. Millar and S. Philcox (eds.), *Some Aspects of the Educational Crisis in the Western Cape in 1980* (Centre for Extra Mural Studies, UCT, 1981), especially T. Fledermann, 'Some Effects of the boycott on the role of classroom teachers', pp. 32-41.

[55] *Cape Times*, 30 July 1985.

[56] 'From Bastions of CNE to the Heart of Resistance', in *Deduct* (UCT Education Faculty), October 1985, pp. 4-5.

unruly "ghetto" school' as a measure of the seriousness of the students. [57] Similarly, a college student was pressed by the interviewer to identify the actual source of his political ideas and beliefs. Yes, he said, the media played a part; so did his family, and pamphlets issued by organisations. COSAS had been a particularly important source of ideas at high school. But more important than any of these (he believed) were those moments when

we had students coming together and we tossed around ideas. . . I think that for me this is the time we got our major ideas, because you have so many different people coming with different ideas. . . You come into contact with pamphlets and all that type of thing. Ah — but the major share is what you get from students because there you have a chance to discuss and that is when you really come out, because having somebody tell you or make a speech or read a pamphlet you just have facts given to you; whereas when you are with fellow students you are able to sort out — you grind out the matter, you know; then you can come to reality.

Secondly, compared to 1980, there appears to have been a far more explicit stress in 1985 upon the direct, practical uses to which an alternative education could be put. These ran from the general ('We must now learn about our true history of struggle, the South African economy, the political system. . . To change the system we need to know how it works') to the specific ('We need knowledge of Mathematics and Physics to make and use more sophisticated implements than petrol bombs. We need history to understand the politics of Liberation.') [58]

'Action, comrades, action!'

Another significant development is by its nature more difficult to document. For the most part it can be described only impressionistically or by inference. This was the impact upon youth/student consciousness of direct, physically dangerous, violent confrontation with state power. As in other cases — Russia or Spain or Latin America — engagement with an authoritarian state engenders a political precocity, produces youthful veterans. Teargas, beatings, and detentions provide a crash course in class struggle. There were thousands, in Cape Town, who learned the practical science of making a petrol bomb; the street sociology of taunting armed soldiers; the pavement politics of pamphlet distribution and slogan painting; the geography of safe houses and escape routes; and the grammar and dialectics of under-cover operations.

In a sense, this tendency is present even without baton-charges or buckshot rounds; it exists in the privations and institutionalised violence of township life. An Eastern Cape clergyman put it thus:

Their frustrations have an educative effect on them. They now study every newspaper they can lay their hands on to see how events will affect them directly, be they political, social or economic issues. In fact, nothing they read, hear or see on TV do they take at face value, but study the media critically. [59]

[57] 'Inside Boycotts', *Ibid.*, pp. 14-15.
[58] Pamphlet issued by Students Revolutionary Front, n.d.
[59] *Evening Post*, 6 July 1985.

A second general point that must be made about the turn to militant direct action is that it stemmed from a political culture that had itself undergone significant changes in recent years. In the Western Cape, as elsewhere in South Africa, the late 1970s and early 1980s saw the proliferation of community organisations. In 1980 and 1981, strikes, consumer boycotts and school boycotts accelerated this process: 85 voluntary associations were formed in GCT between 1980 and 1984. These — Walters and Matiwane have argued — were self-consciously democratic; they also displayed 'a shift towards theoretical understanding rather than blind activism.'[60] (This assessment, while identifying an important dynamic, must be qualified by a recognition of factors which in the Western Cape complicated and even weakened forms of political organisation. These included a factionalised local political culture, the relative weakness of trade union organisation, and a certain lack of continuity or depth in some local structures. These considerations are reviewed more fully in the concluding section below.)

The third quarter of 1984 saw a new peak of intensity in local opposition politics, in the shape of the anti-election campaign. After something of a lull locally in the first half of 1985, politics in GCT entered another highly charged period in July. Calls for 'ungovernability' were echoed at rallies and meetings. Journalist Tony Weaver described the radicalisation of Athlone (a relatively affluent coloured suburb) in these words:

Every block, every school, has its 'action squad', coordinating action, providing direction, helping build petrol bombs and seeking material for barricades. . . Children who have not yet reached puberty tell you 'I wish I had a hand grenade'; teenagers talk of AK-47s, RPG-7s, and bazookas.[61]

Reporting from Hanover Park, another journalist wrote that 'the call taken up by children as young as eight or ten years old was ''Action, comrades, action''.'[62]

As suggested, the political programmes derived from this direct action do not easily find their way into pamphlets or public speeches. They will be more apparent — it seems safe to predict — in the extension in the near future of a more sophisticated internal underground movement. Nevertheless, some echoes of activist radicalism are audible. The work of graffiti artists is an obvious example: 'COMRADES, KILL SADF, SAP OR BE KILLED! THEY ARE VIOLENT MURDERERS' reads a wall in Athlone. A Student Revolutionary Front issued leaflets in 1985 which also capture this mood. One in August spoke of the need to 'build a mass movement which will provide fertile soil for the development of successful armed resistance in both town and country.' Another (October?) proclaimed 'We are Xhosas, Zulus, Coloureds, Indians and Malays no more. We are nothing else but young soldiers fighting a CLASS WAR.'

This mode of activist politics could nurture a political perspective that one might dub 'immediatism': an impatient anticipation of imminent victory, a hubristic assessment of progress made, and a naive underestimation of the resources of the

---

[60] Matiwana and Walters, *Struggle for Democracy*, p. 52.
[61] *Weekly Mail*, 8-14 November 1985.
[62] *Weekly Mail*, 25-31 October 1985.

state. This is not a surprising outcome. The fact that for many young people their political baptism was a heady mix of exhilaration, raw courage, and a sense of group solidarity meant that expectation could easily outrun actuality.

The popular (and ultimately controversial) slogan of 'Liberation before Education' is the best known example of this frame of mind — but anyone who witnessed the rallies and meetings between July and December could cite many others. The same perspective is apparent in several leaflets. 'Yes, the boycott is temporary', ran one: 'But we cannot end it now — not now when we have got the government on its knees. If we end it now, the government will be able to get onto its feet again.' In similar vein, the imposition of the State of Emergency on the Western Cape was assessed thus: 'This apparent show of strength by the state is merely the last kick of a dying animal.' When students held a secret meeting at the end of November, they warned the government to meet their minimal demands 'because the boycott won't remain at this level. . . it will intensify to a great extent.'[63] Less stridently, a student's confidence about the future is a representative voice of 1985:

I am very optimistic. Botha tried to cross the Rubicon. He failed. I tell you I am optimistic that all progressive South Africans will cross the Rubicon and will shape their destiny the way they want.[64]

The political cost of immediatist expectations is that they all too easily feed into demoralisation and disarray when events reveal the balance of forces to be far less favourable to the youthful militants and their allies than had been anticipated.

A development within Western Cape youth/student consciousness that mirrored a country-wide process was a growth of popular support for the ANC. Lodge and others have chronicled the resurgence in recent years of ANC influence and loyalties.[65] Overt, demonstrative allegiance to its emblems, its leaders and its programme was one of the most obvious features in township politics throughout 1985. Compared with — say — the Eastern Cape, where deep reservoirs of loyalty to the movement were tapped, in the Western Cape the enthusiasm for the ANC was frequently a real departure. Historically, the ANC was relatively weak in GCT. Contributing to this were the relatively small proportion of Africans within the population; the tilting of migrant workers towards the PAC; and the entrenchment among coloureds of political organisations critical of the ANC. The upshot was that the ANC commanded less support in GCT than in any other major South African city.

This has changed substantially. In some cases, youth/student support for the ANC rose directly from groupings affiliated with the UDF, with an explicitly 'charterist' position. Thus, in June 1983 an AZASO pamphlet saluted as heroes and martyrs the executed ANC cadres Motaung, Mosololi and Mogoerane; called for a South Africa based on the Freedom Charter; and concluded 'after we have mourned their passing,

[63] Pamphlet issued by Athlone Students Action Committee, September? October? 1985; Pamphlet issued by Thornhill Residents Association and Thornhill Youth, late October/early November, 1985; *Cape Times*, 26 November 1985.
[64] Interview.
[65] T. Lodge, articles in *South African Review One, South African Review Two, South African Review Three* (Johannesburg, 1983, 1984, 1985).

let us mobilise, organise and unite, and take forward the struggle for freedom in our lifetime.' But in 1985 a pro-ANC stance spread rapidly, especially in some DEC schools where it had previously scarcely existed. Press reports of meetings punctuated with cries of 'Viva ANC' were almost as frequent as the graffiti celebrating Mandela and Tambo. Song sheets used at rallies in DEC schools frequently included *Nkosi Sikilele* and other Xhosa songs (plus translations).

Youth/worker alliance: rhetoric, chimera, or objective necessity?

The two most important elements in the forces ranged against the state in the past ten years have been youth-based political resistance and trade union organisation. This is neither an original nor a contentious statement; but it serves to introduce a recurrent theme in the speeches and printed ephemera of 1985 — that student/youth and workers' struggles should be linked. Answers to the questions posed by the issue are being sought both in theory and in practice.

It should be noted at the outset that certain objective factors make a common cultural identity between youth/student and organised worker consciousness relatively easily attainable in South Africa. There is the obvious fact of common racial/national oppression, experienced by black workers and black youth/students alike. There is the enforced propinquity across social divides — by courtesy of the Group Areas Act — of various strata within ethnically demarcated ghettoes. There is the widespread phenomenon of 'first generation students', linking within single families the solidly proletarian and the potential petty bourgeoisie. And finally there is the lived experience of many students: many who complete high school or enter tertiary education can do so only by interrupting their schooling with periods of wage labour.

Even a cursory glance at the leaflets and pamphlets circulating in 1985 reveals the centrality in their discourse of the language of class struggle, class alliances, and working class leadership of the struggle. It is present in the utterances of student/ youth organisations variously aligned and affiliated. In some quarters it was a dominant ideological element well before the 1985 boycotts. 'The battle being waged is between those who want to retain this profit-making system and those who want to overthrow it', ran a SOYA pamphlet of 1984: 'On the one side are the bosses and their supporters, on the other side are the black workers, their children and allies.' On the one hand, SOYA argued that students were objectively working class: 'By and large black students' class position is defined by that of their parents, i.e. working class'; on the other hand, it also recognised that student/youth campaigns were not the same as those undertaken by organised workers: 'The struggle of the students should not be isolated from the struggle of workers.'

Now SOYA, it might be objected, is not a mass organisation; its theoretical position is derived from that of the bodies to which it is affiliated. But very similar analyses were far more widely forthcoming in 1985. In May, before the boycotts began, the Inter-school Coordinating Committee stated that it was 'because of a system where workers are exploited that our fellow students are suffering.'[66]

[66] *Cape Times*, 2 May 1985.

AZASO, a UDF affiliate, defined apartheid as 'a system of racial oppression and economic class exploitation'.[67] The Athlone Students Action Committee said 'We must continue to be PART of the worker struggle − not merely support it in words.' Another pamphlet, issued by half a dozen action committees, argued that the capitalist economy was in crisis and perorated 'Students Unite! A People United will Never be Defeated! Forward to a workers' society free from exploitation and oppression!' (yoking the student, the populist and the workerist positions in close harness).

The African townships Joint SRCs and PAC, in a single paragraph, established the relationship between the state and capital, and identified capital as the enemy:

To enforce the State of Emergency, the security forces are allowed to patrol the townships. They do not patrol but have beaten up and killed hundreds of working class children. The owning class, capitalists, cannot rule on their own, they always look for people to rule on their behalf, that is why there are political parties like ruling Nationalist Party and the PFP. [The] parliament talk shop of Botha and Slabbert is used to win sections of the working masses by promising them a better life under the present system. During times of unrest, when the working people demand more than parliament can offer, the army and police are used to crush the uprisings. Some people argue that the SADF should play a neutral role: to that we say, with the absence of the 'band of armed gangs' Botha and even his masters, Capital, would not be able to rule for a day.[68]

Obviously, using such evidence, one is dealing primarily with the consciousness of activists and leaders of student/youth politics, with those involved in writing and reproducing the pamphlets and handbills. It is impossible to extrapolate from these any accurate claims about rank and file consciousness, or to assess how much of this discourse has been internalised. Such findings await further research − and, of course, will be more fully and concretely revealed in the ebb and flow of political activism in the future.

Having established that many youth/student ideologues in GCT characterised as crucial an effective political alliance between their movements and the organised working class, certain questions pose themselves. How accurate is this perception? Have such alliances been achieved in GCT? Have they been achieved elsewhere? And if so, what have been the enabling factors?

In terms of mounting an effective political challenge, the case for constructing such an alliance is virtually self-evident. The student/youth activists *have* been in the van of popular struggles for a decade − so much so that it sometimes seems 'that these students have been fighting apartheid all by themselves.'[69] At the same time, they do not carry the same social weight, cannot flex the same political muscle, as an organised working class.

Hobsbawm, in the essay cited earlier, states the position lucidly. His reference point was the relationship between students and trade unionists during the Parisian May Days of 1968, but his analysis is directly pertinent to the South African setting.

[67] AZASO leaflet, (August?) 1985.
[68] 'Meet our demands now', pamphlet issued by Parents Action Committee and Joint SRCs.
[69] F. Chikane, 'Effects of the Unrest on Township Children', to be included in a book on childhood in South Africa, edited by S. Burman and P. Reynolds − I am grateful to Sandra Burman for letting me see the typescript of this chapter.

While any convergence of radicalised students and workers in 'a single united left movement' is a source of 'immense' political power (argues Hobsbawm), one cannot take for granted 'that their confluence is automatic, nor that it will occur spontaneously.' If such a junction fails to occur,

the movement of the intellectuals may settle down as one or both of two things: as a powerful and effective reformist pressure group. . . and as a fluctuating radical youth and student movement, oscillating between brief brush fires and relapses into passivity. . . On the other hand, it is also unlikely that the workers will make a successful revolution without the intellectuals, still less against them. They may relapse into a narrow movement. . . militant and powerful within the limits of 'economism'. . . or they may achieve. . . a sort of syndicalism, which certainly envisages and seeks to build a new society, but is incapable of achieving its aims. . . [W]orking people. . . are capable of overthrowing a social order, whereas the intellectuals. . . are not. If a human society worthy of the name is to be built, both need each other. [70]

(The chief amendment that one would move to make this more applicable to the South African case would be to minimise the likelihood of black intellectuals becoming a 'powerful and effective reformist pressure group' on the European model: the alternative — a brush-fire radicalism — seems entirely apt.)

What precisely is the contribution a radicalised intelligentsia, and especially its student wing, can make to organised working class politics? Mandel (like Marx and Lenin) says that what students can offer young workers is 'the product of theoretical production, that is, scientific knowledge. . . a radical critique of the existing society.' [71] More sweepingly (as discussed in Section 1 above) Gramsci saw organic intellectuals not merely as human transmitters of 'scientific knowledge' but as active political agents — 'permanent persuaders' — in working class organisations. Gramsci also stressed the importance of a fissure within 'traditional' intellectuals, so that some of their number would be available as 'organising elements' for the proletariat.

The renascent independent trade union movement in South Africa, during the 1970s, drew upon the practical and theoretical skills of the (tiny) number of intellectuals who took positions as full-time union officers. In the Western Cape, only a handful of the 'veterans' of student activism in 1980/81 have entered trade union work — although where they have, their impact has been considerable. The possibility that the 'class of 1985' will feed into trade unions in greater numbers is already being discussed in some youth/student groupings. The outcome is complicated by the counter-attraction exerted by community or populist organisations.

What of experience elsewhere? It was suggested in Section 1 that the case of Spain was valuable in comparative terms. Not only does it offer the parallel of rapid capitalist development, but also that of the simultaneous re-emergence of student and worker resistance in a non-democratic regime after a period of repression. The phenomena of ideological ferment and the spread of socialist ideas, of intense shop-floor pressure within the factories, and of schools and universities emerging as 'a sub-cultural ghetto' also resonate with contemporary South African history.

[70] Hobsbawm, *Revolutionaries*, pp. 265-6.
[71] E. Mandel, 'The Changing Role of the Bourgeois University', in T. Pateman (ed.), *Counter Course: A handbook for course criticism* (Harmondsworth, 1972), pp. 19, 20.

Maravall asks how one explains the persistence and growth of dissent under an authoritarian regime, and isolates three factors. These are: (a) rapid economic change and attendant social friction; (b) the presence of particular working class communities with 'strong local traditions of working class radicalism'; and (c) the crucial role played in the reorganisation of dissent by underground political parties, more particularly working class organisations: either political survivors or newly created in secret. 'The emergence of the working class and student movements [in the 1960s] was dependent on the underground survival of the parties of the left.'[72] (If one makes the direct comparison, the ANC clearly fulfils some of the functions played by the Spanish underground; equally, in comparison with the Spanish case, it has not so much promoted a socialist political alternative as mobilised under a nationalist banner.)

With particular reference to the Western Cape, Jordi argues convincingly that joint student-community-worker struggles 'while finding often uneasy coordination at a leadership level have lacked an organised mass base'. This has meant that recent struggles in GCT have 'relied consistently and heavily on a militant student/youth initiative.'[73] By comparison with the Transvaal industrial heartland, or Eastern Cape centres like Port Elizabeth or East London, he finds, the involvement of workers through their trade unions in recent community political campaigns has been 'conspicuously absent' in the Western Cape. Greater Cape Town has not yet experienced a political campaign in which youth organisations, trade unions and democratic community bodies were welded together as effectively as in the Transvaal stayaway of November 1984.[74] Nor have youth and community groupings here become as politically imbricated as they have elsewhere — in the Eastern Cape and East Rand, for example.

There are a number of reasons for this, including the relatively undeveloped nature of the trade union movement in the Western Cape; the breach that existed between unions and community organisations in 1980; and the fact that community structures in GCT do not possess the solidarity or organisational depth that they do elsewhere (in itself partly a product of the complex factionalism of the area's politics). For these reasons, the stay-aways and consumer boycotts mounted in GCT recently lacked the 'cumulative impetus provided by more localised community and union action and organisation' that has been enjoyed elsewhere.[75]

In short, it has been argued in this sub-section that alliances between youth/student movements and those of the organised working class are critically important. Theoretical, comparative and local perspectives all point to this conclusion. In the Western Cape, several interlocking factors make its realisation more difficult — but no less necessary.

---

[72] Maravall, *Dictatorship and Political Dissent*, p. 165.

[73] Jordi, 'Parents, Workers, Unite with our Children'.

[74] See Labour Monitoring Group, 'The November Stay-away', *South African Labour Bulletin*, vol. 10, no. 6 (May 1985); more generally, see *ibid.*, vol. 11, nos. 1, 2, and 3.

[75] Jordi, 'Parents, Workers, Unite with our Children'.

Youth/student politics in 1985: Towards an assessment

Through a composite of pamphlets and press reports[76] one can summarise the main strengths and achievements of youth/student political activists in 1985 — as they perceived these themselves. The first and most important gain was that students attained organisational unity: students from different schools in various parts of GCT were linked in joint action. The need for effective organisations had been recognised, and new structures created to achieve this. Secondly, these structures were democratic: 'the ability of the students to democratically control the course of the boycott. . . has been a great achievement'. Thirdly, student political awareness had matured and deepened in several respects. Students 'have realised that their struggle against the educational and political system won't be won if students stand on their own.' They have learned 'that liberation does not lie with one or two leaders, but can only be achieved through long, hard struggle, led by the working class.' They have linked struggles over education with broader political struggles: 'We realise that education can either be an instrument of capitalist domination or of liberation. We must turn our schools into centres of liberation.' To this end, students have challenged the content, format, and goals of their education.

None of these claims is unimportant. All represent political advances. Yet an important qualification must at once be lodged. One way of doing so is simply to quote from a Students-Parents-Workers Manifesto issued by the Committee of 81 — in May 1980. This carried 'a short and incomplete summary of the victories we have won with the boycott'. These included:

Students, parents and workers discussed their grievances together. . . the boycott has created the climate and mood for [a] wider workers' struggle to be intensified. . . The boycott has seen many structures arising. . . We have achieved a high degree of political awareness and consciousness. . . The whole community has been rallied as a unified force. . . It has shown the possibility and desirability of disciplined, planned struggle. The end of unorganised mass protest has arrived. . . We have rocked the state. . . The distortions in our syllabi have been pointed out. We have started on what can be called a deindoctrination process. We want Education for Liberation. . .'[77]

To quote this — with its inevitable sense of *déjà vu* — is not intended to belittle the claims made in 1985, nor those made five years before. Rather, it serves as a reminder of a simple but nonetheless significant feature of student/youth movements: that they are by their nature impermanent and discontinuous. It is difficult for them to sustain 'continuity of activity, organisation, or perhaps even programme and ideology'.[78] Each generation of students (and one is speaking of a four or five year turnover) must, in its political education as in its formal education, repeat many of the lessons that its predecessor learned.

Secondly, even some of the individual claims have to be qualified further. New student umbrella groupings were created — but they also experienced problems of loyalty and cohesion. Student unity did not extend to significant joint action between

---

[76] Especially *Weekly Mail*, 12 September 1985; *Cape Times*, 16 October and 12 November 1985; 'The 1985 School Boycott — organised retreat or demoralised rout', anonymous leaflet, 1985.
[77] 'Manifesto to the People of Azania' issued by the Committee of 81, Cape Town, May 1980.
[78] Hobsbawm, *Revolutionaries*, p. 261.

DET and DEC students. Within DEC schools, where the Department made examinations a show of strength between the state and students (as opposed to more flexible arrangements by the DET) decisions about whether or not to sit the end of year papers created deep divisions. The unity sought across generational lines — between students and their parents — was repeatedly stretched thin, and on occasions frayed. In addition, the importance of schools as a base for mobilisation became a weakness once they were closed by the state: 'the potential for militant pupils to reach the community and agitate. . . was seriously complicated' by the loss of the schools as bases. [79]

Costs of a quite different kind were also incurred during the vehemence and violence of struggle in 1985. Even the resilience and adaptability of the young does not suffice to insulate all of them from trauma. The discipline of the young militants did not — could not — hold all the time:

As an outlet for political anger you see a lot of violence in the classroom. There has been systematic wrecking of classrooms, the kids fight each other at break, the violence has been turned inwards to the schools. . .

said a teacher in November. [80] Another described her school: 'Tears, tears, tears, and more tears. And there's a lot of aggressive behaviour too. There is mass distress. . .' [81]

To identify these actual or potential weaknesses within youth/student political organisations is not, however, to discount their importance or undervalue their achievements. The youth-based resistance that has been the subject of this study engaged more intensively and effectively in political and social struggle than it had before. Simply in terms of courage, ingenuity and commitment, a great deal was demanded: youth activists faced not mere discomforts or reprovals, but the retributive violence of the state. Circumstances at the time that this is written ensure that such qualities will be necessary again.

Secondly, at both a programmatic and an organisational level, educational issues were linked more concretely to broader political objectives. The closure of the schools by Carter Ebrahim served to link the question of *control* of schooling to the rejection of tricameralism and collaboration. The formation and defence of democratic SRCs and the creation of PTSAs provided an embryonic structure for a democratic 'people's education'. [82]

Thirdly, perhaps the most important advance made in 1985 was at the level of consciousness: the maturing recognition within youth/student organisations of an objective necessity for an alliance with an organised working class. Even if this perception, in the Western Cape, remains an expressed goal rather than an achieved reality, the popularisation of the concept during 1985 is hardly to be doubted. The realisation must also be present in the trade union movement; and where it is not

[79] Jordi, 'Parents, Workers, Unite with our Children'.

[80] *Cape Times*, 23 November 1985.

[81] *Argus*, 23 November 1985. (More generally, on the same theme, see Chikane 'The Effects of the Current Unrest'.)

[82] See Z. Sisulu, 'People's Education for People's Power', keynote address to Second National Consultative Conference, National Education Crisis Committee, March 1986.

present, must be fought for. When such an alliance is forthcoming − when it is politically feasible − then the vitality and fervour of black youth politics will be massively augmented by the experience, continuity and weight of the workers' movement.

Finally, this paper has tried to relate the pattern of youth-based struggle in GCT in 1985 to the distinctive aspects of similar movements elsewhere. It has suggested that there is an essential dualism to youth politics: on the one hand, it is characteristically militant and dynamic; on the other hand, by its nature it is short on theoretical sophistication and experience. Youth/student politics in a time of crisis is a hybrid of precocity and immaturity. This dichotomy was observed by Lenin in pre-revolutionary Russia, and by a host of commentators elsewhere.

In South Africa, too, it is precisely this dual nature of youth-based resistance that must be understood. Its strength and vigour are indispensable; its limitations and its weaknesses must be confronted, assessed, and addressed. Youth-based resistance is doubly important to the broader struggle for liberation, democracy, and transformation. Not only are militant cadres recruited from its ranks, but so are intellectuals: those most equipped to provide a theoretical leadership.

Youth has a great deal on its side, not least the future.

SOURCES OF CLASS CONSCIOUSNESS:

SOUTH AFRICAN WOMEN IN RECENT LABOR STRUGGLES*

Iris Berger

The relationship between household labor, wage labor and capitalism has received increasing scholarly attention as part of the
feminist effort to clarify the nature of women's economic activity.
This interest has led to a new awareness of the ways in which household labor sustains the system of capitalist production and to a
deepened understanding of the complex connections between women's
dual spheres of experience – as household workers and as wage laborers. Despite the high level of concern with these issues, certain
received ideas continue to be accepted with insufficient analysis or
examination. One of these is the notion that, because of the split
in eir lives, women industrial workers, do not experience proletarianization as totally or as intensely as men do. Although differing
in emphasis according to the time period and the social formation,
this theory of women's incomplete proletarianization seeks to
explain the low level of women's participation in workers' struggles
by reference to their involvement in reproductive as well as productive activities. Even as full-time wage-earners women continue to
assume responsiblility for household tasks and, more broadly, for
the care and socialization of the next generation of workers. This
division of time and concern, the theory goes, leaves them less
prone to identify themselves solely as workers and therefore less
liable to commit themselves to working class activism. But their
incomplete proletarianization is economic as well as psychological;
for these arguments also suggest that the option of relying on male
incomes for support, if necessary, decreases women's dependence on
their own labor power.

Sheila Rowbotham takes this position in her discussion of European women workers in the nineteenth century. She suggests that "the
particular relationship of the woman to reproduction and consumption
within the family mediated her relationship to commodity production," thereby making women "less liable to organize."[1] She
explains in greater detail:

> Women continued to work in the home, maintaining the
> needs of the family, but working for wages became the
> predominant activity external to family production. The

*I am grateful to the National Endowment for the Humanities and the Social
Science Research Council for providing the funding to support this research.
Neither, of course, bears any responsibility for my conclusions. I also would like
to thank Debbie Gaitskell, Jeanne Penvenne, Karen Sacks and Julie Wells for their
helpful suggestions.

[1]Sheila Rowbotham, *Women, Resistance and Revolution: A History of the Modern
World* (New York, 1972), 113.

wife's work outside the home was therefore an economic supplement to the family income. Women retained certain features of a pre-capitalist labour force. They never fully learned the rules of the new economic game.[2]

Recent studies of women workers in contemporary Third World countries have stressed a similar theme. Diane Elson and Ruth Pearson, writing on women employed in "world market factories," those that produce solely for export to the centers of capitalist production, found a low level of female participation in trade union activities and a lack of workers' or trade union consciousness. Their explanation, based on the idea of women's "secondary status" in the labor market, is similar to that of Rowbotham.[3] A major study of working-class consciousness among Latin American women argues along the same lines that because of women's family roles and their sexual subordination at home, labor force participation alone may be insufficient to foster class consciousness.[4]

Women workers in South Africa also bear heavy reproductive responsibilities, not only for domestic labor, but also for family support. Interviews conducted with female textile workers in Durban in the middle 1970s reported the women's insistence that they assumed the full burden of domestic labor and child-rearing. In the words of one of them, "The woman sees to it that everyone in the family gets food despite that there may be no money available; the man will demand food. This leads the woman to secretly lend money from others. With a small child the mother has to see to it that he is provided with food and clothing." Typically these women rose at 4:30 a.m. in order to catch a 5:15 bus and returned home between 5:30 and 7 p.m., depending on overtime work and the availability of transport. Cooking, child care, and washing and ironing occupied the evening hours, with heavier household work, sewing, and knitting saved for the weekends. The majority of them relied on family members for child care, although some employed unrelated young girls. Migrant workers usually left their children with relatives in the rural areas.[5]

Despite their heavy family involvement, South African women, like those in many other historical settings, have displayed a degree of working-class consciousness that is inconsistent with the idea of semi-proletarianization and suggests a number of problems with the concept. First of all, it fails to distinguish adequately between the economic and the psychological aspects of women's roles.

[2]Rowbotham, *Women*, 113.

[3]Diane Elson and Ruth Pearson, "'Nimble Fingers Make Cheap Workers': An Analysis of Women's Employment in Third World Export Manufacturing," *Feminist Review*, VII (Spring 1981), 102-103, citing a paper by Jane Cardosa-Khoo and Kay Jin Khoo: "Work and Consciousness: the Case of Electronics 'Runaways' in Malaysia," paper presented to the Conference on the Continuing Subordination of Women in the Development Process, Institute of Development Studies, University of Sussex, 1978.

[4]Helen Icken Safa, "Class Consciousness among Working Class Women in Latin America: A Case Study in Puerto Rico," in Robin Cohen, Peter Gutkind and Phyllis Brazier, eds., *Peasants and Proletarians: The Struggles of Third World Workers* (New York and London, 1979), 442-443. I will use the term class consciousness in the way that Safa has defined it on p. 71: "a cumulative process by which women recognize that they are exploited and oppressed, recognize the source of their exploitation and oppression, and are willing and able to organize and mobilize in their own class interests."

[5]Jean Westmore and Pat Townsend, "The African Women Workers in the Textile Industry in Durban," *South African Labour Bulletin*, II, 4 (1975), 27-28, 30.

Secondly, it seems to assume that all women workers are married and have children, failing to take into account the differences in women's ages and family responsibilities. Finally, it ignores aspects of both the work situation and particularly the social formation that may foster or hinder the development of resistance and class consciousness. In South Africa, although women workers are strongly tied to their families, both emotionally and through the demands of domestic labor, a number of factors have helped to foster a militant, politically aware female component within the black working class: the heavy economic responsibility most women bear, the large number of women migrants, particularly among Durban textile workers, who live in single-sex hostels that are densely populated and rigidly controlled, and the strict regulation of black living and working conditions that lends a political dimension to all workers' protest.

The concept of incomplete proletarianization draws on Marx's definition of free wage labor, which he depicts as "free" in the following double sense, "that as a free individual he can dispose [of] his labour-power as his own commodity and that, on the other hand, he has no other commodity for sale".[6] Elson and Pearson, citing this definition to explain women's "secondary status" in the labor market, argue that women are never "free" wage laborers in this classic sense of having no other commodity for sale because they always have the option of obtaining subsistence outside the capitalist labor process in exchange for services "of a sexual or nurturing kind."[7] In South Africa, however, I would contend that this is not the case. Since male wages have been kept deliberately at a level sufficient to support only a single wage-earner, most working class women are unable to rely on male "breadwinners" to satisfy their economic needs and those of their families. Furthermore, the inability of all South African blacks to dispose freely of their own labor power may create a stronger basis for solidarity between men and women than exists elsewhere. The limited possiblity for economic dependence may, therefore, be an important factor in explaining the proletarianized behavior of South African women.

The implied relationship between economic independence and proletarianization gains support from Helen Safa's study of Latin American women. Although she found, in general, a very low degree of working-class identification, she did discover a strong element of class consciousness among women who were household heads. Her analysis stresses, in particular, the high degree of identification with work roles among these women and the importance of the relationships they formed with their co-workers. She writes:

> Women who are heads of households are more prone to develop a stronger commitment to their work role because they become the principal breadwinners for their family. They cannot afford to regard their work roles as temporary or secondary as do most of the married women in the shantytown. This lack of commitment to a work role plays a crucial role in the absence of class consciousness among women in the shantytown, since women never identify with their work role nor stay on one job long enough

[6]Karl Marx, *Capital*, Vol. I (Harmondsworth, 1976), 237, cited in Elson and Pearson, "Nimble Fingers," 96.

[7]Elson and Pearson, "Nimble Fingers," 96.

to develop a relationship with their peers. . . . The
reason is clear: women must rush home after work to care
for children and other household chores, whereas men are
free to join their friends, and, as the survey demonstrated, often meet their best friends through work.

Women who are the sole support of their families are
more likely to develop class consciousness than women
who are still primarily dependent on men to support
them.[8]

In South Africa women have a history of participation in
working-class struggles that dates back, on a small scale, to their
involvement in the Industrial and Commercial Workers' Union and the
Women Workers' General Union of the 1920s, and, on a larger scale,
to the garment and textile organizing of the 1930s.[9] In the early
part of the latter decade, thousands of white and Coloured women in
these newly expanded industries came out on strike in an effort to
stave off wage cuts resulting from the Depression and to gain some
control over their wages and working conditions. During the following years the Garment Workers' Union, particularly in the Transvaal,
became a strong and stable organization, led by the union's male
general secretary, Solly Sachs, but increasingly under the joint
leadership of a strong cadre recruited from the ranks of the workers. Notable among these women were Johanna and Hester Cornelius,
Anna Scheepers, and Dulcie Hartwell. Bettie du Toit, another activist of the period, gained her initial experiences in the textile
industry.

From the late 1930s onwards, women leaders of the garment
workers, joined by organizers with Communist Party affiliations,
succeeded in unionizing large numbers of semi-skilled and unskilled
workers, among them female sweet and tobacco workers, milliners, and
food and canning workers. The Food and Canning Workers' Union (FCWU)
at the Cape, formed and led by Ray Alexander, became a model radical
union that combined action on both economic and political issues
with campaigns on community-oriented concerns such as workers' housing and living conditions. Through its ranks black and Coloured
leaders like Mary Mafeking and Liz Abrahams rose to responsible
positions not only in the union, but also in the Federation of South
African women, the organization that led the massive women's anti-
pass demonstrations of the 1950s. This politicization, however, left
the FCWU vulnerable during the 1950s and early 1960s, as many of its
leaders were banned or banished to remote rural areas.

From World War II on, the garment and textile industries began
to change. The latter expanded enormously and came to rely primarily
on black male labor; only from the middle 1960s, when manufacturers

[8]Safa, "Class Consciousness," 447-448.
[9]For further historical information on women's involvement in workers' strug-
gles, see Ken Luckhardt and Brenda Wall, *Organize or Starve! The History of the
South African Congress of Trade Unions* (London, 1980); Bettie du Toit, *Ukubamba
Amadolo: Workers Struggles in the South African Textile Industry* (London, 1978);
Richard Lapchick and Stephanie Urdang, *Oppression and Resistance: The Struggle of
Women in Southern Africa* (Westport, Conn., 1982); Nancy Van Vuuren, *Women Against
Apartheid: The Fight for Freedom in South African, 1920-1975* (Palo Alto, Calif.,
1979) and Shirene Cadet Carim, "The Role of Women in the Trade Union Movement," UN
Centre Against Apartheid, Notes and Documents, April, 1980 and E.S. (Solly) Sachs,
Rebels' Daughters (London, 1957).

began a campaign to introduce a male-female wage differential, did women begin to re-enter the textile mills in large numbers. In Transvaal garment factories the gradual replacement of white women by black and Coloured women was underway by the mid-1940s. Aided by a legal loophole that union officials discovered, black women gained admission to the registered Garment Workers' Union in 1944 and quickly became staunch union members. By the late 1960s, under the leadership of Lucy Mvubelo and Sarah Chitja, two of the first African women to become shop stewards, the primarily female National Union of Clothing Workers (NUCW) had become largest black union in the country. Unlike the FCWU, which had been progressively weakened by political repression, the NUCW has remained intact by deliberately eschewing politics.

Many of the textile and garment factories that were built in hte 1950s were located in rural "homelands" or in adjacent "border areas." In both cases they drew on destitute, proletarianized rural women for whom even the sub-poverty datum line wages represented an advance over their meager earning potential in the countryside. In one resettlement township of the Ciskei, for example, residents explained that the two factories employed mostly women because "the wages are so low . . . that only they will work there."[10] Throughout this period, however, the vast majority of black women continued to work either in agriculture or domestic service.[11]

The labor activity of the 1970s followed a relatively quiet period born of severe repression during the previous decade. But, despite the small number of major work stoppages between 1960 and 1970, strike activity did persist, especially among migrant workers in the expanding low-wage textile industry. The resumption of workers' protest during the 1970s occurred within a context of continued low wages and steep price increases, especially in the cost of such essential items as food, clothing, and transportation.[12] Furthermore, Africans were legally allowed neither to strike nor to belong to the registered trade unions that alone possessed the right to bargain with their employers. Works committees and liaison committees, designed to voice African grievances, had little power and were limited to single factories; employers found it easy to victimize outspoken critics.

The entire period from 1973 onward was marked by a steadily heightened level of industrial protest, although the largest concentrated strikes clustered during the years 1973-1974 and 1980-

---

[10] *Inquiry*, II (October 1979), 21. As late as 1979, women workers in Babalegi, a "new industrial boom area" in Bophutatswana with over 100 factories, were receiving R 6,90 in weekly wages. See "Babalegi: Exploiters Paradise," *Work in Progress* VIII (May 1979), 32, citing an article by Nadine Hoffman in *Wits Student* , 20 March 1979.

[11] The number of black women in industrial work has increased continually in recent years. According to the *Star* , 9 December 1974, the number employed by Johannesburg industries rose by 100 percent between 1965 and 1973 as compared with an increase of 17.5 percent for black men. In the entire country, figures in the surveys of the South African Department of Manpower for 1969 and 1981 give an increase of 133 percent during this period, from 45,216 to 105,168. It should be noted, however, that the latter figures are incomplete because they exclude areas that had become "independent homelands." The number of Asian and Colored women in industry increased by 47 percent, from 83,199 to 122,386, between 1969 and 1981.

[12] David Hemson, "Trade Unionism and the Struggle for Liberation in South Africa," *Capital and Class*, VI (Autumn 1978), 19.

1981.[13] In between came the three massive stay-at-homes following the Soweto uprising of 1976, an indication of workers' willingness to withdraw their labor to express political grievances. Increasing acceptance of wildcat strikes and organizational efforts that led to a mushrooming of factory committees and unregistered trade unions were characteristic of struggles during the 1970s. As a result of this intensified labor activity, the government-appointed Wiehahn Commission recommended in 1979 that African trade unions be granted official recognition in order to bring them under the control of the existing system of industrial relations.[14] With the new upsurge of strikes in 1980-1981, mass dismissals, penal sanctions against workers and trade unions, and police intervention in labor disputes became increasingly common. The high level of communication and support between striking workers and their surrounding communities that emerged during this unrest led the author of a major study of class struggle in the 1970s to reflect, "It could only be a matter of time and changing conditions before the weapons developed by the workers in their struggle would be turned to political ends."[15]

Women took full part in this revival of militant protest, as strikes swept through garment, textile, and food processing factories. Organizing efforts even spread into the ranks of domestic workers, normally notoriously difficult to unionize.[16] And male trade unionists willingly acknowledged the commitment of their female comrades. A former official of the Textile Workers Industrial Union, writing on the events of the period, noted the "advanced political consciousness" of African women,[17] while during the 1980 textile strike a male shop steward praised the women for having "fought like men."[18]

The typical protests of the period focused primarily on the issues of wages, working conditions, and grievance procedures – particularly the ineffectiveness of management-supported works committees and liaison committees. Differential pay increases were a major issue in the strike of 160 women at Transkei Hillmond Weavers in 1978,[19] while the 850 African women engaged in a wildcat strike

[13]According to South African Government figures, from 1959-1969 there were about 70 work stoppages per year by Africans; in 1973 the Government admitted to 160 in the first three months of the year.

[14]The original recommendations have been amended, as a result of political pressure, to allow the membership of migrant workers and to allow multi-racial unions. Additional changes, however, also place greater restrictions on the political activities of trade unions and attempt to exercise control over unregistered unions. Whether or not to register has been the subject of intense debate within the independent trade union movement over the past few years. The *South African Labour Bulletin* has published the opinions of both sides in this discussion.

[15]D. du Toit, *Capital and Labour in South Africa: Class Struggle in the 1970s* (London and Boston), 1981.

[16]See Interview, "Maggie Oewies Talks About the Domestic Workers Association," *South African Labour Bulletin*, VI, 1 (July 1980), 35-36; Muriel Horrell and others, comps., *A Survey of Race Relations, 1976* (Johannesburg, 1977), 312-313 and *Star* 11/25/74. Even after the recent legal changes, government regulations continued to prohibit domestic workers or farm workers from forming recognized trade unions.

[17]Hemson, "Trade Unionism," 32.

[18]Natal Labour Research Committee, "Control Over a Workforce – the Frame Case," *South African Labour Bulletin*, VI, 5 (December 1980), 38. This article also observes, "Women proved to be the most ardent champions of the strike cause, and were perhaps more united and purposeful than the men."

[19]Carole Cooper, "Details of Strikes During 1978," *South African Labour Bulletin*, VI, 1 (May 1979), 61; Loraine Gordon, and others, comps., *Survey of Race Relations, 1978*, 260.

at the Langeberg canning factory in East London complained of the uncertainty of the amounts of overtime pay to which they were entitled.[20] Pay increases they never had received motivated the January 1980 strike of 1500 textile workers at Butterworth in the Transkei, whereas the need to meet higher transport costs led the 70 women working for a packaging firm in Johannesburg to demand a raise.[21] In almost all of these cases workers also voiced dissatisfaction over the way in which works or liaison committees were handling their grievances. One woman in the Langeberg canning strike, speaking of the liaison committee, explained, "they are now 'ja baas' instead of putting things right." In the Eveready Electrical Company strike in Port Elizabeth in 1978, which led to an international boycott of the company, the dispute centered on the company's refusal to negotiate with the registered union on behalf of some 200 Coloured women workers.[22] At the Sea Harvest fish factory in Saldanha Bay, a strike of 700 women that began in late December 1979 over unsuccessful wage negotiations was the culmination of a series of conflicts over pay, long working hours (often twelve hours a day), unhealthy working conditions, and the union's right to operate freely in the plant.[23] Most strikes were relatively brief and were based on democratic methods of decision-making that prevented employers from singling out leaders for victimization.

A strike in Johannesburg in 1974 offers a typical example of an incident in which a minor dispute led rapidly, and seemingly spontaneously, to an expression of more fundamental grievances. The major issues centered on wages, working conditions, and the kinds of controls exercised over the labor force. At the Turnwright Sweet Factory 300 workers, mainly women, walked out during a dispute over working conditions on August 21, 1974. They had arrived at work at the usual hour of 6:30 a.m., only to find the factory gates shut since the management had decided to open at 6:50 in the future as a security measure. The women first complained that this late opening left them too little time to change clothes and eat before work began at 7:10. But they soon began to shout for wage increases and to complain about their long working hours - 7:10 a.m. to 4:30 p.m. with only a 10 minute break and 25 minutes for lunch - and about the need to clock in and out when they went to the bathroom. Workers also expressed their desire to be represented by the Black Allied Workers' Union.[24]

These examples verify the fact of women's participation in the labor upheavals of the past decade, but they offer little insight

[20] *Daily Dispatch*, 10/4/78. Male workers did not participate in this strike.
[21] *Star*, 9/15/79.
[22] *Survey of Race Relations, 1978*, 261. and Gerhard Maré, "Eveready to Exploit," *Work in Progress* VII (March 1979), 22-29.
[23] "Strike At Sea Harvest," *Work in Progress*, XI (February 1980), 26-27. This summary is intended to highlight some of the major issues that strikes during the period have addressed rather than to be an exhaustive listing of all such incidents. Two other actions involving women workers that merit mention are the strike at the Fattis and Monis factory in Bellville, South Cape which was supported by a nation-wide consumer boycott, and the strike at the Rainbow Chicken factory in Hammarsdale, Natal, both in 1979. For complete listings of workers' actions, see the yearly issues of *Survey of Race Relations* and the "Labour Action" updates in *Work in Progress*. "A View of the 1973 Strikes," RR. 151/73 (Johannesburg, 1973), published by the South African Institute of Race Relations, details strikes and stoppages during that year. *Work in Progress* VII (March 1979) 36-45 covers actions occurring between March 1974 and June 1977.
[24] *Rand Daily Mail*, 8/22/74.

into either the nature or the sources of their class consciousness. Much of the information necessary to understand their position more fully comes from the two areas of the industrial economy with the highest concentration of women workers, garments and textiles.

During March and April 1973, immediately following the Durban strikes, clothing workers staged a number of stoppages.[25] The first two strikes occurred in a "border" area in which the employees were unorganized and received substantially lower wages than their counterparts in the major urban centers. On March 26, undoubtedly spurred by events in nearby Durban, 1,000 workers at the Veka Clothing Co. in Charlestown went on strike for increased wages, leading police to impose a curfew on the nearby township and to prohibit meetings of more than five people. Four days afterward 700 fellow workers at Trump Clothing, also in Charlestown, struck for higher wages in support of the Veka strike. Although both groups returned to work without promise of an increase,[26] these actions represented a significant political awakening in areas in which clothing manufacturers had hoped to maintain a labor force that was not only cheap, but docile. The stoppages of garment workers in and around Johannesburg in March and April 1973 achieved greater success. Fueled by an expected cost of living increase, 4,608 black garment workers took part in some twenty-one work stoppages during a three-week period. With quick intervention by the registered Garments Workers' Union and/or the parallel African body, the National Union of Clothing Workers, the employers usually announced concessions and the workers returned to their jobs; only two of the incidents lasted more than five hours. The years 1980-1982 produced another series of clothing industry strikes on the Witwatersrand culminating, in February and March of 1982, in a strike of 1800 workers in at least 20 factories, all demanding an immediate wage increase of R 3,00.[28]

Garment workers in the largest cities also were involved in other forms of protest that were more anarchistic and more purely political than the 1973 stoppages. During a strike in the early 1970s at a clothing factory in Johannesburg, large numbers of finished garments were slashed, while in another Johannesburg factory an experienced worker took down a fire extinguisher and emptied it onto imported material worth thousands of rands.[29] Garment workers also numbered among the most active supporters of the stay-at-homes that followed the Soweto uprisings in 1976. The clothing industry came to a complete halt during the August protest in the Transvaal, despite the fact that trade union leaders appealed to their members not to withdraw their labor. The 300 African shop stewards, mainly women, probably were responsible for organizing the

[25]These were not the first signs of discontent in the clothing industry during the 1970s, however. In 1971, 26,000 garment workers in the Transvaal engaged in a "work to rule" protest during a deadlock in wage negotiations and in June of that year, thirty-seven Indian women at the Clairwood Clothing Factory were convicted for participating in an illegal strike. This information comes from the Garment Workers' Union Archives, Bcf 2.1 and from "A Study of Strikes During the 1970s," *Work in Progress*, V (November 1978), 111.

[26]*Sechaba*, VII, 6 (June 1973), 9 and VII (July 1973), 9.

[27]L. Douwes Dekker, D. Hemson, J.S. Kane-Berman, J. Lever and L. Schlemmer, "Case Studies in African Labour Action in South Africa and Namibia," in R. Sandbrook and R. Cohen, eds., *The Development of an African Working Class: Studies in Class Formation and Action* (London, 1975), 217.

[28]"Wages in the Clothing Industry," *Work in Progress*, XXIII (June 1982), p. 45.

[29]Institute for Industrial Education, *The Durban Strikes, 1973* (Durban and Johannesburg, 1974), 160.

workers.[30] Women reportedly led the September stay-at-home in the Cape during which the clothing industry, whose workforce of 50,000 was 90 percent female, lost two days of production.[31]

By comparison with the textile industry, garment industry work stoppages were extremely brief. Those in border areas were rapidly repressed, while in the Transvaal well-established procedures for handling disputes were tacitly accepted by employers, the unregistered African union (the National Union of Clothing Workers), and the registered Garment Workers' Union. In the 1973 stoppages, officials of one or both unions intervened immediately. "The existence of an established union such as the NUCW enjoying the confidence of the workers was undoubtedly one reason for the speed in which the disputes were settled."[32] At the same time the activities of the NUCW, in helping members to find work, in administering a burial fund, and in assisting them in such tasks as applying for unemployment and maternity benefits have helped to create a sense of collective identity that favors industrial action when necessary. The union structure itself also has served an important unifying function in an industry built on large numbers of relatively small factories.

Nonetheless, the signs of suppressed anger evident in the instances of industrial sabotage and in the widespread support for the 1976 stay-at-home, against the expressed wishes of union officials, also are explicable. Extremely low wages continue in the industry,[33] despite the union's nominal acceptance, and the inferior position of the NUCW gives African garment workers less than full representation. In several instances after the 1973 strikes Department of Labor officials deliberately excluded the spokesperson of the NUCW from negotiations. On a structural level, the inability to negotiate for its members, except through the representatives of the GWU, has created a dependent relationship between the NUCW and the GWU the details of which were revealed in a series of allegations and denials published in the *Financial Mail* in 1976. The original article, drawn from sources within the union, described the ways in which Anna Scheepers, president of the registered union, allegedly dominated the "sister" African body and influenced the decisions of its leaders. It reported, "She calls the executive in and lectures them like grade school children and then tells them to go back and reconsider. Usually they do."[34]

This "mother-daughter" relationship between the two unions has resulted both from the "understandable caution" of the GWU leaders

[30]Hemson, "Trade Unionism" 32. According to Sarah Chitja, in an interview with Russell Kaplan, shop stewards are elected in the plant in which they work in the presence of union officials. Each one represents from ten to fifty workers. See "Interview with Sarah Chitja, Deputy General Secretary of the National Union of Clothing Workers," *South African Labour Bulletin*, III, 4 (January-February 1977), 58.

[31]See E.C. Webster, "Stay-aways and the Black Working Class since the Second World War - the Evaluation of a Strategy," n.p., n.d., 17, 23; Hemson, "Trade Unionism," 31-32; Counter Information Service, *Black South Africa Explodes*, Anti-Report No. 17 (London, 1977), 40. Whereas the turnout in industry generally was approximately 50 percent, that in the clothing industry ranged from 10-15 percent.

[32]Douwes Dekker, and others, "African Labour Action," 217.

[33]See the wage statistics reported regularly in the annual *Survey of Race Relations*. In 1977, for example, the average monthly wages for the clothing industry as a whole were substantially lower than for any other industry in the country. "Wages in the Clothing Industry" analyzes some of the current reasons for these low wages.

[34]*Financial Mail*, 11/19/76.

and from the continuing dependence of the NUCW leadership.[35] Yet
the independent action of the shop stewards in 1976 suggests a growing resentment of "maternalism," particularly on the part of younger
workers who have entered the industry since the late 1960s. As
second- or third-generation urban dwellers, these women are politically sophisticated and skeptical about supporting a moderate
trade union.[36]

The economic pressures on garment workers, combined with a
racially and sexually biased division of labor, have created yet
another source of discontent among black women. As urban wages in
the industry have risen, capital has tended to expand into rural
areas in order to draw on the large reserves of ultra-cheap non-
unionized labor. The threat of job loss to urban workers has been
continual. And in the urban factories the labor process has operated
to the detriment of black women. Despite their long history of
organization and despite the shortage of white garment workers, they
still occupy the least-skilled jobs in disproportionate numbers. In
the Transvaal in 1973 European men continued to hold the vast majority of the highest paid supervisory positions. Although a surprisingly high percentage of the 120 European women employees (62
percent) earned only R 10 to R 20 a week, 98 percent of the Coloured
women and 99 percent of the African women fell into this category.
Furthermore, black women, 79 percent African and 20 percent
Coloured, held virtually all of the unskilled positions.[37]

On one level, then, the activism of the garment workers has
drawn on the organizational strength generated by membership in an
informally recognized trade union that operates through hundreds of
shop stewards and provides a variety of material benefits to its
members. Yet the protests of the 1970s came from the rank and file
workers, not from union officials, and the spirit that animated them
emerged not as much through the unions as from opposition to existing union leadership. In the eyes of many women, this leadership has
accommodated too readily to an industrial system that hampers the
emergence of strong, independent African unions and that continues
to rely on the exploitation of cheap black labor power.

The textile industry, concentrated around Durban though scattered throughout the low-paying border areas and "homelands," was
among the economic sectors hardest hit during the protests of the
1970s. It operated on a capital-intensive basis that brought together thousands of workers in each mill. Roughly half the textile
workers in Durban were migrants, whose housing in company dormitor-
ies enhanced the possibility of mass action, as did the heavy concentration of ownership by the Frame Company, a vast industrial
empire that in 1973 employed over 22,000 people in factories operating in South Africa, Zimbabwe, Zambia, and Malawi.[38] Women formed

[35]Douwes Dekker, and others, "African Labour Action," 216-217.

[36]Adam Klein, General Secretary of the GWU, 1973-1976, personal communication,
6/8/81.

[37]J.H. Thomas, "The Wage Structure in the Clothing Industry," South African
Institute of Personnel Management and South African Institute of Race Relations,
Johannesburg, January 18-19, 1973.

[38]Rand Daily Mail, 2/6/73. It is interesting to compare this degree of concentration with that in the clothing industry. In the latter, comparatively large firms
with over one thousand workers employ less than 20 percent of the work force, while,
in the textile industry, less than 10 percent of establishments employ nearly 60
percent of the work force. These figures come from Allan Hirsch, "An Introduction to
Textile Worker Organisation in Natal," South African Labour Bulletin, IV, 8
(January-February 1979), 14.

a large part of the workforce throughout the decade, but their numbers increased dramatically between 1973 and 1980 under circumstances that undoubtedly contributed to their willingness to protest, particularly in 1973.

Up until the mid-1960s, strong pressure from the textile workers' union had ensured the unusual policy of paying men and women equal wages. During the middle 1960s, however, the National Textile Manufacturers' Association, under continual pressure from lower priced imports,[39] began an offensive to force employees to accept a male-female wage differential.[40] In 1965 and 1966 the unions resisted their effort to grant women only 75 percent of the wages to be paid after a proposed increase and the NTMA positon won only partial and conditional acceptance by an arbitrator: he agreed to lower wages in certain restricted classes of work provided that the categories in question be "suitably diluted" and that the work assigned to women be clearly specified.[41] By the early 1970s, only 452 of the 3,747 women in the industry were receiving the lower wage - fixed at 80 percent of the male wage.[42] But in 1972 the manufacturers finally won the approval of the Industrial Tribunal for a uniform policy of paying women a wage 20 percent lower than that of men.[43] This ruling undoubtedly accounts for the rising percentage of women in the industry which, in the Frame factories, zoomed from 40 percent to 70 percent during the next eight years.

In addition to receiving lower pay, black women, particularly Africans, have been employed in the lowest-paid, least skilled occupations. Although little information is available on the specific sexual division of labor in the industry, which undoubtedly has changed with the recent increase in the number of female employees, most supervisors are male and women have little chance for advancement. There also seem to be more men than women employed as weavers, a position that offers both a higher wage and a greater degree of control over one's working conditions than is possible for spinners, the other main category of semi-skilled workers.

Despite the large number of women textile workers, the most detailed study of the 1973 strikes, published by the Institute for Industrial Education as *The Durban Strikes, 1973,* leaves many gaps in its information about women. A list of the percentages of workers in each grade of employment contains no breakdown by sex and, more important, the sample of workers interviewed gives information on Indian women, but not on their African counterparts who formed a far greater proportion of the labor force. The main section devoted to women in this discussion concerns the fears about African men that

[39]*Financial Gazette,* 2/9/73 and *Cape Times,* 9/14/74 discuss the continuation of these pressures during the 1970s.

[40]Submission made by the National Textile Manufacturers' Association - Representing the Employer Party to Dr. F.J. Viljoen, Chairman, Industrial Tribunal, Durban, 8th February, 1966.

[41]"Arbitrator's Report and Award," Pretoria, 16th March, 1966.

[42]Wage Proposals by the National Textile Manufacturers' Association as at 8th February, 1972.

[43]*Durban Strikes,* 25. According to the *Financial Gazette,* 2/9/83, the South African textile industry had suffered severely during the eighteen month period preceding the 1973 strikes from a drastic drop in prices worldwide and a 70 percent increase in textile imports, leading the article to characterize the country as "the dumping ground of the world." Between 1960 and 1970, however, Hirsch reports in "Textile Worker Organisation," 30, the average wage per employee increased by 140 percent, while profits grew by 365 percent.

Indian women expressed, thereby conveying the impression that women workers were a main threat to interracial solidarity. Helping to fill this gap in the available information on women workers is a series of interviews conducted with women textile workers in Durban following the strike. Although offering important insights into their concerns, the imprecision of the study, and particularly its lack of reference to the total number of women interviewed, makes it less useful than it might have been.

On January 19, ten days after the strikes began, the first stoppages occurred in the textile industry. The wages throughout the industry were roughly 20 percent lower than those in manufacturing as a whole. At the Frame Cotton Mills in New Germany, male wages apparently had risen by only R 1,00 per week, from R 6,00 to R 7,00, between 1964 and 1972 (not including a R 1,00 attendance bonus). Women at the later date earned R 5,00 with a R 1,00 bonus. But a survey conducted at the Nortex and Seltex Mills in July 1972 revealed that some women were earning only R 3,50 in basic salary.[44] Textile workers came out first not in Durban, but in East London, as work ceased at Consolidated Fine Spinners and Weavers. By January 25 and 26 strikes had spread to the Frame Group, as over 7,000 cotton workers came out on strike at their mill in New Germany. The other adjacent cotton mills followed in quick succession. In at least one of the textile industry stoppages, it was African women, working for D. Pegler and Co. in New Germany, who were first to down their tools.[45] On January 29 the workers at Consolidated Woolwashing and Processing Mills in Pinetown, mainly women rag sorters, came out on strike after the management had ignored a written statement of their grievances presented through a union representative. By that day not a single Frame factory in Natal remained in operation.[46] The strikes in the industry lasted from one to seven days, ending with concessions of R 1 to R 2,50 per week from employers.

These settlements did not end the unrest in the textile industry, however. In April 1973, some 300 Indian and African women working as sorters in a woolwashing and processing firm in the Durban suburb of Pinetown were locked out after striking and then refusing an unspecified pay offer.[47] In July the stoppages spread to women weavers in Umtata, the capital of the Transkei in the eastern Cape.[48] Again, on August 8, some 1,000 workers struck at the Frame Group's Wentex Factory in Durban after 600 workers had lost their jobs in the wake of wage demands.[49] And, by January 1974, 10,000 Durban textile workers in eleven mills were again on strike demanding that the government-ordered increases for new workers in the cotton mills also be extended to employees with seniority.[50]

The textile strikes are interesting from the perspective of women workers because of the degree to which their complaints became

[44]*Durban Strikes*, 23-24.

[45]*Natal Mercury*, 1/30/73.

[46]*Durban Strikes*, 29-31. According to the *Financial Mail*, the parent company of Consolidated Woolwashing, among the lowest paying of the Frame factories, reported an increase of over 70 percent in pretax profits between 1971 and 1972.

[47]*Sechaba*, VII, 4 (April, 1973).

[48]*Sechaba*, VII, 7 (July 1973).

[49]*Durban Strikes*, 16.

[50]*Southern Africa*, VII, 3 (March 1974).

submerged in the wake of other grievances. Although as recently as July 1972 the textile union had included in its demands the removal of wage discrimination against women, this provision rarely was a stated issue in the negotiations that occurred during the strikes. In the IIE report, the issue of a sexual wage differential comes out only once, in the description of negotiations at the relatively progressive firm of Smith and Nephew where the workers demanded a basic wage of R 18 "even if it meant that all workers irrespective of sex and skill be paid that amount."[51] That they settled eventually for a male minimum of R 18 and a female minimum of R 12 was not unconnected with the intimidating presence of carloads of plain-clothes police at the meeting during which the offer was accepted. Not raising the issue of the recently instituted wage differential implied that the strikers tacitly accepted it.

In 1980 another massive strike broke out in the Frame-owned factories in Durban. Beginning among weavers in the Frametex plant and lasting for twelve days, the stoppage was triggered by continuing anger at low wages, the manipulation of the bonus system and the unwillingness of the manager to consult with the liaison committee. Women, who by then comprised 70 percent of the workforce, were involved from the beginning and took an active part in meetings, demonstrations at the bus terminal, and organization at Kranzkloof, the hostel where most of the workers, as migrants, were forced to live. The only grouping of strikers from which they seem to have been excluded was the *impi* or "regiment," which acted as the main strikers' defense force. The following description, based on interviews with participants, summarizes women's activities most succinctly.

> Within 24 hours of its beginning the women workers at Kranzkloof had organized themselves into two groups, one of which was stationed at the main gate, the other at the opposite end of section D. Here they waited for those women workers who were defying the strike, to return from the factories. The latter were then prevented from entering the premises, and only later that night (Friday) after the police dispersed the women strikers with tear gas, were they able to steal back into the hostel. Thereafter the women decided to visit each room which was occupied by one or more strikebreakers. This resulted in violent confrontation, with some of the strikebreakers leaving the Hostel for fear of being attacked. Throughout the strike, the women continued to meet regularly in the Hostel corridors, as well as in the grounds near the bus rank where most of the action took place. Their gatherings were coloured by much discussion, militant chanting and singing.[52]

The militancy of women in these protests undoubtedly draws on the same factors that have fueled and shaped the resistance of their male co-workers - extraordinarily low wages in a time of rapid inflation, rigidly controlled working conditions and a lack of adequate procedures for communicating their grievances. The vast scale

[51] *Durban Strikes*, 35.
[52] "Control Over a Workforce," 38. Unless otherwise indicated the discussion of conditions surrounding the 1980 strikes comes from this source.

of production, with several thousand workers in a single factory, the densely packed hostels in which they reside and the "packed and gregarious" buses on which they ride to and from work have undoubtedly fostered communication and class consciousness among textile workers, male and female alike. The homogeneity of the largely Zulu workforce also figures into discussions of the unrest in Durban.

In addition to their generally disadvantageous position in the labor process, women also have been exploited by management reliance on sexual relations of dominance as a means of enforcing industrial discipline. Male supervisors are given the "marginal capacity" to permit small favors such as permission to go to the bathroom or the "privilege" of sitting down during a bout of menstrual cramps in exchange for sexual favors. Women interviewed after the 1973 strike also complained of more general sexual harrassment at work.

> The women reported that the men workers in their factories have no respect for them. On the factory floor, men ill-treat the women make fools of them, and become vulgar by "touching the women in embarassing parts." Others mentioned that the men assault the women that they work with, one noting that if this is reported to the authorities, the latter take the part of the men.[53]

Women are further pressured and manipulated by policies related to pregnancy. In the Frame factories, prospective female employees who survive a mandatory pregnancy test are then subjected to the continual watchful eye of factory doctors instructed to watch for signs of impending motherhood. Until early 1980 the Frame factories terminated the services of pregnant women, but since then an altered policy ostensibly provides for reemployment eight weeks after confinement. Women workers allege, however, that supervisors retain the arbitrary power to determine whether a woman will be reinstated. Those allowed to return are required to undergo a "retraining" period (which the industry claims to be six weeks and the women claim is actually three months) during which they are excluded from bonuses and overtime work.[54] Instances of coercive intrusion by capital into workers' personal lives appear to be not uncommon in South Africa. In one engineering factory it was discovered in 1970 that African women were being forced to take the pill daily under a nurse's supervision.

Other arbitrary and sometimes humiliating regulations dominate the lives of women textile workers, both in the factories and at the hostel where a majority of them live. Company policy, for example, forbids them from using any company toilet paper or cotton scraps to supplement the single sanitary napkin they are issued. And, while men are frisked for company property at the end of each day, women must go through a special "searching room" where they are more thoroughly scrutinized. Possession of trade union material found during these searches may provide grounds for dismissal.[55]

In Kranzkloof hostel a high degree of paternalism regulates women's daily lives. Whereas men have greater mobility within the area of the hostel, women are largely confined to a fenced-in area

[53]Westmore and Townsend, "African Women Workers," 26.
[54]"Control Over A Workforce," 29-30.
[55]"Control Over a Workforce," 30

that is permanently under guard. The rules are applied more strictly
to them than to men and they are also prohibited from smoking or
drinking in their rooms. Control of their visitors includes a prohi-
bition on having their babies or young children in the hostel. But
the threat of arbitrary expulsion by the superintendent is the
aspect of control that has generated the most bitterness. The women
complained of facing expulsion for questioning unreasonable demands
by the superintendent - such as being selected at random to collect
litter in the corridors, a job others are paid to do. Individuals
are also arbitrarily victimized, with neither investigation nor
recourse to a hearing, for misusing communal facilities. The study
of the 1980 strike concluded: "Because women live in constant fear
of arbitrary expulsion, they have tended to unite in mutual self-
defence against the capricious actions of the authorities. The
solidarity and steadfastness of these women were certainly evident
during the strike."[56]

In the disorder connected with the strike, women's sexual vulnerability became politicized. Female strikers were the target of
youth gangs or *tsotsi*, whose motivation may have been unrelated to
the labor dispute, and of police violence. Since the security and
regulation system at the hostel broke down, non-residents had freer
access, including not only male friends of women residents, but also
groups of youth gangs; numerous incidents of theft and rape were
reported. Other women were raped by non-strikers who then instructed
them to return to work. In one area, women successfully organized
themselves to prevent such attacks, but in another part of the
hostel they were less successful. Women were, therefore, often
forced to flee the hostel to seek accommodation in the nearby
African township of Clermont, frequently in the safest place available - other men's beds. "Once again," according to the 1980 study,
"women found themselves having to choose between the lesser of two
abuses - rape by, or involuntary submission to male coworkers."[57]

Few recent documents from South Africa spell out the ideology
supporting the exploitation of female laborers more fully than the
report that the National Association of Textile Manufacturers
addressed to the Industrial Arbitrator in 1966 as the organization
sought to justify its request for a 25 percent wage differential
between men and women.[58] The authors relied on arguments so standard and stereotyped that they apparently felt little need to sub-
stantiate them - women's alleged physical weakness, their lower
educational attainments, and their minimal financial needs. Yet the
only recent factual study of women textile workers belies these easy
conclusions and supplies data that strongly support the hypothesis
positing a correlation between the level of women's economic responsibility and the degree to which they identify themselves as and act
as proletarianized workers.

The study in question, conducted by the National Institute of
Personnel Research and published in 1973, found a high degree of
financial responsibility among women textile workers - in this case,
predominantly settled residents of a border area in the eastern
Cape. Shattering the myth of the dependent working woman, the survey
found that nearly half (47 percent) were single, 32 percent were
formerly married (including widows, divorcees and women deserted by

---

[56]"Control Over a Workforce," 39
[57]"Control Over a Workforce," 30.
[58]Submission of the NTMA.

their husbands) and only 21 percent were married – a very low percentage considering that 64 percent of the women were between 21 and
35 years old. Although most of these women had no "male breadwinner"
on which to rely, they did not lack dependents. According to the
report, "Many of these women occupied a key role in the households
to which they belonged, for one-quarter of them were household heads
and over one half (52 percent) were the main breadwinners of their
families." Not only were most of the women self-supporting, but they
were, as a group, much better educated than the men employed in the
factory. Furthermore, although the women's absenteeism and turnover
rates were slightly higher than those of men (another contention of
the textile manufacturers), the report judged both figures to be
low, adding that women's high degree of family responsibility as
household heads and as main breadwinners "apparently caused them to
be stable."[59] Significantly, those who were household heads and
those who were married were absent from work more frequently than
those women whose mothers were the household heads. Without citing
direct evidence the report concludes the obvious: "This could well
be caused by the fact that in the latter case the subject's mother
was able to assume domestic responsibilities that otherwise had to
be discharged by wives or female household heads.[60]

Whether or not research in other factories bears out this
picture of women industrial workers as the main source of family
support, there is no doubt about the fact that women work primarily
to sustain their families. An NIPR-related study of garment workers,
which does not distinguish between family heads and main breadwinners, found that 93 percent of women interviewed in a "homeland"
factory and 83 percent of those interviewed in an urban factory
stated that they worked for economic reasons, primarily "to support
or to assist in supporting" their families. Specific needs cited
included food and clothing, education, and transportation. In both
cases, the median number of family members was nine.[61] The
Westmore and Townsend interviews with women workers in Durban also
found a clear consensus that women worked out of economic necessity.
Many of those interviewed were the sole source of family income –
either as widows, divorcees, single women with or without children,
or as women living with men who were unemployed or who worked intermittently.[62] Perhaps not atypical were two other cases reported at
the time of the 1973 strikes: that of Annie Msomi, a sixty-year old

---

[59]The manager of a R 10 million cloth and blanket factory at Butterworth in
the Transkei reported a women's absentee rate of 3 percent compared with a factory
average of 10 percent. Reported in *Star*, 10/9/74. Another study, of a "homeland"
garment factory, found that on days when women were absent they were seeking a
better paying job; they left as soon as they found one. The study is that of Pauline
Clara Masodi Mkalipe, "A Sociological Study of Black Women in the Clothing Industry," unpublished M.A. thesis, University of South Africa, 1979.

[60]S.K. Hall, "An Exploratory Investigation into the Labour Stability and Attitudes of Bantu Women in a Textile Factory," National Institute for Personnel
Research, Johannesburg, September, 1973. The study was based on data collected from
212 workers: ninety-three were interviewed to obtain more detailed demographic and
attitudinal information. Most of the women were settled residents rather than temporary migrants. Sixty-three percent of them had lived for over ten years in the
same place.

[62]Westmore and Townsend, "African Women Workers," 22. Although half of the
women they interviewed lived in the single sex hostels and half in the township of
Clermont itself, they make no distinction between the two groups in reporting their
results.

textile worker who supported a pensioner husband and five grand-
children on R 7,25 a week; R 2 of her wage had to pay for her bus
trip of 32 km each way. Kistanah Naidoo, also a textile worker,
provided for herself and three small children on 7,55 a week.[63]
Although such economic burdens might, in some instances, dictate
caution, that seems not to have been the case for countless women
during the past decade of South African history.

Whether the stereotypical working class wife whose husband
earned a steady, dependable wage ever existed in Europe is debate-
able. She certainly is rare in South Africa where low wages, high
levels of migrant labor, stringent controls on urban migration and
residence and forced resettlement in "homelands" have continuously
threatened the stability of family life. Nonetheless, the persistence of strong extended family networks, often extending to the
provision of child care in the rural areas, and the more limited
reproductive demands on female migrants may create some groups of
women workers with fewer domestic responsibilities than might be
assumed.

In addition to underestimating the variation in women's lives
and thereby failing to account for the impact of economic self-
sufficiency, the idea of semi-proletarianization also tends to
explain the behavior of women workers solely by reference to their
family situations, without considering other aspects of particular
social formations that might lead women to greater militancy as
workers. The close connection between class consciousness and
nationalist consciousness in South Africa undoubtedly influences
women as profoundly as it does men – a fact expressed in women's
overwhelming support for the 1976 stay-at-homes. Throughout the
decade, although the stated grievances of most strikers centered on
their position as workers in a capitalist economy, their struggles
also reflected black discontent in a white-dominated society. One
study of the 1973 strikes in Durban concluded that the enormous wage
increases the strikers demanded, much higher than those to which
they eventually agreed, "must be interpreted as a statement of
rejection, an affirmation of the desire for a quite different
society."[64] *Sechaba*, the magazine of the African National
Congress, reported on the political overtones of the strikes.

> At one [factory] the workers on strike gathered at the
> gates of the factory singing 'Nkosi Sikelele', the
> African National Congress national anthem. At another,
> ... demonstrating strikers were lead, [sic] in a march
> through the streets, by one worker carrying a red flag.
> In yet another cries of "Amandla!" [Power] the A.N.C.'s
> clenched-first [sic] salute were raised at the end of a
> meeting called by the strikers.[65]

The experience of black South African women in recent years,
then, suggests a number of factors that seem to foster class consciousness among women workers. In addition to incredibly low wages
and limits on the right to organize freely, they include: a general
atmosphere of economic and political unrest, a high level of coincidence between economic exploitation and racial oppression, communal
living situations that simultaneously lessen the demands of domestic

[63]*Financial Mail*, 2/2/73.
[64]*Durban Strikes*, 101.
[65]*Sechaba*, VII, 5 (May 1973), 2.

labor and heighten the sense of shared experience, gender-based inequality and harrassment at work, and a high degree of economic self-sufficiency. An aspect of the latter factor that remains to be explored more fully is the division of economic responsibility in the family; based on other African data, it seems likely that even where women are not the main breadwinners, as in the Puerto Rican material, they may assume predominant responsibility for certain central family expenses.

Two conclusions are possible. Either South Africa is an exception to the theory of women's semi-proletarianization or the theory itself is flawed. While South Africa may possess special features, I would argue that these characteristics are not unique and that many conditions likely to foster working-class consciousness among men are just as apt to operate among women. This conclusion is not meant to imply that women's relationship to family is unimportant in shaping their political behavior, but rather that the relationship requires much more precise analysis than most studies to date have done. The South African case, for example, verifies the suggested connection between economic responsibility and political militancy for women. In fact, it may suggest that in the absence of male "breadwinners," where working is a necessity not a choice, the very commitment to family that the theory postulates may demand the political stance of the proletarianized worker. This material also demonstrates a tendency on the part of women to participate actively and readily in sporadic and relatively short-term forms of protest such as strikes and stay-at-homes, although the extent to which their family commitments might interfere with longer term, relatively time-consuming activities such as the day-to-day running of trade unions remains uncertain. South Africa does boast a large number of female trade union leaders.[66] Yet church groups and economically oriented cooperative organizations virtually dominate the scarce spare time of women industrial workers.[67] Perhaps, in view of the limited attention that most unions have devoted to specifically female issues and the multiple demands on women's time, a clear distinction must be made when discussing women between trade union participation and other expressions of class consciousness. Finally, the data suggest that family cannot be viewed simply as a force antithetical to class consciousness; for extended family members in particular, through their assistance with child care and other reproductive tasks, often provide women with the very support networks that enable them to engage in political activism.

[66]Van Vuuren, *Women Against Apartheid,* 96, points out that during the 1970s the general secretaries of nine out of twenty-three African trade unions were women.
[67]"Organising Women?" *Work in Progress* XXI (February 1982), 20-21, citing Jane Barrett, "Knitmore: A Study in the Relationship Between Sex and Class" (B.A. Hons. dissertation, University of the Witwatersrand, 1981.)

Class Formation and Ideology:

The Transkei Region

Duncan Innes
Dan O'Meara

Introduction

The Transkei region of South Africa occupies an area of 16,500 square miles. Its total population in 1970 was just under 2 million - comprised of 715,032 *resident* males; 184,788 males away *at work*; and 1,029,531 females. Of this population 56,761 individuals lived in the urban areas just under half of them (24,838) in the *capital,* Umtata.[1]

On October 26, 1976, *The Transkei* became the first Bantustan to receive its *independence* under the South African Policy of Separate Development. This event has provoked much commentary from various sides, ranging from its *epoch-making* celebration in the National Party press to its dismissal as a fraud by most groups left of the Progressive-Reform Party. The handing over of *power* in a chronically under-developed region to a collection of paid functionaries of the South African state — groups whose political survival since 1960 has rested on the coercion of the Apartheid state — is clearly far removed from the exercise in self-determination claimed by the government, and at this level is tragic farce. Yet this formal transfer of the trappings of power on the 26 October does have a far reaching significance for the defini-tion of the arena in which political action and political organisation occur. To dismiss the event as a sham or as meaningless misses this significance.

Opponents of the Vorster regimes and its Transkei lackeys have long been blinded by the *fraudulence* of the Transkei *independence,* and not yet really confronted its meaning, nor nalysed the new factors it in-troduces in terms of political action and organisation. This paper is a tentative response to some of these problems. It seeks to pose questions for debate rather than present definitive conclusion; to stimulate fresh analysis of the region and its significance, rather than to answer these problems. It poses for itself two broad questions. Firstly, what are the class forces operating within the Transkei region? Secondly,,what alliances do they make within the region, and more particularly, at the level of the South African social formation itself? The paper also makes a few general comments on the ideological mediations of these

69

alliances. Given our tentative aims our arguments are presented in the forms of hypotheses, and the projections which result are similarly speculative.

In attempting to come to terms with class formation within the Transkei region we do not pose the question of whether a capitalist mode of production is dominant within *the Transkei economy*. To do so assumes that there exists such a discreet entity as *the Transkei economy*. It concedes to state ideology the claim that the Transkei region is an autonomous entity, (an *internal colony* to be *decolonised*) and thus further serves to mystify its position within the South African social formation. Rather, we argue, that a capitalist mode of production dominates the South African social formation, of which the Transkei region forms an integral part. The questions posed then of the Transkei refer to the impact on the region of this dominance of a capitalist mode of production over the broad South African social formation.

Implicit in this argument is the assumption that the South African social formation consists in the articulation between a dominant capitalist mode and various subordinated pre-capitalist modes of production. However, whilst it is possible to identify pre-capitalist modes of production within the geographical area known as the Transkei, production relations within the region and within these pre-capitalist modes *are structured by the dominance of the capitalist mode of production* and its imperatives. This is reflected in class relations.

Conditions determining class formation: The Function of the Transkei within the South African social formation as a reservoir of labour.
There are important structural differences between the incorporation of the Transkei region into the social formation pre — and post-1948. The development of the forces of production and capitalist relations of production in South Africa, together with the actions of the state to restructure relations of exploitation after 1948, have transformed the function and nature of this and other *labour reservoirs*. Prior to 1948, labour migrated between pre-capitalist modes of production (which covered the great part of the Transkei region) and the centres of capitalist production. The extension of capitalist relations of production across the South African social formation has proletarianised and/or marginalised the Transkei peasantry (see below), i.e. transformed pre-capitalist relations of production into fully capitalist relations. Displaced from the centres of capitalist production, migrant labour from the Transkei region is contract labour[2] i.e. proletarianised contract labour incorporated in capitalised production relations migrating from the labour reservoirs of the Bantustans to the centres of capitalist production. The role of the state in restructuring relations of exploitation post-1948 is central here, beginning with the 1951 Bantu Authorities Act as a prelude to the 1959 promotion of Bantu Self-Government Act. In distinction to the *normal* capitalist pattern, proletarianised agents are prevented by the state from moving permanently from the rural areas to urban slums. Instead of being located on the fringes of the industrial cities (as was increasingly the pattern in South Africa during the forties), the reserve army of Labour is located by the state in rural areas, and brought into the centres of industrial production, under contract, according to the needs of capital.

70

There is a further aspect to this. Though the relations of production within which the Transkei population is incorporated are thoroughly capitalist, the forces of production in the region are chronically underdeveloped. This paper argues that capitalist production itself cannot develop on any large scale in the Transkei region without the development of these forces of production. This would require massive capital expenditure. Thus, proletarianised agents are forced to sell their labour-power in the centres of capitalist production in the social formation. The underdevelopment of the Transkei region is thus structural, an ongoing process to be maintained in the interests of capital. This under-development will be sustained despite (or probably because of) state intervention though *development* schemes and any general concern about the region's *economic viability*.

In 1974, 257,000 *Transkeians*, or 83 per cent of the Transkei region's male labour potential were employed as migrant labour outside the region. 47,500 males were employed within the region, 20,000 of whom were in the employ of the Transkei *government*..(These 20,000 were employed as follows: Government Departments 14,000; Local Authorities 1700; Public Corporations 2,000; Para-Governmental Agencies 1,000 and the Railways 1,300).[3] Employment in the Transkei is concentrated in the *growth* points of Butterworth and Umtata.

Land Holding and ownership
Under the system of land tenure, land is communally *owned*, but its allocation is under the unchallengeable control of salaried *chiefs and headmen* acting as administrators on behalf of the South African state. The average size of the individual lots, to which every family is supposedly entitled under the provisions of the Glen Grey Act (1894), is between 1 and 2 hectares.

Under this system, *economic ownership of the land is vested in the chiefs*. That is to say, despite the *de jure* common ownership, *de facto* the chiefs have the exclusive right to allocate land within the kinship-group framework, and thus the chiefs have *de facto* control over the means of production and their operation. The question to be answered is whether the *de jure* entitlement to a plot of land, i.e., *access* to the means of production, bestows on the occupants of such small plots *possession* of their means of production. *Possession* here refers to the ability to put these means of production into operation, to produce. If so, i.e., if the bulk of the occupants of the land are able to produce sufficient from these means of production to supply their wants, the question of their class place becomes highly problematic.

The nature of agricultural production in the Transkei region
The concomic owners of the land, the *chiefs and headmen,* are salaried functionaries of the central state. Their function in a redistributive economy has been transformed to the point where they are now the prime agents of state agricultural policy in the region. But what of the structure of rural production?

The findings of a recent survey of 757 rural households in 10 of the region's 26 districts reveal broad trends, supported by other sources.[4] These households could be divided into 4 broad categories:

71

a. those which did no farming at all − 8.4 per cent of the total;
b. those which farmed for home use only − 83 per cent;
c. those which farmed for home use and sale − 8.4 per cent of the total;
d. those which farmed exclusively for the market − 0.1 per cent of the total.[5]

Generalising these findings for the region as a whole (i.e. to indicate broad trends rather than the statistically precise position), only 8.5 per cent of all rural households in the Transkei (categories c & d) ever produce a marketable surplus, of which only 0.1 per cent (category d) has a basis for accumulation − though across the region we would expect this category to be slightly larger. Those households in category c are thus engaged in *intermittent* petty commodity production.

Breaking this down further on the criterion of the adequacy of production to feed the household during the year, the following emerges: the 8.4 per cent producing for home use and sale − category c − are able to feed and reproduce themselves. Breaking down category b − 83 per cent who farmed for home use only: a total of 23 per cent of all rural households are able to feed their members in a *good* year − i.e. their reproduction of the means of subsistence is thus dependent on only the *intermittent* sale of labour-power. (However *reproduction* requires more than mere food. Clothing, bankets, furniture etc., also enter, and the sale of labour-power may be necessary for the purchase of these commodities.) The remainder of category b, or 60 per cent of all rural households, are *never* able to produce sufficient to feed themselves. Their reproduction is thus *totally* dependent on the *continued* sale of labour-power. Such agents are *forced* to sell labour-power in order to subsist.[6] (We have excluded category a − the 8.4 per cent who did no farming at all − from our analysis. These included not only agents totally dependent on remittances from migrant workers; substantial numbers of *marginalised* agents [see below]; but also certain petty bourgeois groups, e.g. teachers etc. Further specification of category a would be necessary before it could be incorporated into the analysis of classes.)

If, as we have argued, approximately 60 per cent of all rural households are dependent for their reproduction on the sale of labour-power, it must then be asked, what of the division of labour within these households? Has it been affected by the extention of capitalist relations of production, and how?

Historically, within both the redistributive system of production and the peasant system of production − which evolved out of the redistributive system through the requirement to produce a surplus for colonial taxation in the 19th Century − *the household* as a production unit spanned more than the two generations of the nuclear family. It was either the extended family, or it incorporated at least three generations under peasant production. Within this production unit, all members performed key roles in the production and reproduction of the means of subsistence and, under the peasant system, the production of surplus product. The productive/reproductive division of labour was not rigidly sexually based (except of course in biological reproduction). The extension of capitalist relations of production has transformed the

72

household division of labour — specifically the roles of second, and even more particularly, first generation women. The bulk of the Transkei region's first and second generation males are absent from the household for long periods as migrant wage labourers in the centres of capitalist production (83 per cent of the region's male labour potential according to the *Financial Mail)* forced to sell their labour-power in order to subsist. Of the Transkei population between the ages 15 and 44 inclusive, 68.3 per cent are women. Though reliable statistics are unobtainable, we would speculate that very many middle or 2nd generation women are similarly in some form of wage employment — though influx control measures operate to regulate the sale of female labour-power even more tightly than that of males. (Recent reports indicate that the majority of the 4,050 workers employed in industry in the Transkei region are in fact women.) Rural production in the region is now virtually exclusively undertaken by women — the burden having fallen particularly heavily on the older (1st) generation women remaining in the Transkei. Thus the number of tasks performed by women has in effect at least doubled. Women, and more particularly older women, have now to perform tasks previously undertaken by males of two generations. This is now essentially *reproductive* work in a dual sense. The extension of capitalist relations of production has transformed the household (as a productive unit) into the servant of capital. Forced to sell labour power in order to subsist, 1st and 2nd generation males and, to a lesser extent, 2nd generation females, now perform the tasks of wage labour. Migrant wage labour in South Africa is paid below the value of its labour-power, i.e., wages insufficient *of themselves* to reproduce that labour-power. Given these wage levels women in the reserves — but particularly the older 1st generation women — are forced to perform not only *reproductory labour* itself (child-care, cooking, cleaning etc.) — the *normal* pattern under capitalism — but have also themselves directly to *produce* the goods necessary for the reproduction of the labour-power of the household (i.e. grow the food, prepare mud for hut walls, thatch for roofs etc.). Under *normal* conditons of capitalism, these would be supplied in the form of wage goods and services, to be paid for out of a wage at the level of the value of labour-power. The peasant and redistributive division of labour in which (biological reproduction aside) the production/reproduction division is not sexually rooted, has been superceeded by the capitalist division of labour, male as wage labourer, female as (unpaid) reproductory labourer. Thus forced to perform both reproductory labour *and* produce the means of subsistance, women in the reserves, particularly older women, become the servants of capital in a dual sense.

Agricultural policy
There have recently been attempts to restructure agriculture in the region, with far reaching consequences for production relations and class formation. This policy has a number of aspects.

Its major aim is to end the practice that (in theory at least) every family in the reserves is entitled to a plot of land. It envisages a drastic reduction in the total number of *small farmers* in all the Bantustans from 500,000 to 50,000.[7] The aim of this reduction is two-fold: Firstly, to create a large proletariat in the Bantustan townships. One

73

of the effects of this policy is to marginalise (see below for definition) producers. Unable to support themselves on the land they are forced to seek work in the centres of industrial production. Such *superfluous appendages* and *illegal* migrants are even expelled from these areas. Hence the notorious practice of forcible removals (or *dumping*) has, with enormous social consequences and human suffering, produced such devastated communities as Limehill, Dimbaza and Stinkwater; secondly, to create a small class of rich peasants/capitalist farmers on now much larger plots of land. Occupation of these plots is on a quit rent basis (i.e. long term leases from the state), making this group dependent on the state.

A secondary aim of agricultural policy in the region is a crude *rationalisation* of agricultural production through the establishment of *betterment* villages. These seek to make more land available through re-siting households, designed to permit a more efficient use of the land. This policy too seems to aim at providing the basis for the development of an independent, rich peasantry.

Agricultural policy aims further at the promotion of ranching through the Xhosa Development Corporation, with *black participation.* Ranching is a highly land extensive operation, promoting, in an already highly overpopulated rural region, the rise of a class of capitalist farmers dependent on state capital.[8]

Other production in the region
At the end of 1974, *manufacturing* within the region employed a mere 4,050 workers most of whom were women (producing matches, timber, veneers, textiles, hardware, furniture and weaving).[9] These, exclusively labour-intensive rather than capital-intensive operations, are concentrated in the growth points of Umtata, and more particularly, Butterworth.

The region's biggest revenue earner is *forestry,* which brings in R 2m pa from 70,000 hectares. The afforested area has trebled since 1961, thereby pushing more people off the land.

The Transkei Development Corporation (TDC) and Bantu Investment Corporation (BIC)
These wholly-owned state corporations function in 2 broad areas: buying out existing white undertakings, mainly trading and farming operations, and leasing and/or selling them to black operators; and creating investment incentives in the region for the re-siting and expansion of industrial undertakings currently centered in the major areas of capitalist production.

The major aim of these corporations, as stated by the Managing Director of the TDC, is to protect white industrialists investing in the region.[10] They therefore continually reproduce the Transkei region in its primary role as a reservoir of labour in the broad South African social formation, whilst simultaneously reproducing the general racial division of labour in various ways. The major incentives offered to white industrialists are exemptions from wage determinations under the Wage Act, i.e., sanctioning even lower wage levels than the barbaric

74

South African norms. (Wages in the Transkei are as much as 50 per cent lower than those paid to black workers for comparable work in the factories in the industrial centres.) In this sense, industry is lured to the Transkei by the inviting prospect of a huge reservior of cheap, docile labour. (Matanzima has made it clear, African trade unions will not be allowed to operate in the region in the forseeable future.) And the racial division of labour is reinforced in other ways. Of the total loans provided by the BIC 1959-1974, e.g. 82 per cent went to white-owned enterprises and only 18 per cent to African undertakings. Only 14 per cent of all applications for loans by Africans were success-ful. The terms of loans to white entrepreneurs are decidedly more favourable than those offered to Africans.[11] Both the TDC and BIC are increasingly linked with Afrikaner capital through such financial institutions as Sanlam, Volkskas and Bonuskor. Any *development* in the region promoted by these two misnomered bodies is designed to further the interests of capital, and to reproduce the subordination of the region's productive forces to capital.

Class formation and alliances
In the light of these questions then, what can we say about class for-mation, class forces and class alliances as they affect the Transkei region's position within the structure of the broader South African social formation. Again, it must be emphasised, we do not claim any definitive status for our conclusions which are presented in the form of hypotheses — designed to stimulate debate.

The central questions revolve around the class determination of people living on the land; of those households which, though producing various amounts from the land, also sell labour-power on a migrant basis: i.e. are they peasants or proletarians? This question must be answered with reference to the categories of economic ownership, possession and commoditisation of labour power as dealt with in the preceding section. That is to say, we must inquire whether these agents control the utili-sation of their means of production (economic ownership); whether they are able to put these means of production into operation — are able to utilise the land on which they live to reproduce themselves (possession); or are forced to sell their labour-power in order to subsist (the commoditisation of labour power).

Hypothesis A:
The trend shown by the general statistics cited on page 4 above, indi-cate that 60 per cent of the population is never able to reproduce itself through rural production. These agents can be divided into 2 categories: firstly, into those considered proletarianised, i.e. *freed* from possession (in the sense defined) of their means of production and forced to sell their labour power in order to subsist. Labour-power, in this case, thus becomes a commodity despite the fact that the household from which such labour-power stems (and in which it is reproduced), is located on land on which some production (for reproduction) occurs; secondly, into those considered marginalised. *Marginalisation* occurs as a *by-product* of the process of proletarianisation i.e. the process of separat-ing producers from their means of production and commoditising their labour power. Thus while the development and extension of capitalist relations of production *frees* agents from their means of

75

production, it leaves a proportion of these without any possibility of functioning in capitalist production. It thus creates a relative *surplus* population: a social category of dispossessed and *broken* individuals, superflous to and discarded by the system which created them. These agents are not incorporated in capitalist production relations (not even part of the reserve army of labour – those on *stand-by* for capital). They exist as a type of rural lumpenproletariat *on the margins* of capitalism, close to starvation and dependent for subsistence on hand-outs, scrounging, theft, prostitution etc. The acute poverty and degradation of such dumping grounds as Dimbaza and Limehill reflects this process.

Hypothesis B:

A numerically small, highly stratified peasantry exists. (A peasantry is distinct from a proletariat in that it retains the ability to put the means of production into operation, i.e. it is able to reproduce itself through production from these means of production. It thus retains *possession* of its means of production. Further, a peasantry is required to provide *a fund of rent* to either the economic/juridicial owners of the means of production, and/or the ruling class. This rent may be in the form of labour, cash or kind. The peasantry are thus incorporated in highly unequal power relations with the central state.)

With reference to the 23 per cent of rural households which are able to feed themselves in a good year – i.e. able to reproduce themselves with only the *intermittent* sale of labour power (see p.4) these are not yet fully proletarianised, but subject to pressures of proletarianization. An index of this is the rapid rise in the number of migrants from the Transkei region seeking to sell their labour-power from 180,000 in 1970 to 250,000 in 1974.[12]

The new agricultural policy – both the enforced reduction of the total number of *small farmers* and the *rationalisation* – intensified this process of proletarianisation and associated marginalisation.

The 8.4 per cent of rural households always able to reproduce themselves through agricultural production and occasionally able to market a variable surplus, form the basis of an independent peasantry, which, under the new agricultural policy, could potentially be transformed into a relatively rich peasantry.

This class fraction is composed mainly of the beneficiaries of state policy *chiefs, headmen* and their clients – i.e. those functionaries of the South African state whose role is to mediate, on behalf of capital, the reproduction of the Transkei region as a reservoir of cheap labour.

The stability of this fraction of the South African peasantry will be determined by the imperatives of capitalist accumulation – and therefore by the pressures of proletarianisation which capital may come to exert on such producers. However, within this fraction there are agents whose relationship with the capitalist state protects them against such pressure; i.e. those whose role in the distribution of land, the exercise of social control and the recruiting of labour (generally the *chiefs* and *headmen*) is necessary for the South African state to fulfill its role as guarantor of the interests of capital in general. Further, the potential size and stability of this fraction, rests secondarily on the success of the new agricultural policy (resettlement and betterment schemes) — itself designed to reproduce the Transkei's labour reservoir function. We would thus hypothesise that while there is little material basis for the development of a stable, rich peasantry in the region, elements of such a class, in particular those agents of the state, will remain. These form the basis of the Transkei National Independence Party's (TNIP) rule in the region.

Hypothesis C:
There exists the potential for the emergence of a very small *class* of capitalist farmers. This refers to the 0.1 per cent of households farming for the market only but may in fact be slightly larger than this figure indicates.

As Colin Bundy has shown,[13] the 1894 Glen Grey Act effectively destroyed the thriving commercial farmers and rich peasants in the Transkei in the period up to the thirties — though a small number of individuals may have survived this process. The promotion of Bantu Self-Government Act (1959) which established the Bantustan policy, created the *conditions* for the re-emergence of such a class. *Land reform* in the region has as its first principle the placement of *selected* black farmers on white farms to be incorporated into the Transkei in areas such as Mount Fletcher, McClear, Ongeluksnek and Indwe. The farms are then owned by the Transkei *state*, and leased out on a quit rent basis. Recent press reports indicate that the Matanzima brothers have secured for themselves two choice such farms.

We would expect then that a new class of capitalist farmers would comprise largely those in the highest echelons of the Transkei government, and their clients — i.e. creatures of Apartheid. This group would thus form the core of a collaborationist bourgeoisie, i.e. a bourgeoisie emerging in the region as the product of the Apartheid state and dependent both on it and its prop, South African capital.

Other Class Fractions: Hypothesis D
Within the region there exist fractions of a small petty bourgeoisie, both in its *traditional* and *new* form. The *traditional* petty bourgeoisie refers to petty commodity producers (shopkeepers, garage owners etc.) who own their means of production yet themselves provide variable portions of the labour embodied in the commodities produced. The *new* petty bourgeoisie refers to those wage earners who neither produce commodities (and hence surplus value) nor exploit labour through the expropriation from and appropriation *to themselves* of surplus value. It includes such supervisory and *mental* labour as teachers, lawyers, bureaucrats etc.

Elements of these fractions were to be found in the region prior to the Promotion of Bantu Self-Government Act (1959), under extreme pressure from the Apartheid regime. African traders etc., were subject to pressures of elimination and no real economic opportunities within the region existed for the new petty bourgeoisie.

77

The 1959 Act created favourable conditions for an expansion of both fractions of this class within the Transkei region. The role of the TDC in buying out locally owned white trading operations and passing them onto blacks has widened the scope for the development of a traditional petty bourgeoisie. Since its inception in 1965, the XDC has bought up 522 white-owned trading stations in the Transkei and neighbouring Ciskei and leased or sold them to Africans to run on their own account. Similarly, the creation of the paraphenalia of an *independent* state in the Transkei, particularly the development of a local bureaucracy, has expanded opportunities for the new petty bourgeoisie in the area. The number of African civil servants in the region below executive level, has thus increased from 1,991 to 4,068 between 1963 and 1973. Similarly, the number of Africans in the police force has risen from 100 in 1963, to 750 in February, 1976.[14]

Yet the expansion of opportunities for both fractions of the petty bourgeoisie under the Apartheid regime, occurs under contradictory pressures. The South African state hands over trading operations, hotels, local administrative functions etc. to these class fractions, but at the same time devalues them as there are no funds for real expansion. Given the under-development of the region's productive forces, the Transkei *government* was only able to generate 32 per cent of its total revenue in 1972/73, or R 9m, from its own resources (taxes, fines, rents, liquor profits, etc). The remainder − R 28m − was provided by the South African state. This financial dependence on the South African state is in fact increasing. In 1974/75, the Transkei government raised only 14 per cent of its total revenue from its own resources − again R 9m −, while the South African state contributed R 64m.

The Transkei *government's* increasing financial requirements stem from the handing over of *control* of services previously adminstered from Pretoria. But the Umtata administration's resources have not expanded with its financial commitments, and in any event they have a limited capacity for expansion. The South African state, under increasing inflationary and arms spending pressures in particular, refuses to supply the funds necessary for the expansion of these commitments. Hence, while on the one hand the interests of both these fractions of the petty bourgeoisie have become increasingly tied to the Apartheid state since 1959, on the other hand, the failure of this state to act decisively in their interests through a commitment to the expansion of existing services and facilities, may generate severe antagonism towards that state. Hence the contradictory nature of the incorporation of these fractions into the social formation has established the possibility of a polarisation of this class in the region. Elements of this fraction of the South African petty bourgeoisie, particularly those in the local bureaucracy, could seek to transform themselves into a bourgeoisie in collaboration with the South African state, and together with the capitalist farmers mentioned above (constituting a *collaborationist bourgeoisie* − defined by its relationship with the South African bourgeoisie, through the capitalist state). Yet, we would argue, the contradictory pressures are such as to permit only a small number successfully to pursue such a policy, and leave the bulk of the petty bourgeoisie in the region in an ambivalent relationship with capital and the state. This too seems to be borne out by aspects of

78

the political practice of such agents. In the 1963 Transkei elections, the opposition Democratic Party (DP) appeared to have the support of the majority of these elements, winning the bulk of the urban constituencies in which they congregate. The 1968 elections saw a marked shift to the TNIP, confirming the recognition of the petty bourgeois position of dependence on the state, while the victories of independents in the areas in 1973 suggest a growing disillusionment with the TNIP and the state's ability to secure the long term interests of this class. Whilst this clearly also reflects the bitter conflict within the DP, both the general trend and this conflict itself over party strategy, reflect these contradictory pressures on the petty bourgeoisie.

Hypothesis E:
A critical question to consider is whether there exist the possibilities for accumulation through production *independent* of *South African* and imperialist capital, and hence the emergence within the region of a Transkeian *national* bourgeoisie, standing in a certain contradiction to South African capital (and which might rally popular opposition to South African capital in the region). The interest displayed by bourgeois social scientists and other commentators in the question of the *economic viability* of the region is in a large part motivated by a need to seek re-assurance on this point — reflected in the United Party claim that the Transkei will become a hotbed of opposition and resistance.

We would argue that no such basis for accumulation and the emergence of a *national* bourgeoisie in the region exists. The development of the productive forces of the region requires massive investment, available only from South African capital, the South African state as its agent, or foreign investment. The injection of capital from any of these sources will in no way establish an *independent* basis for accumulation. As the organisation designed to promote the *development* of the region, the TDC functions as the organ for the creation of a collaborationist, rather than a national, bourgeoisie. For such a class to emerge in the region would rest on a total collapse of links with South African and imperialist capital, and more particularly the full internal development of the region's labour resources. In fact, the reverse is the case: dependence on the South African state and capital has increased, whilst the Transkei's labour resources continue to be drained from the region. The establishment of industries on the Transkei's borders (and those of the other Bantustans) does not alter this latter process, despite their physical proximity to the Transkei, the wealth produced in these factories is appropriated by capital for consumption and/or investment outside the Transkei region.

Possible Alliances
We have argued that the South African state, as the guarantor of South African capitalism (i.e. capital in general, rather than specific fractions of capital), seeks to maintain the Transkei region as a labour reservoir. Such *development* as occurs will be to foster the interests of South African capital and its small groups of Transkei collaborators, and will in no way be allowed to threaten this labour reservoir function of the area. The question of class alliances should be seen in this light. It is

79

incorrect to analyse alliances *within* the region, at the level of the Transkei. These should first be analysed at the level of the South African social formation and then related specifically to the Transkei region. Put another way, the rule of the Matanzima government in the region rests on a series of alliances at different levels: firstly an alliance between the class forces the TNIP represents and the class forces controlling the South African state — i.e. capital; and secondly, an alliance between specific class forces in the region — itself determined by the alliances these various forces make at the level of the South African social formation. We would argue that any attempt to come to terms with both the political significance of Transkeian *independence* for South Africa as a whole, and to understand the nature·and dynamics of *internal* Transkeian politics, must begin at the level of the imperatives of South African capitalism, their mediation by the state, and the impact on the region. It thus transcends the view that Transkeian *independence* and the Bantustan policy generally are *meaningless* and *fraudulent*. While recognising the significance of Bantustan policy for the definition of the limits in which political *and* ideological action and organisation can occur in South Africa, the real changes Transkeian *independence* introduce into this arena should be situated within the determining context, i.e. the imperatives of South African capitalism.

Thus in analysing the question of class alliances in the area, these interests of capital, and the need of capital to forge alliances in order to maintain the relations of exploitation, must be seen as primary. However, while all fractions of the South African bourgeoisie are acutely aware of the need to forge an alliance with *the black middle class* (i.e. the petty bourgeoisie) in order to continue their exploitation of black workers[15] there are substantial and significant differences between factions of that capital on precisely how such an alliance is to be forged, and particularly, the concessions necessary. Thus the Bantustan policy and its concomitants on the one hand, and the Progressive-Reform party's qualified franchise on the other, are both attempts to forge such an alliance to preserve the ability of capital to exploit black workers. This has crucial effects for the nature of the alliances entered into in this case by class forces found within the Transkei region.

Thus, in its attempt to forge alliances with class forces within the region, the South African state seeks to establish firstly an alliance between itself and a collaborationists bourgeoisie — a bourgeoisie which the South African state itself brings into being and maintains in a relationship of dependence. This collaboratonist bourgeoisie consists, secondly, of an alliance *within* the Transkei between the capitalist farmers brought into being by the land policy of the Apartheid state (Hypothesis C above) and elements of the petty bourgeoisie which seek to transform themselves into a bourgeoisie through collaboration with the Apartheid state. Two points must immediately be made here. Firstly, given the contradictory conditons under which the expansion of the petty bourgeoisie occurs within the region, only a small proportion of petty bourgeois agents in the region can be accommodated in such an alliance. Thus the majority of the petty bourgeoisie will remain outside this alliance, or on its fringes. The bulk of this class

80

force will thus at least *be available* for other alliances of various sorts (see below). Secondly, this *internal* collaborationist bourgeois alliance rests on the support of yet another class force dependent on, and agents of, the Apartheid state — the *peasantry* based on the *chiefs, headmen* and their clients, identified in Hypothesis B.

In such a situation we would argue, that given the impossibility of the emergence of a *national* bourgeoisie in the region, there is no possibility of this alliance grouped round the collaborationist bourgeoisie drawing support from either the proletariat or those elements subject to intense pressures of proletarianisation. This paper argues that the collaborationist alliance functions primarily to mediate the exploitation of such groups by South African capitalism. As such, these groups are part of the South African, rather than *Transkeian* proletariat (and peasantry subject to proletarianisation). The potential alliances they forge must be seen in these terms. (There is of course a tiny fraction of the proletariat actually employed in the Transkei itself. The position of this group is structurally that of the South African proletariat as a whole — in that it faces the same trade union restrictions and suffers, in general an even higher rate of exploitation. This fraction of the proletariat thus stands in an antagonistic relationship with South African capital and its collaborationist dependents in the Transkei. Further, the collaborationist bourgois leaders in the region, unlike Buthelezi, have not sought the political support of such workers.

Neither the Transkei *state* nor the general South African capitalist state can *buy off* the proletariat. To do so would demand at the least a form of welfare state and a profound alteration in South African capitalism and the state. Rather, the proletariat must be controlled through its political and ideological division (reinforced possibly through encouraging economic differentiation). At its most obvious, this is seen in the attempts to introduce ethnic divisions — to divide Xhosa from Zulu, etc. Thus the alliances formed by the proletariat based in the Transkei and the peasantry subject to proletarianisation must be seen in terms of such attempts at division and control. Here too, both fractions of the petty bourgeoisie and the divisions within capital over the best means of effecting such division and control become significant.

Given the structure of the system of exploitation in South Africa, significant ambiguities in the experience of such exploitation by producers is introduced, to affect the consciousness of exploitation and hence political and ideological practice. We would argue that though the South African state maintains the sale of labour power on a migrant basis, it is primarily at the points of production themselves — the industrial centres of the Republic — that the contradictions of South African capitalism are most manifest. That is to say, it is here that the exploitation of the proletariat is most acutely experienced *by those agents who themselves produce surplus value,* i.e. the male migrant labourers (and those female labourers similarly involved) and hence determines their consciousness. Yet, classes do not just exist at the points of production. They must reproduce themselves. *The proletariat* refers not just to those aggregate male workers who themselves labour to produce surplus value, but rather to the aggregated basic social units which makes possible the reproduction of the labour power thus expended, i.e. the family or household. As we argued above, the migrant labour system to which workers from the Transkei are subjected, depends on the maintenance of a three-generation household — rather than the two-generation nuclear family *normal* to capitalism. Within the household as the unit of the reproduction of labour-power, we have argued that women are chained to capital in a dual sense. They both perform the reproductory labour and directly produce much of the product necessary for the reproduction of labour-power. However, this double bonding of women of proletarianised households (i.e. households from which the sale of labour power is the sine qua non of its reproduction) is not experienced by them at the points of capitalist production, but on the land itself. Thus this double oppression of women is experienced as a problem of rural, rather than industrial production. Though the link may well be obvious to such women, it is the actual experience of exploitation and oppression which mediates consciousness, and may well be reflected in political and ideological practice.

Thus, we are suggesting that the structure of the relations of production of South African capitalism of themselves introduce ambiguities into the consciousness of the proletariat, with potentially divisive effects for political and ideological practice. While those male and female migrant workers who labour at the centres of capitalist production are likely to see the solution to their poverty in terms of changes in these centres and more particularly in the structure and relations of production, such as occurred, for instance, in Natal in 1973 and after the Soweto killings in 1976, those women who labour in the reserves to reproduce such labour power are more likely to locate the necessary changes in these areas. In particular the oppressive and parasitic function of the *chiefs and headmen* as the functionaries of the Apartheid state is most likely to generate hostility and opposition from these rural producers — the black collaborator class seen by women in particular as the instrument of their exploitation and oppression, and who were the objects of mass popular resistance in the 1950's and '60's.

On the other hand attempts by women to escape the trap of rural impoverishment through the sale of their labour-power at the points of capitalist production are frustrated by apartheid legislation — particularly the pass laws. Hence we are suggesting that the consciousness of women in the reserves who are doubly subject to capital is not mediated solely by the *rural* experience of such subjection, but coloured too by the specific manner in which Apartheid legislation prevents them from moving off the land they no longer *possess* — and their political practice is likely to reflect both aspects in terms of opposition to the collaborationist bourgeoisie and the influx control legislative props of apartheid. We are further suggesting however, that this differential experience of exploitation and oppression by the male and female members of the same proletarian household introudces a structural division at the heart of the proletariat which affects the alliances it might forge and the willingness of this class to organise against capital.

It is this differential experience of capitalist exploitation and its effect on consciousness which partially explains the susceptibility of the

82

proletariat to African nationalism of various forms. The common feature of the urban and rural experience of capitalist exploitation is not overt capital itself. Rather it is *the white man* and *his* oppressive system of apartheid (and particularly the pass laws) which can be seen as responsible for both the urban and rural poverty and degradation of African proletarians of both sexes — and it is through an understanding of *white* oppression that the struggle of women in the reserves and men at the points of production can be linked together. In both cases the appalling poverty induced by capitalist exploitation and the brutal oppression exercised by the capitalist state to mediate such exploitation, can be laid firmly at the door of its racial agents.

This too has significant effects for the proletariat's alliances. For those fractions of the petty bourgeoisie for whom the Apartheid state offers few or no opportunities, the doors of economic advance and political participation are more obviously locked by *the white man* with the key, than by the capitalism which controls its use. This class too is attracted to forms of African nationalism, particularly in its mass form — the petty bourgeoisie allied with the proletariat. Historically this has been its specific response. However, given its position between capital and labour in the class struggle, the petty bourgeoisie firstly tends to see the solutions to its problems in purely political terms — reform in the *political* stuctures rather than changes in the relations of production. Secondly, the petty bourgeoisie is notoriously timid in the presentation of its demands and eager to abandon these when offered concessions. Its aim is not the overthrow of capitalism, but a *fairer* share in its product and changes in its political structures. The willingness of some former militants of the liberation movement to work within the structures of the Apartheid state, exemplifies this point. And as state response to the recent urban revolts indicates, the state seeks to divide the petty bourgeoisie and proletariat so as to prevent a mass movement emerging.

It is here that the divisions between fractions of South African capital over the nature of the concessions to be made to the black petty bourgeoisie are significant. We would argue that the *solution* presented by *Separate Development* is no solution. Though it will create a black collaborationist bourgeoisie, it cannot contain the aspirations of the bulk of the African petty bourgeoisie. While this policy is in force, we would argue that the bulk of this fraction of the South African petty bouregoisie would be susceptible to, and eager to lead, some form of African nationalist alliance with the proletariat. However, were there to be substantial concessions to this class, more particularly along the lines proposed by the Progressive Reform Party, we would argue that these may be sufficiently attractive to this class so as to break this popular alliance. The proletariat would then be substantially isolated. However, that is in the realm of fairly long term speculation. What significance does the above have for the class forces operating within the Transkei region?

In the period since the first Transkei elections in 1963 — after which, despite the electoral victory of the anti-Apartheid Democratic Party, the support from the *chiefs* gave power to Matanzima's TNIP — the organisational and ideological limits of legal political action by blacks

83

at the level of the social formation and within the region itself, have been fixed by the alliance between the collaborationist bourgeoisie and the state. Within the region, an alliance between the prolatariat, the peasantry subject to proletarianisation and the unincorporated elements of the petty bourgeoisie in opposition to the Matanzima regime is likely. However, such an alliance will be (and is) not only subject to extreme repression under Proclamation 400 (as well as the full range of South African repressive legislation) — the recent detention of DP leaders being a case in point — but these class forces within the region appear dispirited and more inclined to define their alliances at the level of the social formation. Thus not till a viable African nationalist alliance re-emerges at this level, are we likely to find a powerful combination between these class forces within the Transkei region.

A Note on Ideology

We wish here to focus very briefly on the possibility of the development of a Transkeian *nationalism* in the region, rooted in the symbols of Xhosa culture and history.

Again, we would suggest that the only class forces with any interest in developing such an ideology are those which we have identified as the collaborationist bourgeoisie. Such an ideology would firstly sanction their collaboration with the South African capitalist state — enabling them to present *independence* as a victory for self-determination and as decolonisation. Secondly, given the social base of TNIP in the *chiefs*, it would give the sanction of traditionalism to their rule — a continuation of Xhosa society after an interruption by white, colonial rule. Given the inability of the collaborationist bourgeoisie to transform itself into a national bourgeoisie and so gain popular support for its class interests (defined as opposed to those of the South African exploiters of the Transkei's labour and resources), attempts by these class forces to develop a nationalist alliance *centred on the Transkei*, is unlikely to find much support from the classes whose exploitation by capital is mediated by the collaborationist bourgeoisie.

Evidence tending to support this view lies in the differing ideological practices of Matanzima and Buthelezi. Though both undoubtedly represent petty bourgeois fractional interests, their respective ideological positions require explanation. Buthelezi seeks to articulate a nationalist ideology by transcending the narrow boundaries of a Kwa Zulu nationalism and appealing to an African nationalism evidenced most recently in a *militant* speech in Soweto. It is only on this basis that a Bantustan leader, formally co-operating with the Apartheid state, can mount popular support for a form of nationalism. Buthelezi espouses an apparently democratic and national ideology precisely because he does not confine his role to that of representative of the collaborationist bourgeoisie, presenting himself instead as the representative of a much broader African, national (aspirant-) bourgeoisie seeking support for this position from working class and peasant groups. As the flood of memoranda from the African Chambers of Commerce, etc. make clear, he is perceived in this role by this class.[16]

84

Matanzima on the other hand rejects this broader African nationalism, functioning as the representative (and leader) of the collaborationist bourgeoisie within a broadly anti-democratic ideological context. Precisely because the material base for the development of a Transkeian nationalism is absent, Matanzima has exhibited a marked reluctance to attempt its development (as opposed to the South African state which has made considerable efforts in this regard). And the collaborationist bourgeoisie's dependence on the South African state renders the development of an anti-South African nationalism virtually impossible (though periodic token attempts to display *independence* are to be expected).

Conclusion

In terms of the argument of this paper, the *independence* of the Transkei is seen essentially as an aspect of state intervention to restructure relations of exploitation within the broad South African social formation. It is designed both to maintain the Transkei region's function as a labour reservoir and to create and extend divisions within and between the proletariat and the petty bourgeoisie. All classes are fracturated according to various criteria — position in the labour process; the historical experience of becoming a class, particularly when race, language and cultural differences impinge on that process of class formation. One of the most potent weapons wielded by capital over labour is the power to play upon these fracturating forces, to intensify and formalise them so as to divide the working class against itself, thereby weakening it in the struggle against capital. One of the main political purposes of the Bantustan policy is to sow racial division amongst the African proletariat, and in this capital and the state are assisted by a collaborationist African bourgeoisie — itself fracturated into Xhosa, Tswana, Zulu, etc. It is the thrust of this paper firstly that such divisions must in the long term prove illusory, that the material base of the collaborationist classes is too weak (unless far-reaching structural changes are introduced to alter the definition of the situation) to implement the policy successfully. Be this as it may, the paper argues secondly that Bantustan policy generally and the *independence* of the Transkei in particular do alter the context in which political and ideological action and organisation occur in South Africa. The illusion of Transkei *independence* must be seen in this light, and its specificity analysed, as the other Bantustans do not automatically have identical effects for class alliances and political and ideological practice.

FOOTNOTES

An earlier draft of this paper was presented at a seminar held at the Centre of International and Area Studies, University of London. We are grateful to all the participants for their extremely useful comments and criticisms. However, we alone are responsible for possible errors of fact and interpretation.

1. Population Census, May, 1970; Report No. 02, 05-01.
2. All migrant labour recruited through officially approved channels (labour bureaux, NRC, etc) is *contract* labour. The official figures for migrant labour cited on p.3 thus refer to contract labour.
3. *Financial Mail*, 16 May, 1975.
4. J. Leeuwenberg, *The transkei: A Study in Economic Regression*, Africa Publications Trust (forthcoming, 1976). We are grateful to the author

85

for permission to utilize the findings of this study. The responsibility for the interpretations placed upon those findings rests with us alone.

5. Ibid., Chapter III, p.6, Table VI.
6. Ibid., Table VII.
7. Deputy Minister of Bantu Administration and Development, *Financial Gazette*, 20 July, 1973.
8. *Financial Mail*, op.cit.
9. Ibid.
10. Quoted Ibid.
11. Barbara Rogers, *Divide and Rule: South Africa's Bantustans*, (London, 1976), p.68.
12. *Financial Mail*, op.cit., and 1970 Census, op.cit.
13. "The Emergence and Decline of a South African Peasantry", *African Affairs*, October, 1972.
14. "Decentralisation: Growth Points, 1974", Department of Planning and the Environment (Johannesburg, 1974) p.XX; *Rand Daily Mail*, 26 February, 1976.
15. Eg. see *Volkshandel*, organ of the *Afrikaanse Handelsinstituut*, June 1976, and Transvaal Chambers of Industry "Blueprint", quoted in *The Star*, 21 August 1976 (Weekend edition).
16. Various appendices to Minutes of Conference of "Eight Black Leaders with the Honourable Advocate B.J. Vorster, M.P. . . . . 22 January, 1975".

86

ACKNOWLEDGMENTS

Denoon, Donald and Adam Kuper. "Nationalist Historians in Search of a Nation: The 'New Historiography' in Dar Es Salaam." *African Affairs* 69 (1970): 329–49. Reprinted with the permission of African Affairs, The Royal African Society. Courtesy of Yale University Sterling Memorial Library.

Wallerstein, I. "Ethnicity and National Integration in West Africa." *Cahiers D'Etudes Africaines* 1 (1960): 129–39. Reprinted with the permission of Editions de l'Ecole des Hautes Etudes et Sciences Sociales. Courtesy of Gregory Maddox.

Sundiata, Ibrahim K. "The Roots of African Despotism: The Question of Political Culture." *African Studies Review* 31 (1988): 9–31. Reprinted with the permission of the African Studies Association. Courtesy of Yale University Sterling Memorial Library.

Metz, Steven. "In Lieu of Orthodoxy: The Socialist Theories of Nkrumah and Nyerere." *Journal of Modern African Studies* 20 (1982): 377–92. Reprinted with the permission of Cambridge University Press. Courtesy of Yale University Sterling Memorial Library.

Goldsworthy, David. "Ethnicity and Leadership in Africa: The 'Untypical' Case of Tom Mboya." *Journal of Modern African Studies* 20 (1982): 107–126. Reprinted with the permission of Cambridge University Press. Courtesy of Yale University Sterling Memorial Library.

Marshall, Judith. "The State of Ambivalence: Right and Left Options in Ghana." *Review of African Political Economy* 5 (1976): 49–62. Reprinted with the permission of Review of African Political Economy Publications Ltd. Courtesy of Yale University Sterling Memorial Library.

Musambachime, Mwelwa C. "Military Violence Against Civilians: The Case of the Congolese and Zairean Military in the Pedicle, 1890–1988." *International Journal of African Historical Studies* 23 (1990): 643–64. Reprinted with the permission of the African Studies Center. Courtesy of Gregory Maddox.

Mazrui, Ali A. "The Social Origins of Ugandan Presidents: From King to Peasant Warrior." *Canadian Journal of African Studies* 8 (1974): 3–23. Reprinted with the permission of the Center for Urban and Community Studies. Courtesy of Yale University Sterling Memorial Library.

Adams, Bert N. "Uganda Before, During, and After Amin." *Rural Africana* 11 (1981): 15–25. Reprinted with the permission of the author and the African Studies Center. Courtesy of Yale University Sterling Memorial Library.

Davidson, Basil. "The Movements of National Liberation." *Tarikh* 6 (1980): 5–19. Courtesy of Yale University Sterling Memorial Library.

Saul, John S. "The Revolution in Portugal's African Colonies: A Review Essay." *Canadian Journal of African Studies* 9 (1975): 315–36. Reprinted with the permission of the Center for Urban and Community Studies. Courtesy of Gregory Maddox.

Markakis, John. "The Nationalist Revolution in Eritrea." *Journal of Modern African Studies* 26 (1988): 51–70. Reprinted with the permission of Cambridge University Press. Courtesy of Yale University Sterling Memorial Library.

Ranger, Terence. "The Death of Chaminuka: Spirit Mediums, Nationalism, and the Guerilla War in Zimbabwe." *African Affairs* 81 (1982): 349–69. Reprinted with the permission of African Affairs, The Royal African Society. Courtesy of Yale University Sterling Memorial Library.

Kriger, Norma. "The Zimbabwean War of Liberation: Struggles Within the Struggle." *Journal of Southern African Studies* 14 (1988): 304–322. Reprinted with the permission of Oxford University Press. Courtesy of Gregory Maddox.

Johns, Sheridan. "Obstacles to Guerrilla Warfare—A South African Case Study." *Journal of Modern African Studies* 11 (1973): 267–303. Reprinted with the permission of Cambridge University Press. Courtesy of Yale University Sterling Memorial Library.

Posel, Deborah. "Rethinking the 'Race-Class Debate' in South African Historiography." *Social Dynamics* 9 (1983): 50–66. Reprinted with the permission of the Centre for African Studies. Courtesy of Yale University Sterling Memorial Library.

Bundy, Colin. "Street Sociology and Pavement Politics: Aspects of Youth and Student Resistance in Cape Town, 1985." *Journal of Southern African Studies* 13 (1987): 303–30. Reprinted with the permission of Oxford University Press. Courtesy of Yale University Sterling Memorial Library.

Berger, Iris. "Sources of Class Consciousness: South African Women in Recent Labor Struggles." *International Journal of African Historical Studies* 16 (1983): 49–66. Reprinted with the permission of the African Studies Center. Courtesy of Yale University Sterling Memorial Library.

Innes, Duncan and Dan O'Meara. "Class Formation and Ideology: The Transkei Region." *Review of African Political Economy* 7 (1976): 69–86. Reprinted with the permission of Review of African Political Economy Publications Ltd. Courtesy of Yale University Sterling Memorial Library.